D0080059

# THE NONVERBAL SELF
## Communication for a Lifetime

**DIANA K. IVY**
*Texas A&M University, Corpus Christi*

**SHAWN T. WAHL**
*Texas A&M University, Corpus Christi*

PEARSON

Boston   New York   San Fransisco
Mexico City   Montreal   Toronto   London   Madrid   Munich   Paris
Hong Kong   Singapore   Tokyo   Cape Town   Sydney

**Acquisitions Editor:** *Jeanne Zalesky*
**Series Editorial Assistant:** *Megan Lentz*
**Marketing Manager:** *Suzan Czajkowski*
**Production Editor:** *Karen Mason*
**Editorial Production Service:** *Elm Street Publishing Services*
**Manufacturing Buyer:** *JoAnne Sweeney*
**Electronic Composition:** *Integra Software Services Pvt. Ltd.*
**Interior Design:** *Elm Street Publishing Services*
**Cover Administrator:** *Kristina Mose-Libon*

For related titles and support materials, visit our online catalog at www.pearsonhighered.com

Copyright © 2009 Pearson Education, Inc.

All rights reserved. No part of the material protected by this copyright notice may be reproduced or utilized in any form or by any means, electronic or mechanical, including photocopying, recording, or by any information storage and retrieval system, without written permission from the copyright owner.

To obtain permission(s) to use material from this work, please submit a written request to Pearson/Allyn and Bacon, Permissions Department, 501 Boylston Street, Suite 900, Boston, MA 02116 or fax your request to 617-671-2290.

Between the time website information is gathered and then published, it is not unusual for some sites to have closed. Also, the transcription of URLs can result in typographical errors. The publisher would appreciate notification where these errors occur so that they may be corrected in subsequent editions.

**Library of Congress Cataloging-in-Publication Data**

Ivy, Diana K.
    The nonverbal self: communication for a lifetime / Diana Ivy, Shawn T. Wahl.
      p. cm.
    ISBN-13: 978-0-205-47481-3   ISBN-10: 0-205-47481-0
    1. Body language.  2. Nonverbal communication.  I. Wahl, Shawn T.  II. Title.
    BF637.N66199 2009
    153.6'9—dc22

                                                   2008031940

Printed in the United States of America

10  9  8  7  6  5  4  3  2  1    11  10  09  08

Photo credits appear on page 456, which constitutes an extension of the copyright page.

For all of us who remain students of
nonverbal communication . . .

# BRIEF CONTENTS

# CONTENTS

■ ■ ■ ■ ■ ▬▬▬▬▬▬▬▬▬▬▬▬▬▬▬▬▬▬▬▬▬▬▬▬▬▬▬▬▬▬

## CHAPTER 2
## Nonverbal Communication Development:
## A Reflexive Approach    24

# PART 2
# Codes of Nonverbal Communication

# CHAPTER 5
# Physical Appearance:
# The Body as Nonverbal Communication     128

---

## CHAPTER 8
## Touch:
## Our Bodies in Contact     245

# CHAPTER 9
## Vocalics:
## Our Voices Speak Nonverbal Volumes    283

# PART 3
# Applications of Nonverbal Communication

# CHAPTER 10
## Nonverbal Communication and the Internet    319

## CHAPTER 11
# Nonverbal Communication in Professional and Educational Contexts 350

## CHAPTER 12
## Nonverbal Communication:
## Gender, Intimate Relationships, and Sexuality    395

# PREFACE

As instructors, typically our question when planning a course is, *What do we want students to know and learn?* Interestingly enough, students often wonder what they're supposed to know and learn from a course as well. Anyone who has ever taught a course in nonverbal communication knows how challenging it is and likely agrees with this claim: The topic of nonverbal communication is supported by a vast, multidisciplinary research base, making it fascinating yet complex to teach and study. Instructors have to make difficult choices about content because there is simply too much material to work through with students over the course of one term.

We have responded to this challenge by developing **an organizing feature** in the form of a **model** (described below and illustrated on the next page) which we believe will help instructors guide students through this new territory. In this text, we provide 12 tightly focused chapters in which the best material—drawn from the research bases of Communication, Psychology, Education, and other disciplines, as well as popular literature—is explored with relevance to our model. We've made difficult choices regarding the content, based on our years of experience teaching courses in nonverbal communication and experimenting with texts written by colleagues across the country. What we've ended up with is what we believe represents the best work in the field, including classic and contemporary research from a variety of methods, as well as popular literature and online contributions. Our goal is to expose students to both the breadth and depth of information regarding nonverbal communication, without overwhelming them.

Nonverbal communication is one of the most grounded, practical, and useful topics within the discipline of communication that a college student will explore. We make every attempt in this book to translate material into meaningful applications for students. We strive in this book to provide a **balance of theory and application**. We believe that the best approach to the instruction of nonverbal communication, as well as the textbooks that serve as tools for conveying that instruction, is to offer students practical ways to *use* information that is based on sound research and theory.

## ■ OUR ORGANIZING DEVICE: THE REFLEXIVE CYCLE OF NONVERBAL COMMUNICATION DEVELOPMENT

We have found that developing an organizing structure or device lends coherence to a textbook. In addition, such a structure helps students make connections between the material and their lives. In Chapter 2 of *The Nonverbal Self*, we introduce the **Reflexive Cycle of Nonverbal Communication Development, a model in five phases** that continues over the lifetime. The model was developed from discussions

## Reflexive Cycle of Nonverbal Communication Development

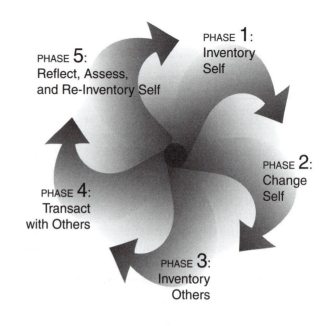

PHASE **1**:
Inventory
Self

PHASE **2**:
Change
Self

PHASE **3**:
Inventory
Others

PHASE **4**:
Transact
with Others

PHASE **5**:
Reflect, Assess,
and Re-Inventory Self

about how people come to learn nonverbal behavior, modify their behavior as they grow and mature, perceive others' nonverbal cues, impact others through their own nonverbal communication, and finally how those behaviors are altered or reinforced as a result of this ongoing process.

Two aspects of **reflexivity** drew us to this principle as a guiding feature for the model in this book: First, *reflexivity* means to refer back to the subject of a sentence, and you'll no doubt notice that we put a good deal of emphasis in this text on the individual, albeit within a social context. A common lay understanding of the study of nonverbal communication is that it involves "reading other people's body language." We spend some time in this book explaining how there is no "language of the body," but many people believe that studying nonverbal communication is merely learning to read other people's cues and interpret them more accurately. To us, this is only part of the picture. To become a skilled, astute perceiver of the nonverbal realm, you must first enhance your awareness of *your own* nonverbal communication—how you come across nonverbally to other people—before you can attempt to fully understand others' nonverbal cues. Our intent to stress this aspect led to the reflexive approach and the development of a cycle model to illustrate it.

Second, another feature of reflexivity is that actions are accomplished automatically rather than purposefully. Having our nonverbal abilities become automatically effective in every situation is a motivating goal to work toward with the realization that we can never reach perfection. A cycle, as opposed to a hierarchical, building-block structure, indicates a repetitive, process goal—**a goal about "becoming," not "arriving."** Improving our nonverbal sending and receiving abilities is a constant process throughout our lifetimes. Through study, experience with diverse people and situations, and conscientious intent to enhance our abilities to send and receive nonverbal signals more accurately, we can work toward such abilities becoming more automatic or reflexive.

The Reflexive Cycle includes the following **five phases**:

*Phase 1: Inventory Self.* This first phase reflects the continuous process of becoming more **aware** of our own nonverbal communication. We have little hope of improving our communication abilities if we're unaware of the current skills we possess, as well as areas we need to work on. So the first challenge the Reflexive Cycle poses is to inventory our own nonverbal behavior—to work toward becoming more aware of how we communicate without or in conjunction with words.

*Phase 2: Change Self.* The second step in the Reflexive Cycle is to make any **changes** to our nonverbal communication that we deem necessary, based on the inventory we completed in Phase 1. This phase involves coming to a decision about those things that are working well, meaning those behaviors we don't want to change or that don't need alteration, as well as those areas that need some work. Students need to understand that, just as many of our nonverbal behaviors have taken time to develop and have become ingrained, it will take time to "un-learn" or alter default or commonly used behaviors.

*Phase 3: Inventory Others.* A course or a book on nonverbal communication tends to make us better "people watchers." Phase 3 of the Reflexive Cycle challenges students to **inventory others' nonverbal behavior** closely, to pay attention to a wider range of cues at a more microscopic level than they're used to doing. The text provides labels for the behaviors students observe, as well as research findings to help them better understand how nonverbal communication functions in social settings.

*Phase 4: Transact with Others.* In Phase 4 we interact with others and mutually affect one another's nonverbal behavior. We prefer to call this process **transaction**, because it implies a shared creation of meaning that occurs in a simultaneous, ongoing manner. We don't exist in a vacuum, but in a social context in which the behavior of others affects the behavior of ourselves. Phase 4 is about communicating with people, verbally and nonverbally, while still maintaining an awareness of nonverbal cues—our own and those other people exude.

*Phase 5: Reflect, Assess, and Re-Inventory Self.* We come full circle in the Reflexive Cycle when we move through Phase 5, which calls upon us to **reflect and assess** the process we've undertaken. An important goal is to be purposeful or mindful in this entire undertaking, this process of understanding nonverbal complexities and applying that understanding to behavior, so that we can reflect on what we've learned, assess triumphs as well as mistakes, and continue to further develop our nonverbal skills.

The cycle is ongoing; we never stop evolving in our understanding and use of nonverbal communication. If we continuously work through the Reflexive Cycle, we believe that we'll be more able to enact nonverbal skills appropriate to varying situations, such that these skills become "second nature." The full model of the Reflexive Cycle is presented in Chapter 2, but **small versions of the cycle** appear at various points throughout chapters, with one or more phases of the cycle highlighted. The highlighting of certain phases means that content corresponding to one or more phases is being discussed in the paragraph or paragraphs adjacent to the icon. We offer the icon reminder simply as a device to reinforce for students the connection between textbook information and different phases in the cycle.

## ■ OVERVIEW OF THE BOOK

The book is organized into three parts. In **Part 1**, Chapter 1 provides context for the study of nonverbal communication within the larger realm of human communication. It also contains the **fundamentals**, in terms of reasons for studying the topic, contrasts with verbal communication, and the basic nature of nonverbal communication. Chapter 2 introduces the Reflexive Cycle of Nonverbal Communication Development and overviews codes of nonverbal behavior that are explored in the second part of the book.

**Part 2** contains seven chapters devoted to the primary **codes** of study within the realm of nonverbal communication: environment; space (proxemics) and territoriality; physical appearance; body movement, gestures, and posture (kinesics); facial and eye expression; touch (haptics); and vocal expression (vocalics). Each chapter covers key information and research related to the code, as well as applications of the information to situations relevant to students' lives.

The final three chapters (**Part 3**) constitute our **applications** section, in which material on nonverbal codes or categories of cues are related to three contexts for communication. Chapter 10 is a cutting-edge treatment of nonverbal communication in Internet exchanges. Probably nothing has impacted the study and enactment of nonverbal cues more than technology, specifically the rising impact of online communication in our culture. Chapter 10 explores communicative aspects that traditionally have been viewed as verbal messages for their nonverbal properties. Chapter 11 examines critical nonverbal cues in two relevant settings for students: professional and educational environments. Finally, Chapter 12 delves into more personal waters, focusing on nonverbal cues relevant to biological sex and psychosocial gender, sexuality, and intimate relationships.

## ■ PEDAGOGICAL FEATURES

We provide **nine pedagogical features** in this book. Each chapter contains two opening features to help instructors deliver course content and to enhance student learning. *Chapter Outlines* detail the organization of each chapter, while *Chapter Objectives* help students prioritize information so that they can learn more efficiently.

For all but the introductory chapters, an opening *Case Study* appears—a brief provocative example to gain attention from readers as they delve into new topics and preview the nature of the discussion that lies ahead. In most chapters, cases represent actual events that either students journaled as a requirement in our nonverbal communication courses or that emerged through class discussion. *Remember* boxes go beyond simple listings of key terms to provide brief definitions for students' review. These boxes appear intermittently within each chapter as a reminder to students of important concepts they will want to retain. Chapters contain *What Would You Do?* boxed features that provide a challenge or dilemma involving nonverbal communication, then pose a question to students as to how they would handle the situation. This feature is designed to help students apply textbook material to real-life experiences. Because nonverbal communication research is prolific and fascinating, we highlight one study or group of studies in the *Spotlight on Research* feature within each chapter. The research chosen for each spotlight box was selected for its cutting-edge qualities, relevance to students' lives, or impact on the field of nonverbal communication.

To close each chapter, we provide a *Summary* section that highlights key information (but doesn't reveal so much that the summary is all a student needs to read!). Next we include *Discussion Starters* that instructors may use as a means of generating class discussions about chapter content, as actual assignments, or as thought provokers for students to consider on their own time. Finally, complete *References* to the research base cited within the text appear at the end of each chapter. Students may find these references useful as they prepare assignments and/or conduct their own research projects. Instructors may use the references to gather additional material for their own research or to supplement instruction.

# INSTRUCTIONAL SUPPLEMENTS

An Instructor's Manual (IM) is provided through Allyn and Bacon, on adoption of the text. The IM contains chapter outlines that can serve as class notes as well as a wealth of additional resources to help you prepare lectures, develop quizzes, and stimulate class discussions.

# ACKNOWLEDGMENTS

This project has certainly been a team effort; thus there are many people to acknowledge and thank. The authors wish to thank the people we've been privileged to work with, including our original editor Brian Wheel, and at Allyn and Bacon Editor-in-Chief Karon Bowers, Acquisitions Editor Jeanne Zalesky, Production Editor Karen Mason, Series Editorial Assistant Megan Lentz, and Marketing Manager Suzan Czajkowski, who all offered great assistance, encouragement, and suggestions. Thanks are also extended to the team at Elm Street Publishing Services, especially Project Editor Amanda Zagnoli.

We are grateful to our colleagues in the field of communication whose advice and encouragement were invaluable throughout the review process of this text. Reviewers include Amanda Brown, University of Wisconsin-Stout; Dwayne Cornelison, Clemson University; Kathleen Czech, Point Loma Nazarene University; Melody Hufman, Amberton University; Julie Mayberry, North Carolina State University; Rebecca Nordyke, Wichita State University; Narissra Maria Punyanunt-Carter, Texas Tech

University; Diana Rehling, St. Cloud State University; Carla Ross, Meredith College; Rebecca Sanford, Monmouth University; Robert J. Sidelinger, West Virginia University; Jason J. Teven, California State University-Fullerton; Amy Lynn Veuleman, McNeese State University; Denise Vrchota, Iowa State University; and Robin Williamson, University of St. Thomas.

We are deeply indebted to Professors Steve and Sue Beebe for their excellent suggestions, willing participation in the formulation of this project and its link to Beebe, Beebe, and Ivy's text, *Communication: Principles for a Lifetime* (Allyn & Bacon), and constant encouragement of us as authors and friends. Thanks also to our colleagues in the Department of Communication and Theatre at Texas A&M University, Corpus Christi, particularly Department Chair Don Luna, Communication Coordinator Kelly Quintanilla, and College of Liberal Arts Dean Richard Gigliotti, for their unwavering support and tolerance of our endless book-writing stories. We are especially grateful to Ashley Billig—research assistant extraordinaire—for her contributions to the research-gathering process, photographic expertise, and assistance with instructional supplements.

Probably no project for the benefit of college students has ever succeeded without the help of college students. We have thousands to thank from the universities at which we've worked over the years for being sources of inspiration for the creation of this book. Students of nonverbal communication deserve our thanks for providing the motivation to write this text and the fuel for a good deal of its content.

Finally, we thank our families and friends for their listening ears, thought-provoking questions, lively discussions, and persistent belief in this book and its authors. Ivy thanks her ever-supportive family, parents Herschel and Carol Ivy, sister Karen Black, nephew Brian Black, niece Sumitra Black, and grandnieces Mackenzie and Sidney Black. They have been constant and generous with their praise for her scholarly achievements. Shawn thanks his mother Evelyn Wahl who was always there to listen and provide support during the writing process, his brothers Larkin Wahl and Shannon Wahl for their confidence and support, and his dearest friends Wesley Citty, Chad Edwards, Autumn Edwards, Chad McBride, and Scott Myers.

Diana K. Ivy
Shawn T. Wahl
*Corpus Christi, Texas*

# ABOUT THE AUTHORS

Diana K. Ivy, PhD, Professor of Communication at Texas A&M University, Corpus Christi, has been teaching communication at the college level for 25 years, including such courses as nonverbal, interpersonal, gender, and instructional communication. She has co-authored two other textbooks, *Communication: Principles for a Lifetime* and *GenderSpeak: Personal Effectiveness in Gender Communication*, both in multiple editions, published by Allyn & Bacon, and has published articles in *Communication Education*, *Southern Communication Journal*, and *Women and Language*. She was Speaker of the Faculty Senate at her university for two years, was awarded Outstanding Gender Scholar of the Year in 2002 by the Southern States Communication Association, has held multiple offices in the National Communication Association, and continues to serve as Archivist for the Women's Caucus of NCA.

Shawn T. Wahl, PhD, Associate Professor of Communication at Texas A&M University, Corpus Christi, has been teaching at the college level for 10 years, with specializations in communication and new media, nonverbal communication, and instructional communication. He has published articles in *Communication Education*, *Communication Research Reports*, *Communication Teacher*, *Journal of Family Communication*, and *Basic Communication Course Annual*. In addition, Shawn serves as Editor of the *Texas Speech Communication Journal*.

# Foundations of Nonverbal Communication

Chapter **1**

## CHAPTER OUTLINE ■ ■ ■ ■ ■

**Nonverbal Communication within a Larger Framework**

**Why Study Nonverbal Communication?**
Nonverbal Messages Communicate Feelings and Attitudes
Nonverbal Messages Are More Believable Than Verbal Ones
Nonverbal Messages Are Critical to Successful Relationships
Nonverbal Messages Serve Various Functions

**Contrasting Verbal and Nonverbal Communication**

**The Nature of Nonverbal Communication**
Nonverbal Communication is Culture-Bound
Nonverbal Communication is Rule-Governed
Nonverbal Communication is Ambiguous
Nonverbal Communication is Multichanneled

**Summary**

## CHAPTER OBJECTIVES ■ ■ ■ ■ ■

After studying this chapter, you should be able to:

1. Contrast communication with human communication.

2. Explain how encoding and decoding function in the communication process.

3. Define verbal and nonverbal communication.

4. Identify and explain the five Communication Principles for a Lifetime, and discuss the role of nonverbal communication within this framework.

5. Provide four reasons for studying nonverbal communication.

6. Describe the six means by which nonverbal communication functions with verbal communication.

7. Offer four ways that verbal communication contrasts with nonverbal communication.

8. Discuss four elements that reveal the nature of nonverbal communication.

"I heard that sigh; is there something wrong with meatloaf, young lady?"

"He's blonde-headed and blue-eyed, and I don't trust him as far as I could throw him."

"I bet you couldn't talk if your hands were tied down."

"You have the most distinctive laugh!"

"Your house always smells so nice, like there's always something good cooking on the stove."

What do these excerpts of conversation all have in common? They all refer to a fascinating form of human communication that occurs without words—nonverbal communication. Think about it for a moment: How do you convey sarcasm? If your roommate comes into the den looking like something the cat dragged in, how would you say to her or him, "You really look great" and convey the sense of sarcasm you feel? You'd probably draw out or elongate the words, emphasize the word "great," and roll your eyes toward the heavens to signify that your roommate looks anything but great. You'd use all of these behaviors to accompany your words, to provide context for how the words are to be interpreted. Your vocal inflections, pacing, and emphasis, accompanied by the eye behavior, would give your roommate the true meaning of your message. You would use nonverbal communication to help get your verbal meaning across accurately. Nonverbal communication is something we use every day as we relate to other people and make our way in the world.

So welcome to the incredible world of nonverbal communication; we're studying one of the most interesting forms of human communication. But before we go further and get more specific, let's back up and define some basic terms. Just what is communication? Communication has been defined in many ways—in fact, one research team counted more than 126 published definitions (Dance & Larson, 1972). Here's the definition we prefer: **Communication** is the process of acting on information (Beebe, Beebe, & Ivy, 2007). A person says or does something, causing others to say or do something in response. From this definition, we can see that communication isn't unique to human beings. If we call out to our dog using its name, it's likely that the dog will perk up, look at us, start wagging its tail, and come over to us. The dog responds to our verbal and nonverbal actions, so communication has occurred. While human-to-dog communication is interesting, it isn't the focus of our study; we're more interested in human-to-human communication.

**Human communication** can be defined as the process of making sense out of the world and sharing that sense with others by creating meaning through the use of verbal and nonverbal messages (Beebe, Beebe, & Ivy, 2007). As human beings, we're driven to make sense out of the world; communication helps us do that. But, unless you're a hermit and completely cut off from the rest of civilization, that's not enough. We're also driven to share our sense of the world with others and receive their responses, so that we repeat the process and are even better equipped to make sense out of our world, share that sense again with others, and so forth. When we share our sense of the world with others, we **encode** our messages with verbal and nonverbal cues, to help others understand what we mean. When the receivers of our messages respond or **decode** our message, we find out if an exchange of meaning has successfully transpired. In one sense, this exchange of message and response is a co-creation of meaning, in that both parties play a role in co-creating a meaningful exchange. While the person initiating the exchange (the sender) can't control how the listener (or receiver) interprets the message, the goal is for the listener to understand the meaning of the message as the sender intended it.

So what are verbal communication and nonverbal communication, and how do they function in this exchange we've just described? **Verbal communication** is the words we choose to use, and, on some occasions, the non-words we use (like "um," "uh-huh," and other vocalizations that aren't really words, but are interpreted as words). Very simply put, **nonverbal communication** includes all those ways we communicate without words. A fancier definition is this: Nonverbal communication is communication other than written or spoken language that creates meaning for someone (Beebe, Beebe, & Ivy, 2007). To make it more complicated, there is one important exception to this definition, which pertains to persons who are deaf. When hearing persons watch deaf persons sign to each other, the signs they use look like nonverbal gestures, but to deaf persons they are actually language—either individual words or phrases—that have direct meanings for receivers of such signs (Fox, 2007). Sign language is verbal communication in exchanges with persons who are deaf.

What kinds of behaviors are included in what we term nonverbal communication? Those behaviors are the focus of this book, but for now, think about this: Our walk, stance, posture, and footsteps are a form of nonverbal communication. What we wear and how we look, move, and gesture, as well as the facial and eye expressions we make, are all included in this fascinating topic we're studying. At what distance do

*Sign language appears as nonverbal communication to people who can hear, but to people who are deaf, signs—and their corresponding body positions and facial expressions—are verbal communication.*

## REMEMBER 1.1

### Basic Terminology in the Study of Nonverbal Communication

| | |
|---|---|
| **Communication:** | Process of acting on information. |
| **Human Communication:** | Process of making sense out of the world and sharing that sense with others by creating meaning. |
| **Encoding:** | Sending verbal and nonverbal cues to help others understand what we mean. |
| **Decoding:** | Receiving and interpreting verbal and nonverbal cues to understand what another person means. |
| **Verbal Communication:** | Words you choose to use. |
| **Nonverbal Communication:** | Communication other than written or spoken language that creates meaning for someone. |

we prefer to stand when talking to people? Our use of space is a form of nonverbal expression, as is the environment we create for ourselves and protect, and the environments we enter into. When we call a close friend on our cell phone, how does he or she know it's us? The sound of our voice—not the words we use—has nonverbal elements related to pitch, rate, volume, and so forth, that become recognizable to those with whom we come into frequent contact. When a friend needs a hug, our touch sends a powerful nonverbal message. All of these behaviors will be studied in depth in this book so that you will have a greater understanding of the role nonverbal communication plays in human interaction.

## ■ NONVERBAL COMMUNICATION WITHIN A LARGER FRAMEWORK

Before going into more detail about the nature of nonverbal communication, we want to situate this topic of study within a larger framework of human communication. Our reason for doing so is this: We believe in five principles that provide the foundation for effective communication. There may be more than five, but these are the ones we believe are most central to human beings' ability to communicate successfully in the world. Our understanding of the nuances of nonverbal communication will be enhanced if we can clearly see how nonverbal communication skill fits into a broader base of communication ability. Our sister book, *Communication: Principles for a Lifetime*, written by Steven Beebe, Sue Beebe, and Diana Ivy (co-author on this nonverbal communication textbook), introduces the five principles and describes how they operate together rather than independently to form the basis of the fundamental processes that enhance communication effectiveness. With permission of these authors, we provide their model of communication principles below.

**FIGURE 1.1  Communication Principles for a Lifetime**

*Source:* Figure reproduced with permission of: Beebe, S. A., Beebe, S. J., & Ivy, D. K. (2007). *Communication: Principles for a lifetime* (3rd ed.). Boston: Allyn & Bacon.

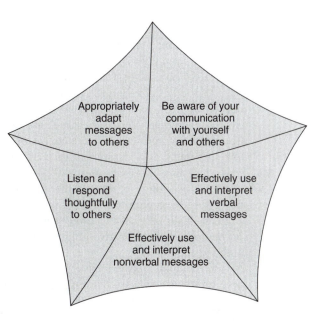

Moving around the model clockwise, Principle 1 is: *Be aware of your communication with yourself and others.* Effective communicators are "present" in the act of communicating, meaning that we develop a keen awareness of ourselves and how we verbally and nonverbally communicate, so as to better understand how we function with others. If we're unaware of how we come across to other people, how can we understand their reactions to us? It takes courage to become more self-aware, especially nonverbally; we must challenge ourselves to be open to feedback from others, even when they make us aware of things that aren't so comfortable.

The second part within this awareness principle is to improve our ability to "catch a clue," meaning that we need to hone our awareness of others' verbal and nonverbal communication. We may already be people watchers, but if we really want to improve we need to take people watching to a whole other level, because we don't communicate in a vacuum, but in a social context. Think of the typical party scene. You go to a party with some friends; you aren't with a date, so you scope the room and notice someone incredibly attractive—someone you'd really like to meet and talk with. But you want to observe the person first before you meet her or him. As you're observing the person, are there any changes in how you look or behave? For many of us, when we're physically attracted, we may feel our heart beating faster, we may turn red in the face and find it hard to make eye contact with the person—or the reverse, find it hard to take our eyes off the person! Do you know what you look like and how you sound when you're attracted to someone? This is what we mean about becoming more aware of yourself as a nonverbal communicator. At the party, the attractive person notices your attention and becomes more aware of you and how you're interacting with people. You notice the person noticing you, then you both notice each other noticing each other—well, you get the picture. All of this "noticing" relates to

Principle 1 of becoming more aware of yourself and others as communicators. Developing your perceptive powers can greatly enhance your communication ability, before you even say a single word.

This takes us to Communication Principle 2 for a Lifetime: *Effectively use and interpret verbal messages.* As we become more aware of ourselves and others, we want to use every tool at our command to communicate effectively and impressively with other people. Verbal messages are created through the tool of language, and the effective communicator selects his or her words wisely. Effective communication also involves accurate interpretations of others' verbal messages because, as we said earlier, interactants must co-create meaning for each other. They must share the meanings of the words they exchange or communication will not be successful. So as communicators, we need to work to make as effective use of our language skills as possible (and work to improve them), while at the same time sharpening our interpretive abilities so that we interpret others' messages as they intended them.

Communication Principle 3 is one you should recognize easily by now—it's the topic we're currently studying: *Effectively use and interpret nonverbal messages.* We believe nonverbal communication skills are so essential to everyday functioning—to personal, relational, and professional success—that we've elevated them for inclusion as one of the five key principles for a lifetime. Do you know people who just can't seem to catch a clue and realize what's happening in a given situation? Most likely, people are unaware of how nonverbal cues function in human interaction. Throughout this book, we share examples in which nonverbal cues are ignored or poorly conveyed, as a means of drawing a contrast with effective nonverbal skill and illustrating the importance of nonverbal awareness.

In the Communication Principles for a Lifetime model, Principle 4 is: *Listen and respond thoughtfully to others.* When students ask us what we believe are the most important communication skills someone can develop, we invariably respond with the five principles for a lifetime. But if pressed to be concise, we highlight these two: nonverbal communication sensitivity toward the self and others; and listening and responding skills. Common sense or past experience might tell you that developing verbal skill is the most important thing, but we believe that common sense is wrong in this case. In our view, the best test of a communicator is how well she or he processes nonverbal information and listens and responds to other people. It's not what we put out in the world that matters most, in terms of interacting with others; it's how we *respond* to other people that separates good communicators from not so good, and merely good communicators from great ones.

The final Communication Principle for a Lifetime, Principle 5, is: *Appropriately adapt messages to others.* It does us little good to process verbal and nonverbal communication—both what we communicate and what we receive from others—if the information isn't put to some kind of use. Back to that party: What if we observe that the person we're attracted to is in the midst of a group of people, but is doing more listening than talking? What if the opposite is going on—the person is the center of attention, talking the most and making everyone laugh? What does that tell us? The person's nonverbal behavior tells volumes, although multiple interpretations of any person's actions exist. How would a savvy communicator react to this situation? Is it more likely that we'll meet the attractive person who's quiet or who's the center of attention in the middle of a group of people? Should we go over and join the group, or wait for a more opportune moment to meet the person and start a conversation? The answers to these questions involve our adaptive powers: our ability to measure or read a situation, assess the verbal and nonverbal communication clues inherent in the situation, and adjust our behavior accordingly for the best possible outcome. What we just described is a tall order. It's not easy to adapt successfully, but it's through our adaptation mistakes and triumphs that we learn, grow, and become more effective communicators.

We trust that the five Communication Principles for a Lifetime provide a framework for studying communication and for working on and improving our abilities. While we explore Principle 3 in depth in this book, it's important to remember where nonverbal skills fall in the general scheme of things—how nonverbal ability doesn't exist independently of other skills that enhance our profile as a communicator. Now that we have situated nonverbal communication within a greater framework, let's explore four reasons for focusing intense attention on the nonverbal realm.

## WHY STUDY NONVERBAL COMMUNICATION?

While it's important, as we stressed earlier, to hone our nonverbal sending and receiving skills, it's also important to realize that we simply cannot be perfect at these tasks. Sometimes students take a nonverbal communication course, like the one you're taking, and assume that they've somehow become completely aware of their own behavior, as well as perfect or near-perfect interpreters of others' behavior. It's unwise and inappropriate to assume that we can become all-knowing or infallible judges of others' nonverbal cues, because human beings are unique, complicated, and ever-changing creatures. What's important is for us to deepen our understanding of nonverbal communication, sharpen our powers of observation, and develop greater skill in interpreting meanings behind our own and others' nonverbal actions. But we must also remain keenly aware of the idiosyncratic, complex nature of nonverbal communication. We all hope to "catch more clues," but we should also avoid making the mistake of believing that we can now magically read people, that our interpretations are always correct. If you aren't fully convinced at this point that nonverbal communication is an important topic to explore, let us provide four explicit reasons for studying this topic.

### Nonverbal Messages Communicate Feelings and Attitudes

If you were really happy and excited about something, how would other people know? Would they know from the words you say or the fact that you're shouting and talking a mile a minute? When you're mad, do you look and act differently than when you're upbeat? Of course you do, unless you have an extremely well-developed poker face. Videotapes or pictures of yourself in different moods can be quite revealing, because your face, body, and voice communicate volumes about what's going on inside of you.

*Nonverbal communication, such as eye contact, facial expressions, and body positions, reveals our emotions and attitudes.*

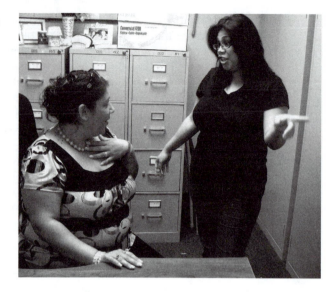

Nonverbal communication is a primary tool for conveying our feelings and attitudes and for detecting the emotional states of others (Argyle, 1988). As one expert in nonverbal research, Albert Mehrabian (1972, 1981) concluded, the most significant source of emotional information is the face, which can channel as much as 55 percent of the meaning of a message. Vocal cues such as pitch, volume, and intensity communicate another 38 percent of the emotional meaning. Thus, approximately 93 percent of how we feel is communicated nonverbally; as little as 7 percent of our emotion is communicated through the words we choose to use. Just realizing those percentages and what they mean is powerful. If we struggle to understand the emotional states of other people (particularly those persons who are really close to us or especially important), we should pay more attention to nonverbal than verbal cues.

## Nonverbal Messages Are More Believable Than Verbal Ones

You're waiting in a reception area to go into the boss's office for a job interview; you really want the job. You're dressed up in an outfit that no doubt makes you uncomfortable, but that gives you the requisite "power look," and are probably sweating a bit, no matter the temperature in the room. You fidget and shift positions in your chair, check for the hundredth time to make sure your resumé is firmly planted in your portfolio, and make endless glances up at the clock on the wall. The receptionist notices your behavior and, in an effort to make small talk and ease the situation, he or she says, "There's no reason to be nervous." You reply, "Oh, I'm not nervous at all. I'm really looking forward to this opportunity." Try as you might to look and sound convincing, do you think the receptionist will believe you?

If the receptionist is a savvy nonverbal communicator, she or he will ignore your verbal protestations, pay attention to your nonverbal cues, and determine, correctly so, that you are nervous about the interview. This example illustrates the fact that nonverbal cues carry the truer weight of a given message than verbal communication, a version of the old adage "actions speak louder than words." Nonverbal communication is both intentional and unintentional, whereas verbal communication is intentional. What we mean by this is that we choose language, even if that choice is accomplished in a split second in our brain. But we may not always choose our nonverbal actions; some actions are innate—they just happen, often leaving us wishing that they didn't happen. For example, most people who blush really wish they didn't, but there's nothing they can do about it once it starts. Perhaps some of you men reading this book may remember a painful experience in middle school, when you wanted to impress a certain someone. When you finally got up the gumption to talk to the person, your voice cracked, going from low to high in an awful instant, no doubt to choruses of laughter from friends nearby. Let's face it: Some things are simply out of our control, and some nonverbal behaviors are no exception. But some forms of nonverbal behavior *are* within our control (like choosing to offer a certain middle-finger gesture to someone who cuts us off in traffic). Nonverbal communication is important to study because, when verbal and nonverbal information contradict, as they often do, the wisest thing to do is to attend to and believe the nonverbal. We shouldn't be distracted by what a person says in such a situation, because the truer message lies in the nonverbal behavior. The more we become aware of this aspect, the more effective communicators we will become.

## What Would *You* Do?

Kelly's had a really rough and very long day; she's finally driving home from classes at the university. All she wants to do is take a hot bath and hit the sheets, but the driver in the car in front of her seems to be really taking his time. He's going about 10 miles *under* the speed limit; Kelly can't get around him because of another car in the lane next to her, so she's frustrated. When she finally gets a break in the traffic, she angrily wheels out of her lane to pass the slow car in front of her. As she gets even with the car, she yells at the driver and gives him the "middle finger salute." Just as her finger is in the air, she realizes that the driver of the car is one of her professors. He looks over, recognizes her, and glares at her. If you were in this situation, *what would you do?*

Would you slow down, get even with your professor's car, and make some kind of signal like "I'm sorry" or laugh like it was all one big joke? Would you speed away, to try to put as much distance between you and your professor and to distance yourself from an embarrassing situation? The next time you saw the professor in class, would you say something or would you remain silent, hoping that the professor didn't recognize you in the car? Would you try to meet the professor during office hours to try to explain your behavior, or would that be drawing undue attention to an already awkward situation?

## Nonverbal Messages Are Critical to Successful Relationships

Ray Birdwhistell is another name you need to know, because, like Albert Mehrabian, he produced fascinating research on nonverbal communication in the early years of its study. Birdwhistell, in his groundbreaking book *Kinesics and Context* (1970), contended that as much as 65 percent of the way human beings convey meaning in our messages is through nonverbal channels. This translates into only about 35 percent of how we get our message across being accomplished through our use of language. A good illustration of how this operates is when we find ourselves attempting to communicate with someone who doesn't speak our language. We become very aware of the importance of nonverbal channels in these situations; we're likely to slow down the pronunciation of our words and use more volume—even though saying words more loudly and slowly won't make us any more intelligible if the person doesn't speak our language! We're also likely to exaggerate head nods and arm and hand gestures, which we hope will translate into some form of meaning for the listener. In these situations, the 65 percent figure is likely to go much higher, as we rely heavily on nonverbal cues to get our message across.

But in situations in which communicators share the same language, nonverbal cues still play a huge role in making impressions on others, which underlies the formation of relationships. In fact, research suggests that we make judgments about other people very quickly, based on nonverbal information (Bert & Piner, 1989). We may decide whether a date is going to be pleasant or dull during the first 30 seconds of meeting our date, before he or she has had time to utter more than "hello." Nonverbal cues are important not only in the early stages of relationships, but also as we maintain, deepen, and sometimes terminate those relationships. The more intimate the relationship, the more we use and understand the nonverbal cues of our partners. Long-married couples often spend less time verbalizing their feelings and emotions to each other than they did when they were first dating; each learns to interpret the other's subtle nonverbal cues. If a spouse is silent during dinner, the other spouse may deduce that the day was a tough one and decide to give the person a lot of space. In fact, all of us are more likely to use nonverbal cues to convey negative messages than to announce our explicit dislike of something or someone (Burgoon, Stern, & Dillman, 1995). We also use nonverbal cues to signal changes in the level of satisfaction with a relationship. When we want to cool things off, we may start using a less vibrant tone of voice and cut back on eye contact and physical contact with our partner; when we want to heat things up, we likely do the opposite (Guerrero & Floyd, 2006).

## Nonverbal Messages Serve Various Functions

Nonverbal cues can work independently or in tandem with verbal language, to convey meaning. First, nonverbal cues can *substitute* for verbal messages. You go to a crowded concession stand at a ballgame; the server can't hear you over the roar of the crowd, so instead of shouting your order for two sodas, you put up two fingers in the air and point to the soda machine to signal what you want. Nonverbal cues function as substitutes for verbal messages.

*How might these guys' gestures and facial expressions complement or extend their words?*

We often use nonverbal actions in connection with words, to *complement* our communication or to clarify or extend the meaning of our words. This complementary function allows us to convey more information, leading to a more accurate interpretation by receivers of our communication (McNeill, 2000). At the concession stand, if you shout your order while holding up two fingers and pointing to the soda machine, the gestures complement the verbal message to make you more understandable to the server. Complementary cues also help color our expressed emotions and attitudes. For example, a long, heavy sigh may reveal how tired or bored we are. The length of a hug while we tell someone we're sorry in a time of great sadness can convey the depth of the emotion we're feeling.

On occasion, our nonverbal cues *contradict* rather than complement our verbal cues. The classic example is a person who has a frowny expression on her or his face, whose arms are crossed defensively across the body, who won't make eye contact and keeps a distance from us, but if asked if he or she is mad, will reply "No; I'm not mad." The body is shouting "I'm mad," but the verbal message is just the opposite. (Like we said earlier, when the verbal and the nonverbal contradict, the wiser approach is to believe the nonverbal.)

Nonverbal behaviors may also serve a *repeating* function. Say you're back at that same concession stand, ordering yet another two sodas. You may shout your order the first time, but upon seeing that the server couldn't hear you, you put up two fingers and point to the soda machine. In this example, you use verbal communication first, followed by a nonverbal signal that repeats the message, thus clarifying the communication that is exchanged.

One of the more fascinating functions of nonverbal communication is its ability to *regulate* conversation. Most conversations occur in a series of turns at talk by the interactants, but just how do we signal we want a turn? Such nonverbal cues as forward body lean, making or breaking eye contact, raised eyebrows, an intake of breath, the utterance of the first few sounds in a word as we try to interrupt or signal that we want to talk, the "uh-huhs" and "um-hms" that we murmur in response to someone

### REMEMBER 1.2

#### Why Study Nonverbal Communication?

- Nonverbal communication is a primary means of communicating feelings and attitudes.
- Nonverbal messages are usually more believable than verbal messages.
- Nonverbal communication is critical in the initiation, development, and sometimes termination of relationships.
- Nonverbal messages can substitute for, complement, contradict, repeat, regulate, and accent verbal messages.

else's communication, raising our hand in a more formal or professional setting—all of these behaviors serve to regulate the flow of conversation (Ekman, 1965).

Finally, nonverbal behaviors often *accent* or provide emphasis for a verbal message. At the loud concession stand, it may take you awhile to get the attention of a server, so you may find yourself shouting your order and waving two fingers in the air so as to get attention and service. Good public speakers learn how to accent their remarks with nonverbal cues that reinforce and add intensity to certain messages in the minds of listeners.

## ■ CONTRASTING VERBAL AND NONVERBAL COMMUNICATION

Verbal and nonverbal communication can be distinguished by several factors. First, verbal communication is *discontinuous*, whereas nonverbal communication is *continuous*. While some people may talk a blue streak, making you think that their verbal communication is continuous, talk actually occurs in a stop-start fashion. However, nonverbal communication occurs continuously; it precedes verbal communication, accompanies it, and continues long after conversations are over. Take your average, benign greeting: You see someone coming your way on a sidewalk and recognize the person as someone you know on campus. As you near, you make eye contact and maybe raise a hand in a friendly waving gesture. Coming within hearing range of one another, you each may say a quick "hello," sustain the eye contact, turn toward each other, pass each other, and then walk away. Nonverbal communication is present throughout this whole exchange, but the verbal exchange was only two words.

A second contrast is this: Verbal communication employs the use of a *language*, with grammar, rules, and syntax (patterns of construction). In school, we studied the proper use of language and rules to follow that make for the clear, appropriate construction of verbal messages. Nonverbal communication is messier than that. Much as people have conducted studies to determine a sort of nonverbal grammar and syntax and to categorize its use into discreet, recognizable, and consistent patterns, such efforts have failed to receive wide support (Birdwhistell, 1970; Dittmann, 1977). Nonverbal communication is simply too complex, too culture- and context-specific, and too idiosyncratic to form into some kind of language.

One of the more interesting efforts to make nonverbal communication into a form of language was contributed by Julius Fast, who wrote the popular book *Body Language* in 1970. Fast contended that certain body gestures, movements, and facial expressions had directly translatable meanings—in all situations, for all persons, across time. If you were savvy and observant enough, you could quickly and easily interpret the meanings of certain nonverbal behaviors. For example, his book instructed men that if a woman was sitting near them with her legs crossed and if she pumped her foot up and down, that meant she was attracted to them. This seems overly simplistic and somewhat ridiculous for our current day and time, but Fast's body language approach caught on within popular culture in the 1970s. His book is still in print today and people still talk about reading someone's "body language."

So let's get something straight right here and now: There is no "language of the body." As we've said, nonverbal communication is too complex, personal, cultural, and contextual to be so easily translated into some sort of language. What if you were standing outside a classroom, waiting to go in for a class, and you had your arms crossed across your chest? What might be the range of interpretations of such a stance? Some observers might think that you were angry and hostile; others might deem you aloof and withdrawn, as though your arms were protecting your body or shielding you from interaction (or invasion) by other people. Some might think nothing of it, believing that you were just comfortable standing that way. Still others might think you were just physically cold; we often cross our arms in front of us when we're cold or we get the shivers. For the women, yet another explanation might be that your bra strap just broke and you're trying to hold things up and together (if you know what we mean). In just this one simple example of a single action, we generated five possible interpretations for the same behavior. So believing that every time we see a nonverbal signal it automatically translates into some direct meaning is just folly.

Another distinction between verbal and nonverbal communication is that language has to be *learned*, while nonverbal behavior is both *learned* and *innate*. Babies babble as they learn to use their vocal mechanisms, but it is a deliberative process to learn a language. A good deal of nonverbal behavior is innate or genetically hard-wired, as evidenced in studies of children who are sensory deprived, meaning that they do not have use of one or more senses. In one line of research, children both blind and deaf responded to stimuli with facial expressions similar to sighted and hearing children. These sensory-deprived children produced patterns of movement, as well as facial expressions related to such emotions as sadness, happiness, anger, disgust, surprise, and fear, similarly to their sighted and hearing counterparts in the studies (Eibl-Eibesfeldt, 1973, 1975; Galati, Miceli, & Sini, 2001; Galati, Scherer, & Ricci-Bitti, 1997; Galati, Sini, Schmidt, & Tinti, 2003). Further evidence favoring the nature part of the nature-nurture debate comes from studies of twins who were separated at birth and raised in different environments, yet many of their nonverbal behaviors, such as walk, posture, gestures, and vocal attributes, such as pitch and tone, were strikingly similar (Bouchard, 1984, 1987; Farber, 1981; Segal, 1999).

## REMEMBER 1.3

### Verbal Communication Versus Nonverbal Communication

| Verbal Communication | Nonverbal Communication |
| --- | --- |
| Discontinuous | Continuous |
| Linguistic | Nonlinguistic |
| Learned | Innate and Learned |
| Left-brain | Right-brain |

However, notice that we say that nonverbal communication is both learned *and* innate, because a good deal of how we communicate nonverbally is learned behavior. Certain gestures, touches, facial expressions, and vocalizations are learned through our culture and upbringing. For example, adults in the 1970s will likely never forget that the index and middle finger, when extended upward together, signal "V is for Victory," mainly because that gesture is so readily associated with former President Richard Nixon. If you're a University of Texas fan, you learn the "hook 'em horns" hand gesture very quickly, but if you're a University of Oklahoma or a Texas A&M fan, you learn equally as quickly to turn that "hook 'em" gesture upside down. A couple of decades ago, most people wouldn't dismiss someone else's communication with the response of "whatever." Prevalent use of this response at the turn of the twenty-first century has taught us to add a vocally higher pitch on the "what" part and a lower pitch on the "ever" part, so that the appropriate sarcasm or tone of dismissal is conveyed. You probably didn't come out of your mother's womb saying "WHATever," in the way that many of our college students say it now. It's interesting to determine which nonverbal expressions we believe are instinctive or innate, versus which ones we've learned over our lifetimes.

A final distinction between verbal and nonverbal is that verbal communication is believed to be processed primarily in the *left hemisphere* of the brain, in which logical, abstract, and analytical thinking reside—thinking that is particularly helpful for the learning and use of language. Nonverbal communication is processed primarily in the *right brain hemisphere*, which tends to be the area in which artistic or creative abilities reside and emotional or affective information is processed (Buck & Van Lear, 2002). These right-brain abilities are particularly well suited to the production and interpretation of nonverbal cues (Andersen, Garrison, & Andersen, 1979; Bowers, Bauer, & Heilman, 1993).

## ■ THE NATURE OF NONVERBAL COMMUNICATION

Many times we've wished we had a dictionary of nonverbal behavior, so that we could simply turn to a page, look up a certain behavior, and find a description of exactly what that behavior means. Such a reference book works well for verbal communication, but no such book exists to help decode nonverbal cues. Below we provide four challenges inherent in the interpretation of nonverbal communication.

## Nonverbal Communication Is Culture-Bound

Is there such a thing as a culturally universal nonverbal cue? Research suggests that humans from every culture smile when they are happy and frown when they are unhappy (Argyle, 1988). They also all tend to raise or flash their eyebrows when meeting or greeting others, and young children in many cultures wave to signal they want their parents, raise their arms to be picked up, and suck their thumbs for comfort (Collett, 1984; Eibl-Eibesfeldt, 1972; Ekman & Friesen, 1971; Hall, 1959, 1966; Shuter, 1976). This body of evidence tells us that some commonality underlies the conveyance of human emotion, yet each culture develops unique ways of displaying and interpreting the expression of emotion.

So this is what we mean when we say that nonverbal communication is culture-bound. It is imperative to take cultural factors into account when deciding which culturally appropriate cues we wish to exhibit and when attempting to interpret the nonverbal cues of members of other cultural groups. As intercultural communication scholars Richard Porter and Larry Samovar (2007) explain, one culture's friendly or polite action may be another culture's obscene gesture. For example, during his second inaugural parade, President George W. Bush displayed the "hook 'em horns" gesture to salute members of the University of Texas marching band as they passed by his stand. According to the Associated Press, a Norwegian newspaper expressed outrage over the gesture, since it is considered an insult or a sign of the devil in Norse culture. In sign language used by and for persons who are deaf, the gesture translates into "bullshit." In Mediterranean countries, the gesture implies that a man is the victim of an unfaithful wife. In Russia, it is considered a symbol for newly rich, arrogant, and poorly educated Russians; in many European countries it serves to ward off the "evil eye"; and in some African nations, it's used to put a hex or curse on another person (Douglas, 2005). Concerns about potential international gaffes led Southern Methodist University to publish a pocket-size guide for its students studying abroad. Tips include sticking out your tongue as a way of saying hello in Tibet; taking your hands out of your pockets when talking with someone in Belgium; and avoiding touching someone's head in Indonesia, where such an action would be considered a serious insult (Adams, 2003; Watch your tongue, 2004).

## Nonverbal Communication Is Rule-Governed

When we say that nonverbal communication is rule-governed, it sounds like there are a lot of do's and don'ts involved, which is a typical connotation for the term *rule*. But what we mean is that expectations or assumptions about appropriate nonverbal behavior are always operating, which most people learn through their culture. (We say *most* because some people raised in the same culture as we are may not have learned the same set of rules.) We may be aware of some of our own rules about nonverbal behavior, but many of these rules we're unaware of *until they are violated*. For example, watch young children who are in the process of learning these culturally rooted rules of behavior.

We may be standing in line at the grocery store and feel something brush past our legs; we look down and realize that a young child has made a bee line for the candy display. She or he didn't care what was in the way (our body); the point was to make the straightest, fastest approach to that candy as possible before being detected by a parent. Imagine the absurdity of an adult doing the same behavior—bumping into us around our kneecaps, in an effort to retrieve some highly desirable candy. Children go through a process, in each culture around the world, of learning rules about appropriate touch and distances to keep from other people, among other lessons. The point about rules in this example is that we may not have known that we have a rule operating about stranger intrusion into our personal space and stranger touch until those rules are violated and we suddenly think, "Hey, something's wrong here."

## SPOTLIGHT on Research

Greeting rituals are fascinating to examine, because they reveal so much about a culture and its people. One greeting ritual that has received attention in nonverbal communication research is the handshake. The research team of Chaplin, Phillips, Brown, Clanton, and Stein (2000) determined characteristics of handshakes, such as strength, vigor, completeness of grip, and duration, that contribute to what they term a *handshake index*. For both women and men, the high index or most positive handshake was strong (but not so strong as to cut off the blood supply), vigorous (containing an appropriate amount of energy), adequate in duration (not too brief or too long), and complete in its grip (a full grip with palms touching).

Next the researchers studied judgments made about people with a high versus a low handshake index. They found that the higher a person's handshake index, the more favorable impression the person made, plus the more extroverted, open to experience, and less shy the person was perceived to be. In addition to these traits, women with high handshake indexes were also perceived to be highly agreeable. Thus, the performance of even a simple symbolic, culturally rooted greeting ritual can have a definite impact on the perceptions people form.

While times have certainly changed, some sex-typed behavior and attitudes still exist regarding the simple handshake ritual. Many female college students admit to being reluctant to extend their hand upon meeting people in social settings, stemming from the belief that handshaking in non-professional settings is a male-only behavior. Rarely does handshaking occur when young women meet other young women or young men socially, unless someone makes a concentrated effort to enact the ritual. (This pattern can be exhibited by women and men from all age groups; we just notice it most often since we work with primarily traditionally aged students on a daily basis.) Most often when men meet each other socially, a handshake is exchanged, but only on rare occasions will a man extend a handshake to a woman in a social setting. What this means is that college students have few opportunities to practice their handshakes before being in a professional setting, where a great deal can be on the line.

As Chaplin and his colleagues' cutting edge research shows, a great deal of information is conveyed through the ritual of the handshake. Sometimes jobs are lost in the first few seconds of an interview, simply because an applicant has a poor handshake. Remember

*(continued)*

**SPOTLIGHT** on **Research** *(continued)*

that the element of trustworthiness—a key impression to give to another person—resides in palm-to-palm contact. The most intimate part of the hand is the palm, so we give of ourselves openly and confidently when we touch palms with someone. If you've ever received a cupped-palm handshake, it can make you feel empty and leave you with feelings of mistrust for the other person. Likewise, a less-than-full grip conveys all sorts of negative messages, the primary one being a lack of respect. Weak, limp handshakes are still prevalent in U.S. culture, much as we'd like to think things have changed. When a man gives a woman a half-handed, weak handshake, it can convey an attitude of believing the woman to be inferior or such a frail flower that she couldn't possibly withstand having her little hand squeezed. This nonverbal greeting, when poorly executed, can communicate condescension and disrespect. We often see college women, in particular, give weak, "wet fish" handshakes to their peers as well as to superiors, like professors and potential employers, and the negative messages conveyed are just as strong.

So let's get this straight: There's nothing inherently feminine in a weak handshake, nor inherently masculine in a strong one. Women and men alike should learn to give a strong, full-handed, palm-to-palm handshake to anyone they meet, regardless of a person's sex, in both professional and social settings, because this ritual speaks volumes about how much we respect ourselves and others. A lack of confidence will definitely manifest itself in a handshake, so that's why it's important to practice what research tells us works best. Practice shaking hands with many different people, and ask them for their honest feedback about what your handshake conveys. You may find that you have some work to do in this area.

Do you want to know more about this study? If so, read: Chaplin, W. E., Phillips, J. B., Brown, J. D., Clanton, N. R., & Stein, J. L. (2000). Handshaking, gender, personality, and first impressions. *Journal of Personality and Social Psychology, 79,* 110–117.

Here's another example that resonates with people these days: Have you been annoyed lately when you pay your hard-earned money to have a night out at a movie theatre, only to be treated to people answering *and carrying on whole conversations* on their cell phones? Or how about those people who talk at full volume to their companions in the theatre, as if they were at home in their living rooms watching TV? Perhaps until this happens to you, you may be unaware that you have a rule operating about appropriate vocalizations in a movie theatre. This example also illustrates the personal, idiosyncratic nature of nonverbal rules, because a rule about appropriate movie theatre behavior is obviously different for those who believe that talking on a cell phone in a movie theatre is perfectly fine. Rules may be broad and sweeping, like a rule about greeting strangers with a handshake instead of another form of more personal touch, or they may be micro-rules, such as the movie theatre rule that applies primarily to only one context.

One of the most prolific nonverbal communication researchers is Judee Burgoon, who developed a fascinating model for how nonverbal communication functions, termed the **expectancy violations model** (Afifi & Burgoon, 2000; Burgoon, 1978, 1983, 1993, 1995; Burgoon & Hale, 1988). We explore this model in more depth in Chapter 4 on proxemics and territoriality, because that was the original focus of the research, but for now let's see how it helps us better understand the rule-governed nature of nonverbal communication. The model suggests that we develop expectations for appropriate nonverbal behaviors in ourselves and others, based on our cultural backgrounds, personal experiences, and knowledge of those with whom we interact. When those expectations (or rules) are violated, we experience heightened arousal (we become more interested or engaged in what's happening), and the nature of our interpersonal relationship with the other person becomes a critical factor as we attempt to interpret and respond to the situation.

One *Seinfeld* episode depicted a person nicknamed the "close talker," because he got too close for most people's comfort when he talked to them. Most people within a given culture adhere to a widely agree-upon rule or expectation as to appropriate conversational distances. But there are those people who don't seem to catch the cultural clue—those who get too close to our face in casual conversation. Burgoon's model says that we register such a nonverbal violation and react in order to adjust to the circumstances. If the violating person is what Burgoon terms a "rewarding" communicator, meaning the person has high credibility, status, and attractiveness (in personality or physicality), we may view the behavior as less of a rule violation and simply adjust our expectations. We may even reciprocate the behavior. However, if the violator is not a rewarding communicator, we will use reactive nonverbal behaviors in an effort to compensate for or correct the situation. So if an attractive, credible, and high-status person stands too close to us while talking, we may adapt to the situation and not think

*The woman on the right, who's reading, may feel that the woman on the left is violating her rule about personal space.*

negatively of the person. If the person has less attractiveness, credibility, and status, we may back away from the person or move to the side so as to increase the conversational distance, break eye contact, and so forth.

Our tendency in a rules violation situation is to attempt to adapt to or correct the violation by nonverbal means before resorting to verbal communication. We're more likely to back away from a "close talker" than to say to her or him, "Please back up; you're violating my personal space." We all violate nonverbal rules from time to time; it is at those moments when we become acutely aware that rules or expectations of appropriateness have a powerful influence on nonverbal communication.

## Nonverbal Communication Is Ambiguous

Most words are given meaning by people within a culture who speak the same language. But the meaning of a nonverbal message is known only to the person displaying it; the person may not intend for the behavior to have any meaning at all. Thus, one aspect of nonverbal communication that makes it complex, albeit fascinating to study, is that it is ambiguous. We can take a course in nonverbal communication, study the research, and hone our people-observing skills, and still be wrong by a mile when we interpret someone's nonverbal communication. For instance, some people have difficulty expressing their emotions nonverbally. They may have frozen facial expressions or monotone voices. They may be teasing us, but their deadpan expressions lead us to believe that their negative comments are heartfelt. Or what about in those situations where someone attempts to deceive us? If we know the person well and know that he or she tends to look us in the eye most of the time, when she or he avoids eye contact with us, does it necessarily mean deception is occurring, or might there be some other explanation? Often it's a challenge to draw meaningful conclusions about other people's behavior, even if we know them quite well.

One strategy that helps us interpret others' nonverbal cues is called **perception checking,** a strategy we mention at other points in this book. It's wise to observe in detail the nonverbal cues in a given situation, make our own interpretation of those cues, and then do one of two things (or both): (1) Run our interpretation by another observer, to get a second opinion or more input before we draw a conclusion (**indirect perception checking**); and (2) Use a more straightforward approach, in which we ask the people we're observing how they feel or what's going on (**direct perception checking**). Remember earlier warnings about not assuming that our interpretation is necessarily the right one; perception checking can enhance the likelihood of our interpretation being more accurate, but it's not a *guarantee* of accuracy.

## Nonverbal Communication Is Multichanneled

Have you ever tried to watch two or more TV programs at once? Some television sets let us see as many as eight programs simultaneously so that we can keep up with three ball games, two soap operas, the latest news, and our favorite sitcom. Like programs on a multichannel TV, nonverbal cues register on our senses from a variety of sources simultaneously. But just as we can pay close attention to only one program at a time

## REMEMBER 1.4

### The Nature of Nonverbal Communication

**Nonverbal communication is...**

| | |
|---|---|
| **... culturally bound:** | Nonverbal behaviors are generated, taught, and understood within the context of the culture in which they occur. |
| **... rule-governed:** | Expectations or assumptions about appropriate nonverbal behavior are always operating, which most people learn through their culture. |
| **... ambiguous:** | Nonverbal behavior is difficult to interpret accurately because the meanings for different actions vary from person to person. |
| **... multichanneled:** | Nonverbal cues register on our senses from a variety of sources simultaneously, but we can attend to only one nonverbal cue at a time. |

on our multichannel TV, we actually attend to only one nonverbal cue at a time, although we can switch our attention very rapidly. Let's take a deception situation again as an example: You wonder if the person you're dating is lying to you about where she or he was the night before, when you were supposed to spend time together (you got stood up). You look for nonverbal clues of deception, like lack of eye contact; eyes shifting back and forth, rather than focusing on one area or on you; hands on the face, particularly the forehead or eyebrow region; a longer-than-usual amount of time the person takes to respond to your questions; lengthier-than-normal explanations, in response to your questions; and nervous energy being expended through the hands and feet. While we can only process one nonverbal signal at a time, just like we can only focus on one TV program at time, we're aware of the cluster or sum total of the behavior being enacted in front of us. One gesture or vocal cue, in isolation, won't tell the whole story, so we gauge the *package* of behavior to determine the veracity of the person's communication. It boils down to this suggestion: Before we try to interpret the meaning of a single nonverbal behavior, we should look for clusters of corroborating nonverbal cues, in conjunction with verbal behavior, to get the most complete picture possible.

## SUMMARY ■ ■ ■ ■ ■

In this chapter, we provided fundamental information pertinent to the study of nonverbal communication. We defined communication, human communication, including the process of encoding and decoding, and then defined verbal and nonverbal communication. Recall this definition: Nonverbal communication is communication other than written or spoken language that creates meaning for someone.

Next we situated our topic of study within a larger framework of human communication—a framework containing five basic principles. Principle 1, *Be aware of your communication with yourself and others*, means that effective communicators develop a keen awareness of ourselves and how we communicate, so as to better understand how we function in interactions with others. We also enhance our awareness of others' verbal and nonverbal communication. Principle 2, *Effectively use and interpret verbal messages*, means using language effectively and impressively with other people. Principle 3 pertains to the topic we're currently studying: *Effectively use and interpret nonverbal messages*. Nonverbal communication skills are essential to everyday functioning. Principle 4, *Listen and respond thoughtfully to others*, speaks to our belief that the truest test of excellent communicators is how well we process information and listen and respond to other people. Finally, Principle 5 is: *Appropriately adapt messages to others*. Adaptability means our ability to measure or read a situation, assess the verbal and nonverbal communication clues inherent in the situation, and adjust our behavior accordingly for the best possible outcome.

In the next section of this chapter, we provided four reasons for studying nonverbal communication. We described nonverbal communication as a primary means of conveying feelings and attitudes. We examined the believability of nonverbal messages compared to verbal messages, and the role nonverbal communication plays in the initiation, development, and sometimes termination of relationships. Finally, we explored how nonverbal messages can substitute for, complement, contradict, repeat, regulate, and accent verbal messages.

While nonverbal and verbal cues often work together, some differences exist in the two modes of communication. First, verbal is discontinuous, whereas nonverbal is continuous, meaning that nonverbal messages are sent non-stop, whether or not someone is talking. Second, verbal communication involves the use of a language, with its own grammar and patterns; nonverbal is nonlinguistic, meaning that it is too individually and culturally based to be viewed as a language. Third, verbal communication is learned, but nonverbal communication is both learned and innate. Finally, verbal communication is processed primarily in the left hemisphere of the brain, while nonverbal communication is processed primarily in the right hemisphere.

In our final section of this chapter, we discussed the culturally bound nature of nonverbal, meaning that nonverbal behaviors are generated, taught, and understood within the context of the culture in which they occur. Nonverbal is also rule-governed; expectations or assumptions about appropriate nonverbal behavior are always operating, which most people learn through their culture. Nonverbal behavior is also ambiguous, in that it is difficult to interpret nonverbal cues accurately because the meanings for different actions vary from person to person. And finally, nonverbal communication is multichanneled: Nonverbal cues register on our senses from a variety of sources simultaneously, but we can attend to only one nonverbal cue at a time.

We trust that your reading of this introductory chapter has provided an understanding of some of the basic terminology and the nature of our topic under study. In the second chapter of this opening section of the book, we explore in more depth some of the generally recognized categories of nonverbal behavior, and then provide a model of how human beings can endeavor to expand our awareness of nonverbal cues, in ourselves and other people, and use that awareness to improve our nonverbal communication skills so as to enhance our personal and professional lives.

## DISCUSSION STARTERS

1. Review the five Communication Principles for a Lifetime provided in this chapter. Do you believe these are the "right" five principles governing human communication? Can you think of some others?

2. If we did not have nonverbal cues, how would human beings communicate their feelings and attitudes to one another? How would we know where we stand in a relationship without our partner's use of nonverbal cues to communicate emotions?

3. When verbal and nonverbal cues contradict, we've advised you to believe the nonverbal because these behaviors often carry the truer weight of a message. But can you think of a situation in which we should pay more attention to verbal than nonverbal cues? When are our words more important than our actions?

4. Discuss the pros and cons of the "body language" approach to studying nonverbal communication.

5. What are some common nonverbal "goofs" or violations that non-natives frequently make when they travel in the United States? That Americans make when they travel abroad? How do these mistakes reveal the culture-bound nature of nonverbal communication?

## REFERENCES

Adams, E. (2003, November 2). Manners can sink international business dealings. *Corpus Christi Caller Times*, K2.

Afifi, W. A., & Burgoon, J. K. (2000). The impact of violations on uncertainty and the consequences for attractiveness. *Human Communication Research, 26*, 203–233.

Andersen, P. A., Garrison, J. D., & Andersen, J. F. (1979). Implications of a neurological approach for the study of nonverbal communication. *Human Communication Research, 16*, 74–89.

Argyle, M. (1988). *Bodily communication* (2nd ed.). London: Methuen.

Beebe, S. A., Beebe, S. J., & Ivy, D. K. (2007). *Communication: Principles for a lifetime* (3rd ed.). Boston: Allyn & Bacon.

Bert, J. H., & Piner, K. (1989). Social relationships and the lack of social relations. In S. W. Duck and R. C. Silver (Eds.), *Personal relationships and social support*. London: Sage.

Birdwhistell, R. L. (1970). *Kinesics and context*. Philadelphia: University of Pennsylvania Press.

Bouchard, T. J., Jr. (1984). Twins reared apart and together: What they tell us about human diversity. In S. W. Fox (Ed.), *Individuality and determinism*. New York: Plenum.

Bouchard, T. J., Jr. (1987). Diversity, development, and determinism: A report on identical twins reared apart. In M. Amelang (Ed.), *Proceedings of the meetings of the German Psychological Association—1986*, Heidelberg, Germany.

Bowers, D., Bauer, R. M., & Heilman, K. M. (1993). The nonverbal affect lexicon: Theoretical perspectives from neuropsychological studies of affect perception. *Neuropsychology, 7*, 433–444.

Buck, R., & Van Lear, A. (2002). Verbal and nonverbal communication: Distinguishing symbolic, spontaneous, and pseudo-spontaneous nonverbal behavior. *Journal of Communication, 52*, 522–541.

Burgoon, J. K. (1978). A communication model of personal space violations: Explication and an initial test. *Human Communication Research, 4*, 129–142.

Burgoon, J. K. (1983). Nonverbal violations of expectations. In J. M. Weimann and R. P. Harrison (Eds.), *Nonverbal interaction* (pp. 77–111). Beverly Hills, CA: Sage.

Burgoon, J. K. (1993). Interpersonal expectations, expectancy violations, and emotional communication. *Journal of Language and Social Psychology, 12*, 30–48.

Burgoon, J. K. (1995). Cross-cultural and intercultural applications of expectancy violations. In R. L. Wiseman (Ed.), *Intercultural communication theory* (Vol. 19, pp. 194–214). Thousand Oaks, CA: Sage.

Burgoon, J. K., & Hale, J. L. (1988). Nonverbal expectancy violations: Model elaboration and application to immediacy behaviors. *Communication Monographs, 55*, 58–79.

Burgoon, J. K., & Jones, S. B. (1976). Toward a theory of personal space expectations and their violations. *Human Communication Research, 2*, 131–146.

Burgoon, J. K., Stern, L. A., & Dillman, L. (1995). *Interpersonal adaptation: Dyadic interaction patterns.* Cambridge, UK: Cambridge University Press.

Chaplin, W. E., Phillips, J. B., Brown, J. D., Clanton, N. R., & Stein, J. L. (2000). Handshaking, gender, personality, and first impressions. *Journal of Personality and Social Psychology, 79*, 110–117.

Collett, P. (1984). History and study of expressive action. In K. Gergen & M. Gergen (Eds.), *Historical social psychology.* Hillsdale, NJ: Erlbaum.

Dance, F. E. X., & Larson, C. (1972). *Speech communication: Concepts and behavior.* New York: Holt, Rinehart, and Winston.

Dittmann, A. T. (1977). The role of body movement in communication. In A. W. Siegman & S. Feldstein (Eds.), *Nonverbal behavior and communication.* Potomac, MD: Erlbaum.

Douglas, J., Jr. (2005, January 23). Outside Texas, "hook 'em horns" gesture has different and unflattering meanings. *Fort Worth Star Telegram,* 2A.

Eibl-Eibesfeldt, I. (1972). Similarities and differences between cultures in expressive movements. In R. A. Hinde (Ed.), *Nonverbal communication.* Cambridge, UK: Royal Society and Cambridge University Press.

Eibl-Eibesfeldt, I. (1973). The expressive behavior of the deaf-and-blind born. In M. von Cranach & I. Vine (Eds.), *Social communication and movement.* New York: Academic Press.

Eibl-Eibesfeldt, I. (1975). *Ethology: The biology of behavior* (2nd ed.). New York: Holt, Rinehart, & Winston.

Ekman, P. (1965). Communication through nonverbal behavior: A source of information about an interpersonal relationship. In S. S. Tomkins & C. E. Izard (Eds.), *Affect, cognition, and personality.* New York: Springer.

Ekman, P., & Friesen, W. V. (1971). Constants across cultures in the face and emotion. *Journal of Personality and Social Psychology, 17*, 124–129.

Farber, S. L. (1981). *Identical twins reared apart: A reanalysis.* New York: Basic Books.

Fast, J. (1970). *Body language.* New York: M. Evans.

Fox, M. (2007). *Talking hands: What sign language reveals about the mind.* New York: Simon & Schuster.

Galati, D., Miceli, R., & Sini, B. (2001). Judging and coding facial expressions of emotions in congenitally blind children. *International Journal of Behavioral Development, 25*, 268–278.

Galati, D., Scherer, K. R., & Ricci-Bitti, P. E. (1997). Voluntary facial expression of emotion: Comparing congenitally blind with normally sighted encoders. *Journal of Personality and Social Psychology, 73*, 1363–1379.

Galati, D., Sini, B., Schmidt, S., & Tinti, C. (2003). Spontaneous facial expressions in congenitally blind and sighted children aged 8–11. *Journal of Visual Impairment and Blindness, 97*, 418–428.

Guerrero, L. K., & Floyd, K. (2006). *Nonverbal communication in close relationships.* Mahwah, NJ: Erlbaum.

Hall, E. T. (1959). *The silent language.* Garden City, NJ: Doubleday.

Hall, E. T. (1966). *The hidden dimension.* New York: Doubleday.

McNeill, D. (2000). (Ed.). *Language and gesture.* New York: Cambridge University Press.

Mehrabian, A. (1972). *Nonverbal communication.* Chicago: Atherton.

Mehrabian, A. (1981). *Silent messages* (2nd ed.). Belmont, CA: Wadsworth.

Porter, R. E., & Samovar, L. A. (2007). An introduction to intercultural communication. In L. A. Samovar & R. E. Porter (Eds.), *Intercultural communication: A reader* (10th ed.). Belmont, CA: Wadsworth.

Segal, N. L. (1999). *Entwined lives: Twins and what they tell us about human behavior.* New York: Dutton.

Shuter, R. (1976). Proxemics and tactility in Latin America. *Journal of Communication, 26*, 46–55.

Watch your tongue; this isn't Tibet. (2004, October 10). *Fort Worth Star Telegram,* 2A.

# Nonverbal Communication Development

## A Reflexive Approach

## CHAPTER OUTLINE ■ ■ ■ ■ ■ ■

## CHAPTER OBJECTIVES ■ ■ ■ ■ ■ ■

After studying this chapter, you should be able to:

1. Explain the concept of reflexivity.
2. Identify the five phases of the Reflexive Cycle of Nonverbal Communication Development.
3. Describe key elements within each of the five phases.
4. Identify and provide examples of the eight codes of nonverbal communication.
5. Discuss key research findings regarding nonverbal communication sending and receiving ability.
6. Identify, define, and provide examples of Mehrabian's three dimensions for interpreting nonverbal cues.

Danielle has an intriguing dilemma: She's really attracted to a guy in one of her classes, but is unsure of what to do—if anything—about her attraction. And this is no ordinary guy. Felipe is an international student, working on a degree in computer

*Do Danielle and Felipe look like they are attracted to each other? Which nonverbal cues reveal attraction?*

science. He comes from a country in which the customs and language are quite different than that found in the U.S., although Felipe speaks very good English. Danielle's attraction is *major*, such that she's finding it hard to concentrate on what her professor and classmates discuss each day, that is, until Felipe jumps into the class discussion. Then she hangs on every word.

She hasn't told anyone about her attraction, but she wonders: Does Felipe even realize I'm in a class with him? Has he noticed me? Do I act somehow differently because of this attraction I feel? I'm sure I act differently in Felipe's presence because I just *feel* different, but can other people tell that I'm attracted to him? Does it show in my actions or can people hear it in my voice? What do I do if Felipe doesn't make a move? Do I make the first move? What *is* the first move?

If Danielle decides that she doesn't want to pursue the object of her attraction and doesn't want Felipe to know she's attracted to him, she will work to suppress any sign that she likes him, so that he and other people won't detect what she feels. But if she wants Felipe to know she's attracted, she will behave in ways that let her interest be known. What exactly *are* those ways? What are appropriate ways in American culture for a young woman to let a young man (from another cultural background, no less) know she's interested, without seeming too aggressive or, worse, promiscuous?

Attraction to another person is a feeling most of us have experienced in our lifetimes, so Danielle's challenge with Felipe is an example that we'll use in this chapter to help us explore how nonverbal communication operates in human behavior. Using Danielle's situation, we'll work from a model we've developed that enhances our understanding of how people come to know themselves better as communicators, how they change and improve their communicative abilities, how they affect others' communication, and then, how they, in turn, are affected by the process of affecting others. Sound complicated? It really isn't once you "unpack" the model, so let's explore this approach to nonverbal understanding and development.

## ■ THE REFLEXIVE CYCLE OF NONVERBAL COMMUNICATION DEVELOPMENT

Nonverbal communication, as we've said before, is a fascinating and complex area of study; you probably know that by now, since you're taking a course in this subject. But you may be wondering: How can I get a handle on this topic? How can I make sense out of all this information and make it useful for me, so that I get something practical out of it, something that can enhance my relationships and improve my life? Those are the perfect questions to ask.

We believe they're perfect questions because—as self-serving as this sounds—we asked them too, as we began envisioning this book. Our challenge was, first, to sift through the vast amounts of information available on the topic of nonverbal communication and to piece it together so that it formed a coherent structure that would make sense to professors and students of nonverbal communication. Second, we wanted to find a way to deliver that information so that its reception had the potential to deepen people's understanding and improve their lives. In a nutshell, those are the goals of this book.

To accomplish those goals, we began by having a frank discussion—as co-authors and nonverbal teacher-scholars—about the last part of our goal: the improvement of people's lives. We talked about out how people come to learn nonverbal behaviors, how and why they make changes in their behavior along the way, how they perceive others' nonverbal cues and interpret them so as to make sense of what's happening around them, how they use their own nonverbal communication to have an effect on others, and then how they are somehow altered (or perhaps reinforced) as a result of this ongoing process. By having this very grounded, purposeful discussion, your textbook authors devised the model you see in Figure 2.1, which we have termed the Reflexive Cycle of Nonverbal Communication Development. This model is central to your developing a sort of relationship with this topic. We encourage you to embrace the model and make it work for you as you continue to deepen your understanding of how nonverbal communication functions and to improve your nonverbal skills as a communicator.

But before we delve into the model, we offer a caution: We don't intend this textbook to appear on the self-help shelves at your local Barnes and Noble (although we'd be delighted if commercial bookstores carried it!). Granted, we choose to offer a grounded approach, meaning that we believe studying nonverbal communication allows for and encourages practical application and that through such study, people can improve their relationships and their lives. But we believe this book to be way more than a self-help handbook. You first need to deepen and broaden your understanding of the complexities of nonverbal communication by becoming familiar with research on the topic. Once you have more knowledge and a better understanding of how nonverbal behavior operates in human communication, you'll be more equipped

**FIGURE 2.1    Reflexive Cycle of Nonverbal Communication Development**

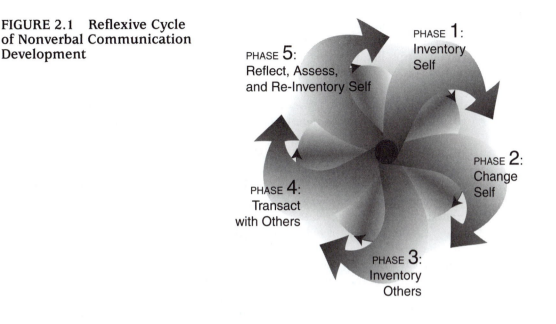

to apply what you've learned, to examine your own nonverbal expression, as well as better prepared to observe and interpret others' nonverbal cues. What we strive for in this book is a balance of theory and practice—an approach that emphasizes skill development based on knowledge and understanding.

In the next few pages, we first examine what is means to be "reflexive," since this property is at the core of the model and is key to your understanding and application of it. Then we explore each phase of the cycle, using Danielle and Felipe's example to help us better understand how the model functions.

## What Does "Reflexive" Mean?

Been to the doctor for a physical lately? If so, your doctor likely banged on your knee cap with one of those rubber mallets to see if you had healthy "reflexes." According to the *Oxford Desk Dictionary and Thesaurus* (1997), a reflex is an action "independent of will, as an automatic response to the stimulation of a nerve" (p. 669). Some nonverbal behaviors are reflexive in that they are automatic responses to stimuli. These behaviors are both innate and learned, but they occur with little or no intentional decision making or forethought. Think about biting down into a lemon that's just been cut in half; does that thought make you cringe? You likely made some sort of facial response (like crinkling the bridge of your nose in revulsion) if you really played out the sensation of biting into that lemon, so your nonverbal response was **reflexive**—accomplished automatically rather than purposefully.

That's the first thing that drew us to viewing nonverbal development as a reflexive cycle, the automatic aspect. Wouldn't it be great if we could learn to produce nonverbal signals and respond to other people with cues that were perfectly appropriate for every circumstance we experience in life? It would be interesting if we could enact those behaviors so seamlessly that it became automatic. For certain, that's an ideal beyond any of our grasps. But if we view it as a goal to work toward, an ideal to approach, realizing that we can never reach perfection, then it becomes an intriguing prospect.

What we describe is a *process* goal, a goal about "becoming," not "arriving." That's why the model is a *cycle*, not a straight line or arrow going upward, indicating that the reflexive process repeats. It's a constant process throughout our lifetimes, as we encounter diverse people and varied situations. Improving our nonverbal effectiveness through study (like you're doing now, taking this course and reading this book), exposure to people and situations, and conscientious intent to enhance our abilities to send nonverbal signals as well as to receive and interpret them from others more accurately, so that we work toward such abilities becoming more automatic or reflexive—that's a practical, encouraging goal that can motivate us over our lifetime.

A second aspect of reflexivity also drew us to this principle as a guiding feature for the model in this book. The dictionary explains that one meaning for the term **reflexive** is "referring back to the subject of a sentence" (p. 669), as in "I, myself, have always wanted to travel to Africa." In this statement, the word "myself" refers back to the subject of the sentence, "I." Note that in the reflexive model, the cycle focuses on the individual. The first part of the title of this text is *The Nonverbal Self.* As we explain each phase of the cycle, you'll see why the self, within a social context, receives so much attention in our exploration of nonverbal communication.

## Phase 1: Inventory Self

Remember Danielle, the student enamored with her classmate, Felipe? One of the first things Danielle was concerned about was this: Does Felipe know that I'm attracted to him? Does it show, to Felipe or other people? These questions reflect the first phase of the Reflexive Cycle—the continuous process of becoming more aware of your own nonverbal communication (see Figure 2.2). We have little hope of improving our communication abilities if we're unaware of the current skills we possess, as well as areas we need to work on. But this becomes a particularly challenging task in the nonverbal realm, because we're unaware of a good deal of our nonverbal communication.

Two of the most prolific scholars in the field of nonverbal communication, whose work we referenced in Chapter 1 and will reference many times throughout this book, are Paul Ekman and Wallace Friesen. Ekman and Friesen (1968) explored the nature of nonverbal communication, characterizing it as behaviors often enacted unconsciously, meaning with little intent. They contended that most people were unaware of the nonverbal cues they produced, thus people's lack of awareness meant that they were unable to make conscious decisions to alter their nonverbal behavior. If we don't realize what we're doing, how can we assess it and possibly change it?

As an example, one of your book authors went to grad school with a student who quickly became tagged the "eye roller," because he rolled his eyes in a "you're so stupid," condescending kind of way after classmates (and sometimes professors) made comments in class. That particular form of nonverbal behavior, at least in U.S. culture, tends to irritate people; let's just say it didn't win the grad student any

FIGURE 2.2    **Reflexive Cycle of Nonverbal Communication Development, Phase 1**

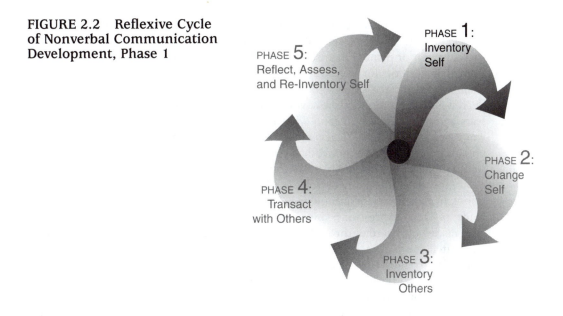

PHASE 5:
Reflect, Assess,
and Re-Inventory Self

PHASE 1:
Inventory
Self

PHASE 2:
Change
Self

PHASE 4:
Transact
with Others

PHASE 3:
Inventory
Others

friends. Finally, after being the recipient of the eye rolling behavior one too many times, one of your book authors asked the student about the behavior, wondering if he realized how it made others feel. The student was actually stunned upon hearing about the eye rolling behavior and the fact that he did it so frequently, typically after classmates' contributions to class discussions. He was completely unaware that he reacted with this particular nonverbal cue, and had to be convinced after several other classmates agreed that, yes, he did roll his eyes often and, yes, it was off-putting. We don't know if he was able to correct this behavior because it was so ingrained in his repertoire, but he was certainly made aware of it and its negative effect on other people.

What we're getting at here is "forewarned is forearmed," meaning that most of us would rather be made aware of how we nonverbally communicate to others than be left in the dark. So the first challenge the Reflexive Cycle poses is to inventory our own nonverbal behavior—to attempt first, on our own, to become more aware of how we communicate without or in conjunction with words.

Our best advice to the student, Danielle, who's attracted to her classmate, Felipe, is to do an honest inventory of her nonverbal behavior, at least as much as she can figure out on her own. During her next class with Felipe, she should make mental notes (or even written ones) of how she's feeling and how she believes she's coming across to others during the class session. She should track such things as feelings of warmth in her skin, meaning that her skin temperature might rise from the activation that feelings of attraction can arouse in us. How about eye contact? Does she look at Felipe at all in class? Does she look at him only when he offers a comment, at times when he's not offering a comment, or does she avoid looking at him altogether, perhaps out of fear that he'll detect her gaze? How close or far away does she sit from where Felipe sits? Research and our own experience has shown that students are very predictable in their choice of seating in a classroom where there is no assigned seating arrangement (Reiss & Rosenfeld, 1980; Roger & Reid, 1982). Once students have spotted a seat or planted themselves next to people they know, they tend not to stray from that position for the entire semester. Does Danielle follow suit, or does she change her seating position to be closer to or farther away from Felipe's chosen seat? Such nonverbal indicators speak volumes about how Danielle feels about Felipe, her fears about her attraction (and what to do, if anything, about it), and how others will react to her if they learn of her attraction. If Danielle really wants to better understand herself as a nonverbal communicator, her first challenge is an honest self-examination or inventory, as we call it.

How does this apply to you? If a friend were to mimic your walk, what would it look like? Is there something particularly striking or memorable about your walk, voice, or facial expressions? Inventory, first, those nonverbal elements that others have made you aware of throughout your life. For a real eye-opener, record yourself and watch the playback; note your posture, your walk, how you tend to sit (e.g., slouched, straight up, legs crossed at the knees or ankles). Record yourself in conversation with someone and note how you use such things as gestures, facial and eye expressions, touch, and tone of voice. Granted, this isn't a "natural" expression of nonverbal behaviors, because the recording is a forced or prescribed event, one

*In Phase 1, Danielle becomes more aware by conducting an inventory of her nonverbal communication.*

for which you know its purpose, but it will give you some insights and a general greater awareness of how you use nonverbal cues to express who you are and to communicate with others.

A second aspect of this inventory activity involves asking others for feedback about your nonverbal behavior. You can make significant changes by conducting your own inventory, but you will no doubt get more useful information if you also ask others for feedback. As a quick example, some people believe that whatever emotion they feel shows up in their facial expressions, like they're an "open book." But when those people ask others about this behavior, they may get different perceptions. Some people may agree that their faces portray their emotions, but others may perceive more of a "poker face." All of this is good information for those of us working on our nonverbal skills. The goal in this phase is to move nonverbal cues more into the realm of the known rather than the unknown, the aware rather than the unaware, so that we operate more consciously as communicators.

As you progress through this course and in the reading of this text, more awareness of your own nonverbal behavior will come to you. But here's our warning to you: Be brave. Being open to learning this much about yourself can be daunting, because there will be bad mixed in with the good. No one is perfect, and you'll no doubt have to confront some behaviors that have developed in you over time that you may not completely understand, much less like and want to continue doing. You may realize, as many of us do, that several of your nonverbal behaviors look and sound a great deal like those of your parents. (This may be horrifying or rather pleasant, depending on your feelings about your parents!) It does take real courage to face yourself honestly, take stock of who you are and how you communicate, be open to others' feedback, even to the point of seeking that feedback, and challenge yourself to make meaningful changes. But realize that awareness is the beginning phase of truly understanding the power of nonverbal communication in our relationships and interactions with others.

## Phase 2: Change Self

The second step in the Reflexive Cycle (see Figure 2.3) is to change our nonverbal communication, based on the inventory we completed in Phase 1. Now when we say change, we also mean to come to a decision about those things that are working well, meaning those behaviors we don't want to change or that don't need alteration. Danielle may discover, once she conducts a purposeful review of her behavior in the class with Felipe, that exactly how she's behaving toward Felipe suits her at this point in time; no changes are needed or comfortable at present. Or she may realize that she's being too obvious about her attraction to Felipe, or perhaps she's being too subtle. Perhaps she asks a trusted classmate if her attraction to Felipe is noticeable, only to learn that no one has noticed any differences in her behavior. Danielle may come to the realization that her subtle behavior is no longer desirable, because it's not going to get Felipe's attention. If Danielle's goal is to get Felipe's attention, to get him to become interested in her, and, ultimately, to test out a relationship with Felipe, then she most likely will have some changes to make in her verbal and nonverbal behavior.

**FIGURE 2.3   Reflexive Cycle
of Nonverbal Communication
Development, Phase 2**

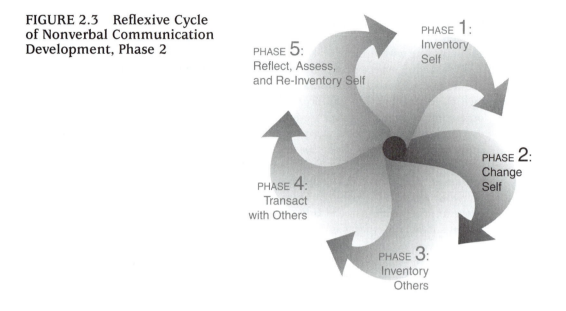

Let's take a simpler, possibly more personal example: Are you one of those people who tends to use a lot of hand gestures in conversation? Do people tell you, "You just couldn't talk at all if your hands were tied together"? By studying nonverbal communication or possibly through common, everyday interaction, you may come to such a revelation and decide that you want to alter this behavior. You inventoried yourself, including putting the feedback from others to good use, and are now working

*In her class with Felipe, Danielle may decide to change her nonverbal communication, depending on a desired outcome she wishes to achieve with Felipe.*

to change something in your nonverbal repertoire. The outcome is that you consciously work to restrict your hand movement when you talk to people.

Just as many of our nonverbal behaviors have taken time to develop—many may have taken a lifetime to develop and become ingrained—it will take time to "un-learn" or alter routine or commonly used behaviors. Some changes in nonverbal communication may pose a great challenge, like our eye-roller friend we described awhile back. Once he was made aware of this particular nonverbal cue and the effect it had on others, he may have made a serious attempt to change this behavior, but how successful he was is unknown. What we're getting at here is that nonverbal change is just downright difficult sometimes. You find out that your voice sounds a certain way (when you thought it sounded altogether different), that you gesture dramatically in conversation, that you shift your weight back and forth nervously when giving a speech, that your voice gets really high in pitch when talking to someone you're attracted to, and so on. These aren't behaviors that can be easily altered overnight, but you can make significant improvements if you put your energy toward real change.

## Phase 3: Inventory Others

Are you a people watcher? Taking a course in nonverbal communication and reading a book on this topic will make you more of a people watcher—at a more microscopic level—than you probably ever deemed possible. In fact, our students in nonverbal communication courses tell us that the course almost "makes them weird," in that they process way more information about people than they did before studying this topic. But they also tell us that the course goes a long way toward improving their skills as communicators, so our hope is that that will happen to you also.

Phase 3 (see Figure 2.4) challenges you to inventory others' nonverbal behavior closely, to pay attention to a wider range of cues at a more microscopic level than

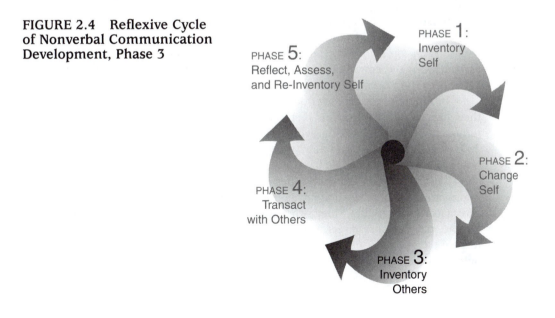

**FIGURE 2.4   Reflexive Cycle of Nonverbal Communication Development, Phase 3**

PHASE 1:
Inventory Self

PHASE 2:
Change Self

PHASE 3:
Inventory Others

PHASE 4:
Transact with Others

PHASE 5:
Reflect, Assess, and Re-Inventory Self

you're used to doing—no matter how fascinated you are, generally, by people. You will likely accomplish this phase **covertly** and **overtly.**

Regarding **covert** observation, you will first want to sharpen your powers of unobtrusive observation. This means that you get out of your own head whenever you have the chance, that you "divorce to self," in that your attention to yourself and your needs are subverted so that you can more carefully clue in to others, and that you appropriately observe the nonverbal behaviors of other people without drawing much or any attention to yourself. Note we said "appropriately." Let's add a caution here, in the form of a quick story: When in grad school, one of your authors remembers hearing the story of a group of students and their teaching assistant (TA) who got into trouble because they played "space invasion in the library." The TA gave his undergraduate students a homework assignment for the unit on nonverbal communication: Students were to invade people's space at the university library in any kind of creative way they could think of, and then record people's verbal and nonverbal reactions. Library officials drew the line and called the communication department to complain when students were hanging out in opposite-sex bathrooms, just to see how people would react when they came in to use the facilities.

Get the point here about appropriateness? It's unethical and inappropriate to manipulate circumstances, to "jack with people's worlds" and make people uncomfortable (or place them in danger) just for the goal of obtaining a greater understanding of nonverbal communication. What Phase 3 challenges you to do is to observe everyday, commonplace behavior—not to create some circumstance in which unordinary behavior might emerge. Since staring is considered rude behavior in U.S. culture, you won't want to take up staring at people as a means of observing their nonverbal behavior. What we mean by honing your covert observational skills is that you develop subtle ways of registering people and their nonverbal behavior. Crowded social spaces are excellent venues for such observation, but you want to seek every opportunity you can find, put on your people-watching hat, and take in the scene around you, noting behaviors you find appropriate and effective and those you do not. And you don't necessarily have to inventory others' behaviors from a distance; you can be actively engaged in a conversation with several people and still clue in to the nonverbal cues flying back and forth. You are a participant in the conversation, but you're also inventorying the fascinating array of behaviors as they occur.

In a more **overt** manner, you may also find occasion to ask people directly about their own nonverbal behavior or the nonverbal behavior of others. This strategy is termed **perception checking,** which we discussed in Chapter 1 (Beebe, Beebe, & Ivy, 2007). It's a useful tool that you're no doubt already using to some extent. Referring to our earlier example, Danielle has perceived some things about Felipe, but she wants to check her perceptions—to bounce her views off of other people—in order to get more information and a better understanding of people and situations. She may ask some classmates very casually, "Hey, what do you think of that Felipe guy in our class?" Or she may be more direct, explaining to friends or classmates that she's attracted to Felipe and then soliciting their opinions of or perceptions about him. This is an ongoing process of becoming more socially competent through inventorying—in as much detail as possible—others' ways of expressing themselves nonverbally. It is said

*Danielle perception checks with her friends to gain information about her situation and about Felipe.*

that "imitation is the sincerest form of flattery," so you may find that others behave in ways that you want to emulate, that you want to adopt certain nonverbal skills others exhibit into your repertoire as a communicator.

## Phase 4: Transact with Others

You've already inventoried yourself in an effort to become more aware of nonverbal cues you give off to others; you've decided what aspects of your nonverbal repertoire you like and want to retain, as well as those things you want to begin to change; and you've sharpened your powers of observation in terms of others' nonverbal communication. In Phase 4 (see Figure 2.5), we interact with others and mutually affect one another's nonverbal behavior. We prefer to call this process **transaction,** because it implies a shared creation of meaning that occurs in a simultaneous, ongoing manner. As compared to verbal communication in which, generally, messages are produced one at a time as interactants take turns at talk, in the nonverbal realm messages are exchanged continuously and the sheer act of exchange shapes the interaction. In this way, people influence one another constantly. We don't exist in a vacuum, but in a social context in which the behavior of others affects the behavior of ourselves. We grow, learn, evolve, and are shaped by our interactions with other people, and they by us.

FIGURE 2.5   **Reflexive Cycle of Nonverbal Communication Development, Phase 4**

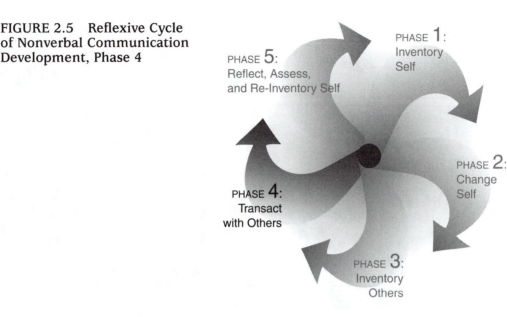

PHASE **1**: Inventory Self

PHASE **2**: Change Self

PHASE **3**: Inventory Others

PHASE **4**: Transact with Others

PHASE **5**: Reflect, Assess, and Re-Inventory Self

As you interact (transact) with other people, you will have an impact on them and they on you, and that's really the whole point of social interaction. So Phase 4 is about communicating with other people, verbally and nonverbally, while still maintaining an awareness of nonverbal cues—yours and those other people exude. We recognize that this is a tall order, because we often become concerned or preoccupied with ourselves in social situations, sometimes just wondering how other people perceive us, whether they like us, whether we sound intelligent or silly, and so forth. It's a challenge sometimes to be engaged in conversation, while at the same time to be aware of what we're putting out nonverbally, much less attend to the nonverbal signals of others. But that's what this process is all about—becoming increasingly aware, on a daily basis, of the critical role nonverbal behavior plays in the process of communicating with others. The more you clue in to how you are nonverbally communicating, how others are nonverbally communicating, and how, in turn, all of that nonverbal communication affects ongoing interaction, the more savvy the communicator you will become.

But here's another caution, one that we alluded to in Chapter 1: It's unwise to go into an interaction believing that you are a perfect reader of others' nonverbals and that you should use your heightened nonverbal awareness to change other people's behavior. If you approach this phase with arrogance or an "I'm studying nonverbal communication and I know all this stuff, so now I can change other people" kind of attitude, you will no doubt be in for some rough times ahead. You may find yourself isolated from other people because they resent your manipulation. We've heard cautions echoed by our professor colleagues across the country, who discuss the need for careful consideration when teaching students about developing nonverbal receiving and interpreting abilities. Some students will take nonverbal perceptual acuity as some kind of gimmick—as a handle that gives them an edge or leg up on the rest of the world. They believe themselves to be such keen observers and interpreters of nonverbal behavior that they simply cannot be wrong in their interpretations, nor misguided in their attempts to change other people. Gaining nonverbal skill should not lead to arrogance or righteous superiority over other people. Does honing your nonverbal observational and interpretive skills give you an edge in life? We believe that it does, but, in the end, you are responsible for changing your own behavior only, such that you become a more evolved communicator.

Let's apply Phase 4 by revisiting the Danielle/Felipe example. Danielle inventoried her own nonverbal behavior regarding her attraction to Felipe, then she started working on some subtle changes in her behavior that she believes will make her a more effective communicator. Next, she inventoried Felipe's nonverbal behavior—overtly and covertly—to try to assess any interest Felipe might have in her, how he interacts with people in general, and so forth. Now she believes she is ready to attempt some kind of exchange with Felipe. As a subtle beginning, Danielle might try to make more eye contact with Felipe, in hopes that he will notice her. She might try to accomplish this by speaking up more in class, following up any comments Felipe makes, trying to draw his attention toward her in class. Her hopes with such behavior is that Felipe takes notice and views her positively, so that he might become interested in developing some sort of relationship with her. In such a nonverbal-only transaction, Danielle's behavior is affected by what she hopes to make happen with Felipe; whether Felipe notices and responds, such that a transaction occurs, is anyone's guess. Felipe might not be as attuned to nonverbal signals as Danielle, so she may decide that more direct contact is necessary, like catching Felipe after class and introducing herself, in the hopes of a good first conversation.

*Danielle's behavior with Felipe reflects Phase 4 of the Reflexive Cycle: Transact with Others.*

### What Would *You* Do?

Shannon is working on an important group project for her communication course—a project worth a large percentage of her final grade. Shannon and most of her group members really want an A on the project, but there's one "problem child" in the group. Her name is Rika and she just has poor communication skills. She rarely makes eye contact with group members when they're discussing their project and, on the rare instance that she actually speaks up, she mumbles and talks so softly that no one can hear her. The group doesn't know how to interpret her nonverbal cues: Either she's really shy and just doesn't know how to interact with people she doesn't know very well, she's intimidated by the other group members, or worse yet, she's a slacker who engages only minimally, letting other group members carry her weight.

If this were your group project and you had a group mate like Rika, *what would you do?* Would you call Rika on her behavior, explaining that her lack of eye contact and unintelligible manner of speaking aren't acceptable? Would you be the comedian, trying something like waving in front of Rika's face to draw her eyes upward, while saying "Yo, I'm up here!" or saying "Eh? What was that? Did you say something?" when she mumbles something in conversation? Or would you try a softer approach, using soothing nonverbal cues to draw Rika into group discussions? This is a tough decision, because it's hard to attempt to correct others' inappropriate nonverbal cues (especially when they're your peers) without seeming superior. But it's also hard to not do anything when something like a huge grade is on the line and someone is pulling the project down.

## Phase 5: Reflect, Assess, and Re-Inventory Self

We come full circle in the Reflexive Cycle when we move through Phase 5 (see Figure 2.6), which calls upon you to reflect and assess the process you've just undertaken. Try to be purposeful or mindful in this entire undertaking, this process of understanding nonverbal complexities and applying that understanding to behavior, so that you can reflect on what you've learned, assess triumphs as well as mistakes, and continue to further develop your nonverbal skills. Remember that the cycle is ongoing; we never stop evolving in our understanding and use of nonverbal communication.

Perhaps Danielle's reflection and assessment might go something like this: Danielle first inventoried her own nonverbal behavior toward Felipe, once she realized she was attracted to him and wanted to do something about that attraction. She observed Felipe in class and talked to some trusted classmates, seeking their perceptions about him. She saw him interact with friends in the student center on campus and took in information about his friends (none of them looked like deviants); she also didn't see him with anyone who looked like a girlfriend, so that was encouraging. Next she decided that her first move toward Felipe (who seemed unaware of her interest in him) would be to catch him after a class session and talk to him about something discussed in class. She introduced herself, resurrected one of Felipe's comments in class, and asked him to tell her more as they walked across campus. She carefully inventoried Felipe's nonverbal behavior, as well as his words, looking for any signs that he might be interested in her or attracted to her too. Detecting Felipe's

**FIGURE 2.6    Reflexive Cycle
of Nonverbal Communication
Development, Phase 5**

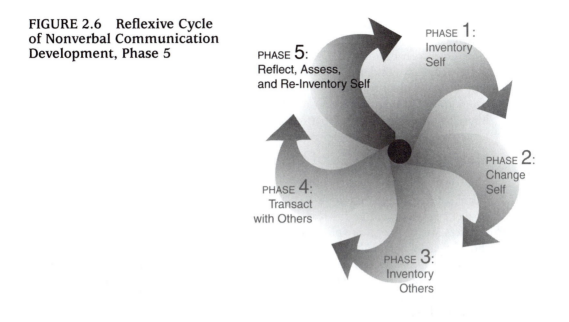

positive response to her, Danielle next chose to extend an offer to Felipe to study together for an upcoming exam in the class they had together. Felipe accepted, and the relationship was off and running. We're happy to say that they're now married and living happily ever after. (Sound like a fairy tale? Not really; it's just an example.)

If Danielle is smart, if she's a person who wants to learn and grow from her experiences, she will enact Phase 5 by overviewing this whole process with Felipe and her attention to nonverbal cues—her own as well as Felipe's. She'll reflect on the nonverbal signals, look for any missteps or missed opportunities, assess whether she did the right thing or if she could have done some things differently, and then continue the process by re-inventorying her nonverbal behavior. If the process works optimally, Danielle will have expanded her nonverbal repertoire of behavior and will be better equipped to cope with and respond to other new situations and people.

Remember that the Reflexive Cycle is a continuous process of moving nonverbal communication out of the "unaware" and into the "aware." One framework, attributed to Abraham Maslow, helps explain what we mean. The framework suggests that people operate at one of four levels:

1. **Unconscious incompetence:** We're unaware of our own incompetence. We don't know what we don't know.
2. **Conscious incompetence:** At this level, we become aware or conscious that we're not competent; we know what we don't know.
3. **Conscious competence:** We're aware that we know or can do something, but it hasn't yet become an integrated skill or habit.
4. **Unconscious competence:** At this level, skills become second nature. We know something or can do something, but don't have to concentrate to be able to act upon that knowledge or draw upon that skill.

If you continuously work through the Reflexive Cycle, we believe that you'll draw closer to the fourth level described above, unconscious competence. You'll be more able to enact nonverbal skills appropriate to varying situations, such that these skills become "second nature." The Reflexive Cycle is a constant process of discovery, but, as we've described it, it's not for the faint of heart. It takes work and a real commitment to improving your ability to nonverbally communicate, but we believe it's well worth the effort and that you're up to the task.

## Making Effective Use of the Reflexive Cycle

Now that you have a greater understanding of each phase in the Reflexive Cycle, let's talk about how to use this model to help you work through the material in this book. A smaller version or icon of the Reflexive Cycle will appear at various points throughout chapters, with one or more phases of the cycle highlighted. The appearance of the icon should signal to you, "Aha, the Reflexive Cycle is in play here." The highlighting of certain phases means that content corresponding to one or more phases is being discussed in the paragraph or paragraphs adjacent to the icon. We offer the icon reminder as simply a device to reinforce for you the connection between textbook information and different phases in the cycle. For example, in the chapter on proxemics (use of space), we ask you to inventory your rules or expectations about space, including such things as how much space you prefer around you in daily interaction, who is allowed to "invade" your space without it being perceived as a violation, and how you react if someone gets

too close to you in conversation. To the side of the paragraphs on this material, you'll see the Reflexive Cycle in icon design, with the first phase "Inventory Self" highlighted, because the text corresponding to the icon focuses on becoming more aware of your own space issues. Pay attention to the presence of the cycle icons as you read, because they will reinforce for you the practical applications we encourage you to make of the information you're learning.

---

### REMEMBER 2.1

| | |
|---|---|
| **Reflexivity:** | actions accomplished automatically rather than purposefully; referring back to the self. |
| **Covert Observation:** | appropriately observing nonverbal behaviors of other people without drawing much or any attention to ourselves. |
| **Overt Observation:** | asking people directly about their own nonverbal behavior or the nonverbal behavior of others. |
| **Perception Checking:** | asking direct or third-person parties for their perceptions, which we can compare to our own. |
| **Transaction:** | shared creation of meaning that occurs in a simultaneous, ongoing manner. |

*(continued)*

## REMEMBER 2.1 *(continued)*

| | |
|---|---|
| **Unconscious Incompetence:** | being unaware of our own incompetence. |
| **Conscious Incompetence:** | becoming aware or conscious of our own incompetence. |
| **Conscious Competence:** | realizing that we know something or can do something, but it has not yet become an integrated skill or habit. |
| **Unconscious Competence:** | knowing we can do something, but not having to concentrate to be able to act upon the knowledge or draw upon the skill. |

## ■ CODES OF NONVERBAL COMMUNICATION

Since human nonverbal behavior is so diverse and vast, the need arises for classifications. Classifications also make this complex topic of nonverbal communication easier to study. The primary categories or **codes** of nonverbal information researchers have studied, and which we'll explore in subsequent chapters in this text, include the following: environment; space and territory; physical appearance; body movement, gestures, and posture; facial expression; eye expression; touch; and vocal expression. Although we concentrate on these codes as they're exhibited in mainstream Western culture, recognize that they're enacted differently in other cultures.

### Environment

Close your eyes and picture your bedroom as it is right now—whether it's a dorm room that you share with someone, the room you've lived in for many years in your parents' house, or a bedroom shared with a spouse. If your professor were to walk into your bedroom right now, what would she or he think about you? Does the room express who you are? What would the state of your closet reveal about you if your professor looked in? These questions all have to do with your creation of and interaction with the physical environment.

What's so great about a corner office with wall-to-wall windows, high atop a skyscraper? It's one of many indications in American culture of high status. In a working world increasingly structured into cubicles, an employee's desk location serves as a symbol of importance (Sandberg, 2003). As one scholar put it, "People cannot be understood outside of their environmental context" (Peterson, 1991, p. 154). Just as we might try to learn the meaning of a word by examining the words surrounding it in a sentence, nonverbal actions are only meaningfully interpreted when context is taken into account (Rapoport, 1982). The environment is important to the study of nonverbal behavior in two ways: (1) The choices we make about the environment in which we live and operate reveal a good deal about who we are, and (2) our nonverbal behavior is altered by various environments in which we communicate.

First, the physical environments in which we function can be seen as extensions of our personality. We may not be able to manipulate all elements of our environment, but to whatever extent we're allowed, we'll put our "signature" on our physical environs. People like to structure and adorn the settings in which they work, study, and reside to make them unique and personal (Gosling, Ko, Mannarelli, & Morris, 2002; Sandalla, 1987). The environments we create for ourselves often speak volumes about those relationships we deem most important (Altman, Brown, Staples, & Werner, 1992; Lohmann, Arriaga, & Goodfriend, 2003). Second, our behavior and perceptions are altered because of the physical environments in which we find ourselves (Maslow & Mintz, 1956; Mintz, 1956). Our body may be more rigid, gestures more restrained, clothing more formal, and speech limited and whispered when we're in a church. (Obviously, this depends on the church.) In contrast, at a sporting event, we move freely, wear comfortable clothing, and scream and applaud wildly.

## Space and Territory

Imagine you're sitting alone at a long, rectangular table in your campus library. As you sit dutifully with your head in a textbook, you're startled when a complete stranger sits directly across from you at the table. Since there are several empty chairs at the other end of the table, you feel uncomfortable because this unknown individual has invaded *your* area. Research over decades has explored the fascinating subject of **proxemics,** or how people (and animals) create and use space and distance, as well as how they behave to protect and defend that space (Hall, 1959, 1966; Krail & Leventhal, 1976; Sommer, 1961).

Every culture has well-established ways of regulating spatial relations. Normally, we don't think much about the rules or norms we follow regarding space, until those rules are violated. Violations can be alarming, possibly even threatening. How physically close we are willing to get to others relates to how well we know them, to considerations of power and status, and to our cultural background (Burgoon, 1978; Burgoon & Jones, 1976).

The study of how people use space and objects to communicate occupancy or ownership of space is termed **territoriality** (Hall, 1966; Lyman & Scott, 1999). You assumed ownership of that table in the library and the right to determine who sat with you. You may have reacted negatively because your sense of personal space was invaded, but also because the intrusive stranger broke a cultural rule governing territoriality.

We announce our ownership of space with **territorial markers**—things and actions that signify an area has been claimed (Goffman, 1971). When you arrive at class, you may put your book bag on a chair while you get up and go across the hall to the "facilities." That book bag signifies temporary ownership of your seat. If you returned to find someone moved your stuff and was sitting in your seat, you'd probably become indignant. The most common form of territorial marker is a lock. We lock our doors and windows, cars, offices, briefcases, televisions (in the form of V-chips), and even our computers so as to keep out intruders. We're increasingly territorial about our very identities.

## Physical Appearance

What do we tend to notice about people when we first see them? Most of us would answer the face, including the person's eyes, but others might answer the person's walk, stance, or general body motion. Generally, before we hear someone's voice or register other nonverbal elements about the person, we've taken in nonverbal cues related to their physical appearance, or physical attributes of the face and body. Thus, appearance is a very important topic to study, since it is generally the first nonverbal cue people perceive about one another. (Obviously, we're talking about face-to-face encounters, not situations where you meet people over the phone or online.)

Many cultures around the world place a high value upon appearance—body size and shape, skin color and texture, hairstyle, and clothing. We realize that we're writing from an American perspective, but it seems as though Americans place an undue emphasis on looks, as we discuss in some depth in Chapter 5. For example, our views of and preferences for government leaders, especially presidents, are affected by their height (Tenner, 2004). College students give higher evaluation ratings to professors whom they deem physically attractive (Montell, 2003). We put such pressure on ourselves and others to be physically attractive that our self-esteem may decline when we realize we cannot match up with some perceived "ideal" (Botta, 1999; Forbes, Adams-Curtis, Rade, & Jaberg, 2001; Wiederman & Hurst, 1998).

Clothing functions primarily to keep us protected, warm, and within society's bounds of decency, but also to convey a sense of our culture (Morris, 1985). Clothing such as baseball caps, baggy pants, and distinctive t-shirts, as well as other appearance aspects, termed **artifacts** (jewelry, tattoos, piercings, makeup, cologne, eyeglasses, and so on) are displays of culture. While we don't believe that "clothes make the man," clothing and artifacts do affect how we are perceived by others (Aune, 1999; Furlow, 1999; Gorham, Cohen, & Morris, 1999; Roach, 1997).

## Body Movement, Gestures, and Posture

Have you ever traveled in a country in which you couldn't speak the language? Or have you tried to converse locally with a person who didn't speak English or who was deaf and didn't read lips? What do you do in these situations? Chances are, you risk looking extremely foolish by using over-exaggerated gestures or slowly and deliberately shouting words the listener can't understand. These responses are nonverbal attempts to compensate for a lack of verbal understanding. Even when we do speak the same language as others, we often use gestures to help us make our point.

**Kinesics** is a general term for the study of human movement, gestures, and posture (Birdwhistell, 1960). (Technically, movements of the face and eyes are contained within this category, but because one's face and eyes can produce such a wealth of information, we discuss them as separate codes.) We have long recognized that our kinesics provide valuable information to others. We develop a certain pattern in our walk, stance, and posture, which becomes easily recognizable by others who come to know us, but which can be affected by our mood and emotions. Have you ever heard someone make reference to how a certain person "carries him/herself"? We know we can't physically "carry ourselves," so this must mean our posture, stance, and movement. Some people carry themselves in ways that convey pride and confidence, while others look as though the weight of the world were on their shoulders. Some people "talk with their hands," meaning that they use a lot of gestures to complement what they're saying, while others prefer using fewer gestures, perhaps viewing them as distracting. The body in motion is a fascinating, complex subset of nonverbal behavior that we study more in depth in Chapter 6.

## Facial Expression

The face is the gallery for our emotional displays (Gosselin, Gilles, & Dore, 1995). Suppose we buy a new expensive gadget and show it to our romantic partner or a friend. Or as an interviewer reads our resumé, we sit in silence across the desk. In both of these situations, we scan the other person's face, eagerly awaiting some reaction. To interpret someone's facial expressions accurately, we need to focus on what the other person may be thinking or feeling. It helps if we know the person well, can see her or his whole face, have plenty of time to observe, and understand the situation that prompted the reaction (Ekman & Friesen, 1975).

As adults, we come to realize that there are times when it's inappropriate and unwise to fully reveal our emotions, such as crying in front of superiors when we've been passed over for promotion or becoming visibly angry when a project doesn't come our way. But there are also times when this learned masking of emotion—the development of a "poker face"—can endanger our relationships. Consider aloof, distant parents who can't separate themselves from their work to enjoy the company of their own children, or romantic partners who complain that they can't tell how their partners feel about them because emotional displays have been squelched. The best approach is a balance of control and spontaneity. We want to stay real and human, to be able to reveal to others what we feel, but there are times when doing so can be inappropriate or damaging.

## Eye Expression

Do you agree that the eyes are the "windows to the soul"? What can people tell about you by looking into your eyes? Are you comfortable making eye contact with most people or only with people you know well? Eye contact is extremely important in U.S. culture, as well as many other cultures around the world. Americans make all kinds of judgments about others—particularly their trustworthiness and sincerity—on the basis of whether they make or avoid eye contact. It's an interesting exercise to inventory your own eye behavior, thinking about when you're apt to look at someone and when you're likely to avert your gaze.

Research shows that eye contact plays a significant role in the judgment of a person's credibility in casual, everyday conversation, but it's particularly critical in a public presentation setting (Beebe, 1974; Napieraliski, Brooks, & Droney, 1995). In the first televised presidential debate, John F. Kennedy appeared comfortable and confident as he made eye contact with television cameras. It seemed as though he was making eye contact directly with the American public. In contrast, Richard Nixon darted his eyes nervously from side to side at times and generally made less eye contact with the camera and the viewing audience. This created a perception that Nixon was shifty, untrustworthy, and lacking credibility (Bryski & Frye, 1979–1980; Davis, 1995; Tiemens, 1978).

## Touch

Touch, or body contact, is the most powerful form of nonverbal communication; it's also the most misunderstood and carries the potential for the most problems if ill used. Consider some moments involving accidental touch. Standing elbow-to-elbow in a crowded elevator or sitting next to a large individual in a crowded airplane, we may find ourselves in physical contact with total strangers. As we stiffen our body and avert our eyes, a baffling sense of shame and discomfort floods over us. Why do we react this way to accidental touching? Normally, we touch to express intimacy. When intimacy is not our intended message, we instinctively react to modify the impression our touch has created (Fisher, Rytting, & Heslin, 1976).

Countless studies on touch, termed **haptics** in research, have shown that human contact is vital to our physical and personal development and well being (Jones & Yarbrough, 1985; Montagu, 1971). The amount of touch we need, initiate, tolerate, and receive depends on many factors. The physical contact evidenced in our family is the biggest influence, because those early experiences shape our views of appropriate and inappropriate touch, and our comfort level in extending touches to others, as well as receiving others' touches. Cultural background has a significant effect as well. Certain cultures are high-contact—meaning that touching is quite commonplace—such as some European and Middle Eastern cultures in which men kiss each other on the cheeks as a greeting. Other cultures are low-contact, like some Asian cultures in which demonstrations of affection are rare and considered inappropriate (Remland, Jones, & Brinkman, 1991, 1995).

## Vocal Expression

Like the face, the voice is a major vehicle for communicating our thoughts and emotions. The pitch, rate, and volume at which we speak and our use of silence—elements termed **paralanguage** or **vocalics**—all provide important clues. Imagine that your spouse, romantic partner, or best friend purchased and modeled a new outfit, asking you what you think. If you really hated the person's new outfit, would you say enthusiastically, "That looks GREAT!"—which could either be an untruth designed to prevent hurt feelings or an expression of sarcasm? Or would you say, "That looks nice" in a halfhearted way? The ability to convey these different reactions is accomplished primarily by the human voice.

The voice reveals our thoughts, emotions, and the nature of our relationships with others, but it also provides information about our self-confidence and knowledge, and influences how we are perceived by others (Hinkle, 2001). Most of us would conclude, as has research, that a speaker who mumbles, speaks very slowly and softly, continually mispronounces words, and uses "uh" and "um" is less credible and persuasive than one who speaks clearly, rapidly, fluently, and with appropriate volume (Burgoon, Birk, & Pfau, 1990; Carli, LaFleur, & Loeber, 1995; Christenfeld, 1995; DeGroot & Motowidlo, 1999; Street, Brady, & Lee, 1984).

## REMEMBER 2.2

### Codes (Categories) of Nonverbal Communication

| | |
|---|---|
| **Environment:** | how people create and behave in spaces. |
| **Space (Proxemics):** | how people create and use proximity and distance; includes behavior to protect and defend space. |
| **Territory:** | cues that indicate ownership and occupancy of space. |
| **Physical Appearance:** | physical attributes of the face and body; typically the first nonverbal cue people perceive in face-to-face situations. |
| **Body Movement, Gestures, and Posture (Kinesics):** | people's use of movements of the body to convey information, emotions, and attitudes. |
| **Eye Expression:** | conveys trustworthiness, sincerity, honesty, and interest. |
| **Facial Expression:** | reveals thoughts and expresses emotions. |
| **Touch (Haptics):** | study of human bodily contact; communicates the nature of the relationship between people. |
| **Vocal Expression (Vocalics):** | communicates emotion and clarifies the meaning of messages through such elements as pitch, rate, and volume. |

## ■ NONVERBAL SENDING AND RECEIVING ABILITY

As we've said throughout this chapter, as well as in Chapter 1, our goal is to help students become more aware of nonverbal communication—nonverbal messages you send to other people, as well as the nonverbal cues others communicate. So this ongoing process involves sharpening both sending and receiving powers. But for a moment, let's consider people beyond ourselves, because we have a prime example within our culture of people whose sending and receiving skills must be at their absolute best—our very safety depends on it.

Unless you've been living under a rock this decade, you know that national security is a prime concern for us all. We live in an increasingly dangerous world, and all too frequently we hear of some threat somewhere to our national security. In response to those threats, a group of ordinary citizens are trained to do extraordinary jobs every day, because they work for the United States' Transportation Security Administration (TSA). First, think about air marshals who undergo rigorous training just to be able to blend in with ordinary passengers on a plane, but who must also be able to assess and respond to dangerous situations instantly. These people's sending abilities must be finely honed so that they convey "normal" nonverbal cues and don't call attention to themselves when they fly right along with the rest of us. Plus, they must be excellent processors of others' nonverbal information, so that they can anticipate a potential threat.

Next, think about the security checkpoint people at the airports. Yes, many of us sigh when we think about how long it often takes to get through airport security so that we can be on our way, but none of us can deny the importance of these security professionals' efforts to protect our safety and, in essence, our freedom and way of life. The TSA employees checking us through security must fine tune their powers of observation also, because they play critical roles in air travel safety.

One TSA training program that was instituted in June of 2003 is called SPOT, short for Screening of Passengers by Observation Techniques. The TSA official website describes this training as utilizing "behavioral observation and analysis techniques to identify potentially high-risk passengers" (Transportation Security Administration, 2008). The training program helps employees focus on passenger behavior, not physical characteristics. A Fox television news segment in September of 2007 reported on the TSA's SPOT training, noting that 270 people had been arrested since 2005 because TSA employees wisely (and accurately) identified their suspicious behavior. According to the news account, employees are trained to look for "red flags" that could indicate deceit or undue anxiety, behavior that reveals a "conflict between the conscious and subconscious," as well as more obvious signs of concealing illegal items or substances in clothing or possessions. Understandably, the TSA isn't more specific in enumerating exactly what behaviors their employees are trained to observe, because that would undermine the very security they work to establish. But as students of nonverbal communication, we can safely deduce that these employees are trained in detecting and interpreting a whole array of nonverbal cues.

Now back to us good old ordinary citizens: How do we become better senders of nonverbal communication, as well as better interpreters of all of the nonverbal cues we receive from others? Let's focus first on sending ability.

## Nonverbal Sending Ability

We've talked at length in this chapter and in Chapter 1 about awareness—developing more awareness of the nonverbal communication we convey to other people. Thus the first step of the Reflexive Cycle is a self-inventory. But some nonverbal signals each of us gives off are beyond our control, such as physical features that communicate unintended messages to observers. Maybe someone's eyes are set closely together, giving us the sense that the person is shifty or not to be trusted. Someone without much of a chin might be deemed lacking in character. A person with large eyes can be seen as naive, and a heavy eye-lidded person can be thought of as sleepy or "out of it." An adult's high, squeaky voice may convey youthfulness, immaturity, and even a lack of intelligence. Someone who speaks with a southern accent may be thought of as a "hick," while someone with a more clipped, stereotypical northern accent may be considered a "snob." A frail body frame may make us think someone is uptight or timid, whereas an overweight body may send signals of laziness and overindulgence. These judgments are rarely fair or accurate, but fair or not, that's the reality. People often make judgments about character, intellect, ability, and personality from such flimsy nonverbal elements as physical appearance. We can't alter the cues that are sent without our control to other people—the unintended consequences of our existence—so let's focus on the nonverbal cues we send that we *can* control or work to improve.

In his review of the topic of nonverbal skill acquisition, scholar Ronald Riggio (2006) discusses nonverbal sending abilities, also called nonverbal encoding skill or nonverbal expressiveness: "The ability to convey nonverbal messages to others, particularly the sending of emotional messages, is a critical skill for social success, and a fundamental component of the larger construct of communication competence" (p. 87). Research has focused more attention on nonverbal receiving ability than sending ability, but some efforts are noteworthy. Prolific nonverbal communication scholar Ross Buck and colleagues (Buck, 1978, 2005; Buck, Miller, & Caul, 1974; Buck, Savin, Miller, & Caul, 1972) developed a slide-viewing technique with this basic setup: Subjects are recorded while viewing and talking about emotion-evoking slides. Then judges who view the recordings attempt to correctly identify the emotion being portrayed by each subject primarily through their facial and vocal expressions. Another approach is to record subjects who are asked to pose in such a way as to convey facially a particular emotion; they may also be asked to read a sentence or phrase, with the intent of conveying facially and vocally a particular emotion. Judges then view the recordings and attempt to correctly identify the emotion being portrayed. One ingenious aspect of these techniques is that they can test both sending (encoding) and receiving (decoding) abilities. Although these approaches were developed in the 1970s, they're still used in research today.

This may elicit a "duh" reaction from you, but one of the best ways to enhance our nonverbal sending ability is to simply engage in the process of daily living, but with an emphasis on the role of nonverbal communication in social interaction. Many people think of communicating as merely talking, but you—as a student of nonverbal communication—realize that verbal messages are only a small part of the communicative encounter. The nonverbal cues will tell you volumes more than the verbal, so focusing on nonverbal broadens your horizons. Experience in different social situations and with different people, especially people from varying cultural backgrounds, is great training if you want to improve in this area. But there are those people who experience what we experience, but never seem to learn anything. The key is to make a concerted effort to *learn something* from every encounter.

As the phrase goes, "watch and learn." Observing role models you think are nonverbally savvy is another excellent way to enhance encoding skills. For example, imagine you've heard a public speaker you thought was excellent. You liked the way the speaker made consistent eye contact with audience members, but wasn't distracted by anyone; the way she or he wasn't tied to notes, but seemed to have the speech "down;" the confident use of gestures to add emphasis to the remarks; and the even  flowing voice that kept the audience in constant attention. Can you try to emulate these winning behaviors the next time you make a presentation? Realize that, as infants, we imitated people's facial movements, especially movements of the mouth; as early as nine months of age, we mimicked our mother's facial expressions, as research by infant specialist Tiffany Field and others attests (Field, 1982; Field, Woodson, Greenberg, & Cohen, 1982; Termine & Izard, 1988). As we grew and learned, we continued to model the nonverbal behaviors of those around us, most importantly, our parents and siblings (Ekman & Friesen, 1967). But that process shouldn't stop just because we're adults and making our independent way in the world.

In addition to experience and role modeling, we need to remain open to other people's feedback about our nonverbal communication. If you exhibited an annoying nonverbal behavior, would you choose to remain oblivious to it, possibly missing out on some social opportunities or potential relationships simply because no one dared bring it to your attention, or would you rather know "what's what" and face the truth about yourself? Which option generates more personal growth?

Other opportunities to expand our nonverbal sending capability include reading books on the subject (like this one), and taking a course or training seminar in nonverbal communication. Role playing is a common activity in a nonverbal communication course or training module. It provides a valuable way for students to experiment with alternative nonverbal cues and to expand their behavioral repertoires in the safe environment of the classroom or training facility—before they try out their new behaviors in other aspects of their lives.

## Nonverbal Receiving Ability

Nonverbal researchers have been prolific on the subject of nonverbal decoding ability for several decades. Various diagnostic tools and tests of nonverbal decoding ability have been developed, but we choose to focus on two of the most prevalent used in past and present research.

In the 1970s, psychologist Robert Rosenthal and colleagues developed the Profile of Nonverbal Sensitivity or, more simply, the PONS test, which is still used in research today (Rosenthal, Hall, DiMatteo, Rogers, & Archer, 1979). One of the original designers of the PONS test describes it as a "standardized audiovisual test of accuracy in understanding the meanings of affective cues conveyed by the face, body, and voice" (Hall, 2005, p. 483). The PONS test is a 45-minute videotape containing a series of audio and video segments to which subjects respond. In each two-second segment, a Caucasian American woman enacts a scene and portrays different affective states (i.e., emotions and attitudes). For example, in one scene, the woman displays a positive feeling of happiness related to seeing a baby; in another scene, she criticizes someone for being late, displaying negative emotions of exasperation and irritation. Eleven scenes were developed—some reveal just the face, some just the body, some with face and body combined, some with no audio, some with audio but with the actual speech content (words) masked, and so forth. When taking the PONS, segments are presented and subjects decode the nonverbal stimuli; in other words, subjects try to decipher what is happening and what emotion is being portrayed in each segment. Subjects' responses are scored for accuracy by type of segment, single channel or multichannel. In a nutshell, the PONS test measures a person's ability to recognize people's emotional or attitudinal states within certain situations.

Research using the PONS test shows that, across various cultures and nationalities, girls and women tend to score higher than boys and men, particularly when it comes to decoding facial expressions. This female advantage extends from grade school through adulthood (Hall, 1984; McClure, 2000; Rosenthal, et al., 1979). The sex difference has been documented by other tests of nonverbal decoding ability as

## SPOTLIGHT on Research

Throughout this book we stress the importance of enhancing your ability to effectively encode and decode nonverbal communication, but what if your brain simply didn't allow you to do this? For a small percentage of the population, processing nonverbal information is nearly impossible, and a learning disability termed Nonverbal Learning Disorder (NLD) is the culprit. The disorder stems from a neurological dysfunction which affects the right hemisphere of the brain, where nonverbal functioning generally occurs (NLD, 2007).

Research in the 1990s and beyond has attempted to better understand this disorder, but efforts have been hampered by the fact that 80 percent of learning disabilities are related to verbal learning—reading, speaking, and listening—and those disabilities receive more research attention. Only relatively recently have psychologists, educators, and medical experts begun to focus on disorders that affect people's (especially children's) ability to send and receive nonverbal messages. According to Liza Little (1999), an RN and a professor of nursing, some characteristics of NLD include the following:

- lack of ability to comprehend nonverbal communication
- significant deficiencies in social judgment and social interaction
- problems in math, reading comprehension, and handwriting
- problems with organization, problem solving, and higher reasoning
- strong verbal and auditory attention and memory skills
- lack of image, poor visual recall
- faulty spatial perception and spatial relations
- lack of coordination
- severe balance problems
- difficulties with fine motor skills
- frequent tantrums, difficulties soothing, easily overwhelmed
- fear of new places and changes in routines
- prone to depression and anxiety as they get older (p. 114)

Little (1999) explains that children with NLD may continue to have difficulty into adulthood; they may actually fare worse over time than children who only have verbal learning disabilities. Of course, many people have both verbal and nonverbal learning disorders. Part of what complicates NLD is that children with the condition find it a challenge to integrate new information into their lives, so they are relatively inflexible when confronted with new and different circumstances. In addition, they often struggle to apply what they learn from one situation to another. Because children with NLD are frequently verbally adept, even precocious, other factors are presumed to be the problem, such as laziness or boredom; thus NLD is often diagnosed late in a child's development (NLD, 2007).

A website on parenting ran a feature on NLD in 2007, so that parents of children with the disorder could better understand it. The website explains:

> One of the most salient consequences of having NLD is the impairment in social functioning. Few of us realize how much of our social interactions are based on our

*(continued)*

understanding of the nonverbal cues of communication. Eye contact, hand gestures, tone of voice, body language, and posture are some of the many signals to which we attend when we speak with someone else. Children who miss the nonverbal cues of communication often feel uncomfortable with their peers and may gravitate toward adults, who admire their broad knowledge, or to younger children, who will gladly take direction from them. (NLD, 2007)

Various treatments have been developed to cope with the disorder, ranging from occupational therapy to social skills training, academic support in weak subjects, and cognitive behavioral therapy or coaching to help with coping skills.

Other research has determined that Asperger's Syndrome, which some experts view as an advanced form of autism, appears to be a severe nonverbal learning disability stemming from neurological abnormality (Brumback, Harper, & Weinberg, 1996). People with Asperger's tend to be uncomfortable in social situations because they have difficulty responding to other people appropriately. They tend to be rejected by people because their nonverbal cues and verbal communication seem disjointed, yet most people with Asperger's are highly functioning verbal communicators. Research continues to search for a better understanding of the causes of Nonverbal Learning Disorder and Asperger's Syndrome, as well as for more effective treatments for the conditions.

If you'd like to read more about these disorders, here are a few sources we recommend:

Maggie Manen's *Understanding Nonverbal Learning Disabilities: A Common-Sense Guide for Parents and Professionals*, published in 2007 by Jessica Kingsley Publishers, London, England.

Steven Nowicki and Marshall Duke's *Helping the Child Who Doesn't Fit In*, published in 1992 by Peachtree Publishers, Atlanta, Georgia.

Kathryn Stewart's *Helping a Child with Nonverbal Learning Disorder or Asperger's Disorder: A Parent's Guide (2nd edition)*, published in 2007 by New Harbinger Publications, Oakland, California.

Pamela B. Tanguay's *Nonverbal Learning Disorder at Home: A Parent's Guide*, published in 2001 by Jessica Kingsley Publishers, London, England.

Sue Thompson's *The Source for Nonverbal Learning Disorders*, published in 1997 by LinguiSystems, East Moline, Illinois.

---

well, with U.S. and non-U.S. subjects alike (Baron-Cohen, Wheelwright, Hill, Raste, & Plumb, 2001; Hall, Murphy, & Schmid Mast, 2006; Horgan, Schmid Mast, Hall, & Carter, 2004). While this is a general trend, other research focusing on specific emotions and nonverbal cues has found that females are less accurate decoders of angry expressions in males (Rotter & Rotter, 1988; Wagner, MacDonald, & Manstead, 1986), as well as nonverbal cues of deception in general (Zuckerman, DePaulo, & Rosenthal, 1981).

Another test of decoding ability, the Diagnostic Analysis of Nonverbal Accuracy or DANVA, was developed and tested by researchers in the 1990s (Nowicki & Carton, 1997; Nowicki & Duke, 1994; Nowicki, Glanville, & Demertzis, 1998;

Nowicki & Mitchell, 1998). This test appears in multiple versions, some of which contain images of Caucasian and African American adults expressing four primary emotions (happiness, sadness, fear, and anger) facially, Caucasian adults expressing the same four emotions vocally, and Caucasian children expressing these emotions facially. People depicted in the DANVA speak the same basic sentence, but try to convey nonverbally a particular emotion. Subjects exposed to the DANVA are scored on the accuracy with which they identify the emotions from the stimuli. Riggio (2006) explains that the DANVA "assesses sensitivity to both visual and auditory cues and increases the range of nonverbal expressions by including the ability to decode both posed and spontaneous expressions of emotions" (p. 82). In contrast, the PONS test only contains posed depictions of emotion, which some scholars believe to be one of its limitations.

Researchers using such measures as the PONS test or the DANVA have detected a trend according to age, in that nonverbal decoding skills generally increase from childhood into adulthood, but plateau as people hit their 20s and 30s (Nowicki & Duke, 1994, 2001; Rosenthal, et al., 1979). One study compared women in their 20s to women in their 60s, and found that the older women scored significantly lower on the PONS test than the younger women, suggesting that age-related changes in memory and attention may affect decoding ability (Lieberman, Rigo, & Campain, 1988). The DANVA continues to be utilized in interesting ways in current research. For instance, one team of researchers administered the test to African American boys diagnosed as severely emotionally disturbed, for greater insight into their aggressive classroom behavior (Cooley & Treimer, 2002). Another study found that students with learning disabilities were less accurate decoders of facial expressions of people appearing in the DANVA than students without learning disabilities (Sprouse, Hall, Webster, & Bolen, 1998).

Beyond research techniques, time and patience improve our receiving ability. If we earnestly want to accurately interpret and sensitively respond to others' non-verbal communication, we must be willing to spend time and effort to develop this skill. You've already learned a good deal about nonverbal communication from reading this chapter, studying this topic in class, and living as many years as you have lived. But enhancing interpretive skills requires, first, an awareness of the importance of nonverbal elements in the communication process. Many people make interpretive mistakes because they overemphasize the words people say.  Verbal communication is important, but remember that the greater portion of someone's total message is conveyed nonverbally. A second requirement is the will-ingness and emotional maturity to make our own behavior secondary to that of someone else. In other words, if we're so wrapped up in ourselves that we can only think about and deal with how *we're* feeling, what *we're* thinking, and what *we* want at a given moment, we can't possibly hope to take in others' nonverbal cues, interpret them accurately, and respond appropriately.

It's also important to remember to take into account the cultural backgrounds of those with whom we communicate, as we discussed in Chapter 1. It's wise to avoid automatically attaching our own cultural frame of reference when we decipher nonver-bal cues. As we've stated, the context within which nonverbal cues are communicated plays an important role. We need to be aware of our surroundings and other situational factors when interpreting the meaning of nonverbal actions. Here's another important point: Be prepared to fail. We all struggle to make sense out of others' actions; no one has this skill down pat. We have to use our interpretive failures to learn lessons we can apply to the next encounter. Beyond these suggestions, we recommend keeping in mind a three-part framework developed by Mehrabian that can help us improve our nonverbal interpretive skills.

## Mehrabian's Framework: Immediacy, Arousal, and Dominance

Albert Mehrabian (1972, 1981), a scholar whose work we cite often in this book, found that we synthesize and interpret nonverbal cues along three primary dimensions: immediacy, arousal, and dominance. Mehrabian believed that you could observe two people talking in a hallway, for instance, and make relatively accurate judgments as to how much they liked each other (if at all), how interested each person was in the conversation, and whether one person was more dominant or in control of the conversation than the other.

Let's begin with the liking part. Why do we like some people and dislike others? Sometimes we can't put a finger on the precise reason. Mehrabian contends that **immediacy**—nonverbal behavior that communicates liking and engenders feelings of pleasure—is a probable explanation. The principle underlying immediacy is simple: We like and respond positively to people who tend to display immediacy cues and we avoid or respond negatively to those who don't. Immediacy cues that show liking and interest include the following (Argyle, 1988):

- *Proximity:* Close, forward lean
- *Body orientation:* Face-to-face or side-by-side position
- *Eye contact:* Eye gaze and mutual eye gaze
- *Facial expression:* Smiling and other pleasant facial expressions
- *Gestures:* Head nods, movement
- *Posture:* Open and relaxed, arms oriented toward others
- *Touch:* Culture- and context-appropriate touch
- *Voice:* Higher pitch, upward pitch

So how do you apply this information to help you improve your nonverbal receiving skills? Think of a social scene you typically go to, like a club, party, or church gathering. You find that you become attracted to someone at that setting. You're introduced to the person and engage in a get-to-know-you kind of conversation. If you're nonverbally savvy, you'll attend to the person's nonverbal cues to determine if the person likes you. Although you can't know for sure that someone's nonverbal behavior translates into liking, immediacy cues can provide some information. Watch for a direct body orientation, as opposed to turning away from you and orienting toward another person or, in general, to the rest of the room. Check out the eye contact, smiling and other pleasant facial expressions, a rising intonation in the voice, and a forward lean toward you, rather than a backward lean which can signal disinterest (Guerrero & Floyd, 2006).

The second component in Mehrabian's framework is **arousal,** but we don't mean sexual arousal; the term simply means stimulation or activation. Arousal prepares the body for action, with such physiological indications as increased heart rate, blood pressure, and brain temperature. Arousal, in this sense, can occur when you drive fast or experience athletic exhilaration. Externally, the face, voice, and movement are primary indicators of arousal. If you detect arousal cues in someone, such as increased eye contact, closer conversational distances, increased touch, animated vocalics, more direct body orientation, and more smiling and active facial expressions, you can conclude with some degree of certainty that the other person is responsive to and interested in you or what you have to say. If the person acts passive or bored, as evidenced by few (or no) arousal cues, you can safely conclude that he or she is uninterested.

The next time you're at a party, become a people-watcher for a moment. Check out which people look interested in the people they're talking to and which ones look bored or like they'd rather be somewhere else, anywhere else. You can tell how people feel about each other—not with absolute accuracy, but with a high degree of certainty—just by looking for arousal cues (LePoire, Duggan, Shepard, & Burgoon, 2002; McGinty, Knox, & Zusman, 2003; Weisfeld & Stack, 2002).

The third dimension of Mehrabian's framework communicates the balance of power in a relationship. **Dominance** cues communicate status, position, and importance. In that conversation in the hallway we proposed earlier, the more dominant or controlling person may exhibit a more relaxed body posture; less direct body orientation to the more submissive person; a downward head tilt; and less smiling, head nodding, and facial animation (Aguinis & Henle, 2001; Hall, LeBeau, Reinoso, & Thayer, 2001; Helweg-Larsen, Cunningham, Carrico, & Pergram, 2004; Schmid Mast & Hall, 2004; Tiedens & Fragale, 2003).

When you attempt to interpret someone's nonverbal communication, realize that a good deal of room for error exists. People are complex, and they don't always send clear signals. But the more you learn about nonverbal communication, the more you become aware of your own communication and the communication of others, the greater your chances of accurately perceiving and interpreting someone's nonverbal message.

### REMEMBER 2.3

#### Mehrabian's Framework for Interpreting Nonverbal Behavior

**Immediacy:**  nonverbal cues that communicate liking and engender feelings of pleasure.

**Arousal:**  nonverbal cues that communicate stimulation or activation.

**Dominance:**  nonverbal cues that communicate status, position, and importance.

# SUMMARY ■ ■ ■ ■ ■

In this chapter, we introduced the Reflexive Cycle of Nonverbal Communication Development, which serves as a structuring device and a learning reinforcement for the rest of the text. This model enhances our understanding of how people come to know themselves better as communicators, how they change and improve their communicative abilities, how they affect others' communication, and then, how they are, in turn, affected by the process of affecting others.

We first examined what it means to be "reflexive," since this property is at the core of the model. We explored reflex action, meaning those behaviors accomplished automatically rather than purposefully, as well as the sense of reflexivity as referring back to the self. The Reflexive Cycle emphasizes the individual within a social context. Then we outlined each phase of the cycle, beginning with Phase 1, Inventory Self, which involves taking stock of our own nonverbal behavior to become more aware of how we communicate without or in conjunction with words. A second aspect of this inventory activity involves asking others for feedback about our nonverbal behavior. We have little hope of expanding or refining our nonverbal abilities if we lack awareness of how we nonverbally communicate to others.

Phase 2 of the Reflexive Cycle is to change our nonverbal communication, based on the inventory we completed in Phase 1. In this phase, we consider our strengths and weaknesses, in terms of our own nonverbal communication, and work to alter those behaviors we believe need changing or to add nonverbal cues to our repertoire. Phase 3 challenges us to inventory others' nonverbal behavior closely, meaning that we pay attention to a wider range of cues at a more microscopic level than we're used to doing. We discussed covert observation, in which we carefully clue in to the nonverbal behaviors of other people without drawing much or any attention to ourselves. We also discussed overt observation, specifically a strategy termed perception checking, in which we ask people directly about their perceptions of their own nonverbal behavior or the nonverbal behavior of others.

In Phase 4, we interact with others and mutually affect one another's nonverbal behavior, a process we termed transaction, because it implies a shared creation of meaning that occurs in a simultaneous, ongoing manner. Through communicative transactions, we grow, learn, evolve, and are shaped by other people, and they by us. Finally, Phase 5 involves reflection and assessment of the entire cycle, our process for understanding nonverbal complexities and applying that understanding to behavior. Remember that the reflexive process repeats; it is a constant cycle throughout our lifetime as we encounter diverse people and varied situations.

In the last half of the chapter, we introduced primary nonverbal communication codes or categories of nonverbal behavior that research has explored. These eight areas include: environment; space and territory; physical appearance; body movement, gestures, and posture; facial expression; eye expression; touch; and vocal expression. A few research findings for each code were outlined to illustrate what we will be exploring more in depth in subsequent chapters.

Finally, we considered research techniques that have been developed to assess people's nonverbal encoding and decoding abilities. We also explored more commonplace ways to enhance our skills as nonverbal communicators, so that we continue to improve our social competence. One specific framework for interpreting nonverbal cues was developed by Mehrabian, and includes three dimensions: immediacy, arousal, and dominance. Nonverbal cues along these lines can reveal a great deal about communicators.

## DISCUSSION STARTERS

1. What does the concept of "reflexivity" mean and how can it be applied to the study of nonverbal communication?

2. Why is the reflexive model structured as a cycle, instead of a straight line or some other configuration? What are the implications of such a structure for the enhancement of nonverbal communication abilities?

3. Work through a personal example—either something you encountered in the past or are presently experiencing—to help you make sense of the Reflexive Cycle of Nonverbal

Communication Development. Does it help you analyze the situation? Are there changes you need to make?

4. What are the eight codes or categories of nonverbal communication? Provide examples of nonverbal behaviors that correspond to the different codes.

5. How can we enhance our encoding and decoding skills as communicators? Why is it important to become more sensitive expressors as well as interpreters of nonverbal cues?

## REFERENCES

Aguinis, H., & Henle, C. A. (2001). Effects of nonverbal behavior on perceptions of a female employee's power bases. *Journal of Social Psychology, 141,* 537–549.

Altman, I., Brown, B. B., Staples, B., & Werner, C. M. (1992). A transactional approach to close relationships: Courtship, weddings, and placemaking. In B. Walsh, K. Craik, & R. Price (Eds.), *Person-environment psychology: Contemporary models and perspectives.* Hillsdale, NJ: Erlbaum.

Argyle, M. (1988). *Bodily communication* (2nd ed.). London: Methuen.

Aune, R. K. (1999). The effects of perfume use on perceptions of attractiveness and competence. In L. K. Guerrero, J. DeVito, & M. L. Hecht (Eds.), *The nonverbal communication reader: Classic and contemporary readings* (2nd ed., pp. 126–132). Prospect Heights, IL: Waveland.

Baron-Cohen, S., Wheelwright, S., Hill, J., Raste, Y., & Plumb, I. (2001). The "Reading the Mind in the Eyes" Test Revised Version: A study with normal adults, and adults with Asperger Syndrome or high-functioning autism. *Journal of Child Psychology and Psychiatry, 42,* 241–251.

Beebe, S. A. (1974). Eye contact: A nonverbal determinant of speaker credibility. *Speech Teacher, 23,* 21–25.

Beebe, S. A., Beebe, S. J., & Ivy, D. K. (2007). *Communication: Principles for a lifetime* (3rd ed.). Boston: Allyn & Bacon.

Birdwhistell, R. L. (1960). Kinesics and communication. In E. Carpenter & M. McLuhan (Eds.), *Explorations in communication: An anthology* (pp. 54–64). Boston: Beacon.

Botta, R. A. (1999). Television images and adolescent girls' body image disturbance. *Journal of Communication, 49,* 22–37.

Brumback, R. A., Harper, C. R., & Weinberg, W. A. (1996). Nonverbal Learning Disabilities, Asperger's Syndrome, Pervasive Developmental Disorder: Should we care? *Journal of Child Neurology, 11,* 427–429.

Bryski, B. G., & Frye, J. K. (1979–1980). Nonverbal communication in presidential debates. *Australian Scan, 7 & 8,* 25–31.

Buck, R. (1978). The slide-viewing technique for measuring nonverbal sending accuracy: A guide for replication. *Catalog of Selected Documents in Psychology, 8,* 62.

Buck, R. (2005). Measuring emotional experience, expression, and communication: The slide-viewing technique. In V. Manusov (Ed.), *The sourcebook of nonverbal measures: Going beyond words* (pp. 457–470). Mahwah, NJ: Erlbaum.

Buck, R., Miller, R. E., & Caul, W. F. (1974). Sex, personality, and physiological variables in the communication of emotion via facial expression. *Journal of Personality and Social Psychology, 30,* 587–596.

Buck, R., Savin, V. J., Miller, R. E., & Caul, W. F. (1972). Nonverbal communication of affect in humans. *Journal of Personality and Social Psychology, 23,* 362–371.

Burgoon, J. K. (1978). A communication model of personal space violations: Explication and an initial test. *Human Communication Research, 4,* 129–142.

Burgoon, J. K., Birk, T., & Pfau, M. (1990). Nonverbal behaviors, persuasion, and credibility. *Human Communication Research, 17,* 140–169.

Burgoon, J. K., & Jones, S. B. (1976). Toward a theory of personal space expectations and their violations. *Human Communication Research, 2,* 131–146.

Carli, L. L., LaFleur, S. J., & Loeber, C. C. (1995). Nonverbal behavior, gender, and influence. *Journal of Personality and Social Psychology, 68,* 1030–1041.

Christenfeld, N. (1995). Does it hurt to say um? *Journal of Nonverbal Behavior, 19,* 171–186.

Cooley, E. L., & Treimer, D. M. (2002). Classroom behavior and the ability to decode nonverbal cues in boys with severe emotional disturbance. *Journal of Social Psychology, 142,* 741–751.

Davis, M. (1995). Presidential body politics: Movement analysis of debates and press conferences. *Semiotica, 106,* 205–244.

DeGroot, T., & Motowidlo, S. J. (1999). Why visual and vocal interview cues can affect interviewers' judgments and predict job performance. *Journal of Applied Psychology, 84,* 986–993.

Ekman, P., & Friesen, W. V. (1967). Head and body cues in the judgment of emotion: A reformulation. *Perceptual and Motor Skills, 24,* 711–724.

Ekman, P., & Friesen, W. V. (1968). Nonverbal behavior in psychotherapy research. *Research in Psychotherapy, 1,* 179–216.

Ekman, P., & Friesen, W. V. (1975). *Unmasking the face.* Englewood Cliffs, NJ: Prentice-Hall.

Field, T. (1982). Individual differences in the expressivity of neonates and young infants. In R. S. Feldman (Ed.), *Development of nonverbal behavior in children.* New York: Springer-Verlag.

Field, T., Woodson, R., Greenberg, R., & Cohen, D. (1982). Discrimination and imitation of facial expressions of neonates. *Science, 218,* 179–181.

Fisher, J. D., Rytting, M., & Heslin, R. (1976). Hands touching hands: Affective and evaluative effects of an interpersonal touch. *Sociometry, 39,* 416–421.

Forbes, G. B., Adams-Curtis, L. E., Rade, B., & Jaberg, P. (2001). Body dissatisfaction in women and men: The role of gender-typing and self-esteem. *Sex Roles, 44,* 461–484.

Furlow, F. B. (1999). The smell of love. In L. K. Guerrero, J. DeVito, & M. L. Hecht (Eds.), *The nonverbal communication reader: Classic and contemporary readings* (2nd ed., pp. 118–125). Prospect Heights, IL: Waveland.

Goffman, E. (1971). *Relations in public: Microstudies of the public order.* New York: Harper Colophon.

Gorham, J., Cohen, S. H., & Morris, T. L. (1999). Fashion in the classroom III: Effects of instructor attire and immediacy in natural classroom interactions. *Communication Quarterly, 47,* 281–299.

Gosling, S. D., Ko, S. J., Mannarelli, T., & Morris, M. E. (2002). A room with a cue: Personality judgments based on offices and bedrooms. *Journal of Personality and Social Psychology, 82,* 379–398.

Gosselin P., Gilles, K., & Dore, F. Y. (1995). Components and recognition of facial expression in the communication of emotion by actors. *Journal of Personality and Social Psychology, 68,* 83–96.

Guerrero, L. K., & Floyd, K. (2006). *Nonverbal communication in close relationships.* Mahwah, NJ: Erlbaum.

Hall, E. T. (1959). *The silent language.* Garden City, NY: Doubleday.

Hall, E. T. (1966). *The hidden dimension.* Garden City, NY: Doubleday.

Hall, J. A. (1984). *Nonverbal sex differences: Communication accuracy and expressive style.* Baltimore: Johns Hopkins University Press.

Hall, J. A. (2005). Meta-analysis of nonverbal behavior. In V. Manusov (Ed.), *The sourcebook of nonverbal measures: Going beyond words* (pp. 483–492). Mahwah, NJ: Erlbaum.

Hall, J. A., LeBeau, L. S., Reinoso, J. G., & Thayer, F. (2001). Status, gender, and nonverbal behavior in candid and posed photographs: A study of conversations between university employees. *Sex Roles, 44,* 677–692.

Hall, J. A., Murphy, N. A., & Schmid Mast, M. (2006). Recall of nonverbal cues: Exploring a new definition of interpersonal sensitivity. *Journal of Nonverbal Behavior, 30,* 141–155.

Helweg-Larsen, M., Cunningham, S. J., Carrico, A., & Pergram, A. M. (2004). To nod or not to nod: An observational study of nonverbal communication and status in female and male college students. *Psychology of Women Quarterly, 28,* 358–361.

Hinkle, L. L. (2001). Perceptions of supervisor nonverbal immediacy, vocalics, and subordinate liking. *Communication Research Reports, 18,* 128–136.

Horgan, T. G., Schmid Mast, M., Hall, J. A., & Carter, J. D. (2004). Gender differences in memory for the appearance of others. *Personality and Social Psychology Bulletin, 30,* 185–196.

Jones, S. E., & Yarbrough, A. E. (1985). A naturalistic study of the meanings of touch. *Communication Monographs, 52,* 19–56.

Krail, K. A., & Leventhal, G. (1976). The sex variable in the invasion of personal space. *Sociometry, 39,* 170–173.

LePoire, B., Duggan, A., Shepard, C., & Burgoon, J. (2002). Relational messages associated with nonverbal involvement, pleasantness, and expressiveness in romantic couples. *Communication Research Reports, 19,* 195–206.

Lieberman, D. A., Rigo, T. G., & Campain, R. F. (1988). Age-related differences in nonverbal decoding ability. *Communication Quarterly, 36,* 290–297.

Little, L. (1999). The misunderstood child: The child with a Nonverbal Learning Disorder. *Journal of the Society of Pediatric Nurses, 4,* 113–121.

Lohmann, A., Arriaga, X. B., & Goodfriend, W. (2003). Close relationships and placemaking: Do objects in a couple's home reflect couplehood? *Personal Relationships, 10,* 437–449.

Lyman, S. M., & Scott, M. B. (1999). Territoriality: A neglected sociological dimension. In L. K. Guerrero, J. DeVito, & M. L. Hecht (Eds.), *The nonverbal communication reader: Classic and contemporary readings* (2nd ed., pp. 175–183). Prospect Heights, IL: Waveland.

Manen, M. (2007). *Understanding Nonverbal Learning Disabilities: A common-sense guide for parents and professionals.* London: Jessica Kingsley Publishers.

Maslow, A. H., & Mintz, N. L. (1956). Effects of esthetic surroundings: I. *Journal of Psychology, 41,* 247–254.

McClure, E. B. (2000). A meta-analytic review of sex differences in facial expression processing and their development in infants, children, and adolescents. *Psychological Bulletin, 126,* 424–453.

McGinty, K., Knox, D., & Zusman, M. E. (2003). Nonverbal and verbal communication in "involved" and "casual" relationships among college students. *College Student Journal, 37,* 68–71.

Mehrabian, A. (1972). *Nonverbal communication.* Chicago: Atherton.

Mehrabian, A. (1981). *Silent messages* (2nd ed.). Belmont, CA: Wadsworth.

Mintz, N. L. (1956). Effects of esthetic surroundings: II. Prolonged and repeated experience in a "beautiful" and "ugly" room. *Journal of Psychology, 41,* 459–466.

Montagu, M. F. A. (1971). *Touching: The human significance of the skin.* New York: Columbia University Press.

Montell, G. (2003, October 15). Do good looks equal good evaluations? *The Chronicle of Higher Education: Career Network.* Available: www.chronicle.com

Morris, D. (1985). *Bodywatching.* New York: Crown.

Napieraliski, L. P., Brooks, C. I., & Droney, J. M. (1995). The effect of duration of eye contact on American college students' attributions of state, trait, and test anxiety. *Journal of Social Psychology, 135,* 273–280.

Nonverbal Learning Disorder. (2007). Available: www.raisingsmallsouls.com/nonverbal-learning-disorder/

Nowicki, S., Jr., & Carton, E. (1997). The relation of nonverbal processing ability of faces and voices and children's feelings of depression and competence. *Journal of Genetic Psychology, 158,* 357–363.

Nowicki, S., Jr., & Duke, M. P. (1992). *Helping the child who doesn't fit in.* Atlanta: Peachtree Publishers.

Nowicki, S., Jr., & Duke, M. P. (1994). Individual differences in the nonverbal communication of affect: The Diagnostic Analysis of Nonverbal Accuracy Scale. *Journal of Nonverbal Behavior, 18,* 9–35.

Nowicki, S., Jr., & Duke, M. P. (2001). Nonverbal receptivity: The Diagnostic Analysis of Nonverbal Accuracy (DANVA). In J. A. Hall & F. J. Bernieri (Eds.), *Interpersonal sensitivity: Theory and measurement* (pp. 183–198). Mahwah, NJ: Erlbaum.

Nowicki, S., Jr., Glanville, D., & Demertzis, A. (1998). A test of the ability to recognize emotion in the facial expressions of African American adults. *Journal of Black Psychology, 24,* 335–350.

Nowicki, S., Jr., & Mitchell, J. (1998). Accuracy in identifying affect in child and adult faces and voices and social competence in preschool children. *Genetic, Social, and General Psychology Monographs, 124,* 39–59.

*Oxford desk dictionary and thesaurus* (American ed.). (1997). New York: Berkley Books.

Peterson, D. R. (1991). Interpersonal relationships as a link between person and environment. In W. B. Walsh, K. H. Craig, & R. H. Price (Eds.), *Person-environment psychology.* Hillsdale, NJ: Erlbaum.

Rapoport, A. (1982). *The meaning of the built environment: A nonverbal communication approach.* Beverly Hills: Sage.

Reiss, M., & Rosenfeld, P. (1980). Seating preferences as nonverbal communication: A self-presentational analysis. *Journal of Applied Communication Research, 8,* 22–28.

Remland, M. S., Jones, T. S., & Brinkman, J. (1991). Proxemic and haptic behavior in three European countries. *Journal of Nonverbal Behavior, 15,* 215–231.

Remland, M. S., Jones, T. S., & Brinkman, J. (1995). Interpersonal distance, body orientation, and touch: Effect of culture, gender, and age. *Journal of Social Psychology, 135,* 281–295.

Riggio, R. E. (2006). Nonverbal skills and abilities. In V. Manusov & M. L. Patterson (Eds.), *The Sage handbook of nonverbal communication* (pp. 79–95). Thousand Oaks, CA: Sage.

Roach, K. D. (1997). Effects of graduate teaching assistant attire on student learning, misbehaviors, and ratings of instruction. *Communication Quarterly, 45,* 125–141.

Roger, D. B., & Reid, R. L. (1982). Role differentiation and seating arrangements: A further study. *British Journal of Social Psychology, 21,* 23–29.

Rosenthal, R., Hall, J. A., DiMatteo, M. R., Rogers, P. L., & Archer, D. (1979). *Sensitivity to nonverbal communication: The PONS test.* Baltimore: Johns Hopkins University Press.

Rotter, N. G., & Rotter, G. S. (1988). Sex differences in the encoding and decoding of negative facial emotions. *Journal of Nonverbal Behavior, 12,* 139–148.

Sandalla, E. (1987). Identity symbolism in housing. *Environment and Behavior, 19,* 569–587.

Sandberg, J. (2003, March 2). Want to know someone's job status? Look at desk location. *Corpus Christi Caller Times,* D4.

Schmid Mast, M., & Hall, J. A. (2004). Who is the boss and who is not? Accuracy of judging status. *Journal of Nonverbal Behavior, 28,* 145–165.

Sommer, R. (1961). Leadership and group geography. *Sociometry, 24,* 99–110.

Sprouse, C. A., Hall, C. W., Webster, R. E., & Bolen, L. M. (1998). Social perception in students with learning disabilities and attention-deficit/hyperactivity disorder. *Journal of Nonverbal Behavior, 22,* 125–134.

Stewart, K. (2007). *Helping a child with Nonverbal Learning Disorder or Asperger's Disorder: A parent's guide* (2nd ed.). Oakland, CA: New Harbinger Publications.

Street, R. L., Jr., Brady, R. M., & Lee, R. (1984). Evaluative responses to communicators: The effects of speech rate, sex, and interaction context. *Western Journal of Speech Communication, 48,* 14–27.

Tanguay, P. B. (2001). *Nonverbal Learning Disorder at home: A parent's guide.* London: Jessica Kingsley Publishers.

Tenner, E. (2004, October 1). Political timber: Glitter, froth, and measuring tape. *The Chronicle of Higher Education,* B12-B13.

Termine, N. T., & Izard, C. E. (1988). Infants' responses to their mothers' expressions of joy and sadness. *Developmental Psychology, 24,* 223–229.

Thompson, S. (1997). *The source for Nonverbal Learning Disorders.* East Moline, IL: LinguiSystems.

Tiedens, L. Z., & Fragale, A. R. (2003). Power moves: Complementarity in dominant and submissive nonverbal behavior. *Journal of Personality and Social Psychology, 84,* 558–568.

Tiemens, R. K. (1978). Television's portrayal of the 1976 presidential debates: An analysis of visual content. *Communication Monographs, 45,* 362–370.

Transportation Security Administration. (2008). Available: www.tsa.gov

Wagner, H. L., MacDonald, C. J., & Manstead, A. S. R. (1986). Communication of individual emotions by spontaneous facial expressions. *Journal of Personality and Social Psychology, 50,* 737–743.

Wiederman, M., & Hurst, S. (1998). Body size, physical attractiveness, and body image among young adult women: Relationships to sexual experience and sexual esteem. *Journal of Sex Research, 35,* 272–281.

Weisfeld, C. C., & Stack, M. A. (2002). When I look into your eyes: An ethnological analysis of gender differences in married couples' nonverbal behaviors. *Psychology, Evolution, and Gender, 4,* 125–147.

Zuckerman, M., DePaulo, B. M., & Rosenthal, R. (1981). Verbal and nonverbal communication of deception. In L. Berkowitz (Ed.), *Advances in experimental social psychology* (Vol. 14). New York: Academic Press.

# Environment as Nonverbal Communication

## Chapter 3

## Our Perceptions and Reactions

## CHAPTER OUTLINE ■ ■ ■ ■ ■

## CHAPTER OBJECTIVES ■ ■ ■ ■ ■

After studying this chapter, you should be able to:

1. Understand how people perceive the environment as a form of nonverbal communication.
2. Increase your awareness of the environments you maintain in personal and professional life.
3. Identify and define the six ways to perceive an environment.
4. Improve your perceptual skills to better understand the expectations that others have about environment.
5. Define chronemics and give examples of how time affects communication.
6. Explain Knapp and Hall's four perceptions of time.
7. Understand the impact of color, sound, lighting, smell, and temperature on human communication.
8. Understand the environment as discussed in popular culture and media.

## CASE STUDY   My "Time" in London

About six months ago I took a trip to London for some relaxation and serious shopping. One day, I grabbed a bite to eat around 11:40 a.m. to beat the lunch crowd and make it to the shops early. After lunch I was ready to start shopping but what happened next shocked me. I went to the shopping strip at about 12:25 p.m. and could not find a shop open. Signs hung in the windows reading *OUT TO LUNCH*. This was odd to me because in U.S. culture we don't close retail stores during lunch. So I stopped a passerby and asked her when stores normally opened after lunch. She informed me that store owners would be back "after they were done." This didn't help me, so I asked another passerby and he informed me that in London, workers can take up to three hours for lunch! They're on a more relaxed schedule than Americans. They're advised to go home, have lunch and spend time with the family, take a nap, and return after they're rested. This blew my mind; nevertheless, I returned to the strip at 2:30 p.m. and commenced my shopping. Time is definitely ruled by culture.

**Paula:**   "Why are you burning all these candles in your office?"

**Wes:**   "I'm trying to get that creepy smell out of here."

**Paula:**   "What creepy smell?"

**Wes:**   "I've noticed that my office still smells like Charlie's cheap cologne. I'm so glad that pathetic guy moved on to another company. I dunno, just the smell of that guy gives me the creeps."

**Paula:**   "I know what you mean. Your clients may notice that old cheap cologne smell and not want to buy a policy from you. The vanilla candles and your new office arrangement are great!"

What does the above situation teach us? The interaction between Paula and Wes relates to an aspect of nonverbal communication called **environment**—the built or natural surroundings that serve as the contexts in which people interact. Can you think of an environment in your personal or professional life that stands out? Some of us may think of our favorite places to eat or hang out with friends. Pubs, bars, coffee houses, diners, and restaurants may come to mind as comfortable environments where we like to have down time or meet others for recreation or friendly conversation. We can also think of environments that are not as comfortable, friendly, or inviting. Imagine this: You go to interview for a new job. The manager who's going to make the final decision to hire you is extremely late. Meanwhile, you're sitting in her or his office waiting. The temperature is quite warm, so you begin to sweat profusely. You also notice an old pizza box on the manager's desk, with crusted remnants of some past meal inside. Would you be excited to start working for this person? How is this office environment going to influence your interview? Do you now even *want* to interview? Will you verbally and nonverbally communicate differently, because of the environmental effects?

People are significantly influenced by environmental factors such as architecture, design, doors, windows, color, lighting, smell, seating arrangements, temperature, and cleanliness (Harris & Sachau, 2005; Jackson, 2005; McElroy, Morrow, & Ackerman, 1983; Morrow & McElroy, 1981; Salacuse, 2005; Teven, 1996; Vilnai-Yavetz, Rafaeli, & Schneider-Yaacov, 2005; Vogler & Jorgenson, 2005; Zweigenhaft, 1976). Whether we're satisfied or dissatisfied with the environment in which we're communicating with friends or interviewing for a new job, it's important to realize that environment is a critical code to examine when studying nonverbal communication.

## ■ ENVIRONMENT AS NONVERBAL COMMUNICATION

 The goal of this chapter is to make you more aware of how people perceive an environment, the control we have over establishing, maintaining, and regulating healthy communication environments, and how these environments influence our communicative decisions in personal and professional life. You may be thinking, How does the environment communicate something about people? The connection between people and environment needs to be made for two reasons: (1) The choices you make about the environment in which you live or work reveal a good deal about who you are, and (2) your nonverbal communication is altered by the environments in which you communicate.

A couple of landmark studies conducted in the 1950s brought our attention to the environment as a nonverbal influence on communication (Maslow & Mintz, 1956; Mintz, 1956). In these experiments, one group of people was placed in a "beautiful" room—a space with adequate lighting, comfortable furniture, and pleasant colors. Another group of people was placed in an "ugly" room—a space with dim lighting, shabby furniture, and dark colors. Each group was asked to rate a series of photographs of people in terms of the attractiveness of the people pictured in the photos. In both studies, the results consistently showed that people in the ugly room took longer to complete their ratings, and they rated the people in the photos as significantly less attractive than people in the beautiful room. Surroundings do make a difference.

As we focus on the environment and physical surroundings in this chapter, we want to emphasize that some environments are already built, but other environments we create or adorn for ourselves (e.g., homes, offices, furniture, decorating choices, colors, smells). In fact, many people maintain an entire repertoire that helps them design a unique and personal environment, complete with such things as lighting, pictures, candles, plants, and music (Gosling, Ko, Mannarelli, & Morris, 2002; Sandalla, 1987). Further, the environments we create for ourselves often speak volumes about those relationships we deem most important, such as creating a highly romantic bedroom so as to signal the importance of private life with a partner or spouse, or enlarging an office to make room for a coworker (Lohmann, Arriaga, & Goodfriend, 2003).

While it's tempting to think about environment as being solely interior, realize that exterior environments also communicate nonverbally. Let's think first about environments we don't create personally—the state capital building or the White House in Washington, D.C., for example. Many college campuses have a central building called Old Main or the Main Building that is connected to student and alumni identity and which serves as a focal or historical point for the campus for many generations (Biemiller, 2007). These buildings communicate something before we even enter, and our verbal and nonverbal communication are affected by those structures when we approach and enter them. While we hate to bring up a sad memory for all of us, the World Trade Center and Pentagon disasters of September 11, 2001, come to mind in this discussion. Horrific crimes were committed that day against our people, as well as important symbols of American prosperity and sovereignty. The site of the two tallest buildings in the country being toppled by a terrorist attack is something we will not soon forget.

Communication scholar Darryl Hattenhauer (1984) helps us understand what he calls the **rhetoric of architecture** by explaining that "architecture not only communicates, but also communicates rhetorically. Churches, shopping malls, doors and stairs—these architectural items not only tell us their meaning and function, but also influence our behavior" (p. 71). Authors of a recent study of environment found that people's motivations to engage in physical activity, such as walking to the grocery store or to work, depend on the condition of sidewalks, roadways, and pedestrian

*What do these buildings at the University of Oxford, England, communicate nonverbally?*

signals on their route (Sallis & Kerr, 2008). Thus, urban planners and transportation specialists give attention to the kinds of external environments that impact human behavior. Have you ever thought about how the built environment on your college campus or neighborhood makes an impact on your everyday decisions? Do you walk, drive, or take a shuttle bus to class? Are some routes you use to navigate your campus more safe and attractive than others? Some of you may live on campus, which allows you to walk to class, while others may commute and face competition for good parking spaces. All of these environmental factors affect our daily experiences, decisions, and communication.

Now that we've discussed such built environments as college facilities, parks, sidewalks, and roads, let's explore some interior environments. Think about banks and financial institutions: A particular environment of professionalism is expected since people who work in these kinds of places take care of money. While many people are shifting their financial management and banking to the Internet, banks in the United States focus on customers who enter local branches wanting a warm and comfortable, yet private environment for conducting financial business. In fact, part of customer satisfaction and establishing a warm environment in the banking business is created by the fresh smell and availability of coffee for any customer who enters the door (Martin, 2006).

Whether it's the exterior look of a building or the interior smell of coffee, we know from the outside construction of a building and the inside "feel" that's established that a certain kind of activity takes place there. Especially in the case of banking, customers expect a comfortable environment, but one that also communicates professionalism and trust. The same is true for your school library. Most of us learned at a very young age that we were expected to be quiet upon entering. We know that people are engaged in the serious business of researching and writing. In other words, when we see or enter a library, we don't think, "It's party time!" The point here is that our communication in a library, church, state capital building, and so forth is likely to be much different than our communication at a local pub, coffee shop, or health club.

Think about environments that you maintain, personally and professionally. What about your bedroom? If someone who didn't know you walked into your bedroom, what perception would she or he have of you? Are your clothes on the floor or put away? Think of other things that may or may not be present in the environment that can serve as nonverbal cues of who you are, what motivates you, whether you're shy or outgoing, and so on. These environmental factors that you create and control serve as nonverbal messages to others who enter, unintentionally or by invitation.

Just as an awareness of those environments we own and operate is important, we also need to become more aware of environments we don't maintain. Think back to the dirty office with pizza boxes. The manager in this example maintains the office where you're going to interview. This environment communicates something about his or her professionalism, credibility, and organizational skills, which leads to **impression management**—the formation of an impression, perception, or view of other (Goffman, 1971; Harris & Sachau, 2005). Remember, you haven't even met this manager yet, so all you have to go by are nonverbal communicative clues. Would this

*Which nonverbal cues do you receive about a person whose closet looks like this?*

be a good place to work? What kind of manager is this person? As you sit in the office, you begin to look around for something to clue you as to what you are about to encounter. Now think more generally about job interviews: Would you want to be interviewed for a job in a cubicle located next to the restroom? You probably wouldn't be interviewed in an environment like this, considering that low-ranking workers tend to sit by restrooms and in high-traffic areas, while higher-ranking managers (who typically do the hiring) get the larger offices with picture windows and private elevators (Farrenkopf & Roth, 1980; Sandberg, 2003). Of course, people want to communicate in comfortable environments, whether they have thought about it before or not. This is especially true when we enter into new communication contexts we're not familiar with and where we don't know what to expect (Jackson, 2005; Teven, 1996).

Now, we don't want to suggest that people with messy offices, apartments, or houses are bad people. In fact, some of your best professors and book authors have messy offices. Perhaps you think of the "mad" or "absent-minded professor" who has books and notes all over the floor. On the other hand, we can think of offices that are extremely warm, comfortable, and inviting. The point is this: The environments created in offices, classrooms, and so forth establish comfortable or uncomfortable communication contexts that influence our perceptions of safety and comfort, as well as the attitude and character of the persons inhabiting the space (Bowen & Kilmann, 1975; Holley & Steiner, 2005; Jackson, 2005; McCroskey & McVetta, 1978; Stires, 1980; Teven, 1996; Winchip, 1996; Wollin & Montagre, 1981).

Your textbook authors have a colleague who immediately came to mind as we were crafting this chapter. As some of you have already experienced, you never know what to expect upon entering faculty offices. Our colleague has a very warm, inviting, and soothing office, furnished with a comfortable couch for students to sit on during conferences. Elegant paintings, green plants, and even a slight smell of incense complement the office decor. Clearly, our colleague has created an environment in which students and coworkers alike feel comfortable. In contrast, think of a professor's office with no pictures, blank white walls, one hard wooden chair behind the desk, and no chairs for students to use. In which type of office would you want to have a conversation? Now that we have established that environment is a form of nonverbal communication, let's focus on some specific human perceptions of environment.

*This is the office of a faculty colleague, Dr. Bilaye Benibo. He uses plants, personal items, and incense to create a warm, inviting, yet professional environment for students and colleagues to visit.*

## REMEMBER 3.1

| | |
|---|---|
| **Environment:** | built or natural surroundings that influence communication. |
| **Rhetoric of Architecture:** | architectural items (e.g., churches, shopping malls, doors, stairs) that have meaning and influence our behavior. |
| **Impression Management:** | formation of a perception or view of another person. |

# ▪ PERCEPTIONS OF ENVIRONMENT

Communication scholars Mark Knapp and Judith Hall (2006) suggest that people perceive their environment in six ways: formality, warmth, privacy, familiarity, constraint, and distance. Let's take a look at each of these perceptions, in terms of people and environment.

## Formality

Have you ever walked into a restaurant and walked right back out again because it was too fancy? Perhaps you've walked into a classroom on the first day and felt extremely nervous. We usually use words like "stuffy" and "serious," or "relaxed" and "casual" to explain our perception of the **formality** of an environment. Think about going on vacation and asking your cab driver for a good restaurant. The types of things the driver may ask are: What are you looking for? What are you in the mood for? We typically respond with the type of food we're hungry for or a place that's popular. But people are interested in the type of atmosphere that a restaurant provides—it's not all about the food. If you've ever walked out of a restaurant, it might not be just because it was more expensive than expected; it might be about the type of environment you desire. Think about your favorite place to eat. Is it formal? casual? relaxed? How does the formality (or lack thereof) influence the way you feel and communicate?

Some of us are church-goers, and people's preferences for church settings vary widely. For some of us, a very ornate, spacious, and formal church creates an environment of reverence that allows us to worship. Others want to get away from the formality often associated with church, so we seek a more informal church setting that allows for a less restricted demeanor. Again, remember that the environment serves as a form of nonverbal communication, but also influences our nonverbal communication within it. Formality is a perception that people have of environment that relates to how comfortably we can behave, in light of our expectations.

## Warmth

In addition to formality, **warmth** is another human perception of environment, meaning that an environment can give off a sense of warmth or coldness. As a perception of environment, warmth goes beyond temperature. Our sense of warmth is about how we perceive and desire a comfortable, welcoming context that is part of our past or current experience. Can you remember a favorite smell from your childhood? Some of you may think of your grandma's house or a cultural tradition. Smells in an environment certainly contribute to our perception of warmth, as can colors and furnishings. In everyday expression, we often hear people talk about the warmth of the home where they grew up or stories of looking forward to going home. After a trip to visit family or a long day at work or school, people often say, "I just want to go home."

Reflect for a moment on environments that you perceive as providing warmth. While the warmth or welcome feeling of grandma's house might make a connection with many of us, it's important to consider other environments that people perceive as warm. For example, many hotel/motel chains focus on marketing the warmth of their room services. For years, Motel 6 used the phrase in its advertising, "We'll leave the light on for you." This phrase (and the "folksy" sound of the voice in the ads) connected customers to the benefits of an affordable motel room that was ready to welcome guests at any time. Higher scale hotels have started to emphasize the warmth of their facilities as well. Customers are provided more than "just a room." In fact, many ad spots for these companies feature some of the comforts of home, such as coffee pots, hair dryers, ironing boards and irons, comfortable bedding, bottled water, mini refrigerators, and high pressure shower heads to make the room more warm and comfortable for business travelers and families on vacation.

In addition to the warmth of individual rooms, hotels and resorts spend a great deal of money on other aspects of their properties. Many casino resorts in cities like Las Vegas emphasize smell, lighting, color, and sound to create a sense of warmth and comfort for customers who wager money on table games, sports book, or slot machines. (Better to lose money in a warm, inviting environment than a stuffy, uncomfortable one!) Certain combinations of wall or curtain color, carpeting, furniture style, sounds, and smells promote human perceptions of warmth, and make people want to linger in the environment.

## Privacy

People also have a perception of **privacy** when it comes to environment. What type of environment do you prefer if you are meeting someone to talk about something important in your life? Do you prefer a crowded, noisy restaurant, a quiet bar, or someone's personal space, like their home or apartment? Ask anyone who's ever worked at a restaurant and she or he will tell you that the booths in the restaurant fill up faster than the tables, mainly because booths offer some semblance of privacy.

To further illustrate privacy as a perception people have of environment, let's turn to a very real example in which a private environment is likely needed. Megan is a lesbian and has been in a same-sex partnership for several years. She is very selective about who she shares her personal life with, but has decided that the feeling and time is right for her to come out to her mom and dad. This is an extremely emotional and sensitive time for Megan, since she has avoided telling her parents about her sexual orientation and committed relationship for some time now. Megan is an only child and has always been close with her family; one family tradition is to go out to eat for special occasions. Megan believes that the best context in which to break the news to her family will be a restaurant—a place where her mom and dad always bond and share exciting news, as well as discuss serious family matters. So Megan needs to choose a restaurant where she can connect with her parents, have a good dinner, and be provided with a communication context that is relatively private, as she does not know how her mom and dad will respond—whether it will be happiness or if tears will flow in confusion and sadness.

As Megan begins to think about the right environment in which to break her news to her family, several factors come to mind. First, she knows that she wants to sit in a booth to provide a sense of privacy in a public space, because the degree of privacy will affect how she communicates to her parents and they to her. Many of us can relate to experiences in which we were in the middle of a room in the spotlight, so to speak. Clearly, Megan does not want to sit in the middle of a crowded restaurant where others can overhear her conversation with her family, so she calls a local restaurant that takes reservations and can guarantee her a booth. Megan's situation teaches us that environment is important. Can you think of a time when you desired privacy? You can probably think of numerous life situations like first dates, talking to an important person about a serious issue, and so forth. These are all cases in which we need to have privacy, so we seek environments that will allow us the privacy we perceive we need. In some situations, privacy is not what we desire; we may want to be noticed and the center of the action in a public place, so with privacy, it's a matter of degree.

## Familiarity

A new karaoke bar is opening in town and your friends want you to meet them there. You enjoy going out for social time and to let loose with your friends, but this time, you're "going where you've never gone before." Karaoke is something you've always avoided because you don't like to sing in public. What's this place going to be like? What kind of crowd goes there? Will you be pressured to sing? When we meet a new person or encounter an unfamiliar environment, our response is cautionary, anxious, and sometimes mechanical. We've all been in situations where we feel like the clod entering through the front door. We're outside our comfort zone and don't know the rituals and norms associated with this unfamiliar environment. Our need for **familiarity** in an environment causes us to ask questions like: Have I been there before? What kind of crowd usually hangs out there? Is it easy to find a seat? Where's the best place to sit? Can I call you when I'm on my way so we can meet up and I won't feel stupid? These questions show us that while we may be open to experiencing new things, we still like to be clued about where we're going and what to expect. Our need for familiarity in an environment leads us to develop favorite hangouts, or to prefer a certain booth or table in the hangout because we enjoy the certainty of knowing what to expect and how to behave in the environment.

*In many restaurants, booths offer customers privacy, which is why booths tend to fill faster than tables.*

## Constraint

Think of a long car trip filled with people you don't like. In many instances, we have to gear ourselves up for experiences we don't want to be in. Human perceptions of **constraint** are psychological. We like to think of this as the "How can I get out of here?" aspect. Beyond the awkward road trip, we might also dread temporary living arrangements, such as having to share a room with friends, colleagues, or family members during a vacation or business trip. In fact, researchers have studied the coping strategies of students living in crowded hostels in Nigeria and found that students coped by staying away from the room and by creating and decorating personal spaces within the environment (Amole, 2005). We can usually think of ways to cope with temporary confinement, such as staying away from the environment as much as possible, going on long walks, listening to music, and so forth. On the other hand, other spaces of confinement are more permanent, such as prisons, rehabilitation clinics, and nursing homes. Most of our perceptions of constraint are shaped by the amount of privacy and space we have available to us.

## SPOTLIGHT on Research

The impressions that others have of us are facts of life that we must deal with and manage in our personal and professional relationships. Beyond the impressions that people form as a result of such things as the kind of car we drive or clothes we wear, cleanliness of living environments seems to be important in U.S. culture, especially as it relates to the impressions we form about people. Many cultures associate cleanliness with family values and the good life, while a lack of cleanliness is associated with poverty.

One fascinating line of research examined the cleanliness of an apartment to see if it would affect visitor impressions of the resident. Researchers Paul Harris and Daniel Sachau (2005) studied living environments of good and poor housekeepers, specifically how visitors perceive people based on their clean or dirty living environments. The results of their study revealed that housekeeping is a cue people use to form impressions of an environment *and* its owners or occupants. Poor housekeepers received lower ratings in the following areas: agreeableness, conscientiousness, intelligence, and femininity. However, they received higher ratings on measures of being open and neurotic. In essence, according to this study, if you're a poor housekeeper, then you're perceived as less intelligent and less feminine (which may be okay if you're male!). The important thing to learn from this research is that people do form perceptions of others based on the clean or dirty environments within which they live and work.

You may be thinking: Why focus on housekeeping in impression formation? As Harris and Sachau's research shows, people do care about environments and look for cues to understand a communication context, as well as the type of people they're communicating with. Let's say that you've invited guests to your house for a party. Is your current state of cleanliness good enough for the party guests? We can think of times when we run for brooms, mops, brushes, and the strongest can of poison to kill the germs and make our place smell fresh and clean. We try to ward off the forces of dirt, bacteria, mold, and mildew. Bravo! When we're finished cleaning, we've transformed our home into a cleaner, fresher, and considerably more presentable environment. Why do we go to all of this trouble—is it because people form impressions of us based on the cleanliness of our home environments? Have you ever altered your living environment to prepare for visitors? Think about those aspects of personal or professional environment that you might modify to impress others.

Do you want to know more about this study? If so, read: Harris, P. B., & Sachau, D. (2005). Is cleanliness next to godliness? The role of housekeeping in impression formation. *Environment and Behavior, 37,* 81–101.

## Distance

While perceptions of constraint are more psychological in nature, our perceptions of **distance** in an environment pertain to physical arrangements, meaning how far something is away from us, where the closest door is located, how many people can fit in a space, and so forth. Take a moment to think about a closed area (e.g., an elevator, a crowded airplane). In such a situation, we often want to avoid intimate or personal connection with others. We do what we can to create distance by avoiding eye

## REMEMBER 3.2

### Knapp & Hall's System: Perceptions of Environment

| | |
|---|---|
| **Formality:** | perception of a place as "serious," "stuffy," "relaxed," or "casual." |
| **Warmth:** | perception of and desire for a comfortable, welcoming context that is part of our current or past experience. |
| **Privacy:** | perception of an environment that is protected from others who may overhear what is said. |
| **Familiarity:** | perception of having been in an environment enough times before that we know what to expect. |
| **Constraint:** | psychological perception related to getting out of or away from an environment. |
| **Distance:** | perception of physical arrangements, for example, how far away something is, where the closest door is located. |

contact, taking shorter or longer routes to avoid saying hello to people, erecting artificial barriers (such as laptop computers on a plane), and closing doors so people don't think we're present. We may also nonverbally indicate how crowded or intimate an environment is by making jokes; looking at our watch, cell phone, or personal belongings; or by being silent and immobile. All of these things combined can serve as our repertoire to communicate when space is limited. How do you communicate in an elevator? Do you avert your eyes from others to avoid conversation or cope with the crowded or claustrophobic environment? Do you stare at the gizmo on the wall that signals which floor you're on?

## ■ REACTIONS TO ENVIRONMENT

Now that we have explained human perceptions of the environment, it's important to consider how people *react* to environment. Have you ever thought about how you personally react to particular environments? Remember that, while environment serves as a form of nonverbal communication, it also affects our communication within it. Nonverbal scholar Albert Mehrabian (1976) studied people's emotional responses to their surroundings; he suggests that people react to environment (which may include the presence of other people in the environment) in the following three ways:

1. *Arousal:* How aroused, stimulated, or energized does an environment make you feel? Does an environment make you want to communicate and be social, or to be quiet and enjoy some "private time"?
2. *Pleasure:* How pleasurable, happy, or satisfied does an environment make you feel? Do you feel positive or negative emotions in the space? Do you want to

linger in the space and enjoy yourself, or do you want out of there as soon as possible?

3. *Dominance:* How dominant or powerful does an environment make you feel? Do you feel in control of the space or does the space control you?

While we hate to overuse the example of the college classroom, we know that it's one setting with which our readers can all relate. So think of a course you're currently taking and the classroom within which the course is delivered. What color are the walls? Are there chalkboards or whiteboards present, and how prominently are they arranged (meaning how much wall space do they take up)? What about multimedia elements in the room—are there large screens available, along with tables or desks with computer and media equipment stacked on or under them? In some college classrooms, professors have to lower a screen for a media presentation, but then raise it again to use the whiteboard underneath it (which we believe is poor design). Some professors don't have wireless remotes for the equipment, causing them to be "glued" to the computer table or cart so that they can work the equipment (again, a design flaw). What's the seating like in this classroom you're imagining? Are seats arranged in a large lecture style, bolted to desks and the floor, such that they're fixed, not movable? What sounds or smells are present? What's the lighting like—any windows?

Now let's use Mehrabian's framework to analyze the room: First, how aroused—visually, verbally, and nonverbally—are you to learn in this setting? Do white walls, cool or cold temperatures, musty smells, and artificial lighting put you to sleep, meaning low arousal? Or do warm colors, comfortable seating, and effective lighting make you more interested in learning? Second, does the seating arrangement feel pleasurable and satisfying, or uncomfortable and confining? How does the seating arrangement and overall size of the room affect your verbal communication—do these elements encourage you to interact in the environment, with both students and your professor? Or do these factors make you feel invisible, like you'd rather do anything but ask a question or volunteer a comment? Finally, how powerful or dominant (meaning in control) do you feel in this classroom environment? Does the environment make you feel like a speck in a sea of students (which can actually make you feel in control), or are you in such a small space that everything you do is easily seen by everyone in the room? If you changed where you sit in the class, would your perception of dominance (your sense of control) be altered?

## REMEMBER 3.3

### Mehrabian's Framework: Reactions to Environment

**Arousal:**      how stimulated or energized an environment makes us feel.

**Pleasure:**     how happy or satisfied an environment makes us feel.

**Dominance:**    how powerful or in control an environment makes us feel.

# ■ PERCEPTIONS OF TIME

We've established that the environment is communicative, in that people have perceptions of and reactions to environment. Another part of the communicative environment is time. You may be thinking: Why in the world is time connected to environment and nonverbal communication? Interestingly, time is something we cannot touch—it's intangible, so to speak. However, time is part of that repertoire of furniture, lighting, colors, sounds, smells, and architecture that make the environment communicative. In fact, time is part of how we experience the environment around us.

In the U.S., we try to make time into something that can be touched, meaning that when we spend our time doing something, we believe we should have something to show for it (e.g., products, materials, outcomes). We don't like it when people waste our time. We do our best to convert time into money. Employers reward employees with "overtime" and keep track of time by requiring their workforce to "clock in" and "punch out." In fact, many corporations send managers and CEOs to time management courses, so they can be productive with their time at work and teach workers to do so as well. Another example that we can perhaps all relate to is "wait time." Have you ever been to a restaurant and had to wait a long time to be seated or to get your food? Researchers Julie Baker and Michaelle Cameron (1996) examined the effects of certain elements (e.g., lighting, color, temperature) within a service environment on customer perceptions of wait time. They discovered that if an environment is pleasing, customers are more tolerant of having to wait longer periods of time than they expected.

Researchers have also examined how efficiently people use time, as in one study conducted at the School of Information and Computer Science at the University of California-Irvine (Morgenstern, 2006). The investigators found that office workers were interrupted every three minutes out of their average eight-hour work day. Given other research that has determined that people can take as long as 25 minutes to regain their concentration after being interrupted, a significant loss of productivity may occur in many workplaces.

Take a moment to think about the numerous indicators of time in our culture. Clocks, watches, timers, beepers, electronic organizers, and scheduling devices are integral parts of our daily experience. Cell phones, pagers, computers, and even our cars and home appliances have clocks displaying the time, which shows how much we care about time in American culture. Some watches show the time in multiple parts of the globe, for those who want to know this information.

Remember, however, that perceptions of time are culturally rooted (Hall, 1959). Many other countries do not view time the way that Americans do, which can lead to cultural misunderstandings (Gonzalez & Zimbardo, 1985). Communication scholar Peter Andersen (2004) explains how perceptions of time can differ in other cultures:

> In the United States and Northern Europe, waiting time for business and social engagements should be kept to a minimum. An American businessman in Latin America might be kept waiting all day for a meeting only to be told to come back tomorrow. This might be a major affront to the American but his Latin American counterpart has no idea this is offensive. (p. 123)

Arriving late to an appointment is generally viewed as inconsiderate and a waste of people's time in American culture, whereas in many other cultures around the world, a less rigid adherence to time constraints is the norm. In such cultures, people conforming to or expecting a rigid time structure may be seen as inflexible and uptight.

## Chronemics

Scholars have studied the communicative aspects of time, termed **chronemics.** Communication researchers Dawna Ballard and David Seibold (2000) help us understand the relationship between time and communication when they state, "Communication creates persons' views and understanding of time, yet our sense of time enables and constrains communication in important ways" (p. 219). Can you think of people who take forever to make a point? These people may simply believe that they need more time to express themselves. On the other hand, some people talk very quickly, rushing through information, such that we have to ask for a pause or clarification. If we're in a hurry and need a quick response, we might feel constrained or disrupted by people who are slower communicators. If we need a detailed explanation and someone rushes the message before there's even time to blink, we may feel disorganized or behind. Thus we may feel alternatively comforted or annoyed by people whose sense of timing differs from ours. Conversations work more effectively if communicators can establish a sort of rhythm, meaning that their timing is in synch.

In a more recent study of chronemics in the workplace, Ballard (2008) contends that the time people spend at work doing such tasks as checking email messages and reading work-related information can have a detrimental impact on job satisfaction, particularly if those tasks aren't considered central to all the other work that needs to get accomplished. Some people believe that email systems—originally intended to help us accomplish our work more efficiently—have actually added to our job duties instead of facilitating them. Spending a lot of time on tasks that seem to take away from our productivity instead of helping us accomplish our work can make us feel out of balance, unfocused, and stressed. Here's an example of a clash of chronemics we think students can relate to—time management in the classroom. Have you ever taken a class with a professor who ignored the time the class was supposed to end, causing you to have to sprint like an Olympian across campus to your next class or to your car to get to work? If you've been in this situation, you know that you start watching the clock in the classroom, your watch, or the readout on your cell phone, anticipating the professor's behavior and becoming agitated, such that you don't listen to the last few minutes of explanation or the announcement of a quiz for the next class session. So here's the main point from this research on chronemics: Time and communication work hand in hand. Time is yet another powerful nonverbal characteristic that can foster as well as constrain communication in a variety of contexts.

Another view of time concerns its **intentional** or **unintentional** use, and how our use of time serves as a form of communication (Dubinskas, 1988; Limaye & Victor, 1991; Schein, 1992). Intentional use of time involves such things as keeping another person waiting in order to communicate dominance or power or to evoke a certain emotion. Perhaps you've slowed down a presentation in order to make a certain required or expected time limit, or sped up the flow of conversation at a meeting so that the meeting could end early. People commonly draft timetables and deadlines for projects at work or home, and how rigidly or successfully they adhere to these timelines communicates volumes about who they are as people. However, many of our uses of time are unintentional communicators, but people still form impressions of us based on how we use time, intentionally and unintentionally. If you're constantly late to meetings or class, if you always arrive early to parties, or if you're usually the last one to leave a gathering, people will form judgments about you based on your use of time. These judgments translate into views about people's personalities or attributes (e.g., hardworking, enthusiastic, lazy, disorganized, rude).

Another approach to chronemics explores time through a cultural lens. In this research, time is viewed as being either **monochronic** or **polychronic** (Hall & Hall, 1990). In a monochronic view, time is almost tangible, as though it were a commodity that could be bought and sold. This perspective of time dominates most American business, as well as such European areas as Germany, Switzerland, and Scandinavia. A polychronic view of time is the opposite of a monochronic view. As one team of researchers describe it, polychronic time is "characterized by the simultaneous occurrence of many things and by a great involvement with people. There is more emphasis on completing human transactions than on holding to schedules" (Hall & Hall, 1990, p. 238).

## Knapp and Hall's Four Perceptions of Time

So we know that time is a nonverbal expression of culture as well as individuality, but how do most people view time? According to Knapp and Hall (2006), people perceive time in the following four ways.

**Time as Location:** References to "perfect timing" or something happening at the "right time" relate to how we expect things to happen in certain moments or locations in time. For example, if you're having an intimate moment with your significant other and the door bell rings, it's probably safe to say that you would think of this as "bad timing." We also use time to organize where we are and what we're going to be doing. For example, some people like to eat dinner exactly at 6 p.m., while others are fine with eating their evening meal anytime between 5 p.m. and 10 p.m.

Have you ever attributed different meanings to the timing of events in your life? For example, if all of your final exams are scheduled in a two-day time period, perhaps you view this timing as punishment. In the same way, we often arrange our schedules and set appointments based on the accomplishment of some time-related goal. Perhaps you've said, "I'm not going out with my friends until I get this paper finished." We use deadlines as incentives because we so greatly look forward to "down time," "personal time," "quality time," and "leisure time" as rewards for our accomplishments.

**Time as Duration:** Another perception we have of time regards how long particular experiences last. We can all likely think of a long car ride that seemed like it took forever to get to the final destination. Kids always ask, "Are we there yet?" Have you had to wait in a long line lately? Perhaps you've been to the doctor and felt like your experience in the waiting room took forever. Oftentimes, when little activity is going on, our perception of time seems to warp or spread out, meaning that a few minutes can feel like an hour. What about short periods of time? Have you ever said or heard any of the following: "How quickly a semester flies by" or "Time flies when you're having fun"? These catchphrases reflect the important role time plays in our lives.

**Time as Intervals:** The period of time between events also influences our perceptions. How we view the amount of time that separates one event from another is associated with the speed of our life. If you're in a long-distance romantic relationship, the amount of time that passes from the last time you were able to have a face-to-face visit to the next time you'll see your partner may be influenced by how busy you are with work, school, or activity in your social network. On the other hand, if you've spent several weekends home alone while your long-distance partner was on a business trip, the feelings of "I haven't seen you for a long time" may emerge more than when your speed of life was moving at a faster pace. To use a different example, college semesters seem to begin and end rather quickly (even when they seem to drag in the middle). Many of us can relate to the summer or winter break "flying by." We often say, "I wish I could have one more week" or "I can't believe it's time to go back to school already."

**Time as Patterns of Intervals:** As we experience a repetition or pattern of intervals of time, we begin to have rhythm or social pulse. This is when we feel on/off, connected/disconnected, in touch/out of touch, and ordered/disordered, to name a few. These feelings make up the cycles of our routines and life experiences. Understanding time as a pattern of intervals is critical to understanding our relationships and social interaction in everyday life. Have you ever said, "We're really in tune with each other" as a way of describing your communication or relational intensity with others in personal

---

### REMEMBER 3.4

| | |
|---|---|
| **Chronemics:** | study of how time is relevant to communication. |
| **Intentional Use of Time:** | use of time for a reason, such as establishing power or dominance over other people. |
| **Unintentional Use of Time:** | use of time to convey information or make attributions about other people. |
| **Monochronic Time:** | view of time as a tangible commodity. |
| **Polychronic Time:** | view of time that places more value on people than schedules. |
| **Time as Location:** | perception of time that organizes where we are and what we're going to be doing. |
| **Time as Duration:** | perception of how long particular experiences last. |
| **Time as Intervals:** | period of time between events that influences our perceptions; how we view the amount of time separating one event from another. |
| **Time as Patterns of Intervals:** | patterns of time, such as feeling connected/disconnected or in touch/out of touch, that indicate what types of predictions we make about our lives. |

---

and professional encounters? If you have, then you've recognized patterns of intervals of time. In the same way, we're sometimes out of tune with other people, sometimes called being "out of synch." We describe this lack of synchrony by saying, "We aren't *on* right now" or "We're not clicking as well on this project as the last one." This lack of synchrony can be accompanied with pausing, silence, and awkward feelings. At any rate, these connected/disconnected or in touch/out of touch patterns can clue us as to what types of predictions to make about our lives, meaning that it is helpful to prepare ourselves to experience these *on* and *off* rhythms in our relationships.

## ■ PERCEPTIONS OF COLOR

The next element of environment important to discuss is color. Researchers have generally categorized colors as being either warm (e.g., red, orange, yellow) or cool (e.g., blue, green). They have found that warm colors are more arousing and, in some cases, more stressful, as opposed to cool colors that are viewed as relaxing and less stressful (Bellizzi, Crowley, & Hasty, 1983).

Three perceptual dimensions of color exist: hue, brightness, and saturation (Arnheim, 1954; Mehrabian, 1976). The word **hue** refers to the modification of a basic color (e.g., bluish green, reddish orange) in an environment, while **brightness** refers to color intensity. Think of when you've been in a really bright room (e.g., bright orange, neon green). Depending on our mood on any given day, we may desire to be in a bright environment. (We sometimes refer to brighter environments such as colorful restaurants as "festive.") On the other hand, we tend to avoid brightness when we're tired or want to relax and even refer to colorful environments we want to avoid as "loud." **Saturation** refers to the amount of color present in an environment. For example, a bright red door might be used to accent a light-colored house, but an entire environment saturated in bright red might not be as appealing. Specifically, a high degree of brightness and a high degree of saturation can promote feelings of agitation, while weak colors (meaning those lacking brightness) promote feelings of calmness regardless of hue (Arnheim, 1954; Mehrabian, 1976). Have you ever been in a situation where the room color stressed you out or made you tired? The effects of color in an environment will vary with its amount and location. Small amounts of a bright or saturated color used as an accent in an otherwise neutral room will not have the same effect as the same color on large areas (Baker & Cameron, 1996).

Scholarly studies have been conducted on the effects of color on human behavior, with sometimes conflicting results. In one line of research, prison behavior in response to the wall color of prisoners' holding cells was studied, with the results being that lighter colors, specifically pink, made prisoners weaker and less aggressive (Pellegrini & Schauss, 1980). Another study found that the color pink, instead of weakening people, actually aroused them (Smith, Bell, & Fusco, 1986). This line of research supports a direct correlation between color of an environment and human behavior.

Another area of research on color focuses on its connection to mood. As detailed in Table 3.1, the results of this line of research show that in the case of some moods, a single color is significantly related, while in other cases, two or more colors promote

*This children's learning environment is filled with color, to stimulate learning and attention.*

a particular mood (Murray & Deabler, 1957; Wexner, 1954). Colors present in works of art have been found to influence human mood in healthcare facilities (Stein, 2006). Scholar Shifra Stein (2008) writes about the Society for the Arts in Health, an organization that "has joined together to promote the idea that viewing or creating art can boost the immune system, alter pain perception, and promote health and well being" (pp. 287–288). Can you think of an experience when the color of an environment was distracting, soothing, or energizing? How did you feel in the environment? Did the color influence your communication?

Researchers have also studied the influence of color on marketing and consumer environments, finding that certain colors match shoppers' expectations and actually enhance sales (Aslam, 2006; Bellizzi & Hite, 1992; Jansson, Marlow, & Bristow, 2004). Is your choice of a shopping environment or your selection of products to purchase influenced by colors in the setting? Do you think that the colors within store environments influence how much or how little you spend? The next time you're shopping, pay attention to the colors present in your favorite stores, since they're a form of nonverbal communication related to environment.

TABLE 3.1    Colors Associated with Moods

| MOOD/TONE | COLOR |
|---|---|
| Exciting/Stimulating | Red |
| Secure/Comfortable | Blue |
| Distressed/Disturbed/Upset | Orange |
| Tender/Soothing | Blue |
| Protective/Defending | Brown, Blue, Black, Purple |
| Despondent/Dejected/Unhappy/Melancholy | Black, Brown |
| Calm/Peaceful/Serene | Blue, Green |
| Dignified/Stately | Purple |
| Cheerful/Jovial/Joyful | Yellow |
| Defiant/Contrary/Hostile | Red, Orange, Black |
| Powerful/Strong/Masterful | Black |

Table adapted and reproduced with permission of: Wexner, L. B. (1954). The degree to which colors (hues) are associated with mood-tones. *Journal of Applied Psychology, 38,* 432–435.

## ■ PERCEPTIONS OF LIGHTING

Lighting also shapes our perceptions of an environment, which in turn influences how we communicate in that environment. Researchers have found that people tend to be less noisy when they're exposed to low lighting and don't get as tired when studying in sunlight compared to artificial light (Maas, Jayson, & Kleiber, 1974; Sanders, Gustanski, & Lawton, 1974). What's your reaction when you enter a dark room as opposed to one that's bright? Think of walking into a dark movie theatre or night club; how do these darker environments make you feel? Does it take you time to adjust? Do you communicate differently in darkness versus light?

Imagine the following situation: Zoe enjoys going to nightclubs with her friend Samantha. On one particular evening, Zoe was approached by a really aggressive man at a club who wanted her to go home with him. What did Zoe do in this hostile situation? She avoided eye contact and didn't respond verbally. Her reaction to this situation actually parallels research on communication and lighting. One study found that the communication of intimate questions by a stranger in a darkly lit environment is perceived as inappropriate, and leads to a lack of verbal response and a significant decrease in eye contact (Carr & Dabbs, 1974). Further, considering that personal safety is a crucial factor influencing the way people live, it's not surprising that more light tends to equate to more safety, while less light suggests danger (Blobaum & Hunecke, 2005). Based on light or the lack of it, we form perceptions of both public and private spaces as either safe or dangerous.

## ■ PERCEPTIONS OF SOUND

Have you ever been to a restaurant with friends and had a difficult time carrying on a conversation because of all the noise? Dishes clanging, tables being cleaned off, and a noisy group at a table close by are just a few contributors to this noisy environment. Noise impacts environment by affecting the way we feel, what we say, and our desire to stay or leave. In fact, nonverbal communication researchers have studied the effects of uncontrollable and unpredictable noise on people and their health, as well as the impact of sound in mental hospitals, stores, college dorms, and classrooms (Cheek, Maxwell, & Weisman, 1971; Glass & Singer, 1973; North, Hargreaves, & McKendrick, 1997; Palmer, 1997; Rabinowitz, 2005; Smith & Curnow, 1966; Weinstein, 1978). Are there certain sounds you believe to be detrimental to your health versus just merely annoying? Are there some sounds that actually improve your health, such as sounds that create relaxation for you or that make you laugh? What constitutes "noise" to you? What actions have you taken to control noise in an environment?

Think of a noisy classroom. The teacher is trying to explain the details of a group assignment and you can't hear the instructions because subgroups of students are talking and digging in their book bags. Would you be distracted in this noisy environment? Would you tell your classmates to be quiet? Would you expect the teacher to say something about the noise or tell them to quiet down? The point we're making here is that sound in the environment *does* matter. People have very real expectations regarding sound.

Let's turn to an example. Jill's preparing to give a presentation to community members and business leaders about the importance of college athletics on her campus. The goal of her presentation is to persuade the audience to financially support a scholarship program for student athletes. Jill has practiced her speech in the college auditorium several times. She's used the sound system before and doesn't feel like she needs to practice with the microphone or do a sound check. (Jill just made a big mistake!) On the evening of the presentation, Jill feels ready to go. After all, she spent some quality time rehearsing and doesn't tend to get nervous in public speaking situations. However, this presentation turns out to be a nightmare. Jill walks up to the podium and pulls the microphone down closer to her mouth. The first sound everyone hears is a loud cracking sound that will not go away. Jill tries to adjust, but the cracking and buzzing only get worse. Several audience members wearing hearing aids must leave the auditorium because the sound is so painful to their ears. Jill is devastated and doesn't know what to do. Finally, a building assistant comes on stage to help. He's able to fix the problem an hour later; in the meantime, Jill's presentation is one big flop.

This example teaches us that noise in the environment can have a significant impact on an audience; it can violate expectations and even drive people out of the environment. A buzzing microphone will certainly ruin a public speaking or performance situation; however, other unexpected sounds can disrupt an environment, like a noisy air conditioner going on and off. Sound in the environment isn't always noticed until it goes away. For examples, filler noises (also called white noise) such as the whirr of a fan, traffic outside, birds singing, and frogs croaking may actually be sounds we desire. In fact, stores like The Sharper Image actually sell sound machines for people who like to hear the sound of water, nature, and storms to help them get to sleep at night. Perhaps you know people who can't sleep at night without their sound machines. Both of your textbook authors have had some noisy travel companions over the years who are professionals at snoring. A hotel stay with one of these characters requires a repertoire of sound devices to cover up the snoring (e.g., fans, ear plugs, headphones, sound machines).

## ■ PERCEPTIONS OF SMELL

Smell is something that many of us spend a good part of our day maintaining. Nonverbal communication scholars use the term **olfaction** to refer to the role of smell in human interaction (Andersen, 2004; Dimitrius & Mazzarrella, 1999; Riley, 1979). Each day Americans take baths and showers, deodorize, brush, floss, gargle, wipe, sanitize, and freshen to cover up natural body odors. If smell wasn't important, we wouldn't buy all of these products and go through all of these activities. Can you think of a neutral smell? It's difficult to think of one. The reason for this is that communication research on olfaction indicates that no neutral scents exist. We either love or hate all kinds of smells that produce automatic reactions. Think of that wonderful smell of homemade donuts, your partner's favorite cologne, your favorite store, or that new car smell that most of us really like. We're connected and attracted to smells we like and are repulsed by smells we dislike. Rotten eggs, spoiled milk, a reeking dumpster, and sweaty clothes are just a few items that we would rather not have to smell too often.

Ever thought about smell and its connection to memory? Some people are distracted by the smell of a hospital, especially if they've lost a loved one or have been hospitalized for a period of time. The smell triggers memories of negative experiences or traumas people have faced. In contrast, the smell of bakeries or coffee shops often promotes a more positive memory of the last time you enjoyed a cinnamon roll or cup of java. Babies use their sense of smell to help them connect to their surroundings.

As with other environmental cues, culture plays a significant role in forming expectations of smell. In the United States, any trace of natural body odor is usually considered to be bad, which is why we spend so much time and money covering ourselves up with perfumes, soaps, lotions, deodorants, and mouthwashes. In fact, if a bad odor is detected in a room or from a person, communication may come to a stop or be very difficult to achieve.

Researcher Robert Baron (1983) studied the impact of artificial scents on the evaluation of job applicants. Male interviewers in his study had more trouble ignoring applicants' smell than female interviewers. In fact, men rated job applicants *lower* in the presence of a scent from cologne or perfume, while women rated job applicants wearing cologne *higher*. We encourage our students not to wear any cologne when interviewing for a job or scholarship, because nervousness or activation in the body enhances the strength of a scent. You could overwhelm an interviewer and lose a job opportunity, all because your cologne was too strong. What if the interviewer is allergic to perfume? These are things we need to think about, because you don't want something like a strong scent of perfume to keep you from a scholarship or dream job.

Smell can be a form of therapy, relaxation, and cleansing of the mind and body. In everyday life we like to refer to the benefits of smell as **aromatherapy.** This type of therapy, which usually involves scented candles or incense, is often used in accord with massage therapy, body wraps, facials, and other products in spas, salons, and resorts. Just this term—aromatherapy—reveals the significance of smell in an environment and its effects on people.

Marketers also use smell to help sell their products. It's not uncommon to find scented cards for new colognes and lotions inserted in newspapers and magazines. As examples, a Tanqueray gin bottle with a pine scent appeared in an ad in *USA Today*; an ad for Rolls Royce used leather-scented strips inserted into magazines. Research indicates that smells influence mood (Baron, 1990; Ehrlichman & Bastone, 1992; Ellen & Bone, 1998; Furlow, 1996; Knasko, 1992) and can affect human judgment (Baron, 1990; Bone & Jantrania, 1992; Spangenberg, Crowley, & Henderson, 1996). Since smell seems to provide marketers with a tool to attract consumers, it's no surprise that brands such as Club Monaco, De Beers, and Ritz Carlton Resorts and Spas have created their own signature scents as an innovative way to make their concepts and brands stand out (George, 2006).

### What Would *You* Do?

Leonard works in accounting at a very prestigious firm. His job is not only to handle tax information but to train the interns on the accounting software. He has been assigned a new intern, Hal, who carries the nickname "The Smelly Guy." Hal happens to have a serious hygiene problem and is an extremely close talker (meaning that he tends to get too close to people's faces when he talks to them). Hal comes in to work in the afternoons after he works out in a gym all morning. Hal sweats profusely and seems completely unaware of his stench. Leonard's stuck between a rock and a hard place because he's required to train all the interns. He's concerned about Hal's effect on clients and coworkers.

Using this story and what you've learned from this chapter about smell and environment, *what would you do*? Would you confront Hal and inform him that the professional environment you work in requires him to shower and have good hygiene? Would you go to your boss and request that he or she take care of the problem? Would you try to suffer through it and teach Hal as fast as you could so that you could move on to the next intern?

## ■ PERCEPTIONS OF TEMPERATURE

The temperature in an environment affects our perceptions and communication, just as the other factors we've considered thus far. Factors that help create temperatures, such as weather, climate, barometric pressure, and seasons, all have an effect (Anderson & Anderson, 1984; Baron, 1972; Baron & Bell, 1976; Griffit, 1970; Griffit & Veithc, 1971). Research into temperature and seasons has examined Seasonal Affective Disorder (SAD), finding that individuals with SAD have recurrent episodes of depression during winter, with remission of the symptoms during summer (Brennen, Hall, Verplanken, & Nunn, 2005). A scholarly focus has also emerged regarding the relationship between heat and aggression. As one example of this kind of research, an analysis of major league baseball games between 1986 and 1988 revealed a strong connection between high temperatures and the number of batters hit by a pitch (Reifman, Larrick, & Fein, 1991). How does temperature influence your behavior? Do you tend to be more aggressive when you are hot and sweaty as opposed to cool and comfortable? If you're too cold or too hot in a classroom, you probably find it difficult to concentrate and learn as much as if you were more comfortable.

Researchers have given specific attention to temperature and climate and have generated the following list of related behavioral changes (Knapp & Hall, 2006):

1. Suicide rates increase in the spring and are the highest in the summer.
2. College students break up with their dating partners at the beginnings and endings of semesters.
3. During the summer, people spend more time with friends.
4. During the summer, assault and rape crimes increase.
5. From July to November, people tend to report less happiness but more activity and less boredom.
6. People use the phone less in the summer than in the winter.

One final topic related to temperature warrants brief discussion, that of your own internal or bodily temperature, which can affect your reactions to temperature in an environment. There's probably no one hotter in the universe than a pregnant woman in her last trimester! Doctors warn expectant mothers not to take overly hot showers or baths or spend time in hot tubs during their pregnancies, because such environments can overheat the mother and the fetus and cause damage to both. Many women experience hot flashes during menopause, a period of time characterized by, among other symptoms, extreme feelings of hot or cold (mostly hot), due to hormonal changes. Not all women experience these shifts in temperature while their bodies are making this change, but the feeling of a sharp rise in internal temperature is a significant phenomenon. These kinds of changes, along with simple fevers associated with infections, can affect how you perceive the temperature of an environment.

Now that we have covered the essentials when it comes to environment as a nonverbal communication code, we would like to promote conversation about how our perceptions, expectations, and decisions about environment are displayed, portrayed, and talked about as everyday necessities.

# ■ ENVIRONMENT IN POPULAR CULTURE AND MEDIA

In this final section of the chapter, we explore the role of environment in popular culture, including media as well as the restaurants we eat in, the homes we live in, what we purchase to decorate them, and what we use to personalize our environment. First, let's explain what we mean by "popular culture." Cultural studies scholar John Fiske (1989) explains that **popular culture** is created by the products of a culture that are owned and made by businesses for the purpose of generating a profit. Examples of popular culture include shopping malls, sporting events, movies, magazines, cell phones, vehicles, virtual communities, furniture, restaurants, amusement parks, and television sitcoms, to name a few. Popular culture consists of many environments in which we spend leisure time with friends and family. Further, popular culture provides consumers with an array of products that shape everyday experiences, both personally and professionally. Let's look further at some examples of popular culture and connect them to our study of nonverbal communication and environment.

## Fast Food Environments

Think of the last time you went for fast food and actually entered the restaurant, rather than using the drive thru. Did you notice the environment? Was it inviting? Did you feel like it was okay to pull out your books and study, lingering over your soda? Probably not! Something as everyday and common as a fast food restaurant serves as a rich example of intentional design driven by the need for customer turnover and corporate profits (Eaves & Leathers, 1991). The next time you visit a  fast food restaurant, pay attention to the facility's design, seating, colors, lighting, smells, sounds, and temperature. You will likely find that the context you're eating in may communicate, "Eat your burger and get out of here!"

Beyond fast food joints, researchers have examined the environmental features of restaurants to determine their effects on customers. Are you willing to pay more money for a meal if there's an entertaining theme, posh decor, or wait staff dressed up like historical figures or entertainers? Communication scholar Emily Langan (1999) investigated two theme restaurants—Hard Rock Café and Planet Hollywood—and found that the allure of entertaining theme restaurants tempts customers to spend more money for a meal, because they think they're getting an entertainment value along with their food. These types of theme restaurants are typically built within commercial centers popular with tourists. Think about people who return from vacation proudly wearing Hard Rock Café and Planet Hollywood t-shirts from the cities they visited. Not only did they pay a higher price for their food, but they also got the t-shirt and the memory of a lot of old guitars and movie paraphernalia.

While the settings of fast food and some theme restaurants encourage us to speed through our meals, pricier restaurants create environments that make diners want to linger over a wonderful meal, perhaps ordering more cocktails or another bottle of wine, enjoying conversation with dessert and coffee (and the expensive price tag to go with it!). The furnishings—often nicer than your own home—make you slow down and take your time, because the seating is likely far more comfortable than that of a fast food place (and because you want to get your money's worth). The colors,

*In fast food restaurants, furniture and decor are typically designed for a quick customer turnover.*

smells, sounds (like music), temperature, and lighting all help create the effect of slowing down time and helping customers escape their normal lives. These kinds of effects are carefully researched and executed for repeat business and maximum profits.

## Home Improvement Shows

After you enjoy your burger and fries or crepes and lobster, head to your dorm room, apartment, or home (recognizing that readers of this text have diverse living situations) you might turn on your television, where you can find a variety of shows that will teach you how to create a posh home environment to show off to your friends and family. While a wide range of shows exists out there, we decided to have some fun by providing our top five television shows that focus on improving home and living environments.

1. *My First Place.* Particularly relevant for college students, this Home and Garden Television (HGTV) show focuses on people who are learning to decorate their first apartment, dorm room, home, townhouse, etc.—the first residence they could call their own, whether they're renting or buying. Emphasis is placed on designing on a budget and space-saving techniques. Specifically, this show reflects the increased attention people place on creating a home environment that serves as a nonverbal symbol of its residents.

2. *Sell This House!* This show on the Arts & Entertainment (A&E) channel focuses on "fixer-upper" strategies that will improve the current state of a person's home and prep it for the real estate market. The hook for this show is that, according to the channel's description, *Sell This House* gets "inside the mind of the buyer and the heart of the seller." Sellers learn of potential buyers' perceptions of their homes, which can be both an enjoyable and painful process. While the home environment isn't talked about in specific nonverbal terms, this show illustrates the importance of creating an attractive home for current owners and prospective buyers.

3. *Extreme Makeover: Home Edition.* Now a primetime hit show on ABC, *Extreme Makeover* features a team of experts that arrives to "save the day" by reconstructing or repairing a family's home. Typically, the lucky family is highly deserving of such an economic windfall, in that they've experienced a tragedy, have a psychologically or medically impaired family member, or perform some sort of outstanding service for their local communities. The new and improved home environment is celebrated as adding to the family's ease and quality of life.

4. *Curb Appeal.* This HGTV show focuses on improving a home's exterior and landscaping, and thus its value to owners. The show claims to help people look at their homes with "fresh eyes," as experts offer homeowners tips for turning great ideas into reality.

5. *Trading Spaces.* Based on the British series *Changing Rooms*, this design show depicts two sets of neighbors who swap houses and renovate one room in each other's homes. Each set of renovators are given a $1,000 budget with only two days to completely redesign their neighbors' room.

## Internet Environments

In the last decade, we've seen an explosion in the amount of time people spend on the Internet. In fact, computer-mediated communication (CMC) researcher Charles Soukup (2004) argues that because people spend so much time at work and in managing face-to-face relationships, they need an extra place to escape the stresses of daily work, family, and public life. We talk more in depth about this topic in Chapter 10, but for now, think about communities of people that form over the Internet, often termed **virtual communities.** Internet spaces that provide chat rooms and other services offer users a "third place" or addition to their public and private spaces. Virtual forums allow people to engage in anonymous communication through which they may change their gender, physical appearance, and occupation, just for starters. Popular online communities, such as MySpace, encourage users to create an environment of personhood where personal and family pictures are posted along with poetry, journals, and listings of personal interests. All of these elements are used to decorate and personalize computerized space.

While the Internet promotes computer-mediated communication in virtual spaces, real spaces such as colleges and universities continue to focus on establishing accessible Internet environments on campus. This is an important trend, since computers, laptops, and wireless Internet access play such an increasingly integral role in the education process at all levels (Worley & Chesebro, 2002). Technology has promoted more flexibility in open spaces with moveable desks and chairs, since so many students are now bringing laptop computers to campus. The days of planning

## REMEMBER 3.5

| | |
|---|---|
| **Hue:** | modification of a basic color (e.g., bluish green, red orange) in an environment. |
| **Brightness:** | intensity of color in an environment. |
| **Saturation:** | amount of color present in an environment. |
| **Olfaction:** | role of smell in human interaction. |
| **Aromatherapy:** | benefits of smell from scented candles or incense used in accord with massage therapy, body wraps, and facials. |
| **Popular Culture:** | products of a culture that are owned and made by businesses for the purpose of generating a profit. |
| **Virtual Community:** | a group of people that forms over the Internet. |

for a large computer lab on campus are changing with the arrival of students like you, the "Net Generation" (Carlson, 2006). Computer labs are still prevalent, but more attention is being given to how Internet environments and the profuse use of technology are changing the way we design and renovate spaces in modern schools, colleges, and universities.

## ■ UNDERSTANDING ENVIRONMENT: APPLYING THE REFLEXIVE CYCLE OF NONVERBAL COMMUNICATION DEVELOPMENT

What significance does environment have in your own life? How much time do you spend thinking about how you create and maintain your personal and professional environments? Are you concerned about the nonverbal signals the environments you maintain send to other people? The first step toward developing your skills and a better understanding of the environment as nonverbal communication is awareness. Again, we ask you to inventory yourself using the following questions: What are your standards regarding your own environment? What are your needs or preferences for the way other people maintain their environment? Do you have expectations or rules about such things as cleanliness, color, or smell? Do these preferences vary depending on whether the environment is personal or professional in nature? Are you aware of the impressions others may form about you based on the environments you create and maintain? How is your verbal and nonverbal communication affected by environment?

Now that you have engaged in an inventory of self regarding environment, it's time to think about making, if necessary, any appropriate changes to improve how you manage these nonverbal cues in your everyday life. This is Phase 2 in the Reflexive Cycle. Ask yourself: Are there some changes I need to make regarding environment (e.g., dirty car, messy office, absence of lighting in my apartment, the cookie dough candle I burn all the time)? If so, how can I make those changes? Perhaps the only thing that needs to change is your awareness of the environments you maintain and how they're perceived by other people.

Beyond engaging in an inventory of self and making appropriate changes, the next step is to inventory others. Can you think of a person who seems to have no awareness of environment? You may be thinking of that "Pig Pen" friend with a messy car or stinky closet. (These are the people who don't get their dorm deposits back when checking out for the summer.) Here's another example: Think of being picked up on a first date. The passenger seat of the car is soiled and empty beer cans cover the floorboard. What kind of first impression does this make? Some people are oblivious to the fact that the environments they maintain are communicative about who they are. They're not aware enough to check with other people (perception checking, a process we discussed earlier in this book) for observations and resulting perceptions of their environments. Still others may be highly aware that their environments communicate themselves to others, so we can learn some lessons for ourselves from these people.

After you have done an inventory of self, changed self, and inventoried others' nonverbal behavior with regard for environment, the fourth phase of the Reflexive Cycle involves interacting with others, trying out the changes you've made or are in the process of making, and observing people as you verbally and nonverbally interact with them. Do people have different reactions to you as a result of any changes you made? For example, people with messy cars might get some recognition for having cleaned things up. As another example, people who are trying to become more organized may draw their coworkers' attention to the fact that they're cleaning up their office and implementing a filing system. It can be interesting to note people's reactions to both subtle and obvious changes in the way we manage environments and how it makes us feel, as well as to gauge our own reactions to changes other people have made related to environment.

In the last part of the cycle, we challenge you to review and assess the whole process, making note of positive and negative aspects, and then begin the cycle again. Remember, the development of communication skills is a never-ending process, as we work to develop our nonverbal abilities on a whole range of topics, not just environment.

## SUMMARY ■ ■ ■ ■ ■

In this chapter, we established environment as a nonverbal communication code and emphasized the need to be aware of our own as well as others' perceptions of environment. The control you have over establishing, maintaining, and regulating healthy communication environments influences your communicative decisions in your personal and professional life. For two reasons, you need to give special attention to environment as a nonverbal communication code: (1) The choices you make about the environment in which you live or work reveal a good deal about who you are, and (2) your nonverbal communication is altered by the environments in which you communicate.

Next we explored six different perceptions people form about environments (formality, warmth, privacy, familiarity, constraint, and distance), followed by ways that we react to the environments we choose or find ourselves in. Remember that arousal (how stimulated or energized an environment can make us feel), pleasure (how happy or satisfied an environment can make us feel), and dominance (how powerful and in control an environment can make us feel) are three different ways people react to environments.

In the next section of this chapter, we discussed chronemics—the study of how time and communication work together—and focused on intentional and unintentional time. We overviewed the different ways that people perceive time—as a location of events, a duration of events, intervals between events, and patterns of intervals.

Then we examined color, sound, and lighting in an environment. The important thing to remember about these nonverbal environmental attributes is that researchers have deemed them influential with regard to human behavior. Colors and sound impact environment by affecting the way we feel, what we say, and our desire to stay or leave. As far as lighting is concerned, people in U.S. culture tend to view places with light as safe environments, while darker environments are more threatening and viewed as higher-risk crime zones.

We then defined olfaction—the role of smell in human interaction. Smell is an important part of how people relate to each other, as well as a key element in the marketing of products. Smell is used to help companies brand themselves with a signature scent that customers remember. Next we explored temperature and seasonal influences on human behavior, noting that people tend to exhibit more aggressive behavior during warmer months than in cooler months. We then turned to a few examples from popular culture and media to show how people in the U.S. are surrounded with environmental factors, including the design of restaurants, home improvement shows on television, and computerized environments on the Internet. Finally, we applied the Reflexive Cycle of Nonverbal Communication Development to our understanding of environment.

# DISCUSSION STARTERS

1. Explain how environment is a form of nonverbal communication.

2. What cues does your living environment reveal about your character, upbringing, and culture? Did you ever consider that so much could be revealed in how you maintain your home environment?

3. Review Knapp and Hall's four perceptions of time and provide an example of each category.

4. Think of how many phrases in American culture relate to time, such as "time flies when you're having fun," and "it's about time."

What does a person's time management nonverbally reveal about her or his character?

5. Do you think the color of a room affects your behavior or mood? What about smells, temperatures, sounds, and lighting? How are your verbal and nonverbal communication affected by these elements?

6. What is your preferred environment for socializing with friends? What kinds of environments are more conducive to friendly conversation? Less conducive? Identify some situations in which you would desire a specific environment for communication.

# REFERENCES

Amheim, R. (1954). *Art and visual perception.* Berkeley: University of California Press.

Amole, D. (2005). Coping strategies for living in student residential facilities in Nigeria. *Environment and Behavior, 37,* 201–219.

Andersen, P. A. (2004). *The complete idiot's guide to body language.* New York: Alpha.

Anderson, C. A., & Anderson, D. C. (1984). Ambient temperature and violent crime: Tests of the linear and curvilinear hypotheses. *Journal of Personality and Social Psychology, 46,* 91–97.

Aslam, M. M. (2006). Are you selling the right colour? A cross-cultural review of colour as a marketing cue. *Journal of Marketing Communications, 12,* 15–30.

Baker, J., & Cameron, M. (1996). The effects of the service environment on affect and consumer perception of waiting time: An analysis of an industrial technology diffusion. *Journal of the Academy of Marketing Science, 24,* 338–350.

Ballard, D. I. (2008). The experience of time at work. In L. K. Guerrero & M. L. Hecht (Eds.), *The non-verbal communication reader: Classic and contemporary readings* (3rd ed., pp. 258–269). Prospect Heights, IL: Waveland.

Ballard, D. I., & Seibold, D. R. (2000). Time orientation and temporal variation across work groups: Implications for group and organizational communication. *Western Journal of Communication, 64,* 218–242.

Baron, R. A. (1972). Aggression as a function of ambient temperature and prior anger arousal. *Journal of Personality and Social Psychology, 21,* 183–189.

Baron, R. A. (1983). Short note: "Sweet smell of success"? The impact of pleasant artificial scents on the evaluations of job applicants. *Journal of Applied Psychology, 68,* 709–713.

Baron, R. A. (1990). Environmentally-induced positive affect: Its impact on self-efficacy, task-performance, negotiation, and conflict. *Journal of Applied Social Psychology, 20,* 368–384.

Baron, R. A., & Bell, P. A. (1976). Aggression and heat: The influence of ambient temperature, negative affect, and a cooling drink on physical aggression. *Journal of Personality and Social Psychology, 33,* 245–255.

Bellizzi, J. A., Crowley, A. E., & Hasty, R. W. (1983). The effects of color in store design. *Journal of Retailing, 59,* 21–45.

Bellizzi, J. A., & Hite, R. E. (1992). Environmental color, consumer feelings, and purchase likelihood. *Psychology and Marketing, 9,* 347–363.

Biemiller, L. (2007, June 8). Take me back to old main. *The Chronicle of Higher Education,* p. A40.

Blobaum, A., & Hunecke, M. (2005). Perceived danger in urban public space: The impacts of physical features and personal factors. *Environment and Behavior, 37,* 465–485.

Bone, P. F., & Jantrania, S. (1992). Olfaction as cue for product quality. *Marketing Letters, 3,* 289–296.

Bowen, D. D., & Kilmann, R. H. (1975). Developing a comparative measure of the learning climate in professional schools. *Journal of Applied Psychology, 60,* 71–79.

Brennen, T., Hall, C., Verplanken, B., & Nunn, J. (2005). Predictors of ideas about seasonal psychological fluctuations. *Environment and Behavior, 37,* 220–235.

Carlson, S. (2006, July 21). The campus of the future: Financially sound and well-designed, with potato-starch cutlery. *The Chronicle of Higher Education,* p. A25.

Carr, S. J., & Dabbs, J. M. (1974). The effect of lighting, distance, and intimacy of topic on verbal and visual behavior. *Sociometry, 37,* 592–600.

Cheek, F. E., Maxwell, R., & Weisman, R. (1971). Carpeting the ward: An exploratory study in environment psychiatry. *Mental Hygiene, 55,* 109–118.

Dimitrius, J., & Mazzarella, M. (1999). *Reading people: How to understand people and predict their behavior—anytime, anyplace.* New York: Ballantine Books.

Dubinskas, F. (1988). Cultural construction: The many faces of time. In F. Dubinskas (Ed.), *Making time: Ethnographies of high-technology organizations* (pp. 170–232). Philadelphia: Temple University Press.

Eaves, M. H., & Leathers, D. G. (1991). Context as communication: McDonald's vs. Burger King. *Journal of Applied Communication Research, 19,* 263–289.

Ehrlichman, H., & Bastone, L. (1992). The use of odour in the study of emotion. In S. Van Toller & G. H. Dodd (Eds.), *Fragrance: The psychology and biology of perfume* (pp. 143–159). London: Elsevier Applied Science.

Ellen, P. S., & Bone, P. F. (1998). Does it matter if it smells? Olfactory stimuli as advertising executional cues. *Journal of Advertising, 27,* 29–39.

Farrenkopf, T., & Roth, V. (1980). The university faculty office as an environment. *Environment and Behavior, 12,* 467–477.

Fiske, J. (1989). *Understanding popular culture.* Boston: Unwin Hyman.

Furlow, F. B. (1996). The smell of love. Reprinted in L. K. Guerrero, J. A. DeVito, & M. L. Hecht (Eds.), *The nonverbal communication reader: Classic and contemporary readings* (1999, 2nd ed., pp. 118–125). Prospect Heights, IL: Waveland.

George, L. (2006, February 13). The sweet smell of shopping. *Maclean's*, p. 55.

Goffman, E. (1971). *Relations in public: Microstudies of the public order*. New York: Harper Colophon Books.

Gonzalez, A., & Zimbardo, P. G. (1985). Time in perspective. Reprinted in L. K. Guerrero, J. A. DeVito, & M. L. Hecht (Eds.), *The nonverbal communication reader: Classic and contemporary readings* (1999, 2nd ed., pp. 227–236). Prospect Heights, IL: Waveland.

Gosling, S. D., Ko, S. J., Mannarelli, T., & Morris, M. E. (2002). A room with a cue: Personality judgments based on offices and bedrooms. *Journal of Personality and Social Psychology, 82*, 379–398.

Glass, D., & Singer, J. E. (1973). Experimental studies of uncontrollable and unpredictable noise. *Representative Research in Social Psychology, 4*, 165.

Griffit, W. (1970). Environmental effects on interpersonal affective behavior: Ambient effective temperature and attraction. *Journal of Personality and Social Psychology, 15*, 240–244.

Griffit, W., & Veithc, R. (1971). Hot and crowded: Influence of population density and temperature on interpersonal affective behavior. *Journal of Personality and Social Psychology, 17*, 92–98.

Hall, E. T. (1959). *The silent language*. Garden City, NY: Doubleday.

Hall, E. T., & Hall, M. R. (1990). Monochronic and polychronic time. Reprinted in L. K. Guerrero, J. A. DeVito, & M. L. Hecht (Eds.), *The nonverbal communication reader: Classic and contemporary readings* (1999, 2nd ed., pp. 237–240). Prospect Heights, IL: Waveland.

Harris, P., & Sachau, D. (2005). Is cleanliness next to godliness? The role of housekeeping in impression formation. *Environment and Behavior, 37*, 81–99.

Hattenhauer, D. (1984). The rhetoric of architecture: A semiotic approach. *Communication Quarterly, 32*, 71–77.

Holley, L., & Steiner, S. (2005). Safe space: Student perspectives on classroom environment. *Journal of Social Work Education, 41*, 49–64.

Jackson, H. (2005). Sitting comfortably? Then let's talk! *Psychologist, 18*, 691.

Jansson, C., Marlow, N., & Bristow, M. (2004). The influence of colour on visual search times in cluttered environments. *Journal of Marketing Communications, 10*, 183–193.

Knapp, M. L., & Hall, J. A. (2006). *Nonverbal communication in human interaction* (6th ed.). Belmont, CA: Thomson/Wadsworth.

Knasko, S. C. (1992). Ambient odor's effect on creativity, mood, and perceived health. *Chemical Senses, 17*, 27–35.

Langan, E. J. (1999). Environmental features in theme restaurants. In L. K. Guerrero, J. A. DeVito, & M. L. Hecht (Eds.), *The nonverbal communication reader: Classic and contemporary readings* (2nd ed., pp. 255–263). Prospect Heights, IL: Waveland.

Limaye, M. R., & Victor, D. A. (1991). Cross-cultural business communication research: State of the art and hypotheses for the 1990s. *Journal of Business Communication, 28*, 277–299.

Lohmann, A., Arriaga, X. B., & Goodfriend, W. (2003). Close relationships and placemaking: Do objects in a couple's home reflect couplehood? *Personal Relationships, 10*, 437–449.

Maas, J., Jayson, J., & Kleiber, D. (1974). Effects of spectral differences in illumination on fatigue. *Journal of Applied Psychology, 59*, 524–526.

Martin, D. (2006, February 2). Slow down and let 'em smell the coffee. *American Banker*, p. 11.

Maslow, A. H., & Mintz, N. L. (1956). Effects of esthetic surroundings: I. Initial effects of three esthetic conditions upon perceiving "energy" and "well-being" in faces. *Journal of Psychology, 41*, 247–254.

McCroskey, J. C., & McVetta, W. R. (1978). Classroom seating arrangements: Instructional communication theory versus student preferences. *Communication Education, 27*, 99–110.

McElroy, J. C., Morrow, P. C., & Ackerman, R. J. (1983). Personality and interior office design: Exploring the accuracy of visitor attributions. *Journal of Applied Psychology, 68*, 541–544.

Mehrabian, A. (1976). *Public spaces and private places*. New York: Basic Books.

Mintz, N. L. (1956). Effects of esthetic surroundings: II. Prolonged and repeated experience in a "beautiful" and "ugly" room. *Journal of Psychology, 41*, 459–466.

Morgenstern, J. (2006, September). We interrupt this magazine.... *O: The Oprah Winfrey Magazine*, pp. 139–140.

Morrow, P. C., & McElroy, J. C. (1981). Interior office design and visitor response: A constructive replication. *Journal of Applied Psychology, 66*, 646–650.

Murray, D. C., & Deabler, H. L. (1957). Colors and mood-tones. *Journal of Applied Psychology, 41*, 279–283.

North, A. C., Hargreaves, D. J., & McKendrick, J. (1997, November 13). In store music affects product choice. *Nature*, p. 132.

Palmer, C. (1997). Hearing and listening in a typical classroom. *Speech and Hearing Services in Schools, 28,* 213–218.

Pellegrini, R. F., & Schauss, A. G. (1980). Muscle strength as a function of exposure to hue differences in visual stimuli: An experimental test of kinesoid theory. *Journal of Orthomolecular Psychiatry, 2,* 144–147.

Rabinowitz, P. (2005). Is noise bad for your health? *The Lancet, 365,* 1908–1909.

Reifman, A. S., Larrick, R. P., & Fein, S. (1991). Temper and temperature on the diamond: The heat-aggression relationship in major league baseball. *Personality and Social Psychology Bulletin, 17,* 580–585.

Riley, J. (1979). The olfactory factor in nonverbal communication. *Communication, 8,* 159–168.

Salacuse, J. (2005). Your place or mine? Deciding where to negotiate. *Negotiation, 11,* 3–5.

Sallis, J. F., & Kerr, J. (2008). Physical activity and the built environment. In L. K. Guerrero & M. L. Hecht (Eds.), *The nonverbal communication reader: Classic and contemporary readings* (3rd ed., pp. 270–286). Prospect Heights, IL: Waveland.

Sandalla, E. (1987). Identity symbolism in housing. *Environment and Behavior, 19,* 569–587.

Sandberg, J. (2003, March 2). Want to know someone's job status? Look at desk location. *Corpus Christi Caller Times,* p. D4.

Sanders, M., Gustanski, J., & Lawton, M. (1974). Effect of ambient illumination on noise level of groups. *Journal of Applied Psychology, 59,* 527–528.

Schein, E. H. (1992). *Organizational culture and leadership.* San Francisco: Jossey-Bass.

Smith, E., Bell, P. A., & Fusco, M. E. (1986). The influence of color and demand characteristics on muscle strength and affective ratings of the environment. *Journal of General Psychology, 113,* 289–297.

Smith, P. C., & Curnow, R. (1966). "Arousal hypothesis" and the effects of music on purchasing behavior. *Journal of Applied Psychology, 50,* 255–256.

Soukup, C. (2004). Multimedia performance in computer-mediated community: Communication as a virtual drama. *Journal of Computer-Mediated Communication* [Online], *9(4).* Available: http://jcmc.indiana.edu/vol9/issue4/soukup.html

Spangenberg, E., Crowley, A., & Henderson, P. (1996). Improving the store environment: Do olfactory cues affect evaluations and behaviors? *Journal of Marketing, 60,* 67–80.

Stein, S. (2006). Communicating with color. Reprinted in L. K. Guerrero & M. L. Hecht (Eds.), *The nonverbal communication reader: Classic and contemporary readings* (2008, 3rd ed., pp. 287–288). Prospect Heights, IL: Waveland.

Stires, L. (1980). Classroom seating location, student grades, and attitudes: Environment or self selection? *Environment and Behavior, 12,* 241–154.

Teven, J. J. (1996). The effects of office aesthetic quality on students' perceptions of teacher credibility and communicator style. *Communication Research Reports, 13,* 101–108.

Vilnai-Yavetz, I., Rafaeli, A., & Schneider-Yaacov, C. (2005). Instrumentality, aesthetics, and symbolism of office design. *Environment and Behavior, 37,* 533–551.

Vogler, A., & Jorgensen, J. (2005). Windows to the world, doors to space: The psychology of space architecture. *Leonardo, 38,* 390–399.

Weinstein, N. D. (1978). Individual differences in reactions to noise: A longitudinal study in a college dormitory. *Journal of Applied Psychology, 63,* 458–466.

Wexner, L. B. (1954). The degree to which colors (hues) are associated with mood-tones. *Journal of Applied Psychology, 38,* 432–435.

Winchip, S. (1996). Academic environments: Internal analysis. *College Student Journal, 30,* 340–345.

Wollin, D. D., & Montagre, M. (1981). College classroom environment: Effects of sterility versus amiability on student and teacher performance. *Environment and Behavior, 13,* 707–716.

Worley, D., & Chesebro, J. (2002). Goading the discipline towards unity: Teaching communication in an Internet environment—A policy research analysis. *Communication Quarterly, 50,* 171–191.

Zweigenhaft, R. (1976). Personal space in the faculty office: Desk placement and the student-faculty interaction. *Journal of Applied Psychology, 61,* 529–532.

# Proxemics

## Our Use of Space

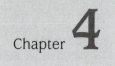
Chapter 4

## CHAPTER OUTLINE ■ ■ ■ ■ ■

**Proxemics as Nonverbal Communication**
Physical Versus Psychological Space
Hall's Zones of Space

**Factors Influencing the Management of Space**
Cultural Background
Sex and Sexual Orientation
Age
Status
Physical Characteristics
Characteristics of the Relationship
Subject Matter
Setting

**Territoriality**
Types of Territory
Territorial Violation, Invasion, and
Contamination

Classroom Environments as Student
Territory

**Crowding and Density**

**Privacy Management: A Different View
of Proxemics**
Communication Privacy Management
People with Disabilities
Bartenders
Teacher Privacy Management
Internet Chat Rooms as Private Spaces

**Understanding Proxemics: Applying the
Reflexive Cycle of Nonverbal
Communication Development**

**Summary**

## CHAPTER OBJECTIVES ■ ■ ■ ■ ■

After studying this chapter, you should be able to:

1. Define proxemics.

2. Identify Hall's four zones of space and the kind of communication that typically occurs
within each zone.

3. Increase your awareness of the factors influencing people's proxemic behavior.

4. Improve your perceptual skills to better appreciate the spatial boundaries of others.

5. Define territoriality, identify the three types of territories, and provide examples of each type.

6. Explore the various ways people protect and defend their territories from violation, invasion,
and contamination.

7. Know the difference between crowding and density.

8. Outline the various ways that people nonverbally cope with high density, crowded conditions.

9. Understand the relationship between privacy and proxemics.

10. Identify and define the four types and four dimensions of privacy.

11. Understand the basic components of Communication Privacy Management theory.

> "I felt dirty! He totally violated my personal space bubble."
>
> "She invades my space all the time."
>
> "I still love you, but I just really need some space!"

What do these statements have in common? They all relate to an aspect of nonverbal communication called **proxemics**—the way that distance and space play a communicative

## CASE STUDY   Attack of the Space Invader

I moved to New York from New Jersey after I landed a great job at an architectural firm. My first day on the job I worked late, trying to prove that I wasn't a slacker and that I could hold my own. While I was making copies in the workroom, I began to feel that I wasn't alone. Out of the corner of my eye, I saw dark shoes and grey slacks move closer towards me, but I couldn't make myself turn around. In a matter of seconds I began to review in my mind the self-defense techniques I learned from a class I took. I decided to swing around and attack the person who was now so close that I could feel his or her slacks touching my calves. When I whipped around, I found my boss, Mr. Tompkins, up in my face, smiling at me. My fists were clenched and my heart dropped because if what I thought was going to happen actually did happen, I knew that I would be moving back to New Jersey. Before I could react further, Mr. Adler, the district boss, walked in. Mr. Tompkins rushed over to him and then I saw it—he stood equally close to Mr. Adler! My new boss wasn't an attacker or harasser; he just didn't respect or was completely unaware of other people's personal space.

As the months passed, whenever I interacted with Mr. Tompkins, I felt like I was sitting in the front row of a movie theatre. It was difficult to concentrate on what he was saying; I found myself counting the tiny lines around his eyes. After working there for four months, Mr. Tompkins and his wife, Barbara, invited me over to their house for a barbeque. It came up during the course of conversation that he had been "accidentally" sprayed with mace by people on three different occasions in Central Park. The Tompkins were laughing about it, seemingly unaware that a three-time event couldn't have been an accident.

After that dinner, I decided to talk to my boss about his being an extremely "close talker" (like they called it in that *Seinfeld* episode). After all, I couldn't with a clear conscience allow this man—a really good boss—to continue invading people's space and interacting with people in a way that could get him into hot water. Besides, I wasn't anxious to be in another situation where I could count his pores. I picked my moment—a time when we could have a private conversation—and explained the situation to him as gently as I could. To his credit, at first he was embarrassed, but then receptive. He said he'd try to work on it, and he has actually changed his "space invading" ways. We laugh about it today, but there were some really awkward moments when I first started working there.

role in our everyday life. As you've moved through life, you've likely met a wide range of people who either have no awareness of others' personal space needs or who we think of as distant or hard to get to know. Either way, how we manage our own personal space, the awareness we have of others' personal space, and ultimately how we interact with others are important as we continue our study of nonverbal communication.

## ▪ PROXEMICS AS NONVERBAL COMMUNICATION

The goal of this chapter is to make you more aware of proxemics as a key code of nonverbal communication. You may be thinking: How do distance and space communicate something nonverbally? The connections between people, space, and distance need to be made for three reasons: (1) The preferences we have regarding distance and space in which we live or work reveal a good deal about who we are as people, (2) our verbal and nonverbal communication is impacted by distance and space, and (3) we use metaphors of distance and space to talk about our interpersonal relationships as they develop, redefine, or come to an end (Derlega, Metts, Petronio, & Margulis, 1993; Derlega, Wilson, & Chaikin, 1976; Hays, 1984, 1985; Matthews, Derlega, & Morrow, 2006; Petronio, 1991, 2000, 2002; Rawlins, 1983, 1994; Rose, 1984; Rose & Serafica, 1986; Rosenfeld & Kendrick, 1984; Rubin & Shenker, 1978).

*What does the space between these two women signify to you nonverbally?*

## Physical Versus Psychological Space

Imagine you're standing at an ATM trying to get some cash. You swipe or insert your card, then punch in your personal identification number (PIN). But you become aware that someone behind you is standing too close; he or she could actually see what numbers you punch in and thus, get your PIN. This violation of your personal space gives you the creeps. In a situation like this, our space is violated, making us feel surveyed, threatened, and unsafe. Ever been in a situation like this? Has anyone ever stood too close to you in line somewhere less threatening, like a sporting event or concert? We've all had experiences like these at one time or another and these instances remind us of the powerful force of proxemics at play. The space within which we communicate, as well as how we feel about that space, influence our communicative decisions.

As we begin to explore this fascinating topic, it's important to contrast physical space with psychological space. **Physical space** refers to where we communicate and how we interact within a given space, as well as how much space is available. We know from the environment chapter that physical spaces serve as a form of nonverbal communication; plus they have a profound effect on the people who communicate within them. **Psychological space** is the impact of space on our attitude, mood, and emotionality. An easy way to understand psychological space is to consider how you respond or think about particular situations, like being confined to a small room (like trapped in an elevator), being backed into a corner, or having a "space invader" stand too closely to you at an ATM. Can you think of a situation in which your psychological space got the best of you? How did the experience impact your attitude, mood, and emotion?

## Hall's Zones of Space

Anthropologist Edwin T. Hall (1959, 1963, 1966, 1968, 1983) has helped us understand proxemics by providing a classification of spatial zones, sometimes referred to as conversational distances (see Figure 4.1). Hall's first zone is **intimate space,** measuring zero to one-and-one half feet between communicators, which is considered the most personal for communication. Our intimate space is reserved for those who are emotionally close to us, such as dear friends, sexual partners, and spouses. At times when we get stuck in a crowd or busy elevator, we're reminded that people may be in our intimate space by necessity, not invitation.

Hall's second zone is **personal space**—one-and-one half to four feet of space between communicators. The conversations we have with our family and friends usually take place within this zone. The third zone is **social space**—four to twelve feet of distance between communicators. Social space is illustrated in professional life and in most educational contexts. Group interactions also tend to take place within social space. The fourth and final zone is **public space,** which is twelve feet and beyond. Public space generates communication that usually is not personal in nature. In fact, when speakers present in a meeting room or auditorium, the audience is typically at least twelve feet away. (Of course, the distance varies according to the physical setting, the occasion, and the preferences of the speaker.)

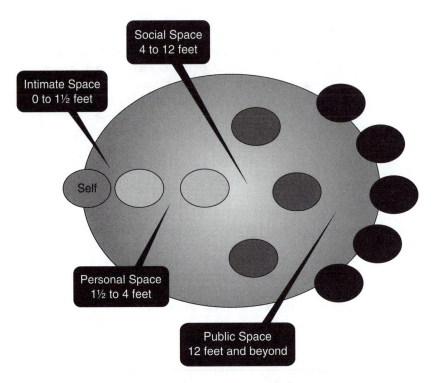

**FIGURE 4.1    Edwin T. Hall's Four Zones of Space**

Figure reproduced with permission of: Hall, E. T. (1966). *The hidden dimension.* New York: Doubleday.

An understanding of spatial zones is important to your everyday nonverbal communication competency. Look at Figure 4.1 again and reflect on how your use of spatial zones varies across the many relationships you have in your life. While proxemics plays a communicative function that helps shape the perceptions and interactions we have with others in U.S. culture, we must also remember that expectations and use of space vary as we interact with members of other cultures. In fact, nonverbal

---

 **REMEMBER 4.1**

| | |
|---|---|
| **Proxemics:** | the way distance and space play a communicative role in everyday life. |
| **Physical Space:** | where we communicate and how we interact within a given space, as well as how much space is available. |
| **Psychological Space:** | effect of space on attitude, mood, and emotionality. |
| **Intimate Space:** | zero to one-and-one half feet of space between communicators; considered the most personal range for communication. |

*(continued)*

## REMEMBER 4.1 *(continued)*

| | |
|---|---|
| **Personal Space:** | one-and-one half to four feet of space between communicators; conversations with family members and friends usually take place within this zone. |
| **Social Space:** | four to twelve feet of space between communicators; social space is utilized in professional life and many social contexts. |
| **Public Space:** | twelve feet and beyond; usually not personal in nature. |

scholar Judee Burgoon and colleagues suggest that the distance we manage in our communication with others is based on our cultural and personal expectations (Burgoon, 1978; Burgoon & Jones, 1976).

## ■ FACTORS INFLUENCING THE MANAGEMENT OF SPACE

Why do you stand a certain distance from people in conversation? Are you perfectly comfortable in the middle seat in an airplane, with a stranger on either side of you? Why might you cozy up to one person, but keep your distance from another? Why do some people get too close in conversation, while others seem to stay farther away than you're used to? According to research, certain factors influence how we manage our own personal space and how we use proxemics when we relate to other people in everyday life (Sommer, 2002).

### Cultural Background

As we said in Chapter 1, some nonverbal behaviors are innate, such as facial expressions that have universal application and interpretation, as Charles Darwin (1872/1965) argued. But many more nonverbal cues are learned as we experience life within our cultural settings. Thus, cultural background is a key factor that contributes to our understanding of nonverbal cues and our acquisition of them, and space management is no exception (Manusov, 1997; Matsumoto, 2006; Smeltzer, Waltman, & Leonard, 1991). Culture is perhaps the most profound factor of those we cover in this section of the chapter, given that we learn appropriate expectations and proxemic behaviors within our cultural context (Barry, 2002; Beaulieu, 2004; Huff, 2001; Li, 2001; Li & Li, 2007; Shuter, 1976; Watson, 1970). Hall's (1966) zones of space are culturally rooted, as are many, if not all, of our beliefs about appropriate nonverbal cues. Hall (1968, 1983) contended that a major distinguishing factor among cultural groups was their proxemic behaviors.

Let's consider two interesting studies to help illustrate this point. One line of research examined the use of space in Japan, which contains dense urban areas in which space is at a premium (Altman, 1975). In Japanese culture, specific types of spaces are given specific meanings because of the value placed on space. For example, street intersections are named rather than streets, because intersections are more important in Japanese daily life than streets. Rooms are identified according to their function, with structures built to enhance a room's functionality, such as movable walls and room dividers that can transform a space. The research also examined the Japanese people's tendency to miniaturize objects, producing such things as bonsai plants, because of their cultural sense of space. As a second example, Hall (1966) observed Arab cultures for their use of proxemics, noting significant differences between how Arabs and Westerners view public space and conversational distance. Arabs do not seek privacy in public space, preferring to converse intimately in public and viewing less-than-intimate conversations as rude behavior. The intimate behaviors include close distances between people, direct and continuous eye contact, and frequent touch.

Think about Americans, with their cultural variations *within* U.S. culture that relate to proxemics. While someone growing up in the plains states or in Texas might prefer wide, open spaces where you can see the entire horizon, someone growing up in New York City might be uncomfortable with all that space, preferring the density and rhythms of a bustling city and tight living conditions that are more familiar. These environments and the cultural customs that come with them affect our proxemic expectations and behavior.

## Sex and Sexual Orientation

Are men and women really from different planets? Doubtful. However, when we consider the influence that sex has on our personal space management, distinctive communication patterns emerge (Baxter, 1970; Evans & Howard, 1973; Fisher & Byrne, 1975; Gifford, 1982; Hall, 2006; Li & Li, 2007). We talk more in depth about this topic (and a whole range of cues) in Chapter 12 on sex/gender, sexual orientation, and relationships, but for now, consider a few examples. For one, it seems to be socially appropriate in U.S. culture for women to sit next to each other at a movie theatre, bar, or restaurant. Yet, when we shift our focus to men, some social force seems to exist that tells men it's less than appropriate to sit right next to each other. Men can and do sit this way, but it may cause some discomfort or lead men to feel that they have to joke their way through the behavior. In fact, research documents the trend for American women's personal space to be smaller than that afforded to men, and for women's space to be invaded more frequently than men's (Hall, 2006; Henley, 2001; Spain, 1992). Studies show that female dyads tend to stand and sit closer together than male dyads, with the male–female dyad standing and sitting the closest (Aiello & Jones, 1971; Hall, 2006; Mehrabian & Diamond, 1971). Have you ever seen a group of men at a movie theatre who insist on having one seat between each other to provide more space? One explanation we've heard for this behavior (from men we've questioned at a movie theatre, plus our students) is that men are just larger in size and, thus, need more space than most women. Do you buy that? Might there be another reason?

It could be that more space tells everyone in the movie theatre that these men aren't gay. Their spatial choices may communicate, "Look at us; we're straight." Of course, some men *do* sit next to each other at a movie. Does this mean that they're more secure with their sexuality? While some cultures are more prohibitive than the United States regarding sexual orientation (like some Middle Eastern cultures), other cultures are more open (Freitas, Kaiser, & Hammidi, 1996). In the U.S., homophobia is still prevalent, although our culture has made some strides on this front. But the primary explanation we hear for men's spatial behavior relates to homophobia—a fear of being perceived or labeled gay. Most women don't have to deal with this perception, because the latitude of acceptance about women's behavior tends to be wider than men's. If two women sit closely in a public setting, even moving more closely to whisper to each other, most people don't observe this behavior and think, "They must be lesbians." But many men are concerned that their nonverbal behavior will cause people to perceive them as gay (whether they're gay, straight, bisexual, or transgender), and proxemics is one of the most prominent codes that factors into such perceptions.

## Age

Researchers continue to explore the effects of age on a range of nonverbal cues (Feldman & Tyler, 2006). Evidence indicates that age does influence the management of space (Naus & Eckenrode, 1974; Sinha & Nayyar, 1995; Smith, Reinheimer, & Gabbard-Alley, 1981; Webb & Weber, 2003). Children have a need for affection and typically want to be close to their parents. We hear stories from parents whose children want to sleep in the same bed with mom and dad. Of course, this desire for kids to be around their parents all the time changes with development. For example,

*Parents and children often come into close proximity, especially in the early years of a child's development.*

toddlers reach an age when they want to venture out from mom or dad's grasp; it's common to see a parent chasing after some wayward two-year-old who's enjoying a public adventure. Further in life, junior high and high school students establish more and more space between themselves and others, particularly family members, as they form and clarify a sense of self. First dates, kisses, sexual experiences, communication with boyfriends and girlfriends, and so on tend to be private experiences for adolescents that happen at a distance from the family. At times, such exploration can be painful to a parent who misses the hugs and closeness of a child who's trying to find her or his own way in the world.

As we continue on into adulthood, some of us establish closer proxemics with a partner or spouse than with family members or friends, but for others it's the exact opposite—we may feel closer to (and exhibit closer distances when communicating with) our friends than anyone else. In terms of elders and proxemics, research is mixed. While some studies have found that elderly people's space is readily invaded by others, especially caretakers who help elders do things for themselves (much like helping children), other research shows that people often avoid touch and put greater distances between themselves and elders, to the elders' physical and psychological detriment (Kramer & Gibson, 1991; Tank Buschmann, Hollinger-Smith, & Peterson-Kokkas, 1999; Tobin & Gustafson, 1987). While many people give elders a wider berth than they do younger people or their peers, perhaps believing that the elders' frailty demands more space to maneuver, others assume that elderly people can't take care of themselves, so they invade their space to tend to them. Perhaps we should all think about how we behave with our elders, in terms of proxemics and other nonverbal cues, and consider what we will want when we become elderly.

## Status

As we discuss in Chapter 5 on physical appearance, certain physical characteristics communicate messages of status, power, and dominance in U.S. culture, one being height. Research has been consistent over four decades in terms of the connection between height, credibility, and status (Egolf & Corder, 1991; Elman, 1977; Roberts & Herman, 1986; Vrij, 2001). Other aspects related to appearance, such as expensive attire, personalized and expensive accessories, and good grooming all contribute to perceptions of high status, which, in turn, affect the management of space.

A person's status within society affects proxemic behavior in two ways: (1) A high status person's use of space tends to differ from people with lower status, and (2) differences can be found in how others manage space in a high status person's presence. In their review of this topic, nonverbal scholars Judee Burgoon and Norah Dunbar (2006) explain:

> Powerful people have access to more space, larger territories, and more private territories, which also afford their occupants or owners great insulation from intrusion by others and more space in which to display other visible indications of their status and power. They may display more territorial markers, have easy access to others, and may have others' access regulated by gatekeepers—people such as receptionists who can prevent intrusions. In addition to access to space, dominance may also be expressed by taking up more physical space (i.e., a combination of enlarging one's size and occupying more space). (p. 289)

In the first sense we mentioned above, higher status people tend to operate in larger "bubbles" of personal space than lower status people and to invade others' space more readily (Carney, Hall, & Smith LeBeau, 2005; Hall, Coats, & Smith LeBeau, 2005; Remland, 1981). Think about officials and celebrities you've seen on TV or in person, or bosses you've worked for, especially ones who held high status or a lot of power within the organization. Compared to people holding less status, those celebs or bosses probably took up more personal space, were less likely to have their personal space invaded by others, and were more likely to invade the space of lower status people. In essence, their status made them freer to take and use more space than people with less status. This may not be fair or right, but it does seem to be the norm in U.S. culture. People who are perceived to have a lot of power, and typically the wealth that comes along with it or that helped create their image, often move about in private or concealed transportation that insulates and protects their space (like limousines with darkened windows or private planes). Many have an entourage—other people who act as buffers to prohibit anyone but a chosen few from entering into the zone of space around the power person. Sometimes a security detail or entourage stems more from a necessity for personal safety than to show power. But the example of celebrities who are free to walk the red carpet and stop to talk to whomever they please versus the fan who's crammed up in some bleachers or held at a distance by ropes, barriers, and security guards, bears out the proxemic difference.

This brings us to the second effect we mentioned, which goes along with the first: Not only do high status people operate in more personal space, they're also afforded more space by others. Unless you have no manners or are an aggressive reporter trying to get a statement from a public official, you're probably not going to cozy up to a high status person and get in his or her face. That's considered too aggressive and downright rude in our culture. Most of us back off in the presence of a powerful person. It's fairly easy to spot this trend in action: Go to a courthouse or other public building in which city officials work or have their offices and watch a high-ranking public official move about in the lobby of the building. It's common to see a high status person walk toward an area that's dense with people and the people will actually pull back from the space, allowing the higher status person more room. We've seen this happen at elevators in simple situations in which professors (who we don't believe to be high status, just typically older!) are given more space by students while waiting for an elevator, as well as inside the elevator car.

## Physical Characteristics

Some of the information in this section may overlap with the previous one, because in U.S. culture as well as other cultures around the world, the physical characteristics of height and weight are connected with status, as are other appearance factors such as clothing, artifacts, and certain aging cues (Burgoon & Dunbar, 2006). Research on this topic isn't extensive, but some evidence shows that height affects how people manage space, with shorter people being more likely to use and invite others into smaller interpersonal distances than taller people (Caplan & Goldman, 1981). In addition, people who are considered overweight by cultural standards are generally afforded more personal space than people who are not overweight (Lerner, Venning, & Knapp, 1975; Venturini, Castelli, & Tomelleri, 2006).

Do you see evidence of these research trends in your daily life? Have you observed that shorter people are more likely to interact at closer spaces than tall people? What happens when a very tall person and a very short person have a conversation—whose approach to space usually rules? Do you see these people try to adjust to the height difference, like by sitting down, so that the space in which a conversation takes place becomes more manageable and equitable? What about in the weight arena—do you see evidence of the differences research alludes to? Are you likely to make more space for an overweight or obese person coming toward you? We don't necessarily believe this to be discriminatory or purposeful behavior, although we realize that intentional nonverbal cues of isolation or disapproval are often communicated. But obese people often talk about feeling ostracized by people's reactions to their appearance—from avoiding touch to discontinuing eye gaze to increasing distance.

We talk more about people with disabilities in the privacy management section of this chapter, but research over a couple of decades shows that people who do not have physical disabilities tend to use greater distances when talking to people with disabilities. However, over time, as a conversation progresses, the distance generally decreases (Braithwaite, 1991; Kleck, 1969; Kleck, Buck, Goller, London, Pfeiffer, & Vukcevic, 1968; Kleck & Strenta, 1985). In one study of space afforded blind people, researchers found that people gave a blind person using a white cane six times as much space as they gave a blind person who did not use a cane (Conigliaro, Cullerton,

*Our friend, Wonda Wilson, occasionally notices that people adjust their use of space around her because she's in a wheelchair.*

Flynn, & Rueder, 1989). Some people are cautious when approaching people in wheelchairs, affording them more space because of the disability and their means of getting around. Some of this distancing behavior is understandable—if you've ever tried to help someone in a wheelchair maneuver to enter a classroom or exit an elevator, you know what we mean. But some distancing is discriminatory, as though the sight of someone with a disability is unnerving and the added space serves to protect or insulate the able-bodied person from the reality of disabled bodies. Think about your own behavior in this regard and see if you need to make some changes.

## Characteristics of the Relationship

Use your common sense and experience to consider these questions: Who tends to exhibit closer interpersonal distances—friends or intimates (like sexual partners)? Friends or coworkers? Friends or strangers? You've probably decided that the more intimate the relationship, meaning the better people know each other, the more comfortable they are using closer proxemics when interacting. If that's your conclusion, you're right! Research shows that conversational distances are affected by the type of relationship interactants have, meaning that friends tend to talk at a more intimate distance than strangers; friends talk more closely than coworkers (unless the coworkers happen to also be friends); and intimate partners, such as dating or married partners, maintain closer interpersonal distances than other combinations of people (Andersen, Guerrero, & Jones, 2006; Bell, Kline, & Barnard, 1998; Guerrero & Floyd, 2006; Muehlenhard, Koralewski, Andrews, & Burdick, 1986).

## Subject Matter

Imagine you're having dinner with a close friend. As you shove down the chips and salsa, you chat about your day, what's going on at school and work, and so forth. Then, before your huge platter of fajitas can arrive, your friend leans in toward you across the booth, takes her or his voice down to a whisper, opens his or her eyes wide, and says, "Guess what I heard about our friend so and so?" In anticipation of a juicy story, you respond by leaning in toward your friend, decreasing the distance between the two of you so that you can better hear the interesting news. You're "all ears," as the phrase goes, and don't really want the food to come until you've heard the "scoop." Your proxemic behavior has just been influenced by the subject matter under discussion.

While this sounds sort of intuitive, like a "duh" kind of moment, research has actually examined this very thing—the effects of topic of conversation on proxemic behavior. Scholar Robert Sommer (1961) studied proxemics in conversation, but insisted that subjects use impersonal topics, because he knew that the intimacy level of the topic would affect how subjects positioned themselves. Other studies have focused on such elements as proxemic movements (forward and backward lean by people in conversation) that mark critical segments of an interaction, such as beginning and ending phases and topic shifts (Erickson, 1975), as well as the effects of receiving positive feedback (like praise) or negative information (like an insult) on proxemic behavior (Leipold, 1963). In the latter study, subjects distanced themselves from people who gave negative information, such as an insult, whereas they used shorter distances with people who gave praise. In situations where we're placed in "close quarters" with people we barely know or have just met, conversation can be sparse or, at best, superficial because of the awkwardness of the situation (Schulz & Barefoot, 1974). That's why people rarely talk on elevators, unless they get on with someone they know.

## Setting

This factor is fairly obvious, because we all know that the environment or setting for an interaction affects our behavior. For example, the presence or absence of noise in a setting often affects proxemic behavior. In a social situation, such as a club in which loud music is playing, we might move closer to someone and lean in to talk, not because we're attracted or interested, but simply because we can't hear the person talk over the roar of the music and other people's conversations unless we get really close. Perhaps you find yourself in a setting where people are whispering, which makes you curious, so you move closer to them so you can overhear their conversation. If there's too much space and interaction is a challenge, we're likely to work to change the physical setting so that communication can occur. We see this behavior a lot in classrooms, where some students will position themselves in the first couple of rows in a lecture hall—not because they want to brown nose the teacher or because they're necessarily enraptured by the topic of the course, but because they simply find they can hear and focus better (and learn more) when they reduce the distance between themselves and the instructor (Richmond, 1997).

## ▪ TERRITORIALITY

Another concept related to our study of proxemics is **territoriality**—our sense of ownership of an object, a particular space, a person, or even time. This territory is OURS (or at least we come to think of it as ours) and personal, special, possibly even expensive (e.g., gifts that cost a lot of money, such as jewelry or a new computer). We want our territory to be safe from intrusion by unwelcome outsiders or strangers, and we will use our best verbal and nonverbal means of defending it from those we perceive as invaders. What territory is YOUR territory? Perhaps you're thinking of personal possessions such as purses, book bags, laptop computers, palm pilots, cell phones, or even your room or home. More than likely, you work to protect those objects and prevent those places you regard as your territory from being tarnished or invaded. What about people as territory? Maybe the thought of people as territory is distasteful to you, but we probably all know people who view their boyfriend or girlfriend as their own private territory, and they become seriously forceful when they believe they're territory is being invaded or violated. (Some people are territorial about their pets!) Many of us are protective of our time, defending any hard-fought "private time" to extremes, because it's such a precious commodity in our lives. A simple phone call from a solicitor during our personal time can be met with severe frustration. Let's first consider a helpful way of classifying territory, then take up the topic of territorial invasion.

*As children develop, so does their sense of territoriality.*

## Types of Territory

Prominent researchers have contributed to our knowledge of territoriality. First, consider communication scholar Irwin Altman's (1975) three types of territories: (1) primary, (2) secondary, and (3) public. Extent of ownership is the key factor that separates one type of territory from the other. **Primary territories** (e.g., homes, bedrooms, vehicles) have a clear owner; access by others is limited. Clear rules or barriers function to protect the territory from invasion or intrusion, such as locks, access codes, and passwords. Because of unwanted invasion, owners tend to protect their primary territory with intense emotion and, in some cases, aggression.

**Secondary territories** are important, but not as important to the owner nor as exclusive as primary territories. A secondary territory generally is not owned by anyone, but people develop a sense of ownership over the space. Examples include the family pew at a church, someone's parking place (not labeled with his/her name, but seen as owned by the person because she or he commonly parks there), a favorite barstool or booth at a commonly frequented restaurant, and a practice field or court in a gym where teams practice or scrimmage. Since we know that we don't really own these spaces, we often use **territorial markers** as nonverbal signals to others that the space is taken or reserved. Markers may include such possessions as notebooks or clothing, other objects in the environment that can be manipulated to "save" a place (like tilting a chair against a table at a dinner), or decorations like ribbons and bows across church pews at weddings, signifying that those rows are reserved for family members. Conflicts often arise over secondary territories because people may have different interpretations of who has the right to enter or occupy the space. If you have a favorite hangout, for example, and a group of visitors from out of town "invades" that hangout, such that you can't sit where you normally sit or do what you normally do in the hangout, you may feel some animosity as a result. You have no real right of ownership, but you *feel* that the space is yours.

**Public territories** are those spaces open to anyone for temporary ownership, and these areas typically do not arouse feelings of invasion in us. A city bus or subway, a public library, a beach, parks, streets, public buildings like courthouses, and walkways are public territories. But these territories can still be invaded, such as when someone turns their music up too loud on a public bus, causing everyone else to have to "appreciate" their musical tastes, or when someone pulls a gun at a courthouse or behaves in an inappropriate or unlawful way, violating the expectations or laws governing the space. An invasion of public space usually has to be extreme for someone's sense of territoriality to be evoked.

Sociologist Erving Goffman (1971) provides us with what he calls the "eight territories of self" as a means of classifying the spaces we experience around us:

1. *Personal space* is territory that we reserve as ours and that we protect and defend vigorously from intrusion. Examples include a home office, closet, or bedroom.
2. *Stalls* are spaces that have designated boundaries for individual use. Study rooms in a university library, phone/Internet cubicles, public restroom stalls, and parking spaces are some of the more obvious examples of this form of space.
3. *Use space* describes those areas close to our occupied surroundings that we need in order to perform certain daily tasks. Examples include check-out areas at grocery stores, hotel check-in counters, slot machines in casinos, spaces people need for the purpose of smoking cigarettes, or areas people use to take their turns during a bowling match, golf tournament, or other event.
4. *Turns* represent spaces that are governed by social norms and expectations. We often hear reference to people "waiting for their turn" in line at the hotdog stand or coffee shop. When turns are violated, people tend to get angry and frustrated because they expect their territorial claims to be respected and honored.
5. *Sheaths* pertain to our skin, artifacts, and clothing we use to cover and protect our bodies. While clothing and artifacts (e.g., eyeglasses, makeup) protect and adorn the body and provide privacy, we may choose to forego that privacy by wearing clothing that reveals our summer tan or the hard work we accomplished at the gym with our personal trainer (e.g., six pack abs or "guns" for arms).
6. *Possessional territory* refers to the use of personal possessions to mark or claim our surroundings, like we mentioned when we defined territorial markers. At movie theatres, sporting events, concerts, and picnics, people like to mark their territory with personal possessions such as blankets, hand bags, clothing, water bottles, and so forth. In the college classroom, students who want to sit next to each other often use personal possessions to mark other desks in their surroundings as territory for friends who have not yet arrived to class. You may have a particular spot in the library or student center that you mark and protect, so that you limit who comes into that space.
7. *Informational preserves* pertains to a means of protecting information we deem private and that others aren't welcome to view. Personal computers, checkbooks, diaries, information posted to our MySpace page or sent to our email accounts, and traditional mailboxes are examples of information territory. Do you have information that you don't want your roommates or family members viewing?

The information you're thinking of likely points to one or several of your informational preserves.

8. *Conversational preserves* are locations in which we talk about intimate or private matters. Can you think of certain topics that you don't want others to hear you discuss in public? Private or personal information that we choose to disclose to others tends to be shared in locations reserved for such an exchange. Some dating or married couples may request a booth when dining out because they want to have conversational preserve surrounding their discussion. You can probably think of times when people have said, "Let's go someplace where we can talk privately."

---

## REMEMBER 4.2

**Territoriality:**  our sense of ownership of an object, a particular space, a person, or even our time.

**Primary Territory:**  territory that has a clear owner and rules or barriers that serve to mark or protect the territory from invasion.

**Secondary Territory:**  territory that is not as important to the owner nor as exclusive as primary territory; space that one does not own, but over which one develops a sense of ownership.

**Territorial Marker:**  a nonverbal signal to others that a space is taken or reserved.

**Public Territory:**  space that is open to anyone for temporary ownership.

---

## Territorial Violation, Invasion, and Contamination

Another important aspect of understanding our nonverbal behavior with regard for proxemics involves how we protect territory from encroachment. Three types of encroachment are typically viewed as negative: violation, invasion, and contamination (Lyman & Scott, 1967). **Violation** is the most general category of the three, and it means the use of or intrusion into primary territory—usually particular spaces or objects that we view as our personal belongings—without our permission. Parents who go through their teenager's room looking for empty beer bottles or tobacco products exemplify a violation of territory. You can probably relate to the story of an infamous roommate who violates your personal territory by using your expensive shampoo or who surfs the Internet on your computer when you're out for the evening. One of our students complained of a roommate who violated their computer by downloading pornographic images and neglecting to remove them before they left school!

**Invasion** is an intense and typically permanent encroachment that is driven by an intention to take over a given territory. The original owner of the territory is often forced out during or after the invasion. Several levels of invasion are important to understand. The first level is large in scale, such as when one country invades another with the intention of taking over to expand its land mass and power. A second level, smaller in scale but still powerful, is exemplified when groups or individuals take over a situation or even a conversation, such as when gangs take over or mark territories

## SPOTLIGHT on Research

Parking places are often viewed as secondary territory; even though people's names may not be printed on certain spots, they tend to park in the same spots, so they develop a sense of ownership over them. They can get irritated, possibly irate when someone else parks in "their" spot. But what about those parking lots where spaces aren't designated or even considered secondary territory—where it's "every person for themselves"? If you've ever been late to class because you were "trolling" a campus lot for someone to leave so you could get their spot, only to have someone cut you off and whip into a space you were headed for or felt entitled to, you're likely to get really frustrated, perhaps even mad. So just how do people nonverbally communicate or negotiate space in public parking lots? Are aggressive parking lot drivers viewed as "space invaders"?

Researchers Rubank and Juieng (1997) examined territorial behavior in parking lots. They looked at many factors, but the purpose of their study was to find out whether or not people in a public setting would use their temporary ownership of a parking lot to retaliate against people they perceived to be intruding on their claimed parking space. Rubank and Juieng wanted to see if people who no longer needed the parking space would display territorialism by taking extra time to leave, even though the spot no longer held any value to them. They predicted that even though the spot was no longer useful, drivers would feel their control and status threatened by an "intruder."

The findings of the study revealed, first, that the number of people in a car was associated with the amount of time it took a driver to exit; drivers departed more quickly when alone than when they had passengers in the car. Rubank and Juieng also found that male drivers in their study had more passengers in their vehicles than female drivers, and that African Americans had more passengers than Caucasian drivers. However, no difference was found for either sex or race in the amount of time taken to exit a parking place. Pertaining to their primary purpose for conducting the study, Rubank and Juieng found that drivers did show evidence of territorialism about parking places—even those they were leaving—in that they took more time to exit a parking place when in the presence of an "intruding" car than when no car was seen waiting for the spot.

How aware are you of your driving behavior in parking lots? Do you see a parking space as your territory? Have you ever had a confrontation over something like a parking space or another form of secondary territory? You can learn a lot about your own view of territory by considering how you manage something as simple as parking.

Do you want to know more about this study? If so, read: Rubank, R. B., & Juieng, D. (1997). Territorial defense in parking lots: Retaliation against waiting drivers. *Journal of Applied Social Psychology, 27,* 139–148.

with painted symbols, staking out their turf. Yet another level, which is more subtle, can be seen in public places where settings are intruded upon. Perhaps you've experienced a situation in which you were enjoying some solitude at a public park or beach, when someone or a group of people arrived and suddenly your solitude was gone.

**Contamination** is a type of encroachment in which someone's territory is tarnished with noise or impurity. Maybe you've heard someone complain, "They came to the party late and trashed the place!" Contamination is about doing something to a

*Which type of territorial invasion is operating in this photo?*

territory that symbolizes your presence, such as leaving cigarette butts and beer bottles in someone's backyard, or wearing someone's sweater and returning it reeking of perfume or smoke. As another example, contamination occurs when neighbors allow their little pack of dogs to come over into our yard and leave us fecal presents that we don't find until it's time to mow the lawn. (That example hits a little close to home—literally.)

The ways that we defend our territory vary in style and intensity. Knapp and Hall (2006) provide the following questions to help us analyze territorial infractions:

1. Who violated our territory?
2. Why did she or he violate our territory?
3. What type of territory was it?
4. How was the violation accomplished?
5. How long did the encroachment last?
6. Do we expect further violations in the future?
7. Where did the violation occur?

We may believe that a violation is severe at first, but when we answer the first question (who did it?), we may find out that it was someone we really like or are close to, so the offense is more forgivable than if someone else did it. Or we may learn that someone has a really good reason for the invasion, so we don't feel as violated once we find out why the incident occurred.

## Classroom Environments as Student Territory

Students can be very protective of their classrooms, which is often surprising to teachers. Some students react negatively when people are in their classrooms who aren't supposed to be there. If you attend the same college for several years and tend to have

## REMEMBER 4.3

### VIC—The Lousy Roommate

One of our students, Ian Samples, gave us an easy way to remember the material in this chapter about territorial encroachment, and we thought we'd pass it along to you. Here's the story of Vic, the lousy roommate.

Imagine that you come back to your apartment one night and Vic is on your laptop computer, working on a paper. Vic has a perfectly good computer of his own in his room, but for some reason, he's using yours. When you ask Vic about this—why he went into your room, got your laptop out of your book bag, and started using it without permission—Vic explains that he wanted to watch TV in the living room while working on his paper. Since his computer wasn't portable, he used your laptop instead. We know this type of encroachment to be a **violation** of personal territory.

But not only is Vic working on your laptop, he's sitting in *your* chair while he works and watches TV. You brought that chair from home, it's your favorite chair, and you *always* sit in it—not Vic, or anyone else for that matter. Yet here Vic is, sitting in your chair using your laptop. We recognize this type of encroachment as **invasion.**

To make matters worse, Vic decided he was hungry while working on his paper (on your laptop) and sitting in your favorite chair, so he helped himself to some crackers in the kitchen. The problem is, you now have cracker crumbs all over the keyboard of your laptop computer, down in some of the cracks around the keys, along with Vic's greasy fingerprints on your keyboard. Strike three for Vic! Not only has he violated your territory, he's invaded your space and **contaminated** it with his food and greasy hands.

Vic is the worst kind of roommate, but his name helps us remember the three types of encroachment:

**V** = **violation:**   the use of someone's primary territory without permission.

**I** = **invasion:**   an intense and typically permanent encroachment of territory that is driven by an intention to take over the territory.

**C** = **contamination:**   the tarnishing of someone's territory with noise or impurity.

your major classes in the same rooms, you can view those spaces as your secondary territory and become protective and defensive of them, as though they belonged to you, your close friends, and favorite teachers. Students can even become territorial about whole campus buildings, like a fine arts facility where the theatre or music students hang out or the gym or field house where student athletes work out, practice, and gather. You may come to feel like a campus area is your "home away from home" because you spend so much time there.

How many of us have walked into a room on the first day of class to stake out a good seat? Perhaps some of us have even saved a spot close by for a friend, or maybe we've used our book bags or laptops to make it look like someone will be sitting in the seat next to us, only to reserve the area for more arm and leg room. Some teachers prefer to assign seats to make roll checking easier, while some will ask students to change their seating arrangements periodically (which usually doesn't go over well).

*What Would <u>You</u> Do?*

Miranda was in the grocery store when she turned from her cart to look for a new brand of shampoo. She was temporarily distracted, so she didn't notice when a woman and her daughter started looking through the contents of her shopping cart. When Miranda turned back to her cart she saw the two "invaders" move her bread out of the way in order to dig deeper into her cart. When she called attention to what they were doing, they looked up, startled but not particularly embarrassed, then muttered to each other and walked away. Miranda quickly checked her cart to see if anything was missing, thinking to herself that she was glad she had her purse on her shoulder. Did the people simply mistake the cart for theirs? Did they see something interesting and want to check it out more closely, or were they trying to somehow rip her off?

*What would you do* if you were Miranda? Would you ignore the situation or shake it off and go on about your business? Would you confront the "invaders" and try to find out what they were doing, call the store manager, or take legal action? What would you do if you were the mother or daughter, facing an irritated Miranda? How would you explain or defend your violation of territory? What type of territory is a cart full of groceries that you haven't yet paid for? What type of space invasion does this example illustrate?

Our point is this: Students can be touchy about classroom space and territorial about where they sit.

What kinds of territorial markers might you use in a classroom? Certainly personal objects such as purses, book bags, laptop computers, and books and notebooks come to mind. But students also tend to view their desk or seat—that almighty throne where you sit each class period—as their own personal territory. If you want to have some fun, arrive to class early next time, sit where another student usually sits, and see what happens. We bet it won't be pretty.

## ■ CROWDING AND DENSITY

Have you ever been in a situation where your personal space was violated simply because the crowd at a sporting event or concert was too large? Our individual perceptions of crowding tend to vary from one person to the next. The study of density and crowding gained popularity in the 1960s, as some people became concerned about an increasing world population (Erlich, 1971). For example, one classic study was conducted in Norway on rats to determine how they reacted to the overpopulation of a given space. Over time, the rats responded in negative, dramatic ways to their overcrowded conditions, leading to concerns about how human beings would behave in crowded, overpopulated situations (Calhoun, 1962). Of course, over the years scholars have debated the wisdom of generalizing from rats to humans (Freedman, 1979; Judge, 2000; Judge & de Waal, 1993).

To stay focused on our study of nonverbal communication, let's establish some definitions related to crowding and density. **Crowding** is a psychological reaction to a perception of spatial restrictions. Perhaps you know someone who doesn't like to travel to large cities simply due to the number of people and buildings there. When we think about large cities, it's important to not confuse crowding with **density,** defined as the number of people or objects in a space that have the potential to restrict or interfere with people's activities and the achievement of their goals (Machleit, Eroglu, & Powell Mantel, 2000). Many people who live in high density areas, such as major cities, learn over time to adjust to the constant invasion and disruption of their personal space. One way to remember the difference between these two related concepts is to recall the discussion in the first few pages of this chapter about physical and psychological space. Density is a physical dimension, whereas crowding is a psychological reaction based on perception. You may be in a small space with lots of other people (high density), yet you don't feel crowded because you're comfortable with the place and the people. Conversely, you may be in a wide-open space, but the people you're with, the occasion, or the topic under discussion make you feel crowded and like you want "outta there." Researchers have studied this distinction, finding that individual perceptions of life in high density areas have more to do with people's daily experiences than the physical environments within which they live and work (Carey, 1972; Galle, Grove, & McPherson, 1972; Sommer, 1969).

How do people cope with high density? According to Knapp and Hall (2006), people cope in the following ways:

1. They spend less time with other people. For example, they engage in shorter conversations or exchanges with people because the perception becomes, over time, that there are just too many people to deal with.
2. They ignore or avoid low-priority interactions, like those that might occur on the street, a city bus, or a subway. Sometimes avoiding the pleasantries that people can use to greet one another in less dense, slower-paced areas (like small towns) can lead people to judgments that people in big cities are unfriendly, when actually the density of the setting contributes to the behavior.
3. They shift the responsibility for some transactions. They're aware of the time and complexities of living in a high density area, so this awareness affects their behavior. For example, they take responsibility to get the correct change for a bus, relieving bus drivers of this task so as not to bog down entry onto the bus.
4. They simply block others out and become more restrictive about who they choose to connect and interact with. For example, many use attendants to guard apartment buildings. The high density of an environment can cause people to ignore homeless people on the street or to generally pay less attention to their surroundings.

## ■ PRIVACY MANAGEMENT: A DIFFERENT VIEW OF PROXEMICS

Beyond the basics of proxemics as a key nonverbal communication code, let's now turn our attention to privacy, which we all know is an important commodity in everyday life. You may not have thought of it this way, but we use proxemic terms, like space and distance, to understand and articulate the status of relationships in our lives. The following statements bear this out: "I feel really close to her." "We've grown apart." "He's been really distant over the past few weeks." Beyond using space and distance to talk about and process what happens in our relationships, we also make decisions about what private information to reveal and conceal based on how close or connected we feel to a given friend, family member, or partner.

**Privacy** is "an interpersonal boundary-control process, which paces and regulates interaction with others" (Altman, 1975, p. 12). Several aspects of privacy are important to understand because of their relevance to our study of nonverbal communication. **Desired privacy** refers to the amount of contact we desire from others, while **achieved privacy** is the actual degree of contact that results from interaction with others. Altman explains that if "the desired privacy is equal to the achieved privacy, an optimum state of privacy exists. If achieved privacy is lower or higher than desired privacy—too much or too little contact—a state of imbalance exists" (pp. 10–11). Can you think of a time when you had the desire to be around your friends and family? Can you think of other

*What does this office door—slightly open—communicate nonverbally about the person who inhabits the space?*

times when you didn't want people around you at all? These instances when we restrict and seek interaction can be explained by thinking about privacy as a **dialectic process,** or an interplay between opposing forces, with varying balances of opening and closing the self to others.

Categories of privacy are helpful to our understanding of this topic as well; let's overview four types of privacy that have emerged in research and that help frame our discussion (Westin, 1970):

1. **Solitude** occurs when a person is completely alone and isolated from other people and cannot be seen by others.
2. **Intimacy** refers to two or more people who are able to reduce distractions from outsiders in order to enhance personal contact in their relationship.
3. **Anonymity** occurs when people are able to hide their identity from others and avoid observation even though they're in a public space.
4. **Reserve** refers to a person's ability to signal that he or she doesn't want to disclose information that is potentially embarrassing.

In addition to these privacy categories, Burgoon (1982) provides dimensions of privacy, which may be preferable to the above typology, in that people rarely experience

---

### REMEMBER 4.4

| | |
|---|---|
| **Crowding:** | a psychological reaction to a perception of spatial restrictions. |
| **Density:** | the number of people or objects in a space that have the potential to restrict or interfere with people's activities and the achievement of their goals. |
| **Privacy:** | an interpersonal boundary-control process, which paces and regulates interaction with others. |
| **Desired Privacy:** | amount of contact desired from others at a given point in time. |
| **Achieved Privacy:** | actual degree of contact that results from interaction with others. |
| **Dialectic Process:** | instances in which we restrict and seek interaction; an interplay between opposing forces; different balances of opening and closing the self to others. |
| **Solitude:** | when a person is alone and isolated from other people and cannot be seen by others. |
| **Intimacy:** | when people are able to reduce distractions from outsiders in order to enhance personal contact. |
| **Anonymity:** | the ability to hide identity from others and avoid observation, even in public spaces. |
| **Reserve:** | when a person is able to signal that he or she does not want to disclose information that is potentially embarrassing. |

complete privacy or a complete lack of privacy. Instead, people experience various degrees of privacy, described as follows:

1. **Physical privacy** is the degree to which someone is physically inaccessible to others.
2. **Social privacy** occurs when an individual or group opts to withdraw from social interaction.
3. **Psychological privacy** refers to people's ability to exercise control over the expression of their thoughts and feelings.
4. **Information privacy** pertains to people's ability to prevent the collection and distribution of information about themselves or their social networks without their knowledge or permission.

## Communication Privacy Management

The leading privacy scholar in the communication discipline, Sandra Petronio (2000, 2002, 2007), developed **Communication Privacy Management (CPM)** theory as a way of better understanding how we establish rules about privacy and manage privacy using spatial metaphors. As you study this information within this chapter on proxemics, it may help to think of privacy as your own little, personal box of space—it's not a physical space, but an intangible entity that you hold dear. You develop rules about your little space, in terms of what you consider private, who has access to you and your private information, how you select those people you want to share private information with, how you actually go about sharing that information, what you expect the sharing of private information to do for (or to) a relationship, how you protect your privacy from intrusion by unwanted others, and so forth. Our privacy rules are in constant motion, as we keep things in and let things out, as we draw people in, but keep others out. Privacy is important to us all, even those of us who believe ourselves to be fairly open with most people, because without privacy we lose control over who has access to us, who knows what about us, and what they to do with that information. Because privacy is so important, we develop rules about how to manage it in our lives and relationships and tend to talk about it in spatial metaphors, like when someone says "My husband and I have grown apart" or "You're distancing yourself from me. Is something wrong?"

Petronio (2002) suggests that private information is a form of **self-disclosure,** defined as the sharing of information that people cannot learn about us unless we reveal it to them. Self-disclosure is a building block toward intimacy in a relationship, so how we handle the disclosure of private information is critical to the success of any relationship. As we've said, Petronio uses the metaphor of spatial boundaries to delineate the role of private information in relationships. Boundaries act as rules for managing privacy, meaning that we often "draw a line" on what information we will and will not share with people. For example, an instructor may place a symbolic spatial boundary around information about his or her personal life—a boundary that cannot be transcended by students. Many faculty believe that sharing private information with students is inappropriate and that it can confuse the relationship between teacher and student. Sometimes students attempt to push that boundary, asking inappropriate questions about an instructor's opinions or personal life. As another example, you may think it's perfectly fine to ask people about a medical condition they have or what medications they're on. You may believe that such questions show interest and that you'd like to learn more about living with such a condition. But many of us were raised believing that this sort of questioning is intrusive and "none of our business." Many people feel that details about their health are private matters, not to be shared with much of anyone. If you ask questions about areas people deem private, you may bump your head right up against a privacy boundary (which doesn't feel good) and be negatively evaluated as a result.

Petronio's principles have been utilized to examine the management of private information in various contexts. For example, researchers have used CPM theory to better understand the following: the disclosure of HIV-testing information and AIDS prevention (Green & Serovich, 1996; Yep, 1992, 1993); relational bonding between fathers and children (Petronio & Bradford, 1993); efforts to control negative outcomes of private disclosures (Petronio & Bantz, 1991); instances of embarrassment (Petronio, Olson, & Dollar, 1989); the revelation of private gender-related information (Petronio, Martin, & Littlefield, 1984); how privacy functions in small groups (Petronio & Braithwaite, 1987); and privacy issues for persons with disabilities (Braithwaite, 1991). In this body of work, researchers have focused primarily on privacy in face-to-face relational contexts and have highlighted the concerns of balancing the "private" with the "public." Some research applications of CPM theory warrant further discussion.

## People with Disabilities

Have you ever had social contact with a person who has a disability? Some of us probably have family members who are living with disabilities. Others can think of social situations in which we tried to avoid staring at a person with a disability at the shopping mall or in an elevator. Or perhaps we've been overly helpful such that we call too much attention to someone's disability and not enough attention to the person *as a person*. Communication scholar Dawn Braithwaite is one of the leading researchers of communication about and among people with disabilities. In one of her studies (Braithwaite, 1991), she examined how people with disabilities are challenged when it comes to managing private information about their disability, because able-bodied people tend to ask personal, often embarrassing questions, as though a person's disability were an appropriate topic of conversation like a shirt one wears or a book one's reading. Some of these questions include how a person became disabled, how a person with a disability goes about her or his everyday life, and so forth. Can you think of experiences you have had with people with disabilities? Have you breached a person's privacy boundary by asking questions or drawing too much attention to a disability?

## Bartenders

Another example to help explain communication privacy management is how bar patrons communicate with bartenders. Have you ever been or do you have a friend who is a bartender? Both authors of this book bartended as we worked our way through college and we both agree that there is something magical about how comfortable people feel to self-disclose private information to bartenders. We've seen too many bottles of beer lead anyone to talk openly about their private information. However, most bartenders will tell you that people—under the influence or not—are quite willing to disclose information about their most personal affairs. Cheating, financial problems, health concerns, and depression are just the beginning of a long list of private issues that bartenders get to listen to. What is it about the context of a bar that makes people more open with their private information? Is there something about the way most bars are situated spatially that sets up a more comfortable location to disclose private information? Is there something anonymous about self-disclosing personal information to a bartender?

## Teacher Privacy Management

As we've stated, people use space and distance to help them better understand and talk about their relationships; the same is true for teacher–student relationships (Mazer, Murphy, & Simonds, 2007; McBride & Wahl, 2005; Rawlins, 2000). (By "teacher–student" relationship, we don't mean to imply anything romantic or sexual; we simply mean the connection between teachers and students for the purposes of education.) In quick review of key concepts discussed in the past few pages, beyond using space and distance to talk about and process what's going on in our relationships, we also make decisions about how to balance private information we wish to reveal and that which we wish to conceal. These decisions are based primarily on how emotionally close or connected we feel to someone.

In the educational context, instructors deal with this balance every day. **Teacher Privacy Management (TPM)** pertains to those instances in which teachers make decisions about what private information they want to reveal or conceal in the process of creating a comfortable classroom for learning to take place. These decisions help teachers avoid the negative ramifications of inappropriate revelations and protect their personal lives outside the classroom (McBride & Wahl, 2005). When teachers talk about "boundaries" and establishing appropriate "distances" from their students, they use nonverbal proxemic terms to help guide their behavior. We've probably all heard stories in the media about teachers who didn't use good judgment in establishing and maintaining boundaries between themselves and their students. These are the tales of lawsuits and damaged lives.

## Internet Chat Rooms as Private Spaces

Increasingly, people turn to chat rooms and online message systems to meet romantic partners and friends (Edwards, Edwards, Qing, & Wahl, 2007; Ellison, Steinfield, & Lampe, 2007; Mazer, Murphy, & Simonds, 2007; McCown, Fischer, Page, & Homant, 2001; Merkel & Richardson, 2000; Parks & Roberts, 1998; Tidwell & Walther, 2002; Tucker, 2006; Ventura, 2005; Walther, 1992, 1994, 2007). Something about the anonymous nature of the Internet seems to empower people and give them the comfort to express extremely private matters (e.g., dating, intimacy, and sexual activity) in virtual realms (cyberspace) for the purpose of forming connections—connections that

## REMEMBER 4.5

| | |
|---|---|
| **Physical Privacy:** | degree to which someone is physically inaccessible to others. |
| **Social Privacy:** | when an individual or group opts to withdraw from social interaction. |
| **Psychological Privacy:** | people's ability to exercise control over the expression of their thoughts and feelings. |
| **Information Privacy:** | people's ability to prevent the collection and distribution of information about themselves or their social networks without their knowledge or permission. |
| **Communication Privacy Management (CPM):** | theory that explains how we manage privacy using spatial metaphors. |
| **Self-Disclosure:** | the sharing of information that people cannot learn about us unless we reveal it to them. |
| **Teacher Privacy Management (TPM):** | teacher decisions about what private information they want to reveal or conceal. |

sometimes grow into face-to-face relationships. Do you have a friend who has dated someone they've met online? What are the advantages and disadvantages of establishing relationships through chat rooms, emailing, or other forums like MySpace or Facebook? Do you view Internet chat rooms as public or private spaces? The Internet raises a series of questions that are important to think about, with regard for space and privacy management (Allen, Coopman, Hart, & Walker, 2007; Lee & Wahl, 2007; Soukup, 2004, 2006). Because of the growing fascination with and use of online communication, the topic of nonverbal communication and the Internet will be explored extensively in Chapter 10.

## ■ UNDERSTANDING PROXEMICS: APPLYING THE REFLEXIVE CYCLE OF NONVERBAL COMMUNICATION DEVELOPMENT

Have you ever thought about how you manage space in your own life? The first step to developing your skills and a better understanding of proxemic behaviors as a code of nonverbal communication is awareness. Just like we asked you to do for environment in the last chapter, we ask you to inventory yourself using the following questions: What standards or expectations do you have regarding space management? What are your needs or preferences regarding the way other people use space? Do you have expectations or rules about such things as a personal space bubble or comfort zone? Do these judgments vary depending on who the person is or whether your relationship with the person is personal or professional in nature? Are you aware of the impressions others may have about you based on the way you use and manage space?

Now that you have engaged in an inventory of self regarding proxemics, it's time to think about making, if necessary, any appropriate changes to improve how you manage these nonverbal cues in your everyday life. This is Phase 2 in the Reflexive Cycle. Ask yourself: Are there some changes I need to make regarding my own proxemic behaviors (e.g., too close, too distant, space violations, invasions of territory, reactions to encroachment)? If so, how can I make those changes? Perhaps the only thing that needs to change is your level of awareness about how your uses of space are perceived and interpreted by other people.

Beyond engaging in an inventory of self and making any appropriate changes, the next step is to inventory others. Can you think of a person who seems to have no awareness of space and distance? You may be thinking of a friend who gets too close to you in conversation, stands too far away during conversation, or who has a sensitive space bubble. These people may lack self-monitoring skills (the ability to be aware of one's own appropriateness in social situations) or may simply have no realization of how negatively their use of space is viewed by others. Think about a simple social situation, like a gathering of some friends, as well as the person you're dating. Your significant other doesn't sit next to you at the gathering; when you attempt to get the person to sit by you, he or she blows you off, which embarrasses you in front of your friends. How should you react? Is it time to end this relationship or ask your significant other to simply catch a clue? How might you sensitively find out what's going on?

Some people are oblivious to the fact that their use of space communicates something to other people about their attitude or level of interest. They aren't aware enough to consult with other people for their observations and resulting interpretations of their use of space. We need to be aware that our use of space sends nonverbal signals to other people. Sometimes we get clues from other people who react to our use of space to give us a sense as to what message we're sending (e.g., "Back off!", "Why are you getting so close?"). If someone was uncomfortable with or offended by your use of space, would you notice? What nonverbal signals would the person send? How might you respond in such a situation?

After you have done an inventory of self, changed self, and inventoried others' nonverbal behavior, the fourth phase of the Reflexive Cycle involves interacting with others, trying out the changes you've made or are in the process of making, and observing people as you verbally and nonverbally interact with them. Do people have different reactions to you, as a result of any changes you made? For example, some people who tend to distance themselves from others may come to be seen as more friendly if they get closer in conversation. As another example, some people who are trying to become more sensitive to the way they manage space may be recognized for not getting so close or being inappropriate. It can be interesting to note people's reactions to both subtle and obvious changes in your use of space and how that makes you feel, as well as to gauge your own reactions to changes in others' use of space.

In the last part of the cycle, the challenge is to review and assess the whole process, making note of positive and negative aspects, and then begin the cycle again. The Reflexive Cycle of Nonverbal Communication Development is an ongoing process, one that helps us work to develop and improve our nonverbal sending and receiving abilities.

## SUMMARY ■ ■ ■ ■ ■

Proxemics is a fascinating code of nonverbal communication that reveals a lot about how people feel about one another. In this chapter, we defined proxemics as the way that distance and space play a communicative role in our everyday life. Space can be physical or psychological. The different zones of communicative space or conversational distances include intimate, personal, social, and public. As we develop nonverbal communication skills in everyday life, it's important to consider cultural background, sex, sexual orientation, age, status, physical characteristics (such as having a disability), characteristics of the relationship between interactants, the subject matter of conversation, and the setting for an interaction. All of these factors can influence our proxemic behavior.

Next we discussed territoriality, defined as our sense of ownership of an object, a particular space, a person, or even time. Three major types of territory were examined in this chapter—primary, secondary, and public. We protect and defend our territory from violation (the use of territory without our permission) and from invasion (an intense and typically permanent encroachment that is driven by an intention to take over territory). The final type of threat to territory that we discussed was contamination—a form of encroachment in which someone's territory is tarnished with noise or impurity. We discussed classrooms and campus buildings as settings in which students can become territorial.

We explored crowding and density as two elements within the study of proxemics that affect our verbal and nonverbal communication. Crowding can be defined as a psychological reaction to a perception of spatial restrictions, while density refers to the number of people or objects in a space that have the potential to restrict or interfere with people's activities and the achievement of their goals.

Then we addressed the fascinating and important topic of privacy, turning to Communication Privacy Management theory to help explain the connection between proxemics and privacy. We often use spatial metaphors to better understand and communicate about our relationships. Managing our privacy by establishing and maintaining boundaries in our relationships is important as we develop connections with people over time. We encourage you to consciously be aware of yourself and others regarding nonverbal communication needs, expectations, and desires for privacy. The more we understand ourselves in relation to others regarding distance and space in both personal and professional life, the better prepared we will be to enter new relationships or to strengthen existing ones.

Finally, we applied the Reflexive Cycle of Nonverbal Communication Development to proxemics, so that we can become more aware of our own spatial behavior as well as that of others, in order to make any changes we deem necessary that will help make us more effective communicators. We should keep the following steps of the cycle in mind to improve our nonverbal communication: inventory self, make any appropriate changes to self, inventory others, and combine the inventory and changes of self with what you learn about others, as you move in and out of human interaction. This process involves such questions as: What are our own spatial and distance-based needs, as well as the needs of those with whom we communicate? Are we too close? Are we too far away? Have we just invaded someone's territory? If so, how can we make things right? This critical assessment enables us to develop more awareness of self in terms of space, distance, and privacy expectations, needs, and desires. Further, the assessment enables us to enhance our nonverbal communication for a lifetime.

## DISCUSSION STARTERS

1. Can a space that a person doesn't own be personal? What about the contents of your shopping cart, your favorite table at a restaurant, or a parking space? Provide some examples of physical versus psychological space.

2. What are the three types of territory? What kinds of territorial markers are you likely to use to delineate your space? How do you react when someone invades your space?

3. Explain the three types of encroachment represented by VIC, the lousy roommate. What verbal and nonverbal responses will each type of encroachment generate in you?

4. What's the difference between crowding and density? Can you feel crowded in a non-dense space? Not crowded in a high density space? How does that work?

5. We spent a good deal of time discussing privacy in this chapter. Think about your own privacy needs and expectations, then think of a time when your privacy was violated by someone. Was it an invasion of your private space or of your private information? How did the invasion make you feel and how did you react?

## REFERENCES

Aiello, J. R., & Jones, S. E. (1971). Field study of the proxemic behavior of young school children in three subcultural groups. *Journal of Personality and Social Psychology, 19*, 351–356.

Allen, M. W., Coopman, S. J., Hart, J. L., & Walker, K. L. (2007). Workplace surveillance and managing privacy boundaries. *Management Communication Quarterly, 21*, 172–200.

Altman, I. (1975). *The environment and social behavior.* Thousand Oaks, CA: Brooks/Cole.

Andersen, P. A., Guerrero, L. K., & Jones, S. M. (2006). Nonverbal behavior in intimate interactions and intimate relationships. In V. Manusov & M. L. Patterson (Eds.), *The Sage handbook of nonverbal communication* (pp. 259–277). Thousand Oaks, CA: Sage.

Barry, D. T. (2002). An ethnic identity scale for East Asian immigrants. *Journal of Immigrant Health, 4*, 87–94.

Baxter, J. C. (1970). Interpersonal spacing in natural settings. *Sociometry, 33*, 444–456.

Beaulieu, C. M. J. (2004). Intercultural study of personal space: A case study. *Journal of Applied Social Psychology, 34*, 794–805.

Bell, P. A., Kline, L. M., & Barnard, W. A. (1998). Friendship and freedom of movement as moderators of sex differences in interpersonal distancing. *Journal of Social Psychology, 128*, 305–310.

Braithwaite, D. O. (1991). "Just how much did that wheelchair cost?": Management of privacy boundaries by persons with disabilities. *Western Journal of Speech Communication, 55*, 254–274.

Burgoon, J. K. (1978). A communication model of personal space violations: Explication and an initial test. *Human Communication Research, 4,* 129–142.

Burgoon, J. K. (1982). Privacy and communication. In M. Burgoon (Ed.), *Communication yearbook 6* (pp. 206–249). Beverly Hills, CA: Sage.

Burgoon, J. K., & Dunbar, N. E. (2006). Nonverbal expressions of dominance and power in human relationships. In V. Manusov & M. L. Patterson (Eds.), *The Sage handbook of nonverbal communication* (pp. 279–297). Thousand Oaks, CA: Sage.

Burgoon, J. K., & Jones, S. B. (1976). Toward a theory of personal space expectations and their violations. *Human Communication Research, 2,* 131–146.

Calhoun, J. B. (1962). Population density and social pathology. *Scientific American, 206,* 139–148.

Caplan, M. E., & Goldman, M. (1981). Personal space violations as a function of height. *Journal of Social Psychology, 114,* 167–171.

Carey, G. W. (1972, March/April). Density, crowding, stress, and the ghetto. *American Behavioral Scientist,* 495–507.

Carney, D. R., Hall, J. A., & Smith LeBeau, L. (2005). Beliefs about the nonverbal expression of social power. *Journal of Nonverbal Behavior, 29,* 105–123.

Conigliaro, L., Cullerton, K., Flynn, K., & Rueder, S. (1989). Stigmatizing artifacts and their effect on personal space. *Psychological Reports, 65,* 897–898.

Darwin, C. (1872/1965). *The expression of emotion in man and animals.* London: J. Murray. (Reprinted in 1965, Chicago: University of Chicago Press).

Derlega, V. J., Metts, S., Petronio, S., & Margulis, S. T. (1993). *Self-disclosure.* Newbury Park, CA: Sage.

Derlega, V. J., Wilson, J., & Chaikin, A. L. (1976). Friendship and disclosure reciprocity. *Journal of Personality and Social Psychology, 34,* 578–582.

Edwards, C., Edwards, A., Qing, Q., & Wahl, S. T. (2007). The influence of computer-mediated word-of-mouth communication on student perceptions of instructors and attitudes toward learning course content. *Communication Education, 56,* 255–277.

Egolf, D. B., & Corder, L. E. (1991). Height differences of low and high job status female and male corporate employees. *Sex Roles, 24,* 365–373.

Ellison, N., Steinfield, C., & Lampe, C. (2007). The benefits of Facebook "friends": Social capital and college students' use of online social network sites. *Journal of Computer-Mediated Communication, 12,* 1143–1168.

Elman, D. (1977). Physical characteristics and the perception of masculine traits. *Journal of Social Psychology, 103,* 157–158.

Erickson, F. (1975). One function of proxemic shifts in face-to-face interaction. In A. Kendon, R. M. Harris, & M. R. Key (Eds.), *Organization of behavior in face-to-face interaction.* Chicago: Aldine.

Erlich, P. R. (1971). *The population bomb.* New York: Ballantine Books.

Evans, G. W., & Howard, R. B. (1973). Personal space. *Psychological Bulletin, 80,* 334–344.

Feldman, R. S., & Tyler, J. M. (2006). Factoring in age: Nonverbal communication across the life span. In V. Manusov & M. L. Patterson (Eds.), *The Sage handbook of nonverbal communication* (pp. 181–199). Thousand Oaks, CA: Sage.

Fisher, J. D., & Byrne, D. (1975). Too close for comfort: Sex differences in response to invasions of personal space. *Journal of Personality and Social Psychology, 32,* 15–21.

Freedman, J. L. (1979). Reconciling apparent differences between the responses of humans and other animals to crowding. *Psychological Review, 86,* 80–85.

Freitas, A., Kaiser, S., & Hammidi, T. (1996). Communities, commodities, cultural space, and style. *Journal of Homosexuality, 31,* 83–107.

Galle, O. R., Grove, W. R., & McPherson, J. M. (1972). Population density and pathology: What are relations for man? *Science, 176,* 23–30.

Gifford, R. (1982). Projected interpersonal distance and orientation choices: Personality, sex, and social situation. *Social Psychology Quarterly, 45,* 145–152.

Goffman, E. (1971). *Relations in public: Microstudies of the public order.* New York: Harper Colophon Books.

Green, K. L., & Serovich, J. M. (1996). Appropriateness of disclosure of HIV-testing information: The perspective of PWA's. *Journal of Applied Communication Research, 24,* 50–65.

Guerrero, L. K., & Floyd, K. (2006). *Nonverbal communication in close relationships.* Mahwah, NJ: Erlbaum.

Hall, E. T. (1959). *The silent language.* Garden City, NJ: Doubleday.

Hall, E. T. (1963). A system for the notation of proxemic behavior. *American Anthropology, 65,* 1003–1026.

Hall, E. T. (1966). *The hidden dimension.* Garden City, NJ: Doubleday.

Hall, E. T. (1968). Proxemics. *Current Anthropology, 9,* 83–108.

Hall, E. T. (1983). Proxemics. In A. M. Katz & V. T. Katz (Eds.), *Foundation of nonverbal communication: Readings, exercises, and commentary* (pp. 5–27). Carbondale: Southern Illinois University Press.

Hall, J. A. (2006). Women's and men's nonverbal communication: Similarities, differences, stereotypes, and origins. In V. Manusov & M. L. Patterson (Eds.), *The Sage handbook of nonverbal communication* (pp. 201–218). Thousand Oaks, CA: Sage.

Hall, J. A., Coats, E. J., & Smith LeBeau, L. (2005). Nonverbal behavior and the vertical dimension of social relations: A meta-analysis. *Psychological Bulletin, 131,* 898–924.

Hays, R. B. (1984). The development and maintenance of friendship. *Journal of Social and Personal Relationships, 2,* 74–98.

Hays, R. B. (1985). A longitudinal study of friendship development. *Journal of Social and Personal Relationships, 4,* 909–924.

Henley, N. M. (2001). Body politics. In A. Branaman (Ed.), *Self and society: Blackwell readers in sociology* (pp. 288–297). Malden, MA: Blackwell.

Huff, J. L. (2001). Parental attachment, reverse culture shock, perceived social support, and college adjustment of missionary children. *Journal of Psychology and Theology, 29,* 246–264.

Judge, P. G. (2000). Coping with crowded conditions. In F. Aureli & F. B. M. de Waal (Eds.), *Natural conflict resolution* (pp. 129–154). Berkeley: University of California Press.

Judge, P. G., & de Waal, F. B. M. (1993). Conflict avoidance among rhesus monkeys: Coping with short-term crowding. *Animal Behavior, 46,* 221–232.

Kleck, R. E. (1969). Physical stigma and task-oriented interaction. *Human Relations, 22,* 51–60.

Kleck, R. E., Buck P. L., Goller, W. L., London, R. S., Pfeiffer, J. R., & Vukcevic, D. P. (1968). The effect of stigmatizing conditions on the use of personal space. *Psychological Reports, 23,* 111–118.

Kleck, R. E., & Strenta, A. C. (1985). Physical deviance and the perception of social outcomes. In J. A. Graham & A. M. Kligman (Eds.), *The psychology of cosmetic treatments.* New York: Praeger.

Knapp, M. L., & Hall, J. A. (2006). *Nonverbal communication in human interaction* (6th ed.). Belmont, CA: Thomson/Wadsworth.

Kramer, B. J., & Gibson, J. W. (1991). The cognitively impaired elderly's response to touch: A naturalistic study. *Journal of Gerontological Social Work, 18,* 175–193.

Lee, R., & Wahl, S. T. (2007). Justifying surveillance and control: An analysis of the media framing of pedophiles and the Internet. *Texas Speech Communication Journal, 32,* 1–15.

Leipold, W. E. (1963). *Psychological distance in a dyadic interview.* Unpublished doctoral dissertation, University of North Dakota.

Lerner, R. M., Venning, J., & Knapp, J. R. (1975). Age and sex effects on personal space schemata toward body build in late childhood. *Developmental Psychology, 11,* 855–856.

Li, S. (2001). How close is too close? A comparison of proxemic reactions of Singaporean Chinese to male intruders of four ethnicities. *Perceptual and Motor Skills, 93,* 124–126.

Li, S., & Li, Y. (2007). How far is far enough? A measure of information privacy in terms of interpersonal distance. *Environment and Behavior, 39,* 317–331.

Lyman, S. M., & Scott, M. B. (1967). Territoriality: A neglected social dimension. *Social Problems, 15,* 237–241.

Machleit, K. A., Eroglu, W. A., & Powell Mantel, S. (2000). Perceived retail crowding and shopping satisfaction. Reprinted in L. K. Guerrero & M. L. Hecht (Eds.), *The nonverbal communication reader: Classic and contemporary readings* (2008, 3rd ed., pp. 191–202). Prospect Heights, IL: Waveland.

Manusov, V. (1997). Stereotypes and nonverbal cues: Showing how we feel about others during cross-cultural interactions. Reprinted in L. K. Guerrero & M. L. Hecht (Eds.), *The nonverbal communication reader: Classic and contemporary readings* (2008, 3rd ed., pp. 314–320). Prospect Heights, IL: Waveland.

Matsumoto, D. (2006). Culture and nonverbal behavior. In V. Manusov & M. L. Patterson (Eds.), *The Sage handbook of nonverbal communication* (pp. 219–235). Thousand Oaks, CA: Sage.

Matthews, A., Derlega, V. J., & Morrow, J. (2006). What is highly personal information and how is it related to self-disclosure decision making? The perspective of college students. *Communication Research Reports, 23,* 85–92.

Mazer, J., Murphy, R., & Simonds, C. (2007). I'll see you on Facebook: The effects of computer-mediated teacher disclosure on student motivation, affective learning, and classroom climate. *Communication Education, 56,* 1–17.

McBride, M. C., & Wahl, S. T. (2005). "To say or not to say": Teachers' management of privacy boundaries in the classroom. *Texas Speech Communication Journal, 30,* 8–22.

McCown, J., Fischer, D., Page, R., & Homant, M. (2001). Internet relationships: People who meet people. *CyberPsychology and Behavior, 4,* 593–596.

Mehrabian, A., & Diamond, S. G. (1971). Seating arrangement and conversation. *Sociometry, 34,* 281–289.

Merkel, E., & Richardson, R. (2000). Digital dating and virtual relating: Conceptualizing computer-mediated romantic relationships. *Family Relations, 49,* 187–193.

Muehlenhard, C. L., Koralewski, M. A., Andrews, S. L., & Burdick, C. A. (1986). Verbal and nonverbal cues that convey interest in dating: Two studies. Reprinted in L. K. Guerrero & M. L. Hecht (Eds.), *The nonverbal communication reader: Classic and contemporary readings* (2008, 3rd ed., pp. 353–359). Prospect Heights, IL: Waveland.

Naus, P. J., & Eckenrode, J. J. (1974). Age differences and degree of acquaintance as determinants of interpersonal distance. *Journal of Social Psychology, 93,* 133–134.

Parks, M., & Roberts, L. (1998). Making MOOsic: The development of personal relationships on line and a comparison to their off-line counterparts. *Journal of Social and Personal Relationships, 15,* 517–537.

Petronio, S. (1991). Communication boundary management: A theoretical model of managing disclosure of private information between marital partners. *Communication Theory, 1,* 311–335.

Petronio, S. (2000). *Balancing the secrets of private disclosures.* Mahwah, NJ: Erlbaum.

Petronio, S. (2002). *Boundaries of privacy: Dialectics of disclosure.* New York: State University of New York Press.

Petronio, S. (2007). Translational research endeavors and the practices of communication privacy management. *Journal of Applied Communication Research, 35,* 218–222.

Petronio, S., & Bantz, C. (1991). Controlling the ramifications of disclosure: "Don't tell anybody but. . . ." *Journal of Language and Social Psychology, 10,* 263–269.

Petronio, S., & Bradford, L. (1993). Issues interfering with the use of written communication as a means of relational bonding between absentee, divorced fathers and their children. *Journal of Applied Communication, 24,* 181–199.

Petronio, S., & Braithwaite, D. O. (1987). I'd rather not say: The role of personal privacy in small groups. In M. Mayer & N. Dollar (Eds.), *Issues in group communication.* Scottsdale, AZ: Gorsuch Scarisbrick.

Petronio, S., Martin, J., & Littlefield, R. (1984). Prerequisite conditions for self-disclosure: A gender issue. *Communication Monographs, 51,* 268–273.

Petronio, S., Olson, C., & Dollar, N. (1989). Privacy issues in relational embarrassment: Impact on relational quality and communication satisfaction. *Communication Research Reports, 6,* 216–225.

Rawlins, W. K. (1983). Openness as problematic in ongoing friendships: Two conversational dilemmas. *Communication Monographs, 30,* 1–15.

Rawlins, W. K. (1994). Being there and growing apart: Sustaining friendships during adulthood. In D. J. Canary & L. Stafford (Eds.), *Communication and relational maintenance* (pp. 275–294). San Diego: Academic Press.

Rawlins, W. K. (2000). Teaching as a mode of friendship. *Communication Theory, 10,* 5–26.

Remland, M. (1981). Developing leadership skills in nonverbal communication: A situational perspective. *Journal of Business Communication, 18,* 18–31.

Richmond, V. P. (1997). *Nonverbal communication in the classroom: A text, workbook, and study guide.* Acton, MA: Tapestry Press.

Roberts, J. V., & Herman, C. P. (1986). The psychology of height: An empirical review. In C. P. Herman, M. P. Zanna, & E. T. Higgins (Eds.), *Physical appearance, stigma, and social behavior: The Ontario symposium* (Vol. 3). Hillsdale, NJ: Erlbaum.

Rose, S. M. (1984). How friendships end: Patterns among young adults. *Journal of Social and Personal Relationships, 1,* 267–277.

Rose, S., & Serafica, F. C. (1986). Keeping and ending casual, close and best friendships. *Journal of Social and Personal Relationships, 3,* 275–288.

Rosenfeld, L. B., & Kendrick, W. L. (1984). Choosing to open: An empirical investigation of subjective reasons for self-disclosing. *Western Journal of Speech Communication, 48,* 326–343.

Rubank, R. B., & Juieng, D. (1997). Territorial defense in parking lots: Retaliation against waiting drivers. *Journal of Applied Social Psychology, 27,* 139–148.

Rubin, Z., & Shenker, S. (1978). Friendship, proximity, and self-disclosure. *Journal of Personality, 46,* 1–11.

Schulz, R., & Barefoot, J. (1974). Nonverbal responses and affiliative conflict theory. *British Journal of Social and Clinical Psychology, 13,* 237–243.

Shuter, R. (1976). Proxemics and tactility in Latin America. *Journal of Communication, 26,* 46–52.

Sinha, S. P., & Nayyar, P. (1995). Perception of crowding among children and adolescents. *Journal of Social Psychology, 135,* 263–268.

Smeltzer, L., Waltman, J., & Leonard, D. (1991). Proxemics and haptics in managerial communication. Reprinted in L. K. Guerrero & M. L. Hecht (Eds.), *The nonverbal communication reader: Classic and contemporary readings* (2008, 3rd ed., pp. 184–190). Prospect Heights, IL: Waveland.

Smith, M. J., Reinheimer, R. E., & Gabbard-Alley, A. (1981). Crowding, task performance, and communicative interaction in youth and old age. *Human Communication Research, 7,* 259–272.

Sommer, R. (1961). Leadership and group geography. *Sociometry, 24,* 99–110.

Sommer, R. (1969). *Personal space: The behavioral basis of design.* Englewood Cliffs, NJ: Prentice-Hall.

Sommer, R. (2002). Personal space in a digital age. In R. B. Bechtel and A. Churchman (Eds.), *Handbook of environmental psychology* (pp. 647–660). New York: Wiley.

Soukup, C. (2004). Multimedia performance in computer-mediated community: Communication as a virtual drama. *Journal of Computer-Mediated Communication* [Online], *9(4)*. Available: http://jcmc.indiana.edu/vol9/issue4/soukup.html

Soukup, C. (2006). Computer-mediated communication as a virtual third place: Building Oldenburg's great good places on the world wide web. *New Media and Society, 8*, 421–440.

Spain, D. (1992). *Gendered spaces.* Chapel Hill: University of North Carolina Press.

Tank Buschmann, M. B., Hollinger-Smith, L. M., & Peterson-Kokkas, S. E. (1999). Implementation of expressive physical touch in depressed older adults. *Journal of Clinical Geropsychology, 5*, 291–300.

Tidwell, J. C., & Walther, J. B. (2002). Computer-mediated communication effects on disclosure, impressions, and personal evaluations: Getting to know one another one bit at a time. *Human Communication Research, 28*, 317–348.

Tobin, S. S., & Gustafson, J. D. (1987). What do we do differently with elderly clients? *Journal of Gerontological Social Work, 10*, 107–121.

Tucker, A. (2006, June 25). Is he your boyfriend? Check Facebook. *The Baltimore Sun: Knight-Ridder Tribune.*

Ventura, J. (2005, February 14). More and more people are turning to the Internet to find a perfect match. *Baton Rouge Advocate*, p. D1.

Venturini, B., Castelli, L., & Tomelleri, S. (2006). Not all jobs are suitable for fat people: Experimental evidence of a link between being fat and "out-of-sight" jobs. *Social Behavior and Personality, 34*, 389–398.

Vrij, A. (2001). Credibility judgments of detectives: The impact of nonverbal behavior, social skills, and physical characteristics on impression formation. *Journal of Social Psychology, 133*, 601–610.

Walther, J. (1992). Interpersonal effects in computer-mediated interaction: A relational perspective. *Communication Research, 19*, 52–90.

Walther, J. (1994). Anticipated ongoing interaction versus channel effects on relational communication in computer-mediated interaction. *Human Communication Research, 20*, 473–501.

Walther, J. (2007). Selective self-presentation in computer-mediated communication: Hyperpersonal dimensions of technology, language, and cognition. *Computers in Human Behavior, 20*, 2538–2557.

Watson, O. M. (1970). *Proxemic behavior: A cross-cultural study.* The Hague: Mouton.

Webb, J. D., & Weber, M. J. (2003). Influence of sensory abilities on the interpersonal distance of the elderly. *Environment and Behavior, 35*, 695–711.

Westin, A. (1970). *Privacy and freedom.* New York: Atheneum.

Yep, G. (1992). Communicating the HIV/AIDS risk to Hispanic populations: A review and integration. *Hispanic Journal of Behavioral Science, 14*, 403–420.

Yep, G. (1993). Health beliefs and HIV prevention: Do they predict monogamy and condom use? *Journal of Social Behavior and Personality, 8*, 507–520.

# Physical Appearance

## Chapter 5

## The Body as Nonverbal Communication

## CHAPTER OUTLINE ■ ■ ■ ■ ■

**Physical Appearance as a Nonverbal Communication Code**

**Physical Attractiveness**
   The Impact of Physical Attractiveness
      on Our Culture

**The Body**
   Body Type, Shape, and Size
   Weight
   Height and Status
   The Disabled Body
   Skin Color
   Body Smell
   Hair

**Clothing**
   Functions of Clothing
   Expressions of Personality and Culture
   Dressing to Connect with Others

**Artifacts**
   Jewelry
   Eyeglasses
   Makeup

**Modifying the Body**
   Piercings
   Tattoos
   Cosmetic Procedures
   The Televisual Makeover
   The Trouble with Normalization

**Understanding Physical Appearance: Applying the Reflexive Cycle of Nonverbal Communication Development**

**Summary**

## CHAPTER OBJECTIVES ■ ■ ■ ■ ■

After studying this chapter, you should be able to:

1. Understand how people perceive physical appearance as a form of nonverbal communication.

2. Improve your understanding of how physical appearance impacts your perception of others, as well as your awareness and management of your own physical appearance.

3. Explain the difference between attraction and attractiveness.

4. Identify and describe Sheldon's body types, along with their corresponding psychological characteristics.

5. Understand the role that clothing and artifacts play in nonverbal communication.

6. Define homophily.

7. Discuss various forms of body modification and how normalization affects our view of these forms of nonverbal communication.

## CASE STUDY   Is Body Image "Shaping" Our Future?

As a first year teacher, I find myself observing every aspect of my work environment—the interactions of administration, faculty, staff, and the students. I want to make sure I don't miss any opportunity to be a more successful educator. About two months ago, something started to surface. A few of my female students began to disappear before my eyes. Not in a magical way, but in a physical way. These girls are in ballet classes outside of school and are auditioning for the upcoming play, *The Nutcracker*. Upon further observation, I noticed that when we'd return from lunch, each of the three girls would separately ask to go to the restroom. I would remind them to do this on the way to class, but with our new lunch schedule, they only have about three minutes to go to their locker and return to class before they are counted tardy. I would give in and allow them to go.

Last week, the girls were caught in the restroom vomiting. A passing teacher noticed that one girl was on the look-out in the restroom doorway and the other two were making themselves vomit. I was completely dumbfounded when I was informed of the situation. How could I be so blind? All of the signs were there but I didn't put it all together!

Each girl was asked to write a statement about the issue separately. They were not allowed to speak to each other and had to write it in the office before they were sent home that day. Each of them wrote similar statements, basically stating how they were too fat to be ballerinas, that they needed to lose weight to be cast in the play, and that "everyone" knows the beautiful people in magazines are not "fat." I know that eating disorders are very serious, and that they can stem from concerns about controlling one's own life, rather than from an obsession with appearance, but probably like many other educators who are aware of the problem, I found myself stumped as to how to help.

**Evelyn:**   "Have you seen our new boss?"

**Genie:**   "No, what does he look like?"

**Evelyn:**   "He's really handsome and professional looking."

**Genie:**   "Well, it's about time they hired someone who actually looks good. The other two executives didn't last around here because they just didn't have the image."

**Evelyn:**   "Exactly!"

What does the above conversation teach us? Evelyn and Genie reveal the importance of **physical appearance**—the way our bodies and overall appearance nonverbally communicate to others and impact our view of ourselves in everyday life. You may be thinking: How can physical appearance or the way someone looks be communicative? That's not a bad question, which is why this chapter addresses physical appearance as a nonverbal communication code. Have you ever thought about how you avoid or are drawn to people who look a certain way? Think about how much time out of each day you spend grooming yourself: How does my hair look? Does this dress make me look fat? Will people be able to see sweat rings if I wear this shirt? Should I use more hair spray? Should I tuck my shirt in or leave it out? Am I wearing too much perfume? Do these jeans make my butt look good? Am I sexy? All of these questions relate to **body image**—the view we have of ourselves and the amount of mental energy we put into our physical appearance.

While the energy level varies from person to person as to how much we care about our looks, some of us constantly think about how we look. The term **image fixation**—a high degree of concern an individual has about his or her physical appearance—can promote a constant comparison of self to others and an intense desire to look better. Let's take a moment to think about image fixation. To what degree do we compare ourselves to other people? Do we desire to always improve our looks or is it healthy to reach a point where we're satisfied? The amount of energy and preoccupation we have about physical attractiveness reveals how relevant image fixation is in our lives. Many of us care a great deal about physical appearance, first, because it communicates something about us as people, which other people respond to. Second, while most of us would agree that other qualities of a person are more important, appearance influences our interest in getting to know other people or our motivation to avoid them.

People are significantly influenced by aspects of physical appearance such as body shape, size or weight, height, skin color, smell, hair, clothing, and artifacts (like makeup or eyeglasses) (Amsbary, Vogel, Hickson, Oakes, & Wittig, 1994; Barber, 2001; Bonamici, Herman, & Jarvis, 2006; Carney, Hall, & LeBeau, 2005; Masip, Garrido, & Herrero, 2004; Roach, 1997; Rosenfeld & Plax, 1977; Schmid Mast & Hall, 2004). Take a moment to reflect on all the opportunities that exist to buy a product that claims to make your body look better. From grocery store aisles featuring low fat foods, to late night infomercials persuading consumers to transform their bodies with products like Tai Bo, Bowflex, and Total Gym, to Jessica Simpson offering her reflections on the wonders of Proactiv Solution, it doesn't take long to realize that physical appearance is an important aspect of people's lives in the U.S. While we still taut the greater significance of "inner beauty," outer beauty warrants discussion.

In turn, the emphasis on looks causes us to think about the consequences for people who don't look good. Are they going to get their dream job? Will they ever be asked out on a date? Are they going to find a life partner who will love them forever? Whether we focus on our own physical appearance or tend not to give it much attention, it's important to realize that physical appearance is a critical code to examine when studying nonverbal communication.

## ■ PHYSICAL APPEARANCE AS A NONVERBAL COMMUNICATION CODE

The goal of this chapter is to make you more aware of the role that physical appearance plays in your everyday life. You may be thinking: How can physical appearance communicate something nonverbally? The connection between physical appearance and nonverbal communication needs to be made for two important reasons: (1) The decisions we make to maintain or alter our physical appearance reveal a great deal about who we are, and (2) the physical appearance of other people impacts our perception of them, how we communicate with them, how approachable they are, how attractive or unattractive they are, and so on. As we move forward in this chapter, we examine physical appearance as nonverbal communication in two ways. First, we emphasize the reality of physical appearance that nonverbal communication research illustrates—summed up easily by the simple statement, "How we look *does* matter." Second, because we know that physical appearance is so powerful, we also explore the fears associated with the level of attention paid to physical appearance in U.S. culture.

We don't have to look too hard to find a television show, exercise product, skin cream, or surgical procedure tempting us to change our natural body (Allatson, 2004; Deery, 2004; Gallagher, 2004; Mason & Meyers, 2001; Moorti & Ross, 2004; Pearson & Reich, 2004; Waggoner, 2004). We're not advising people *not* to take care of themselves or *not* to work to look good, but part of our purpose here is to expose and critique some aspects of physical appearance and the pressure to achieve a certain standard that create turmoil in people's lives. Such aftereffects as the rise in eating disorders and elective cosmetic surgery highlight a culture of body customization that goes against us accepting our natural bodies and that can engender low self-esteem (Ackerman, 2006; Haines & Neumark-Sztainer, 2006; Hardy, 2006; Jaffe, 2006; Taras & Potts-Datema, 2005).

## ▓ PHYSICAL ATTRACTIVENESS

Before delving further into this topic, an important distinction needs to be made between *attraction* and *attractiveness*. **Attraction** is grounded in the study of interpersonal relationship development. It refers to how we are drawn toward other people interpersonally, spiritually, emotionally, physically, and/or sexually for possible friendship, dating, love, partnership, and marriage (Mulvey, 2006). Attraction is a powerful force in the development of human relationships, but it isn't nonverbal communication per se; it's a psychological variable (Bugenthal, 2005; Montepare, 2005; Noller, 2005). In contrast, **physical attractiveness** is a culturally derived perception of beauty formed by features of our appearance such as height, weight, size, shape, and so on. In other words, a mental picture emerges of physical appearance that dictates what *is* and *is not* attractive. The distinction between the two terms is this: You may be attracted to someone you believe to be physically attractive, *or not*. Some people are *attractive*, but we're not *attracted* to them—understand the difference? Thus, while attraction is interesting, in this chapter we choose to focus on physical appearance as a form of nonverbal communication, realizing its role in attraction.

In most cultures, including U.S. culture, people have a particular mental picture of physical features (e.g., weight, size, shape) that define beauty (Venturini, Castelli, & Tomelleri, 2006). Key issues related to the topic of physical attractiveness include sex differences and the influence of culture, both of which will be examined in this chapter. For example, scholars contend that American women feel more pressure than men to be physically attractive (Adams, 1977; Dohnt & Tiggemann, 2006; Harrison,

Taylor, & Marske, 2006; Steese, Dollette, Phillips, Hossfeld, Matthews, & Taormina, 2006). Perceptions of what constitutes attractiveness vary widely by culture (Bloomfield, 2006; Cunningham, Roberts, Barbee, Druen, & Wu, 1995; Darling-Wolf, 2003, 2004; Furnham, McClelland, & Omer, 2003; Keenan, 1996).

You might be wondering: What is the impact of physical attractiveness—our own and others'—on the communicative process? Do attractive people have an advantage over unattractive people? While these questions will take this whole chapter to address, one aspect of physical attractiveness to mention here is the **halo effect**—people's tendency to attribute positive qualities to physically attractive people (Dion, Berscheid, & Walster, 1972; Hatfield & Sprecher, 1986; Zakahi, Duran, & Adkins, 1994). What this means is that just because someone is perceived to be good looking, he or she is also likely to be perceived as credible, successful, and personable—which might be far from the truth if we were to get to know the person. Nonverbal scholars Guerrero and Floyd (2006) explain that attractiveness is important to individuals and their relationships because "attractive people are benefited in numerous ways and penalized in others" (p. 57).

## The Impact of Physical Attractiveness on Our Culture

Reflect on how important physical attractiveness is in your own life. Are there certain decisions you've made based on physical attractiveness? Let's consider an example. J.R. is a manager at a new bar and grille called *Perky Perks*, opening up close to campus. The establishment will have a sports theme and the primary investors want to attract a young college crowd. One of the investors has made it clear to J.R. that he wants all young women hired as bartenders and servers to have nice "booties and boobs." While J.R. doesn't publicize this fact, he has decided to hire only attractive young women who will look good in mini-skirts and cut-off tops. While we may find this example disturbing and J.R.'s hiring practice sexist, this kind of hiring practice does exist. In this example, we can see that physical attractiveness will be an advantage for any of the applicants who fit the desired employee look.

**Interviewing and Hiring.** While physical appearance is a focus for J.R. in his hiring process, ethical or not, his example shows us one case in which physical attractiveness does have an effect on hiring. In fact, physical attractiveness often serves as an advantage when applying for a job, especially a high profile job, and being hired at a higher salary or wage (Cash, Gillen, & Barnes, 1977; Dipboye, Arvey, & Terpstra, 1977; Hamermesh & Biddle, 1994; Marlowe, Schneider, & Nelson, 1998). With an increasing emphasis on being physically attractive and communicating a professional image in the job search process, more and more employers seek employees who have a certain look that they believe will build business (Nai-kuo, 2005; Pante, 2006; Thornbory & White, 2006; White, 1995). Unfortunately, people deemed overweight and unattractive are often viewed as unsuitable for certain jobs, which points to the problems and fears connected to physical appearance that we examine in a subsequent section of this chapter (Venturini, Castelli, & Tomelleri, 2006).

**Educational Settings.**    In addition to getting a job, physical attractiveness affects educational contexts. For example, students viewed as attractive by their peers tend to be more popular (Bahad, 2001); attractive teachers are perceived by students to be more approachable (Rocca & McCroskey, 2001); and students give higher evaluations to professors whom they deem physically attractive (Montell, 2003). The physical attractiveness of college professors seems to matter to students, since some of you rate your professors as attractive or unattractive on popular websites like RateMyProfessor.com. Users have the option of rating a teacher's physical attractiveness by putting a chili pepper next to the name of an instructor, signifying her or him as "hot" (Edwards, Edwards, Qing, & Wahl, 2007). Think about the professors teaching your courses this semester. Are they "hot" or "not"? What's the verdict? (Until the semester ends and grades are in, you may want to keep your ratings to yourself or use one of the online rating communities that allows for anonymous postings.) Perhaps some of us are chuckling right now—this is a fun topic. However, when you think about it, the notion of evaluating your teacher's attractiveness is pretty obnoxious. Take a moment to think about the fears and emotional struggles people, including some of your teachers, have with self-esteem, confidence, and their physical appearance. Is it right for the insecurities many teachers battle every day and carry into classrooms to be judged and exposed by a simple click of a mouse?

*Should the physical attractiveness of a job appplicant affect her or his chances of landing a job?*

**Dating, Partnering, and Marriage.**  Physical attractiveness impacts our dating, partnering, and marriage decisions. If you were asked whether you would rather marry, partner with, or date a person who ranks low on physical attributes versus high, what would you say? Nonverbal communication researchers have explored this question over several decades to learn more about the effects of physical attractiveness on dating, partnering, and marriage. In studies, men were more likely to reject women who were not physically attractive, while women weren't as concerned as men about physical attractiveness when thinking about a potential partner. Men tended to want partners who were more physically attractive than themselves, while women reported that they were more likely to marry men who were similar to themselves in level of physical attractiveness (Walster, Aronson, Abrahams & Rohmann, 1966; Wilson & Nias, 1999).

Research shows that we tend to seek out partners we perceive to be equal to us in attractiveness—a phenomenon called the **matching hypothesis** (Bar-Tal & Saxe, 1976; Forbes, Adams-Curtis, Rade, & Jaberg, 2001). Think about couples you see around you each day: Don't most of them "match" in terms of physical attractiveness? While we may think people are attractive who are more beautiful than we perceive ourselves to be, research shows that we tend to connect with people we perceive to be on our "level." When we see "mismatched" couples, we often make all kinds of inferences about their personalities, financial success, sexual prowess, or motives for being in the relationship. So why do people tend not to seek out the best looking partners? One explanation is the risk of rejection. To avoid unwanted rejection, people tend to select a person similar to themselves in physical attractiveness to date, partner with, or marry (Hinsz, 1989; Kalick & Hamilton, 1986).

## REMEMBER 5.1

| | |
|---|---|
| **Physical Appearance:** | how a person's body and overall appearance communicates a view of self to others. |
| **Body Image:** | view of ourselves and the amount of mental energy we put into our physical appearance. |
| **Image Fixation:** | high degree of concern about physical appearance. |
| **Attraction:** | grounded in the study of interpersonal relationships; how we are drawn toward other people interpersonally, emotionally, physically, sexually, and/or spiritually for possible friendship, dating, love, partnership, and marriage. |
| **Physical Attractiveness:** | culturally derived perception of beauty formed by features such as height, weight, size, shape, and so on. |
| **Halo Effect:** | tendency to attribute positive personality qualities to physically attractive people. |
| **Matching Hypothesis:** | tendency to seek out dating and marital partners we perceive to be equal to us in physical attractiveness. |

Take a moment to think about first dates. (Even if you're married or in a committed partnership, we encourage you to think back to your dating days.) Is physical attractiveness an important factor in your decision to go on a first date? What about a second date? We recognize that situations exist in dating and marriage in which physical attractiveness is not always the determining factor for relationship initiation and development. However, studies have established that physical attractiveness does impact dating and marriage decisions. Research indicates that, if a perception of attractiveness is not present initially between two people, the chances of having successful dating and marriage outcomes decrease (Berscheid & Walster, 1978; Guerrero & Floyd, 2006).

# ■ THE BODY

The appearance of our body helps others form perceptions and stereotypes, as well as decisions about how to communicate with us (Bodenhausen & Macrae, 1998; Forbes, Adams-Curtis, Rade, & Jaberg, 2001). In this section, we examine how our bodies play a role in our overall physical appearance, as a code of nonverbal communication. Our study of the body includes type, shape, size, weight, height, disability, skin color, body smell, and hair. Let's move forward and get more familiar with how the body sends nonverbal signals.

## Body Type, Shape, and Size

Does the shape or size of people's bodies influence communication? Have you ever avoided interaction with another person because of the size or shape of her or his body? Whether you've thought about this before or not, the general size and shape of our bodies does communicate something nonverbally. In fact, scholars developed a system called **somatyping** that classifies people according to their body type (Sheldon, 1940, 1954; Sheldon, Stevens, & Tucker, 1942). While much criticism has been made of somatyping over the years, nonverbal communication researchers typically reference the system in the study of physical appearance and body type.

Refer to Figure 5.1 as we discuss the various body types. The first is the **ectomorph.** People classified as ectomorphs (ectos) are usually thin, bony, and tall. Ectomorphs appear fragile-looking; they usually have flat chests and limited muscular development. The second body type is the **mesomorph.** Mesomorphs (mesos) generally have a triangular body shape with broad shoulders and a tapering at the hip; they are muscular with a good balance between height and weight, and are usually described as athletic in appearance. The third body type is the **endomorph.** People classified as endomorphs (endos) typically have bodies that are rounded, oval, or pear-shaped; they are usually heavy-set or stocky, but not necessarily obese.

Can you think of people or characters in popular culture, media, sports, and so on that reflect the three categories? Borat, Abraham Lincoln, Ichabod Crane, and Pee Wee Herman are appropriate examples of the ectomorphic or tall and skinny body type—sometimes referred to as lanky or a "long, tall drink of water." Brad Pitt,

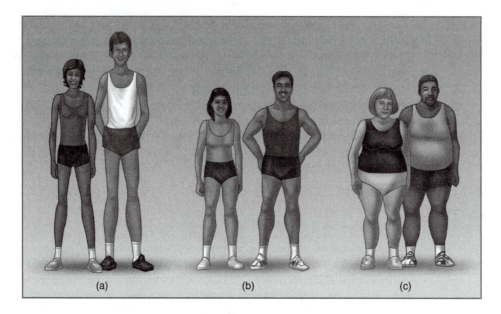

**FIGURE 5.1    Sheldon's Body Types**

Figure reproduced with permission of: Lilienfield, S. O., Lynn, S. J., Namy, L. L., & Woolf, N. J. (2009). *Psychology: From Inquiry to Understanding.* Boston: Allyn & Bacon.

Tim Duncan, Kelly Ripa, Michael Phelps, and Laila Ali are appropriate examples of the mesomorphic or athletic body type. Danny Devito, Santa Claus, Rosie O'Donnell, Tony Soprano, and Jason Alexander (who played George on *Seinfeld*) have endomorphic characteristics. What about you—what category reflects your body type?

According to Sheldon's (1940) theory, each body type has a corresponding psychological type (see Figure 5.1). The ectomorphic body is associated with the psychological type called **cerebrotonic,** described as tense, awkward, careful, polite, and detached. Mesomorphs are connected to the psychological type called **somatonic,** which reflects dominant, confident, energetic, competitive, assertive, enthusiastic, and optimistic attributes. For endomorphs, the corresponding psychological type is called **viscerotonic,** described as slow, sociable, emotional, forgiving, and relaxed. Researchers suggest that our body shapes correspond with the psychological descriptions, so check out Figure 5.1 again. Do the body types and corresponding psychological types describe you? While the body and psychological types may ring true to some of our self-descriptions more than others, remember that, for the most part, people do make judgments of others based on body type (Portnoy, 1993; Staffieri, 1972; Wells & Siegal, 1961).

Another system for judging body shape, primarily applied to women, is the **waist-to-hip ratio.** Research suggests that an ideal female body has a 0.70 waist-to-hip ratio, meaning that for a woman to be considered proportional, her waist size should be 70 percent of her hip size (Singh, 1993, 1995, 2004; Streeter & McBurney, 2003). One study sought to determine if the 0.70 waist-to-hip ratio represented an attractiveness stereotype in other cultures. Male and female subjects from different

## REMEMBER 5.2

### Sheldon's Body Classifications & Personalities

**Somatyping:**    system that classifies people according to their body type.

| Body Type | Personality |
|---|---|
| **Endomorph:** person with a rounded, oval, or pear-shaped shaped body; usually heavy-set or stocky, but not necessarily obese. | **Viscerotonic:** slow, sociable, forgiving, and relaxed. |
| **Mesomorph:** person with a triangular body shape, i.e., broad shoulders and tapering at the hip; muscular and proportioned by height and weight; usually described as athletic. | **Somatonic:** dominant, confident, energetic, competitive, assertive, enthusiastic, and optimistic. |
| **Ectomorph:** person who is thin, bony, and tall; fragile-looking, with a flat chest and limited muscular development | **Cerebrotonic:** tense, awkward, careful, polite, and detached. |

parts of the world, including the U.S., agreed that women with a higher waist-to-hip ratio (above 0.70) were less physically attractive than women with lower waist-to-hip ratios (Singh, 2004). As a surprising additional finding, subjects in this study also believed that attractive women were less faithful to their husbands or partners than unattractive women.

Preferences for body types do vary from culture to culture, especially for women (Furnham, McClelland, & Omer, 2003). In North American and Western European cultures, for example, mesomorphic or ectomorphic body types are preferred since food is more abundant in these areas and physical exercise is optional (Symons, 1979). However, some ethnic groups within the same culture may exhibit variation in their body type preferences. For example, in one study black Americans rated larger women as more attractive than white Americans (Cunningham et al., 1995). In cultures where food is abundant (e.g., the U.S. where exercise and diet peddling are multi-billion dollar industries), people have to work out and watch what they eat to maintain the preferred mesomorphic and ectomorphic body types. In these cultures, being thin and in shape signals that people have the time and money to eat right and be on a fitness plan. In contrast, cultures in which the food supply is limited prefer people, especially women, with endomorphic body types because their weight is a sign of wealth and prosperity (Guerrero & Floyd, 2006).

## Weight

Body weight is a nonverbal cue, even if you haven't ever thought of it that way. We've established that perceptions about body type vary from culture to culture, but so do perceptions of weight (Furnham, McClelland, & Omer, 2003). In many cultures around the world, body weight isn't the obsession it is in the United States. Increased pressure from the media, advertisers, and companies who want to make a buck off of people's weight insecurities contribute to the problem (Hargreaves & Tiggemann, 2002). In fact, a TV news broadcast announced that technology giant Hewlett Packard has developed a new camera with a "slimming feature." The camera actually reduces the middle and enlarges the outside edges of a picture, a technique that can take 10 pounds off of people's appearance in photos (MSNBC, 2006). (We can hear you all rushing right out to buy one.) The media constantly portray young, thin, attractive people doing all kinds of amazing things and becoming successful, while overweight characters are ridiculed. Media provide a barrage of "perfect bodies" with the message that we, the viewers, must do all we can to lose weight and become fit or we will be unlovable or unacceptable in society. The amount of media pressure on this one nonverbal cue is enormous (Cottle, 2003; Flynn, 2004; Martin & Gentry, 2005; Myers & Biocca, 1992). In addition, the growing and very real problem of **obesity**—the medical term for being significantly overweight—and its detrimental effects on health lead Americans to spend a lot of time listening to messages or reading books about weight loss, thinking about how they can lose weight, or attempting to lose weight.

Most women in the U.S. are not happy with their current weight and have a strong desire to be thin—a reality fueled by the media (Feingold & Mazzella, 1998; Koch, Mansfield, Thurau, & Carey, 2005). According to the Women's Sports Foundation in 2006, 56 percent of American women said that they were on a diet. Eve Ensler, author of *The Vagina Monologues*, believes the following:

> Body hatred has been defined as a personal problem. But it is a social problem, a political problem, a cultural problem. It is not accidental or incidental. It is induced, injected, and programmed. We Americans like to tell ourselves we are free, but we are imprisoned. We are controlled by a corporate media that decrees what we should look like and then determines what we have to buy in order to get and keep that look. We are controlled by our mother's idea of how we are supposed to look, and our father's idea. We are controlled by other women's ideas. (2006, p. 216)

The obese woman in our culture is often ridiculed and cut off from opportunities because she's perceived as lazy, slow, and unattractive (Harris, Harris, & Brochner, 1982; Larkin & Pines, 1979; Venturini, Castelli, & Tomelleri, 2006). Obese women are perceived as having bad attitudes and are often described as "fat and bitchy," while overweight men are perceived as being "funny and jolly," like Santa Claus (Richmond, McCroskey, & Hickson, 2008). Women tend to be denied the more positive "fat and jolly" description afforded to men. The ideal weight for women adheres to a smaller, more rigid standard compared to men, meaning that men can carry more extra weight than women before they are deemed heavy or overweight. Perhaps some of us can think back to parents and family members who embraced the "growing boys" attitude. When male children eat too much and gain weight, it's more often accepted because they're "growing boys," but the pressure on girls not to grow too much is significant. While the country is increasingly concerned with juvenile obesity (and its connection to a whole host of health problems, chiefly diabetes), gender differences are still prevalent. In many American homes, it's okay for men and boys to eat a lot of food because it's seen as fuel to support their hard work, while women and girls who may work just as hard are encouraged to eat lightly so they don't gain weight.

While women continue to face longstanding social pressure to be thin, men are increasingly feeling the pressure to stay fit and young looking by enrolling in diet and fitness programs (Feingold & Mazzella, 1998; Koch et al., 2005). Unfortunately for both men and women, **eating disorders**—clinically diagnosed or undiagnosed disorders, such as bulimia and anorexia nervosa—emerge from an obsessive desire to control one's weight. Given the amount of media attention and obsession with weight in our culture, is it any wonder that eating disorders are a problem?

## Height and Status

**Evelyn:** "Have you seen the new shift leader?"

**Genie:** "No, what does he look like?"

**Evelyn:** "Oh my gosh, girl; he's tall, dark, and handsome!"

**Genie:** "Wow......"

**Evelyn:** "Come with me; I'll show you his schedule so you'll know when he's working."

Physical appearance is important to Evelyn and Genie, like it is to most of us. What does their conversation reveal about preferences for height, as a nonverbal cue? Heterosexual women in American culture tend to like men who are tall and handsome. Tall is still preferable to short, in general, especially when it comes to men in our culture, and that can be a pressure or self-esteem downer for men who struggle with their lack of height. Americans' views of and preferences for government leaders, especially presidents, are affected by their height; in fact, voters have elected the taller of the presidential candidates in almost every contest in the twentienth and twenty first centuries (Tenner, 2004). Many of us can remember our parents telling us to "stand tall." Reflect on those reminders; your parents coached you on posture because standing up straight makes you look taller. Research over four decades consistently shows that perceptions of more height equate with more credibility, status, power, and dominance (Egolf & Corder, 1991; Elman, 1977; Lechelt, 1975; Roberts & Herman, 1986; Stabler, Whitt, Moreault, D'Ercole, & Underwood, 1980; Vrij, 2001). Posture is even more important in a public speaking situation in which an audience (live or mediated) is looking at you and judging your credibility (Andersen, 2004; Beebe, Beebe, & Ivy, 2007).

Height in women is a bit of a mixed bag: Some people believe that the same judgments of enhanced credibility and status apply to tall women as to tall men. But some

*What kind of comments might these two students receive from other people about their height?*

women—especially those who gained above average height in their puberty years, when they towered over boys their age—see it as a disadvantage, socially and professionally. They may intimidate male bosses, coworkers, and dates simply because of a height advantage. We don't believe this is appropriate, but for some tall women, it's a reality they face.

## The Disabled Body

Since we're discussing the body as a nonverbal cue, have you ever considered the communicative properties of the disabled body? Some of you reading this text live with a physical disability every day; others of us understand the issues from a distance, because we have a family member or friend with a disability. Still others have no experience with people with physical disabilities at all. Usually, the knowledge or clue that a person is living with a disability is based on their physical appearance, but this is not always the case (Braithwaite & Thompson, 2000). We remember a student who constantly took flak for having a handicapped sticker on his car and parking in handicapped spots at the university. This student was a very tall man who walked with a confident stride and appeared to have no physical disability. Turns out he had a degenerative joint disease—one that would leave him seriously impaired within a few short years—and his doctors said that the shorter the distances he walked, the better.

We all need to think about nonverbal communication between able-bodied people and people with disabilities. Consider some social situations where able-bodied people avoid making eye contact with people with disabilities, such as at a shopping mall, in elevators, in college classrooms, or at a doctor's office. Many of us were taught "it's not nice to stare," but it's also not nice to deny someone with a disability the same kind of eye contact we give able-bodied people. On this issue, one of our students who's in a wheelchair told us that she frequently gets ignored in restaurants when she goes out to eat with her friends. Servers look to her dinner companions to provide her order, as if she was mute—not just in a wheelchair—and thus unable to order for herself. On those rare occasions when she gets asked for her order, waitpersons make less eye contact with her than with other people at the table, as though they're uncomfortable even looking at her. Another possible explanation she offers is that servers feel they'll be perceived as

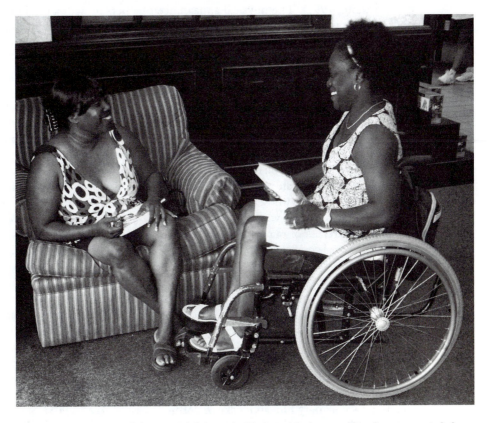

*When communicating with a person who's in a wheelchair, positioning oneself on the same vertical plane (i.e., being seated) facilitates interaction.*

staring at a disabled person, rather than just giving normal eye contact. How many of us able-bodied people change our nonverbal behavior toward people with disabilities, thinking we're being polite, when we're actually being anything *but* polite?

Another example emerged from an observation the male co-author of your text made when he recently got onto an airplane. A gentleman in a wheelchair was poised at the top of the jet bridge, waiting for an airline employee to help him get seated on the plane. As the employee walked toward the man and began to stick out his arms, as though to lift him, the man waved him off and said, "Don't you go grabbing at me!" The man wanted the employee to respect his situation and wait to be instructed as to how to help him, rather than assuming he would have to pick the man up and assist him onto the plane, like he did for other passengers with disabilities.

All of us—able-bodied and disabled—need to be more aware of our verbal and nonverbal communication with people with disabilities. People with disabilities are challenged when it comes to managing information about their disability; communication with them is often triggered by indications of disability (Braithwaite, 1991). The physical appearance of a person with a disability can lead us to make assumptions about what they're capable of doing as well as how we should communicate with them verbally and nonverbally (Braithwaite, 1990, 1996; Braithwaite & Braithwaite, 1997; Braithwaite & Thompson, 2000). We may also need to be clued as to what a person with a disability needs or expects of us, as the airplane example suggests.

What interactions have you had with people with disabilities? When you talk to people in a wheelchair (assuming you're not in one yourself), do you tower over them, making them look up the whole time, or do you find a way to stoop or sit down on their level, so the conversation occurs at a more parallel height? Do you get louder when you speak to blind people, if you even speak at all? Do you get louder when you speak to deaf persons or over-enunciate your words (which actually impedes lip reading)? If you walked to class with someone whose legs were in braces or who relied on permanent crutches, would you think to slow your pace to match theirs? Whether we are able-bodied or disabled, an awareness of our nonverbal communication with people with disabilities enhances our social competence and prepares us for meaningful and respectful relationships.

## Color

Color is an important dimension of physical appearance that has communicative potential, as much as we would like to downplay it. Much attention has been given to racial and ethnic issues in the last century due to racism and stereotypes based on skin color (Keenan, 1996). In fact, an episode of *The Oprah Winfrey Show* illustrated the still-prevalent discriminatory perceptions people have about skin color. One of Oprah's guests was an 18-year-old high school girl named Kiri Davis, who made a documentary film about skin color in America (Davis, 2005). She interviewed several of her friends for their self-perceptions about appearance, and replicated an experiment from 50 years ago in which African American children were presented with two identically-dressed baby dolls—one with black skin and one with white. The children were asked which baby doll was the nicest and why, as well as which doll they looked like. The children overwhelmingly viewed the white baby doll as being nicer than the black doll because "white was good," even while selecting the black doll as the one that looked like them.

Oprah interviewed the documentarian and other guests, but one person was especially memorable: She interviewed an African American woman whose greatest concern when she became pregnant was that her child would have dark brown skin, just like hers. She'd experienced a great deal of ruthless teasing and discrimination as a child as well as an adult, and hoped her son wouldn't have to suffer through the same thing. Indeed her baby did have just as dark a skin tone as she, and he grew up being tormented, mostly by his lighter-skinned African American peers, to the point that he struggled with depression and thoughts of suicide. The conclusion reached in the documentary and Oprah episode was this: While we've made some strides, if you think we're past skin color discrimination in America, think again. Unfortunately, people in the U.S. and other countries around the world are still categorized, stereotyped, and discriminated against based on the color of their skin (Bloomfield, 2006; Boswell, 2005; Darling-Wolf, 2004).

In addition to perceptions of skin color related to ethnicity, we react to skin color in other ways. For example, if a Caucasian looks too pale, we may think the person is sick or not taking care of himself or herself. People who blush or have a natural reddish tone to their skin can be perceived as embarrassed (or heavy drinkers), while a red neck on a person can communicate anger.

Now let's talk about attempts to modify skin color by tanning—a practice ridiculed by darker-skinned individuals and warned against by dermatologists, but still enjoyed by many people. Tanning is big business in America! Besides the use of products for tanning, many spas and salons offer tanning services. Tanning salons—businesses offering "fake" tanning—have been around a long time but are still popping up everywhere, offering tanning beds, spray-on tans, and creams and lotions that help get your skin color at the exact level of "bronzing" you desire. There's even a pill you can take that tans you from the inside out, meaning it alters your body chemistry to turn your skin a darker color. Clearly, skin color impacts the perceptions we have of ourselves and other people, and serves as yet another cue of nonverbal communication.

## Body Smell

A pleasant body smell is something that many of us spend part of our day attending to and maintaining. In fact, most of us think of smell as part of our physical appearance; we may say "I'm going home to clean up," which usually means we're going to shower and make ourselves smell better to prepare for being around others. Those of us who live in a hot climate, as both authors of your textbook do, become especially sensitive to this issue. For women and men alike, it's a balancing act in terms of how much scent, body powder, cologne, or perfume to use, since smell is an integral part of our overall appearance.

Can you think of a neutral smell? We first talked about this in Chapter 3 on environment, and you may recall that the research on **olfaction** (the role of smell in human interaction) indicates that no neutral scents exist (Andersen, 2004; Dimitrius & Mazzarrella, 1999; Riley, 1979). Each day Americans take baths and showers, deodorize, brush, floss, wipe, sanitize, and freshen to cover up natural body odors. If smell wasn't important, we wouldn't buy all of these products and go through all of these activities. We use our scent to attract others and to be perceived positively by them, for the purposes of making impressions and developing relationships (Furlow, 1999).

Research on olfaction is fascinating; studies have found a connection between perfume scent, evaluations of job applicants, and perceptions of physical attractiveness (Aune, 1999; Baron, 1983). While a subtle whiff of perfume might cause someone to be more physically attracted to you, it's that "subtle" part that's important. We encourage students not to wear cologne when interviewing for a job, scholarship, internship, and the like, because nervousness or activation in the body enhances the strength of a scent. You could overwhelm an interviewer and lose a job opportunity, all because your cologne was too strong. You might think about this for social situations as well; your cologne might increase in effect on a first date, due to nerves, when at home before the date it smelled "just right." At any rate, smell and scent are key nonverbal cues related to physical appearance, so it's important to be mindful of the decisions you make in managing your body smell in both personal and professional situations.

As we've mentioned regarding other aspects of physical appearance, culture plays a huge role in forming expectations of smell. In the U.S., any trace of natural body odor or sweat is considered bad. That's why we spend so much time and money covering ourselves up with soaps, perfumes, lotions, deodorants, and mouthwashes. In fact, if a bad odor is detected in a room or from a person, communication may come to a stop or be very difficult to achieve. But in an increasingly "global village," body odor becomes a complicated issue. You may find yourself working overseas or with people from another country or culture in which the emphasis on body smell is not the same as it is in the U.S. In some cultures, the predominant food people eat causes their skin to have a smell that people from another country aren't familiar or comfortable with. In these cases, it's not bad body odor—it's just something cultural that an outsider may not understand or adopt.

We've heard of some difficult situations in which American employees struggled with what they considered to be a "smelly coworker," but what should you do in these instances? There are no simple solutions, but some general advice about functioning effectively cross-culturally may be helpful here: If you're the visitor, meaning you're not in your home country, then "do as the Romans do," as the saying goes, which means that you really don't have the right to insist that members of other cultures adapt to your standards. However, it's appropriate to apply that guideline equally to members of other cultures who work and live in the U.S. If you struggle with a coworker's smell and that person lives and works in American culture, then you may have a legitimate reason for concern. Again, the best approach is to apply common sense and sensitivity here, because we're suggesting taking action (either gently confronting the person, talking to a supervisor about the problem, or seeking counsel from someone in human relations) in *extreme* situations where productivity or company image is affected, not minor irritations, occasional problems, or instances in which someone might use smell as a way to hurt a colleague when the issue with him or her is something else.

## Hair

Are you a short-haired, long-haired, or no-haired person? What preferences do you have in terms of the length of your own hair? What length of hair do you find attractive in other people? Do you like blondes, brunettes, or red heads? These questions introduce another important feature of the body connected to our physical appearance—it's all about the hair.

**Hair Color.** Many of us have formed perceptions of other people because of the color of their hair. We've heard "blonde jokes" and perhaps made the statement, "She's a dumb blonde." What can we learn from these comments? Right or wrong, we do form impressions of other people based on hair color. In addition to our perception of other people's attractiveness, we tend to evaluate personality and intelligence based on hair color. People with blonde hair, especially women, are stereotyped as less intelligent or "ditzy," while people with red hair are perceived as hot tempered or filled with anger. As we've discussed, people with brown or dark hair, especially men, are included in the more positive descriptions of being "tall, dark, and handsome." Take a moment to think about the perceptions you have of people based on their hair color. Do you associate red hair with anger? Blonde hair with less intelligence?

Blonde, brown, and red tend to be the most typical colors you associate with hair. Ah, but that reflects the youth of many of our readers. What about grey hair—something many of you don't have to think about, but will have to some day? A highly successful industry—one consumed with hair dyeing, streaking, and highlighting—continues to attract consumers who wish to alter or mask this particular nonverbal cue of physical appearance. While some believe that hair dyeing is the number one most useful and affordable anti-aging process around, once again, we see evidence of an American culture that glorifies youthfulness and disdains the natural aging process. Men are catching up to women in this arena, given the increasing popularity of such products as Grecian Formula for Men, which some men apply to their hair, mustaches, and beards in order to turn back the clock. "Washing away the grey" can take years off a person's appearance, but what statement does that make about the person and the culture within which she or he lives? Should people feel pressured to cover up their age?

Let's talk about the more "creative" uses of hair dye. Both of your authors remember their mothers pointing out to them egregious misuses of hair dye that could be found just about anywhere at any time of the day; however, times have really changed on this front. Many of our college students view their hair as just another blank canvas upon which to display their "art." We've seen large streaks of color corresponding to the particular holiday at the time, pink and purple mohawks, one student who had a bleached yellow (yellow, not blonde) spiked hairstyle that reminded us of the crown on the Statue of Liberty, and many other colorful forms of self-expression. Many male and female students alike now enjoy adding highlights to their hair, to give them that "just-surfed look." What non-verbal cues do these hair-dyeing processes communicate about a person? Do they communicate "free spirit," "over-commercialization," or "weirdo," from your perspective? If you're a person who likes to experiment with your hair color, you may or may not consider this tendency to be an act of nonverbal communication, but this aspect of physical appearance has communicative power, just like the many others we discuss in this chapter.

**Hair Length (Quantity).**   Do you like short or long hair, both on yourself and others? Hair length or quantity of hair is another factor to consider as part of our overall physical appearance. The advice to men about hair and looks is mixed. Some younger men who want to be viewed as more mature are advised by hair stylists to let their hair grow out in order to avoid showing a baby face (Masip, Garrido, & Herrero, 2004). The male co-author of your textbook likes to keep his hair short (military style). When he was going to interview for a job, his hair stylist told him that it would be better not to cut his hair so short because he would look like a high school kid to potential employers. While the times continue to change regarding hair length and credibility, still the predominant position or most conservative approach is for men with longer hair (below the collar) to cut or trim their hair for job interviews so that they'll be viewed as professional, serious, and credible. Of course, it depends on the job and the workplace, because some interviewers for high tech jobs would rather the men look like many of their employees, which often includes long hair, informal clothing, and so forth.

Women with long hair are often perceived as having sex appeal. However, professional women often cut their hair to a shorter length to enhance their credibility and downplay their sexuality; some pull their hair up or back while at work and let it down at home. As we've said, perceptions about hair length in the workplace are changing, but just be aware that women with long hair in professional settings may still be resented by their female colleagues and viewed as incompetent and less intelligent by men (Dimitrius & Mazzarella, 1999; Korda, 1975).

As we explore hair length and the influence it has on physical appearance, it's important to think about hair loss. What impact does hair loss have on physical appearance? Men and women who live with baldness or lose their hair due to medical conditions or treatments (like chemotherapy) may turn to medication, extreme comb-overs, hairpieces or plugs, hair replacement surgery, baseball caps, and so on to cover up their hair loss. Hair loss products and services represent a multimillion dollar industry in the U.S. While some people want to hide their hair loss at all costs, others embrace the bald look, such as Chris Daughtry, a contestant on Season 5 of *American Idol*, who believes that his bald head contributes to his rocker image.

*What do hair length and facial hair communicate to you nonverbally?*

**Body Hair.**    In U.S. culture, it's expected that women shave their arm pits and legs. However, in many other cultures around the world, women don't shave these areas and their looks are positively regarded. Americans also have interesting rules or expectations about men's body hair—chest, arm, leg, and pubic hair are acceptable (to most people), but not back hair. How arbitrary is *that*? You may agree with this rule, but did you ever think about where that rule came from? Because of such illogical expectations, again another multimillion dollar industry has developed that is devoted to altering our physical appearance. Salons and medical spas offer waxing services and laser removal procedures to keep hair away; do-it-yourself kits are also available in any drugstore, if you're that brave. Probably one of the best scenes depicting one man's pressure to wax his body hair comes from the movie *The 40-Year Old Virgin*, in which lead actor Steve Carrell actually had some of his own chest hair waxed and removed, to add realism (and pain) to the scene.

**Facial Hair.**    Medications, hormones, and genetics can cause women to grow facial hair, which is often viewed negatively because facial hair is linked with masculinity. Men's and women's perceptions of men with facial hair vary. For example, research shows that women tend to view bearded men positively, but men tend to feel more tense and anxious around men with facial hair than those who are clean shaven (Barber, 2001). According to some perceptions, the more facial hair a man has, the more he's seen as masculine, mature, hard-working, confident, and dominant. On the other hand, clean shaven men tend to be viewed by women as youthful, sleek, and vigorous. One drawback for bearded men, at least in U.S. culture, is that they can be perceived as less trustworthy, like they're hiding something (Dimitrius & Mazzarella, 1999; Kalick, Zebrowitz, Langlois, & Johnson, 1998).

---

**REMEMBER 5.3**

**Waist-to-Hip Ratio:** body measurement of the waist in proportion to the hips.

**Obesity:** medical term for being significantly overweight.

**Eating Disorders:** clinically diagnosed or undiagnosed conditions (e.g., bulimia, anorexia nervosa) related to eating behavior.

**Olfaction:** role of smell in human interaction.

**Preening Behavior:** nonverbal cue sent to potential courtship partners to let them know it's okay to approach and initiate conversation.

---

**Hair Manipulation.** Perhaps some of us have noticed people who touch or manipulate their hair. What nonverbal message does this send? Hair manipulation may impact the impression others have of us. People taking public speaking classes, especially the women, tend to touch or adjust their hair while speaking. Students also mess with their hair a great deal while taking tests, so touching our hair can be a way for some of us to adapt to high anxiety situations. Hair manipulation can also be a nonverbal cue of attraction, termed **preening behavior**—nonverbal cues sent to potential courtship partners to let them know it's okay to approach us and initiate conversation. Consider the following example: Monique is sitting at the end of a bar sipping a martini. She notices a nice looking gentleman (Charlie) enter the room with his friends. Monique is attracted to Charlie's physical appearance and is interested in talking more intimately with him, so she begins to run her fingers through her long hair and smell the tips of her curls, while making eye contact with Charlie. Monique's use of her hair to attract Charlie illustrates preening behavior—she sends him a nonverbal cue to approach her.

## CLOTHING

One of the ways we manage our physical appearance is by making decisions about our clothing. You might be thinking, How does clothing communicate nonverbal messages? Let's first examine the most common functions of clothing, then explore how clothing is a nonverbal cue related to appearance.

### Functions of Clothing

Clothing does communicate something nonverbally to people in our daily interactions (Pante, 2006; Rainey, 2006; Roach, 1997; Rosenfeld & Plax, 1977; Thornbory & White, 2006). According to communication scholars Knapp and Hall (2006), attire provides the following functions:

1. *Decoration:* We use clothing to decorate our bodies for everyday exhibition, because we know clothing sends nonverbal messages to others. A t-shirt that

supports a certain cause or group is a form of body decoration. We also decorate ourselves with clothing for special occasions, like costume parties, holidays, weddings, formal outings, and sporting events.

2. *Protection:* Another function of clothing is protection from intrusion or natural elements, such as inclement weather. If you've ever done yard work or even simple construction without gloves, you know the punishment your hands take. In some occupations, certain attire is required because it protects the body from harm (e.g., hard hats, back braces, eye protectors, masks, plastic gloves, bulletproof vests, hazardous material suits).

3. *Sexual Attraction:* Situations in which we want to be noticed and appear sexually attractive to other people can influence our decisions about clothing. Going out on a romantic date, having a special evening at home with our partner, or going out to a club with friends are a few situations in which our clothing choices may be designed to promote sexual attraction. It's fine to want to look and feel sexy so that other people notice, but we all know that we have to strive for balance and not go so far with our clothing and behavior as to make other people uncomfortable or create a negative impression of ourselves.

4. *Concealment:* We also use clothing as a general means of modesty, meaning that in most, if not all cultures, the body is covered, even minimally. The function of concealment also means that we use clothing to hide or mask certain features of the body. During job interviews, applicants may wear long sleeves to hide tattoos, dark colored clothing that camouflages extra weight, or over-sized

*What does this person's choice of t-shirt communicate about him nonverbally?*

clothing so that a slender build is not as evident. For an interesting bit of research on concealment, check out how U.S. military uniforms have evolved over past decades, from the green camouflage worn in the jungles of Viet Nam during that conflict, to the tan, desert-like camouflage worn in more recent Middle Eastern conflicts.

5. *Group Identification:* Sporting events, campus gatherings, and political rallies exemplify a few social contexts in which people wear clothing to celebrate and publicize their group identification. Many of us have sports jerseys in our closet, because we're proud to be affiliated with and support our favorite teams. Some of us are members of a campus group, political party, or club; when we attend such groups' events, we may be encouraged to wear clothing to nonverbally indicate our affiliation. Schools have their reasons for creating dress codes, such as reducing cliques and gangs, allowing students to concentrate on schoolwork rather than socializing, and fostering a professional atmosphere which can enhance morale (Garcia Hunter, 2004). But these codes can actually build student cohesion and group identity. Proponents of school dress codes argue that they're "great equalizers;" students of lower socioeconomic backgrounds feel more connected, since they're not compared to other students wearing expensive clothes that communicate their higher status (Santos-Garza, 2004).

6. *Persuasion:* How can clothing persuade people? Researchers have studied the impact of clothing on persuading others to comply (e.g., follow directions, fundraise, pick up garbage, deposit money in parking meters) (Lawrence & Watson, 1991). Research results indicate that a police officer in uniform directing traffic is more likely to get people to comply with her or his instructions than someone not in uniform (Young, 1999). We're also more persuaded to donate money when approached by someone in uniform than someone not in uniform. Firefighters, police officers, and members of the military are highly successful fundraisers for special causes; their uniforms symbolize their service and communicate credibility, both of which are very persuasive.

7. *Display of Status:* Clothing also nonverbally communicates status. Studies over several decades have examined people's responses to high status clothing—clothing that communicates achievement, professionalism, or financial success (Lefkowitz, Blake, & Mouton, 1955; Long, Mueller, Wuers, & Khong, 1996; Schiavo, Sherlock, & Wicklund, 1974). In such studies, people dressed in high status clothing were observed for their effects on others' compliance (e.g., obeying or defying traffic signals, accepting or ignoring leaflets, donating or rejecting requests for money, giving directions). In most studies, well-dressed people affected other people's behavior; they also received better responses than poorly dressed people. However, Long, Mueller, Wuers, and Khong (1996) found no differences in responses to well dressed or sloppily dressed people who asked strangers for money. Because of the perceived connection between clothing and status, some establishments have strict dress codes and bouncers who select customers who look good enough to enter the establishment.

## Expressions of Personality and Culture

Clothing is also a nonverbal expression of our personality and culture. We may wear a t-shirt that expresses a way of life or an attitude; that choice of clothing has communicative power. Think of all the t-shirts you see around your college campus that depict humorous messages about drinking or pot smoking; what message do those shirts send? Let's take a moment to consider a short of list of some outrageous messages we've seen on t-shirts and sweaters. What type of personality is someone trying to express by wearing a t-shirt that says, "Spank Me," "For Sale," "I Taste Good," "Reject from the Thelma & Louise School of Etiquette," or "I'm out of estrogen and I have a gun!"?

Nonverbal scholars Rosenfeld and Plax (1977) studied the connection between clothing and personality and suggest the following four relationships:

1. *Clothing Consciousness:* People who have this type of personality feel like everyone is watching them; it's important to them for others to notice what they're wearing.
2. *Exhibitionism:* Some people enjoy wearing skimpy clothes that show off their bodies. They're likely to wear inappropriate clothing in all kinds of settings, not just professional or formal ones.
3. *Practicality:* Many people wear clothes for simplicity, comfort, and practicality rather than for looking good or exhibiting their personality traits.
4. *Designer:* Some people dress in a manner that reveals that they would love to be clothing designers. These folks tend to dress in the trendiest clothing possible.

In addition to expressions of personality, clothing also communicates and celebrates our cultural beliefs. The brightly colored gowns and matching headpieces worn by some African women, the beautiful saris (draped dresses) many Indian women wear, and the beaded outfits and elaborate feather headdresses displayed by leaders of Native American tribes are but a few examples of cultural expressions of clothing. In some cultures, women are expected to keep their heads covered, while in the Jewish culture, traditionally the men wear kipot (Jewish hats). Many Jewish people wear kipot only while praying or studying religious texts, but more traditional Jews wear kipot for the entire day. One of the most extreme examples of cultural clothing comes from news footage of women in Afghanistan during the Taliban rule, who were forced to cover themselves in public from head to toe; the images of those blue buhrkas are seared in our minds.

## Dressing to Connect with Others

In addition to clothing as a nonverbal expression of personality and culture, some of us dress a certain way because we feel that other people are going to like us more because of our clothing selection. Can clothing influence popularity? In fact, clothing can be beneficial to our interpersonal relationships. When we achieve **homophily** with others, or a perceived similarity in appearance, background, and attitudes, our relationships and level of popularity in other people's eyes is enhanced. We tend to like people whom we

---

**REMEMBER 5.4**

| | |
|---|---|
| **Decoration:** | how we decorate our body for celebrations and special occasions. |
| **Protection:** | how we use clothing to protect our body from intrusion or harm. |
| **Sexual Attraction:** | ways that clothing helps draw sexual attention from others. |
| **Concealment:** | how clothing helps us conceal features of our body we don't want others to see. |
| **Group Identification:** | clothing that allows us to communicate or celebrate a group we identify with or connect to. |
| **Persuasion:** | ways that clothing influences others' behavior. |
| **Status:** | how clothing communicates social and professional class. |
| **Homophily:** | perceived similarity in people's appearance, background, and attitudes that benefits relationships. |

---

perceive to be similar to us and this includes similarity in what clothes we wear. But the need for homophily can create pressure—peer pressure to conform and become trendy, seeking clothing that reflects current fashion trends (which can put pressure on the pocketbook as well). Some level of social appropriateness or fitting in is understandable, but we also encourage the "different drummer" in each of us.

One example of homophily and appearance comes from the world of work, where "casual Friday" and the act of dressing down on the job are becoming increasingly prevalent (Averyt, 1997). Business professor William McPherson (1997) describes this trend:

> There is a hostile takeover trend that's threatening to change the very nature of American business. Corporate America is changing the way it dresses. Students who are preparing for careers in business must be made aware of this change. Just as American culture as a whole has undergone a series of clothing revolutions from tie-dyed shirts in the 1960s to bell-bottom pants in the 1970s to yuppie sweaters in the 1980s, so too has the American workplace begun its own fashion revolution. (p. 134)

As we've said, it's important to dress professionally for a job interview because potential employers often make judgments of candidates' suitability within the first few minutes of the interview (Kaiser, 1997). But once you've landed the position you can adjust your dress to express more homophily with your coworkers. If everyone where you work dresses down or casually on Fridays and you don't, what nonverbal message might that send?

## ▪ ARTIFACTS

In addition to clothing, **artifacts** such as jewelry, eyeglasses, cologne, and makeup are temporary or mobile aspects of physical adornment that provide clues about our personalities, attitudes, and behaviors and that nonverbally communicate something about us to other people (Amsbary et al., 1994; Breitenbach, 2005; Roberti & Storch, 2005; Tiggemann & Golder, 2006). You might think of a piercing or tattoo as an artifact or form of body decoration. However, we prefer to think of it this way: Artifacts are temporary—you can take off your jewelry or wash makeup off your face. While some tattoos, like henna tattoos, are temporary, most are permanent. Most piercings are permanent, unless you happen to have a hole that goes without jewelry for a long time and the tissue grows back. So in most situations, piercings and tattoos are permanent, thus we prefer to view them as body modifications and discuss them in the next section of this chapter. For now, let's consider a few categories of artifacts and how they communicate nonverbally.

## Jewelry

The most common artifact that comes to mind is jewelry. How many of us are wearing jewelry this very second, as we explore this topic? Rings, bracelets, anklets, watches, cufflinks, necklaces, earrings, nose rings, pins, and so on are examples of jewelry many of us wear on a daily basis. What nonverbal message does jewelry send? Wedding rings serve as a great example of how jewelry can inform us nonverbally about other people. If we're out on the town with friends for a fun evening and notice an attractive person across the room, one clue to figure out their availability is to look for a ring on the person's finger. If we notice a ring, we're led to believe that our person of interest isn't available. On the other hand, if we don't see a ring, it may be okay to approach, buy the person a drink, and ask for a phone number. However, we suggest caution here, in that some married men in the U.S. do not own or wear wedding rings, while many, if not most, married women do.

Take a moment to think about how jewelry communicates nonverbally. How does jewelry communicate status? Does a Rolex watch communicate a different image than a Swatch? A different message is certainly sent by diamonds versus rhinestones. What does too much jewelry communicate—possible compensation for insecurity about attractiveness? Some people in U.S. culture and in other parts of the world like to wear crosses, typically as necklaces or lapel pins. Should you assume that everyone who wears a cross is a member of the Christian faith? Was this the image Madonna wanted to communicate when she wore multiple crosses while singing "Like a Virgin"? As another example, after the attacks on the U.S. on September 11, 2001, many people began wearing American flag pins on their clothing—many still do. If you saw someone wearing such a pin, would you necessarily assume that she or he was a patriot? a conservative? What messages do these tiny details send, nonverbally?

## Eyeglasses

In addition to jewelry, eyeglasses (including sunglasses) also send nonverbal messages. For example, people who wear glasses are often perceived as more intelligent and honest, but also more nerdy than those without glasses. You've probably heard the old rhyme, "Boys don't make passes at girls who wear glasses," but is this still the case? Women with glasses may be viewed as brainy or studious, but glasses are also fashion statements. Popular eyeglass styles and shapes seem to change constantly. For awhile, large-shaped eyeglasses were in style, then it wasn't long before the skinnier shapes and no-rim glasses began being viewed as hip and cool.

The way people use and wear eyeglasses also sends nonverbal signals. For example, people who chew on their glasses may be perceived as nervous and tense. People who push their eyeglasses up in their hair or onto their forehead may send a signal that they're willing to be approached—they attempt to make direct eye contact without the distraction of glasses. Just as we mentioned about hair color, eyeglasses can be seen as an artifact of the aging process. Many people with perfect eyesight in their youth find themselves needing glasses, contacts, or reading glasses when they reach their forties or fifties. People who wear reading glasses are interesting to watch; they often use their glasses when trying to articulate or emphasize an important point, in conversation as well as in public speaking situations.

Then there are those people who wear sunglasses inside of buildings (like Jack Nicholson and Bill Cosby). What nonverbal message does this behavior send? One message is that the wearer doesn't want anyone to see how bloodshot their eyes are, which could be an indication of alcohol or substance use. Another interpretation is that the wearer is covering up a black eye, which is often a telltale sign of physical abuse. Yet another view is that it allows wearers control over other people—they can see your eyes, but you can't see theirs. Or perhaps they simply believe it makes them look cool. Teachers, trainers, or anyone in a public speaking situation may find audience members wearing sunglasses to be hostile, threatening, or bored. The distraction to the speaker comes from the fact that you don't know who or what they're looking at, if they're interested, or even awake! There's something unsettling about not being able to see someone's eyes, at least in American culture.

## Makeup

Speaking of billion dollar industries, we could go on forever about the cosmetics industry, but we won't. Just realize that some critics suggest that contemporary beauty practices (like the application of makeup) are done *by* women, not *for* women, meaning that the real beneficiaries of all the stuff women put on their faces are the sex industry, cosmetic surgeons, and the fashion and cosmetics industries (Jeffreys, 2005).

Given that, let's take a moment to examine cosmetics and the nonverbal messages sent by people wearing them. Makeup is a common artifact worn primarily by women and increasingly by men in American culture. Stage makeup or cultural uses of cosmetics (like war paint for rituals) are their own unique categories, but everyday makeup applied in the extreme is of interest to us for the nonverbal signals it sends. Unwittingly, some women use makeup products that just look downright odd, but we agree that the perception of odd is in the eye of the beholder. But extreme shades of eye shadow (especially in opposition to one's skin color); overly drawn, dramatic eyebrows with no resemblance to nature; dark colored or overdone applications of blush (such that a person looks punched in the jaw); dark lip-liners that don't match the lipstick; and extreme shades of lipstick (that can alternately make someone look ghostly or also like they've been punched) draw undue attention and can send the wrong signals. Overdone makeup is, to many people, reminiscent of prostitutes.

Now, lest you think your authors old fogies who prefer conservative makeup, think again. We appreciate this form of body decoration just like the next person, but we think it's important to consider what message makeup sends nonverbally—something many people forget to do before they leave the house. Granted, sometimes we don't want to send a signal at all—we just want to cover up a zit or discoloration so not to attract attention to ourselves. But an extreme use of this artifact can send a signal of insecurity, trying too hard to be noticed, or a general lack of self-awareness. Another  factor that adds confusion to the mix is some men's reactions to women's makeup: Often heterosexual men will say they prefer a natural look, meaning women wearing little to no makeup. But these same men will crane their necks and risk bodily injury to check out a woman wearing heavy makeup, as though the makeup nonverbally signals that the woman wants attention and the men are obliged to give it to her.

Men's use of makeup is a controversial subject. Clinique was one of the first companies to develop a line of men's cosmetics, although men have been slow to embrace such usage. For some reason, bronzers are pretty well accepted, but illogically enough, typically they're not viewed as a form of makeup by the men who wear them. But with the acceptance now of the metrosexual (a media-generated description of heterosexual men who are more concerned with their appearance than the stereotypical straight man), cosmetic products for men are gaining acceptability (Flocker, 2003; Mullen, 2003). If you can easily tell that a man is wearing makeup, what nonverbal signal does that send? What kinds of judgments do you make about his personality?

## ■ MODIFYING THE BODY

In this chapter, our purpose was to cover the reality of physical appearance; we said upfront, "looks do matter." We've explored some aspects of physical appearance, as well as their effects on human behavior. But we do have some fears or reservations associated with this complex topic. Physical appearance has become so important in our culture that waves of people talk on a daily basis about **body modification,** meaning the more permanent methods of changing the way we look (Covino, 2004; Davis, 1995, 2003; Frasure, 2003; Heyes, 2007; Oliver, 2006; Pitts, 2003). The number of people getting tattoos, piercings, and cosmetic procedures has increased dramatically in recent years (Blum, 2003; Selwyn Delinsky, 2005). In 2005, nine million cosmetic procedures were performed on women in the U.S., with breast augmentation as the most prevalent (American Society of Plastic Surgeons, 2006). In 2003, 91 percent of women who had breast augmentation surgery said that they did it because they "wanted to look better without clothes" (American Society for Aesthetic Plastic Surgery, 2006, p. 39). For Asian and Asian American women, the fastest-growing and most common cosmetic procedure creates a crease over each eye, since most Asians do not have extra skin or creases that make their eyes look larger. In a typical year, more than $400 million is spent on Retin-A and similar treatments to erase lines, wrinkles, and other indications of aging (American Society of Plastic Surgeons, as in Duke, 2003). What's at stake here?

We don't want to suggest that people should *not* care about how they look or *not* strive for good health. Instead, we want to talk about the *need* to modify ourselves, this process of customizing our bodies to match up to some idealized beauty standard. We know our readers are adults and can make up their own minds about body modification, but the constant pressure to improve our physical appearance can take a toll on our emotional stability and warp our priorities in life. You've probably seen or read about people, mostly women, who are addicted to cosmetic surgery—those who have multiple surgeries but are still never happy with the way they look. There's actually a term for this problem; Body Dysmorphic Disorder (BDD) is a preoccupation with a bodily defect and a propensity toward cosmetic surgery (Mulkens & Jansen, 2006). Our concerns and fears about body modifications, including piercings, tattoos, and cosmetic procedures, don't stem from worries about "going under the knife" or a fear of botched medical procedures. The real danger is the increasing dissatisfaction with our natural selves, fostered by the constant talk about enlarging, reducing, buffing, bulking, filling, piercing, whitening, suctioning, tattooing, and tightening various parts of the body. As we explore this important topic, consider the pros and cons of body modification, thinking about what you believe you'll gain if you modify your body in these ways. We first examine piercings and tattoos as forms of body modification that have nonverbal communicative power; then we address the cosmetic procedure issue.

## Piercings

Very simply, **piercings** are holes in the skin created for the purposes of wearing jewelry and expressing oneself. They are an ancient and increasingly popular form of body modification, sometimes viewed as body art, that can send nonverbal messages (Riley & Cahill, 2005). For some people, there's no limitation as to the location of the piercing. One study distinguished non-intimate piercing locations (e.g., ears, eyebrows, lips, bellybutton, nose, tongue) from intimate locations (e.g., nipples, penis, vagina) and explored characteristics of people choosing to receive intimate piercings (Caliendo, Armstrong, & Roberts, 2005). People with intimate piercings described themselves as young, well educated, less likely to get married, of sexual orientations that included heterosexual, homosexual, and bisexual, and as having had initiated sexual activity at an earlier age than the average person in the U.S. population. Their purposes for getting intimate piercings included uniqueness, self-expression, and sexual expression.

In a similar line of inquiry, a group of researchers attempted to learn college students' motivations for getting body piercings (of all types), as well as their sources of influence (Armstrong, Roberts, Owen, & Koch, 2004). Results indicated that the majority of students in the study held a positive image of body art, viewed it as a form of self-expression and a way to be unique, and reported that friends (not family) were major influences on their decision to acquire body art. Other research into piercing has examined the following: piercing and a higher incidence of suicide attempts (Hicinbothem, Gonsalves, & Lester, 2006); the relationship between engaging in healthy behaviors and the likelihood of getting tattoos and piercings (Huxley & Grogan, 2005); the correlation between piercing and mental health (Stim, Hinz, &

Brahler, 2006); how piercing relates to masculine development (Denness, 2005); and tattooing and body piercing as risk-taking behaviors and self-harm, just as eating disorders are considered risky behavior and a means of harming oneself (Claes, Vandereycken, & Vertommen, 2005; Preti, Pinna, Nocco, & Mulliri, 2006). One final study we want to mention: Scholar Nancy Swanger (2006) examined the perceptions of college recruiters and human resource managers toward interviewees who had visible body modifications; almost 90 percent of recruiters and managers viewed the tattoos and piercings of interviewees negatively. We understand that you want to be true to yourself on a job interview, but you can still be true to yourself while camouflaging, rather than flaunting, your tattoos and removing jewelry from some of your piercings (including earrings on men), given the potential for employers to view these body modifications negatively.

Some of us have body piercings (beyond our ears); many of us have friends who do. Do you believe that body piercing is now seen as a common, acceptable practice in U.S. culture, rather than something only punk rockers used to do? Do you believe it's a form of self-expression or self-mutilation? What does the presence of body piercings communicate nonverbally? Does it send a message that the wearer is a free spirit, a risk taker, or an insecure trend seeker? Eye contact is one nonverbal cue that is disturbed for us by the presence of nose piercings. While we accept students' forms of self-expression (within reason), we simply find it hard to maintain eye contact with students who wear studs or, worse, hoops in their noses—it's just hard to look anywhere else but the nose!

## Tattoos

In addition to body piercings, **tattoos**—temporary or permanent ink messages and symbols placed on the body—are also an increasingly popular form of body modification (Gloss, 2005; Tiggemann & Golder, 2006). While tattooing used to be viewed as an act of deviance (something only soldiers, convicts, bikers, and drunken people did), today's tattoos are often planned in advance and well thought out, in terms of both design and body location (Forbes, 2001, Selvin, 2007). All sorts of people now get tattoos—people you wouldn't expect to have them. Some people get tattoos in tribute to other people; for example, the former director of our campus women's center got a tattoo on her shoulder in honor of her best friend who died of cervical cancer (Williamson, 2007). One piece of advice: Try to avoid tattooing the name of your current love interest on your body; we hate to be pessimists, but you might live to regret that decision.

What nonverbal signals are sent by someone who has a visible tattoo? Is the person an exhibitionist, a risk taker, a sadist (a lover of pain), or just a free spirit who views her or his body as a blank canvas, ready for artistic expression? Here's another question for you: What nonverbal signals are sent by someone who gets a tattoo on a part of their body that she or he can't see—that only others can see? A few years back a friend had a large sunflower (about six by six inches) tattooed on her lower back. We found this interesting because obviously she could only see the tattoo in a mirror—why get a tattoo mainly for other people to see? Perceptions of tattooed people certainly have changed over the past couple of decades, since the

**SPOTLIGHT on Research**

Have you ever looked around and noticed the number of people who have tattoos and body piercings? On some college campuses, the number of students with these body modifications have become the majority. What goes through your mind when you see people with sleeves of tattoos and enough metal to set off a detector? What thoughts do you have about those people's behaviors, personalities, and attitudes? One might assume someone with tattoos and piercings is probably a risk taker or looking for some excitement or attention. These characteristics might explain why people get tattoos or piercings. However, recent research suggests possible emotional explanations.

A recent study examined the association between body modification, anxiety, and depression within a group of college students. Researchers Roberti and Storch (2005) studied a group of undergraduates and noted which ones had a tattoo or piercing. (Female ear piercings were not counted as body modifications.) Out of the total number of students, 65 percent had at least one tattoo or body piercing. Each student completed questionnaires regarding their experiences with depression in the past week and anxiety in general. Results of these tests showed that anxiety and depression levels in people with body modifications were much higher than in people without modifications. People with multiple tattoos or piercings scored higher on both questionnaires.

Psychological factors such as depression and anxiety may reveal motivations for some students to acquire tattoos and piercings, meaning that some students may opt to alter their bodies as a form of self-medication instead of seeking professional counseling. But if a majority of students have these modifications, that would seem to indicate that they're more socially acceptable and don't necessarily reflect psychological distress. However, Roberti and Storch noted that student distress may cause a person to be less assertive in seeking help. In order to fit in with their peers, lower their anxiety, or lessen their depression, some students opt for getting a (or another) tattoo or piercing.

It's likely that many of you reading this may have tattoos and piercings—some noticeable, some not. Maybe your body is covered with ink that's hidden beneath your clothes. If so, you may be thinking that your desire for a tattoo or piercing had nothing to do with depression or anxiety. But what, exactly, motivated you to alter your body in this way? Consider what others think about you when they see your piercings or tattoos, because we know that others form impressions of us based on our physical appearance. These impressions often relate to how people think we act and feel. Next time you see someone with a body modification, stop and think about what impression that appearance gives you. Is she or he expressing individuality? boredom? anxiety? Might she or he be depressed and simply needed a change?

For more information about this study, read: Roberti, J. W., & Storch, E. A. (2005). Psychosocial adjustment of college students with tattoos and piercings. *Journal of College Counseling, 8,* 14–19.

days of the "tattooed lady" who was considered a carnival freak. A lot of people used to look down on someone with a tattoo, especially a tattooed woman. Even though today's tattoos are more generally accepted, watch out for that job interview if you have a visible tattoo.

*Tattoos and piercings are increasingly popular and normalized physical adornments, which serve as forms of nonverbal communication.*

### What Would *You* Do?

The company you work for has asked you to conduct interviews for a receptionist position that just became available. After reviewing 25 resumés, you've narrowed the field down to five individuals. You've contacted all five applicants and set up interviews. You interview each person and at the end of the day you can't decide between a nice young lady named Bianca and a nice young gentleman named Charles. Bianca has impressed you to the point that you feel she's almost overqualified for the position. She arrived 15 minutes early for the interview, was dressed professionally, has three years experience as a receptionist, and was extremely personable. She has three visible tattoos—one above her chest area, one on her ankle, and one on her arm. Charles has an impressive resumé (but not much experience), a good work ethic, and answered most of the questions satisfactorily. Charles has no visible tattoos and could be trained to fill this position.

Using this story and what you've learned from this chapter about physical appearance, *what would you do*? Would you hire Bianca or Charles? Would you take physical appearance into consideration for the job? Is it more important to find the right candidate with the most experience or someone who looks the part and can be trained? Would you hire Bianca under the condition that she finds a way to conceal all of her tattoos? Or would you hire Charles and take time to mold him into the employee you want him to be?

## Cosmetic Procedures

Have you ever watched an episode of *Nip/Tuck*, then thought about getting cosmetic surgery for yourself? If you're someone who would never get a full-out surgery, what about cosmetic procedures like Botox injections, varicose vein or stretch mark removals, or collagen injections in your lips? Beyond having fat sucked from your hips or getting breast implants, a whole series of procedures are now advertised by cosmetic surgeons, laser spas, and salons across the world. Below are some of the most popular procedures of body modification today:

1. *Breast Augmentation:* the number one most common cosmetic procedure in the U.S., a process of enlarging the breasts through the insertion of implants.
2. *Liposuction:* a process of suctioning fat from the body.
3. *Gastric Bypass or Banding Surgery:* medical procedures that partition a part of the stomach, thus reducing the amount of food a person is able to consume, with rapid, major weight loss as the main result.
4. *Botox:* an injection of a toxic substance that temporarily paralyzes muscles and skin tissue, typically applied to the forehead and around the eyes, for the purposes of tightening skin on the face, reducing wrinkles, and making people look younger.
5. *Body Wrap:* a temporary body modification related to water weight, available at many salons and medical spas, in which clients are wrapped tightly in material (sometimes cellophane) and placed into warming beds for the purpose of ridding the body of water and toxins and generating weight loss.
6. *Laser Treatments:* lasers applied to the face or other areas of the body marred by acne or skin discolorations, so as to produce a more consistent skin tone.
7. *Facelift:* a surgical procedure in which the skin on the face (and sometimes neck) is detached, lifted up, and reattached to defy the natural aging effects of gravity and to create a tighter, more youthful looking face.

While we don't want to get into an argument about the pros and cons of such body modification procedures and treatments, we do want to ask a question: What nonverbal signals are sent when someone alters their physical appearance in such ways? Some people who have liposuction or gastric bypass surgery may be criticized because they didn't attempt to lose weight or tighten fatty places the "old-fashioned way" (diet and exercise). But many people *have* tried repeatedly to lose weight or tone up after losing considerable weight, and results just aren't possible for them. For some morbidly overweight people, their knees or lungs can't manage exercise programs, and gastric bypass or banding surgeries actually save their lives. So we realize that this is a complicated and emotional issue.

But what about the procedures that attempt to "turn back the hands of time"? Are signs of aging so horrifying that people feel the need to inject themselves with a toxic substance so that they can paralyze their foreheads, to the point that they're unable to reveal emotions in their faces? Have you seen people after (even weeks after) a facelift, when they're taking pain pills around the clock and look like they were beaten in the face with a baseball bat? What does it say, nonverbally, about people who elect to endure such procedures, all for the sake of looking younger? What about adolescents and teenagers who want cosmetic surgery, like to redo their noses or strengthen their chins? Is this appropriate? A lot of times we judge people who have cosmetic procedures as insecure, shallow, and vain. However, with such procedures becoming more readily available and affordable, and with more and more people having them, some of us may have begun to change our thinking about this topic—perhaps deciding that these procedures must be okay and healthy, since so many people like us are having them done . . . perhaps we might think about having a little nip or tuck done ourselves, after all, no one's perfect. Is there danger in such thinking?

## The Televisual Makeover

A lot of the stigma of getting a cosmetic or medical procedure is removed or lessened because millions of viewers can watch it happening, courtesy of the televisual makeover, an offshoot of home makeover shows (Deery, 2004; Tait, 2007; Weber, 2005). As psychotherapist Irene Rosenberg Javors (2004) explains, "Television as a medium offers us enough of a safe distance from reality to allow us to witness it as passive viewers without having to risk anything" (p. 35). Makeover culture has become a major focus in the U.S. in recent years, in part because of numerous TV shows (e.g., *The Swan, Dr. 90210, Ten Years Younger, The Biggest Loser*), websites, and magazines that focus on losing weight and transforming the body (Allatson, 2004; Covino, 2004; Davis, 1995, 2003; Frasure, 2003; Gallagher, 2004; Heyes, 2007; Mason & Meyers, 2001; Moorti & Ross, 2004; Oliver, 2006; Pearson & Reich, 2004; Waggoner, 2004).

Two shows that best illustrate the televisual makeover aired in the early 2000s, but are no longer on the air: ABC's *Extreme Makeover* (the version preceding the home edition) and Fox's *The Swan. Extreme Makeover* featured people who were awarded free extensive cosmetic surgery, along with dental and dermatological procedures to change their looks (and supposedly boost their self-esteem) in rapid time. Most also worked with a trainer and nutritionist, to assist in the "transformation." We're not sure why the program went off the air, but it might be related to medical liability—some people featured on the show may have experienced medical problems afterward or may have been unhappy with the results of their procedures or how they were portrayed. The other, more egregious televisual makeover show was *The Swan*; this show is also no longer on the air (Flynn, 2004). The premise was to take a few women who presented their "sob stories" to judges and the viewing public, pick a winner (the one with the saddest story), transform her through cosmetic procedures, and then present her to friends, family, and the TV viewing audience at what's now become known as "the big reveal." If that wasn't enough, at the end of the season, the transformed women from each episode came together (in evening gowns, no less) and competed—pageant-style—for the top prize, the winner being the one who had most transformed herself from an "ugly duckling" into a "swan." The uproar and outcry over this show was enough to cause Fox to cancel it after only two seasons.

Feminist media scholar Cressida Heyes (2007) explains that the televisual makeover show's goal is to "revolutionize appearance, in the course of which the participants' lives, and even their very selves, will also be transformed" (p. 20). Today's ease of transforming ourselves into someone else could be viewed as dangerous. One of the biggest problems with shows like *Extreme Makeover* is that patients' emotions and concerns aren't addressed at all or with any depth; there's no room for trouble or fear in this fantasy world of change. Heyes (2007) further suggests that, particularly at "the reveal," children are often uncomfortable with their parent's new look, but friends and family save the day by arguing that "if the participant is doing what makes her or him happy, then it can't be wrong" (p. 24). But is it wrong?

## The Trouble with Normalization

We recognize the allure of televisual makeover shows, past and present, and understand the magical and fantasy-like quality to these shows that can be quite inviting and inspiring. After all, seeing a frog converted into a prince overnight is always going to have some entertainment value. At the same time, our fear about this physical appearance fetish or compulsion is that shows like these and other forms of persuasion bring the process of modifying our bodies into a normal part of conversation. The expectation to transform ourselves and be the best we can be becomes an *everyday message*. **Normalization**—the process of making a viewpoint or action about something such a normal and everyday part of reality that it can't be questioned— benefits the cosmetic surgery and procedures industries. It destigmatizes cosmetic surgery, making it a more acceptable part of daily life and less the exception than the norm (Brooks, 2004; Davis, 1995, 2003). Normalization also allows features of the televisual makeover story to come to life as we are encouraged to place ourselves in the characters' shoes in the show, and try to make ourselves meet impossible standards (Heyes, 2007; Tait, 2007).

Some of the research we reviewed in the piercings and tattoos sections deal with this normalization phenomenon. One study of attitudes toward body piercings found that people now perceive this form of body modification to be normative, meaning that it's now so commonplace to see people of all ages with piercings that the practice goes without question (Koch, Roberts, Armstrong, & Owen, 2004). The more something becomes accepted or normalized, the less we question it or think to ask: Is this good for me? Why am I even considering doing this? Some voices, particular those of feminist scholars, urge us to expose normalization and examine the demons we're chasing by all of this motivation to alter our natural bodies. Scholars like Kathy Davis, Victoria Pitts, Virginia Blum, and Sheila Jeffreys, whose work we cite in this chapter, approach this topic from different angles, but with the same level of concern about what people, particularly young women, are doing to their bodies.

You may be thinking: What's the problem? What's the trouble with all of this attention to physical appearance? (If you think that, you've been affected by normalization.) Here's one problem: These everyday messages and stories create turmoil in people's lives and can adversely affect health, evidenced by the rising statistics of eating disorders, depression, drug and alcohol abuse, and cosmetic surgery (Ackerman, 2006; Haines & Neumark-Sztainer, 2006; Hardy, 2006; Jaffe, 2006; Taras & Potts-Datema, 2005). Normalizing a culture of body modification and undergoing procedures—whether they're related to weight loss, use of steroids to bulk up body mass, piercings and tattoos, cosmetic alterations and the like—may give us feelings of increased self-esteem and confidence, but those highs tend to be fleeting, not lasting.

## REMEMBER 5.5

**Artifacts:** temporary aspects of physical adornment other than clothing (e.g., jewelry, eyeglasses, cologne, makeup) that provide clues about our personalities, attitudes, and behaviors and that nonverbally communicate something about us to other people.

**Body Modification:** more permanent methods of changing physical appearance (e.g., piercings, tattoos, cosmetic procedures).

**Piercings:** form of body modification created by putting holes into skin, for the purposes of wearing jewelry.

**Tattoos:** form of body modification involving temporary or permanent ink messages and images placed on the body.

**Normalization:** process of making a viewpoint or action such a normal and everyday part of reality that it can't be questioned.

At the end of the day, you're still the same person *inside.* If you think that losing weight will make you a new person, just talk to people who've lost a lot of weight; many of them will tell you that they still have problems—*different* problems perhaps, but problems nonetheless.

 Please understand: We're not trying to preach to you or tell you what to do with your own body, but we ask that you take some time to reflect on your own personal realities of physical appearance, as a form of nonverbal communication, presented in this chapter. Balance or weigh those realities against the risks, fears, and problems created by a culture of unrealistic expectations and impossible standards, and then use your best judgment.

## UNDERSTANDING PHYSICAL APPEARANCE: APPLYING THE REFLEXIVE CYCLE OF NONVERBAL COMMUNICATION DEVELOPMENT

 Have you ever thought about how you manage physical appearance in your own life? How much time do you spend thinking about your physical appearance? Recall our discussion of the Reflexive Cycle of Nonverbal Development in Chapter 2. The first step to developing your skills and a better understanding of physical appearance as nonverbal communication is awareness. Regarding physical appearance, we ask you to inventory yourself using the following questions: What standards do you have regarding your own appearance? What are your needs or preferences regarding the physical appearance of other people? Do you have expectations or rules about looks? Do these judgments vary depending on who the person is or whether the relationship is personal or professional? Are you aware of the impressions others may have about you based on your physical appearance?

Now that you have engaged in an inventory of self regarding physical appearance, it's time to think about making, if necessary, any appropriate changes to improve how you manage physical appearance as nonverbal communication in everyday life. This is Phase 2 in the Reflexive Cycle. Ask yourself: Are there some changes I need to make regarding my physical appearance, perhaps with regard for cleanliness, attire, jewelry, hair, or weight? If so, how can I make those changes? Perhaps the only thing that needs to change is your attitude about your physical appearance; perhaps you need to work on being less self-critical and accepting yourself more as you are physically.

Beyond engaging in an inventory of self and making appropriate changes, the next step is to inventory others. Can you think of a person who seems to have no awareness of their physical appearance? Images of a sloppy friend who wears wrinkled clothes (the same ones, for days in a row) and practices bad hygiene may come to mind. These people may lack high levels of image fixation or self-monitoring skills (the ability to be aware of our appropriateness in social situations). Probably they could care less about how they look. Now think about being picked up for a first date: The person you're going out with shows up with his or her clothes soiled and it's apparent that she or he hasn't showered. What kind of first impression does this make? Some people are oblivious to the fact that their physical appearance communicates something about who they are. They aren't aware enough to perception check with other people for their observations and resulting perceptions about appearance. While we agree that U.S. culture's overemphasis on appearance is a problem, we acknowledge the importance of learning to live effectively in a social context. We need to be aware that the physical appearance we maintain (or not) sends nonverbal signals to other people. Sometimes we get clues, such as "business casual" or "professional attire" on an invitation, to give us a sense as to what's expected of our physical appearance. But many times our judgment and experience, and that of others, are relied upon to help us make decisions about appearance. Our physical appearance for a pool party should be different than for a formal dinner or professional interview. If someone was uncomfortable with or offended by your physical appearance, would you notice? What nonverbal signals would the person send? How might you respond in such a situation?

After you have done an inventory of self, changed self, and inventoried others' nonverbal behavior, the fourth phase of the Reflexive Cycle involves interacting with others, trying out the changes you've made or are in the process of making, and observing people as you verbally and nonverbally interact with them. Do people have different reactions to you, as a result of any changes you made? For example, some people who've lost a lot of weight can't handle the different way people respond to them; sometimes this effect is so pronounced and uncomfortable that it drives them to gain the weight back. As another example, some men decide to shave their beards and mustaches, just for a change; when they interact with people after changing this form of their appearance, most people notice that something is different (e.g., "you look younger;" "have you lost weight?"), but they can't put their finger on what has changed. It can be interesting to note people's reactions to both subtle and obvious changes in your physical appearance and how that makes you feel, as well as to gauge your own reactions to changes in others' appearance. In the last part of the cycle, we challenge you to review and assess the whole process, making note of positive and negative aspects, and then begin the cycle again. Remember, the development of communication skills is a never-ending process, as we work to develop our nonverbal abilities on a whole range of topics, not just physical appearance.

## SUMMARY ■ ■ ■ ■ ■

In this chapter, we established physical appearance as a nonverbal communication code and emphasized the need to be aware of our physical appearance as well as how we respond to the physical appearance of other people. For two reasons, we need to give special attention to physical appearance as a nonverbal communication code: (1) The decisions we make to maintain or alter our physical appearance reveal a great deal about who we are, and (2) the physical appearance of other people impacts our perceptions of them, how we communicate with them, how approachable they are, how attractive or unattractive they are, and so on.

Next we defined physical attractiveness—a culturally derived perception of beauty, formed by such bodily features as height, weight, size, shape, and so on—and explored the effects of physical attractiveness in contexts like interviews and hiring decisions, educational settings, and dating and marriage. We also introduced the matching hypothesis, which explains our tendency to seek romantic partners whom we perceive to be equal to us in physical attractiveness.

We then discussed somatyping, meaning the classification of people according to body type. Further, we covered three different body types—endomorphs, meso-morphs, and ectomorphs—and the personality characteristics and types (viscerotonic, somatonic, and cerebrotonic) associated with each. The next few sections on physical appearance examined weight, height, as related to status, and the disabled body for their ability to communicate something about us nonverbally. We then explored other features of the body (skin color, body smell, and hair) for the important role they play in physical appearance, and defined olfaction as the role of smell in human interaction. Next we studied clothing as a form of nonverbal communication and its various functions (decoration, protection, sexual attraction, concealment, group identification, persuasion, display of status, and expressions of personality and culture). We then defined homophily as a perceived similarity in appearance, background, and attitudes that enhance our interpersonal relationships, and discussed how clothing can serve to connect us to others. The last topic in this section was an examination of artifacts (jewelry, eyeglasses, cologne, makeup) and what they communicate about us nonverbally to other people.

The final section explored the complex topic of body modification, including discussions of piercings, tattoos, cosmetic procedures, and televisual makeover shows prevalent in media that create in us or reinforce a need to alter our bodies. We presented the problem of normalization—making something in society so everyday and commonplace that it goes without question—in relation to people's motivations for modifying their bodies. Finally, we closed the chapter by applying the Reflexive Cycle of Nonverbal Communication Development to our understanding of physical appearance. We encouraged reflection as a way of exposing the normalization rampant in our culture and calling into question the constant striving to enhance our appearance.

## DISCUSSION STARTERS

1. Explain how physical appearance is a form of nonverbal communication. What does your overall physical appearance communicate about you to others?

2. What is the difference between physical attraction and attractiveness? Do you believe that you can find people physically attractive, but not be attracted to them?

3. Review Sheldon's three body types and relate them to figures in popular media. Do you think the comparison of body types to personality traits is appropriate or helpful?

4. Think of how many self-improvement products exist in the U.S. related to physical appearance, especially to weight loss or gain. Make a list of these products and discuss the ones that might actually help someone, versus products that are bogus. Do you feel compelled or pressured to use these products?

5. What do you think about the discussion of the disabled body presented in this chapter?

Have you ever thought about this aspect of nonverbal communication? How might your nonverbal cues change with persons with disabilities, now that you know more about this topic?

5. Looking at the various functions of clothing provided in this chapter, consider your own strategies or preferences for the way you dress in various social situations. Are you more likely to dress for comfort and protection, rather than to express your personality? How is your clothing a form of nonverbal communication about you?

6. We talked a good deal in this chapter about body modification, in specific, piercings, tattoos, cosmetic procedures, and the problem of normalization. Have your views on body modification changed as you've gotten older and have been exposed to different kinds of situations? What nonverbal cues do you receive about people who have piercings and/or tattoos?

## REFERENCES

Ackerman, B. (2006). The dangers of Body Dysmorphic Disorder: Discover the dangers associated with this unhealthy behavior. *American Fitness*, 24–26.

Adams, G. R. (1977). Physical attractiveness research: Toward a developmental social psychology of beauty. *Human Development, 20*, 217–239.

Allatson, P. (2004). *Queer Eye*'s primping and pimping for Empire et al. *Feminist Media Studies, 4*, 208–211.

American Society for Aesthetic Plastic Surgery. (2006, June). O-zone. *O: The Oprah Winfrey Magazine*, 39.

American Society of Plastic Surgeons. (2006, June). O-zone. *O: The Oprah Winfrey Magazine*, 39.

Amsbary, J., Vogel, R., Hickson, M., Oakes, B., & Wittig, J. (1994). Smoking artifacts as indicators of homophily, attraction, and credibility: A replication. *Communication Research Reports, 11*, 161–167.

Andersen, P. A. (2004). *The complete idiot's guide to body language*. New York: Alpha.

Armstrong, M. L., Roberts, A. E., Owen, D. C., & Koch, J. R. (2004). Toward building a composite of college student influences with body art. *Issues in Comprehensive Pediatric Nursing, 27*, 277–295.

Aune, R. K. (1999). The effects of perfume use on perceptions of attractiveness and competence. In L. K. Guerrero, J. A. DeVito, & M. L. Hecht (Eds.), *The nonverbal communication reader: Classic and contemporary readings* (2nd ed., pp. 126–132). Prospect Heights, IL: Waveland.

Averyt, L. (1997, August 31). Casual-attire Fridays are spreading to rest of week in many companies. *Corpus Christi Caller Times*, pp. A1, A6.

Bahad, E. (2001). On the conception and measurement of popularity: More facts and some straight conclusions. *Social Psychology of Education, 5*, 3–29.

Barber, N. (2001). Mustache fashion covaries with a good marriage market for women. *Journal of Nonverbal Behavior, 25*, 261–272.

Baron, R. A. (1983). Short note: "Sweet smell of success"? The impact of pleasant artificial scents on the evaluations of job applicants. *Journal of Applied Psychology, 68,* 709–713.

Bar-Tal, D., & Saxe, L. (1976). Perceptions of similarity and dissimilarity of attractive couples and individuals. *Journal of Personality and Social Psychology, 33,* 772–781.

Beebe, S. A., Beebe, S. J., & Ivy, D. K. (2007). *Communication: Principles for a lifetime* (3rd ed.). Boston: Allyn & Bacon.

Berscheid, E., & Walster, E. H. (1978). *Interpersonal attraction* (2nd ed.). Reading, MA: Adams Media Corporation.

Bloomfield, S. (2006, January 16). The face of the future: Why Eurasians are changing the rules of attraction. *Independent on Sunday* (London), p. 3.

Blum, V. L. (2003). *Flesh wounds: The culture of cosmetic surgery.* Berkeley: University of California Press.

Bodenhausen, G. V., & Macrae, C. N. (1998). Stereotype activation and inhibition. In J. R. Wyer (Ed.), *Advances in social cognition* (Vol. 11, pp. 1–52). Mahwah, NJ: Erlbaum.

Bonamici, K., Herman, S., & Jarvis, P. (2006, January 23). Decoding the dress code. *Fortune,* 130–131.

Boswell, R. (2005, October 8). You know, eh, most national stereotypes don't stand up: Researchers find perceptions "highly mistaken." *The Calgary Herald,* p. A3.

Braithwaite, D. O. (1990). From majority to minority: An analysis of cultural change from able bodied to disabled. *International Journal of Intercultural Relations, 14,* 465–483.

Braithwaite, D. O. (1991). "Just how much did that wheelchair cost?": Management of privacy boundaries by persons with disabilities. *Western Journal of Speech Communication, 55,* 254–274.

Braithwaite, D. O. (1996). "I am a person first": Different perspectives on the communication of persons with disabilities. In E. B. Ray (Ed.), *Communication and disenfranchisement: Social health issues and implications* (pp. 257–272). Mahwah, NJ: Erlbaum.

Braithwaite, D. O., & Braithwaite, C. A. (1997). Understanding communication of persons with disabilities as cultural communication. In L. W. Samovar & R. Porter (Eds.), *Intercultural communication: A reader* (8th ed., pp 154–164). Belmont, CA: Wadsworth.

Braithwaite, D. O., & Thompson, T. L. (2000). *Handbook of communication and people with disabilities: Research and Application.* Mahwah, NJ: Erlbaum.

Breitenbach, S. (2005, November 12). Tattoos and piercings can keep young people from jobs. *The Frederick News-Post.*

Brooks, A. (2004). Under the knife and proud of it: An analysis of the normalization of cosmetic surgery. *Critical Sociology, 30,* 207–239.

Bugenthal, D. (2005). Interdisciplinary insights on nonverbal responses within attachment relationships. *Journal of Nonverbal Behavior, 29,* 177–187.

Caliendo, C., Armstrong, M. L., & Roberts, A. E. (2005). Self-reported characteristics of women and men with intimate body piercings. *Journal of Advanced Nursing, 49,* 474–484.

Carney, D. R., Hall, J., & LeBeau, L. (2005). Beliefs about the nonverbal expression of social power. *Journal of Nonverbal Behavior, 29,* 105–123.

Cash, T. F., Gillen, B., & Burns, S. (1977). Sexism and "beautism" in personnel consultant decision making. *Journal of Applied Psychology, 62,* 301–310.

Claes, L., Vandereycken, W., & Vertommen, H. (2005). Self-care versus self-harm: Piercing, tattooing, and self-injuring in eating disorders. *European Eating Disorders, 13,* 11–18.

Cottle, M. (2003). Turning boys into girls. In A. Alexander & J. Hanson (Eds.), *Taking sides: Clashing views on controversial issues in mass media and society* (7th ed., pp. 68–74). Guilford, CT: McGraw-Hill/Dushkin.

Covino, D. C. (2004). *Amending the abject body: Aesthetic makeovers in medicine and culture.* Albany: State University of New York Press.

Cunningham, M. R., Roberts, A. R., Barbee, A. P., Druen, P. B., & Wu, C. (1995). "Their ideas of beauty are, on the whole, the same as ours": Consistency and variability in the cross-cultural perception of female physical attractiveness. *Journal of Personality and Social Psychology, 68,* 261–279.

Darling-Wolf, F. (2003). Media, class and western influence in Japanese women's conceptions of attractiveness. *Feminist Media Studies, 3,* 153–172.

Darling-Wolf, F. (2004). Sites of attractiveness: Japanese women and westernized representations of feminine beauty. *Critical Studies in Media Communication, 21,* 325–345.

Davis, K. (1995). *Reshaping the female body: The dilemma of cosmetic surgery.* New York: Routledge.

Davis, K. (2003). *Dubious equalities and embodied differences: Cultural studies on cosmetic surgery.* Lanham, MD: Rowman and Littlefield.

Davis, K. L. (2005). *A girl like me.* Documentary film.

Deery, J. (2004). Trading faces: The makeover show as primetime "infomercial." *Feminist Media Studies, 4*, 211–214.

Denness, B. (2005). Tattooing and piercing: Initiation rites and masculine development. *British Journal of Psychotherapy, 22*, 21–36.

Dimitrius, J., & Mazzarella, M. (1999). *Reading people: How to understand people and predict their behavior— anytime, anyplace.* New York: Ballantine.

Dion, K., Berscheid, E., & Walster, E. (1972). What is beautiful is good. *Journal of Personality and Social Psychology, 24*, 285–290.

Dipboye, R. L., Arvey, R. D., & Terpstra, D. E. (1977). Sex and physical attractiveness of raters and applicants as determinants of résumé evaluation. *Journal of Applied Psychology, 62*, 288–294.

Dohnt, H., & Tiggemann, M. (2006). The contribution of peer and media influences to the development of body satisfaction and self-esteem in young girls: A prospective study. *Developmental Psychology, 42*, 929–936.

Duke, L. N. (2003, August 10). Boomers attempt to cling to young looks. *Corpus Christi Caller Times*, p. A14.

Edwards, C., Edwards, A., Qing, Q., & Wahl, S. T. (2007). The influence of computer-mediated word-of-mouth communication on student perceptions of instructors and attitudes toward learning course content. *Communication Education, 56*, 255–277.

Egolf, D. B., & Corder, L. E. (1991). Height differences of low and high job status female and male corporate employees. *Sex Roles, 24*, 365–373.

Elman, D. (1977). Physical characteristics and the perception of masculine traits. *Journal of Social Psychology, 103*, 157–158.

Ensler, E. (2006, June). Belly dancing. *O: The Oprah Winfrey Magazine*, 216–218.

Feingold, A., & Mazzella, R. (1998). Gender differences in body image are increasing. *Psychological Science, 9*, 190–195.

Flocker, M. (2003). *The metrosexual guide to style: A handbook for the modern man.* Cambridge, MA: DeCapo.

Flynn, G. (2004, April 23). Self-hate crime: Misogynistic makeover show *The Swan* is one ugly duckling. *Entertainment Weekly*, 69.

Forbes, G. B. (2001). College students with tattoos and piercings: Motives, family experiences, personality factors, and perceptions by others. *Psychological Reports, 89*, 774–786.

Forbes, G. B., Adams-Curtis, L. E., Rade, B., & Jaberg, P. (2001). Body dissatisfaction in women and men: The role of gender-typing and self-esteem. *Sex Roles, 44*, 461–484.

Frasure, S. (2003). The agent within: Agency repertoires in medical discourse on cosmetic surgery. *Australian Feminist Studies, 40*, 27–44.

Furlow, F. B. (1999). The smell of love. In L. K. Guerrero, J. DeVito, & M. L. Hecht (Eds.), *The nonverbal communication reader: Classic and contemporary readings* (2nd ed., pp. 118–125). Prospect Heights, IL: Waveland.

Furnham, A., McClelland, A., & Omer, L. (2003). A cross-cultural comparison of ratings of perceived fecundity and sexual attractiveness as a function of body weight and waist-to-hip ratio. *Psychology, Health and Medicine, 8*, 219–230.

Gallagher, M. (2004). *Queer Eye* for the heterosexual couple. *Feminist Media Studies, 4*, 223–226.

Garcia Hunter, O. (2004, July 18). Goodbye, grunge… and freedom of expression, according to CCISD students facing new dress code. *Corpus Christi Caller Times*, pp. A1, A8.

Gloss, M. (2005, June 8). Body art. *Telegraph Herald— Dubuque*, p. A10.

Guerrero, L. K., & Floyd, K. (2006). *Nonverbal communication in close relationships.* Mahwah, NJ: Erlbaum.

Haines, J., & Neumark-Sztainer, D. (2006). Prevention of obesity and eating disorders: A consideration of shared risk factors. *Health Education Research, 21*, 770–782.

Hamermesh, D. S., & Biddle, J. E. (1994). Beauty and the labor market. *American Economic Review, 84*, 1174–1194.

Hardy, L. (2006). Fighting student obesity in school. *The Education Digest, 7*, 25–26.

Hargreaves, D., & Tiggemann, M. (2002). The effect of television commercials on mood and body dissatisfaction: The role of the appearance-schema activation. *Journal of Social and Clinical Psychology, 21*, 287–308.

Harris, M. B., Harris, R. J., & Brochner, S. (1982). Fat, four-eyed and female: Stereotypes of obesity, glasses, and gender. *Journal of Applied Psychology, 6*, 503–516.

Harrison, K., Taylor, L., & Marske, A. (2006). Women's and men's eating behavior following exposure to ideal-body images and text. *Communication Research, 33*, 507–529.

Hatfield, E., & Sprecher, S. (1986). *Mirror, mirror…: The importance of looks in everyday life.* Albany: State University of New York Press.

Heyes, C. J. (2007). Cosmetic surgery and the televisual makeover: A Foucauldian feminist reading. *Feminist Media Studies, 7*, 17–32.

Hicinbothem, J., Gonsalves, S., & Lester, D. (2006). Body modification and suicidal behavior. *Death Studies, 30*, 351–363.

Hinsz, V. B. (1989). Facial resemblance in engaged and married couples. *Journal of Social and Personal Relationships, 6,* 223–229.

Huxley, C., & Grogan, S. (2005). Tattooing, piercing, healthy behaviours and health value. *Journal of Health Psychology, 10,* 831–841.

Jaffe, E. (2006). Deadly disorder. *Science News, 170,* 52–53.

Jeffreys, S. (2005). *Beauty and misogyny: Harmful cultural practices in the west.* London: Psychology Press.

Kaiser, S. B. (1997). Women's appearance and clothing within organizations. Reprinted in L. K. Guerrero & M. L. Hecht (Eds.), *The nonverbal communication reader: Classic and contemporary readings* (2008, 3rd ed., pp. 74–81). Prospect Heights, IL: Waveland.

Kalick, S. M., & Hamilton, T. E. (1986). The matching hypothesis reexamined. *Journal of Personal and Social Psychology, 51,* 673–682.

Kalick, S. M., Zebrowitz, L. A., Langlois, J. H., & Johnson, R. M. (1998). Does human facial attractiveness honestly advertise health? Longitudinal data on an evolutionary question. *Psychological Science, 9,* 8–13.

Keenan, K. (1996). Skin tones and physical features of blacks in magazine advertisements. *Journalism and Mass Communication Quarterly, 73,* 905–912.

Knapp, M. L., & Hall, J. A. (2006). *Nonverbal communication in human interaction* (6th ed.). Belmont, CA: Thomson/Wadsworth.

Koch, P., Mansfield, P., Thurau, D., & Carey, M. (2005). "Feeling frumpy": The relationships between body image and sexual response changes in midlife women. *Journal of Sex Research, 42,* 215–223.

Koch, J. R., Roberts, A. E., Armstrong, M. L., & Owen, D. C. (2004). Religious belief and practice in attitudes toward individuals with body piercing. *Psychological Reports, 95,* 583–586.

Korda, M. (1975). *Power: How to get it, how to use it.* New York: Ballentine.

Larkin, J. C., & Pines, H. A. (1979). No fat persons need apply: Experimental studies of the overweight and hiring preference. *Sociology of Work and Occupations, 6,* 312–327.

Lawrence, S. G., & Watson, M. (1991). Getting others to help: The effectiveness of professional uniforms in charitable fund-raising. *Journal of Applied Communication Research, 19,* 170–185.

Lechelt, E. (1975). Occupational affiliation and ratings of physical height and personal esteem. *Psychological Reports, 36,* 943–946.

Lefkowitz, M., Blake, R., & Mouton, J. (1955). Status factors in pedestrian violation of traffic signals. *Journal of Abnormal and Social Psychology, 51,* 704–706.

Long, D. A., Mueller, J. C., Wyers, R., & Khong, V. (1996). Effects of gender and dress on helping behavior. *Psychological Reports, 78,* 987–994.

Marlowe, C. M., Schneider, S. L., & Nelson, C. E. (1998). Gender and attractiveness biases in hiring decisions: Are more experienced managers less biased? *Journal of Applied Psychology, 81,* 11–21.

Martin, M. M., & Gentry, J. W. (2005). Stuck in the model trap. In A. Alexander & J. Hanson (Eds.), *Taking sides: Clashing views on controversial issues in mass media and society* (8th ed., pp. 52–61). Dubuque, IA: McGraw-Hill/Dushkin.

Masip, J., Garrido, E., & Herrero, C. (2004). Facial appearance and impressions of credibility: The effects of facial babyishness and age on person perception. *International Journal of Psychology, 39,* 276–289.

Mason, A., & Meyers, M. (2001). Living with Martha Stewart Media: Chosen domesticity in the experience of fans. *Journal of Communication, 51,* 801–823.

McPherson, W. (1997). "Dressing down" in the business communication curriculum. *Business Communication Quarterly, 60,* 134–146.

Montell, G. (2003, October 15). Do good looks equal good evaluations? *The Chronicle of Higher Education: Career Network.* Available: http://chronicle.com

Montepare, J. (2005). Marking the past and forging the future in nonverbal research: The importance of forming relationships. *Journal of Nonverbal Behavior, 29,* 137–139.

Moorti, S., & Ross, K. (2004). Reality television: Fairy tale or nightmare? *Feminist Media Studies, 4,* 203–205.

MSNBC. (2006, June 7). Television broadcast.

Mulkens, S., & Jansen, A. (2006). Changing appearances: Cosmetic surgery and Body Dysmorphic Disorder. *Netherlands Journal of Psychology, 62,* 34–41.

Mullen, J. (2003, July 25). Hot sheet. *Entertainment Weekly,* 12.

Mulvey, K. (2006, January 23). Love and the laws of attraction: Express yourself. *The Express,* p. 31.

Myers, P. N., Jr., & Biocca, R. A. (1992). The elastic body image: The effect of television advertising and programming on body image distortions in young women. *Journal of Communication, 42,* 108–133.

Nai-kuo, H. (2005, August 28). Physical appearance an important factor in job hunting: Survey. *Central News Agency* (Taiwan).

Noller, P. (2005). Attachment insecurity as a filter in the decoding and encoding of nonverbal behavior in close relationships. *Journal of Nonverbal Behavior, 29,* 171–176.

Oliver, E. J. (2006). *Fat politics: The real story behind America's obesity epidemic.* New York: Oxford University Press.

Pante, R. (2006). Image builds business. *Today's Chiropractic, 34,* 73–75.

Pearson, K., & Reich, N. (2004). *Queer Eye* fairy tale: Changing the world one manicure at a time. *Feminist Media Studies, 4,* 229–231.

Pitts, V. (2003). *In the flesh: The cultural politics of body modification.* New York: Palgrave Macmillan.

Portnoy, E. J. (1993). The impact of body type on perceptions of attractiveness by older individuals. *Communication Reports, 6,* 101–108.

Preti, A., Pinna, C., Nocco, S., & Mulliri, E. (2006). Body of evidence: Tattoos, body piercing, and eating disorder symptoms among adolescents. *Journal of Psychosomatic Research, 61,* 561–566.

Rainey, A. (2006). Tress for success. *The Chronicle of Higher Education, 52,* p. A6.

Richmond, V. P., McCroskey, J. C., & Hickson, M. L. III. (2008). *Nonverbal behavior in interpersonal relations* (6th ed.). Boston: Allyn & Bacon.

Riley, J. (1979). The olfactory factor in nonverbal communication. *Communication, 8,* 159–168.

Riley, S. C. E., & Cahill, S. (2005). Managing meaning and belonging: Young women's negotiation of authenticity in body art. *Journal of Youth Studies, 8,* 261–279.

Roach, K. D. (1997). Effects of graduate teaching assistant attire on student learning, misbehaviors, and ratings of instruction. *Communication Quarterly, 45,* 125–141.

Roberti, J. W., & Storch, E. A. (2005). Psychosocial adjustment of college students with tattoos and piercings. *Journal of College Counseling, 8,* 14–19.

Roberts, J. V., & Herman, C. P. (1986). The psychology of height: An empirical review. In C. P. Herman, M. P. Zanna, & E. T. Higgins (Eds.), *Physical appearance, stigma, and social behavior: The Ontario symposium* (Vol. 3). Hillsdale, NJ: Erlbaum.

Rocca, K., & McCroskey, J. (2001). The interrelationship of student ratings of instructors' immediacy, verbal aggressiveness, homophily, and interpersonal attraction. *Communication Education, 48,* 308–316.

Rosenberg Javors, I. (2004). Reality TV: Escape from reality? *Annals of the American Psychotherapy Association, 7,* 35.

Rosenfeld, L., & Plax, T. (1977). Clothing as communication. *Journal of Communication, 27,* 24.

Santos-Garza, V. (2004, August 1). School code is dressed in stress. *Corpus Christi Caller Times,* p. C1.

Schiavo, R. S., Sherlock, B., & Wicklund, G. (1974). *Psychological Reports, 34,* 245–246.

Schmid Mast, M., & Hall, J. A. (2004). Who is the boss and who is not? Accuracy judging status. *Journal of Nonverbal Behavior, 28,* 145–165.

Selvin, M. (2007, July 15). More workers have something up their sleeve. *Corpus Christi Caller Times,* p. 3D.

Selwyn Delinsky, S. (2005). Cosmetic surgery: A common and accepted form of self-improvement? *Journal of Applied Social Psychology, 35,* 2012–2028.

Sheldon, W. H. (1940). *The varieties of human physique: An introduction to constitutional psychology.* New York: Harper & Brothers.

Sheldon, W. H. (1954). *Atlas of men.* New York: Harper.

Sheldon, W. H., Stevens, S. S., & Tucker, S. (1942). *The varieties of temperament: A psychology of constitutional differences.* New York: Harper & Row.

Singh, D. (1993). Adaptive significance of female physical attractiveness: Role of waist-to-hip ratio. *Journal of Personality and Social Psychology, 65,* 293–307.

Singh, D. (1995). Female judgment of male attractiveness and desirability for relationships: Role of waist-to-hip ratio and financial status. *Journal of Personality and Social Psychology, 69,* 1089–1101.

Singh, D. (2004). Mating strategies of young women: Role of physical attractiveness. *Journal of Sex Research, 41,* 43–54.

Stabler, B., Whitt, K., Moreault, D., D'Ercole, A., & Underwood, L. (1980). Social judgments by children of short stature. *Psychological Reports, 46,* 743–746.

Staffieri, J. R. (1972). Body build and behavioral expectancies in young females. *Developmental Psychology, 6,* 125–127.

Steese, S., Dollette, M., Phillips, W., Hossfeld, E., Matthews, G., & Taormina, G. (2006). Understanding girls' circle as an intervention on perceived social support, body image, self-efficacy, locus of control, and self-esteem. *Adolescence, 41,* 55–74.

Stim, A., Hinz, A., & Brahler, E. (2006). Prevalence of tattooing and body piercing in Germany and perception of health, mental disorders, and sensation seeking among tattooed and body pierced individuals. *Journal of Psychosomatic Research, 60,* 531–534.

Streeter, S. A., & McBurney, D. H. (2003). Waist-hip ratio and attractiveness: New evidence and a critique of a "critical test." *Evolution and Human Behavior, 24,* 88–98.

Swanger, N. (2006). Visible body modification (VBM): Evidence from human resource managers and recruiters and the effects on employment. *Journal of Hospitality Management, 25,* 154–158.

Symons, D. (1979). *The evolution of human sexuality.* New York: Oxford University Press.

Tait, S. (2007). Television and the domestication of cosmetic surgery. *Feminist Media Studies, 7,* 119–135.

Taras, H., & Potts-Datema, W. (2005). Obesity and student performance at school. *Journal of School Health, 75,* 291–295.

Tenner, E. (2004, October 1). Political timber: Glitter, froth, and measuring tape. *The Chronicle of Higher Education,* pp. B12-B13.

Thornbory, G., & White, C. (2006). How to project a professional image. *Occupational Health, 58,* 24.

Tiggemann, M., & Golder, F. (2006). Tattooing: An expression of uniqueness in the appearance domain. *Body Image, 3,* 309–315.

Venturini, B., Castelli, L., & Tomelleri, S. (2006). Not all jobs are suitable for fat people: Experimental evidence of a link between being fat and "out-of-sight" jobs. *Social Behavior and Personality, 34,* 389–398.

Vrij, A. (2001). Credibility judgments of detectives: The impact of nonverbal behavior, social skills, and physical characteristics on impression formation. *Journal of Social Psychology, 133,* 601–610.

Waggoner, C. (2004). Disciplining female sexuality in *Survivor. Feminist Media Studies, 4,* 217–220.

Walster, E. V., Aronson, E., Abrahams, D., & Rohmann, L. (1966). Importance of physical attractiveness in dating behavior. *Journal of Personality and Social Psychology, 4,* 508–516.

Weber, B. (2005). Beauty, desire, and anxiety: The economy of sameness in ABC's *Extreme Makeover. Genders [Online], 41.* Available: www.genders.org/g41

Wells, W. D., & Seigal, B. (1961). Stereotyped somatotypes. *Psychological Reports, 2,* 77–78.

White, S. E. (1995). A content analytic technique for measuring the sexiness of women's business attire in media presentations. *Communication Research Reports, 12,* 178–185.

Williamson, R. W. (2007). Personal communication, March 7.

Wilson, G., & Nias, D. (1999). Beauty can't be beat. In L. K. Guerrero, J. A. DeVito, & M. L. Hecht (Eds.), *The nonverbal communication reader: Classic and contemporary readings* (2nd ed., pp. 101–105). Prospect Heights, IL: Waveland.

Women's Sports Foundation. (2006, June). O-zone. *O: The Oprah Winfrey Magazine,* 39.

Young, M. (1999). Dressed to commune, dressed to kill: Changing police imagery in England and Wales. In K. K. Johnson & S. J. Lennon (Eds.), *Appearance and power.* New York: Oxford University Press.

Zakahi, W. R., Duran, R. L., & Adkins, M. (1994). Social anxiety, only skin deep? The relationships between ratings of physical attractiveness and social anxiety. *Communication Research Reports, 11,* 23–31.

# Kinesics

## Body Movement, Gestures, and Posture

Chapter **6**

## CHAPTER OUTLINE ■ ■ ■ ■ ■

**Do the Locomotion**

**Stand Up for Yourself**
Mehrabian's Postural Analysis
Scheflen's Dimensions of Posture
Status and Dominance

**Walk the Walk**

**Be Seated**

**More Than a Gesture**
Ekman and Friesen's Kinesic Categories
Gestures and Culture

**Applications of Kinesics Research**
Such a Flirt
Kids and Kinesics

**Understanding Kinesics: Applying the Reflexive Cycle of Nonverbal Communication Development**

**Summary**

## CHAPTER OBJECTIVES ■ ■ ■ ■ ■

After studying this chapter, you should be able to:

1. Define kinesics.
2. Explain Mehrabian's analysis of body movement related to posture, and the primary nonverbal cues related to his two dimensions.
3. Identify Scheflen's three dimensions of body movement related to posture, and the primary nonverbal cues related to each dimension.
4. Contrast the terms self-synchrony and interactive synchrony.
5. Describe the relationship between stance, height, and status/dominance.
6. Understand how factors such as culture, sex, and status contribute to the development of an individual style of walking.
7. Discuss research findings related to female and male sitting behavior.
8. Identify, define, and provide examples of each of Ekman and Friesen's five kinesic categories.
9. Overview primary cultural differences related to the use of gestures.
10. Discuss major findings related to kinesic research on flirting and the communication of attraction.
11. Discuss major findings related to kinesic research on pre-linguistic children's acquisition of gestures, a form of sign language between parents and children.

172

## CASE STUDY   Observations from a Job Interview

I *really* wanted this job I'd learned about from my campus career center; I was getting ready to graduate with my bachelor's degree and was nervous about landing that first post-college job. Fortunately, my resumé and cover letter got me in the door and landed me an interview—me and about 20 other people, who all arrived for the interview on the same day at the same time! Rather than let this unnerve me (and make me view the interviewers as poor planners), I decided to make the waiting room outside the location for the interview my own little nonverbal laboratory. (Having just completed a course in nonverbal communication, the info was fresh in my mind and my powers of observation were sharp.)

First, there was the obvious nervousness in the room—the kind you could cut with a knife. Since the number of people was greater than the seating in the room allowed, many people posted themselves up against the walls of the room. Among all the newly suited applicants, I detected a range of nervousness based on nonverbals. A few people seemed hardly fazed at all by the event and the fact that so many people seemed to be sharing the space for the same reason. Their body postures were more relaxed and they didn't exhibit the usual "nervous Nellie" behaviors, like fidgeting or shifting in their seats or positions against the wall. Others seemed as nervous as I felt, shifting continually in our chairs, adjusting our clothing and hair, and rifling through our bags for some undetermined, but very crucial, slip of paper. A couple of people managed some small talk and tense smiles, but most kept to themselves. It was as though they viewed everyone in the room as the potential enemy, destined to take their dream job.

In the next phase, a perky administrative assistant came into the waiting area and announced that the interviews would begin—in groups of three applicants at a time. You could see the confusion and disappointment in everyone's faces (including, I assumed, in mine), as shoulders sloped, positive facial expressions turned downward, and eye contact started flitting about the room as people tried to let go of their expectations about a private interview and start processing what was about to happen.

To make a long story short, the group interview experience was one I'll never forget, but not one I wish to ever repeat. While the awkwardness of having a team of interviewers question three job candidates at one time generated some interesting nonverbal cues, it was just too much. It felt really unprofessional, once I had time to reflect on what happened. In the end, I was glad I didn't get what at one time seemed like my dream job, because if that was the way the interview was handled (so casually), I didn't want to work for those people anyway.

## ■ DO THE LOCOMOTION

Have you ever heard someone's footsteps coming down a hall and thought to yourself, "Oh, good; that's Bob coming this way. I need to talk to him"? Or perhaps you thought, "Uh oh; that's Mary coming and if I'm not busy, she'll talk my head off for an hour. Better get on the phone quickly." We may not readily think of it this way, but our footsteps are a form of nonverbal communication that others can detect and interpret.

If we're having a really bad day, our footsteps can sound heavy, as though we're trudging around, carrying the weight of the world on our shoulders. Conversely, if we're having a particularly great day, we probably walk with a "spring in our step." Footsteps are but one nonverbal cue within the larger category of body motion, which is one element within the larger category of nonverbal behavior known as kinesics.

In Chapter 2, we defined **kinesics** as the study of human movement, gestures, and posture (Birdwhistell, 1960). As we explained in that chapter, technically, movements of the face and eyes are considered kinesics, but because one's face and eyes can produce a vast amount of information, we discuss them as separate codes in other chapters. Raymond Birdwhistell is considered the "father of kinesics," so we are grateful for his work that forms the foundation for how kinesics has been studied and is still studied today (1960, 1967, 1970, 1974).

Research shows that sensitivity to body movement and the ability to decode kinesics can emerge as early as four to six months of age, so we can see that an understanding of kinesics is important (Feldman & Tyler, 2006). The way our body moves; the way we gesture with our hands, arms, shoulders, and, occasionally, with our torso, legs, and feet; as well as how we walk, stand, and carry ourselves are powerful nonverbal clues about us (Argyle, 1969; Richmond, McCroskey, & Hickson, 2008). Based on genetics, physiological development, psychological characteristics, and upbringing, within the context of the culture into which we were born and in which we live, we develop certain patterns in our walk, stance or posture, and use of gestures. These patterns become easily recognizable by others who come to know us, but they can be affected by our mood and emotions (Coulson, 2004; Ekman, 1969). In this chapter, we explore kinesics for what this set of behaviors reveals about the individual, and we examine research that can help us become better interpreters of others' kinesics.

## ■ STAND UP FOR YOURSELF

Ever heard one of your parents say, "Stand up straight!"? As annoying as that command may be, our parents are right. In American culture as well as many other cultures abroad, an upright yet relaxed body posture is attached to many attractive attributes, such as confidence, positivity, and high self-esteem (Guerrero & Floyd, 2006). We make personality judgments based on something as subjective as posture, so it's worth thinking about. How aware are you of your posture? Do you tend to stand in a dominant position, or does your stance typically give off signs of weakness, timidity, or low self-esteem? How greatly is your posture affected by your mood and emotions? Did you know that, according to one researcher, the human body is capable of producing 1,000 steady postures (Hewes, 1957)?

## Mehrabian's Postural Analysis

Albert Mehrabian is a major contributor to our understanding of many nonverbal behaviors, among them kinesics. His work on posture set an early standard for nonverbal research (1968, 1969a, 1969b, 1972, 1981). Mehrabian contended that two

*What can you interpret about the interaction between these two women, just based on their stance and posture?*

primary dimensions of posture exist, through which we communicate our attitudes and feelings to others. The first dimension he termed **immediacy,** which refers to the degree of perceived physical or psychological closeness between people (Mehrabian, 1966). The more immediacy behaviors we exhibit, generally the more we like someone or are interested in what the person has to say or conveys nonverbally. Postural cues related to immediacy include forward lean of the body, symmetric positioning (meaning that arms or legs are in correspondence with the general body position), and a direct body orientation (meaning that the body is positioned towards someone, rather than in an indirect or side configuration).

    **Relaxation** is Mehrabian's second dimension, which refers to a backward lean of the body, asymmetric positioning, rocking movements, and reduced tension in the body, specifically the arms and legs. Mehrabian suggested that a keen observer of nonverbal behavior could tell how much interest, liking, and activation occurred among people just by watching their posture, positioning, and body movement. In a related study, nonverbal researchers Afifi and Johnson (1999) found that a normal or relaxed posture was perceived to be more affectionate than a stiff, formal posture.

## Scheflen's Dimensions of Posture

Nonverbal scholar Albert Scheflen has contributed significantly to our understanding of the role of posture and other kinesic behaviors in human interaction (Scheflen, 1974; Scheflen & Scheflen, 1972). This line of research identified three dimensions of posture: (1) inclusiveness/noninclusiveness; (2) face-to-face/parallel; and (3) congruence/incongruence. These are dimensions, which means they represent a range of behavior or postural tendencies. Let's explore each of these for what clues these nonverbal behaviors provide.

**Inclusiveness/noninclusiveness** refers to the degree to which a person's body posture includes or excludes one person, relative to other people. Imagine you're at a party, observing a man and woman sitting on a couch. If the woman exhibits highly inclusive nonverbal cues, she will arrange her body and posture in such a way as to focus her attention on the man, to the exclusion of other people on the couch or in near vicinity. Such a behavior indicates a high degree of liking and interest. Conversely, if she is not interested in or dislikes the man, she will arrange her posture in such a way as to exclude the man, but not the other people on the couch or in the vicinity. Maybe you've seen someone carry on a conversation with people on a couch or in a crowded booth or table at a restaurant, skipping the person right next to them, and talking over him or her to get to the people at the other end of the couch or table. Talk about sending a definite negative signal!

*The woman's body position indicates her interest in the man.*

*Both people's body position indicates interest.*

The second dimension is termed **face-to-face/parallel,** and refers to the degree to which two people face each other directly versus at each other's sides, with their shoulders in a line (a parallel position). Back to the man and woman sitting on the couch: If they like each other, they're more likely to assume a face-to-face position, turning their body postures inward toward each other, even though a couch is more conducive to side-by-side seating than face-to-face. If the two people are unfriendly or dislike each other, they're more likely to assume a parallel posture than a face-to-face one. (They probably wouldn't be on the couch together at all, but you get the point.) Face-to-face body postures tend to indicate mutual involvement and some level of intimacy. Sometimes the nature of a task is more often the cause for body postures, rather than liking or showing interest; for example, reading or watching television involves more parallel positioning than face-to-face. In such instances, posture may not tell us much about the relationship between the people we're observing.

Scheflen's third dimension is termed **congruence/incongruence,** which refers to the degree of mirroring or imitation of the behavior between two or more people. What if, when the woman on the couch arranged her body posture directly toward the man, the man didn't arrange his posture to match hers? If you were observing such an interaction, you might conclude that the woman was interested and attracted, but the man wasn't. In a high congruence situation, one person's behavior is imitated by another; in a

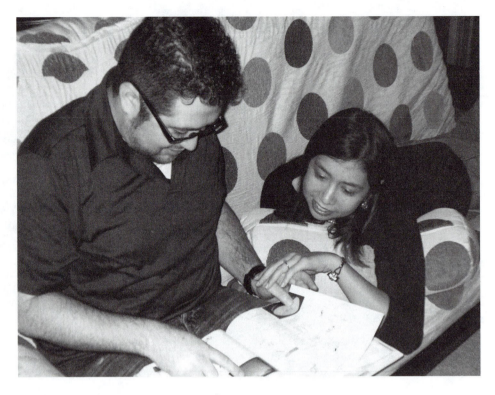

*Are these positions congruent or incongruent?*

low congruence (or incongruent) situation, behaviors will not be mirrored. In some such situations, one person may assume a position completely opposite another's, revealing incongruence (as well as little attraction and little liking). Scheflen reminds us that the wise interpreter of nonverbal communication will observe a range of behaviors over time to get the fullest picture of a situation possible. We can make interpretive mistakes (and social blunders) if we jump too quickly to a conclusion about a situation or a person's behavior based on nonverbal cues in isolation and out of context.

Scholars have described Scheflen's third dimension in terms of **synchrony** (Condon, 1976; Condon & Ogston, 1966; Kendon, 1987; Knapp & Hall, 2006). Synchrony can emerge in two forms: First, **self-synchrony** refers to a person's coordination of speech and body movement or how coordinated a person is in her or his own behavior, meaning that verbal communication and nonverbal movements and expressions work together in synch, to produce a fluid outcome. Perhaps you've seen someone who "can't walk and chew gum"? The problem might be a case of poor self-synchrony. Communication theorists Janet Beavin Bavelas and Nicole Chovil (2006) study how a person's speech, facial expressions, and body movement, such as gesturing, coordinate to produce meaning in face-to-face interactions. A second form of synchrony is **interactive synchrony**, which focuses on the coordination of speech and body movement between at least two speakers. Interactive synchrony has also been termed "the chameleon effect," "mimicry" (Lakin, Jefferis, Cheng, & Chartrand, 2003, p. 145), "social rhythm" (Knapp &

Hall, 2006, p. 246), and "postural echo" (Do you know?, 2006, p. 40). This type of synchrony is a particularly fascinating phenomenon for the keen eye to observe when it appears people are in rhythm, mirroring one another's movements unintentionally. One application of interactive synchrony can be found in the food service industry, where wait staff are often trained to lean down toward or squat by diners' tables, in an effort to put themselves more at the same level as their customers. A study conducted by the Center for Hospitality Research at Cornell University's School of Hotel Administration found that wait staff who introduced themselves to diners while squatting down by the table or booth increased their tips by 3 percent, on average (Rush, 2006).

## Status and Dominance

The relationship between posture, dominance, and status has also been the subject of much research (Aguinis & Henle, 2001; Aguinis, Simonsen, & Pierce, 1998; Aries, Gold, & Weigel, 1983; Burgoon, 1991; Carney, Hall, & Lebeau, 2005; Cashdan, 1998; Ellyson & Dovidio, 1985; Henley, 2001; Schmid Mast & Hall, 2004; Tiedens & Fragale, 2003). Social psychologist David Johnson (2006) contends, "individuals with high status and power may engage in a dominance display by puffing themselves up to full size, stiffening their backs, tightening their brows, thrusting their chins forward, and leaning toward the challenger in an attempt to convince others of their power" (p. 199). A common stance often connected to dominance is a spread-legged stance with the hands on the hips, called the **arms akimbo** position (Andersen, 2004; Armstrong & Wagner, 2003). Hands on the hips may indicate frustration rather than dominance. A variation of this position involves the arms crossed across the chest, which is a comfortable position for many people, but which can signal irritation and inapproachability. Interestingly enough, the high-status stance we describe tends to be more of a male position than a female one, because a spread-legged stance on a woman would send a different signal than when enacted by a man. However, as communication scholar Peter Andersen (2004) points out, reversing the hand position such that the thumbs point forward and the fingers go backward on the hips, along with a bit of a frontal pelvic tilt, changes the message significantly. This simple change in placement of the hands is more indicative of a woman's position than a man's, at least in American culture (and we can *never* forget the effects of culture on all nonverbal behavior), and it tends to soften the sense of dominance in the stance.

However, dominant nonverbal behaviors aren't always correlated with high status behaviors. Consider the job interview situation, in which an interviewer tends to be much more relaxed than a job applicant who puts herself or himself on the line to get hired. Internationally recognized communication consultants Audrey Nelson and Susan Golant (2004) explain: "The more restricted, tight, pulled in, and tense, the less power we have. This is evident during a job interview. The interviewer is in a power position, relaxed and at ease; the interviewee looks like a private in the military, sitting in a straight-backed, full-attention position" (p. 171).

One position that illustrates a relaxed yet dominant style and that conveys self-confidence is called "the cape and crown," which simply means lifting up the arms and placing the hands on the back of one's head, sometimes in conjunction with a hip tilt. People can enact this kinesic behavior in a seated position, perhaps leaning back in a chair or with their feet elevated. The position is considered more of a male behavior than female, however it is quite common among female celebrities like Beyoncé, because it conveys an "I'm in charge; I'm royalty" message (Soll, 2007, p. 18). It can also accentuate a person's head, making the person look larger or more dominant than other people, with the sharp angles of the elbows as cues of aggression.

We discussed height in Chapter 5 on physical appearance. As we suggested there, since height is associated with confidence, extroversion, and high status in American culture, it's important to make the most of our height by standing as erectly as possible, without looking like we're in a body cast (Egolf & Corder, 1991; Elman, 1977; Lechelt, 1975; Roberts & Herman, 1986; Stabler, Whitt, Moreault, D'Ercole, & Underwood, 1980). This is particularly important when we're in a public situation in which an audience (live or mediated) is looking at us and judging our credibility (Andersen, 2004; Beebe, Beebe, & Ivy, 2007). When making a presentation, remember the positive impressions people form related to good posture and animation. An effective presenter will evidence good posture, while at the same time incorporating body movement (animation) into her or his presentation. Standing completely still can make a speaker look rigid, boring, and detached from the situation at hand (Beebe & Beebe, 2006; Fatt, 2000; Gallo, 2005). While a minimal level of forward body lean conveys confidence and interest, a backward lean may indicate nervousness or a fear of the audience (Burgoon, Birk, & Pfau, 1990). Try to avoid leaning too much on a podium or resting your body on a table top (if seated while speaking) unless such a move is done minimally to create drama or for some other intended effect. Most microphones on stands are adjustable, plus mics are sophisticated enough now to pick up a voice without the speaker having to stoop down to speak closely to be heard.

## REMEMBER 6.1

| **Kinesics:** | study of human movement, gestures, and posture. |
|---|---|
| **Immediacy:** | degree of perceived physical or psychological closeness between people. |
| **Relaxation:** | backward lean of the body, asymmetric positioning, rocking movements, and reduced tension in the body. |
| **Inclusiveness/ Noninclusiveness:** | degree to which a person's body posture includes or excludes one person, relative to other people. |
| **Face-to-Face/ Parallel:** | degree to which two people face each other directly versus at each other's sides, with their shoulders in a line (a parallel position). |
| **Congruence/ Incongruence:** | degree of mirroring or imitation of the behavior between two or more people. |
| **Self-Synchrony:** | coordination of speech and body movement enacted by one person. |
| **Interactive Synchrony:** | coordination of speech and body movement between at least two speakers. |
| **Arms Akimbo:** | hands on the hips position, often indicating dominance or frustration. |

# WALK THE WALK

What celebrities or historical figures have memorable walks? The first person to come to your authors' minds—given that we're older than the traditionally aged college student—is John Wayne. Perhaps John Wayne was before your time—*way* before for some of you—but you've no doubt seen at least a clip from one of his famous movies. Or perhaps you remember the actor Nathan Lane trying to mimic Wayne's walk in the movie *The Birdcage*? Marilyn Monroe's walk, with her famous sashay of the hips, is certainly memorable. How we walk is one of the most personal and long-lasting elements within our nonverbal repertoire, but it's often one of the most overlooked.

While adults don't typically retain memories from our infancies, we know from research and observation that the vast majority of babies crawl before they learn to walk, so let's think about crawling for a moment. As Andersen (2004) explains, crawling is a "milestone in a baby's development," in that it's the "baby's new window to the world" (p. 92). This first level of body movement exploration is critical. Andersen recommends that parents get down on all fours and crawl with their babies as a way to create rapport and see the world from their baby's angle.

Before most children begin to walk, they begin pulling up on objects. In other words, they "cruise," which Andersen describes as the behavior of standing while holding on to furniture or other structures (or sometimes a parent's pants leg), as a means of steadying themselves in an upright position (p. 92). Andersen suggests that the action of cruising marks a transition from infancy into childhood. And we've all probably witnessed—in person or through watching a television show or movie—those all important first steps a child takes. The wobbly steps and lurching arms, often resembling Frankenstein, are comical and thrilling to watch, as well as highly significant in a child's development. Parents' reactions to the inevitable tumbles children take during this phase are critical, because an overly emotional reaction can frighten a child and make her or him fearful to try to walk again. A more calm, "you're okay" response to a fall is actually helpful, in that it tempers the child's reactions and lessens the fear of trying again. It also helps keep the parents more calm while the child is learning to control his or her body movements. The name "toddler" is derived from the toddling from side to side effect that most children exhibit as they learn to walk. Even in these very early and basic body movements, we see the importance of learning to accurately read nonverbal cues and respond appropriately.

Less is known or written about how we develop into our adult styles of walking, but consider the idiosyncracy of the walk—meaning that each person has his or her own unique walk. Some categories emerge, because the behaviors are more obvious and prevalent, like someone who walks with a slumped shoulder/head down/low-to-the-ground method of moving the feet, almost in a shuffling manner. (We've probably all seen these people on campus. Maybe you *are* one of these people.) Some people bounce when they walk, while others seem to glide like their feet don't actually hit the ground, as though some other rule of gravity applies to them. Still others sort of schlep from side to side when they walk, creating an inefficient but easily recognizable gait. Some people move their arms a lot when they walk; others look almost as though their upper body and arms aren't attached to their lower body.

■ ■ ■ ■ ■

## ?

### *What Would You Do?*

Your friend has *terrible* posture. He doesn't actually *walk*; he sort of shuffles. Most of the time his head is down, his shoulders slump to the ground such that you marvel at how he keeps his book bag up on them. His hair is always in his eyes, blocking people's view of his face, and his clothes are beyond baggy, blocking people's view of his body. In general, nonverbally he's sort of shut off. When he gives presentations in classes, well, they're pretty pathetic. All of his nonverbal cues scream, "Please get me down from this podium and hey world, leave me alone." And yet, you—his good friend—know that he's a really great guy and could be a great friend to lots of people. He's just very unaware of the vibe his nonverbal behaviors communicate to other people. And he's not one of those "I don't care what other people think" kind of people either; he honestly struggles with how hard it is for him to make friends and get dates. Most people simply think he's a freak.

*What would you do* in this situation? Are you your brother's keeper, meaning do you take it on yourself to help your friend become more aware of, and possibly change, his nonverbal communication? We're not suggesting that you pull a *My Fair Lady* effect here, in which you accomplish a makeover just to make yourself feel good for "saving" some poor schmoe. But what is the appropriate response when you see your friend puzzled or possibly hurting over his own isolation? Is it your place to try to help your friend onto a path of heightened nonverbal awareness, given your belief that this kind of self-awareness is a positive thing?

As we alluded to earlier, our culture, as well as our genetic profile, physiological features, upbringing, and psychological characteristics all shape the way we walk and stand. It can be downright eerie if we come to realize that we walk or stand just like our mother or father. One of your co-authors had a humorous revelation in her 30s: In a conversation in which she was standing sort of in a circle with her grandmother, mother, and sister, she looked down and realized that all four women were standing exactly alike—one foot toward the front, the other pointed out to the right side. Anyone observing this interaction might have thought some grand choreographer was teaching the women synchronized movement.

Of course, a person's culture has an effect on walking behavior. An upright carriage, with the head held high, shoulders squared, and a wide stride and a quick pace, conveys confidence and positivity in American culture, but in some Asian cultures this style of walking may convey arrogance, a lack of politeness and respect for others, and lower status. As one example of research on this topic, Montepare and Zebrowitz (1993) observed the gait of persons in the United States and Korea. In their research, older Americans walking with a slow gait were not perceived as being dominant, but older Koreans walking with the same slow gait were perceived as being dominant in Korean culture. The researchers attributed the difference, in part, to the higher level of esteem placed on elders in Korean culture, compared to American culture.

Some generalizations have been made about the sexes and their ways of walking, such that some believe a person's sex can be determined by simply observing their walk. Andersen (2004) suggests that men's bodies are somewhat motionless while walking, with the hips and torso staying frontward, the feet moving about one foot apart in stride, and the arms swinging significantly. In contrast, Andersen explains that "women add motion to their locomotion," in that they have more swing or side-to-side motion in their walks (p. 92). Women's hips move more than men's, mostly due to the fact that women tend to put one foot in front of the other when walking, which engages the hip action. Nonverbal scholars Hickson, Stacks, and Moore (2004) describe sex differences in walking as follows:

> Research of male and female postures has shown that American women give off gender signals by bringing their legs together, keeping their upper arms close to their trunks, carrying their pelvises rolled forward, and presenting their entire bodies as moving wholes. American men, however, tend to keep their legs rolled slightly back, and present their trunks as moving independently from the arms and hips. (p. 233)

The pace at which we walk is also a fascinating nonverbal aspect to observe and study, because some people believe pace correlates with power and status. However, the verdict is out on this phenomenon; consider your own experience. Do higher status or "power" people tend to walk faster, as though they've got many places to be, lots to do, tons of people wanting to meet them, and they're cutting every meeting too closely? Or do higher status people tend to move more leisurely because, simply put, they *can*. Their time is more their own, so they can control the pace of their movement because much in their lives is in their control. If you watch a busy office complex, you will likely see the lower employees on the totem pole scurrying around to retrieve things for their bosses, while their bosses wouldn't be caught dead "scurrying." Instead, they may stroll, causing associates around them—particularly those of lower status—to slow down to match their pace. With this behavior, as well as many others we describe in this book, the higher status person calls the nonverbal shots; lower status people are expected to adapt their nonverbals to parallel or remain subordinate to the higher status person's.

Research has also examined nonverbal behaviors associated with victimization (Gunns, Johnston, & Hudson, 2002; Messakappa & Andersen, 1996; Murzynski & Degelman, 1996). Social scientific experiments as well as interviews with imprisoned criminals reveal that a weak walking style sends a cue of vulnerability to a would-be mugger or attacker. A weak walking style involves a lack of arm swing, short steps, and a slow pace, while a strong walking style involves longer strides, swinging arms, and a quickened pace. The latter style conveys confidence to victimizers, and this line of research has found that confident walkers rank near the bottom of potential targets of crime.

At times, other people may cause us to alter our normal gait, and our ability to adapt to others' nonverbal behaviors becomes critical. For example, you see a friend on campus and really need to give her or him a message, but the person is dashing off to class. You very likely will match the pace of that person's movement so as to be able to deliver your message. If you don't match the pace and you slow your friend down, the response may be negative and you may come away with an odd feeling about the exchange. However, at times we may feel the need to slow someone down, to get their full attention, and to accomplish our goals—for both our sake and theirs.

# ■ BE SEATED

We know that you may be overwhelmed at this point with the level of detail—the sheer number of nonverbal cues the body is capable of communicating. But try to stave off that sense of being overwhelmed to simply view what we're studying as complex human behavior that is actually quite amazing. We're not expected to catch every clue every time someone nonverbally expresses themselves, but a realistic goal—after taking this class and reading this book—is to sharpen our powers of observation, as well as expand our awareness of how we come across to others, so that we put our enhanced understanding of nonverbal communication to the fullest use possible.

We include sitting behavior in this chapter because people tend to do a lot of sitting (some more than others). You can tell a lot about people and their relationships simply by observing where and how they sit. Sex differences in sitting behavior are easily detectable in American culture. Typically, men assume open sitting positions, meaning that the legs are often extended and spread apart rather than close together. A man is more likely to cross his leg over his knee in a 90-degree angle to the floor, while a woman is more likely to cross her legs at the knee with the crossed leg hanging down, or to cross her legs at the ankles (Andersen, 2004; Hall, 1979, 1984). (Some of this sex difference in sitting tendencies may relate back to advice many a girl got

*These students exhibit the typical male and female sitting behavior.*

from her mother—remember the lesson about keeping your legs together? We don't mean to be crude, but this particular piece of advice is still prevalent today.) We've also seen some of our female students get into the most pretzeled positions in their seats in classrooms, accomplished only through repeated Pilates classes!

Perhaps you're familiar with Young Life, a Christian ministry prevalent in American high schools. Many Young Life meetings involve sitting on the floor, since they often take place in halls or open spaces without chairs. Plus, chairs can make a setting too formal—something Young Life tries to avoid. If you have been in such a setting or find yourself on the floor with a large group of people, note the sex differences in sitting behavior. Oftentimes, men will stretch themselves out to the point they may actually lie on the floor, perhaps with their heads resting on their elbows, whereas women tend to sit straight up on the floor, often cross-legged or on their knees so that they take up less space and look "ladylike."

Some nonverbal scholars believe that sitting tendencies have more to do with power and status than a person's sex, given that higher status persons are afforded more personal space and can more easily spread themselves out in relaxed body positions than lower status persons (Mehrabian, 1981; Mehrabian & Friar, 1969). But the findings are parallel, since men still tend to hold more power (in terms of economic wealth, ownership of property, and assumption of higher positions of leadership and authority) in American society.

 Watch how several men will sit on a couch together, particularly if there's not enough room for each man to cross his leg in the 90-degree fashioned we described. Typically one or more of the men will adapt, so that no one's feet or legs touch the others'. Attribute it to homophobia in American culture or a simple adjustment made because of physical size, but the phenomenon can be readily detected from simple observation.

## ■ MORE THAN A GESTURE

In Chapter 1 we defined nonverbal communication and mentioned one exception to the definition, in particular reference to hand and arm gestures. Here's a quick review: When communicating through sign language with people who are deaf, the signs look like nonverbal gestures to people who can hear. But to people who are deaf (and those hearing people who know sign language) these gestures, and the accompanying body posture and facial and eye expressions, are actually language. They are either individual words or phrases that have direct meanings for receivers of such signs. Sign language is verbal communication in exchanges with persons who are deaf. For the most part in this section of the chapter, we examine gestures—movements of the head, arms, hands, fingers, torso, legs, and feet—as nonverbal expressions.

### Ekman and Friesen's Kinesic Categories

Various scholars and researchers have proposed models for analyzing and coding kinesics, just as exist for spoken or written language (Birdwhistell, 1970; Leathers & Eaves, 2008). In one of their most comprehensive contributions to nonverbal research, Ekman and Friesen (1969) classified movement and gestures according to how they function in human interaction. Let's explore the five categories of kinesics provided by Ekman and Friesen: emblems, illustrators, affect displays, regulators, and adaptors.

**Emblems.**    Nonverbal cues that have specific, widely understood meanings in a given culture and that may actually substitute for a word or phrase are called **emblems.** Just as the American flag is an emblem that is a symbol of the United States, some gestures emerge to become easily translatable within societies. What are some famous nonverbal gestures that have become emblematic over time? One such gesture is the index and middle finger up in the air, palm facing out, which could be interpreted as the number two, as a symbol for peace, or for "V" as in victory (famous with cheerleaders and politicians). In the 1970s the irony was obvious, in that President Nixon vigorously used the "V for Victory" sign—even as he boarded a helicopter on the White House lawn after he resigned the presidency—while at the same time Viet Nam war protestors used the sign as an emblem of peace.

As we said, emblems have widely understood meaning, but note that we didn't say *universally* understood meanings. Only a few gestures have been found to have virtually the same meaning for members of any culture, anywhere, across time (Axtell, 1998; Matsumoto & Yoo, 2005). Three gestures that have the widest generalizability cross-culturally include the pointing gesture, in which one uses the index finger of a hand in a motion to draw attention in a certain direction. Another is a "come here" gesture and the third is its opposite, the "stay away" gesture. The signal of "come here" involves moving one or both palms toward the body, with the back of the hands facing outward, to signal an approach is wanted or acceptable. The converse or "stay away" gesture involves the palms of the hands facing out, with the backs of the hands toward the body. We have no way of knowing that members of every culture throughout history have used these basic gestures and interpreted them in the same way, but they are presumed to be the closest to universal as researchers have uncovered.

As an example of a gesture that can become emblematic for a co-culture (a subgroup within a larger culture), consider the many hand and arm signals colleges and universities develop in conjunction with their mascots and athletic teams. One of the most well known is the "Hook 'em Horns" gesture at the University of Texas. The gesture is made by extending the arm upward, turning the palm outward, and extending only the index and little finger upward, as though in the shape of longhorns. Occasionally this sign is confused with a similar one in American Sign Language, which adds an extension of the thumb outward to mean "I love you." Take away the index finger from this configuration and we have a sign many surfers and rockers use. People who signal pilots on aircraft carriers, referees and umpires at sporting events, choral and orchestral conductors, and traffic cops are examples of individuals who must rely on carefully negotiated and learned sets of emblematic gestures to accomplish their duties.

It's wise to use emblematic gestures with caution because, as we've warned with regard to other forms of kinesics, emblems emerge or are negotiated within cultures. Without cultural sensitivity, our nonverbal behaviors may offend whole groups of people unintentionally. Something as seemingly universal as a pointing gesture can be used in a culturally specific way to mean something different than we expect. As an example, during his second inaugural parade, President George W. Bush displayed the "Hook 'em Horns" gesture to salute the University of Texas marching band as they passed by his

*Pointing gesture*

*"Come here" gesture*

*"Stay away" gesture*

*"Hook 'em horns" gesture*

stand. According to the Associated Press, a Norwegian newspaper expressed outrage over the gesture, since it is considered an insult or a sign of the devil in Norse culture. In sign language, the gesture translates into "bullshit." In some Mediterranean countries, the gesture implies that a man is the victim of an unfaithful wife. In Russia, it is considered a symbol for newly rich, arrogant, and poorly educated Russians; in many European countries it serves to ward off the "evil eye;" and in some African nations, it's used to put a hex or curse on another person (Douglas, 2005). Concerns about potential international gaffes led Southern Methodist University to publish a pocket-size guide for its students studying abroad. Tips include sticking out our tongue as a way of saying hello in Tibet; making certain to take our hands out of our pockets when talking with someone in Belgium; and avoiding touching someone's head in Indonesia, where such an action would be considered a serious insult (Adams, 2003; Watch your tongue, 2004).

**Illustrators.**   We frequently accompany a verbal message with nonverbal **illustrators** that either complement, contradict, or accent a verbal message (Beattie & Shovelton, 1999; Streeck, 1993). Occasionally, an illustrator will substitute for or repeat a verbal message. This category reflects simple, everyday movements, including facial expressions, that we often enact without really thinking about it. Have you ever seen someone give another person directions over the phone to a location? With the prevalence of cell phones nowadays, it's easy to spot people in all kinds of locales giving directions, mainly because they often use complementing gestures. If the person says, "You'll go down a big hill, then turn on the first street on the right," the person most likely will make the arm movement for downhill, then move her or his arm toward the right, even though the

*Choral conductors rely on arm and hand gestures, along with facial expressions and body positions, to convey nonverbal cues to singers.*

caller at the other end of the phone conversation can't see these movements. Research shows that illustrating gestures are frequently used to complement verbal messages, and that using gestures enhances people's recall of a message in face-to-face settings (Cohen & Harrison, 1973; Stevanoni & Salmon, 2005; Woodall & Folger, 1985).

Yawning while proclaiming we're not tired is an example of a nonverbal illustrator that contradicts the verbal message. What do you look like when you're mad? How do you nonverbally behave, especially in a situation where you don't want people to know that you're mad? We've seen people who we *know* are angry—complete with arms crossed over the chest, restricted facial expressions, and rigid body posture—but who insist they're not angry. We learned in Chapter 1 that when nonverbal and verbal communication contradict, we should attend more heavily to the nonverbal cues, since they more often carry the truer weight of the message.

Successful public speakers use accenting illustrators to great effect, meaning that the gestures are well chosen, well timed, and used sparingly. A gesture—such as pounding the podium—if used excessively, can actually work against the dramatic effect the speaker wants to accomplish because the repetition takes away from the gesture's ability to accent or emphasize the speaker's words or phrases. In some situations, a verbal message can't be heard, isn't appropriate or possible to convey, or simply isn't the most desirable way to communicate; in such situations, illustrators are handy. For example, we're at a crowded ballpark and there's too much noise to convey to the hot dog stand workers what we want, so instead of shouting our order, we point at the food and hold up some fingers to indicate how many we want. This is a substitution function of an illustrating gesture. Or perhaps after shouting our order and not being heard, we point and hold up a number of fingers, such that these gestures serve a repeating function for the verbal message.

Our use of illustrators are related to many things, according to Ekman and Friesen (1972). They suggest the following:

> When a person is demoralized, discouraged, tired, unenthusiastic, concerned about the other person's impression, or in a nondominant position in a formal interaction and setting, the rate of illustrators is less than is usual for that person. With excitement, enthusiasm about the topic or process of communication, when in the dominant role in a formal interaction, or in a more informal interaction where there is little concern about the impression being conveyed, a person uses more illustrators. When difficulty is experienced in finding the right words, or when feedback from the listener suggests he is not comprehending what is being said, illustrators increase. (as in Guerrero, DeVito, & Hecht, 1999, p. 50)

**Affect Displays.**    Nonverbal gestures, postures, and facial expressions that communicate emotion are called **affect displays.** Beginning in 1872, when Charles Darwin systematically studied the expression of emotion in both humans and animals, and continuing through decades of research, scientists have realized that nonverbal cues are the primary ways we communicate emotion (Coulson, 2004; Darwin, 1872/1965). Facial expressions, posture, and gestures reveal our emotions. Think about it: If we've just broken up with a romantic partner and are sad about the relationship ending, are we more likely to reveal the sadness we feel through our nonverbal cues or walk up to a group of friends and say, "I just broke up with so-and so and I'm really sad about it"? Granted, we might make such a statement but, typically, the nonverbal cues arrive first and are then accompanied by the verbal messages.

Our face tends to express which *kind* of emotion we're feeling, while our body reveals the intensity or how *much* of the emotion we're feeling. If we're happy, for example, our face may telegraph our joy to others. The movement of our hands, the openness of our posture, and the speed with which we move tell others just how happy we are. Likewise, if we're depressed, our face likely reveals our sadness or dejection, unless we're very practiced at masking our emotions. Our slumped shoulders and lowered head indicate the intensity of our despair.

**Regulators.**    **Regulators** control the interaction or flow of communication between people. When we're eager to respond to a message, we're likely to make eye contact, raise our eyebrows, open our mouth, take in a breath, and lean forward slightly. When we do not want to be part of the conversation, we do the opposite: We tend to avert our eyes, close our mouth, cross our arms, and lean back in our seats or away from the verbal action.

Next time you have a staff meeting at your job or a meeting for a student club in which one person—typically the president or chair of the club—runs the meeting, note both the subtle and more obvious nonverbal regulators present in the meeting. Typically, the lead person, highest-ranking officer, or boss begins the meeting by virtue of his or her status. At more formal gatherings or with larger groups, people tend to look to the group's leader, attempt to make eye contact, use an open facial expression, and offer the nonverbal gesture of raising their hands to be given a chance to speak. An unspoken but generally known rule is operating in such a setting, but we've probably all participated in situations in which people didn't know about the rule. These people may blurt out their contributions without using any nonverbal indications that they want to participate, often to the dismay of other people present at the meeting, sometimes to their own embarrassment. When approaching such a setting, especially as a new member, watch and learn. If we observe other people's nonverbal cues so that we learn the informal, unspoken rules that govern the interaction *before* we verbally participate, we'll fit in with the group more effectively and make a more positive impression on the people there.

Some people believe that regulators are the glue that hold conversations together—the little head nods, vocal expressions (such as "um" and "uh-huh"), facial expressions, body postures (especially leaning in), and eye contact that people come to expect when they engage in conversation. When we don't receive these sorts of nonverbal cues from a conversational partner, we may have a negative reaction and believe that our listener isn't listening to us at all. In one study of kinesic behaviors of successful job interviewees, nonverbal scholars Forbes and Jackson (1980) determined that candidates who received jobs evidenced more nonverbal regulators—direct eye contact, smiling, head nodding, and head shaking—than those interviewees who did not receive jobs.

**Adaptors.**    As professors, we know that our students prefer to bolt the classroom as soon as they've finished an exam, but as a nonverbal experiment, the next time you finish a test and some of your classmates are still in the room finishing theirs, stick around and watch the nonverbals. You'll see examples of nervous tension in the bodies of your classmates—frequent shifts of posture in chairs, hair twirling, pencil chewing or tapping on desktops, running the hands through the hair repeatedly, and long stares up at the ceiling (hoping for a vision of the right answer)—because most students exhibit some sort of nonverbal signal of test anxiety. Then there's the thigh shaker. Some students can make one of their legs quiver up and down at a very high speed, and they don't usually realize they're doing it. These are examples of **adaptors**—nonverbal behaviors that help us to satisfy a personal need, cope with emotions, and adapt to the immediate situation.

Perhaps part of our clothing is cutting off our circulation; what do we do? Announce to the people around us that we have a clothing issue, or adapt to the situation with some sort of nonverbal behavior? Many women will agree that bras are a pain—always creeping up the back, straps falling off the shoulders, or pinching in a variety of important places. We've never seen a woman stand up and announce that she needs a bra adjustment, but we've seen plenty who correct these situations nonverbally. These behaviors—adjusting our clothes, makeup, hair, eyeglasses, and so forth; fidgeting nervously with our hands and feet; and interacting nonverbally with our environment—reveal our attempts to normalize situations and to make ourselves feel more comfortable and able to function effectively.

## Gestures and Culture

Scholar Roger Axtell (1998) in his book, *Gestures: Do's and Taboos of Body Language around the World*, examines in depth many cultural effects on nonverbal kinesic behavior.

He begins by exploring the simple greeting ritual, enacted quite differently across the globe. Americans tend to think that everyone shakes hands when greeting, but this is not the case. In India and Thailand, people place their hands in a praying position in front of their chests and bow to the person they are greeting, with the translation being "I pray to God for you." This gesture can also mean "thank you" and "I'm sorry," which can be confusing for non-natives. Older generations in some Middle Eastern countries perform a greeting in which the right hand sweeps upward, touching first the heart, then the forehead, and then up and outward, accompanied by a slight head nod, known as the *salaam*.

Some greetings are more physical than others: Eskimos bang each other on the head or shoulders, while Polynesian men who don't know one another embrace and rub each other's backs. Maori tribespeople in New Zealand rub noses as a sign of friendship; some East African tribes' greeting consists of spitting at each other's feet, while Tibetan tribesmen stick their tongues out at each other (Axtell, 1998). Axtell deems the bow, evidenced in many eastern countries, primarily Japan, as the most "courtly" of all greetings. When Westerners visit these countries, a slight bow is recommended as a sign of courtesy and respect for the customs of the country. The higher the status of the person we're bowing to, the lower the bow should be. The lower status person (the visitor to the country, in this case) bows first. And interpreting the bow as a sign of subservience is incorrect, according to Axtell; to the Japanese, a bow signals respect and humility, not lowered status. Again, when moving to another culture or traveling across the globe we should do our homework. It's wise to research the customs and traditions of the countries we're moving to or visiting, pay attention to nonverbal differences in particular, and adapt our behavior appropriately so that we can communicate effectively.

## REMEMBER 6.2

### Ekman & Friesen's Categories of Movements & Gestures

| Category | Definition | Example |
|---|---|---|
| Emblems | Behaviors that have specific, generally understood meanings | A hitchhiker's raised thumb |
| Illustrators | Cues that accompany verbal messages and provide meaning | A speaker pounding on a podium to emphasize a point |
| Affect Displays | Expressions of emotion | Leaning toward someone to indicate attraction |
| Regulators | Cues that control and manage the flow of communication | Nodding the head while listening |
| Adaptors | Behaviors that help you adjust to your environment | Chewing your fingernails, indicating nervousness |

# APPLICATIONS OF KINESICS RESEARCH

Many applications of the basic research on kinesics have emerged in past decades, and work is still being done in this area. In this section, we overview two areas of research that couldn't be more different.

## Such a Flirt

What do you look like when you're attracted to someone? How do you behave if you want the other person to know you're attracted? Even if you're married or in some other form of committed relationship, perhaps you find it interesting to think about how people flirt or show attraction and interest in one another. Nonverbal research into the phenomenon of flirting has produced some intriguing findings (Abrahams, 1994; Grammer, 1990; Grammer, Kruck, Juette, & Fink, 2000; Renninger, Wade, & Grammer, 2004; Singh, 2004; Whitty, 2004). One study found 52 gestures and nonverbal behaviors that heterosexual women use to signal their interest in men. Among the top nonverbal flirting cues were smiling, surveying a crowded room with the eyes, using more forward body lean, and moving closer to the object of one's affection (Knox & Wilson, 1981; Moore, 1985). Research has found that heterosexual men tend to view flirting as a more sexual behavior than women do, and men often misinterpret women's friendly behaviors as signs of sexual attraction and interest (Abbey, 1982; Koeppel, Montagne, O'Hair, & Cody, 1999). The likelihood for this kind of misinterpretation becomes enhanced as alcohol consumption increases (Abbey, Zawacki, & Buck, 2005; Delaney & Gluade, 1990).

Another body of research along these lines has examined **quasi-courtship behavior,** those nonverbal actions we consciously and unconsciously exhibit when we are attracted to someone (Grammer, Knuck, & Magnusson, 1998; Scheflen, 1965). The first stage of quasi-courtship behavior is *courtship readiness*. When we are attracted to someone, we may alter our normal pattern of eye contact, suck in our stomach, tense our muscles, and stand up straight. The second stage includes *preening* behaviors, which includes combing our hair, applying makeup, straightening our tie, pulling up our socks, and double-checking our appearance in the mirror. Research shows that women tend to preen more than men (Daly, Hogg, Sacks, Smith, & Zimring, 1983). In stage three, we demonstrate *positional cues*, using our posture and body orientation to be seen and noticed by another person, as well as to position ourselves to prevent invasion by a third party. We intensify these cues in the fourth stage, termed *appeals to invitation*, using close proximity, exposed skin, open body positions, and direct eye contact to signal our availability and interest. The next time you're in a social setting, watch for these nonverbal cues and try to detect who's in to who.

## Kids and Kinesics

While many of you do not yet have children of your own, some of you are parents, and you may be aware of the extraordinary work that has been done over the past decade with children and gestures. Other organizations may be at work in this area, but perhaps the most well known is Kindermusik, in which educators teach parents to sign with their hearing children who have not yet acquired language skills. Some of the specific

SPOTLIGHT on Research

In this chapter on kinesics, one of the topics we've explored is hand gestures. Here's a question for you: Are hand gestures beneficial or distracting in conversation? Is it a matter of degree, meaning how many gestures are used to help get the message across? Is it the type of gesture that makes the difference, rather than the frequency?

In our nonverbal communication classes, we occasionally do this exercise with students. We send four student volunteers out into the hallway, keeping a fifth student up in front of the classroom. We explain that we're going to give the student directions to a restaurant in another city, directions that the student will have to give to the first of his or her classmates out in the hall, then the second student will direct the third, and so on. The point is to see how the communication gets distorted in the re-telling. In our directions, we include hand gestures that accompany such details as "you're going to take a wide curve left where the two highways intersect" and "you'll go down a steep hill, then the turn to the restaurant's street will be quickly on your right when you come up the hill." The exercise is increasingly hilarious as instructions are re-told. Inevitably, verbal instructions given with accompanying hand gestures are accurately transmitted across the student volunteers, but instructions without accompanying hand gestures become increasingly inaccurate and distorted as they continue to be relayed.

We recently came across a study that formalized our classroom experience, but that involved children instead of adults. Psychologists Stevanoni and Salmon (2005) explored the role of gestures in children's recall of an experience. Specifically, a group of six-year olds participated in an event created by the experimenters—a "pirate visit" in which children got to make a treasure map, compete for a key, and find hidden treasure. The children were interviewed two weeks later and were asked to recall the event.

Children who were instructed to use gestures when recalling and explaining their experience to another person remembered more about the event and were more accurate in their remembrances than children whose gestures were restricted. In addition, the gestures the children used conveyed more information in tandem with their verbal accounts of events than non-gesturing children. So perhaps we should all re-think advice to children about limiting their movements!

Do you want to know more about this study? If so, read: Stevanoni, E., & Salmon, K. (2005). Giving memory a hand: Instructing children to gesture enhances their event recall. *Journal of Nonverbal Behavior, 29*, 217–233.

programs include "Sign and Sing" and "Signing Smart," which combine song and playful interaction for parents and children (aged six months to three years) in an effort to help children learn 50 various signs from American Sign Language (ASL). These programs build on finger plays related to songs children typically learn, such as "This Little Piggy," and parents begin to substitute signs in other songs as well as in interactions with children. As Kindermusik websites suggest, these activities "speed a child's language development, ease frustration, enhance long-term learning abilities," and improve motor skills—more specifically, they "strengthen fingers for zipping zippers and using scissors" (Kindermusik of the Woodlands.com, 2006; 3bees.org, 2006).

We've provided some photos for you of a mother and daughter engaged in signing. This is a unique application of kinesics, specifically the use of gesturing so that parents and pre-linguistic children can better communicate. In the first photo, the child indicates to her mother that she wants more food by moving the index fingers and thumbs together. In the second photo, the mother makes the hand gesture for "ball" while saying the word out loud to the child. If you look closely, you can see that the child is saying the word out loud also, while her hands are beginning to move into the shape of the many balls in front of her. In the final photo the sign for book is being taught, with the mother shaping the child's hands for her, reinforcing the object that is in front of them.

A study conducted by Signing Smart co-founders Michelle Anthony and Reyna Lindert claimed the following: "Hearing children who know signs learn language almost twice as fast. As early as 11–14 months old, hearing children exposed to sign language put sentences together faster than non-signing children, who do not begin to combine words into short sentences, such as 'Da-da car,' until the average age of 20 months" (Kindermusik of the Woodlands.com, 2006). Many parents involved in such efforts are certain that their children learn to express themselves verbally more quickly and effectively than children who don't learn signs (West, 2007). But as far as we've been able to determine, research on long-term effects of experience with parent-child signing have yet to be conducted, so we don't yet know if children who signed before they learned language end

*This gesture means "more, please."*

*The mother gestures "ball" as she teaches her daughter to communicate.*

*Here, the mother teaches her daughter the sign for "book."*

---

### REMEMBER 6.3

| | |
|---|---|
| **Quasi-Courtship Behavior:** | nonverbal actions we consciously and unconsciously exhibit when we are attracted to someone. |
| **Courtship Readiness:** | first stage of quasi-courtship behavior, in which we begin to alter our normal nonverbal patterns. |
| **Preening:** | second stage of quasi-courtship behavior, in which we attend to our appearance and make adjustments. |
| **Positional Cues:** | third stage of quasi-courtship behavior, in which we use posture and body orientation to draw attention from the other person. |
| **Appeals to Invitation:** | fourth stage of quasi-courtship behavior, in which we use more obvious and direct nonverbal cues to signal availability and interest. |

---

up having better communication skills as adolescents and adults than those who did not. Suffice it for now to say that such efforts as Sign and Sing are enhancing parent–child communication, which can only bode well for an individual's future development.

## ■ UNDERSTANDING KINESICS: APPLYING THE REFLEXIVE CYCLE OF NONVERBAL COMMUNICATION DEVELOPMENT

Have you thought about your own kinesic behavior, including your walk, stance, posture, and use of gestures? As you will no doubt recognize by now, the Reflexive Cycle begins with an inventory of self. The first step to develop your skills and a better understanding of the role of kinesic behavior in human interaction is to look at yourself. What tendencies do you have in terms of kinesics? Do you move and gesture just like one of your parents? Were you taught anything specific about hand gestures or movement, in general? Do you use certain gestures because your friends use them?

One of your authors remembers a situation that arose while teaching public speaking in which a male student seemed very "tight" in front of an audience. This particular student barely moved during a speech performance and used few, if any, gestures. When asked about his lack of movement, he explained that when he was growing up, especially in his middle school years, he became self-conscious about his physicality and the possibility of looking clumsy. (He grew tall quickly and lacked coordination.) His parents told him not to move too much and to try to keep his arms by his sides, so that he wouldn't risk appearing clumsy in front of his peers and teachers. While his well-meaning parents believed that this advice would help their son's confidence and smoothness when communicating with other people, the advice had a more long-lasting and pronounced effect than his parents could have realized. Once this young man grew into his body and matured, he needed to learn how to loosen up and to move and gesture freely, especially because movement in a public speaking situation (or even conversationally) helps reduce nerves and creates more visual interest for listeners.

So are you one of those people who can't talk without moving your hands? Or do you use gestures seldom and view people negatively who move a lot in conversation? Are there kinesic behaviors you'd like to change? Once you've surveyed your own behavior in terms of kinesics and decided if you have some changes to make or not, it's time to inventory others' kinesic behaviors. The next time you're in a social situation with lots of people, do some keen nonverbal observation. How do people stand, move, and gesture in social settings? Note the variation in these behaviors across people, because some people move a lot, while others move very little.

Your next step in the Reflexive Cycle is to interact with others, enacting any kinesic changes you've decided are appropriate, and to detect how your nonverbal behaviors transact with others' behaviors in everyday conversation. Do the kinesic behaviors you exhibit coordinate with others' or are they in opposition? How do the kinesics reveal or express what is transpiring in conversation?

After you have inventoried yourself, begun to make changes in your kinesic behavior, inventoried others' kinesics, and engaged in mutual transaction of behavior (such that your nonverbal cues affect other people and theirs affect you), your final step is to evaluate the whole process. What did you learn about your own and others' body movements that you believe make you a better communicator? Again, the reflexive process takes an honest assessment of yourself, the willingness to change, keen observational skills, and a sense of "communicator adventure," as you put your new behaviors into action, transact with others, note the results, and re-evaluate.

## SUMMARY ■ ■ ■ ■ ■

In this chapter, we explored kinesics—the study of human movement, gestures, and posture. Kinesics includes the way our body moves; the way we gesture with our hands, arms, shoulders, and, occasionally, with our torso (or trunk), legs, and feet; and how we walk, stand, and carry ourselves.

Specifically, we examined posture for what it reveals nonverbally about a person. We overviewed Mehrabian's research, which suggests that two dimensions of posture exist—immediacy and relaxation—through which we communicate our attitudes and feelings to others. Scheflen's research identified three dimensions of posture: (1) inclusiveness/noninclusiveness; (2) face-to-face/parallel; and (3) congruence/incongruence. These dimensions help us observe nonverbal behavior and analyze people's attitudes and feelings about others as they interact. In related research, we also explored nonverbal synchrony, a coordination of speech and movement within one person (self-synchrony) and across people in an interaction (interactive synchrony, also referred to as "social rhythm"). This section concluded with an examination of nonverbal kinesic cues of status and dominance.

The second major topic of study was walk, in terms of how our walk is influenced by our culture, genetic profile, physiological features, upbringing, and psychological characteristics. Specific attention was paid to cultural and sex/gender differences regarding walking behavior. We include sitting behavior in this chapter because it is a common position for people across various cultures. Plus, we can tell a lot about people and their relationships simply by observing where and how they sit.

In the third major section of this chapter, we explored gestures, first by reviewing Ekman and Friesen's kinesic categories as a system for organizing and understanding kinesic behavior. Then we examined how gestures vary according to culture, with suggestions about studying native customs when traveling or relocating out of our home culture. Two applications of kinesics research were provided to better understand how research enhances our understanding of the role of kinesics in our overall nonverbal behavior. First, flirting behavior was described in nonverbal terms, with current research results provided. Second, new programs involving parents and pre-linguistic children learning sign language were discussed, once again as evidence of the powerful role of nonverbal communication in human development. Finally, we worked through the Reflexive Cycle as it applies to kinesics, encouraging students to carefully inventory their own kinesics as well as to keenly observe the kinesics of others to better understand transactions in which they engage on a daily basis.

## DISCUSSION STARTERS

1. What cues does your posture reveal about your character, upbringing, culture, and specific emotions and mood? Did you ever consider that so much could be revealed in how you carry yourself?

2. Think of how many phrases in American culture relate to walking, such as "walk the walk/talk the talk," and "walk on the wild side." What makes a person's walk memorable and worthy of imitation?

3. What is your preferred sitting position and what does it reveal about you to others? How can we detect emotions, such as nervousness and anxiety, through people's sitting behavior?

How is the kinesic behavior of sitting related to proxemics (the use of space)?

4. Review Ekman and Friesen's kinesic categories and provide examples of each of the five categories of gesture.

5. How are gestures and culture related? What can you tell about a given culture by studying its gestures? How can you go about learning gestures in another culture?

6. What are some of the pitfalls related to kinesic behaviors and flirting? How easily can some kinesics be misperceived in a flirtatious context?

## REFERENCES

3bees.org. (2006). [Online]. Available: www.3bees.org/signlanguage.

Abbey, A. (1982). Sex differences in attributions for friendly behavior: Do males misperceive females' friendliness? *Journal of Personality and Social Psychology, 42,* 830–838.

Abbey, A., Zawacki, T., & Buck, P. O. (2005). The effects of past sexual assault perpetration and alcohol consumption on reactions to women's mixed signals. *Journal of Social and Clinical Psychology, 24,* 129–157.

Abrahams, M. F. (1994). Perceiving flirtatious communication: An exploration of the perceptual dimensions underlying judgments of flirtatiousness. *Journal of Sex Research, 31,* 283–292.

Adams, E. (2003, November 2). Manners can sink international business dealings. *Corpus Christi Caller Times,* p. K2.

Afifi, W. A., & Johnson, M. L. (1999). The use and interpretation of tie signs in a public setting: Relationship and sex differences. *Journal of Social and Personal Relationships, 16,* 9–38.

Aguinis, H., & Henle, C. A. (2001). Effects of nonverbal behavior on perceptions of a female employee's power bases. *Journal of Social Psychology, 141,* 537–549.

Aguinis, H., Simonsen, M. M., & Pierce, C. A. (1998). Effects of nonverbal behavior on perceptions of power bases. *Journal of Social Psychology, 138,* 455–469.

Andersen, P. A. (2004). *The complete idiot's guide to body language.* New York: Alpha.

Argyle, M. (1969). *Social interaction.* London: Methuen.

Aries, E. J., Gold, C., & Weigel, R. (1983). Dispositional and situational influences on dominance behavior in small groups. *Journal of Personality and Social Psychology, 44,* 779–786.

Armstrong, N., & Wagner, M. (2003). *Field guide to gestures: How to identify and interpret virtually every gesture known to man.* Philadelphia: Quirk Books.

Axtell, R. E. (1998). *Gestures: Do's and taboos of body language around the world.* New York: John Wiley & Sons.

Beattie, G., & Shovelton, J. (1999). Mapping the range of information contained in the iconic hand gestures that accompany spontaneous speech. *Journal of Language and Social Psychology, 18,* 438–462.

Beavin Bavelas, J., & Chovil, N. (2006). Nonverbal and verbal communication: Hand gestures and facial displays as part of language use in face-to-face dialogue. In V. Manusov & M. L. Patterson (Eds.), *The Sage handbook of nonverbal communication* (pp. 97–115). Thousand Oaks, CA: Sage.

Beebe, S. A., & Beebe, S. J. (2006). *Public speaking: An audience-centered approach* (6th ed.). Boston: Allyn & Bacon.

Beebe, S. A., Beebe, S. J., & Ivy, D. K. (2007). *Communication: Principles for a lifetime* (3rd ed.). Boston: Allyn & Bacon.

Birdwhistell, R. L. (1960). Kinesics and communication. In E. Carpenter & M. McLuhan (Eds.), *Explorations in communication: An anthology* (pp. 54–64). Boston: Beacon.

Birdwhistell, R. L. (1967). Some body motion elements accompanying spoken American English. In L. Thayer (Ed.), *Communication: Concepts and perspectives* (pp. 53–76). Washington: Spartan.

Birdwhistell, R. L. (1970). *Kinesics and context: Essays on body motion communication.* Philadelphia: University of Pennsylvania Press.

Birdwhistell, R. L. (1974). The language of the body: The natural environment of words. In A. Silverstein (Ed.), *Human communication: Theoretical explorations* (pp. 203–220). New York: John Wiley & Sons.

Burgoon, J. K. (1991). Relational message interpretations of touch, conversational distance, and posture. *Journal of Nonverbal Behavior, 15,* 233–259.

Burgoon, J. K., Birk, T., & Pfau, M. (1990). Nonverbal behaviors, persuasion, and credibility. *Human Communication Research, 17,* 140–169.

Carney, D. R., Hall, J. A., & Lebeau, L. S. (2005). Beliefs about the nonverbal expression of social power. *Journal of Nonverbal Behavior, 29,* 114–118.

Cashdan, E. (1998). Smiles, speech, and body posture: How women and men display sociometric status and power. *Journal of Nonverbal Behavior, 22,* 209–228.

Cohen, A. A., & Harrison, R. P. (1973). Intentionality in the use of hand illustrators in face-to-face communication situations. *Journal of Personality and Social Psychology, 28,* 276–279.

Condon, W. S. (1976). An analysis of behavioral organization. *Sign Language Studies, 13,* 285–318.

Condon, W. S., & Ogston, W. D. (1966). Soundfilm analysis of normal and pathological behavior patterns. *Journal of Nervous and Mental Disease, 143,* 338–347.

Coulson, M. (2004). Attributing emotion to static body postures: Recognition accuracy, confusions, and viewpoint dependence. *Journal of Nonverbal Behavior, 28,* 117–139.

Daly, J. A., Hogg, E., Sacks, D., Smith, M., & Zimring, L. (1983). Sex and relationship affect social self-grooming. *Journal of Nonverbal Behavior, 7,* 183–189.

Darwin, C. (1872/1965). *Expression of emotions in man and animals.* London: Appleton; reprinted, University of Chicago Press.

Delaney, H. J., & Gluade, B. A. (1990). Gender differences in perception of attractiveness of men and women in bars. *Journal of Personality and Social Psychology, 16,* 378–391.

Do you know? (2006, June). *Martha Stewart's Living,* 40.

Douglas, J., Jr. (2005, January 23). Outside Texas, "Hook 'em Horns" gesture has different and unflattering meanings. *Fort Worth Star Telegram,* p. 2A.

Egolf, D. B., & Corder, L. E. (1991). Height differences of low and high job status female and male corporate employees. *Sex Roles, 24,* 365–373.

Ekman, P. (1969). Non-verbal leakage and clues to deception. *Psychiatry, 32,* 88–106.

Ekman, P., & Friesen, W. V. (1969). The repertoire of nonverbal behavior: Categories, origins, usage, and coding. *Semiotica, 1,* 49–98.

Ekman, P., & Friesen, W. V. (1972). Hand movements. Reprinted in L. K. Guerrero, J. DeVito, & M. L. Hecht (Eds.), *The nonverbal communication reader: Classic and contemporary readings* (1999, 2nd ed., pp. 48–52). Prospect Heights, IL: Waveland.

Ellyson, S. L., & Dovidio, J. F. (1985). Power, dominance, and nonverbal behavior: Basic concepts and issues. In S. L. Ellyson & J. F. Dovidio (Eds.), *Power, dominance, and nonverbal behavior* (pp. 1–27). New York: Springer-Verlag.

Elman, D. (1977). Physical characteristics and the perception of masculine traits. *Journal of Social Psychology, 103,* 157–158.

Fatt, J. P. T. (2000). It's not what you say, it's how you say it. *Communication World, 16,* 37–40.

Feldman, R. S., & Tyler, J. M. (2006). Factoring in age: Nonverbal communication across the life span. In V. Manusov & M. L. Patterson (Eds.), *The Sage handbook of nonverbal communication* (pp. 181–199). Thousand Oaks, CA: Sage.

Forbes, R. J., & Jackson, P. R. (1980). Nonverbal behavior and the outcome of selection interviews. Reprinted in L. K. Guerrero, J. DeVito, & M. L. Hecht (Eds.), *The nonverbal communication reader: Classic and contemporary readings* (1999, 2nd ed., pp. 82–89). Prospect Heights, IL: Waveland.

Gallo, C. (2005, November 17). Actions do speak louder than words. *Business Week* [Electronic version].

Grammer, K. (1990). Strangers meet: Laughter and nonverbal signs of interest in opposite-sex encounters. *Journal of Nonverbal Behavior, 14,* 209–235.

Grammer, K., Knuck, K. B., & Magnusson, M. S. (1998). The courtship dance: Patterns of nonverbal synchronization in opposite sex encounters. *Journal of Nonverbal Behavior, 22,* 3–25.

Grammer, K., Kruck, K., Juette, A., & Fink, B. (2000). Nonverbal behavior as courtship signals: The role of control and choice in selecting partners. *Evolution and Human Behavior, 21,* 371–390.

Guerrero, L. K., & Floyd, K. (2006). *Nonverbal communication in close relationships.* Mahwah, NJ: Erlbaum.

Gunns, R. E., Johnston, L., & Hudson, W. M. (2002). Victim selection and kinematics: A point-light investigation of vulnerability to attack. *Journal of Nonverbal Behavior, 26,* 129–158.

Hall, J. A. (1979). Gender, gender roles, and nonverbal communication skills. In R. Rosenthal (Ed.), *Skill in nonverbal communication: Individual differences* (pp. 32–67). Cambridge, MA: Oelgeschlager, Gunn, & Hain.

Hall, J. A. (1984). *Nonverbal sex differences: Communication accuracy and expressive style.* Baltimore: Johns Hopkins University Press.

Henley, N. M. (2001). Body politics. In A. Branaman (Ed.), *Self and society* (pp. 288–297). Malden, MA: Blackwell.

Hewes, G. W. (1957). The anthropology of posture. *Scientific American, 196,* 123–132.

Hickson, M., III., Stacks, D. W., & Moore, N. J. (2004). *Nonverbal communication: Studies and applications* (4th ed.). Los Angeles: Roxbury.

Johnson, D. W. (2006). *Reaching out: Interpersonal effectiveness and self-actualization.* Boston: Allyn & Bacon.

Kendon, A. (1987). On gesture: Its complementary relationship with speech. In A. W. Siegman & S. Feldstein (Eds.), *Nonverbal behavior and communication* (2nd ed.). Hillsdale, NJ: Erlbaum.

Kindermusik of the Woodlands.com. (2006). [Online]. Available: www.kindermusikofthewoodlands.com

Knapp, M. L., & Hall, J. A. (2006). *Nonverbal communication in human interaction* (6th ed.). Belmont, CA: Thomson/Wadsworth.

Knox, D., & Wilson, K. (1981). Dating behaviors of university students. *Family Relations, 30,* 255–258.

Koeppel, L. B., Montagne, Y., O'Hair, D., & Cody, M. J. (1999). Friendly? Flirting? Wrong? In L. K. Guerrero, J. DeVito, & M. L. Hecht (Eds.), *The nonverbal communication reader: Classic and contemporary readings* (2nd ed., pp. 290–297). Prospect Heights, IL: Waveland.

Lakin, J. L., Jefferis, V. W., Cheng, C. M., & Chartrand, T. L. (2003). The chameleon effect as social glue: Evidence for the evolutionary significance of nonconscious mimicry. *Journal of Nonverbal Behavior, 27,* 145–161.

Leathers, D. G., & Eaves, M. H. (2008). *Successful nonverbal communication: Principles and applications* (4th ed.). Boston: Allyn & Bacon.

Lechelt, E. (1975). Occupational affiliation and ratings of physical height and personal esteem. *Psychological Reports, 36,* 943–946.

Matsumoto, D., & Yoo, S. H. (2005). Culture and applied nonverbal communication. In R. E. Riggio & R. S. Feldman (Eds.), *Applications of nonverbal communication* (pp. 255–277). Mahwah, NJ: Erlbaum.

Mehrabian, A. (1966). Immediacy: An indicator of attitudes in linguistic communication. *Journal of Personality, 34,* 26–34.

Mehrabian, A. (1968). Inference of attitudes from the posture, orientation, and distance of a communicator. *Journal of Consulting and Clinical Psychology, 32,* 296–308.

Mehrabian, A. (1969a). Measures of achieving tendency. *Educational and Psychological Measurement, 29,* 445–451.

Mehrabian, A. (1969b). Significance of posture and position in the communication of attitude and status relationships. *Psychological Bulletin, 71,* 359–372.

Mehrabian, A. (1972). *Nonverbal communication.* Chicago: Atherton.

Mehrabian, A. (1981). *Silent message: Implicit communication of emotions and attitudes* (2nd ed.). Belmont, CA: Wadsworth.

Mehrabian, A., & Friar, J. T. (1969). Encoding of attitude by a seated communicator via posture and position cues. *Journal of Consulting and Clinical Psychology, 33,* 330–336.

Messakappa, D., & Andersen, P. A. (1996, November). *Nonverbal cues of crime victims: Perceptions of convicted criminals.* Paper presented at the meeting of the Western States Communication Association, Pasadena, CA.

Montepare, J. M., & Zebrowitz, L. A. (1993). A cross-cultural comparison of impressions created by age-related variations in gait. *Journal of Nonverbal Behavior, 17,* 55–68.

Moore, M. M. (1985). Nonverbal courtship patterns in women: Context and consequences. *Ethology and Sociobiology, 6,* 237–247.

Murzynski, J., & Degelman, D. (1996). Body language of women and judgments of vulnerability to sexual assault. *Journal of Applied Social Psychology, 26,* 1617–1626.

Nelson, A., & Golant, S. K. (2004). *You don't say: Navigating nonverbal communication between the sexes.* New York: Prentice-Hall.

Renninger, L. A., Wade, T. J., & Grammer, K. (2004). Getting that female glance: Patterns and consequences of male nonverbal behavior in courtship contexts. *Evolution and Human Behavior, 25,* 416–431.

Richmond, V. P., McCroskey, J. C., & Hickson, M. L. III. (2008). *Nonverbal behavior in interpersonal relations* (6th ed.). Boston: Allyn & Bacon.

Roberts, J. V., & Herman, C. P. (1986). The psychology of height: An empirical review. In C. P. Herman, M. P. Zanna, & E. T. Higgins (Eds.), *Physical appearance, stigma, and social behavior: The Ontario symposium* (Vol. 3). Hillsdale, NJ: Erlbaum.

Rush, C. (2006). *The mere mortal's guide to fine dining.* New York: Broadway Books.

Scheflen, A. E. (1965). Quasi-courtship behavior in psychotherapy. *Psychiatry, 28,* 245–257.

Scheflen, A. E. (1974). *How behavior means.* New York: Gordon and Breach.

Scheflen, A. E., & Scheflen, A. (1972). *Body language and the social order.* Englewood Cliffs, NJ: Prentice-Hall.

Schmid Mast, M., & Hall, J. A. (2004). Who is the boss and who is not? Accuracy of judging status. *Journal of Nonverbal Behavior, 28,* 145–165.

Singh, D. (2004). Mating strategies of young women: Role of physical attractiveness. *Journal of Sex Research, 41,* 43–54.

Soll, L. (2007, February 9). The best of bad pits. *Entertainment Weekly,* 18.

Stabler, B., Whitt, K., Moreault, D., D'Ercole, A., & Underwood, L. (1980). Social judgments by children of short stature. *Psychological Reports, 46,* 743–746.

Stevanoni, E., & Salmon, K. (2005). Giving memory a hand: Instructing children to gesture enhances their event recall. *Journal of Nonverbal Behavior, 29,* 217–233.

Streeck, J. (1993). Gesture as communication I: Its coordination with gaze and speech. *Communication Monographs, 60,* 275–299.

Tiedens, L. Z., & Fragale, A. R. (2003). Power moves: Complementarity in dominant and submissive nonverbal behavior. *Journal of Personality and Social Psychology, 84,* 558–568.

Watch your tongue; this isn't Tibet. (2004, October 10). *Fort Worth Star Telegram,* p. 2A.

West, M. (2007, September 9). Learning to communicate: Babies may talk sooner if they learn to sign. *Corpus Christi Caller Times,* p. 6B.

Whitty, M. T. (2004). Cyber-flirting: An examination of men's and women's flirting behaviour both offline and on the Internet. *Behaviour Change, 21,* 115–126.

Woodall, W. G., & Folger, J. P. (1985). Nonverbal cue context and episodic memory: On the availability and endurance of nonverbal behaviors as retrieval cues. *Communication Monographs, 52,* 320–333.

# Face and Eyes

## Revealing, Modifying, and Deceiving

## CHAPTER OUTLINE ■ ■ ■ ■ ■

## CHAPTER OBJECTIVES ■ ■ ■ ■ ■

After studying this chapter, you should be able to:

1. Understand facial and eye behavior as key codes of nonverbal communication.
2. Identify contrasting elements between the innate versus the learned perspective, in terms of the acquisition and development of facial expressions.
3. List and describe four facial management techniques.
4. Identify and explain Ekman and Friesen's eight categories of facial expressions.
5. Review the Facial Action Coding System and explain its use in assessing emotion in each region of the face.
6. Discuss common procedures of facial modification.
7. Identify three influences of eye behavior and explain how each nonverbally operates in every-day conversation.

8. Provide ten purposes of eye behavior and explain how each nonverbally operates in everyday conversation.

9. List and explain six forms of eye behavior.

10. Discuss common procedures of eye modification.

11. Identify key research findings regarding facial and eye behavior and deception.

## CASE STUDY  Mr. Winker

After eight months at my first post-college job, I felt confident in my abilities as an employee and coworker. All of my coworkers seemed to like me and my supervisors gave me nothing but positive feedback on my performance. I had developed personal relationships with several coworkers and often spent time with them on weekends.

One guy in another department had a reputation for being the company's resident flirt. He was young, attractive, confident, charming, and personable. He was always invited to the gatherings outside of work and got along well with everyone. One evening, on a rare occasion when he wasn't at the company gathering, a new hire in his department told me she felt uncomfortable around him. She said he was too flirtatious, often smiling and winking in her direction. I told her that was just his flirty personality and that he did that with everyone, including supervisors, family, and clients. I told her to confront him if she didn't feel comfortable and that he would totally understand and correct the problem.

The following week, all of us received an email from the director reminding us of the no-tolerance policy on sexual harassment in the workplace. I wondered if something had happened with my colleagues. In the break room, some people were talking about the email that had been received by the entire staff and taking guesses as to who was involved in the complaint. Everyone guessed it was "Mr. Winker." I thought back to the new hire and her comments to me the previous weekend. Surely she hadn't mistaken his winking and smiling as sexual harassment!

Sure enough, that afternoon "Mr. Winker" was put on administrative leave, pending an investigation into the allegations against him. Supervisors began calling us into their offices one by one, questioning our relationship with him and if we'd ever observed anything unprofessional. One by one, we all confirmed his propensity to wink during conversations, but we said that no suggestive innuendo or inappropriate comments were ever made. His winking wasn't directed to one individual either; rather, it was a natural communicative trait he was probably used to using for years.

After investigating the harassment allegations against him, "Mr. Winker" was cleared to return to work. Before coming back to the office, he was sent to a seminar on sexual harassment, while the entire staff went to a workshop on appropriate conduct in the workplace. His winking had caused an uproar in the corporation! Something most of us saw as natural and inoffensive was seen by the newer staff member as sexual harassment. "Mr. Winker" was totally oblivious to how his eye behavior had affected his coworker, to the point of making her uncomfortable around him.

After completing the seminar, "Mr. Winker" came back to work. The allegations served as a harsh lesson to him. What may be a natural, friendly wink to one person may be considered sexual harassment by another.

# ■ FACIAL AND EYE BEHAVIOR AS NONVERBAL COMMUNICATION

**Wanda:** "Did you see the look on her face?"

**Jackie:** "Yeah, she was totally offended by Ruben's comment."

**Wanda:** "You could tell by the look in her eye that she was about to explode."

**Jackie:** "Oh, I know!"

This brief conversation illustrates that facial and eye behaviors influence the perceptions we have of others' emotions, attitudes, and desires. We rely on facial and eye behavior to clue us about what other people are thinking or, more important, feeling (Mendolia, 2007). The reason we place an emphasis on the feeling aspect is because many people trudge through life hurting others' feelings by using lackluster facial and eye responses that communicate the following messages: "He doesn't care about what I'm saying," "She isn't listening to me," "He thinks I'm stupid," and "I'm not important." Obviously, violations or misuses of the other nonverbal communication codes you're studying in this class and reading about in this book can lead to hurt feelings and relational tensions with friends, partners, and even social acquaintances (Hall, Murphy, & Schmid Mast, 2006). Yet, there's a special power of the human face and eyes that sends positive messages of joy and affirmation, which is why we rely on them so much in our everyday communication (Krumhuber, Manstead, & Kappas, 2007; Zebrowitz, 2006; Zebrowitz, Bronstad, & Lee, 2007).

Perhaps you've heard the expression, "The eyes are the windows to the soul" or "There's nothing more comforting than a familiar face." Even in everyday service encounters at coffee shops, pubs, grocery stores, and restaurants we evaluate facial and eye behavior as part of the customer service we experience (Pugh, 2001). Take a moment to think about the typical customer service survey: What types of questions are usually included in these surveys? Typical items include "Was the associate friendly?" "Were you treated with respect?" "Did our associates greet you with a smile?" and "Did your sales clerk have a positive attitude?" When we fill out one of these satisfaction surveys, we're reminded that facial and eye behavior in service situations mold our experiences as positive or negative, satisfied or dissatisfied. Our point is this: Facial and eye behaviors are critical to the study of nonverbal communication. So in this chapter, we focus on facial and eye behavior as significant nonverbal codes. Let's begin by examining facial behavior and its important role in our overall communication.

# ■ SIGNIFICANCE OF FACIAL BEHAVIOR

By some estimates, attributed primarily to nonverbal scholar Ray Birdwhistell (1974), the human face is capable of producing more than 250,000 expressions. What an incredible ability! Computer-generated imaging technology, a rapidly growing trend in film and video gaming, continues to evolve in its potential to emulate this human ability (Waxman, 2006). The human face is so important in communication that it has become, according to communication theorists Domenici and

Littlejohn (2006), "a symbol of close personal interaction" (p. 10). They suggest that "we use expressions such as 'face to face,' 'face time,' 'in your face,' and 'saving face.' In other words, the metaphor of face is powerful in bringing many aspects of personal communication to the fore" (p. 10). You might want to check out a fascinating website entitled DataFace, which is devoted to the study of the face and its ability to express emotions; the URL is face-and-emotion.com/dataface. The authors of the site describe it as being "for people who want to know more about the human face, whether they are casual observers or professional analysts of the face."

Your face is connected to your public identity; it's the *you* presented to others in everyday encounters. Scholar Erving Goffman (1967) wrote about this presentation of self in everyday life, explaining how face can be "lost," "maintained," "protected," or "enhanced." This approach has been incorporated by communication scholars into a concept known as **facework,** defined as "a set of coordinated practices in which communicators build, maintain, protect, or threaten personal dignity, honor, and respect" (Domenici & Littlejohn, 2006, pp. 11–12). Consider the times when you've thought about how you or someone else could "save face" in an embarrassing or awkward situation.

Take a moment to think about what another person's face tells you about her or him. What emotion is she expressing? How is he feeling? Is your friend surprised to see you? Did your audience find your presentation entertaining or were they bored to tears? As we begin to think about how much the human face clues us about what's going on, it's quite amazing, to say the least. But how do we acquire our facial abilities in the first place?

## ■ ACQUISITION AND DEVELOPMENT OF FACIAL EXPRESSION

Nonverbal communication scholars have debated for many years how facial expressions are formed. The main point in the debate has been whether facial expressions are innate, learned, or both. **Innate behavior,** as related to the face, means that facial expression is biological or an ability that comes with humans at birth. In contrast, **learned behavior** means that our facial expressions are acquired through cultural, social, and family experiences over time. Do you think your facial expressions are a natural part of who you are as a person? Have you learned how to express happiness, sadness, and other emotions as you've grown and matured? Other factors to consider are social and cultural influences. Do people from various cultural and social experiences exhibit different facial behavior than you, leading you to believe that facial expressions are "made" not "born"? These questions are important for reflection as we study the nonverbal dimensions of the face.

### Evolution and Natural Selection: The "Born" Perspective

Charles Darwin (1872/1965) is famous for his theory of **evolution,** or how species change and adapt over time. From Darwin's perspective, facial expressions are acquired

*Charles Darwin studied facial expressions of animals as a means of better understanding human facial expressions.*

through evolution and **natural selection,** meaning that organisms best suited to survival in an environment will thrive and pass on their genetic advantages to future generations. Darwin was interested in how facial expressions of animals served as survival mechanisms that evolved along with other physical characteristics. That is to say, he believed that facial movements were animals' primary form of expression before other communication skills emerged; thus facial movements evolved because they were necessary for basic survival. Darwin contended that higher order primates also used facial expressions to communicate emotions, feelings, and attitudes.

While Darwin's observations of facial expressions in animals are interesting and important to consider, our focus is on the nonverbal dimensions of the human face. Researchers conducting observations of children have found evidence that human facial behaviors are, in fact, inborn or genetically derived (Eibl-Eibesfeldt, 1970, 1972; Grossman & Kegl, 2007; Spackman, et al., 2005). This line of research has shown that basic facial expressions of emotion (e.g., sadness, anger, disgust, fear, surprise, and happiness) produced by able-bodied children can be observed in children who are born deaf and blind. Since children with these disabilities aren't able to see or hear, the chance of them learning how to express emotions from family or social experiences is minimal or non-existent, since humans learn primarily through auditory and visual channels (Grossman & Kegl, 2007; Spackman, Fujiki, Brinton, Nelson, & Allen, 2005).

The ultimate nonverbal communication assignment would be to travel the globe and document facial expressions across cultures. Do you think you would find

*What does the expression on this woman's face communicate about her nonverbally?*

"universal" facial expressions? Or do you think culture influences facial expressions in humans? A bit of both? Studies provide evidence that facial expressions are, in fact, similar across cultural boundaries, thus strengthening the "nonverbal cues as innate" stance (Elfenbein, 2006; Grossman & Kegl, 2007; Matsumoto, 1989, 1992; Matsumoto & Ekman, 1989; Spackman, et al., 2005; Weitz, 1974).

## External Factors: The "Learned" Perspective

In addition to evolution and natural selection, another aspect of our study of the non-verbal dimensions of the face is **external factors**—influences on our facial expressions that come from environment, social norms, and culture. While a great deal of research suggests that human facial expressions are innate characteristics, we can probably all agree that we learn how to act in relation to social contexts. For example, young children are often taught how to behave for certain situations. One of the authors of this text recently observed parents instructing their young child to "act like a big girl" during the process of security agents screening a family at a check point in Chicago's Midway Airport. The little girl stood up straight and shifted her smiling facial expression into a serious one, reminding us all that "security is not a laughing matter." As children develop, they're often coached by family members and teachers about what facial expression is appropriate for a particular emotion and situation (Ekman & Friesen, 1967). Children can learn at very early ages to mask disappointment and other emotions that register in their facial expressions in order to appear more socially appropriate or to comply with what an adult desired or expects. In one study, one group of preschool and elementary children were presented with new toys, while another group of children were presented with broken, used toys. The children (some of whom were as young as two-and-a-half years) who got the disappointing toys registered disappointment and confusion on their faces, but quickly masked those emotions, put smiles on their little faces, and thanked the researchers for the presents (Cole, 1986).

## Innate and Learned

A final perspective on the acquisition of facial expression important to review is a combined perspective, that is, that facial behavior is both innate and learned. Many nonverbal communication scholars agree with this position (Ekman & Friesen, 1969a, 1969b, 1975; Ekman, Friesen, & Ellsworth, 1972). Some facial expressions that we're born with are closely associated with our six primary emotions: sadness, anger, disgust, fear, surprise, and happiness. We may be born able to express these emotions on our faces, but with experience we learn different facial expressions or more nuanced ways of communicating (and sometimes masking) what we feel.

As a baby is born into the world, he or she feels free to express emotions without management or holding back. But over time, as the baby grows into adulthood, she or he becomes socialized and trained to control the expression of emotions based on the context. We learn what is socially appropriate and accepted in terms of expressive behavior. For example, a teacher may get irritated at several students in the back of a classroom who are talking. Rather than expressing that irritation through the flash of a facial expression, the teacher may mask the emotion and choose to ignore the disruption until after class, fearing an emotional outburst will throw off the rhythm of the class and only make the situation worse. As another example, we quickly learn in life that it's okay to laugh at jokes and have fun in certain situations. But as an audience member in a public speaking situation, part of our ethical responsibility is to not laugh or poke fun at a speaker who gets disorganized or sounds odd due to communication anxiety. In various situations, we learn (or we *hope* that we learn) to adapt our behavior in order to act appropriately in the situation. Put simply, people are born with the ability to express the primary emotions through facial and bodily expressions. But as we mature, we are expected to adapt our nonverbal expressions and mold them to what is appropriate in a given communication and cultural context (Newcombe & Lie, 1995; Russell & Bullock, 1985; Wagner, MacDonald, & Manstead, 1986).

We could argue that a smile is an innate behavior, given evidence that sensory-deprived children produce smiles comparable to children who do not have such impairments. But different types of smiles exist, including genuine and forced smiles; some of these expressions are learned as adaptations of the basic smile (Hugenberg & Sczesny, 2006; Krumhuber, Manstead, & Kappas, 2007; Schmidt, 2006). Many of us no doubt remember those annoying photographers in years past who asked us to look at the camera and smile. **Genuine smiles** are unconscious and uncontrolled—the kind a photographer will try to capture so that a picture reflects who we really are (Krumhuber & Kappas, 2005). The **Duchenne smile** (named after a French specialist in anatomy), also termed a **felt smile,** engages the muscles around the eyes as well as the muscles around the lips that cause the corners of the mouth to move upward; these smiles send the following positive messages: "Good to see you," "Let's play," or "Let's be friends" (Ekman, Davidson, & Friesen, 1990; Fridlund & Russell, 2006). Smiling is said to make people feel better. Thus, when we're smiling, we may feel happier, which communicates happiness to other people in our environment (Hall, Horgan, & Carter,

*Genuine smile*    *Fake smile*

2002; Heisel & Mongrain, 2004; Krumhuber & Kappas, 2005; Pell, 2005a, 2005b; Pugh, 2001). But when our smiles are forced and conscious, we often plaster a **fake smile** on our faces, which involves a less wide expression than a genuine smile (generally speaking), with possibly a forced baring or gritting of the teeth (Ekman & Friesen, 1982). Fake smiles can damage how others view us in social situations, while genuine smiles promote social relationships and convey honest emotions to other people (Shimamura, Ross, & Bennett, 2006; Yamamoto & Suzuki, 2006).

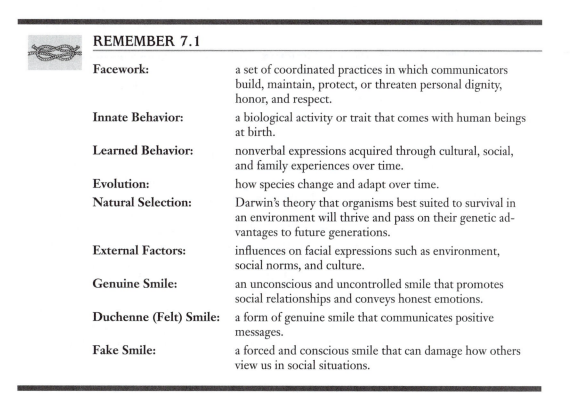

### REMEMBER 7.1

**Facework:** a set of coordinated practices in which communicators build, maintain, protect, or threaten personal dignity, honor, and respect.

**Innate Behavior:** a biological activity or trait that comes with human beings at birth.

**Learned Behavior:** nonverbal expressions acquired through cultural, social, and family experiences over time.

**Evolution:** how species change and adapt over time.

**Natural Selection:** Darwin's theory that organisms best suited to survival in an environment will thrive and pass on their genetic advantages to future generations.

**External Factors:** influences on facial expressions such as environment, social norms, and culture.

**Genuine Smile:** an unconscious and uncontrolled smile that promotes social relationships and conveys honest emotions.

**Duchenne (Felt) Smile:** a form of genuine smile that communicates positive messages.

**Fake Smile:** a forced and conscious smile that can damage how others view us in social situations.

# ■ MANAGING FACIAL EXPRESSIONS

We've established that the face communicates basic human emotions. The question we explore in this section is: How do people manage their facial expressions? You may not have ever thought of facial expressions as something needing to be "managed," but what we mean is that we have some degree of control over what we express on our faces. While some expressions happen quickly and innately (like opening the eyes widely and raising the eyebrows when surprised), for other expressions we have a choice. In some situations and for some emotions, facial expression is purposeful. So, in addition to having a basic understanding of the emotions communicated by the face, we need to be aware of how we manage our face in everyday life. Because of social norms and communication expectations, it's important to understand emotional expression and how it varies situationally (Buck, 1984, 1988, 1993, 1994; Sato & Yoshikawa, 2007).

Stemming from the work of nonverbal scholars Paul Ekman and Wallace Friesen (1969a, 1969b, 1975), facial management techniques are categories of behavior that help us determine the appropriate facial response for any given situation. To begin our study of facial management, let's review the four most common techniques: neutralization, masking, intensification, and deintensification.

**Neutralization.**    **Neutralization** is the first facial management technique, which refers to the process of using facial expression to erase or numb how we really feel. People who neutralize their facial expressions are often referred to as having a poker face. If you watch *The World Series of Poker* on television, you don't have to look too hard to find a player engaged in the neutralization of her or his facial expressions. In fact, many poker players use caps, sunglasses, and costumes as part of their attempt to neutralize their true emotions cued by the face. Another example of the poker face can be seen in the remake of the movie *Casino Royale*, in which the James Bond character (played by Daniel Craig) participates in a poker match with millions of dollars at stake—even more of a reason to be in the know when it comes to facial management!

**Masking.**    The next facial management technique we use in certain social contexts is **masking**—concealing the expressions connected to a felt emotion and replacing them with expressions more appropriate to the situation. Here's an example: Over the past few weeks Cindy and Megan have studied hard for a huge history exam. They share the goal of earning at least a B on the exam. When their professor passes out the exam scores, Cindy's face lights up and she immediately bursts with joy in response to earning an A. When Megan receives her grade and realizes that she has only earned a D, she's extremely disappointed and initially feels anger and envy toward Cindy since they studied together. When Cindy expresses happiness about her good grade, Megan masks her facial expression of disappointment, thus suppressing her feelings about her own grade, and congratulates Cindy. Take a moment to think about experiences you've had that led you to mask your facial expressions and emotions. Is masking a technique that comes easily for you or is it difficult to pull off?

**Intensification.**    The next facial management technique is called **intensification**— the use of a facial expression that reveals an exaggeration of how we feel about something. For example, Joel is really nervous about meeting the parents of his partner, Sam. Joel isn't used to disclosing his sexual orientation to people he doesn't know well, so meeting his partner's family is causing a lot of anxiety. When Joel is introduced to Sam's parents, he intensifies his smile to send a message of happiness and pleasure. He's glad to meet them, as a turning point in his relationship with Sam, but feels a pressure to intensify his smile since he's meeting them for the first time and the situation feels awkward. Perhaps you can think of other situations in which social pressure requires or leads to an exaggerated facial expression.

**Deintensification.**    The final facial management technique is **deintensification**— the reduction of intensity of our facial expression of a particular emotion due to social or cultural expectations. In U.S. culture, men are not conditioned to express intense feelings of sadness, fear, or worry. Televised sporting events like football, baseball, and basketball games often show close-up shots of members of the losing team sitting on the bench looking forlorn, in order to capture a sense of their emotion. In the 2007 NFC wildcard game, Dallas Cowboys quarterback Tony Romo fumbled the field goal snap that resulted in a last second playoff loss to the Seattle Seahawks. The cameras zoomed in on Romo to capture his expression of emotion in response to making a huge mistake that contributed to his team's defeat. While some athletes mask what they're feeling during a game, match, or meet, others simply "let it all hang out" for the cameras. Men in U.S. culture are allowed some emotion, but not too much since their role is often to keep it together so they can maintain their toughness—a key element often associated with masculinity. Thus, many men tend to deintensify their facial expressions of sadness or grief, as well as joy, to meet what they perceive social expectations to be.

Deintensification is also exemplified by people in leadership positions. Someone in charge of a business, team, classroom, or the like is usually expected to keep his or her emotions held in check. If a manager is angry about the way a customer is behaving, she or he must deintensify any emotional display in order to remain calm and professional. Again, the sporting arena is prime territory to see this technique in action. Think about how coaches respond to the media after winning or losing a game. Of course the winning coach is going to be happy about the win, but deintensification of facial expressions of elation are often accompanied by references to what the team could have done better, what needs to be done to keep up the success, and so forth. On the other hand, the losing coach no doubt feels terrible, but tries to deintensify facial expressions of sadness or anger so as to talk calmly about what went wrong and what needs to be done for the next game. Winning and losing also apply to people in leadership positions, who are expected to remain poised and professional in the best of times, as well as the worst of times. In sum, good communicators know what face to wear given the constraints of the communicative situation.

---

**REMEMBER 7.2**

**Ekman & Friesen's Facial Management Techniques**

| | |
|---|---|
| **Neutralization:** | facial expressions that erase or numb how we really feel. |
| **Masking:** | concealing the expressions connected to a felt emotion and replacing them with expressions more appropriate to the situation. |
| **Intensification:** | use of a facial expression that reveals an exaggeration of how we feel about something. |
| **Deintensification:** | reduction of intensity of a facial expression related to a particular emotion due to social or cultural expectations. |

---

## Ekman and Friesen's Classification of Facial Expressions

In addition to facial management techniques, Ekman and Friesen and colleagues created a classification system for facial expressions (Ekman & Friesen, 1969a, 1969b; Ekman, Friesen, & Tompkins, 1971). Let's review their eight different styles of facial expressions, understanding that many, if not all, of these styles are subconscious to the communicator.

1. *The Withholder:* With this style of facial expression, the face does not exhibit any states of emotion (the ultimate poker face). Facial movement is restricted.
2. *The Revealer:* Opposite of the withholder, the face tells all, with little doubt as to how the person feels.
3. *The Unwitting Expressor:* A person tries to mask an emotion, but "unwittingly" the emotion is revealed through facial expressions, which may surprise the communicator.
4. *The Blanked Expressor:* In this style, the communicator believes an emotion is being conveyed, but no one else can see it.
5. *The Substitute Expressor:* This style of facial expression displays an emotion other than what the communicator thinks is being portrayed. The substitute expressor thinks a message of sadness is being sent, for example, while others interpret the facial expression as related to a different emotion.
6. *The Frozen-Affect Expressor:* In this style, part of an emotion is displayed at all times, meaning that a characteristic or feature of the face translates to an emotion in the minds of viewers. For example, someone whose mouth naturally turns down at the corners can be perceived to be frowning and sad all the time.
7. *The Ever-Ready Expressor:* In this style, a communicator tends to display one general facial expression as a response to almost any situation, no matter the emotion being felt. For example, the ever-ready expressor smiles whether receiving good or bad news.

8. *The Flooded-Affect Expressor:* These communicators feel a particular emotion and that emotion "floods" their face with a certain expression; they rarely look neutral when they're emotional. For example, if a person has registered anger on her or his face, a situation that might evoke a different emotion doesn't cause the look of anger to go away.

What's your style of facial expression? Do any of the styles listed above ring a bell? Take a moment to review the styles and try to think of a friend, family member, or classmate who resembles these styles of facial expression. While this list is useful in the general classification of styles of facial expressions, it's important to remember that we rarely display only one emotion at a time on our faces. In other words, our emotions aren't one dimensional; we may register several emotions and express them on our faces at the same time. These multiple facial expressions are called **affect blends.** In addition, in some situations, we may try to be neutral in our expression, but one portion of the face reveals how we feel. This phenomenon is known as a **partial**—an emotion that registers in a single area of the face, while other facial areas are controlled. One other form of facial expression is interesting, while we're on the subject of styles and controlled versus spontaneous expressions. In their classic study, researchers Haggard and Isaacs (1966) detected dramatic, rapid changes of expressions flashing across their subjects' faces, which they termed **micromomentary facial expressions.** These expressions can be at odds with what a person says, but the researchers believe that they are truer indicators of an emotion before that emotion is masked, if an observer is quick enough to detect them.

## Facial Action Coding System (FACS)

How does one go about locating and evaluating facial expressions? Ekman and Friesen designed a process called the **Facial Action Coding System (FACS)** that separates the face into three regions (see Figure 7.1): eyebrows and forehead; eyes and eyelids; and lower face, including the cheeks, nose, and mouth. Using Ekman's six primary emotions (see Table 7.1), researchers have learned to classify particular emotions in terms of where they emerge on the face (Atkinson, Tipples, Burt, & Young, 2005; Boucher & Ekman, 1975; D'Acremont & Van der Linden, 2007; Ekman & Friesen, 1975; Johnson, Ekman, & Friesen, 1975; Kalick, Zebrowitz, Langlois, & Johnson, 1998; Mendolia, 2007). Let's explore each region of the face to see what's communicated nonverbally.

**FIGURE 7.1    Three Regions of the Face**

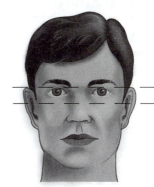

1. Eyebrows and Forehead

2. Eyes and Eyelids

3. Lower Face: Cheeks, Nose, and Mouth

*Sadness*

*Anger*

*Disgust*

*Fear*

*Happiness*

*Surprise*

## TABLE 7.1    Ekman and Friesen's Six Basic Emotions Revealed by the Face

| EMOTION | FACIAL LOCATION |
|---|---|
| **Sadness** | Eyes and eyelids |
| **Anger** | Forehead, mouth, brows, and cheeks |
| **Disgust** | Multiple areas of face, including bridge of the nose |
| **Fear** | Eyes and eyelids |
| **Happiness** | Lower facial region; eyes and eyelids |
| **Surprise** | All facial regions (brows/forehead, eyes/eyelids, and lower face) |

**Eyebrow and Forehead.**   The first region of the face includes the eyebrow and forehead region, which can communicate a variety of messages. For example, lowering the brows can be viewed as a frown, a signal of disappointment or anger. In contrast, raising the brows can signal interest or surprise. At the more extreme level, brow raises can communicate amazement, surprise, or fear. One brow raised, also known as the **cocked eyebrow,** while keeping the other brow still can be a sign of questioning or confusion. **Knitted eyebrows** (both brows down towards the nose and eyes) can signal pain, illness, anxiety, or frustration. **Flashing eyebrows** (both brows raised and lowered quickly) can signal flirtation (sometimes sexual) or a friendly greeting, depending on the situation. Have you ever been distracted by someone's eyebrow movement? If so, what was your reaction? Did you view the eyebrow behavior as positive or negative? Take a moment to think about your own eyebrow behavior. Review the terms in this section and think about your use of them in social situations.

**Eyes and Eyelids.**   While we examine ways in which we use our eyes to nonverbally communicate more thoroughly in the last half of this chapter, it's important to mention the eyes here since they're part of Ekman and Friesen's regions of the face. The U.S. is a visually oriented culture; estimates suggest that 80 percent of the information we take in is accomplished visually (Brown & Lloyd-Jones, 2006; Messaris, 2003; Morris, 1985). The human eyes and eyelids are critical to everyday functioning, such as protection from environmental factors (e.g., wind, dust, sunlight) and recognition of faces and objects. In addition to basic functions, our eyes and eyelids are used to nonverbally communicate with others. For example, the eye is used to **wink**—quickly closing and opening one eye at another person. The ways in which people interpret and evaluate winking has been studied by nonverbal communication scholars (Lindsey & Vigil, 1999). Researchers suggest that winking is perceived as positive or negative depending on the situation. Similar to flashing eyebrows, winking can signal flirtation or serve as a cue that someone is joking around (Whitty, 2004). Take a moment to think about your own experiences with winking. What's your reaction when another person winks at you? Does it depend on the situation and the person? Have you ever winked at another person and received a negative response? Winking at someone you like is generally accepted in social situations, but we recommend you avoid winking in professional situations as it could make others feel uncomfortable and even harassed, as alluded to in the opening case study.

**Cheeks.**   Do you have a friend or loved one with a light complexion whose face turns red in response to embarrassment? Nonverbal behaviorist Desmond Morris (1985) explains that the lower facial region typically reveals the true emotions that people experience. The flushing of the cheeks you've likely observed on other people or that you may evidence yourself, primarily triggered by shame, embarrassment, or self-consciousness, is explored in nonverbal communication research (Asendorpf, 1990; Costa, Dinsbach, Manstead, & Pio Enrico, 2001; Fridlund & Russell, 2006; Keltner, 1995; Keltner & Buswell, 1997). The pattern of blood rushing into the cheeks varies, depending on whether an emotion of anger or embarrassment is felt. Specifically, reddening associated with anger tends to spread throughout the face, while reddening in embarrassment is more subtle and confined to a smaller region of the face.

**Nose.**   Another important region of the human face is the nose. Take a moment to think about life without a nose. It's hard to imagine, isn't it? You wouldn't be able to smell and breathing would be extremely difficult. Some view the nose as a protector of the eyes and a filter against dust and debris. Similar to the mouth, many cultural groups use a variety of methods to modify or decorate the nose. Celebrities like Michael Jackson and Ashlee Simpson spend large sums of money on cosmetic surgery to perfect their nose (Davis, 2003b). You may not think that your nose communicates much, but its size and shape send signals to others, warranted or not. Some people have a perky "button" nose, often conveying youthfulness; others have a large, bulbous nose which may send a different kind of signal to an onlooker. Plus, the bridge of the nose is integral to facial expression; it's a primary area for conveying the emotion of disgust, as we typically wrinkle the bridge of the nose when we confront a disgusting stimulus.

**Mouth.**   The human mouth is used for a wide variety of actions, such as talking, smiling, laughing, frowning, kissing, singing, screaming, eating, drinking, and even smoking. Clearly, the human mouth is one of the most active body parts and, at the same time, it's used to express a variety of emotions such as surprise, happiness, fear, anger, boredom, and sadness, to name a few. In fact, since the mouth is so important in terms of location on the face as well as the functions it serves, members of cultural groups often

## REMEMBER 7.3

| | |
|---|---|
| **Affect Blends:** | expressing several emotions at the same time on the face. |
| **Partial:** | an emotion in a single area of the face while other facial areas are controlled. |
| **Micromomentary Facial Expressions:** | dramatic, rapid changes of facial expressions. |
| **Facial Action Coding System (FACS):** | a research coding system that examines the face in three regions: eyebrows and forehead; eyes and eyelids; and lower face (e.g., cheeks, nose, and mouth). |
| **Cocked Eyebrow:** | one brow raised while the other is still. |
| **Knitted Eyebrows:** | both brows down toward the nose and eyes. |
| **Flashing Eyebrows:** | both brows raised and lowered quickly. |
| **Wink:** | quickly closing and opening one eye at another person. |

modify the appearance of the mouth with tattoos, piercings, color, and cosmetic procedures, such as collagen injections (Darling-Wolf, 2003, 2004; Davis, 1995, 2003a, 2003b; Deery, 2004; Denness, 2005; Heyes, 2007; Holliday & Cairnie, 2007; McCurdy & Lam, 2005).

## ■ MODIFYING THE FACE

In the previous sections of this chapter, we reviewed the nonverbal dimensions of face and discussed how central facial expressions are to human communication. Because the face is so important to people across cultures, we've started to see increases in the amounts of money spent on facial modification so that people can achieve what their culture views as "ideal" (Caliendo, Armstrong, & Roberts, 2005; Holliday & Cairnie, 2007; Mulkens & Jansen, 2006). In Chapter 5 on physical appearance, we discussed some personal and social consequences of **body modification,** meaning the more permanent methods of changing the way we look (Heyes, 2007; Oliver, 2006). Here, we refine our focus to **facial modification,** that is, more permanent methods of changing the face. To be clear, we're not talking about people who suffer disfigurement from birth defects, car wrecks, fires, or other catastrophes in which their faces are damaged or malformed. Surgeries that can improve the functioning of a person's disfigured face or help make someone feel like she or he fits in or functions more effectively in society are not the subject of our discussion. Our focus is the alteration of the face for which the key motivation is to enhance perceptions of attractiveness.

Similar to body modification, the cosmetic surgery industry offers an array of procedures and products that enable people to change each region of the face, including the nose, cheeks, chin, eyes, and forehead (Davis, 2003a, 2003b; Holliday & Cairnie, 2007). One basic perception of attractiveness relates to **facial symmetry,** meaning a face that is equally proportioned in size and shape. Research shows that in U.S. culture, as well as many other cultures around the world, equally proportioned or symmetrical faces are viewed as highly attractive (Cunningham, Barbee, & Philhower, 2002; Grammer & Thornhill, 1994). Some cosmetic procedures are aimed at simply achieving greater symmetry in the face.

You've no doubt heard or read stories of celebrities and non-celebrities alike who attempt to correct a facial "flaw" (from their perception) or try to "turn back the hands of time" by modifying their faces, either through surgery or cosmetic procedures. Some procedures do enhance appearance and possibly even health, such as facial peels or laser techniques that reverse the effects of sun damage. But you've probably also heard the tragic outcomes of some of these surgeries and procedures, like the people who become addicted to facial and body modification, such that after multiple procedures they end up looking less than human, or people who die from complications of surgery, like singer Kanye West's mother who died in 2007 after a cosmetic surgical procedure. Below we provide some of the most common facial modification procedures. While more women than men in the U.S. undergo facial modification procedures, the number of men seeking to alter their facial features is on the increase (American Society for Aesthetic Plastic Surgery, 2006).

1. *Rhinoplasty:* This is the technical term for nose surgery. Originally developed to correct breathing problems in youth, the nose is broken and reshaped to a preferred size.
2. *Botox:* This procedure consists of an injection of a toxic substance that temporarily paralyzes muscles and skin tissues, typically applied to the forehead and around the eyes, for the purposes of tightening the skin on the face, reducing wrinkles, and making people look younger.
3. *Laser Treatments:* Lasers are applied to the face or other areas of the body marred by acne or skin discolorations, to produce a more consistent skin tone.
4. *Facelift:* This is a complex surgical procedure in which the skin on the face (and sometimes the neck) is surgically detached, lifted up, and reattached to defy the natural aging effects of gravity and to create a tighter, more youthful looking face.
5. *Collagen Injections:* Some people, especially women, wish to create more fullness in their lips, which have a tendency to thin and flatten with age. They undergo this procedure in which collagen is injected into the lips to create a fuller, more youthful look (at least for the few months the effect lasts).
6. *Chin Implants:* Some people believe that they have a "weak chin," a chin that recedes or doesn't balance their nose, or they simply don't like their profiles. To correct this they opt for a procedure in which material or a "bridge" of sorts is implanted into their existing chin to make the chin more prominent.

We've already mentioned celebrity Michael Jackson in this chapter—he often comes to mind in discussions of cosmetic surgery since he has had extensive work done to alter his facial features and skin color. Feminist scholar Kathy Davis (2003b) writes that Michael Jackson "has had at least four rhinoplasties as well as numerous fine tuning operations. The result is a fragile, pointed nose, whittled away to almost nothing, that gives his face a skeletal look" (p. 81). Davis continues, "Jackson has also had a cleft put in his chin, cheek implants, his lower lip thinned and probably some face-lifting" (p. 82). Jackson exemplifies both the pressure people often feel to change the way they look physically, as well as the growing number of men choosing to undergo cosmetic procedures (Holliday & Cairnie, 2007).

Procedures designed to make ethnic minorities look more Caucasian or members of other cultures appear more American or western are controversial, but occur with such frequency that they actually have a categorical label now—**ethnic cosmetic surgery** (Davis, 2003b). Davis (2003b) discusses this issue, suggesting that "while a white person may be free to experiment with her or his appearance—and this includes indulging in the surgical fix—the same experiment takes on a different meaning when undertaken by people of color or the ethnically marginalized" (pp. 83–84). Davis contends that "cosmetic surgery for people of color or the ethnically marginalized is about 'race,' while cosmetic surgery for white Anglos is about beauty" (p. 84). Whether any sort of facial feature is a point of cultural pride or something one desires

*Like it or not, physical appearance of the face plays a role in professional as well as personal contexts.*

to change depends on the individual. One recent international trend is for wealthy Iranian women to get their noses "fixed" to enhance their beauty. In fact, the U.S. cosmetic surgery industry now targets the growing community of Iranian exiles for this form of facial modification.

No doubt, the face is a powerful instrument of communication. From the acquisition and development of human facial expressions to the ways we manage facial expressions when we communicate to cosmetic procedures, the face is a critical code

---

### REMEMBER 7.4

| | |
|---|---|
| **Body Modification:** | more permanent methods of changing the way the body looks. |
| **Facial Modification:** | more permanent methods of changing the face. |
| **Facial Symmetry:** | a face that's equally proportioned in size and shape. |
| **Ethnic Cosmetic Surgery:** | medical procedures that make members of ethnic minority groups look more western or Caucasian. |

### What Would _You_ Do?

Imagine that you and a friend are working at the same place for the summer. Your jobs are in the sales department of a local electronics store. After a few weeks on the job, as customers are waiting for your help, you direct them to your friend for assistance. They all stay in your area, waiting for you to assist them. A few make comments to you about your friend's behavior towards customers and that they would rather wait for you. You know your friend to be a really nice and friendly person, so you figure the customers must have her confused with someone else.

At a weekly meeting with your supervisor, you're notified that your friend has the lowest sales numbers out of the entire staff at the store. You, on the other hand, have excelled in sales and are up for a promotion. Your friend's job is in jeopardy, so you have been asked to shadow her and give her tips on how you've managed to climb the ladder in such a short time. After only a few hours, you realize the problem: Your friend is not aware of the rude, unfriendly facial expressions she's giving people! While working in the computer department, she rolls her eyes at people who ask simple questions about their systems. She rarely smiles or makes eye contact when approaching a customer, and for the most part looks bored with her work.

Using this scenario and what you have learned from this chapter about the importance of facial expressions and eye behavior in nonverbal communication, _what would you do?_ Would you tell your friend that her nonverbal expressions are a turn-off to customers? How can you give her this feedback about her nonverbal cues without hurting her feelings? How could she use her face and eyes to reflect her normally friendly personality to customers?

within our study of nonverbal behavior. Now it's time to turn our attention in part two of this chapter to a very important subset of the face: the eyes. Our eyes are enormous conveyors and processors of nonverbal communication, so let's explore this topic in depth.

## SIGNIFICANCE OF EYE BEHAVIOR

In this section we review the study of eye behavior, also known as **oculesics,** which includes eye contact, eye movement, and other functions of the eye. As we stated earlier, estimates indicate that 80 percent of the information in our everyday surroundings is taken in visually, despite other human communicative behaviors such as talking, listening, moving, and touching (Morris, 1985). Particularly in American culture, we feel connected to other people if eye contact is established, believing that the eyes truly are "the windows to the soul." That's why eye behavior is emphasized in basic communication courses (Beebe, Beebe, & Ivy, 2007) and has been a central topic within the study of nonverbal communication for many years (Argyle & Dean, 1965; Argyle & Ingham, 1972; Argyle, Ingham, Alkema, & McCallin, 1973; Argyle, Lefebvre, & Cook, 1974; Ashear & Snortum, 1971; Bakan, 1971; Bakan & Strayer, 1973; Barlow, 1969; Baron-Cohen,

Wheelwright, & Jolliffe, 1997; Droney & Brooks, 2001; Everett, Olmi, Edwards, & Tingstrom, 2005; Guerrero & Floyd, 2006; Manusov & Patterson, 2006). Communication scholar Steve Beebe (1974) studied the influence of eye contact on judgments of speaker credibility and found that the best speakers connect with their audiences in a variety of ways, the primary one being through eye contact. Let's begin our study of eye behavior as a key code of nonverbal communication by examining its influences and purposes.

## Influences of Eye Behavior

It's helpful to think of eye behavior in terms of its influence on the social interactive process. The first influence of eye behavior is its powerful ability to stimulate **arousal**—a positive or negative reaction in response to another person. To clarify, we don't mean *sexual* arousal here, but more in the vein of activation or some sort of reaction to visual stimuli. We all experience some degree of arousal when we see another person. The arousal may be extremely positive in response to someone we like and haven't seen for awhile. On the other hand, we may experience negative arousal if we cross paths with someone who gets on our nerves.

Another influence of eye behavior relates to **salience,** meaning that what we do with our eyes is more noticeable than other actions of the face and body. Simply put, the eyes really matter in social interaction and are critical to our study of nonverbal communication. Our eyes play a central role in developing relationships with others, as well as managing everyday communicative needs such as attention getting, listening, and showing interest (Gueguen & Jacob, 2002; Guerrero & Floyd, 2006). Take a moment to reflect on the power of eye behavior in your everyday life. Even in the most mundane social encounters, like at the grocery store, eye behavior helps us manage politeness and common courtesy. One example would be the awkward moment of almost running over another person with your shopping cart. As you hold the cart back, you make quick eye contact, squeeze out a smile, and mumble a quick "excuse me." This approach works most of the time and gets us out of social predicaments. Of course, some of us may practice a more intense, second option: avoid eye contact, don't smile, get that cart out of the way, and move on to the dairy section.

The third influence of eye behavior is **involvement**—the need to interact with another person even if it's a simple eye acknowledgement or head nod. A good example of this is when we pass by a stranger on campus. We don't know the person and haven't had class with him or her before, but as we approach there's some form of energy that gets us to be involved with the person, even if only for a second or two. Some of us may view ourselves as shy and perhaps even avoidant when it comes to strangers. Yet, there's usually some sort of involvement, even if it's a head nod or grunt, promoted by even the briefest of eye contact. It's quite common to see students, particularly male students, acknowledge each other's presence by making brief eye contact, coupled with the "chin lift" move, which together translate into the ever-popular "What's up?" greeting. In the HBO series, *Curb Your Enthusiasm*, one episode featured what the lead character, Larry David, called the "stop and chat." The scene showed several people passing each other on the sidewalk in front of a café. Larry saw

---

### REMEMBER 7.5

**Oculesics:**    the study of eye behavior including eye contact, eye movement, and other functions of the eye.

**Arousal:**    a positive or negative reaction to another person.

**Salience:**    the fact that what we do with our eyes is more noticeable than other actions of the face and body.

**Involvement:**    a need to interact with other people, even through a simple acknowledgement of eye contact or a head nod.

---

someone he knew—someone who obviously wanted to stop and say hello, but Larry didn't want this simple social encounter, so he avoided eye contact and kept moving. Larry found out later that the person he eluded on the sidewalk was mad at him for avoiding the "stop and chat."

## Purposes of Eye Behavior

In addition to influences of eye behavior, nonverbal communication researchers have explored its various purposes (Kendon, 1967). As we review ten purposes of eye behavior below, reflect on how you use your eyes to see if the purposes connect with your personal experience.

1. *Recognizing others:* One of the most basic functions of the eye is to help us recognize other people, objects, places, and so forth. Those of us who have the privilege of sight often take this ability for granted, until we find ourselves groping about in a suddenly dark room or when we emerge into the sunlight from a dark location, or until an injury or illness takes away our sight. In these situations we likely gain a big dose of empathy for people who are visually impaired, and we marvel at how they learn to cope with their circumstances in a culture that emphasizes visual stimuli, even in its language. (Think about how many times a sighted person might say "I see what you mean" or "I'm not blind to what's going on here.") However, medical research has detected a rare condition in which sighted people can't recognize others, termed prosopagnosia or, more commonly, face blindness (Hewitt, 2007). People who suffer from this malady have no problems with their eyesight, but their brains are impaired such that they can't remember what people look like, even members of their own families.

2. *Scanning:* Another primary function of eye behavior is to scan the environment and social situations, typically checking for physical safety and social comfort. A good example is scanning a busy movie theatre to find an open seat or hunting through a crowd for people you know. Another more social use for the scanning function relates to flirting. When we come into a social setting, like a club or

party, we're likely to scan the area (and the people within the area) with our eyes, whether or not we came to the event alone. Such scanning helps us get "the lay of the land," as well as seek out interested parties to talk to, where refreshments are located, whether anyone has noticed our arrival, and so forth. Scanning is often a precursor to flirting (Collett, 2004; Grammer, Kruck, Juette, & Fink, 2000; Muehlenhard, Koralewski, Andrews, & Burdick, 1986; Renninger, Wade, & Grammer, 2004).

3. *Thinking (Cognitive Activity):* Eye behavior reflects **cognitive activity**— the use of the brain for memory recall and information processing (Bakan, 1971; Bakan & Strayer, 1973). Researchers measure **conjugate lateral eye movements (CLEMs)**— involuntary eye movements to the left or right that reveal brain activity or thought processes—while asking subjects thought-provoking questions that require them to use different parts of their brain (Theeuwes, Kramer, Hahn, & Irwin, 1998). When people move their eyes to the left, it's thought to reflect activity in the right hemisphere of the brain, and vice versa. So by tracking eye behavior you get a "window" into brain activity. Have you ever seen yourself on videotape? If you've ever been interviewed by a reporter or watched a recording of yourself, you'll likely notice that your eye movement signals cognitive activity when you're trying to remember or describe something.

4. *Decreasing physical and psychological distance:* As we've discussed elsewhere in this book, **nonverbal immediacy cues** communicate approachability, availability, closeness, and warmth (McCroskey, Richmond, & McCroskey, 2006). Eye contact is a key immediacy behavior, in that it can decrease the physical and psychological distance between people, such as often occurs between speakers and audiences in a public communication setting (Beebe, 1974; Beebe & Beebe, 2006; Mehrabian, 1971).

5. *Regulating interaction:* Eyes also function to **regulate** interaction, meaning that nonverbal cues are sent with the eyes to let another person know whether a conversation is going to start, continue, or come to an end (Duncan, 1972). People generally take turns at talk in a conversation (termed, logically, **turn-taking**), and eye contact, along with other nonverbal cues, helps cue the behavior. This process is a subset of **interaction management,** or how people use verbal and nonverbal communication to conduct or manage their conversations (Guerrero & Floyd, 2006). We examine turn-taking more thoroughly in the Chapter 9 on vocal nonverbal cues, but it's also pertinent to our study of eye behavior. The eyes help us manage interaction by letting us know when it's okay to speak or respond. Further, broken eye contact usually cues that a conversation is over. Trying to continue a conversation after eye contact is broken can be annoying or perceived as negative by the person wanting to move on to another appointment or someone who's more interesting.

6. *Establishing and defining relationships:* We use eye gaze to connect with others, and then to help define and manage those relationships. If we make eye contact and connect, a relationship is likely to be initiated. If we avoid eye contact and don't connect, a relationship has less chance of forming. While eye gaze is critical to establishing and maintaining relationships, it's important

to avoid staring—giving too much eye contact or looking at another person in a way that is viewed as socially inappropriate. If you're interested in establishing a relationship with someone, you're likely to make a lot of eye contact with that person, but if the eye contact isn't returned, indicating that the feeling isn't mutual, you may be accused of staring.

7. *Displaying power:* In addition to regulating interaction, eye behavior can be used as a **power display**—a nonverbal means of indicating dominance over another person (Dovidio & Ellyson, 1985; Droney & Brooks, 2001). You've probably heard of the "stare-down" or "staring match" that can be a fun game for children, but it can also cause conflict among adults striving for interpersonal superiority. We mentioned general staring earlier, but the **power stare** occurs when someone narrows the eyelids (almost into a squint) and maintains eye contact with someone without blinking as an assertion of authority (Tannen, 2006). You often see two boxers at a pre-bout press conference or just before a match begins engaged in a mutual power stare in an attempt to

*Eye behavior helps us connect with others and establish relationships.*

psych out their opponent and establish their dominance. People who are being stared at usually respond in one of two ways: (1) They either stare back to send a signal that the power stare from the other person isn't working and they're not going to back down, or (2) they avoid eye contact altogether to escape potential conflict. Another phenomenon related to power displays is termed the **visual dominance ratio,** or the amount of eye contact we make when we're talking to someone, versus the amount of eye contact we make when we're listening to that person (Ellyson, Dovidio, & Fehr, 1981). In face-to-face conversation, the general expectation is to engage in mutual eye gaze, with brief breaks away, when both speaking and listening. But some people make steady eye contact only when they're talking; they break eye contact and look elsewhere the majority of the time someone else is talking, and this behavior can communicate dominance. It can also be quite irritating if you're the person giving steady eye contact, which signals your attention, but your conversational partner is looking everywhere but you. It can make you feel undervalued and invisible.

8. *Expressing emotions:* The eyes also function to express emotions—in fact some experts suggest that emotions are most readily detected from eye behavior, meaning that if you want to know how someone's feeling, watch their eyes. When people have lost a loved one and have been mourning, the eyes have a certain tired or watery look from crying and exhaustion as a byproduct of the grieving process. It's likely hard for the person to maintain eye contact, because the body just won't respond like it normally does. Or perhaps you see a friend at some distance; you can tell that something's up, but can't tell what emotion the person is feeling until he or she gets closer and you can focus on the eyes. As we said in Chapter 6 on body movement, the face and eyes will tell you *which* particular emotion is being felt, while the body will tell you *how much* emotion is being felt.

9. *Excluding:* Eye behavior can be used for **exclusion**—the process of closing others out from the action or from conversation. If you've ever intentionally focused on a person, but been aware that someone else is waiting to speak with you or attempting to join the conversation, then you've likely used eye gaze that prevented or excluded the other person from the conversation. Closing others out isn't always done with mean intention or disrespect. Sometimes our conversations are personal in nature or related to business—contexts that make it awkward to include another person.

10. *Monitoring feedback:* You're at a staff meeting and a coworker tells an off-color joke. He or she looks around the room, trying to detect what other people thought of the joke because no one's laughing. An uncomfortable silence fills the room and people avoid making eye contact with the coworker who told the joke. What's going on here? We use our eyes to monitor the feedback we receive from other people, which is an important function. In the example, people's lack of eye gaze with the jokester, in tandem with their lack of vocalizations (laughter) and negative facial expressions, should clue the person that her or his joke was not well received.

## REMEMBER 7.6

| | |
|---|---|
| **Cognitive Activity:** | eye behavior that signals brain use for memory recall and information processing. |
| **Conjugate Lateral Eye Movements (CLEMs):** | involuntary eye movements to the left or right that signal brain hemispheric activity. |
| **Nonverbal Immediacy Cues:** | nonverbal cues of approachability, availability, closeness, and warmth that decrease psychological and physical distance between people. |
| **Regulating:** | eye behavior that lets other people know whether a conversation will begin, continue, or come to an end. |
| **Turn-Taking:** | a structure for conversation and a means of studying or tracking conversations for the purpose of analysis. |
| **Interaction Management:** | how people use verbal and nonverbal communication to conduct or manage their conversations with others. |
| **Power Display:** | a nonverbal means of indicating dominance over another person through the use of sustained eye contact. |
| **Power Stare:** | a narrowing of the eyelids (almost into a squint) and the maintenance of eye contact without blinking, as a means of establishing dominance. |
| **Visual Dominance Ratio:** | amount of eye contact made when talking to someone, versus the amount of eye contact made when listening to the person. |
| **Exclusion:** | the use of eye behavior to close others out from conversation. |

# ■ FORMS OF EYE BEHAVIOR

Forms of eye behavior have been studied and defined by many nonverbal communication scholars over time (Argyle & Cook, 1976; Argyle & Ingham, 1972; Callahan, 2000; Doherty-Sneddon & Phelps, 2005; Droney & Brooks, 2001; Ellsworth, 1975; Exline, 1963; Exline & Fehr, 1982; Monk & Gale, 2002; Rhys, 2005). While the common term for looking at people or things is eye contact, the research term is **gaze,** defined as looking at someone or something in any given context. A subset of gaze is **mutual gaze** which occurs when two people look at each other, either in the eyes or within the region of the face (Monk & Gale, 2002). In U.S. culture, parents teach their children to "look people in the eye," encouraging mutual gaze as an eye behavior reflective of respect and confidence. In other cultures, mutual eye gaze is a sign of disrespect, such as in some Asian cultures where greeting rituals involve bowing, lowering the head, and eye gaze avoidance.

Another form of eye behavior is the **one-sided look,** a gaze or look towards another person that's not reciprocated. In other words, you may look in the direction of another person to get her or his attention or initiate conversation; if he or she does not look back, your eye gaze is one-sided and **gaze aversion** has occurred. Gaze aversion is usually *intentional* in the sense that the person who avoided eye contact is usually aware of the behavior (Doherty-Sneddon & Phelps, 2005). Gaze aversion is sometimes confused with **gaze omission**—an *unintentional* avoidance of eye contact. A reason usually exists for gaze aversion, such as disinterest, dislike, embarrassment, conflict avoidance, and so forth. But gaze omission can reflect shyness, being preoccupied or distracted in one's thinking, or simply being raised without lessons about the importance of eye contact, nor role models who enacted it appropriately. Can you think of situations in which you've used gaze aversion? A variety of factors can influence people to avert their eye gaze, including low self-esteem, embarrassment, and discomfort over the potential for conflict (Droney & Brooks, 2001; Levine & Sutton-Smith, 1973; Mobbs, 1968; Modigliani, 1971; Rhys, 2005; Stass & Willis, 1967; Stephenson & Rutter, 1970). Another interesting phenomenon related to the eyes is **civil inattention,** which occurs when two people share the same space or cross paths, but simply acknowledge each other with a quick look or glance without starting a conversation (Cary, 1978a, 1978b; Goffman, 1967; Zuckerman, Miserandino, & Bernieri, 1983). Perhaps you've seen this behavior in elevators, crowded hallways at school, or in subways, buses, or other forms of public transportation.

Our gaze behavior influences the perceptions other people have of us (Burgoon, Coker, & Coker, 1986; Greene & Frandsen, 1979; Turkstra, 2005). In fact, those of you preparing for job interviews should take note of your eye behavior. If you exhibit gaze aversion, your credibility and attractiveness may be harmed in the employment interview process (Burgoon, Manusov, Mineo, & Hael, 1985; Burkhardt, Weider-Hatfield, & Hocking, 1985). Likewise, if you stare at someone who's interviewing you, rather than make and break eye contact in succession (typical of interactions in the U.S.), you may be perceived negatively as well. Sometimes it's difficult to manage our gaze behavior when we're nervous, but the more we think about it and prepare ahead of the event, the better we're likely to behave (Callahan, 2000). Whether rehearsing a presentation or holding a simple conversation, be aware of eye behavior

## REMEMBER 7.7

### Forms of Eye Behavior

| | |
|---|---|
| **Gaze:** | looking at someone or something in any given social context. |
| **Mutual Gaze:** | occurs when two people look at each other, either in the eyes or within the region of the face. |
| **One-Sided Look:** | a gaze or look towards another person that is not reciprocated. |
| **Gaze Aversion:** | looking in the direction of another person, but not receiving the person's gaze in response. |
| **Gaze Omission:** | unintentional avoidance of eye contact. |
| **Civil Inattention:** | when people share the same space or cross paths and simply acknowledge each other with a quick look or glance without starting a conversation. |

that may cause your listeners to perceive you as untrustworthy, incompetent, or boring (Beebe & Beebe, 2006; Beebe, Beebe, & Ivy, 2007).

## Pupil Dilation: Size Matters

A cable television show airing in November of 2007 leads us to the following question: Are you *Gay, Straight, or Taken*? (We recognize that you may identify as bisexual or have other ways of expressing your sexual identity, but you get the point.) If you're not taken, are looking, or are perfectly content with your personal life, but curious about how eye behavior relates to sexual orientation, read on.

**Pupil dilation** occurs when the eyes dilate (increase in size or open more widely) or constrict (decrease in size or begin to close), and this phenomenon can actually tell us something nonverbally about another person. Communication researchers have studied human pupil dilation under a variety of conditions for several decades and have reported some interesting findings (Bakan, 1971; Burkhardt, Weider-Hatfield, & Hocking, 1985; Goldwater, 1972; Hess, 1968, 1975a, 1975b; Hess & Petrovich, 1987; Hess & Polt, 1964; Pettijohn & Tesser, 2005). In general, positive visual images stimulate pupil dilation, as though the eye were trying to take in more of a positive stimulus. In the 1960s when research on pupil dilation was "hot," in one study, men's pupils dilated when they looked at pictures of women and women's pupils dilated when they viewed pictures of men; however, women's pupils also dilated upon seeing pictures of newborn babies (Hess & Polt, 1960). Research with gay men found that their pupils dilated when they looked at pictures of men (Hess, Seltzer, & Shlien, 1965). One use of these findings was made by relationship "experts" at the time, who suggested that if you wanted to find out if someone was attracted to you, watch their pupils for dilation. This was really hard to do, since it required people to get up in the face of someone to check out their pupils; plus, it turned out to be an unreliable predictor of attraction. To make our understanding

SPOTLIGHT on Research
_____

Physical appearance has been, and still is, a fascination among nonverbal communication researchers. For years scholars have researched how physical attributes lead to generalizations about people. The shape of the eye has become the object of recent studies involving attitudes and behaviors. Specifically, when people are threatened or in need, to whom do they turn for help? Are people drawn to certain types of faces in these situations, like the baby-faced "warm" person or the more stern "mature"-faced person? Research by Pettijohn and Tesser explores these questions.

Large eyes, round cheeks, small noses, and full lips are characteristics of the neotenous or "baby-faced" appearance. In 1999, Pettijohn and Tesser first proposed the environmental security hypothesis, which suggested that as a threat in our environment increases, we tend to seek help from others who have more mature facial features (e.g., smaller eyes, thinner lips), as opposed to those who look less likely to be able to help us in a dire situation. We feel more comfortable with people with mature faces because those faces convey strength, power, and control. This isn't to say that baby-faced people aren't liked; they are often perceived as fun, agreeable, caring, and honest, but also naïve. In a situation where threat is involved, Pettijohn and Tesser's (2005) more recent study suggests that rather than having a neotenous person with us, we want someone who appears physically stronger, more in control, and more likely to know how to respond to the situation.

This preference is mostly unconscious, according to the research. When we're threatened, we don't specifically think to ourselves "I need to find someone with smaller eyes for help!" Rather, the eye shape in accord with other facial characteristics conveys a sense of security and affects our behavior.

These findings have implications for our culture. The next time you see a cosmetic surgery TV show in which someone is changing her or his facial appearance, think about this article. As people have their eyelids lifted or foreheads Botoxed, for example, what unconscious attitudes might people form about their new appearance? Will judgments of their ability to handle a dangerous or threatening situation be altered, in correspondence with their more youthful appearance?

Do you want to know more about this study? If so, read: Pettijohn, T. II., & Tesser, A. (2005). Threat and social choice: When eye size matters. *Journal of Social Psychology, 145,* 547–570.

_____

of this phenomenon even more confusing, a more recent study detected pupil dilation among people in less-than-positive situations. People who were being deceptive evidenced pupil dilation, which researchers concluded occurred because of the stimulation in the brain typically associated with lying (DePaulo, Lindsay, Malone, Muhlenbruck, Charlton, & Cooper, 2003).

When some of this early research hit the popular press in the 1960s and 1970s, advertisers attempted to make use of the findings by enlarging the appearance of models' eyes in ads. The approach did not produce increased ad sales, thus the fad fell out of favor quickly. It's important to remember that environmental conditions such as the brightness of lighting have an effect on pupil size. So it's unwise to conclude that someone is attracted to you if her or his pupils dilate during a conversation with you. Attraction might be occurring, but so could deception!

## ■ MODIFYING THE EYES

In the second part of this chapter, we've reviewed some nonverbal dimensions of eyes. Certain parts of the face and eyes are so important to people across cultures that we've started to see increases in the amount of money spent on cosmetic surgery and other procedures to accomplish **eye modification**—permanent and temporary changes to the eyes (Caliendo, Armstrong, & Roberts, 2005; Holliday & Cairnie, 2007; Mulkens & Jansen, 2006). Just as for body and facial modification, the cosmetic alteration industry offers a menu of surgeries, procedures, and products that enable people to change the appearance of their eyes. For Asians and Asian Americans (predominantly women), the fastest-growing and most common cosmetic procedure is a process that creates a crease over the eye, since most Asians do not have extra skin or creases that make their eyes look more prominent (McCurdy & Lam, 2005). Double eyelid surgery or **upper blepharoplasty** on people of Asian descent makes their eyes look wider and more western, providing another example of ethnic cosmetic surgery that we discussed earlier in this chapter (Davis, 2003b; Kaw, 1993, 1994). While the popularity of eyelid surgery among Asian Americans is often

*Cosmetic surgery on Asian Americans to make their eyes look more Western is on the rise. What's your view of this trend?*

attributed to western influence, it's important to note that many Asians and Asian Americans view an alert and bright-eyed look as aesthetically desirable (Kaw, 1993, 1994; McCurdy & Lam, 2005). Eyelid surgery is an increasingly popular procedure, but other methods of enhancing or modifying the eye have been developed over time and are still available; we describe some of these below.

1. *Eyelift:* In this surgical procedure, skin around the eye (and sometimes forehead) is detached, lifted up, and reattached to reduce wrinkles, swelling, and appearances of bags under the eye.

2. *Eye cosmetics:* Most students are familiar with the array of products that can enhance the appearance of the eye, but you might be surprised to realize that more men (not just rock stars) are drawn these days to eye cosmetics, such as applications of mascara, eyeliners, and eyebrow pencils. Fairly recently, a process of tattooing permanent makeup such as eye liner and brow color has become popular.

3. *Eye creams:* History is replete with miracle creams that are said to naturally or chemically make the eyes look younger and more rested. (One of the more popular over-the-counter products is Preparation-H, a cream used to treat hemorrhoids, which can tighten the skin around the eye!) The effectiveness of these products varies, but expensive eye creams (as well as inexpensive cucumbers) are readily available and commonly used in medical and day spas.

4. *Fake eyelashes:* Fake eyelashes are an enormously profitable product within the cosmetic industry; such lashes can be attached as an extension of or replacement for the natural eyelash. But before thinking that only stage actors and drag queens use these, it's important to realize that such a product can be helpful in enhancing the self-esteem of people whose eyelashes (as well as other facial and body hair) have fallen out due to chemotherapy or medical conditions.

5. *Eyeglasses:* We all know that eyeglasses (including sunglasses) are primarily used to enhance vision, but they also modify the overall appearance of the face and eyes. People who wear glasses are often perceived as highly intelligent and honest, but also more "nerdy" or "bookish" than those who don't wear glasses. Sunglasses can be an effective way to cover up bloodshot, blackened, or crying eyes and to protect the eyes from sunlight, but we all know their primary utilities: making a fashion statement and looking cool.

6. *LASIK surgery:* This is one of the most popular and effective laser techniques that helps correct human vision so that eyeglasses or contacts aren't needed.

7. *Colored contacts:* Contact lens companies a few decades ago began producing dramatically colored soft contact lenses that could temporarily modify eye color, allowing people to experiment and express different parts of their personalities. This innovation was quite a fad, but like many fads, it isn't seen much anymore because, as good a product as the contacts were, people still saw them as fake and sometimes formed negative perceptions of people wearing them.

8. *Eyebrow piercings:* We cover the topic of piercings thoroughly in Chapter 5, but suffice it here to say that piercing the eyebrow and even the sensitive skin around the eye is more commonly seen today than in past decades, as a form of body adornment and personal expression.

These examples of eye modification give you a sense of the time and money that many people spend on this activity. What's your perception of friends who modify their eyes and eye area with colored contacts, piercings, eyeglasses, or cosmetic procedures? If you've engaged in eye modification, did you view this activity as a form of nonverbal expression? How have people responded to this change in your appearance?

# ■ LYING EYES (AND FACES): NONVERBAL CUES OF DECEPTION

One of the more fascinating applications of research on facial and eye behavior is the exploration of deception cues. Think for a moment about some stereotypical behaviors associated with lying: avoiding eye contact, looking down at the floor, shuffling the feet, fidgeting, clearing the throat, stammering to get words out, and using lots of filled pauses like "um" and "er." We explore the major vocal cues of deception in Chapter 9, but here we focus on facial and eye cues that research has examined in connection with deception.

Before we begin this section, let us offer a couple of things to keep in mind: First, deception is a complex business. Deceptive behavior involves a multitude of verbal and nonverbal cues, so it's important not to use this information as a sure-fire way of catching people in lies. It's not that simple. Just because someone exhibits a behavior we describe here as a deception cue doesn't necessarily mean that deception is happening; it *might* be happening, but it's wise to avoid jumping from nonverbal cue to judgment too quickly. Another complicating factor is that when information about deception cues becomes public and well known, many liars will change their behavior. For example, remember the old adage about liars not being able to look people in the eye when lying? Once that information became readily known as a dead giveaway that someone was lying, people who were intent on deceiving others changed that behavior. People who are good at getting away with deception can look you straight in the eye and lie to your face. Finally, deception cues are idiosyncratic, meaning that people exhibit deceptive behavior in unique ways within their cultural contexts. Deception will manifest itself differently across cultural groups, so be careful in generalizing too much from the research. That's true of everything we study in nonverbal communication, but it's critical to remember when focusing on something that can be as detrimental to relationships as deception.

In recent decades, communication researchers have become increasingly interested in identifying a range of **deception cues,** defined as nonverbal indications of dishonesty (DePaulo, et al., 2003; Ekman, 1991, 1996, 2001; Ekman, O'Sullivan, & Frank, 1999; Park, Levine, McCornack, Morrison, & Ferrara, 2002; Vrij, 2000). These deception cues exist within a larger framework known as **Interpersonal Deception Theory (IDT),** which helps identify and explain the verbal and nonverbal behavior of deceivers (Buller & Burgoon, 1996; Jensen & Burgoon, 2008). Research has shown that deceptive communicators are prone to **leakage,** meaning that their deception makes itself known in some sort of nonverbal behavior, typically beyond their control (Ekman & Friesen, 1969a; Knapp, 2008; Zuckerman, DePaulo, & Rosenthal, 1981). Studies on deception leakage have focused on the sending of deceptive verbal and nonverbal messages, as well as how receivers detect deception in others (Park, et al., 2002; Stromwall, Hartwig, & Granhag, 2006; Vrij, 2006b).

## Deceptive Facial Behavior

One facial behavior that has been the subject of study with regard for deception is smiling, but studies have produced inconsistent results. While DePaulo et al.'s (2003) review of many studies on the topic found no relationship between smiling and deception, in other studies deceivers smiled less than truth tellers (Granhag & Stromwall, 2002; Vrij, 2006a). Ekman and Friesen (1982) suggest that truthtellers are more likely to evidence Duchenne (or felt) smiles, whereas deceivers will use fake smiles.

Adaptors in the form of self-touches and fidgeting have also been linked with deception (Caso, Maricchiolo, Bonaiuto, Vrij, & Mann, 2006; Caso, Vrij, Mann, & De Leo, 2006). One such adaptor that involves the face occurs when a deceiver covers her or his mouth with the hand while talking, as if to say, "This is only half true" or "I'm not proud of what's coming out of my mouth." It may also be an attempt to muffle what's being said so as to somehow, irrationally, mute the lies. In other instances, deceivers will cover their eyebrows or other parts of the face, perhaps in an effort to create a barrier between themselves and their receivers or shield themselves from someone's wrath when they've been caught in a lie.

## Deceptive Eye Behavior

Like we said, breaking or being unable to sustain eye gaze is commonly believed to indicate deception, but research has not determined a consistent pattern. Some studies have detected decreased eye contact when people lie (Hirsch & Wolf, 2001; Hocking & Leathers, 1980), but others have found an increase in eye gaze, possibly due to deceivers trying to compensate for their deception by making more eye contact than expected (DePaulo, et al., 2003; Zuckerman, DePaulo, & Rosenthal, 1981). Our best advice is this: While most chronic liars will develop the ability to engage in mutual gaze while lying to someone, most of us aren't able to pull this off. So one eye behavior to watch for or consider when we wonder about someone's truthfulness is gaze avoidance. If someone can't meet our eye and maintain eye contact, we're justified in thinking about why. Another behavior is the conjugate lateral eye movements (CLEMs) we discussed earlier. The expression "shifty eyes" wasn't coined for nothing, so we may rightfully become alarmed or suspicious when we see someone's eyes shifting from side to side in interaction. Again, such a behavior may have many root causes, deception being only one of them.

While some sources have suggested that rapid or frequent eye blinking is associated with deception, research is also mixed on this front. One scholar who studied nonverbal behavior among criminal suspects found that eye blinking actually slowed during deceptive attempts because of all the brain activity occurring at the time (Vrij, 2004). However, other studies have found that the rate of blinking increases among people attempting to deceive (DePaulo, et al., 2003; Kraut, 1980; Zuckerman & Driver, 1985).

*What does the young woman's gaze aversion to the man communicate nonverbally?*

Here's a useful generalization regarding detecting deception in another person: Compare what you see and hear from a person against what is normal behavior for him or her. It's important to get a baseline of behavior, meaning a sense of how someone typically behaves, then look for aberrations—the odd facial expression, a strange tone in the voice, a change in patterns of eye contact, and so forth. Again, you don't necessarily know for sure that deception is occurring in these instances, but it's a possibility, one that you can pursue further to find out what's happening.

## Familiarity, Suspicion, and Deception Detection

Since deception can be deadly for a relationship, most of us are motivated to understand how our coworkers, friends, family members, and intimate partners view deception, as well as what verbal and nonverbal behaviors they tend to use when they deceive, *if* they deceive. (We grant that some people are bent on telling the truth and avoiding deception in all circumstances.) Start with yourself—are you aware of your own behavior when you try to deceive someone? Now, you may say that you aren't very deceptive, that you don't like deception and so you try to be truthful most of the time. If that's your stance, good for you, but we also recognize different levels of lies, beginning with the "little white lie," ranging up to the "big whopper." Most of us are taught that lying isn't right, so if and when we choose to lie, we register some sort of activation in the body, meaning that the added energy it takes to be untruthful reveals itself somewhere (what we earlier called "leakage"). It's an interesting and eye-opening exercise to think about how deception cues might "leak" from you.

Then think about others' behavior, particularly the behavior of those who are emotionally closest to you. If the person you love the most in the world deceived you, would that deception more likely be enacted verbally, nonverbally, or through a combination of behaviors? Granted, it depends on the lie. For example, if you came into the room wearing the most horrible outfit possible and asked your best friend how you looked, if your friend chose to lie and said that you looked great, that level of lie probably wouldn't take much effort, nor be too readily detectable from nonverbal cues. But in those instances where the "big whopper" of a lie gets told, how do people you know behave? What nonverbal cues emerge?

Research has examined the impact of familiarity and suspicion on deception detection, finding two interesting, yet competing trends: First, we may be better able to detect deception in someone we know well because we know what to look for. That relates back to what we said earlier about getting a baseline of information. As we continue to know someone better, we know how she or he typically behaves, so we can compare normal behavior with behavior we think might be deceptive and go from there. Once our suspicion has been aroused, research says that intimate partners or friends are fairly accurate detectors of deception (Comadena, 1982; McCornack & Parks, 1986, 1990; Stiff, Kim, & Ramesh, 1992). However, a second view is that familiarity hampers our ability to detect deception, because we presume that people are telling us the truth (often called a "truth bias") or because we wish to remain "blissfully ignorant," as one scholar puts it (Collett, 2004, p. 287). We don't really want to think about someone we love deceiving us, so we presume truthfulness, don't notice cues to the contrary, or attempt to distract ourselves from deception cues. Or we will attribute a change in behavior to *any other possible thing*, so as to avoid thinking that someone we care about is lying to us (Millar & Millar, 1995). In these cases, our familiarity (and trust in those we care about) actually blinds us to the reality of deception.

## REMEMBER 7.8

| | |
|---|---|
| **Pupil Dilation:** | an increase or decrease in size of the pupils of the eyes. |
| **Eye Modification:** | permanent or temporary methods of changing the eyes. |
| **Upper Blepharoplasty:** | a surgical procedure that modifies the eyelids, primarily performed on Asians and Asian Americans. |
| **Deception Cues:** | nonverbal indications of dishonesty. |
| **Interpersonal Deception Theory (IDT):** | theory that helps explain verbal and nonverbal behavior of deceivers. |
| **Leakage:** | nonverbal cues outside of a deceiver's control that signal dishonesty. |

## ■ UNDERSTANDING FACIAL AND EYE BEHAVIOR: APPLYING THE REFLEXIVE CYCLE OF NONVERBAL COMMUNICATION DEVELOPMENT

Have you ever thought about how you manage facial and eye behavior in your own life? How much time do you spend thinking about your facial and eye behavior? The first step to developing your skills and a better understanding of these behaviors as nonverbal communication is awareness. Again, we ask you to inventory yourself using the following questions: What standards do you have regarding facial and eye behavior for yourself? What are your needs or preferences regarding facial and eye cues of other people? Do you have expectations or rules about such things as smiling or staring? Do these judgments vary depending on who the person is or whether your relationship with the person is personal or professional in nature? Are you aware of the impressions others may have about you based on your facial and eye behavior?

Now that you have engaged in an inventory of self regarding facial and eye signals, it's time to think about making, if necessary, any appropriate changes to improve how you manage these nonverbal cues in your everyday life. This is Phase 2 in the Reflexive Cycle. Ask yourself, Are there some changes I need to make regarding my facial and eye behavior (e.g., frowning, smiling, eye rolling, gaze aversion, staring)? If so, how can I make those changes? Perhaps the only thing that needs to change is more of an awareness of how your facial and eye behavior are perceived by other people.

Beyond engaging in an inventory of self and making appropriate changes, the next step is to inventory others. Some people are oblivious to the fact that their facial and eye behavior communicate something to other people about their attitude or level of interest. Can you think of people who seem to have no awareness of what they do with their face or eyes? You may be thinking of a friend who rolls her or his eyes all the time, a coworker who avoids eye contact, or a classmate who has a fake smile. These people may lack self-monitoring skills (the ability to be aware of our appropriateness in social situations) or the ability to honestly assess their own nonverbal communication. In addition, they aren't aware enough to perception check with other people for their observations and resulting interpretations of their facial and eye cues. Other people are very well aware of how they come across to others, in terms of facial and eye behavior; perhaps they've actually worked on these cues, so these are the people we can learn from.

After you have done an inventory of self, changed self, and inventoried others' nonverbal behavior, the fourth phase of the Reflexive Cycle involves interacting with others, trying out the changes you've made or are in the process of making, and observing people as you verbally and nonverbally interact with them. Do people have different reactions to you, as a result of any changes you made? For example, some of you who don't smile much may stand out to other people as being friendly if you try to smile more or just generally maintain a more positive facial expression. As another example, some of you who are trying to become better listeners by working on your eye contact may get feedback from others that they appreciate how well you listen to them, or that they appreciate your empathy. It can be interesting to note people's reactions to both subtle and obvious changes in your facial and eye behavior and how that makes you feel, as well as to gauge your own reactions to changes in others' behavior.

In the last part of the cycle, we challenge you to review and assess the whole process, making note of positive and negative aspects, and then begin the cycle again. We've said it before and we'll say it again: The development of nonverbal communication skills is a continuous process, as we work to develop and hone our nonverbal abilities in an effort to become more effective communicators.

## SUMMARY ■ ■ ■ ■ ■

In this chapter, we established facial and eye behavior as nonverbal communication and emphasized the need to be aware of these important nonverbal cues, as well as how we respond to the facial and eye cues of other people. The first part of the chapter reviewed the significance of facial behavior. We explored different viewpoints on facial expression acquisition and development, including evolution, natural selection, external factors, and innate versus learned perspectives. We also reviewed facial management with a focus on Ekman and Friesen's four management techniques of neutralization, masking, intensification, and deintensification.

Next we examined the Facial Action Coding System (FACS)—a technique that separates the face into three regions for study: eyebrows and forehead; eyes and eyelids; and lower face, including the cheeks, nose, and mouth. We discussed facial modification, which refers to more permanent methods of altering the appearance of the face.

In the next section of this chapter, we explored the significance of eye behavior in nonverbal communication and the influences of eye behavior, including arousal, salience, and involvement. Further, we overviewed ten purposes of eye behavior: recognizing others; scanning; thinking; decreasing physical and psychological distance; regulating interaction; establishing and defining relationships; displaying power; expressing emotions; excluding; and monitoring feedback.

The next few sections focused on different forms of eye behavior, beginning with key terms related to gaze or general looking behavior. We explored research findings on pupil dilation, which occurs when the eyes dilate or constrict in response to stimuli. This section closed with a discussion of the complex topic of eye modification, in which we provided a listing of cosmetic procedures and products that enable people to modify their eyes. We provided research results regarding common facial and eye behaviors associated with deception. Research has produced mixed findings regarding ways to detect deception through attention to facial and eye behavior, but some common deception cues include fake smiling, facial adaptors, avoiding eye contact, and frequent and rapid blinking. This chapter ended with a brief discussion of the effects of familiarity and suspicion on the ability to detect deception among persons who are close to us emotionally.

## DISCUSSION STARTERS

1. Explain how facial and eye behavior is a form of nonverbal communication. What do your facial and eye cues nonverbally communicate about you to others?

2. Take a moment to think about how we use the metaphor of face in everyday life. What are some other common uses of facial metaphors that come up in conversation?

3. Review the difference between innate and learned behavior, with regard for facial expressions. Do you think your facial expressions are innate, learned, or a combination of both?

4. Looking at the various eye behaviors presented in this chapter, what is the most interesting to you? Take a moment to review gaze aversion. What experiences have you had with gaze aversion, gaze omission, and civil inattention?

5. In both of the primary sections of this chapter, we explored various methods of modifying the face and eyes. What reactions do you have to these techniques or processes? Have you ever thought about having a cosmetic procedure done to modify your face or eyes? If so, what's the reasoning behind your decision? Have you ever viewed this kind of process as something that could affect your nonverbal communication?

6. We explored the role of facial and eye cues in the communication of deception. What are the most central facial and eye behaviors deceivers exhibit? How skilled do you think you are at detecting deception in other people? Does your ability change when it comes to people who are emotionally close to you?

## REFERENCES

American Society for Aesthetic Plastic Surgery. (2006, June). O-zone. *O: The Oprah Winfrey Magazine*, 39.

Argyle, M., & Cook, M. (1976). *Gaze and mutual gaze.* Cambridge, UK: Cambridge University Press.

Argyle, M., & Dean, J. (1965). Eye contact, distance and addiliation. *Sociometry, 28*, 289–304.

Argyle, M., & Ingham, R. (1972). Gaze, mutual gaze and proximity. *Semiotica, 6*, 32–49.

Argyle, M., Ingham, R., Alkema, F., & McCallin, M. (1973). The different functions of gaze. *Semiotica, 7*, 19–32.

Argyle, M., Lefebvre, L., & Cook, M. (1974). The meaning of five patterns of gaze. *European Journal of Social Psychology, 4*, 125–136.

Asendorpf, J. (1990). The expression of shyness and embarrassment. In W. R. Crozier (Ed.), *Shyness and embarrassment: Perspectives from social psychology* (pp. 87–118). Cambridge, UK: Cambridge University Press.

Ashear, V., & Snortum, J. R. (1971). Eye contact in children as a function of age, sex, social and intellective variables. *Developmental Psychology, 4*, 479.

Atkinson, A. P., Tipples, J., Burt, D. M., & Young, A. W. (2005). Asymmetric interference between sex and emotion in face perception. *Perception and Psychophysics, 67*, 1199–1213.

Bakan, P. (1971). The eyes have it. *Psychology Today, 4*, 64–67, 96.

Bakan, P., & Strayer, F. F. (1973). On reliability of conjugate lateral eye movements. *Perceptual and Motor Skills, 36*, 429–430.

Barlow, J. D. (1969). Pupillary size as an index of preference in political candidates. *Perceptual and Motor Skills, 28*, 587–590.

Baron-Cohen, S., Wheelwright, S., & Jolliffe, T. (1997). Is there a "language of the eyes"? Evidence for normal adults, and adults with autism or Asperger Syndrome. *Visual Cognition, 4*, 311–331.

Beebe, S. A. (1974). Eye contact: A nonverbal determinant of speaker credibility. *Speech Teacher, 23*, 21–25.

Beebe, S. A., & Beebe, S. J. (2006). *Public speaking: An audience-centered approach* (6th ed.). Boston: Allyn & Bacon.

Beebe, S. A., Beebe, S. J., & Ivy, D. K. (2007). *Communication: Principles for a lifetime* (3rd ed.). Boston: Allyn & Bacon.

Birdwhistell, R. L. (1974). The language of the body: The natural environment of words. In A. Silverstein (Ed.), *Human communication: Theoretical explorations* (pp. 203–220). New York: John Wiley & Sons.

Boucher, J. D., & Ekman, P. (1975). Facial areas and emotional information. *Journal of Communication, 25*, 21–29.

Brown, C., & Lloyd-Jones, T. J. (2006). Beneficial effects of verbalization and visual distinctiveness on remembering and knowing faces. *Memory and Cognition, 34*, 277–286.

Buck, R. (1984). *The communication of emotion.* New York: Guilford.

Buck, R. (1988). Nonverbal communication: Spontaneous and symbolic aspects. *American Behavioral Scientist, 31*, 341–354.

Buck, R. (1993). Emotional communication, emotional competence, and physical illness: A developmental-interactionist view. In H. C. Traue & J. W. Pennebaker (Eds.), *Emotion, inhibition, and health.* Seattle: Hogrefe & Hubner.

Buck, R. (1994). Social and emotional functions in facial expression and communication: The readout hypothesis. *Biological Psychology, 38*, 95–115.

Buller, D. B., & Burgoon, J. K. (1996). Reflections on the nature of theory building and the theoretical status of interpersonal deception theory. *Communication Theory, 6*, 311–328.

Burgoon, J. K., Coker, D. A., & Coker, R. A. (1986). Communicative effects of gaze behavior: A test of two contrasting explanations. *Human Communication Research, 12*, 495–524.

Burgoon, J. K., Manusov, V., Mineo, P., & Hael, J. L. (1985). Effects of gaze on hiring, credibility, attraction and relational message interpretation. *Journal of Nonverbal Behavior, 9*, 133–146.

Burkhardt, J. C., Weider-Hatfield, D., & Hocking, J. E. (1985). Eye contact contrast effects in the employment interview. *Communication Research Reports, 2*, 5–10.

Caliendo, C., Armstrong, M. L., & Roberts, A. E. (2005). Self-reported characteristics of women and men with intimate body piercings. *Journal of Advanced Nursing, 49*, 474–484.

Callahan, P. E. (2000). Indexing resistance in short-term dynamic psychotherapy (STDP): Change in breaks in eye contact during anxiety (BECAS). *Psychotherapy Research, 10*, 87–99.

Cary, M. S. (1978a). The role of gaze in the initiation of conversation. *Social Psychology, 41*, 269–271.

Cary, M. S. (1978b). Does civil inattention exist in pedestrian passing? *Journal of Personality and Social Psychology, 36*, 1185–1193.

Caso, L., Maricchiolo, F., Bonaiuto, M., Vrij, A., & Mann, S. (2006). The impact of deception and suspicion on different hand movements. *Journal of Nonverbal Behavior, 30*, 1–19.

Caso, L., Vrij, A., Mann, S., & De Leo, G. (2006). Deceptive responses: The impact of verbal and nonverbal countermeasures. *Legal and Criminological Psychology, 11*, 99–111.

Cole, P. M. (1986). Children's spontaneous control of facial expression. *Child Development, 57*, 1309–1321.

Collett, P. (2004). *The book of tells.* London: Bantam.

Comadena, M. E. (1982). Accuracy in detecting deception: Intimate and friendship relationships. In M. Burgoon (Ed.), *Communication yearbook 6* (pp. 446–472). Beverly Hills, CA: Sage.

Costa, M., Dinsbach, W., Manstead, A. S. R., & Pio Enrico, R. B. (2001). Social presence, embarrassment, and nonverbal behavior. *Journal of Nonverbal Behavior, 25*, 225–240.

Cunningham, M. R., Barbee, A., & Philhower, C. L. (2002). Dimensions of facial physical attractiveness: The intersection of biology and culture. In G. Rhodes & L. A. Zebrowitz (Eds.), *Facial attractiveness* (pp. 193–238). Westport, CT: Ablex.

D'Acremont, M., & Van der Linden, M. (2007). Memory for angry faces, impulsivity, and problematic behavior in adolescence. *Journal of Abnormal Child Psychology, 35*, 313–324.

Darling-Wolf, F. (2003). Media, class and western influence in Japanese women's conceptions of attractiveness. *Feminist Media Studies, 3*, 153–172.

Darling-Wolf, F. (2004). Sites of attractiveness: Japanese women and westernized representations of feminine beauty. *Critical Studies in Media Communication, 21*, 325–345.

Darwin, C. (1872/1965). *The expression of emotion in man and animals.* London: J. Murray. (Reprinted in 1965, Chicago: University of Chicago Press).

Davis, K. (1995). *Reshaping the female body: The dilemma of cosmetic surgery.* New York: Routledge.

Davis, K. (2003a). *Dubious equalities and embodied differences: Cultural studies on cosmetic surgery.* Lanham, MD: Rowman and Littlefield.

Davis, K. (2003b). Surgical passing: Or why Michael Jackson's nose makes "us" uneasy. *Feminist Theory, 4*, 73–92.

Deery, J. (2004). Trading faces: The makeover show as primetime "infomercial." *Feminist Media Studies, 4,* 211–214.

Denness, B. (2005). Tattooing and piercing: Initiation rites and masculine development. *British Journal of Psychotherapy, 22,* 21–36.

DePaulo, B. M., Lindsay, J. L., Malone, B. E., Muhlenbruck, L., Charlton, K., & Cooper, H. (2003). Cues to deception. *Psychological Bulletin, 129,* 74–118.

Doherty-Sneddon, G., & Phelps, F. G. (2005). Gaze aversion: A response to cognitive or social difficulty? *Memory and Cognition, 33,* 727–733.

Domenici, K., & Littlejohn, S. W. (2006). *Facework: Bridging theory and practice.* Thousand Oaks, CA: Sage.

Dovidio, J. F., & Ellyson, S. L. (1985). Patterns of visual dominance behavior in humans. In S. L. Ellyson & J. F. Dovidio (Eds.), *Power, dominance, and nonverbal behavior* (pp. 129–150). New York: Springer-Verlag.

Droney, J. M., & Brooks, C. I. (2001). Attributions of self-esteem as a function of duration of eye contact. *Journal of Social Psychology, 133,* 715–722.

Duncan, S. D., Jr. (1972). Some signals and rules for taking speaking turns in conversations. *Journal of Personality and Social Psychology, 23,* 283–292.

Elfenbein, H. A. (2006). Learning in emotion judgments: Training and the cross-cultural understanding of facial expressions. *Journal of Nonverbal Behavior, 30,* 21–36.

Eibl-Eibesfeldt, I. (1970). *Ethology: The biology of behavior.* New York: Rinehart & Winston.

Eibl-Eibesfeldt, I. (1972). Similarities and differences between cultures in expressive movement. In R. A. Hinde (Ed.), *Nonverbal communication* (pp. 207–283). Lincoln: University of Nebraska Press.

Ekman, P. (1991). Who can catch a liar? *American Psychologist, 46,* 913–920.

Ekman, P. (1996). Why don't we catch liars? *Social Research, 63,* 801–817.

Ekman, P. (2001). *Telling lies* (3rd ed.). New York: W. W. Norton.

Ekman, P., Davidson, R. J., & Friesen, W. V. (1990). The Duchenne smile: Emotional expression and brain physiology: II. *Journal of Personality and Social Psychology, 58,* 342–353.

Ekman, P., & Friesen, W. V. (1967). Head and body cues in the judgment of emotion: A reformulation. *Perceptual and Motor Skills, 24,* 711–724.

Ekman, P., & Friesen, W. V. (1969a). Nonverbal leakage and clues to deception. *Psychiatry, 32,* 88–106.

Ekman, P., & Friesen, W. V. (1969b). The repertoire of nonverbal behavior: Categories, origins, usage, and coding. *Semiotica, 1,* 49–98.

Ekman, P., & Friesen, W. V. (1975). *Unmasking the face: A guide to recognizing emotions from facial cues.* Englewood Cliffs, NJ: Prentice-Hall.

Ekman, P., & Friesen, W. V. (1982). Felt, false, and miserable smiles. *Journal of Nonverbal Behavior, 6,* 238–252.

Ekman, P., Friesen, W. V., & Ellsworth, P. (1972). *Emotion in the human face: Guidelines for research and an integration of findings.* New York: Pergamon Press.

Ekman, P., Friesen, W. V., & Tompkins, S. S. (1971). Facial affect scoring technique: A first validity study. *Semiotica, 3,* 37–58.

Ekman, P., O'Sullivan, M., & Frank, M. G. (1999). A few can catch a liar. *Psychological Science, 10,* 263–267.

Ellsworth, P. C. (1975). Direct gaze as a social stimulus: The example of aggression. In P. Pliner, L. Krames, & T. Alloway (Eds.), *Nonverbal communication of aggression* (pp. 53–76). New York: Plenum Press.

Ellyson, S. L., Dovidio, J. F., & Fehr, B. J. (1981). Visual behavior and dominance in women and men. In C. Mayo & N. M. Henley (Eds.), *Gender and nonverbal behavior.* New York: Springer-Verlag.

Everett, G. E., Olmi, D. J., Edwards, R. P., & Tingstrom, D. H. (2005). The contributions of eye contact and contingent praise to effective instruction delivery in compliance training. *Education and Treatment of Children, 28,* 48–62.

Exline, R. V. (1963). Explorations in the process of person perception: Visual interaction in relation to competition, sex, and need for affiliation. *Journal of Personality, 31,* 1–20.

Exline, R. V., & Fehr, B. J. (1982). The assessment of gaze and mutual gaze. In K. R. Scherer & P. Ekman (Eds.), *Handbook of methods in nonverbal behavior research* (pp. 91–135). Cambridge, UK: Cambridge University Press.

Fridlund, A. J., & Russell, J. A. (2006). The functions of facial expressions. In V. Manusov & M. L. Patterson (Eds.), *The Sage handbook of nonverbal communication* (pp. 299–319). Thousand Oaks, CA: Sage.

Goffman, E. (1967). *Interaction ritual: Essays on face-to-face behavior.* New York: Pantheon.

Goldwater, B. C. (1972). Psychological significance of pupillary movements. *Psychological Bulletin, 77,* 340–355.

Grammer, K., Kruck, K., Juette, A., & Fink, B. (2000). Nonverbal behavior as courtship signals: The role of control and choice in selecting partners. *Evolution and Human Behavior, 21*, 371–390.

Grammer, K., & Thornhill, R. (1994). Human (homo sapiens) facial attractiveness and sexual selection: The role of symmetry and averageness. *Journal of Comparative Psychology, 108*, 233–242.

Granhag, P. A., & Stromwell, L. A. (2002). Repeated interrogations: Verbal and nonverbal cues to deception. *Applied Cognitive Psychology, 16*, 243–257.

Greene, J. O., & Frandsen, K. D. (1979). Need-fulfillment and consistency theory: Relationships between self-esteem and eye contact. *Western Journal of Speech Communication, 43*, 123–133.

Grossman, R. B., & Kegl, J. (2007). Moving faces: Categorization of dynamic facial expressions in American Sign Language by deaf and hearing participants. *Journal of Nonverbal Behavior, 31*, 23–38.

Gueguen, N., & Jacob, C. (2002). Direct look versus evasive glance and compliance with a request. *Journal of Social Psychology, 142*, 393–396.

Guerrero, L. K., & Floyd, K. (2006). *Nonverbal communication in close relationships.* Mahwah, NJ: Erlbaum.

Haggard, E. A., & Isaacs, F. S. (1966). Micromomentary facial expressions as indicators of ego mechanisms in psychotherapy. In L. A. Gottschalk & A. H. Auerback (Eds.), *Methods of research in psychotherapy.* New York: Appleton-Century-Crofts.

Hall, J. A., Horgan, T. G., & Carter, J. D. (2002). Assigned and felt status in relation to observer-coded and participant-reported smiling. *Journal of Nonverbal Behavior, 26*, 63–81.

Hall, J. A., Murphy, N. A., & Schmid Mast, M. (2006). Recall of nonverbal cues: Exploring a new definition of interpersonal sensitivity. *Journal of Nonverbal Behavior, 30*, 141–155.

Heisel, M. J., & Mongrain, M. (2004). Facial expressions and ambivalence: Looking for conflict in all the right faces. *Journal of Nonverbal Behavior, 28*, 35–52.

Hess, E. H. (1968). Pupillometric assessment. In J. M. Shlien (Ed.), *Research in psychotherapy.* Washington, DC: American Psychological Association.

Hess, E. H. (1975a). The role of pupil size in communication. *Scientific American, 233*, 110–112, 116–119.

Hess, E. H. (1975b). *The tell-tale eye.* New York: Van Nostrant Reinhold.

Hess, E. H., & Petrovich, S. B. (1987). Pupillary behavior in communication. In A. W. Siegman & S. Feldstein (Eds.), *Nonverbal behavior and communication* (2nd ed.). Hillsdale, NJ: Erlbaum.

Hess, E. H., & Polt, J. M. (1960). Pupil size as related to interest value of visual stimuli. *Science, 132*, 349–350.

Hess, E. H., & Polt, J. M. (1964). Pupil size in relation to mental activity during simple problem solving. *Science, 143*, 1190–1192.

Hess, E. H., Seltzer, A. L., & Shlien, J. M. (1965). Pupil response of hetero- and homosexual males to pictures of men and women: A pilot study. *Journal of Abnormal Psychology, 70*, 165–168.

Hewitt, B. (2007, December 24). When every face is unfamiliar. *People*, 107–110.

Heyes, C. J. (2007). Cosmetic surgery and the televisual makeover: A Foucauldian feminist reading. *Feminist Media Studies, 7*, 17–32.

Hirsch, A. R., & Wolf, C. J. (2001). Practical methods for detecting mendacity: A case study. *Journal of the American Academy of Psychiatry and the Law, 29*, 438–444.

Hocking, J. E., & Leathers, D. G. (1980). Nonverbal indicators of deception: A new theoretical perspective. *Communication Monographs, 47*, 119–131.

Holliday, R., & Cairnie, A. (2007). Man made plastic: Investigating men's consumption of aesthetic surgery. *Journal of Consumer Culture, 7*, 57–78.

Hugenberg, K., & Sczesny, S. (2006). On wonderful women and seeing smiles: Social categorization moderates the happy face response latency advantage. *Social Cognition, 24*, 516–539.

Jensen, M. L., & Burgoon, J. K. (2008). Interpersonal deception theory. In L. K. Guerrero & M. L. Hecht (Eds.), *The nonverbal communication reader* (3rd ed., pp. 421–431). Long Grove, IL: Waveland.

Johnson, H. G., Ekman, P., & Friesen, W. V. (1975). Communicative body movements: American emblems. *Semiotica, 15*, 335–353.

Kalick, S. M., Zebrowitz, L. A., Langlois, J. H., & Johnson, R. M. (1998). Does human facial attractiveness honestly advertise health? *Psychological Science, 9*, 8–13.

Kaw, E. (1993). Medicalization and racial features: Asian American women and cosmetic surgery. *Medical Anthropology Quarterly, 7*, 74–89.

Kaw, E. (1994). Opening faces: The politics of cosmetic surgery and Asian American women. In N. Sault (Ed.), *Many mirrors: Body image and social relations* (pp. 241–265). New Brunswick, NJ: Rutgers University Press.

Keltner, D. (1995). Signs of appeasement: Evidence for the distinct displays of embarrassment, amusement, and shame. *Journal of Personality and Social Psychology, 68,* 441–454.

Keltner, D., & Buswell, B. N. (1997). Embarrassment: Its distinct form and appeasement function. *Psychological Bulletin, 122,* 250–270.

Kendon, A. (1967). Some functions of gaze-direction in social interaction. *Acta Psychologica, 26,* 22–63.

Knapp, M. L. (2008). *Lying and deception in human interaction.* Boston: Pearson Allyn & Bacon.

Kraut, R. E. (1980). Humans as lie detectors: Some second thoughts. *Journal of Communication, 30,* 209–216.

Krumhuber, E., & Kappas, A. (2005). Moving smiles: The role of dynamic components for the perception of the genuineness of smiles. *Journal of Nonverbal Behavior, 29,* 3–24.

Krumhuber, E., Manstead, A. S., & Kappas, A. (2007). Temporal aspects of facial displays in person and expression perception: The effects of smile dynamics, head-tilt, and gender. *Journal of Nonverbal Behavior, 31,* 39–56.

Levine, M. H., & Sutton-Smith, B. (1973). Effects of age, sex and task on visual behavior during dyadic interaction. *Developmental Psychology, 9,* 400–405.

Lindsey, A., & Vigil, V. (1999). The interpretation and evaluation of winking in stranger dyads. *Communication Research Reports, 16,* 256–265.

Manusov, V., & Patterson, M. L. (2006). *The Sage handbook of nonverbal communication.* Thousand Oaks, CA: Sage.

Matsumoto, D. (1989). Face, culture, and judgments of anger and fear: Do the eyes have it? *Journal of Nonverbal Behavior, 13,* 171–188.

Matsumoto, D. (1992). American-Japanese cultural differences in the recognition of universal facial expressions. *Journal of Cross-Cultural Psychology, 23,* 72–84.

Matsumoto, D., & Ekman, P. (1989). American-Japanese cultural differences in intensity ratings of facial expressions of emotion. *Motivation and Emotion, 13,* 143–157.

McCornack, S. A., & Parks, M. R. (1986). Deception detection and relationship development: The other side of trust. In M. L. McLaughlin (Ed.), *Communication yearbook 9* (pp. 377–389). Newbury Park, CA: Sage.

McCornack, S. A., & Parks, M. R. (1990). What women know that men don't: Sex differences in determining the truth behind deceptive messages. *Journal of Social and Personal Relationships, 7,* 107–118.

McCroskey, J. C., Richmond, V. P., & McCroskey, L. L. (2006). Nonverbal communication in instructional contexts. In V. Manusov & M. L. Patterson (Eds.), *The Sage handbook of nonverbal communication* (pp. 421–436). Thousand Oaks, CA: Sage.

McCurdy, J. A., & Lam, S. M. (2005). *Cosmetic surgery of the Asian face* (2nd ed.). New York: Theime.

Mehrabian, A. (1971). *Silent messages.* Belmont, CA: Wadsworth.

Mendolia, M. (2007). Explicit use of categorical and dimensional strategies to decode facial expressions of emotion. *Journal of Nonverbal Behavior, 31,* 57–75.

Messaris, P. (2003). Visual communication: Theory and research. *Journal of Communication, 53,* 551–556.

Millar, M. G., & Millar, K. (1995). Detection of deception in familiar and unfamiliar persons: The effects of information restriction. *Journal of Nonverbal Behavior, 19,* 69–84.

Mobbs, N. (1968). Eye contact in relation to social introversion/extroversion. *British Journal of Social and Clinical Psychology, 7,* 305–306.

Modigliani, A. (1971). Embarrassment, facework and eye-contact: Testing a theory of embarrassment. *Journal of Personality and Social Psychology, 17,* 15–24.

Monk, A. F., & Gale, C. (2002). A look is worth a thousand words: Full gaze awareness in video-mediated conversation. *Discourse Processes, 33,* 257–278.

Morris, D. (1985). *Body watching.* New York: Crown.

Muehlenhard, C. L., Koralewski, M. A., Andrews, S. L., & Burdick, C. A. (1986). Verbal and nonverbal cues that convey interest in dating: Two studies. Reprinted in L. K. Guerrero & M. L. Hecht (Eds.), *The nonverbal communication reader* (2008, 3rd ed., pp. 353–359). Long Grove, IL: Waveland.

Mulkens, S., & Jansen, A. (2006). Changing appearances: Cosmetic surgery and Body Dysmorphic Disorder. *Netherlands Journal of Psychology, 62,* 34–41.

Newcombe, N., & Lie, E. (1995). Overt and covert recognition of faces in children and adults. *Psychological Science, 6,* 241–245.

Oliver, E. J. (2006). *Fat politics: The real story behind America's obesity epidemic.* New York: Oxford University Press.

Park, H. S., Levine, T. R., McCornack, S. A., Morrison, K., & Ferrara, M. (2002). How people really detect lies. *Communication Monographs, 69,* 144–157.

Pettijohn T. II., & Tesser, A. (2005). Threat and social choice: When eye size matters. *Journal of Social Psychology, 145,* 547–570.

Pell, M. D. (2005a). Nonverbal emotion priming: Evidence from the "facial affect decision task." *Journal of Nonverbal Behavior, 29,* 45–73.

Pell, M. D. (2005b). Prosody-face interactions in emotional processing as revealed by the facial affect decision task. *Journal of Nonverbal Behavior, 29,* 193–215.

Pugh, D. (2001). Service with a smile: Emotional contagion in the service encounter. *Academy of Management Journal, 44,* 1018–1027.

Renninger, L. A., Wade, T. J., & Grammer, K. (2004). Getting that female glance: Patterns and consequences of male nonverbal behavior in courtship contexts. *Evolution and Human Behavior, 25,* 416–431.

Rhys, C. S. (2005). Gaze and turn: A nonverbal solution to an interactive problem. *Clinical Linguistics and Phonetics, 19,* 419–431.

Russell, J. A., & Bullock, M. (1985). Multidimensional scaling of emotional facial expressions: Similarity from preschoolers to adults. *Journal of Personality and Social Psychology, 48,* 1290–1298.

Sato, W., & Yoshikawa, S. (2007). Enhanced experience of emotional arousal in response to dynamic facial expressions. *Journal of Nonverbal Behavior, 31,* 119–135.

Schmidt, K. L. (2006). Movement differences between deliberate and spontaneous facial expressions: Zygomaticus major action in smiling. *Journal of Nonverbal Behavior, 30,* 37–52.

Shimamura, A. P., Ross, J. G., & Bennett, H. D. (2006). Memory for facial expressions: The power of a smile. *Psychonomic Bulletin and Review, 13,* 217–222.

Spackman, M. P., Fujiki, M., Brinton, B., Nelson, D., & Allen, J. (2005). The ability of children with language impairment to recognize emotion conveyed by facial expression and music. *Communication Disorders Quarterly, 26,* 131–143.

Stass, J. W., & Willis, F. N., Jr. (1967). Forms of defensive looking: A naturalistic experiment. *Journal of Nervous and Mental Disease, 145,* 261–271.

Stephenson, G. M., & Rutter, D. R. (1970). Eye contact, distance and affiliation: A re-evaluation. *British Journal of Psychology, 61,* 251–257.

Stiff, J. B., Kim, H. J., & Ramesh, C. (1992). Truth biases and aroused suspicion in relational deception. *Communication Research, 19,* 326–345.

Stromwall, L. A., Hartwig, M., & Granhag, P. A. (2006). To act truthfully: Nonverbal behavior and strategies during a police interrogation. *Psychology, Crime, and Law, 12,* 207–219.

Tannen, D. (2006, August). Every move you make. *O: The Oprah Winfrey Magazine,* 175–176.

Theeuwes, J., Kramer, A. F., Hahn, S., & Irwin, D. E. (1998). Our eyes do not always go where we want them to go: Capture of the eyes by new objects. *Psychological Science, 9,* 379–385.

Turkstra, L. S. (2005). Looking while listening and speaking: Eye-to-face gaze in adolescents with and without traumatic brain injury. *Journal of Speech, Language, and Hearing Research, 48,* 1429–1441.

Vrij, A. (2000). *Detecting lies and deceit: The psychology of lying and its implications for professional practice.* Chicester, UK: John Wiley and Sons.

Vrij, A. (2004). Why professionals fail to catch liars and how they can improve. *Legal and Criminological Psychology, 9,* 159–181.

Vrij, A. (2006a). Challenging interviewees during interviews: The potential effects on lie detection. *Psychology, Crime, and Law, 12,* 193–206.

Vrij, A. (2006b). Nonverbal communication and deception. In V. Manusov & M. L. Patterson (Eds.), *The Sage handbook of nonverbal communication* (pp. 341–359). Thousand Oaks, CA: Sage.

Wagner, H. L., MacDonald, C. J., & Manstead, A. S. R. (1986). Communication of individual emotions by spontaneous facial expressions. *Journal of Personality and Social Psychology, 50,* 737–743.

Waxman, S. (2006, October 15). Cyberface: A new technology makes animated figures as expressive as SAG members. *The New York Times,* pp. 2, 14.

Weitz, S. (1974). *Nonverbal communication: Readings with commentary.* New York: Oxford University Press.

Whitty, M. T. (2004). Cyber-flirting: An examination of men's and women's flirting behavior both offline and on the Internet. *Behavior Change, 21,* 115–126.

Yamamoto, K., & Suzuki, N. (2006). The effects of social interaction and personal relationships on facial expressions. *Journal of Nonverbal Behavior, 30,* 167–179.

Zebrowitz, L. A. (2006). Finally, faces find favor. *Social Cognition, 24,* 657–670.

Zebrowitz, L. A., Bronstad, M., & Lee, H. K. (2007). The contribution of face familiarity to ingroup favoritism and stereotyping. *Social Cognition, 25,* 306–338.

Zuckerman, M., DePaulo, B. M., & Rosenthal, R. (1981). Verbal and nonverbal communication of deception. In L. Berkowitz (Ed.), *Advances in experimental social psychology* (pp. 1–59). New York: Academic Press.

Zuckerman, M., & Driver, R. E. (1985). Telling lies: Verbal and nonverbal correlates of deception. In A. W. Siegman & S. Feldstein (Eds.), *Multichannel integrations of nonverbal behavior* (pp. 129–148). Hillsdale, NJ: Erlbaum.

Zuckerman, M., Miserandino, M., & Bernieri, F. (1983). Civil inattention exists—in elevators. Reprinted in L. K. Guerrero & M. L. Hecht (Eds.), *The nonverbal communication reader* (2008, 3rd ed., pp. 130–138). Long Grove, IL: Waveland.

# Touch

## Our Bodies in Contact

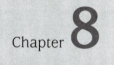
Chapter 8

## CHAPTER OUTLINE ■ ■ ■ ■ ■

## CHAPTER OBJECTIVES ■ ■ ■ ■ ■

After studying this chapter, you should be able to:

1. Define haptics as a nonverbal communication code.

2. Understand the touch ethic, in terms of how it is formed and how it affects our everyday nonverbal communication with others.

3. Describe touch deprivation and explain the importance of touch for infants, children, adolescents, and the elderly.

4. Identify Heslin's five categories of touch and provide examples of touches that apply to each category.

5. Identify Jones and Yarbrough's six meanings of touch and provide examples of touches that apply to each category.

6. Review expectancy violation theory as applicable to touch.

7. Define location, duration, and intensity as three ways to gauge the appropriateness of a touch.

8. Describe current applications of haptics research.

245

## CASE STUDY Don't Wanna Hold Your Hand

This is going to sound really weird, but I just hate holding hands with someone! When I got my first boyfriend in junior high, the big thing was to walk down the hallways at school holding hands, so everyone knew we were a couple. It was sort of a status symbol to have a boyfriend at that time, so holding hands was one way to show off your guy.

But it always felt gross to me—sweaty palms clasped, rocking back and forth as we walked. Invariably my boyfriend had a different stride or way of walking than I, because during junior high, like most girls, I was taller than most boys my grade. I took longer steps naturally, but when you hold hands with someone, you're supposed to walk in synch. It's not cool to walk faster than your boyfriend!

I don't have a problem shaking hands with people in professional or social settings, so it's not like I'm repulsed by touch. But even with dates in college, I try to avoid the hand holding thing, especially at a movie theatre when you can get stuck holding someone's hands for *hours*. It just seems to me like the insides of the hands—the palms—are a pretty intimate area on a person's body, so you need to be really comfortable with how you extend your palms to other people and for how long. I guess I just have some picky rules about how hands are supposed to touch and what messages are sent through the hands.

"That guy had a really weak handshake—that 'wet fish' kind; I wouldn't hire him to work here."

"I went on a first date with this girl and she was *all over me*. Sometimes that's okay, but this time it bugged me."

"My husband's family is *very* affectionate. It was awkward for me at first, since my family isn't all that 'touchy,' but now I'm used to it."

What do these comments have in common? They're about the most powerful, yet most misunderstood nonverbal communication code of all: touch. The study of touch among humans is often referred to as **haptics;** less often you may hear a reference to **tactile behavior, tactics,** or **zero proxemics.** In this chapter, we explore this important code of nonverbal communication, beginning with an examination of its power.

## ■ THE POWER OF TOUCH

A baby is crying in a back room of a house; what happens? The parents may decide that letting the baby cry itself to sleep is the best thing, but most parents will go into the room, touch or pick up the baby, and try to calm it so it can sleep. Your friend has just learned that a family member is seriously ill; how do you comfort your friend? You might sit with the person, let her or him cry it out, and possibly extend a hug for support and sympathy. A team has just won a championship; what are you likely to see? Probably you'll see lots of high fives, hugs, and slaps on the back or rear end.

What's common to these examples is that each illustrates the significant role of touch in everyday human interaction.

Out of the five human senses, touch develops first (Montagu, 1978). As we said in the introduction, touch is the most powerful of all the codes, yet also the most misunderstood among the realm of nonverbal behavior. Think about it: The other codes (e.g., proxemics, facial expressions, eye gaze, vocalics), don't involve physical contact. They *can* involve contact, but we can establish eye contact with someone without touching, make a facial expression without touching, and so on. Touch is accomplished when one person's body comes into contact with another person's body. Granted, proxemics may involve touch, if the distance between people is small enough (zero proxemics). But typically when contact is made, the nonverbal code of touch becomes the primary element for analysis. When we allow someone to touch our bodies (including faces, heads, and extremities), that extension of one person to another is a powerful form of communication. Touch is also the most volatile nonverbal behavior, because if rules regarding touch are not followed or expectations are violated, serious consequences arise. We talk more about this aspect in a subsequent section, but for now think about how people form rules for touch and what happens when those rules aren't clearly explained or followed.

We also contend that touch is the most misunderstood code of nonverbal communication, in that a sender's meaning behind a touch may not correspond with a receiver's interpretation of the touch. This kind of incongruence happens frequently, in all kinds of settings and within all kinds of relationships. Sometimes a

*What do these simple touches communicate nonverbally about the relationship between these two people?*

misunderstanding is small and of relatively minor consequence. For example, two men shake hands and one places a hand on the forearm or elbow of the other while shaking. From the first man's perspective (sender of the touch), the hand to elbow touch simply adds warmth or emphasis to the handshake. But from the receiver's perspective, the elbow touch might be interpreted as a dominance cue, as though the sender wanted to convey his status. Even a simple ritualized greeting can evoke different interpretations of the touch involved. At other times a misunderstanding about touch can cause a major offense or rift, such as in cases in which a coworker or boss thinks his or her touch is a sign of friendliness, while the recipient of the touch deems it sexual harassment.

We talk more later about this "misunderstood touch" aspect, because it has a powerful effect on how we interact with people, but for now consider how many relationships have either not gotten off the ground or have ended, simply because of a misunderstanding over touch or the lack of touch. Some people have cold, distant fathers, and the lack of touch they received growing up causes them to be cautious around men in both adolescence and adulthood. Other people have doting mothers—those who touch, protect, or cradle their children too much—which can also lead to negative consequences later in life. These are just a couple of examples that illustrate our contention that misunderstandings between people are more likely to emerge in respect to the touch nonverbal code than others.

## ■ TOUCH ETHIC

 Think for a moment about your approach to or philosophy of touch. What purpose do you believe touch serves in human interaction, in general? What rules or expectations do you have about your own touching behavior toward others, as well as how others can touch you? What kinds of touches do you observe people giving one another that you deem acceptable or unacceptable? One way to prompt this kind of thinking is to ponder those touches you *don't* like. We probably all have a list like this, even if we've not thought much about it—touches we find intrusive, irritating, or distracting. For example, the opening case study for this chapter was about a woman who didn't like holding hands with her boyfriend or date. What touches annoy you? Make you nervous? Does it depend on the person offering the touch? The situation? Your mood? Are there some touches that are appropriate for other people, but inappropriate for you? How did you develop your expectations regarding touch?

These questions all pertain to something we call the **touch ethic** or people's beliefs about and preferences for touch. The touch ethic encompasses our rules about appropriate and inappropriate touch, our expectations as to how people will receive our touch as well as extend touch to us, whether we are a "touchy" person or not (how much touch we're comfortable with), and how we actually behave regarding touch. The touch ethic develops early in life and remains fairly constant; however, it can change during our lifespan because of our relationships and experiences.

The primary influence on our touch ethic is our family of origin; secondary influences include extended family members and peers. What did you observe, experience, and learn about touch while growing up? If you grew up in a two-parent family, you mostly likely observed your parents' touch—how often they touched; where they touched (environmental as well as body location); what parts of their bodies they used; if touch from one parent to another was accepted, reciprocated, or rejected; and so forth. You registered how your parents and siblings touched you and how you touched them. Our earliest experiences with touch—even touch as infants—impact the touch ethic in the most profound way. If you grew up fighting, wrestling, or rough-housing with parents or siblings, these forms of aggressive touch are components of your touch ethic as well.

Our touch ethic may change over time, meaning that if you grew up in circumstances involving touch that you later, as an adult, deem inappropriate or not preferable, your touch ethic will evolve to accommodate that change of view. Perhaps you accepted some forms of touch as a kid, but those touches seemed inappropriate, unwelcome, or just physically unfeasible as you got a bit older, like sitting on a parent's lap. Parents often lament the passage their children and adolescents experience when they feel they're too old for goodnight kisses or hugs. The kids would rather *die* than be kissed or touched by their parents in front of their friends. Heterosexually speaking, we can probably remember a time when kissing or touching a member of the opposite sex was gross (because they had "cooties"). But as our bodies and emotions evolved and hormones raged, we began to change our views about contact with members of the opposite sex—contact that we began to deem interesting or wonderful. Gays and lesbians sometimes describe this same process, but with a different result: Kissing or touching an opposite-sex person may have continued to seem gross or it simply didn't feel to the homosexual person like it seemed to feel to heterosexuals. Same-sex touching during childhood and adolescence was, for a lot of people, confusing and turbulent territory.

Our touch ethic may change because we fall in love. If our romantic partner's touch ethic differs from ours, we may find that our rules or expectations evolve to match our partner's, or vice versa. Sometimes "unnatural" or dramatic events cause a shift in the touch ethic. For example, a child who grew up in a loving home with her or his parents, but who was physically or sexually abused by an extended family member or family friend, is likely to have the touch ethic seriously altered because of the experience. Tragedies or sad situations, like a serious illness of a loved one, can alter the touch ethic as well, as people use touch to comfort one another. Someone who isn't that comfortable with touch may suddenly seek the comfort of someone else's shoulder, as a way of coping with a difficult or traumatic experience.

 We encourage you to take some time to think about your own touch ethic, using the questions we posed earlier, before pushing further into this chapter. Beyond this self inventory, consider touch in a variety of encounters: touch with strangers, such as in a crowded elevator or airplane; parent-child touch; professional touches with coworkers, bosses, and clients; and touch among intimates. Do the touches you receive from others function in accord with your touch ethic? If so, then these relationships are probably positive and affirming. However, an inspection of touch as a nonverbal communication code operating within your relationships can reveal how you feel about the relationship—whether it's satisfying or stagnant and whether any change is necessary.

## ■ TOUCH AND HUMAN DEVELOPMENT

We heard somewhere that human beings need at least 12 hugs each day to be psychologically stable. If that's true, we know a lot of unstable people out there, because many of us do not receive 12 hugs a day. Research shows that women who receive several hugs a day from their husbands have lower blood pressure than women who do not receive this kind of affection (Love your life, 2007). In addition, research shows that people's brain activity, specifically their fear response, revealed on an MRI is altered when they hold a loved one's hand during the scan (Coan, Schaefer, & Davidson, 2006). Psychologist Sidney Jourard believes that the U.S. is a touch-starved country; he cites examples such as going out of our way not to bump into people and being embarrassed when we accidentally touch someone, such as might happen in a crowded environment (Jourard, 1964, 1966). Compared to other parts of the world, like Europe and Latin America, U.S. culture is restrictive in its approach to and beliefs about touch (Burgoon & Saine, 1978). Anthropologist Desmond Morris (1967, 1969) critiques the way that Americans hire "licensed touchers," like massage therapists and beauticians, to provide human contact.

But the U.S. is not alone on this front: A study reported in a Canadian newspaper suggested that Canadians suffer from "touch deficit" because a third of the population regularly go an entire day without any human contact (Harris, 2005). The explanation for the Canadian lack of touch was an increased emphasis on social boundaries, changes in sex roles, and more reliance on electronic communication. Whether you're a Canadian or an American who doesn't get your 12 hugs a day, the point is this: Human beings need physical contact with one another in order to survive and thrive. Since most of what we discuss in this chapter relates to touch in adulthood, let's take a moment to examine the importance of touch in the human development of infants and children, and then at the end of life, among members of American society who are the most touch-deprived.

### Infancy and Childhood

When we hear of abandoned babies or abused children, we're reminded of some of the worst aspects of our society. We're emotionally moved by the thought of a helpless infant or child being denied human contact or being given the wrong kind of contact, because we know how important touch is to the development and well being of the most vulnerable among us. Research shows that depriving infants and children of touch can retard their mental, physical, and emotional development; cause them to be sickly, socially maladjusted, quiet, and overweight; and can even kill them (Andersen, 2004; Arnold, 2002; Montagu, 1971, 1978; Stack & Arnold, 1998). Touching premature infants who undergo incubation in the early hours of their lives is critical to their development and to the establishment of a successful parent-child relationship (Feldman, Eidelman, Sirota, & Weller, 2002; Lappin, 2005). Research shows that children who experience abundant positive touch while growing up tend to be warm, affectionate, and confident adults (Burgoon, Buller, & Woodall, 1996; Jones, 1994; Jones & Brown, 1996; Weiss, 1990).

While it is beyond our scope to review the vast literature on touch and infant/child development, one area of research is particularly interesting. Have you heard of infant massage? It's been around awhile, but has been steadily gaining popularity as an effective parenting technique and a way to enhance parent-child bonding. Research has explored some of the benefits of this unique form of parent-infant touch. One of the leading scholars is Tiffany Field (2000), who researches the positive relationship between infant massage and health. We know the benefits of general touch between parents and infants, but a purposeful massage goes beyond simple holding, cradling, or touching of a baby. Caressing a baby's skin using appropriate pressure has been shown to assist in premature infant weight gain, mental development, and motor coordination (Field, 1995a, 1998, 2000; Schneider, 1996). It also serves as an expression of love; provides meaningful parent-child exchanges, particularly for fathers who might not normally touch their babies as often as mothers; and can actually help mothers who suffer with postnatal depression (Cullen, Field, Escalona, & Hartshom, 2000; Dellinger-Bavolek, 1996; Onzawa, Glover, Adam, Modi, & Kumar, 2001). Instructional videotapes and DVDs are available that teach parents how to provide this helpful form of touch to their children (Danna, 1999).

## Touch Deprivation: Adolescents to Elders

While touch to infants and children has been studied, especially the effects of **touch deprivation** (lack of physical contact between people), the role of touch in adolescent and adult development is also an interesting subject. Touch deprivation has been linked to alienation, depression, and violence (Trenholm, 2001). Anthropological research from the 1970s examined primitive cultures and touch deprivation, finding that infants and adolescents who experienced limited physical contact evidenced high levels of adult violence (Prescott, 1975). In a cross-cultural study of adolescents and touch, Tiffany Field (the "guru" of infant massage) found that adolescents who received less physical affection in their preschool years were more aggressive and even violent in their adolescent years (Field, 2002). In a related study, Field (2005) discovered that adolescents who underwent massage therapy had fewer suicidal thoughts and less depression. Another group of researchers studied touch deprivation and body image among women with eating disorders; they found that women with eating disorders revealed greater body image concerns, but also perceived themselves as touch deprived, both currently and in their childhood (Gupta, Gupta, Schork, & Watteel, 1995). These findings underscore the importance of human contact to our basic well-being. But what about the end of the age spectrum?

It's a fact: Unless we die at an early age, we're all going to be elderly someday. Unfortunately, in U.S. culture, elderly people aren't revered like they are in other cultures, such as in many Asian cultures in which the elder members of society are held in high esteem and respected for their wisdom and experience. It's sad, but true, that elderly people tend to be the most alienated and touch-deprived segment of American society. Psychotherapist Maggie Turp (2000) explains:

> As we move into late adulthood, our "tactile" circumstances change. We are less likely to have young children to attend to. We are less likely than previously to be in a sexual relationship. If we lose a longstanding and affectionate partner, we lose the touch experiences that were a part of that relationship and they are not easy to replace. Activities involving vigorous movement, which, because of the overlaps between touch and movement, might to some degree substitute for touch experience, are also likely to diminish. And if we experience a narrowing of our social world, then touch equivalents such as gaze will also be less available to compensate for deficits of physical touching. (p. 68)

While elders may need more touch from others, like being helped out of a chair or attended to medically, these touches tend to be functional, not affectionate. Elders may be granted latitude whey they extend touch to others—few of us would reject the handshake or hug of an elderly person, even someone we don't know—but they tend to receive less touch, other than what is necessary to help them function physically.

Part of the reason for the touch deprivation is our perception of elderly people as frail; perhaps we fear touching or hugging them because we think we might hurt them. In some cases, our fears are reasonable, because many elderly are frail, but do we forget that light hugs or other types of touches are possible? Does a hug have to be a bear hug to count as a meaningful touch? A more honest explanation for touch deprivation is this: Some people are put off by the physical appearance of elderly persons. This sounds harsh, but if you ask people to dig down into their heart of hearts, a negative perception of elder appearance, combined with a fear of aging and becoming infirm, lead some people to distance themselves from elderly persons and avoid physical contact with them. What's more interesting is that this is a *learned* behavior, because children, for the most part, aren't put off by the appearance of elderly persons. They're just as likely to approach an elder as they would anyone else.

More research is being done on touch deprivation among the elderly. In one study of infant massage, grandparents were trained in massage techniques and, as an unexpected byproduct, the grandparents reported less anxiety, improved mood, and less depression as a result of contact with the infants (Field, 1995b). Other research has been conducted in clinical settings, such as one study of an urban adult day care center in which staff members touched elderly residents, in combination with eye contact and positive verbal cues. Residents offered more verbal responses and had better attitudes as a result of the contact (Kramer & Gibson, 1991). Researchers have also found that touch, as a form of social support, has a therapeutic effect on elderly people suffering from depression (Tank Buschmann, Hollinger-Smith, & Peterson-Kokkas, 1999). A study of gerontological social workers revealed that the workers believed that interactivity and touch were important, as a way of showing caring for elderly patients (not just for functional purposes) (Tobin & Gustafson, 1987).

*Touch is important to us throughout our lifetime.*

But there's a difference in the touch we receive from a social worker or medical professional, rather than a friend or loved one, isn't there?

Just like infant massage, a technique called intergenerational massage provides nurturing and health-enhancing touch to elderly people (Ward, Duquin, & Streetman, 1998). Again, the touch such a massage provides is from a worker or clinician to an elder patient, but the purpose of providing more contact is still a worthy one. Another interesting attempt to reduce elderly people's touch deprivation is pet therapy, sometimes termed animal-facilitated therapy (Colombo, Dello Buono, Smania, Raviola, & De Leo, 2006; Darrah, 1996). Usually this therapy comes in the form of animals being loaned to elder-care facilities, so that the patients can have contact with the animals. The presence of animals in nursing homes and other elder-care facilities has been shown to lower elder patients' blood pressure (Allen, 2003) and create an atmosphere of domesticity, meaning that elders are reminded of home when they interact with animals, which can do wonders for their attitudes and moods (Savishinsky, 1992).

### REMEMBER 8.1

| | |
|---|---|
| **Haptics (Tactile Behavior, Tactics, Zero Proxemics):** | study of touch among people. |
| **Touch Ethic:** | beliefs about and preferences for touch. |
| **Touch Deprivation:** | lack of physical contact between people. |

# ■ TYPES OF TOUCH

Several different systems for categorizing touch have been developed to help us better understand this complex code of nonverbal communication. We've selected a couple to review with you, so that you can better gauge your own touching behavior toward others, as well as their contact with you.

## Heslin's Categories

Social psychologist Richard Heslin (1974) provides for us one of the best means of classifying touch behavior. His categories appear below, which range from distant and impersonal to close and intimate.

1.  *Functional/Professional:* These touches serve a specific function, usually within the context of a professional relationship, and are generally low in intimacy (even if the contact is with an intimate part of the body). Examples include a doctor giving a patient a physical exam, a massage therapist working out the kinks in someone's neck, and a beautician giving a customer a makeup demonstration.
2.  *Social/Polite:* Touches associated with cultural norms, such as handshakes, hugs, and kisses as greeting and departure rituals fall under this category. Again, these touches indicate fairly low intimacy within a relationship.
3.  *Friendship/Warmth:* People use touch to show their non-romantic emotion and affection toward one another. Close friends may hug, exchange kisses on the cheek, or pat one another on the back to show their liking and connection. Men may offer a handshake with a half hug (or free arm around the shoulder, pulling the other person in a bit closer) to show affection and friendship. Like other categories, friendship/warmth touches will be enacted differently across cultures.
4.  *Love/Intimacy:* These touches are highly personal and intimate, as people communicate strong feelings of affection toward one another. Hugs may last longer or may involve more of the body in contact than hugs between friends; kisses may be on the lips rather than on the cheek. While typically thought of within the context of romantic relationships, other loving relationships, such as those between family members, may involve these touches as well.
5.  *Sexual Arousal:* These touches are extremely intimate and typically target the sexual zones and organs of the body for the purpose of sexual arousal. If people engaged in this kind of touching also love each other, then touches in the Love/Intimacy and Sexual Arousal categories often overlap.

The next time you're out at a club, party, restaurant, or some other social event, become an astute people watcher, applying what you're learning about nonverbal communication. It's fascinating to hone in on one code of nonverbal behavior at a time, such as the touch that passes between people. Say you're at a restaurant and you see a romantic couple at another table or booth. First, besides our telling you they're a romantic couple, can you tell that they're "more than friends"? How is the touching

*The handshake is an important form of touch between people.*

behavior of friends different than that of people who are sexually attracted to each other? Can you tell if this couple is on their first date? Been together a long time? If they're sitting on the same side of a booth, chances are that the relationship is in the early stages, when the thrill of the new romance causes us to want close proximity and the opportunity to touch. (This interpretation applies more to heterosexual than homosexual couples, whose touch behaviors are often constrained by society's view of their relationship.) If a couple has been together awhile, the need or desire to touch publicly usually diminishes; partners are more likely to sit across from one another at a booth or table, rather than side by side. Touch may become more formalized, such as in heterosexual couples where the man may escort the woman to and from the restaurant with his hand on the small of her back. If a couple has been together a long time, little touch will likely pass between them, other than functional touches (like getting salad dressing off of a partner's clothing) or ritualized ones, like offering a hand as a partner gets out of a booth. Research tells us that affection is critical to the formation and continuance of a successful relationship and the development of intimacy (Andersen, 2008; Andersen, Guerrero, & Jones, 2006; Keeley, 2005; Pendell, 2002; Prager, 1995). But we don't mean to suggest that a lack of public touching means a relationship is in trouble. People have very personalized rules for touch behavior (the touch ethic), especially when they find themselves in view of other people, and these rules evolve over time (Guerrero & Andersen, 1999).

An interesting line of research documents sex differences in perceptions of touch. Scholar Antonia Abbey (1982, 1987, 1991) conducted fascinating research with consistent results that showed that, among heterosexuals, men tend to misinterpret women's touches as being more intimate than women intend. In terms of Heslin's categories, the biggest discrepancy occurs between the Friendship/Warmth and Love/Intimacy categories. Abbey found that men often interpret women's touches as indications of love and intimacy (or general romantic interest and attraction), leading to sexual arousal, rather than as friendship or warmth as intended. The research of Abbey and others shows that this trend is more than a stereotype (Guerrero & Andersen, 1999; Heslin & Alper, 1983; Heslin, Nguyen, & Nguyen, 1983). Watch an old romance movie and you'll no doubt see a scene in which the male leading man gets "fresh" with the female leading character, causing her to slap his face or pull away and declare that her touch had no romantic intentions. The same misperception problem occurs today, would you agree? Granted, it's more complicated than this, because some men believe that women send mixed signals regarding intimacy. Women may intend to be flirtatious, but when men read more serious intent into the touches and other nonverbal behaviors and want to pursue the encounter, women may back off and contend that they were just "being friendly." These are complicated relational waters.

We'd like to briefly share an interesting bit of classroom discussion from a few semesters back on this very subject of women, men, and perceptions of touch. The heterosexual men in this particular interpersonal communication class were quite open about touches they appreciated from women, touches they didn't like, and the complexity of interpreting a woman's touch. To the education of the women in the room, these college men explained that a touch on their knee meant something entirely different than a touch on their thigh. Many of the women were floored over the fact

## REMEMBER 8.2

### Heslin's Categories of Touch

| | |
|---|---|
| **Functional/Professional:** | non-intimate touches that serve a specific function, usually within the context of a professional relationship. |
| **Social/Polite:** | touches associated with cultural norms that indicate fairly low intimacy within a relationship. |
| **Friendship/Warmth:** | touches that show non-romantic emotion and affection. |
| **Love/Intimacy:** | highly personal and intimate touches that communicate feelings of romantic affection. |
| **Sexual Arousal:** | extremely intimate touches that typically target the sexual zones or organs of the body for the purpose of sexual arousal. |

that a few inches upward or downward on a man's leg would send such different signals. But, apparently, to these men anyway, a knee touch was "safe"—an indication of a friendship/warmth touch—but when a woman touched a man's thigh, that signaled sexual interest and, as one male student put it, "got a whole different ball rollin.'" Do the views expressed in this exchange match your experience?

## Jones and Yarbrough's Meanings of Touch

Communication scholars Jones and Yarbrough (1985) provide a system that helps us understand the various meanings behind a touch. The six most meaningful categories of touch are as follows:

1. *Positive Affect (Affectionate) Touches:* These touches indicate a degree of liking or positivity toward another person. Such touches can convey messages of support, appreciation, inclusion, sexual interest, and affection. When college roommates reunite after not seeing each other over the summer, they are likely to hug or, more often the case with men, do the "handshake, pat on the back, half hug" thing.
2. *Playful Touches:* These touches include both playful affection and playful aggression subcategories. They convey teasing or joking between people, and may include mildly aggressive touch such as wrestling or rough-housing, tickling, grabbing, pinching, and so forth. Parents and children often engage in this form of touch as a means of expressing affection.
3. *Control Touches:* These touches are used to gain compliance from someone, to get someone's attention, or to engender a response. The touch is persuasive, meaning that it conveys a person's influence or attempt to control a situation or others' behavior. If two men go to shake hands and one puts his free hand on the shoulder of the other, this touch can be interpreted as a dominance or controlling nonverbal cue.
4. *Ritualistic Touches:* Touch is an important component of many everyday rituals. We generally think of these kinds of touches as being associated with greeting and departure rituals, such as you're likely to see at an airport.
5. *Task-Related Touches:* In order to accomplish a specific task, often touch is required, so these touches serve an instrumental function. For example, a dentist has to come into contact with the face and mouth area in order to examine the teeth. A limo driver or bellhop may offer a hand of assistance to someone exiting a car.
6. *Accidental Touches:* These touches are unintentional and, thus, meaningless, according to Jones and Yarbrough. Think of a crowded airplane with narrow seats, when it's likely that passengers' arms or hips might come into contact during a flight. When people get on an already crowded elevator, people at the back may bump into one another as everyone adjusts to the cramped conditions.

We should note that Jones and Yarbrough's categories of touch can overlap. Let's use the dentist example again: A dentist will likely touch your face and mouth

## REMEMBER 8.3

### Jones & Yarbrough's Meanings of Touch

| | |
|---|---|
| **Positive Affect (Affectionate) Touches:** | touches that indicate a degree of liking or positivity toward another person. |
| **Playful Touches:** | touches that convey teasing, joking, or mild aggression between people. |
| **Control Touches:** | touches used to gain compliance, get someone's attention, or generate a response. |
| **Ritualistic Touches:** | touches typically associated with rituals, such as greetings and departures. |
| **Task-Related Touches:** | touches that serve an instrumental function, meaning those that help accomplish a task. |
| **Accidental Touches:** | unintentional and meaningless touches. |

during an examination of your teeth, but what if you feel some pain as a result and raise up off of the exam chair? The dentist may touch your shoulder or arm to try to gently settle you back down into the chair so that the exam can continue. Is this touch task-related or controlling? The point is that it doesn't really matter which category a touch fits into; the categories should be used to better understand common meanings behind touches you see and experience in everyday life. Try to be more observant of the touches you see around you, both those that are extended to you and touches that emerge between other people. See if you can match the touches you observe to the various categories, to help you better understand what these touches mean within human interaction.

## ■ GAUGING THE APPROPRIATENESS OF TOUCH

This is a tricky topic, because everyone has their own standards or rules about the appropriateness or inappropriateness of touch. To tackle this tricky topic, let's first revisit a theory that helps us understand the role of touch in everyday life.

### Expectancy Violations Theory

Communication scholar Judee Burgoon and various colleagues developed **expectancy violations theory,** a model or explanation that helps explain how nonverbal communication functions in everyday interaction (Afifi & Burgoon, 2000; Burgoon, 1978, 1983, 1993, 1995; Burgoon & Hale, 1988). We introduced this model in Chapter 1, but it has particular relevance for our discussion of touch. You may remember that, according to the model, we develop expectations for appropriate nonverbal behaviors in ourselves and others, based on our cultural backgrounds, personal experiences, and knowledge of those with whom we interact. When those expectations are violated, we become more engaged in what's happening and the nature of our relationships becomes a critical factor as we attempt to interpret and respond to situations.

As we explore appropriate and inappropriate touch in this section, we can see how this model relates because it pertains to actions people believe are in violation of some rule or expectation for both private and public behavior. But here's an important point: We contend that the ramifications for a violation in the realm of touch are more serious than for other codes of nonverbal behavior. It's one thing to stand too close to someone when talking—the example of an expectancy violation we provided in Chapter 1. But it's another thing to touch someone in the wrong place on his or her body or to touch inappropriately in a given situation. Bodily contact is more intrusive and personal than a proxemic violation, an inappropriate gesture, or staring.

First, let's consider a relatively benign example to illustrate how the model applies to touch. What's your view of PDAs? (No, we don't mean the electronic gadgets that allow people to email and text their friends; here we refer to "public displays of affection.") If you're out to dinner with some friends and you look over at another table or booth and a couple sitting there is making out, what are you likely to think? If you think their affection in public is inappropriate, how come the couple doesn't agree? There's probably no sign on the door of the place that says "No Kissing Allowed," so what leads you to decide that this touch is inappropriate? Might you attempt to correct the couple's behavior by shouting "get a room!" or would you just try to ignore them and go on with your evening? (Sometimes ignoring inappropriate behavior is hard to do.) If the same display of affection occurred in a dark nightclub, would you see it as a violation like you did in the restaurant? The location or context within which behavior occurs plays an important role in your interpretation of events.

**Tie signs** are nonverbal behaviors that not only express affection between people, but also signal the status of the relationship to other people (Morris, 1977). Making out is an extreme example of a tie sign; others include holding hands, walking arm in arm or with one person's arm around the other's shoulders, touching each other's faces, and so forth. Some people will claim that they engage in this form of touching simply to convey affection, but they shouldn't forget that their behavior exists in a social context, one in which the touch communicates volumes to onlookers about the nature of the relationship, as well as about people's touch ethic (Guerrero & Andersen, 1999).

According to the expectancy violations model, we register nonverbal violations and react in order to adapt to the circumstances. If the violating person is what Burgoon terms a "rewarding" communicator, meaning the person has high credibility, status, and attractiveness (in personality or physicality), we may view the behavior as less of a violation and simply adjust our expectations. We may even reciprocate or mimic the behavior. However, if the violator is not a rewarding communicator, we're likely to use reactive nonverbal behaviors in an effort to compensate for or correct the situation. Back to the nightclub example: If the people you see making out are attractive, credible, and of high status, you might adapt to the situation and not think negatively of them. In fact, you might decide, temporarily, that your rules about PDAs could relax for this situation. However, if the people engaging in

*If you were an observer of this couple, what might you assume about their relationship, as a consequence of their touch?*

intimate touch have less attractiveness, credibility, and status, you may back away from them or leave the scene, deeming their behavior a violation of your expectations for appropriateness.

One more thing about this theory: Our tendency in a rules violation situation is to attempt to correct the violation nonverbally before resorting to verbal communication. We're more likely to try to disregard or ignore a minor inappropriate touch, like an overly enthusiastic handshake, than to say to someone, "Please don't grip my hand so hard when we shake hands." We're more likely to glare at the making-out couple or laugh and point at them than to actually say something to them to correct their behavior.

Now consider a more dire example: A college student attends a campus party after a long week of studying and writing papers—she just needs to blow off steam and have some fun. She meets an attractive guy at the party, flirts with him a bit, then decides she's tired and wants to head back to the dorm to call it a night. The guy she's been flirting with offers to walk her home, since it's dark and walking with an escort would be safer than walking alone. They get back to her dorm room, he starts to make out with her (instead of offering a simple goodnight kiss), and well, you probably know where we're going from here. The situation goes from bad to worse, with the woman saying no and being ignored, and the end result is date rape. (We don't use this example lightly and don't mean to insinuate that all college men and women behave this way, but you know as well as we do what a problem sexual assault is on many college campuses.) In this situation, to call the sexual assault an expectancy violation sounds like we're sanitizing the event, but we're trying to make a point about how touch violations carry more negative sanctions than other nonverbal codes. Relational touch that degenerates into sexual assault or domestic violence represents, as one team of scholars puts it, "the darkest side of haptic communication" (McEwan & Johnson, 2008, p. 232).

## Appropriateness: Location, Duration, and Intensity

Before delving further into the topic of appropriate touch, here's a disclaimer: It's all about the *who*. Your rules or expectations about touch mostly depend on *who* touches you, *who* you touch, and the nature of the relationship between the two of you. People mean everything in this realm, because a touch from one person can mean one thing and be received positively, while the exact same touch from someone else can be terribly wrong and received negatively. For example, researchers have examined how people who experience expectancy violating touches in their platonic friendships account for or explain those touches (Floyd & Voloudakis, 1999). A touch that normally occurs between lovers, when exchanged between friends, can be incredibly awkward.

### What Would *You* Do?

Marisa works part-time at the campus library and, for the most part, she likes her job. It's quiet, offers flexible hours, and she gets to catch up on studying during slow times. Well, she likes her job except for one thing: her supervisor. He's a graduate student who works at the library while finishing his master's degree, and he's only a few years older than Marisa. She cringes when he comes near her while she's working, because she just knows he's going to circle around her desk, reach for her shoulders, and give her the old inappropriate backrub.

    Her boss must think a backrub is completely appropriate touch between a supervisor and an employee because he does it all the time, never wondering if Marisa appreciates the touch. Marisa knows he's married, so she doesn't think the backrubs are flirtatious or sexual at all, but they're bewildering. His actions embarrass Marisa and make her feel disrespected. Sometimes when she sees her boss coming toward her and she anticipates the usual backrub, she gets up from her desk and makes herself busy, so she can avoid the unwanted touch.

    *What would you do* in Marisa's situation? Would you continue the diversionary tactics, such as getting up from your desk before a supervisor could put his or her hands on your shoulders, or would you quit the job? Would you report the unwanted touch to your supervisor's supervisor? Would you say something to your boss's face, explaining to her or him that you find the backrubs inappropriate and asking him or her to refrain from touching you, or would that just be too weird or scary? Do you deem the supervisor's backrubs a form of sexual harassment on the job?

Besides using expectancy violation theory to help you understand how non-verbal communication functions, three aspects related to touch can help you gauge its appropriateness. The first is **location,** which we mean in two senses: First, the location on the body where contact is made has a significant impact on whether we deem a touch appropriate or inappropriate. At some point in your life, you've probably heard the unfortunate comparison of touch exploration to the game of baseball (i.e., getting to first or second base, scoring a home run), but the metaphor does help illustrate our point about the importance of body location in a judgment of touch appropriateness. Each of us has rules or expectations about touch, like the earlier example of our male students who explained the difference between a touch on the knee versus one on the thigh. Even if you're a "free spirit"—someone who believes that he or she isn't judgmental or doesn't operate according to rules—you *do* have rules or expectations about how people are supposed to treat each other, but may not have ever thought about it this way. Socially speaking, you have rules about who can touch you, when, where on your body, and in what setting. Maybe you're involved in a romantic relationship, but believe abstinence is best for you right now; to you—at this point in your life and development—sexual activity with your partner may only involve kissing and petting, but not intercourse or oral sex. That's considered a rule or expectation about intimate touch—who can touch you when and where on your body. Such a rule must be respected and adhered to by your intimate partner(s).

The second sense of location with regard to touch means the setting or context within which the touch occurs. Recalling our earlier PDA example, many of us were raised to believe that intimate touching, like making out or petting, should only be done in private—never in public, not even a party where other people are around. Others of us have different rules, meaning any form of touch is okay, any time and any place. (Comedian Billy Crystal used to joke that women needed a reason to have sex; men just needed a place.) But think of other examples: When you meet a date's or partner's parents for the first time, should you merely shake hands with them or hug them? Does this vary, depending on whether it's the mother or the father you're meeting? Are there different expectations for women versus men in this instance, meaning, is it less of a violation for a woman to hug people upon meeting them than a man? If you do extend a touch that's received as inappropriate, should you say something or just remember never to do that again?

The next aspect related to appropriateness is **duration,** meaning how long a touch lasts. Touches can be fleeting or long-lasting, but you indeed have rules about this too. Gynecological or prostate exams can seem to take *forever*, as though you were in a time warp. These situations pose a paradox—non-intimate touches extended to our most intimate areas of the body—so they can be confusing and uncomfortable. If doctors are wise and well trained, they'll do all they can to reduce the discomfort their unwelcome touch causes and get the exams over with quickly. As a less awkward example, consider the basic embrace: A long hug communicates more emotion or intense affection than a short hug (Floyd, 1999; Guerrero & Floyd, 2006).

When we refer to the **intensity** of a touch, we mean the power, force, or concentration of bodily contact. Your female co-author of this book doesn't care for horror films and waited several years after *The Exorcist* came out before going to see a screening of the movie on the campus where she was employed at the time. After viewing a gruesome scene which included the lead character's head doing a 360 on her body, she looked down and realized that her hand formed a "death grip" on the thigh of the man sitting next to her. She also realized that the man she'd touched was one of the professors on campus who taught religion—a mild-mannered, happily married gentleman, who thankfully didn't make her feel like a loon for grabbing his thigh in the theatre.

Our emotions generally influence the amount of intensity we put into a touch. If you're anxious about a job interview, you might grip a bit harder when you shake hands with your potential employer. If you're nervous about kissing your date good night on a first date, you might miscalculate the amount of pressure to apply to the lips. We occasionally see men give each other bear hugs—hugs with more than normal intensity—as a way of covering possible embarrassment over the fact that their bodies are coming into contact. Sometimes between men, the greater the intensity of the contact—whether it's a hug, high five, handshake, or punch on the upper arm—the greater the insecurity or discomfort over the very act of same-sex touching or the greater the need to show dominance.

A final note on the appropriateness of touch: Try to be an effective observer of nonverbal communication; put more simply, register people's reactions to your touch. As nonverbal scholar Peter Andersen (2004) suggests, you can usually tell if people like your touch or not by their nonverbal reactions, not by what they say. If you're unsure of a reaction, it's fine to simply ask a question like, "I'm sorry; was my grip too strong in that handshake?" In romantic encounters, observing someone's reaction to your touch is critical. Even better, as nerdy as it sounds, is to have a conversation about touch—specifically the touch ethic, meaning what the person thinks is appropriate, what she or he likes, dislikes, and so forth. Better to risk this kind of conversation early on than to extend a touch that isn't appreciated and have the relationship come to a screeching halt.

## REMEMBER 8.4

| | |
|---|---|
| **Expectancy Violations Model:** | model that suggests that we develop expectations for appropriate nonverbal behaviors in ourselves and others; when expectations are violated, we experience heightened arousal and the nature of our relationships becomes critical. |
| **Tie Sign:** | nonverbal behaviors that express affection between people and also signal the status of the relationship to others. |
| **Location:** | area of the body where physical contact is made; setting or context within which a touch occurs. |
| **Duration:** | how long a touch lasts. |
| **Intensity:** | power, force, or concentration of bodily contact. |

# ■ APPLICATIONS OF HAPTICS RESEARCH

Many interesting applications of the research on haptics continue to emerge as we seek to better understand this powerful, yet complicated code of nonverbal communication. Here we overview briefly some provocative topics of research on touch.

## Culture and Touch

As with other nonverbal communication codes, touch is culturally rooted, which means that we should interpret the meaning of a touch only within its appropriate cultural context. One of the most prolific nonverbal scholars to study the effects of culture is Edwin T. Hall (1966, 1981), who believes that cultures can be distinguished according to two categories of nonverbal behavior: the distances at which members of a given culture interact (proxemics) and the touch that occurs between members (haptics). With regard for haptics, Hall terms those cultures exhibiting frequent touching **contact cultures,** while those exhibiting infrequent touch are **noncontact cultures.** Contact cultures include Latin America, India, France, and Arab countries (Kras, 1989; Ruch, 1989); noncontact cultures include Germany and northern-European nations, North America, and many Asian countries, such as China, Japan, Korea, Indonesia, and Malaysia (Barnlund, 1989; Kim, 1977; Ruch, 1989). Other research supports Hall's findings (DiBiase & Gunnoe, 2004; Klopf, Thompson, Ishii, & Sallinen-Kuparinen, 1991). For example, Morris (1971, 1977) observed that people in Anglo-Saxon (non-contact) cultures engage in far less everyday, casual touch and are more restrictive in their public touching than people in Mediterranean and Latin cultures.

Cultural distinctions can be easily noted in the greetings members of different cultural groups give to one another (Axtell, 1998). For example, French Canadian greetings look a lot like those Americans use (handshakes for men, brief hugs for women); Puerto Rican women often grasp each other's shoulders and kiss both cheeks when greeting, and Italian women offer the double cheek kiss as well. Saudi Arabian men shake right hands to greet each other, and may also place their left hands on each other's shoulders while kissing both cheeks (Hickson, Stacks, & Moore, 2004).

We have a memorable example that relates to this topic of culture and haptics, dating back to a year in which the summer Olympics were held. We can't remember the exact year of the games, but it was before the breakup of the Soviet Union, when that country was a powerhouse in gymnastics. A discussion was sparked in a nonverbal communication course that was in session the summer the Olympics aired, with some of our very American students saying that they were appalled at the behavior of the male Soviet gymnasts and their coaches. When each male gymnast finished his routine, he did the traditional "arms up in the air in a V, feet together" signal to the judges that he was finished, then bounded off the mat into the open arms of his male coach, and the two men exchanged a brief kiss on the lips. Our students weren't the only ones to notice and comment on this "outrageous" and "gross" behavior. American sportscasters covering the gymnastic events took note, but were more careful than our students not to criticize the Soviet public display of affection. Granted, the context of a sporting event changes how we interpret touches, because it's more acceptable for men to pat each other's rear ends after a good play on the football field than in the produce section of the grocery store. But our American students felt that the Soviet men's behavior was just "wrong." Were our students just showing their **ethnocentricity** (a belief that one's cultural practices are correct and superior to that of other cultures) or was there some **homophobia** (a fear of being labeled homosexual or a general dislike of homosexuals) inherent in their responses? Our students didn't have the same reaction when female gymnasts of various cultures showed affection for their female and male coaches, so what do you think was operating here?

While the contact/noncontact cultural distinction is interesting and helpful, we have to be careful about applying it too generally. Subsequent research shows that the distinction may be too simplistic (McDaniel & Andersen, 1998; Remland, Jones, & Brinkman, 1991, 1995). In a study of Central and South American cultures (often lumped together as Latin American), touch behavior was quite different across cultural groups (Shuter, 1976). We have to be careful also with such distinctions among European cultures; while French, Greek, and Italian men tend to be demonstrative with their affection for one another, British men rarely show their affection in such ways (Morris, 1971). Not all Middle Eastern citizens view and exhibit touch the same way either; in some countries, men embrace and kiss each other on both cheeks, while in other countries a handshake or more formal greeting is the norm.

## Offering Comfort

This may not be the most pleasant exercise that we've asked you to do, but it's important. No one likes funerals, but we ask you to imagine or think back to a time when you grieved the death of someone—perhaps not a person particularly close to you, but someone close enough that you attended the funeral or memorial service, then gathered at someone's home after the service. (If you haven't had this experience, try to think of something comparable.) What do you recall seeing at the gathering after the service? Most likely you saw lots of examples of touch behavior, even if you didn't register it consciously as such at the time. Were people hugging, holding each other and crying, patting hands or backs, or extending other kinds of comforting touches to each other? When emotions run high, people tend to reach out to each other and make bodily contact, but not everyone. Some people don't want to be physically close or in contact with other people when they're grieving, and we have to be sensitive to this and not impose our will or needs on people like this. It's important for us not to judge people who are in a grieving process, because each of us grieves differently.

One of the most prolific scholars to study the communication of emotional support is Brant Burleson, whose research has explored verbal and nonverbal means of offering comfort to people in emotional distress (Burleson, 1982, 1985, 1994; Burleson, Albrecht, & Sarason, 1994; Burleson & Goldsmith, 1998; Burleson & Samter, 1985). Burleson (2003) contends that the communication of comfort and emotional support is critical to relationships, and that such behavior can help people establish, maintain, and even repair close relationships. His research shows that people who are able to provide emotional support for others are perceived as more likable, popular, and socially attractive than people who cannot extend this kind of support to others.

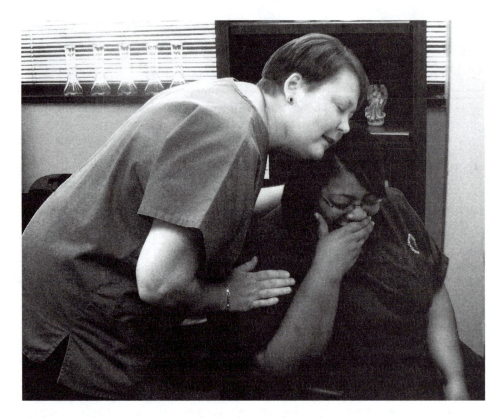

*At times, a touch can convey support and caring in a way that words cannot.*

Touch is an important way we express comfort and emotional support to one another (Guerrero & Floyd, 2006). One team of researchers in the 1980s interviewed women who had recently given birth, for their views on touch during labor (Stolte & Friedman, 1980). Overwhelmingly, the women viewed touches they received during labor positively. They reported supportive feelings from being touched on the hand by their husbands, family members, and nurses, but negative feelings from being touched by physicians on their abdomen or pelvic area. Jones and Yarbrough (1985), whose categories of touch we reviewed earlier in this chapter, found that people often used touch in the form of patting or touching someone's arm, shoulder, or hand to offer support and comfort. Hugs tended to be reserved for situations that involved more emotional or serious distress.

Another study asked college students about the nonverbal comforting behavior they might offer if their roommate was going through a breakup with a romantic partner (Dolin & Booth-Butterfield, 1993). Most students said that they would use some form of touch to comfort their roommate; hugs, pats, and arms around the shoulders were among the top responses from students. Interestingly, women in this study said that they were likely to offer a hug to comfort someone, while men were more likely to use a pat than a hug. Again, as we've said for all the topics within this chapter, the appropriateness of extending a touch depends on the situation and the people involved. Sensitivity and a keen awareness of the power of nonverbal cues are important in situations where an offer of comfort could make a lot of difference.

## Touch within Marriage

Earlier in this chapter we discussed the importance of touch in relationships, specifically romantic or intimate relationships. But research has uncovered some trends regarding touch within the marital relationship. First, Heslin and colleagues conducted studies on touch by asking subjects, "What does it mean to you when a close person of the opposite sex touches a certain area of your body in a certain manner?" The researchers specifically examined type of touch, using Heslin's five categories; location of touch on the body; and the sex of subjects (Nguyen, Heslin, & Nguyen, 1975, 1976). In general, married people in these studies held a positive view of touch, but associated touch more with sexual activity than unmarried subjects. Men and women were significantly different in their views of the meanings of touch to certain areas of their bodies, but in general, married people were more likely than unmarried people to link touches to sexual arousal than other categories (friendship/warmth, love intimacy).

Nonverbal scholars Guerrero and Andersen (1991, 1994) studied touch within intimate relationships and determined that people in long-term relationships, like marriages, touched each other less frequently and less intimately than people who were working to establish a romantic relationship or to repair one that was in trouble. The authors of the studies explain that *quantity* of touch appears to be more important when trying to get a relationship off the ground or back on track, while *quality* of touch becomes more important over the long haul of a relationship. A subsequent study found similar results: Men and women in heterosexual, romantic, ongoing relationships reported that touch between themselves and their partners increased during the time they moved from casual dating to serious dating, but decreased when they moved from serious dating to marriage (Emmers & Dindia, 1995). A more recent study on affection within relationships found that dating partners reported receiving more verbal and nonverbal affection than did marital partners (Punyanunt-Carter, 2004).

What gives? Should we enjoy touch while we're dating, then give up on it once we get married? While other research posits that when key nonverbal cues (like eye contact) diminish within a relationship, so does the level of satisfaction (Noller, 1980), studies of marital partners suggest that satisfaction with the relationship isn't affected much by a change or decrease in touching behavior. Is it possible that, what with the busy-ness of marital life and the same-ness of one's partner, the importance of touch diminishes or affection becomes routinized, such that it is relegated to the realm of occasional sexual activity? That may be true, but then it's interesting that TV talk shows that offer help to overly busy and stressed out married couples often give them free romantic getaway vacations, so that they can reenergize their relationship and "reconnect."

Do the research results on affection and long-term relationships ring true for you, either in your own experience or what you've observed in others? We would agree that it seems like touching is more frequent and possibly more important to couples who are in the beginning stages—the "throes" of being in love—than couples in long-term rela-tionships. Think of our earlier restaurant example, where we described a couple making out in a booth of a restaurant. Can you imagine a married couple behaving like this? We recently observed a married couple at a restaurant—they were like a well-oiled machine. (We assumed they were married because of their wedding bands.) They sat opposite each other at a table (four-top), went right to their menus without speaking or making eye contact, ordered their meals quickly, didn't talk or make eye contact before their meals were served, ate their meals in basic silence, paid their check, and left. They never touched and probably said only a couple of sentences to each other the whole hour they were in the restaurant. Now, should we make a judgment that this marriage is in trouble or merely comfortable? Do these people take each other for granted or simply operate smoothly as a team? Perhaps this couple doesn't need touch or affection as a sign that they love each other, but then again, the relationship may be on its last legs and headed for divorce.

The point for all of us is this: What we see and the interpretations we make about what we see don't always match the reality within a relationship. We shouldn't be too quick to judge the quality of other people's relationships by certain observable nonverbal cues, because nonverbal communication is complicated, like we've said all along in this book. If you're a single person in the dating world, it's unwise to impose your perspectives of appropriate affection as a template for how all couples should behave, since each of us have different touch ethics and because relationships can be quite different in private versus within range of someone's watchful eye. But if you're in a marriage or other long-term committed partnership, you might want to take some time to think about the presence or absence of critical nonverbal cues, especially touch. Your relationship might be generally satisfying, but could it be improved simply by increasing the amount or type of affection you show your partner? Might you choose to revive the important role of affection as connection and comfort—affection that doesn't signal or lead to sexual activity?

## Sex, Gender, and Touch

In order to understand the complex research on the effects of sex and gender on touch behavior, it's important to first comprehend the difference between the two terms— sex and gender. Briefly, **sex** refers to a biological distinction of being born female or male, while **gender** is a culturally constructed, complex designation that encompasses biological sex, psychological gender (masculine, feminine, androgynous—a blend of masculine and feminine traits), attitudes about roles the sexes should assume in society, and sexual orientation (e.g., heterosexual, homosexual, bisexual, transgender) (Ivy & Backlund, 2008). Most studies of touch among women and men have focused on biological sex, with an occasional examination of psychological gender (Floyd & Morman, 2000; Morman & Floyd, 1999; Rane & Draper, 1995).

Over several decades of research, results are consistent: Touch seems to be more a woman's "realm" than a man's. As one team of researchers put it, women have a "greater theoretic bandwidth of appropriate affectionate behaviors" than do men (Floyd & Morman, 1997, p. 292). Researchers who conducted studies in the U.S. from the 1970s through the 2000s conclude the following: (1) Women express more nonverbal affection than men; (2) women receive more touch, from both men and other women, than men; (3) women engage in more frequent and more intimate same-sex touch than men; (4) women are more comfortable with touch in general, and same-sex touch in specific, than men; (5) women in heterosexual stable or married relationships are more likely to initiate touch than their male partners; and (6) women perceive themselves as being more affectionate than men (Andersen & Leibowitz, 1978; Bombar & Littig, 1996; Burgoon & Walther, 1990; Derlega, Lewis, Harrison, Winstead, & Costanza, 1989; Emmers & Dindia, 1995; Floyd, 1997, 2000; Floyd & Morman, 1997; Greenbaum & Rosenfeld, 1980; Hall & Veccia, 1990; Jones, 1986; Major, Schmidlin, & Williams, 1990; Roese, Olson, Borenstein, Martin, & Shores, 1992; Wallace, 1981; Willis & Rawdon, 1994). In fact, in their book on nonverbal communication in close relationships, Guerrero and Floyd (2006) state, "To our knowledge, no published research has found that men, at any age or in any context, express more affection than women do" (p. 96).

Some of these same researchers have tried to determine what's at the root of the differing touch behavior of men and women, with most agreeing that homophobia in American culture is the primary culprit. Say, for example, you see two women holding hands as they walk through a shopping mall somewhere in the U.S. Are you likely to jump to the conclusion that they're lesbians or might you simply think that they're good friends or sisters, comfortable with expressing their affection and connection in public? Now picture two men doing the same thing—holding hands as they window shop. What interpretation comes to mind first? For one thing, you're far less likely to see two men holding hands in public (other than in gay bars or other primarily homosexual gatherings) than two women, but you're more likely to assume the men are gay than merely affectionate friends. The scrutiny on men in our society is far greater than on women regarding expressions of affection. Women aren't likely to have their femininity called into question because of affection they express to others, but men face this kind of pressure daily. Homophobia leads men—straight, gay, and bisexual— to seek covert means of expressing affection and affiliation with one another, because the negative sanctions associated with more overt expressions are serious (Morman & Floyd, 1998; see the Spotlight on Research box for more information on this topic). So before assuming that women are just better than men at expressing their emotions and affection through touch, consider the societal constraints that have operated for a very long time and that continue to affect this form of nonverbal communication.

## Immediacy: Touch between Teachers and Students

While we've all probably heard national news stories about sordid sexual affairs between teachers and underage students, that's not the focus of this section. A more common problem or challenge is the everyday type of touch that can occur between teachers and students in educational settings.

In Chapter 11, we discuss nonverbal communication in the workplace and educational environments and, more specifically, **immediacy,** defined as behavior that enhances psychological and physical closeness between people (Mehrabian, 1971). We explore **teacher nonverbal immediacy** or the use of nonverbal cues (e.g., vocal expressiveness, smiling, gestures, eye contact, relaxed body position, movement around the classroom, and appropriate touch) to signal to students a teacher's approachability, availability, closeness, and warmth. Research shows that teacher immediacy has a positive impact on student attitude and learning (Frymier, 1993; Menzel & Carrell, 1999; Rocca & McCroskey, 1999). Some positive effects of teacher immediacy include the creation of a more open classroom environment, greater student enjoyment of the subject matter, more frequent student–teacher and student–student communication, and enhanced learning opportunities because students' attention spans increase (Christophel, 1990; McCroskey, Richmond, & McCroskey, 2006; Moore, Masterson, Christophel, & Shea, 1996; Powell & Harville, 1990; Richmond, McCroskey, & Hickson, 2008).

## SPOTLIGHT on Research

Professor of communication Kory Floyd of Arizona State University is an affectionate kind of guy. Floyd, a leading nonverbal communication scholar, has studied the expression of human affection for more than a decade. Rather than focusing on one piece of published research for this feature, as is our approach in other chapters, for the topic of touch we're going to spotlight Floyd's program of research that has enlightened our understanding of touch between parents and children—more specifically, fathers and sons.

Floyd and various colleagues have examined how affection expressed or denied by fathers predicts how men will show affection to their own sons. In 2000, Floyd and Morman examined two hypotheses for their predictions about expressions of affection: (1) the modeling hypothesis, which predicts that a parent's positive behavior will be replicated in a child's own parenting skills; and (2) the compensation hypothesis, which predicts that a parent's negative behavior will be compensated for in a child's parenting skills. (In other words, when you hear someone say "I'll never treat my own kids like my dad treated me," that statement reflects a desire to compensate for bad fathering when one has children of one's own.) Floyd and Morman combined the two hypotheses into a hybrid theory of affection, because they found that men were most affectionate with their own sons when they had fathers who were either highly affectionate (modeling hypothesis) or highly unaffectionate (compensation hypothesis). In other words, men who become fathers are likely to show affection to their own sons based on how their fathers treated them.

Next in this line of research was the first of what Floyd termed Human Affection Exchange studies (Floyd, 2001). This study delved more deeply into the connection between father–son affection and men's expressions of affection with their own sons, but with a focus on heterosexual versus homosexual/bisexual men. Floyd found that, in general, men in the study communicated more affection to their own sons than they reported receiving from their fathers; in addition, heterosexual men received more affection from their fathers than did men identifying themselves later in life as homosexual or bisexual. Another fascinating result was that the communication of affection was more often accomplished covertly, meaning indirectly through service activities than direct verbal (e.g., saying "I love you") or nonverbal means (e.g., hugging), a finding that corroborates earlier research (Morman & Floyd, 1998). Men tend to express affection for other men by doing things like helping each other with projects or giving each other tickets to sporting events. Sometimes people criticize or make fun of male friendship

*(continued)*

**SPOTLIGHT** on Research *(continued)*

because positive feelings between men are often expressed differently than between female friends or cross-sex friends. But this research teaches us that we shouldn't be quick to judge the quality or importance of a friendship just because the affection isn't expressed like we expect or experience.

Floyd's subsequent studies found the following: (1) the presence of a cultural shift in fatherhood, away from an authoritarian, emotionally detached father to a more involved, nurturing father, with positive outcomes in the quality of men's relationships with their fathers, as well as their own sons (Morman & Floyd, 2002); (2) fathers tend to extend more physical affection to their biological sons than to stepsons or adopted sons, and they extend more affection to their sons than the sons show toward the fathers (Floyd & Morman, 2003); (3) fathers' awareness of their sons' sexual orientation is associated with the amount of affection fathers extend (Floyd, Sargent, & Di Corcia, 2004); (4) sons with siblings often believe that they must compete for a finite amount of affection their fathers can extend to them (Floyd & Morman, 2005); and (5) the amount of affection a person can express to others is associated with the body's ability to handle stress (Floyd, 2006a).

We can learn a great deal from Kory Floyd's continuing research into patterns of affection within key relationships. Do you want to know more about this line of research? If so, check out this book: Floyd, K. (2006b). *Communicating affection: Interpersonal behavior and social context.* New York: Cambridge University Press.

Touch between teachers and students is a sensitive topic, given what we now know about sexual harassment in educational environments. Research over a couple of decades has investigated the effects of college teachers' touch on students' perceptions of teachers, with mixed results. Scholars Steward and Lupfer (1987) studied touch in teacher–student conferences, and found that students who were touched on the arm by their teachers during private conferences perceived those teachers to be more capable, understanding, interesting, and friendly than those students who were not touched in the study. In the decade of the 1990s, nonverbal scholars conducted a study manipulating the immediacy behavior of an instructor and measuring the resulting effects on student learning (Comstock, Rowell, & Bowers, 1995). Researchers set up three conditions: low immediacy, moderate immediacy, and high or excessive immediacy. In the excessive category, the instructor moved about the classroom, occasionally touching students' shoulders. Students responded negatively to excessive immediacy and positively to moderate immediacy, which did not involve touch. The results of these two studies seem contradictory, but let's remember that one study used the context of a private conference while the other took place during a class session in a lecture hall. In addition, the teacher's movement as part of the excessive immediacy condition in the second study may have affected students' ratings more than the teacher's touch toward students.

Yet another study investigated several teacher immediacy behaviors and found that students perceived teacher touch to be potentially sexually harassing (Mongeau &

*Is this teacher's touch on the student's arm appropriate?*

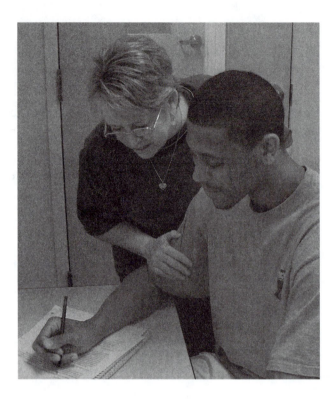

Blalock, 1994). Communication scholars Lannutti, Laliker, and Hale (2001) applied expectancy violation theory to teacher–student touch and found that teachers who were perceived as non-rewarding (i.e., low in credibility, status, and attractiveness) and who touched students on the thigh, as compared to the arm, were the most negatively evaluated, especially by female students. This is yet another tricky area within the realm of touch, because professors often want to comfort students who come to them, upset about something in their lives or disappointed about their grades, and touch is a primary form of comforting behavior. But professors worry about the possible negative effects of extending any form of touch to a student. Just as we've advised for other contexts that may involve touch, people in educational settings—especially those in positions of authority—have to be extremely careful with touch, given that it is the most powerful, yet most complex of all the codes of nonverbal communication.

## Power and Status

In other codes chapters of this book, we describe nonverbal cues that communicate power and status. For example, we explore several status cues related to the environment (e.g., corner offices, expensive furniture, the appearance of gatekeepers to buffer the boss from the public), the physical appearance cue of height, kinesic cues of stance and posture, and ways people use their voices to command attention and influence others. It follows, then, that certain touch behaviors work in tandem with other cues to communicate power and status (Hall, Coats, & LeBeau, 2005).

Research has shown that powerful people tend to initiate touch toward others, but generally they don't receive touch from lower status people unless it comes in the form of reciprocation or a formalized greeting, like a handshake (Hall, 1996; Henley, 2001; Nelson & Golant, 2004). Let's say that an employee enters her or his boss's office for a meeting. If the boss extends his or her hand for a handshake with the employee, the employee should reciprocate because that's expected and proper behavior in American culture. But if the boss also places the free hand on the employee's shoulder, should the employee do the same—put her or his free hand on the boss's shoulder? In general, the answer is no, because, like we've said elsewhere in this chapter, a hand on the shoulder touch can be viewed as a dominance behavior, so the employee most likely should not reciprocate this touch.

Typically, higher status people are afforded more liberty in initiating touch, so lower status people are advised to wait for nonverbal cues from higher status people. It's hard to imagine a situation in which a lower status person would initiate an unprovoked touch toward a boss—like giving a boss a hug or a slap on the back. Such nonverbal actions would not likely go over well, but of course it depends on the situation and the organizational climate. It's commonplace in many organizations for bosses to initiate touch with employees. But these days, more than ever, that touch has to be appropriate, professional, and non-intimate or else you could be looking at a charge of sexual harassment (Lee & Guerrero, 2001; Smeltzer, Waltman, & Leonard, 1991).

High status people also have more prerogative to violate nonverbal expectations, because it is less likely that their actions will be perceived negatively than if a

## REMEMBER 8.5

| | |
|---|---|
| **Contact Cultures:** | cultures exhibiting frequent touch. |
| **Noncontact Cultures:** | cultures exhibiting infrequent touch. |
| **Ethnocentricity:** | belief that one's cultural practices are correct and superior to that of other cultures. |
| **Homophobia:** | a fear of being labeled homosexual or a general dislike of homosexuals. |
| **Sex:** | a biological distinction of being born female or male. |
| **Gender:** | a culturally constructed complex designation that encompasses biological sex, psychological gender, attitudes about roles the sexes should assume in society, and sexual orientation. |
| **Immediacy:** | behavior that enhances psychological and physical closeness between people. |
| **Teacher Nonverbal Immediacy:** | use of nonverbal cues to signal to students a teacher's approachability, availability, closeness, and warmth. |

low status person does the same thing (Dunbar, 2004). For example, what if your boss came into the workplace one day looking disheveled and upset, suddenly started crying, and reached out to you for comfort? Would you provide the boss with a supportive embrace or arm around the shoulder? While the situation would no doubt be startling and awkward, such behavior would likely evoke different responses and interpretations if a low status person did the same thing—crumpling into a sobbing heap in the boss's arms. We know this example is extreme, but think about it for a moment: Powerful people are afforded more benefit of the doubt, verbally and nonverbally, than less powerful people.

## ■ UNDERSTANDING HAPTICS: APPLYING THE REFLEXIVE CYCLE OF NONVERBAL COMMUNICATION DEVELOPMENT

Applying the Reflexive Cycle to your touch behavior can be eye-opening, because it's likely that you haven't thought all that much about how, when, and where you touch other people, as well as how you view or process the touch you receive. It's important to work through the cycle because touch is such a powerful nonverbal cue, with significant rewards when it's extended appropriately and serious sanctions when it's done inappropriately.

Since the first step in the cycle is self-awareness, let's address some questions: What's your touch ethic? What kinds of touches do you like and dislike to give, as well as receive? For example, you may not be a massage person; the thought of paying someone to rub your neck may seem like the last thing you want to do. How much of your touch ethic comes from what you observed and experienced with your parents and siblings? How comfortable are you with touching other people? Perhaps you're comfortable touching only those people you know well, keeping touch ritualized with strangers or new people you meet. Or perhaps you're fairly "touchy" with people in general. What rules do you have about appropriate touch across situations, locations, and people? This inventory of your touch ethic should take some time, because it affects all the other steps in the cycle.

Once you've inventoried your touch ethic and behavior, you may have identified some areas you want to improve or change. Maybe you're nervous in romantic situations and don't know what kinds of touch are appropriate, in terms of showing someone that you're attracted to him or her. You'd like to loosen up and show more affection, but don't want to seem "grabby" or "clingy." There's no magic trick to this; you just have to be brave and take a risk (within what's socially appropriate, of course) to try and change your touch behavior with people. Another idea is to have a conversation about touch with a group of friends, to gauge how they view the topic. You can have this conversation also with a date or romantic partner, as we suggested earlier in the chapter, so that you learn what kind of touch the person finds desirable and appropriate. In some of our communication courses, we have students practice professional handshakes with one another, because even this simple form of touch can use some practice. It's surprising, but often the case that many college men haven't had much experience shaking hands with a woman, so the practice is generally appreciated by our students.

As another example connected with the second step of the cycle, perhaps you are too "touchy," meaning that you tend to touch people when you talk to them—anybody, everybody. Someone who cares about you may tip you off about this or perhaps a statement to this effect shows up on an evaluation of you at work. You don't want someone thinking that you "just can't keep your hands to yourself," so if someone lets you know that your frequency of touch is too much or inappropriate, you'll want to work to change that behavior.

The third phase of the Reflexive Cycle involves inventorying others' touch behavior. If you really want to become savvy when it comes to touch, become more of a people watcher because you'll learn a lot from observing other people. You've no doubt seen this in movies: The suave guy approaches a woman or a group of women in a social scene while his buddies look on, noting the smooth way he makes connections, especially physical ones. We're not suggesting you observe people and merely copy what they do, because touch is more complex than this, but you can get some pointers from watching other people, noting things that work as well as the negative consequences of inappropriate touch.

Your next step in the Reflexive Cycle is to interact with others, enacting any haptic changes you've decided are appropriate, and gauge how your nonverbal behaviors transact with others'. If you change your handshake, for instance, do people at work notice? Do potential employers react any differently because of such a change? We've seen some of our students decide to start shaking hands with more professors and classmates, because they like the mature tone such a touch sets. This behavior almost always receives a positive response. Just remember that a purposeful change in touch behavior, because it involves bodily contact, is likely to register significantly with people, so be prepared for this.

So you've inventoried yourself, begun to make changes in your touch behavior, inventoried others' approaches to touch, and engaged in mutual transaction of behavior (such that your touch impacts other people and theirs impacts you). Now the final phase of the Reflexive Cycle involves an evaluation of the whole process. What did you learn about your own and others' touch behavior that makes you a better communicator? We've said it before and we'll say it again: The reflexive process includes a courageous inventory of yourself (your background and upbringing, behavior, and attitudes), a willingness to experiment and attempt some change, keen observational skills of others' behavior, and more social experience, as you put your new behaviors into action, transact with others, note the results, and re-evaluate.

## SUMMARY ■ ■ ■ ■ ■

This chapter was devoted to haptics—the study of human touch—as a powerful code of nonverbal communication. We began by discussing how touch is a complex and powerful nonverbal cue, because unlike other codes, touch involves bodily contact between people. We then explored the touch ethic, meaning our beliefs about and preferences for touch, because the touch ethic affects how we touch other people, as well as how we interpret their touch toward us.

Next, we delved into the topic of the role of touch in human development, beginning with research on the importance of touch to infants and children. We then discussed the detrimental effects of being deprived of touch, especially for elder adults in American society, who tend to be the most touch deprived among us.

Because touch is such a complicated nonverbal code, category systems have been developed to help us understand and study it. We first overviewed Heslin's categories, which include Functional/Professional, Social/Polite, Friendship/Warmth, Love/Intimacy, and Sexual Arousal types of touch. Research indicates that problems arise when men view women's touches as indications of love/intimacy or sexual arousal, but women intend their touches to indicate merely friendship. A second category system helps us understand the meanings behind certain touches; Jones and Yarbrough offer six primary meanings for touch: positive affect (affectionate), playful, control, ritualistic, task-related, and accidental touches.

In the next section of this chapter, we examined ways we can gauge the appropriateness of touch, including touches we extend to other people and touches we receive from them. Expectancy Violations Theory helps us understand this phenomenon, because violating someone's expectations regarding bodily contact can have serious consequences. We also explored location, duration, and intensity of touch which offer clues about appropriateness.

We outlined some of the many applications of haptics research, beginning with a discussion of touch as a culturally rooted nonverbal behavior. Touches like hugs, pats on the hand or back, and arms around the shoulder are often used to comfort or show support for people who are in need. We examined the complicated topic of touch within ongoing, committed relationships, because behavioral patterns of touch seem to change depending on the stages of a relationship a couple experiences. Research shows that quality of touch appears to be more critical for marriage, as opposed to quantity of touch that is so important in new relationships.

Scholars have explored sex differences in touch behavior, finding that women touch people in general more often and more intimately than men; women also receive more touches from both men and women. One explanation for this phenomenon that has consistently received support in research is that homophobia in society affects men's touching behavior, causing them to look for covert means of conveying affection for fear that their masculinity and sexual orientation will be called into question.

Another interesting application of haptics research concerns educational environments. We discussed teacher nonverbal immediacy in general, and teacher-to-student touch in specific, for its effects on the teacher–student relationship and on student learning. Our last application of haptics research pertained to touch behaviors that reveal a person's power or status. Powerful, high-status people have more free rein with regard for touch than low-status people, but touch in professional settings needs to be expressed carefully, because of the potential for such actions to be interpreted as sexual harassment. Finally, we applied the Reflexive Cycle of Nonverbal Communication Development to the code of touch, in terms of inventorying your own touch behavior, making any necessary changes, observing and inventorying others' use of touch, transacting with other people and understanding how touch operates within interaction, and finally, re-examining the whole process so that you can become a more effective communicator.

## DISCUSSION STARTERS

1. Think of ways that touch has power. Why do we suggest that bodily contact is the most powerful code of nonverbal communication, as compared to eye contact or proxemics?

2. When we asked the question in this chapter, "What is your touch ethic?" were you able to respond? What lessons did you learn from your parents and siblings regarding appropriate touch as you were growing up? Have you ever been in a romantic relationship that changed your touch ethic?

3. Discuss the merits of pet therapy and intergenerational massage, as means of extending touch to elderly persons in our society who tend to be touch deprived.

4. How can people get the meanings of touch confused, such as interpreting someone's friendship/warmth touch (Heslin category) as an indication of love or romantic interest? Can category confusion alter a person's touch ethic?

5. Why do people seem to have such varying views about the appropriateness of touch?

Recall a situation in which either you or a friend viewed someone's touch as inappropriate, but the other person thought the touch was perfectly acceptable. How can this kind of perceptual difference exist?

6. If someone were to touch you inappropriately, either because of location, duration, or intensity, how would you react? Would you be more likely to ignore the behavior, correct it nonverbally, or say something to the inappropriate toucher?

7. From either your travels or knowledge of other cultures, describe some cultural differences in touch behavior. If someone makes a cultural gaffe in the form of an inappropriate touch, what's the best way to handle the situation?

8. Have you worked with people who use touch as a means of conveying their power or status? How do you cope with workplace touches that can best be interpreted as "power play"? How might inappropriate touches in the workplace be construed as sexual harassment?

## REFERENCES

Abbey, A. (1982). Sex differences in attributions for friendly behavior: Do males misperceive females' friendliness? *Journal of Personality and Social Psychology, 42,* 830–838.

Abbey, A. (1987). Misperception of friendly behavior as sexual interest: A survey of naturally occurring incidents. *Psychology of Women Quarterly, 11,* 173–194.

Abbey, A. (1991). Misperception as an antecedent of acquaintance rape: A consequence of ambiguity in communication between men and women. In A. Parrot & L. Bechhofer (Eds.), *Acquaintance rape: The hidden crime* (pp. 96–111). New York: Wiley.

Afifi, W. A., & Burgoon, J. K. (2000). The impact of violations on uncertainty and the consequences for attractiveness. *Human Communication Research, 26,* 203–233.

Allen, K. (2003). Are pets a healthy pleasure? The influence of pets on blood pressure. *Current Directions in Psychological Science, 12,* 236–239.

Andersen, P. A. (2004). *The complete idiot's guide to body language.* New York: Alpha.

Andersen, P. A. (2008). *Nonverbal communication: Forms and functions* (2nd ed.). Long Grove, IL: Waveland.

Andersen, P. A., Guerrero, L. K., & Jones, S. M. (2006). Nonverbal behavior in intimate interactions and intimate relationships. In V. Manusov & M. L. Patterson (Eds.), *The Sage handbook of nonverbal communication* (pp. 259–277). Thousand Oaks, CA: Sage.

Andersen, P. A., & Leibowitz, K. (1978). The development and nature of the construct touch avoidance. *Environmental Psychology and Nonverbal Behavior, 3,* 89–106.

Arnold, S. L. (2002). *Maternal tactile-gestural stimulation and infants' nonverbal behaviors during early mother-infant face-to-face interactions: Contextual, age, and birth status effects.* Unpublished master's thesis, Concordia University, Montreal, Quebec, Canada.

Axtell, R. E. (1998). Initiating interaction: Greetings and beckonings across the world. Reprinted in L. K. Guerrero, J. A. DeVito, & M. L. Hecht (Eds.), *The nonverbal communication reader: Classic and contemporary readings* (1999, 2nd ed., pp. 395–405). Prospect Heights, IL: Waveland.

Barnlund, D. C. (1989). *Communicative styles of Japanese and Americans: Images and realities.* Belmont, CA: Wadsworth.

Bombar, M. L., & Littig, L. W. (1996). Babytalk as a communication of intimate attachment: An initial study in adult romances and friendships. *Personal Relationships, 3,* 137–158.

Burgoon, J. K. (1978). A communication model of personal space violations: Explication and an initial test. *Human Communication Research, 4,* 129–142.

Burgoon, J. K. (1983). Nonverbal violations of expectations. In J. M. Weimann and R. P. Harrison (Eds.), *Nonverbal interaction* (pp. 77–111). Beverly Hills, CA: Sage.

Burgoon, J. K. (1993). Interpersonal expectations, expectancy violations, and emotional communication. *Journal of Language and Social Psychology, 12,* 30–48.

Burgoon, J. K. (1995). Cross-cultural and intercultural applications of expectancy violations. In R. L. Wiseman (Ed.), *Intercultural communication theory* (Vol. 19, pp. 194–214). Thousand Oaks, CA: Sage.

Burgoon, J. K., Buller, D. B., & Woodall, W. G. (1996). *Nonverbal communication: The unspoken dialogue* (2nd ed.). New York: McGraw-Hill.

Burgoon, J. K., & Hale, J. L. (1988). Nonverbal expectancy violations: Model elaboration and application to immediacy behaviors. *Communication Monographs, 55,* 58–79.

Burgoon, J. K., & Saine, T. (1978). *The unspoken dialogue: An introduction to nonverbal communication.* New York: Houghton Mifflin.

Burgoon, J. K., & Walther, J. B. (1990). Nonverbal expectancies and the evaluative consequences of violations. *Human Communication Research, 17,* 232–265.

Burleson, B. R. (1982). The development of comforting communication skills in childhood and adolescence. *Child Development, 53,* 1578–1588.

Burleson, B. R. (1985). The production of comforting messages: Social-cognitive foundations. *Journal of Language and Social Psychology, 4,* 253–273.

Burleson, B. R. (1994). Comforting messages: Features, functions, and outcomes. In J. A. Daly & J. M. Wiemann (Eds.), *Personality and interpersonal communication* (pp. 305–349). Newbury Park, CA: Sage.

Burleson, B. R. (2003). Emotional support skills. In J. O. Greene & B. R. Burleson (Eds.), *Handbook of communication and social interaction skills* (pp. 551–594). Mahwah, NJ: Erlbaum.

Burleson, B. R., Albrecht, T., & Sarason, I. G. (1994). *The communication of social support: Messages, interactions, relationships, and community.* Thousand Oaks, CA: Sage.

Burleson, B. R., & Goldsmith, D. J. (1998). How the comforting process works: Alleviating emotional distress through conversationally induced reappraisals. In P. A. Andersen & L. K. Guerrero (Eds.), *Handbook of communication and emotion: Research, theory, applications, and contexts* (pp. 246–280). San Diego: Academic.

Burleson, B. R., & Samter, W. (1985). Consistencies in theoretical and naive evaluations of comforting messages. *Communication Monographs, 52,* 103–123.

Christophel, D. M. (1990). The relationships among teacher immediacy behaviors, student motivation, and learning. *Communication Education, 39,* 323–340.

Coan, J. A., Schaefer, H. S., & Davidson, R. J. (2006). Lending a hand: Social regulation of the neural response to threat. *Psychological Science, 17,* 1032–1039.

Colombo, G., Dello Buono, M., Smania, K., Raviola, R., & De Leo, D. (2006). Pet therapy and institutionalized elderly: A study on 144 cognitively unimpaired subjects. *Archives of Gerontology and Geriatrics, 42,* 207–216.

Comstock, J., Rowell, E., & Bowers, J. W. (1995). Food for thought: Teacher nonverbal immediacy, student learning, and curvilinearity. *Communication Education, 44,* 251–266.

Cullen, C., Field, T., Escalona, A., & Hartshom, K. (2000). Father-infant interactions are enhanced by massage therapy. *Early Childhood Development and Care, 164,* 41–47.

Danna, T. M. (1999). Video review: Gentle Touch infant massage. *Journal of Prenatal and Perinatal Psychology and Health, 13,* 315–317.

Darrah, J. P. (1996). A pilot survey of animal-facilitated therapy in Southern California and South Dakota nursing homes. *Occupational Therapy International, 3,* 105–121.

Dellinger-Bavolek, J. (1996). Infant massage: Communicating love through touch. *International Journal of Childbirth Education, 77,* 34–37.

Derlega, V. J., Lewis, R. J., Harrison, S., Winstead, B. A., & Costanza, R. (1989). Gender differences in the initiation and attribution of tactile intimacy. *Journal of Nonverbal Behavior, 13,* 83–96.

DiBiase, R., & Gunnoe, J. (2004). Gender and culture differences in touching behavior. *Journal of Social Psychology, 144,* 49–62.

Dolin, D. J., & Booth-Butterfield, M. (1993). Reach out and touch someone: Analysis of nonverbal comforting responses. *Communication Quarterly, 41,* 383–393.

Dunbar, N. E. (2004). Dyadic power theory: Constructing a communication-based theory of relational power. *Journal of Family Communication, 4,* 235–248.

Emmers, T. M., & Dindia, K. (1995). The effect of relational stage and intimacy on touch: An extension of Guerrero and Andersen. *Personal Relationships, 2,* 225–236.

Feldman, R., Eidelman, A. L., Sirota, L., & Weller, A. (2002). Comparison of skin-to-skin (kangaroo) and traditional care: Parenting outcomes and preterm infant development. *Pediatrics, 110,* 16–26.

Field, T. (1995a). Massage therapy for infants and children. *Journal of Developmental and Behavioral Pediatrics, 16,* 105–111.

Field, T. (Ed.) (1995b). *Touch in early development.* Hillsdale, NJ: Erlbaum.

Field, T. (1998). Touch therapy effects on development. *International Journal of Behavioral Development, 22,* 779–797.

Field, T. (2000). Infant massage therapy. In C. H. Zeanah (Ed.), *Handbook of infant mental health* (2nd ed., pp. 494–500). New York: Guilford.

Field, T. (2002). Violence and touch deprivation in adolescents. *Adolescence, 37,* 735–749.

Field, T. (2005). Touch deprivation and aggression against self among adolescents. In D. M. Stoff & E. J. Susman (Eds.), *Developmental psychobiology of aggression* (pp. 117–140). New York: Cambridge University Press.

Floyd, K. (1997). Communicating affection in dyadic relationships: An assessment of behavior and expectancies. *Communication Quarterly, 45,* 68–80.

Floyd, K. (1999). All touches are not created equal: Effects of form and duration on observers' perceptions of an embrace. *Journal of Nonverbal Behavior, 23,* 283–299.

Floyd, K. (2000). Affectionate same-sex touch: The influence of homophobia on observers' perceptions. *Journal of Social Psychology, 140,* 774–788.

Floyd, K. (2001). Human affection exchange: I. Reproductive probability as a predictor of men's affection with their sons. *Journal of Men's Studies, 10,* 39–50.

Floyd, K. (2006a). Human affection exchange: XII. Affectionate communication is associated with diurnal variation in salivary free cortisol. *Western Journal of Communication, 70,* 47–63.

Floyd, K. (2006b). *Communicating affection: Interpersonal behavior and social context.* New York: Cambridge University Press.

Floyd, K., & Morman, M. T. (1997). Affectionate communication in nonromantic relationships: Influences of communicator, relational, and contextual factors. *Western Journal of Communication, 61,* 279–298.

Floyd, K., & Morman, M. T. (2000). Affection received from fathers as a predictor of men's affection with their own sons: Tests of the modeling and compensation hypotheses. *Communication Monographs, 67,* 347–361.

Floyd, K., & Morman, M. T. (2003). Human affection exchange: II. Affectionate communication in father-son relationships. *Journal of Social Psychology, 143,* 599–612.

Floyd, K., & Morman, M. T. (2005). Fathers' and sons' reports of fathers' affectionate communication: Implications of a naive theory of affection. *Journal of Social and Personal Relationships, 22,* 99–109.

Floyd, K., Sargent, J. E., & DiCorcia, M. (2004). Human affection exchange: VI. Further tests of reproductive probability as a predictor of men's affection with their adult sons. *Journal of Social Psychology, 144,* 191–206.

Floyd, K., & Voloudakis, M. (1999). Attributions for expectancy violating changes in affectionate behavior in platonic friendships. *Journal of Psychology, 133,* 32–48.

Frymier, A. B. (1993). The impact of teacher immediacy on students' motivation: Is it the same for all students? *Communication Quarterly, 42,* 454–464.

Greenbaum, P. E., & Rosenfeld, H. M. (1980). Varieties of touching in greetings: Sequential structure and sex-related differences. *Journal of Nonverbal Behavior, 5,* 13–25.

Guerrero, L. K., & Andersen, P. A. (1991). The waxing and waning of relational intimacy: Touch as a function of relational stage, gender, and touch avoidance. *Journal of Social and Personal Relationships, 8,* 147–165.

Guerrero, L. K., & Andersen, P. A. (1994). Patterns of matching and initiation: Touch behavior and touch avoidance across romantic relationship stages. *Journal of Nonverbal Behavior, 18,* 137–153.

Guerrero, L. K., & Andersen, P. A. (1999). Public touch behavior in romantic relationships between men and women. In L. K. Guerrero, J. A. DeVito, & M. L. Hecht (Eds.), *The nonverbal communication reader: Classic and contemporary readings* (2nd ed., pp. 202–210). Prospect Heights, IL: Waveland.

Guerrero, L. K., & Floyd, K. (2006). *Nonverbal communication in close relationships.* Mahwah, NJ: Erlbaum.

Gupta, M. A., Gupta, A. K., Schork, N. J., & Watteel, G. N. (1995). Perceived touch deprivation and body image: Some observations among eating disordered and non-clinical subjects. *Journal of Psychosomatic Research, 39,* 459–464.

Hall, E. T. (1966). *The hidden dimension* (2nd ed.). Garden City, NY: Anchor/Doubleday.

Hall, E. T. (1981). *Beyond culture.* New York: Doubleday.

Hall, J. A. (1996). Touch, status, and gender at professional meetings. *Journal of Nonverbal Behavior, 20,* 23–44.

Hall, J. A., Coats, E. J., & LeBeau, L. S. (2005). Nonverbal behavior and the vertical dimension of social relations: A meta-analysis. *Psychological Bulletin, 131,* 898–924.

Hall, J. A., & Veccia, E. M. (1990). More "touching" observations: New insights on men, women, and interpersonal touch. *Journal of Personality and Social Psychology, 59,* 1155–1162.

Harris, M. (2005, September 27). Survey finds Canadians increasingly out of touch: 44% want more physical contact in their lives. CanWest News Service, for *National Post* (Canada), p. A2.

Henley, N. M. (2001). Body politics. In A. Branaman (Ed.), *Self and society: Blackwell readers in sociology* (pp. 288–297). Malden, MA: Blackwell.

Heslin, R. (1974). *Steps toward a taxonomy of touching.* Paper presented at the meeting of the Midwestern Psychological Association, Chicago, IL.

Heslin, R., & Alper, T. (1983). Touch: A bonding gesture. In J. M. Weimann & R. P. Harrison (Eds.), *Nonverbal interaction* (pp. 47–75). Beverly Hills: Sage.

Heslin, R., Nguyen, T. D., & Nguyen, M. L. (1983). Meaning of touch: The case of touch from a stranger or same-sex person. *Journal of Nonverbal Behavior, 7,* 147–157.

Hickson, M., III., Stacks, D. W., & Moore, N-J. (2004). *Nonverbal communication: Studies and applications* (4th ed.). Los Angeles: Roxbury.

Ivy, D. K., & Backlund, P. (2008). *GenderSpeak: Personal effectiveness in gender communication* (4th ed.) Boston: Allyn & Bacon.

Jones, S. E. (1986). Sex differences in touch communication. *Western Journal of Speech Communication, 50,* 227–241.

Jones, S. E. (1994). *The right touch: Understanding and using the language of physical contact.* Cresskill, NJ: Hampton.

Jones, S. E., & Brown, B. C. (1996). Touch attitudes and touch behaviors: Recollections of early childhood touch and social self-confidence. *Journal of Nonverbal Behavior, 20,* 147–163.

Jones, S. E., & Yarbrough, A. E. (1985). A naturalistic study of the meanings of touch. *Communication Monographs, 52,* 19–56.

Jourard, S. (1964). *The transparent self.* New York: Van Nostram-Reinhold.

Jourard, S. (1966). An exploratory study of body-accessibility. *British Journal of Social and Clinical Psychology, 5,* 221–231.

Keeley, M. P. (2005). The nonverbal perception scale. In V. Manusov (Ed.), *The sourcebook of nonverbal measures: Going beyond words* (pp. 93–103). Mahwah, NJ: Erlbaum.

Kim, K. (1977). Misunderstanding in nonverbal communication: America and Korea. *Papers in Linguistics, 10,* 1–22.

Klopf, D. W., Thompson, C. A., Ishii, S., & Sallinen-Kuparinen, A. (1991). Nonverbal immediacy differences among Japanese, Finnish, and American university students. *Perceptual and Motor Skills, 73,* 209–210.

Kramer, B. J., & Gibson, J. W. (1991). The cognitively impaired elderly's response to touch: A naturalistic study. *Journal of Gerontological Social Work, 18,* 175–193.

Kras, E. S. (1989). *Management in two cultures: Bridging the gap between U.S. and Mexican managers.* Yarmouth, ME: Intercultural.

Lannutti, P. J., Laliker, M., & Hale, J. L. (2001). Violations of expectations and social-sexual communication in student/professor interactions. *Communication Education, 50,* 69–82.

Lappin, G. (2005). Using infant massage following a mother's unfavorable neonatal intensive care unit experiences: A case study. *RE:view, 37,* 87–95.

Lee, J. W., & Guerrero, L. K. (2001). Types of touch in cross-sex relationships between coworkers: Perceptions of relational and emotional messages, inappropriateness, and sexual harassment. *Journal of Applied Communication Research, 29,* 197–220.

Love your life in 30 seconds. (2007, May). *O: The Oprah Winfrey Magazine*, 208.

Major, B., Schmidlin, A., & Williams, L. (1990). Gender patterns in social touch: The impact of setting and age. *Journal of Personality and Social Psychology, 58*, 634–643.

McCroskey, J. C., Richmond, V. P., & McCroskey, L. L. (2006). Nonverbal communication in instructional contexts. In V. Manusov & M. L. Patterson (Eds.), *The Sage handbook of nonverbal communication* (pp. 421–436). Thousand Oaks, CA: Sage.

McDaniel, E., & Andersen, P. A. (1998). International patterns of interpersonal tactile communication: A field study. *Journal of Nonverbal Behavior, 22*, 59–73.

McEwan, B., & Johnson, S. L. (2008). Relational violence: The darkest side of haptic communication. In L. K. Guerrero & M. L. Hecht (Eds.), *The nonverbal communication reader* (3rd ed., pp. 421–431). Long Grove, IL: Waveland.

Mehrabian, A. (1971). *Silent messages*. Belmont, CA: Wadsworth.

Menzel, K. E., & Carrell, L. J. (1999). The impact of gender and immediacy on willingness to talk and perceived learning. *Communication Education, 48*, 31–40.

Mongeau, P. A., & Blalock, J. (1994). Student evaluations of instructor immediacy and sexually harassing behaviors: An experimental investigation. *Journal of Applied Communication Research, 22*, 256–272.

Montagu, M. F. A. (1971). *Touching: The human significance of the skin*. New York: Columbia University Press.

Montagu, M. F. A. (1978). *Touching: The human significance of the skin* (2nd ed.). New York: Harper & Row.

Moore, A., Masterson, J. T., Christophel, D. M., & Shea, K. A. (1996). College teacher immediacy and student ratings of instruction. *Communication Education, 45*, 29–39.

Morman, M. T., & Floyd, K. (1998). "I love you, man": Overt expressions of affection in male-male interaction. *Sex Roles, 38*, 871–881.

Morman, M. T., & Floyd, K. (1999). Affectionate communication between fathers and young adult sons: Individual- and relational-level correlates. *Communication Studies, 50*, 294–309.

Morman, M. T., & Floyd, K. (2002). A "changing culture of fatherhood": Effects on affectionate communication, closeness, and satisfaction in men's relationships with their fathers and their sons. *Western Journal of Communication, 66*, 395–411.

Morris, D. (1967). *The naked ape: A zoologist's study of the human animal*. London: Jonathan Cape.

Morris, D. (1969). *The human zoo: A zoologist's classic study of the urban animal*. New York: Random House.

Morris, D. (1971). *Intimate behavior*. New York: Random House.

Morris, D. (1977). *Man watching: A field guide to human behavior*. New York: Abrams.

Nelson, A., & Golant, S. K. (2004). *You don't say: Navigating nonverbal communication between the sexes*. New York: Prentice Hall.

Nguyen, T., Heslin, R., & Nguyen, M. L. (1975). The meanings of touch: Sex differences. *Journal of Communication, 25*, 92–103.

Nguyen, T., Heslin, R., & Nguyen, M. L. (1976). The meaning of touch: Sex and marital status differences. *Representative Research in Social Psychology, 7*, 13–18.

Noller, P. (1980). Gaze in married couples. *Journal of Nonverbal Behavior, 5*, 115–129.

Onzawa, K., Glover, V., Adam, D., Modi, N., & Kumar, R. C. (2001). Infant massage improves mother-infant interaction for mothers with postnatal depression. *Journal of Affective Disorders, 63*, 201–207.

Pendell, S. D. (2002). Affection in interpersonal relationships: Not just a "fond or tender feeling." In W. B. Gudykunst (Ed.), *Communication yearbook 26* (pp. 70–115). Thousand Oaks, CA: Sage.

Powell, R. G., & Harville, B. (1990). The effects of teacher immediacy and clarity on instructional outcomes: An intercultural assessment. *Communication Education, 39*, 369–379.

Prager, K. J. (1995). Nonverbal behavior in intimate interactions. Reprinted in L. K. Guerrero, J. A. DeVito, & M. L. Hecht (Eds.), *The nonverbal communication reader: Classic and contemporary readings* (1999, 2nd ed., pp. 298–304). Prospect Heights, IL: Waveland.

Prescott, J. W. (1975). Body pleasure and the origins of violence. *Futurist, 9*, 64–74.

Punyanunt-Carter, N. M. (2004). Reported affectionate communication and satisfaction in marital and dating relationships. *Psychological Reports, 95*, 1154–1160.

Rane, T. R., & Draper, T. W. (1995). Negative evaluations of men's nurturant touching of young children. *Psychological Reports, 76*, 811–818.

Remland, M. S., Jones, T. S., & Brinkman, H. (1991). Proxemic and haptic behavior in three European countries. *Journal of Nonverbal Behavior, 15*, 215–232.

Remland, M. S., Jones, T. S., & Brinkman, H. (1995). Interpersonal distance, body orientation, and touch: Effects of culture, gender, and age. *Journal of Social Psychology, 135,* 281–298.

Richmond, V. P., McCroskey, J. C., & Hickson, M. L. III. (2008). *Nonverbal behavior in interpersonal relations* (6th ed.). Boston: Allyn & Bacon.

Rocca, K. A., & McCroskey, J. C. (1999). The interrelationship of student ratings of instructors' immediacy, verbal aggressiveness, homophily, and interpersonal attraction. *Communication Education, 48,* 308–316.

Roese, N. J., Olson, H. M., Borenstein, M. N., Martin, A., & Shores, A. L. (1992). Same-sex touching behavior: The moderating role of homophobic attitudes. *Journal of Nonverbal Behavior, 16,* 249–259.

Ruch, W. V. (1989). *International handbook of corporate communication.* Jefferson, NC: McFarland.

Savishinsky, J. S. (1992). Intimacy, domesticity, and pet therapy with the elderly: Expectation and experience among nursing home volunteers. *Social Science and Medicine, 34,* 1325–1334.

Schneider, E. (1996). The power of touch: Massage for infants. *Infants and Young Children, 5,* 40–55.

Shuter, R. (1976). Proxemics and tactility in Latin America. *Journal of Communication, 26,* 46–52.

Smeltzer, L., Waltman, J., & Leonard, D. (1991). Proxemics and haptics in managerial communication. Reprinted in L. K. Guerrero, J. A. DeVito, & M. L. Hecht (Eds.), *The nonverbal communication reader: Classic and contemporary readings* (1999, 2nd ed., pp. 184–191). Prospect Heights, IL: Waveland.

Stack, D. M., & Arnold, S. L. (1998). Changes in mothers' touch and hand gestures influence infant behavior during face-to-face interchanges. *Infant Behavior and Development, 21,* 451–468.

Steward, A. L., & Lupfer, M. (1987). Touching as teaching: The effect of touch on students' perceptions and performance. *Journal of Applied Social Psychology, 17,* 800–809.

Stolte, K., & Friedman, H. (1980). Patients' perceptions of touch during labor. *Journal of Applied Communication Research, 8,* 10–21.

Tank Buschmann, M. B., Hollinger-Smith, L. M., & Peterson-Kokkas, S. E. (1999). Implementation of expressive physical touch in depressed older adults. *Journal of Clinical Geropsychology, 5,* 291–300.

Tobin, S. S., & Gustafson, J. D. (1987). What do we do differently with elderly clients? *Journal of Gerontological Social Work, 10,* 107–121.

Trenholm, S. (2001). *Thinking through communication.* Boston: Allyn & Bacon.

Turp, M. (2000). Touch, enjoyment and health: In adult life. *European Journal of Psychotherapy and Counselling, 3,* 61–76.

Wallace, D. H. (1981). Affectional climate in the family of origin and the experience of subsequent sexual-affectional behaviors. *Journal of Sex and Marital Therapy, 7,* 296–396.

Ward, C. R., Duquin, M. E., & Streetman, J. (1998). Effects of intergenerational massage on future caregivers' attitudes toward aging, the elderly, and caring for the elderly. *Educational Gerontology, 24,* 35–46.

Weiss, S. J. (1990). Parental touching: Correlates of a child's body concept and body sentiment. In K. E. Barnard & B. T. Brazelton (Eds.), *Touch: The foundation of experience* (pp. 425–459). Madison, CT: International Universities Press.

Willis, F. N., & Rawdon, V. A. (1994). Gender and national differences in attitudes toward same-gender touch. *Perceptual and Motor Skills, 78,* 1027–1034.

# Vocalics

## Our Voices Speak Nonverbal Volumes

Chapter 9

## CHAPTER OUTLINE ■ ■ ■ ■ ■

**Production of Voice**

**Properties and Qualities of the Voice**
  Vocal Properties
  Vocal Qualities
  Vocalizations

**Applications of Vocalics Research**
  Pausing and Silence
  Turn-Taking in Conversation

  Interruptions and Overlaps
  Vocal Indications of Deception

**Understanding Vocalics: Applying the Reflexive Cycle of Nonverbal Communication Development**

**Summary**

## CHAPTER OBJECTIVES ■ ■ ■ ■ ■

After studying this chapter, you should be able to:

1. Define vocalics (paralanguage) as a nonverbal communication code.

2. Understand the difference between verbal and vocal communication.

3. Identify the major anatomical contributors to voice production and explain their primary functions.

4. List and describe five properties and three qualities of the voice.

5. Define vocalizations and explain how they serve as nonverbal communication.

6. Identify three types of pauses and give examples of how each emerges in conversation as well as public speaking situations.

7. Discuss positive and negative uses of silence, including self-silencing.

8. Identify four categories of turn-taking and explain how each nonverbally operates in everyday conversation.

9. Contrast interruptions with overlaps in conversation, and explain how each can reflect dominance.

10. Provide the four most common types of vocal cues associated with deception and offer examples of each.

283

## CASE STUDY   Be My Little Baby

My friend, Amy, just has one of those voices—you know, the kind that sounds like she's five years old when she's actually 21?! When I first met Amy in biology lab, I thought she was faking, because her voice sounded so high and strange that I just couldn't believe it could be natural. But after hanging out with Amy for a few months, I realized that she wasn't faking—her voice just sounded really young. On my cell phone, in particular, Amy's voice sounded even higher and more child-like, making it harder than ever to understand her. When Amy finished her degree and was getting ready to walk through graduation, her parents came to campus for the occasion and I got to meet them. Imagine my shock upon meeting Amy's mom who had just as babyish a voice as Amy! We talked about this in my nonverbal communication class, so I guess voices really can be passed down genetically, or at least modeled after in the home.

One night when some friends and I were all celebrating (code for partying), and Amy was among us, I got up the nerve to ask her about her voice. To make a long story short, the whole group ended up laughing so hard we cried, that's how funny Amy's stories were about encounters with people who responded in weird ways to her voice. She told us about having the most trouble on the phone, when salespeople constantly ask to speak to her mother because they don't believe Amy is an adult.

I've had some fun over the months I've known Amy, watching guys respond to her voice. Some are drawn to it, as though it were hyper-feminine. I've actually seen guys help her with her chair, carry her books to class or to her car, and do other little gestures that remind me of how you'd behave around a child. Amy doesn't see it this way—she just thinks the guys are being nice—but until guys get to know her and get used to the voice, they act differently (in my opinion). I wonder if Amy will have trouble landing a job. Let's just hope she doesn't have to go through a phone interview to get a job, because in person her maturity and intelligence comes through. But over the phone, it's a whole different story.

(Ring tone . . . .)

"Hello?"

"Hey; what's up?"

"Hey you; nothin's up. What's up with you?"

"Same old boring stuff. [Sigh] Nothing to report. [Pause] Just thought I'd see what you were doin'. Talk to you later."

"Okay, later."

This is an excerpt from a typical telephone conversation, but here's a question for you: How did the person answering the phone know who was on the other end of the line (other than looking at caller i.d. or the readout on a cell phone)? No names were mentioned, but the exchange indicates obvious familiarity. How do you recognize your best friend or a family member over the phone? You know the person's voice, right? Most of us don't have a voiceprint machine (spectrogram) handy, which creates a visual image of a person's speech. Human beings (those who aren't hearing impaired) have the wonderful capability to learn to recognize all kinds of people by the sound of their voices. This happens in particular when we are infants and our eyes can't quite focus on people's faces yet; we rely on sounds more than visual images in those early days of development. What's funny, however, is that often we don't recognize our own voices when we hear them on recordings, or we may feel that the recording is distorted. That's because the voice we hear inside our own head isn't the voice others hear. The true voice is the one we project to others, so with the sophistication of today's technology, recordings accurately capture and reproduce our voice.

The voice is a miraculous mechanism, one which we explore in this chapter as a code of nonverbal communication. Now don't get confused: This chapter focuses on *vocal* aspects, not *verbal* ones—there's a difference. Verbal means words, either written or spoken. Vocal means the sounds we make that accompany words or non-words (like "uh-huh") that have communicative power. You've no doubt heard the phrase "It's not *what* you say, but *how* you say it." When you study *how* people express themselves through their voices, you study **vocalics,** sometimes referred to as **paralanguage.**

Besides being able to identify someone from his or her voice, you can also come to detect physical, emotional, and attitudinal states through **tone of voice** (sometimes referred to as **prosody**), meaning all the elements that the human voice

*Vocal cues over the phone become important when other nonverbal cues cannot be detected.*

can produce and manipulate. That's another subject we explore in this chapter—how we vary aspects of our voices to create tone, which clues people as to what we're thinking and feeling. For example, you've probably heard a parent say, "Don't use that tone of voice with me"—perhaps as you were growing up and testing the boundaries of your parents' patience. Or maybe you can tell if someone isn't feeling well, if they're sad or angry, or if they're expressing sarcasm, just by paying attention to that all important tone in their voice.

If you have the physical ability to hear and speak, you use your voice (as well as a whole host of other nonverbal cues) to help convey the meaning behind what you say (Tusing, 2005). When you think about it, we would all be in big trouble as communicators if our voices didn't have the capacity to shape our words. How would we convey a question, if not for our ability to raise our pitch at the end of a series of words? When we teach children to do things, we tend to slow down the rate of our instructions, so as to give children time to comprehend the meaning of our messages. If someone tends to interrupt us too often, we increase our volume and rate of speaking, hoping to communicate to the interruptor, "Hey, don't break in; I'm talking here!" So you can see how important a function vocalics play in everyday interaction. Let's begin our discussion of this important nonverbal code with a cursory understanding of the anatomical mechanism that produces the voice.

## ▇ PRODUCTION OF VOICE

We rely primarily in this section on the work of communication scholar Lynn Wells (2004), author of *The Articulate Voice*, and sociologist Anne Karpf (2006), who wrote *The Human Voice: How This Extraordinary Instrument Reveals Essential Clues about Who We Are*. You may not tend to think of your voice as an instrument, but it is something capable of producing sound, just like a tuba or guitar. Karpf and Wells both explain that voice production isn't accomplished by a single organ, but a process of combining different body parts into a sequence. Karpf states, "We speak with our body: almost every part of it is called upon to make a voice, including the back" (p. 23). Wells suggests "the human anatomical structure and the physical processes involved in producing voice form an amazing interlocking system" (p. 18). As you'll note in Figure 9.1, the primary vocal organs are the trachea, larynx (including vocal folds or cords), pharynx, nose, jaw, and mouth (including the soft palate, hard palate, teeth, tongue, and lips). Our lungs are critical to voice production as well, since the voice is "audible air." As Karpf puts it, "the process by which we breathe in order to live also, with minor changes, provides the energy for speech" (p. 23).

Our breathing is altered when we speak; we breathe in quickly and exhale slowly, so that the breath will carry our statements. As we take in air through the pharynx (throat), down into the trachea (windpipe), and into our lungs, we then expel that air by contracting our diaphragms. The air goes back up the trachea to the larynx (colloquially referred to as the voice box) which controls the flow of air between the lungs and the throat. At this point, the air meets an obstacle—the vocal folds (cords). The central space or slit between the folds, through which air passes, is

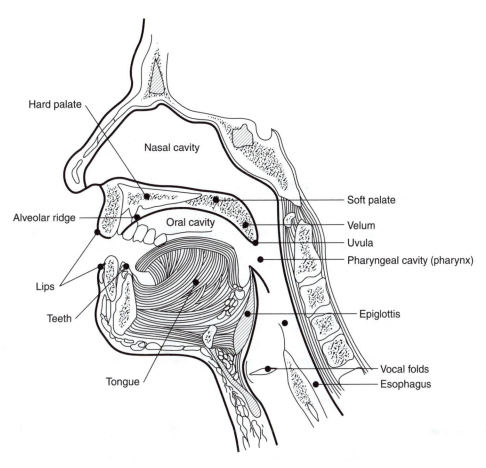

**FIGURE 9.1    Anatomy of the Voice**

Figure reproduced with permission of: Wells, L. K. (2004). *The articulate voice: An introduction to voice and diction* (4th ed.). Boston: Allyn & Bacon.

termed the glottis. These elastic vocal folds act like a pair of curtains, opening and closing, as they control the flow of air. In the closed position, the folds operate to prevent the passage of foreign matter, such as food and drink, into the trachea (Lessac, 1997). When air meets the folds rushing through the glottis, the folds vibrate and sound is produced. That sound is a succession of bursts of air, more like a buzz or a hiss. According to Karpf (2006), "If the voice emerged straight out of the larynx, it would make a poor, thin sound. It needs to resonate, and the characteristics of the buzz or frequency are shaped by what happens to the air once it has passed through the vocal folds into the rest of the vocal tract" (p. 25). Once air has made the vocal folds vibrate, the jaw, tongue, teeth, lips, and nasal and oral cavities take over and contort the process to produce the desired sound. (Well, sometimes we make desired sounds; if you've ever sung a flat note, you know that not all sounds are desirable or controllable.) So there you have it—a brief explanation of voice production.

The process of producing sound is more complicated than this of course, but for our interests, we at least now understand the basic mechanism. More important to our discussion is the role of voice production in human communication.

## ■ PROPERTIES AND QUALITIES OF THE VOICE

In 2005, Felicity Huffman was nominated for an Oscar for Best Actress for her role as a transsexual in the film *Transamerica*. In an interview included with the DVD of the movie, Huffman describes how altering her voice to sound like a man in the process of a sex change was her biggest challenge. She worked against her own higher-pitched, feminine voice in an effort to produce a masculine sound. But in one of the opening scenes of the movie, she tries to raise the pitch of her character's voice to sound more feminine, as part of her character's transformation into a woman.

Some aspects of the voice are anatomical and therefore basically unchangeable, such as the physical dimensions of the vocal folds, which control the range of pitches a person can produce. In general, women cannot physically produce the same low notes as men with bass voices. There are limits to what the voice can do, because of our anatomy and physiology. But many aspects of voice production are changeable, and that's what gives us variety as speakers (Leathers & Eaves, 2008). First, let's consider **vocal properties,** meaning aspects of the voice that can be purposefully altered to create meaning within our nonverbal communication repertoire.

### Vocal Properties

What do you sound like when you're mad? Do you get loud? Do you speed up when making your argument? If you're asked a question in class by a professor and you're unsure of the answer, how differently do the sounds come out of your mouth as you try to answer, compared to times when you answer with confidence? You probably speak more quietly and with some hesitation when unsure, possibly throwing in an "um" or "er" along the way. These are examples of vocal properties in action which, believe it or not, can be controlled and manipulated.

**Pitch.**    **Pitch** is defined as the "falling or rising tone heard in the voice: It creates our voice's melody" (Karpf, 2006, p. 35). As young children, when our bodies (and voices) are developing, we produce higher pitches. But as we age and our hormones change, our voices change. If you're male, do you remember battling the change in your voice around puberty, most likely during your middle school years? This was but one of a myriad of embarrassments boys experienced during puberty—those unpredictable moments when your voice could suddenly go into a yodel. The vocal effects of puberty are more subtle for girls, but all of our voices deepen and our voice capacity diminishes over the years as our bodies experience significant changes (Hummert, Mazloff, & Henry, 1999; Kooijman, Thomas, Graamans, & de Jong, 2007).

You have a general or average pitch to your voice, sometimes referred to as habitual or usual pitch (Wells, 2004). If you want to know what it is, just say "mm-hmm" (the equivalent of yes) out loud. The normal or typical way you say "mm-hmm" reveals the most comfortable or average pitch of your voice, termed the **fundamental frequency** (Hirano, Tanaka, Fujita, & Terasawa, 1991; Riding, Lonsdale, & Brown, 2006; Zraick, Gentry, Smith-Olinde, & Gregg, 2006). We all have a pitch range, meaning that we can produce low pitches (slowly vibrating vocal folds) to high pitches (quickly vibrating vocal folds), and some people have a wider pitch range than others. For example, pop singer Mariah Carey is known for a tremendous range of pitches she can sing, including such high pitches that it almost sounds like an orchestral instrument made the sound instead of a human voice. If you're familiar with the song "Ole' Man River" from the classic musical *Showboat*, you know that only a man with a deep bass voice can accomplish that song (as it was meant to be sung). In general, men can produce more low pitches than women, and women can produce more high pitches than men (Krolokke & Sorensen, 2006; Tracy, 2002). But scholarly evidence suggests that vocal sex differences are more about what's acceptable in society than what anatomy and physiology can produce (Brownmiller, 1984; Graddol & Swann, 1989). Some research indicates that women and men have equal abilities to produce high pitches, but that men have been socialized not to use higher pitches lest they sound feminine (Henley, 2001; Kramer, 1977; Pfeiffer, 1985).

While you have limitations in the range of pitches your voice can produce, you can extend your range with practice (Wells, 2004). Voice teachers will help you find your ideal pitch range—pitches you can hit the best and with ease—and then they will work to extend your range upward and downward on the scale, to help you develop more flexibility in what you can sing (or say) (Ruark, 2007). Actress and model Kathy Ireland got tired of being perceived as ditzy or unintelligent because of her baby-like voice, so she hired a vocal coach and worked to lower her normal speaking voice.

You may hear a shift in pitch from low to high when adults talk to infants, children, the elderly, pets, and romantic partners, a vocalization often called baby-talk (sometimes referred to as "motherese" or "parentese"). Nonverbal scholars Guerrero and Floyd (2006) define baby-talk as "a vocalic pattern characterized by high modal pitch and high pitch variance, and exaggerated, highly simplified, and often repetitive speech" (p. 92). The shifting pitch may represent an expression of affection or an offer of care or comfort (Floyd & Ray, 2003; Grieser & Kuhl, 1988; Trainor, Austin, & Desjardin, 2000; Zebrowitz, Brownlow, & Olson, 1992). However, particularly in communication with elderly people, baby-talk can be interpreted as condescending, patronizing, and disrespectful (Andersen, 2004; Caporael, 1981). Baby-talk has been detected across cultures, genders, and age groups, since even children and adolescents often shift into higher voices when talking to infants or animals (Bombar & Littig, 1996; Ferguson, 1964; Shute & Wheldall, 1989; Toda, Fogel, & Kawai, 1990).

Patterns of pitch are termed **intonation,** described by sociolinguist Sally McConnell-Ginet (1983) as "the tune to which we set the text of our talk" (p. 70). It's important to develop intonation that's interesting to listeners and that conveys your personality. For example, in U.S. culture, we associate seriousness, confidence, and credibility with lower intonation, and flightiness and insecurity with higher intonation (Nelson & Golant, 2004). So if you want to be taken seriously when you speak, you'll want to work on using lower pitches available to you and not letting your voice rise too high, lest you be seen as overemotional, erratic, or deceptive.

However, using a pattern of low pitches or one consistent pitch can be problematic as well—this reflects a problem in **vocal variety,** also termed **inflection** (Nelson & Golant, 2004). Research shows that monotone voices are generally perceived as unpleasant, while vocal variety is received more positively (Buller & Burgoon, 1986). In our teaching of public speaking over the years, we've noticed that many students—particularly the men—tend to go monotone during presentations. A monotone voice occurs most often because of nervousness, but it belies an inflection problem, meaning that the speaker isn't varying her or his pitches to create vocal interest.

If you have a monotone problem or just want to increase your vocal variety, you can receive instruction from a vocal coach or you can record yourself, listen to or watch the recording, and work on how you sound. One of the best ways to improve is to read to children. Most children will insist that you "do the voices" when you read stories or nursery rhymes out loud to them, and this can be a great way to experiment with your pitch range. However, here's a caution: Taken too far, highly varied intonation can be irritating and sound "sing-songy," such as is often evidenced in television news reporters, who believe that they have to make their voices jump around to create more interest or drama for their stories. Karpf (2006) discusses this tendency in news casting, comparing today's trends with former long-time CBS news anchor Dan Rather, whose monotone

*Speaking with vocal variety when reading to children not only helps sustain their attention, but helps them develop their own vocal pitch.*

voice communicated "gravitas and decency," along with "trust and authority" (p. 37). Karpf suggests that "most American news-broadcasting voices today arch and buck, changing pitch for what seems like capricious reasons. Pitch now seems dissociated from meaning, and has become part of corporate style instead" (p. 37).

## SPOTLIGHT on Research

One vocal property we explore in this chapter is pitch. Would it interest you to know that researchers for decades have studied what voice pitches are more attractive than others? In the 1970s, teams of researchers began to investigate the possibility that certain intonation patterns exhibited in male voices were sexier and more attractive to women than others (Brown, Strong, & Rencher, 1973, 1974; Tuomi & Fisher, 1979). Researchers in the eighties and nineties found that voices lower in fundamental frequency (voices that, on average, were lower pitched than others) were more attractive to women (Barber, 1995; Dabbs & Mallinger, 1999). In general, research determined that women tended to prefer male voices that sounded mature, dominant, and strong, and these voices were lower in average pitch (Zuckerman, Miyake, & Elkin, 1995).

Our spotlight research for this chapter comes from Riding, Lonsdale, and Brown (2006) who studied attractiveness in the male voice, in terms of fundamental frequency (average pitch) and variance of fundamental frequency, or how much a man varies the pitches in his voice while speaking. These scholars used recordings produced by male college students who answered the question, "How did you choose your major?" The recordings were manipulated so that male voices were low, medium, or high in general pitch and men used little vocal pitch variety (monotone), medium variety, or high variety. Fifty-four female college students then listened to samplings of the recordings and responded to a list of questions about the speakers. Some of the questions were "Would you like to get to know this person?", "Would this person be romantic?", and "Would you consider this voice attractive?"

Riding et al. found that, similar to research three decades prior, male voices using medium and low average pitch were deemed most attractive by female subjects in the study. Women perceived that men with these pitch ranges in their voices were more socially attractive, considerate, kind, and likeable than men exhibiting more high-pitched voices. While other studies found a relationship between variance of pitch in the voice and attractiveness, Riding et al. did not find this association. Women were not necessarily more drawn to men's voices that included pitch variety than to men whose voices were more monotone.

If you're male, think about the average pitch of your voice compared to your male friends' voices. Is your voice one that people would classify as high, medium, or low in general pitch? Do you sound like George Clooney, Brad Pitt, or Mickey Mouse? Have you noticed women being drawn to guys with lower pitched voices, as compared to those with higher pitched voices? If you're female, what male voices draw you more than others? Now before you think we're disparaging some of our male readers, we do realize how arbitrary this whole topic sounds. Physical strength and, more importantly, strength of character and personality should and do predominate in people's impressions of the overall strength of a man.

*(continued)*

**SPOTLIGHT on Research** *(continued)*

But studies on vocal pitch, such as the one we highlight here, are fascinating in how they reveal subtle nonverbal cues associated with perceptions of masculinity and femininity in our culture.

Do you want to know more about this study? If so, read: Riding, D., Lonsdale, D., & Brown, B. (2006). The effects of average fundamental frequency and variance of fundamental frequency on male vocal attractiveness to women. *Journal of Nonverbal Behavior, 30,* 55–61.

---

**Rate.**   The **rate** of your speech simply means the pace at which sounds are uttered. According to Karpf (2006), the average speaking rate (which she calls **tempo**) of an American or British adult is 120 to 150 words per minute, or around 6 syllables per second. Primarily, your rate of speech reflects your upbringing, meaning what you tended to hear and pattern after at home. Our families have the earliest and most significant impact on our vocal characteristics, as well as our nonverbal communication development in general (Berry, 2001). Does anyone who knows your family tell you that you talk like your mother, father, or a sibling? Genetics plays a role in this phenomenon, but having similar vocal patterns as family members has more to do with nurture (the environment within which you were raised) than nature (genetics) (Karpf, 2006).

Another factor affecting general speech rate is what region of the country you are raised in (Wells, 2004). It's more than a stereotype that people raised in the southern part of the United States tend to speak more slowly than people in the north or Midwest (Nelson & Golant, 2004; O'Sullivan, 2005). The stereotype enters in when people deem southerners less intelligent, simply because they tend to speak more slowly than northerners. With all the transplantation in the U.S.—meaning that many people move around and live in various regions of the country—the dichotomy of northern versus southern speaking styles may be disappearing. One theory attributes regional differences in speaking rates to the weather, meaning that if it's hot most of the year where people live, they're likely to move and speak more slowly, because it's just too hot to be in a rush. Likewise, if you're cold, you're not going to dawdle in conversation, because you have to take in too much cold air to speak. (Sounds crazy, but it's an interesting theory. However, we don't know how the theory applies to northern and southern California!)

Our voices (and ears) are highly adaptable. Ever traveled to England, heard British people speak, and picked up properties of their way of speaking, only to be laughed at when you returned home and talked to your friends? What you hear often transfers to how you speak, and this is true of speech rate. For example, if one of your friends comes up to you very excitedly and starts spilling his or her good news, you're likely to adopt that same rate when you respond, just because speech properties are "catching." Likewise, if you're speaking normally or hurriedly and a friend is sad or down, when that person speaks to you in a slower rate of speech (a telltale sign of negative emotion), you'll likely slow your rate to correspond with your friend's. Sometimes this tendency is referred to as **synchrony,** when people's nonverbal cues mirror one another (Beavin Bavelas & Chovil, 2006; Lakin, Jefferis, Cheng, & Chartrand, 2003).

Rate is significantly affected by emotion, and this effect is often hard to control (Buller, 2005; Cruttenden, 1986; Dimitrius & Mazzarella, 1999; Ellgring & Scherer, 1996; Izard, 1991; Karpf, 2006; Scherer, 1986; Segrin, 1998). When nervous, you're more likely to increase your rate of speaking, which can be a dead giveaway. If you're aware that this tends to happen to you and you don't want your nerves revealed, then you'll need to practice to control this tendency, so that listeners (e.g., job interviewers, audiences, a would-be date) don't detect any nervousness from your speech rate. Karpf (as in Fuller, 2006) suggests that, when people are angry, their speech rates max out at 200 vibrations per second. She describes how, according to historical experts, Adolph Hitler's average rate while giving speeches was 228 vibrations per second. In fact his vocal aggression was so closely associated with his power that American spies tried to find ways to slip female hormones into his food, in attempts to slow him down and diminish perceptions of powerfulness.

Research shows that people with slower speaking rates are often judged as being colder, weaker, less truthful, less knowledgeable, less trustworthy, less clever, less competent, and less persuasive than faster speakers (Apple, Streeter, & Krauss, 1979; Burgoon, Birk, & Pfau, 1990; Feldstein, Dohm, & Crown, 2001; Laver & Trudgill, 1979; Miller, Maruyama, Beaber, & Valone, 1976; Street & Brady, 1982; Woodall & Burgoon, 1983). This may not be fair, but it seems to be the case in U.S. culture. Persuasiveness becomes especially critical to political candidates and leaders whose ability to sway the masses through the power of their voices, among other nonverbal cues, is critical to their success (Goethals, 2005). Research has determined that an appropriate speech rate is an essential paralinguistic cue for successful job interviewing (DeGroot & Motowidlo, 1999).

As with pitch, vocal variety creates interest, so it's important to learn to vary your rate to create a desired effect. We work with public speakers to help them change their speech rates to be dramatic, to make sure that their audience gets the intended message, to create a special effect, or just to keep the audience awake. Whether in conversation or a presentation, maintaining a constant rate of speaking, especially when combined with a monotone pitch, can be deadly for listeners.

**Volume.**    Simply defined, **volume** (sometimes called **intensity**) refers to the softness or loudness of your voice. Karpf (2006) suggests that the average conversational volume for speakers standing about three feet apart is 60 decibels. Quiet speech ranges from 35–40 decibels, while shouting rises to about 75 decibels. As a way to gauge these amounts, since you're not likely to have a decibel meter handy, Karpf explains that rustling leaves average 10 decibels of sound, loud music averages 80 decibels. If you're exposed to 120 decibels of sound, a sensation will be created in your body that is like a touch; beyond 120 decibels, you will feel physical pain.

Volume is another vocal property that you can vary to your advantage, unless you have a hearing loss. Some people who experience hearing losses—whether they know they have a hearing loss or not—speak in louder tones so as to hear themselves, but this can be offputting to listeners who feel like people are barking at them. Some people speak so loudly in conversation that it can send you running for a human mute button.

In general, louder voices are associated with confidence, assertiveness, and boldness, while softer voices are associated with low self-esteem, timidity, and passivity (Nelson & Golant, 2004; Wells, 2004). However, softer voices can also indicate a

*Our colleague, Dr. Kelly Quintanilla, effectively modulates her vocal pitch, rate, and volume to enhance student attention in the classroom.*

calm self-assurance, suggesting that someone doesn't feel the need to get loud to control a conversation; the hushed tones dominate because of their sheer contrast with other people's volume (Dimitrius & Mazzarella, 1999).

In an article published in *The Chronicle of Higher Education*, Professor of English at Assumption College James Lang (2007) explores methods classroom lecturers can use to enhance student attention and, subsequently, their learning of course material. Lang describes the tendency for most speakers to begin a sentence with adequate volume, only to let the sound trail off toward the end of the sentence. He explains that this tendency is natural, given, as Karpf (2006) addressed, we expel breath as we speak. We have more breath when we start a sentence than when we finish it. But Lang warns, "Unfortunately, the structure of many English sentences leaves crucial bits of meaning until the end of a sentence" (p. C2). Speakers may actually impede their listeners' attention and recall because they fail to sustain or vary their volume to add emphasis to key words or phrases.

Like we said for other vocal properties, for most of us, volume is affected by our emotions and attitudes (Karpf, 2006). While we tend to associate raising the voice or shouting with dominance and displays of anger, some of us get very, very quiet when we're angry (Andersen, 2004; Guerrero & Floyd, 2006; Scherer & Oshinsky, 1977; Shaver, Schwartz, Kirson, & O'Connor, 1987). Later in this chapter we talk about the communicative power of pauses and silence; for now just realize that our volume is affected by our emotional states, but the particular effect is individualized. Some people never shout; others get loud only when they're very happy. Still others tend not to alter their volume much above or below their normal intensities of speaking, no matter their emotional state.

In Chapter 1, we provided several functions of nonverbal communication or ways that nonverbal cues work with verbal communication to create a message. One of those functions was **accenting**—the use of nonverbal cues to emphasize or draw special attention to a verbal message (Ekman, 1965). Volume in the form of an extreme increase or decrease is one of the prime vocal properties that we use to accent verbal messages. While volume is controllable, it takes a lot of work to alter volume because, first, people are often unaware that they speak too softly or loudly and, second, many people won't take the time and energy to break such a long-term habit. But you can work to achieve a louder voice for those occasions that demand it (like making speeches where there are no microphones or the equipment fails) or a softer voice (so that only those people you want to hear you actually hear your whispers). Parents often work with their children to develop their "inside voices" versus their "outside voices," so that they function appropriately in social settings.

**Articulation and Pronunciation.**    **Articulation** (also called **enunciation**) refers to how *distinctly* you speak while **pronunciation** refers to how *correctly* you speak, according to a dictionary's indication of proper pronunciation (Wells, 2004). If you have trouble understanding what someone says, the problem may be that she or he slurs words, drops syllables, emphasizes the wrong syllables, or mumbles—articulation errors. It might also be that the person doesn't speak words correctly—pronunciation errors. For example, some people say "pasketti" instead of "spaghetti" and "sim-yoo-lar" instead of "similar," which are pronunciation problems. If they say "pasketti" and "sim-yoo-lar" crisply and cleanly, they articulate just fine, but pronounce these words incorrectly. Someone who mumbles "spaghetti" when asked what he or she wants for dinner pronounces the word correctly, but articulates it poorly. Both are nonverbal vocalic problems that can cause confusion in listeners and lead to a breakdown in communication.

Our physical health and emotions come into play in this area. When we are overly tired or just don't feel well, our articulation may be affected. For the female co-author of this book, her family members can always tell when she's tired because her voice tends to get soft and she mumbles instead of clearly articulating words. What happens to your articulation when you feel certain emotions? Is it easier to speak clearly when you're happy and in a good mood than when you're angry or annoyed?

Articulation and pronunciation are the most easy to change of all the vocal properties, but, like other changes, they take concentrated effort. You may simply not know that you pronounce certain words incorrectly until someone notices and says something to you. The male co-author of this book has trouble pronouncing the word "anonymity"—granted, a tough word to say because of all the vowels. He can say "anonymous" perfectly, but avoids the other form of the term. Are there words you learned and grew up using that you mispronounce? How did you discover the mispronunciation and correct the problem? A college education is great for improving your pronunciation and expanding your vocabulary (as well as many other things).

## Vocal Qualities

Some qualities of the voice are physiologically based and a challenge to change, such as the condition of your vocal folds or your ability to breathe to assist your

## REMEMBER 9.1

| | |
|---|---|
| **Vocalics (Paralanguage):** | study of how people express themselves through their voices. |
| **Tone of Voice (Prosody):** | all the qualities that the human voice can produce and manipulate. |
| **Vocal Properties:** | aspects of the voice that can be purposefully altered to create meaning. |
| **Pitch:** | falling or rising tone heard in the voice. |
| **Fundamental Frequency:** | most comfortable or often-used pitch of the voice. |
| **Intonation:** | patterns of pitch. |
| **Vocal Variety (Inflection):** | varying the pitches used in speaking. |
| **Rate (Tempo):** | pace at which sounds are uttered. |
| **Synchrony:** | when people's nonverbal cues mirror one another. |
| **Volume (Intensity):** | softness or loudness of the voice. |
| **Accenting:** | the use of nonverbal cues to emphasize or draw special attention to a verbal message. |
| **Articulation (Enunciation):** | how distinctly a person speaks. |
| **Pronunciation:** | how correctly a person speaks, according to a dictionary's indication of proper pronunciation. |

voice production. But other qualities can be invoked (or faked) to achieve a certain communication goal, or they become habit because you've spoken that way over time. In this section, we explore **vocal qualities,** characteristics of the voice that develop subtly and more as habits than conscious choices. More vocal qualities exist than the three we discuss in this section, but these are the three we deem most interesting and common in human voices.

**Breathiness.**   No matter what age you are or what movies you grew up watching, no voice in U.S. culture is more recognizable for its breathiness than Marilyn Monroe's. If you've seen footage of Monroe's tribute to President Kennedy at his birthday celebration, when she sang "Happy Birthday," it looked like she might have passed out on each phrase, so much breath escaped her body (Nelson & Golant, 2004). The physiological explanation for **breathiness** in the voice is this: The glottis (space between the vocal folds) narrows but lets through more air than we normally use to make sounds and, as a result, the vocal folds vibrate but don't fully close (Poyatos, 1993). In essence, breathiness has to do with an overabundance of air moving through almost-closed vocal folds. Breathiness is associated with femininity in American culture, and with other stereotypical traits such as helplessness, sexiness, and childishness. However, Karpf (as in Fuller, 2006) suggests that men and women alike exhibit breathiness in the voice when sexually aroused, because hormones alter the amount and form of mucus in the larynx, which leads to that out-of-breath sound.

Just as we've seen for other aspects of the voice, our emotions and attitudes can be conveyed through how much or how little breath escapes when we speak. For example, have you ever had a nightmare and tried to scream or cry out, only to feel like you couldn't get any breath to come through your throat? Sometimes, when we're really excited, it's hard to "catch our breath," meaning that our anatomical functioning associated with producing the breath we need to make sound is impaired. As we struggle for air and to get the mechanism going, we may make breathy vocalizations until we're more fully functional.

**Raspiness.**   We most often think of the vocal quality of **raspiness** as hoarseness or a gravelly sound in the voice. Some experts call it a throaty or guttural quality, which works well if you're speaking German, but not so well when speaking English (Wells, 2004). The makers of the Head-On headache remedy know that their ads are irritating, but they also know how successfully they sell the product. The second wave of these ads made fun of the first wave, with one ad in particular depicting a man with the raspiest voice we've ever heard. In the ad, he says, "Head-On, apply directly to the forehead. Head-On, I hate your commercials, but your product is *amazing*," as he reaches a croakingly low note on the word "amazing." Another famous raspy voice belongs to actor Harvey Fierstein, probably most notable for his role on Broadway as the mother (!) of the central character in the musical *Hairspray*.

Raspiness in the voice involves an overabundance of friction on the vocal folds caused by forcing too much air through the mechanism, and it can be created for dramatic effect. Some cheerleaders develop raspiness due to constant abuse of their voices, but these conditions tend to be fleeting. But if raspiness persists, it is more likely due to excessive phlegm, dryness because of an illness, or the presence of nodes (inflamed, roughened tissues) that may develop on the folds over time (Wells, 2004). Constant inflammation of the vocal folds because of illness, smoking, straining, or other irritations can engender raspiness in the voice over the long haul. Professional singers who overtire their voices or whose style involves straining to reach high notes can develop voice problems, which can force some of them out of the business or at least cause them to take the keys of their songs down as they age and continue to perform.

**Nasality.**   A punch line to a joke goes "Would you like some *whine* with that cheese?" When we refer to **nasality** in the voice, we mean when air is trapped or too heavily contained in the nasal cavities, instead of resonating through all the structures, and then that air is pushed or squeezed out to form a whiny sound (Wells, 2004). Nasality can also be caused by a physical defect, such as a deviated septum. Perhaps the actress Fran Drescher (formerly of the TV show *The Nanny*) best embodies what we call a nasal or whiny voice. Nasality is similar to a quality termed "twang" in research on vocal disorders, which voice experts Lombard and Steinhauer (2007) describe as the "bright, brassy, ringing voice quality commonly heard in country-western singing, witch-cackling, a child's 'nya, nya' taunt, and is equated often with duck quacking" (p. 295). These researchers investigated the use of a "twang technique" to treat people with chronic hypophonic (weak and breathy) voices. (Since both of your textbook authors hail from Texas, we're quite familiar with "twang.")

Research isn't extensive on nasality and the perceptions that we make of people with nasal voices, but in general nasal voices aren't deemed attractive. For three decades, psychologist Miron Zuckerman and various colleagues have studied what makes voices attractive. This line of research has determined that attractive voices are more varied (meaning non-monotone), more resonant, lower in pitch (for men only), and less nasal (Zuckerman & Driver, 1989; Zuckerman, Hodgins, & Miyake, 1990; Zuckerman & Miyake, 1993). Subsequent studies have produced consistent results, in that nasal voices in adults as well as infants as young as three months are received negatively by listeners (Bloom, Moore-Schoenmakers, & Masataka, 1999; Bloom, Zajac, & Titus, 1999).

## Vocalizations

As we've said, the human voice is a marvelous mechanism, capable of producing a multitude of nonverbal sounds to help generate meaning. Another category of sounds is termed **vocalizations,** meaning non-words or sounds not tied to speech, including those that can substitute for speech. As nonverbal communication scholar Michael Argyle (1988) explains, "Vocalizations consist of sounds, of different frequencies and intensities, put together in different sequences. Some of these are encoded and de-coded as meaningful speech, while others express emotions or interpersonal attitudes, or convey information about the sender" (as in Guerrero, DeVito, & Hecht, 1999, p. 135). Consider the many messages or responses you can convey using sounds, but not words. Use the examples below to get you thinking:

| | |
|---|---|
| **Questioner:** | "Hey, are you hungry? Want something to eat?" |
| **Responder:** | "Mm-hmm." |
| **Questioner:** | "Man, that test was HARD. Did you think so?" |
| **Responder:** | "Unh-uh. Guess I studied more than you." |
| **Questioner:** | "That guy is HOT." |
| **Responder:** | "Hmmmm. I don't know; maybe." |
| **Questioner:** | "I wiped out on that last wave; check out my foot—is it swollen?" |
| **Responder:** | "Geeez; that looks painful." |

In each of these examples, the response contains a non-word or vocalization that has a fairly universal interpretation (at least among English speakers). We learn these vocalizations and the inflections that accompany them fairly easily growing up, recognizing them as other forms of nonverbal vocal communication that help get our point across. Author of *The Complete Idiot's Guide to Body Language* Peter Andersen (2004) terms these vocalizations "linguistic shortcuts" or conversation regulators, meaning that they are often used as responses while listening to people talk (p. 202). Nonverbal scholar Albert Mehrabian (1981) calls them "verbal reinforcers" (p. 45). Most of the time such vocalizations are heard as supportive responses that aren't commonly interpreted as interruptions or attempts to get a turn at talk, unless done in rapid succession, which can signal people to speed up what they're saying or to stop so we can say something. These vocalizations can stand alone, but they often accompany words, as evidenced in the examples above.

Another common vocalization is the **filled pause,** which we talk more about later in this chapter. But for now, realize that we often use vocalizations like "um" and "er" to fill the space when we pause, typically as a way of covering the silence and giving us time to think of what to say or encouraging someone else to speak. While filled pauses are common, they're much more acceptable in conversation than in public speaking. In everyday conversation, usually we don't focus on or register the amount of fillers we or someone else uses. But when ours is the only voice a group of listeners hears, as in a presentation or broadcast, an "um" or "er" becomes obvious and can distract listeners, undermine our credibility, and detract from our overall effect.

Other vocalizations are quite individualistic and can have nonverbal communicative power for listeners. Nonverbal scholars Knapp and Hall (2006) provide the following list: "laughing, crying, whispering, snoring, yelling, moaning, yawning, whining, sighing, and belching" (p. 374). Argyle (1988) adds grunting to the list. These are sounds the voice can produce that have meaning for listeners, but that aren't verbal communication.

Do people tell you that you have a great laugh? We tend to remember people with distinctive laughs, because it's fun to try to make them laugh, just to see and hear them do it. For example, some people laugh with their mouths open, but no sound comes out or all you hear is a wheeze as the air rushes out; some people snort when they laugh. Other people produce "belly laughs," which sound robust and hearty and generally

*A laugh is a form of vocalization that can reveal information about a person.*

make everyone around them break into laughter as well. Each of us is capable of producing different kinds of laughs, meaning that laughter is versatile. While something might make you roar with side-splitting laughter, other stimuli will elicit from you high-pitched giggles. Then there's the snicker. There's really no way to explain or write out the snicker, but we all know what it sounds like, right? It's mostly accomplished with air through the nose, but it involves the throat as well, and it sends a message.

It probably won't surprise you to know that researchers have actually studied the communicative properties of laughter (Grammer, 1990; Martin & Kuiper, 1999; Provine, 2000). Laughter has been studied for its specific rhythms, duration, and changes in fundamental frequency (Kipper & Todt, 2003), for its impact on attitudes and emotions of listeners (Owren & Bachorowski, 2003), and to determine if laughter evoked by media occurs differently than laughter that erupts in social contexts (Vettin & Todt, 2004).

Have you noticed that we seem to have lost the art of the whisper these days? We really notice this the most when we're in a movie theatre, irritated by the loud conversations all around us, the people answering and *actually talking* on their cell phones while the film is showing, and people who have to comment on everything coming across the screen. (Especially irritating are those people who see a movie for the second time, who have to alert everyone around them when the "good" or "scary parts" are coming.) Is whispering considered a female-only appropriate behavior? Some of our male students say that whispering isn't manly, unless you're whispering private things ("sweet nothings") into the ear of someone you care about. Then it's extremely manly, right?

One last thing about vocalizations: Try to become more aware that you're nonverbally communicating when you use a vocalization, because this is probably something you've not thought about before. We've seen students stretch dramatically and yawn vocally (*very* vocally) while class is going on and, while students say they don't mean anything by it, such nonverbal signals can convey boredom or other negative things to your professors and classmates. Likewise, some students let out a big ole'

---

**REMEMBER 9.2**

| | |
|---|---|
| **Vocal Qualities:** | characteristics of the voice that develop subtly, more as habits than conscious choices. |
| **Breathiness:** | overabundance of air rushing through the vocal folds. |
| **Raspiness:** | hoarseness or a gravelly sound in the voice. |
| **Nasality:** | whiny sound produced when air is trapped or too heavily contained in the nasal cavities, instead of resonating through all the structures. |
| **Vocalization:** | non-word or sound not tied to speech, including those that can substitute for speech. |
| **Filled Pause:** | vocalization like "um" and "er" that fills a pause, typically as a way of covering silence and giving communicators time to think of what to say, or to encourage others to speak. |

sigh right during a professor's lecture. Now we realize that lecturers aren't scintillating and captivating all the time, but please avoid the huge sigh—the one that communicates nonverbally that you'd rather be anywhere than in class.

## ■ APPLICATIONS OF VOCALICS RESEARCH

Many interesting applications of the research on vocalics continue to emerge, as social scientists and music scholars try to better understand the fascinating mechanism of the voice. Here we briefly overview some provocative topics of research on this code of nonverbal communication.

### Pausing and Silence

Let's first consider the **pause**—generally known as a temporary stop in speech, sometimes referred to as a **vocal hesitation.** The more all-encompassing term for this aspect of vocalics is **fluency,** meaning how continuously we produce sound as communicators. Actually, spontaneous speech is a disfluent activity, meaning that it's discontinuous and fragmented. We may have moments when our vocalizations flow—those are the moments we remember the most, when we sound impressive, glib, and convincing. But even in those flowing moments, we pause between statements. We need pauses to get the intake of breath necessary to produce speech, and we use them before, during, and after speech. Pauses vary in length; some are very brief and almost undetectable, while others are lengthy and unbearable. Ever heard of the "pregnant pause"? That's a term for a long pause filled with emotion or suspense.

Research suggests that pausing behavior may be related to (1) emotions, because people who are depressed tend to pause in their speech more than people who aren't depressed (Karpf, 2006), and (2) the complexity of a message, meaning that pausing may be more necessary when delivering a complex message than a simple one (Greene & Ravizza, 1995). Pausing and silence are culturally rooted nonverbal behaviors. A judgment of how short or long a pause should take depends on one's culture. For example, a typical pause in Japanese culture can last as long as eight seconds, in comparison to about one second on average for Americans (Karpf, as in Fuller, 2006). In general, Americans have little tolerance for silence (Remland, 2003).

Three different types of pauses are at your disposal as a communicator. Like we mentioned earlier in this chapter, some pauses include vocalizations (**filled pauses**) like "um" or "er." These often occur when communicators wish to maintain their turn at talk, indicate that they'd like someone else to talk (a trailing off technique), or hesitate during conversation or while giving a presentation. One study examined the detrimental effect of filled pauses in presentations and found that listeners perceive filled pauses to be indications of anxiety and a lack of preparation on a speaker's part (Christenfeld, 1995). In addition, while filled pauses create better impressions in listeners than silent pauses, a style of no pauses at all (except between sentences where short pauses are expected) is received the most positively by listeners.

**Silent pauses** are breaks in speech that carry no sound; sometimes they're used on purpose, but sometimes not. Sometimes they emerge because we're stumped, flabbergasted, emotional, or reluctant to say anything. A third type of pause is the **audible pause** (sometimes known as an audible gasp), in which air is taken in and speech is disrupted. In some instances, the audible pause may substitute for speech. For example, what if a total stranger came up to you and asked your weight? You might draw in a quick breath, revealing your shock or surprise at the question, and then stumble out some kind of response. When speech is disrupted by a sigh, that sigh can also be viewed as a form of audible pause, but with air being expelled rather than drawn in.

A pause is often purposeful; it can be used as a stall tactic by a receiver of a request when the receiver doesn't want to comply with the request (Roberts, Francis, & Morgan, 2006). Pauses can create dramatic effect in a presentation or set up a punch line for a joke. Many politicians and actors learn to use pauses effectively. In fact, trained stage actors are taught to "pause for applause" or "hold for laughs," because if they continue with dialogue over an audience's reaction, they'll ruin the enjoyment of the laughter, cut the applause short, or cause the audience to miss the next few lines.

Pauses tend to be fairly short, but if any of you have ever received the "silent treatment" from a loved one, you know that silence can seem like forever. Very simply, **silence** is defined as the absence of sound. Some people feel that they need lots of words and nonverbal messages to communicate, while others think "silence is golden." People have been long-fascinated with silence: A classic Simon and Garfunkel song refers to the "Sounds of Silence"; you've probably heard of "suffering in silence" and a reference to a police or military "code of silence." Karpf (2006) suggests that silence is the "most culturally bound aspect of communication" (p. 189). She provides multiple examples of cultural uses of silence, which can cause difficulties when members of different cultures attempt to communicate and interpret one another's silence.

You may have never thought of silence as a form of nonverbal communication, but it is one of the most powerful ways to register protest or get your point across, nonverbally (Jaworski, 1993). In their book on nonverbal communication in intimate relationships, Guerrero and Floyd (2006) describe the downside of silence, those instances when it is "intimidating and threatening," such as in response to conflict (p. 158). A couple can be in the heat of an argument when one partner simply stops talking *and* listening. While silence may seem like the best thing to do in the heat of battle—you've probably been taught the wisdom of "holding your tongue"—it can be a power play or stall tactic, which can bring conflict resolution to a screeching halt. Guerrero and Floyd discuss common ways that silence manifests itself in close relationships: "failing to acknowledge a relational partner's presence, giving a partner the silent treatment, failing to respond to a partner's question, or ignoring someone's suggestions or requests" (p. 158). Relational silence can heighten a person's frustration, which can then escalate into isolation (with partners not even speaking to each other for days or perhaps *ever again*), and can generate feelings of disrespect, resentment, and neglect (Bruneau, 1973; Knapp & Vangelisti, 2005). However, conflict scholar Alexia Georgakopoulos (2004) suggests that avoidance and silence as conflict management strategies aren't necessarily negative; silence can effectively promote peace in relationships that experience conflict.

*This gesture requesting silence is common in the U.S., as well as other countries.*

Educators have studied silence in the classroom, from the "hushing" technique teachers use with students to the choice that students make, from elementary to college levels, when they maintain silent postures in classrooms (Rendle-Short, 2005; Thornberg, 2006). Psychiatrists and pediatricians have examined a form of silence termed selective mutism, a complex childhood disorder (Anstendig, 1998; Cohan, Price, Stein, 2006). On the positive side, silence has been studied for its role in therapeutic conversations, meaning the ways therapists use silence in their counseling sessions as well as respond to silence from their patients (Ladany, Hill, Thompson, & O'Brien, 2004; MacDonald, 2005). In some contexts, silence can communicate respect for authority, such as in a meeting with your boss when you let the higher status person speak first, thus breaking the silence (Burgoon, Buller, & Woodall, 1996). Sometimes it can be really nice to find someone you can just *be* with, without talking; silence can indicate comfortability between people.

One of the more interesting lines of research into silence as nonverbal communication explores **self-silencing,** defined as the inhibition of self-expression (Schuessler Harper, 2004, p. vi). Silencing the Self theory first emerged from research with clinically depressed adult women, who reported that they constantly refrained from expressing their beliefs and opinions to their husbands or significant others. As a result, they experienced depression, low self-esteem, a morphing of identity into the kind of wife or partner they believed to be socially and culturally acceptable, and a lack of trust in their own opinions (Jack, 1991). Psychologist Schuessler Harper (2004) suggests that self-silencing can become a necessary and constant "preservation tool" and that men and women alike exhibit this behavior (p. 12). The focus of Schuessler Harper's research was adolescent dating couples who reported self-silencing behavior. Those members of couples who revealed that they frequently self-silenced, particularly during conflict with their partners, evidenced the following, as compared to non self-silencers: (1) greater levels of depression, (2) earlier ages of transitioning into their first experience with sexual intercourse, (3) greater discomfort when they tried to refuse offers of sexual activity from their partners, and (4) poor overall communication with their partners.

Think about your own use of silence: Have you been in situations when you've self-silenced, out of a perception that at that moment, you needed to hold your tongue? What caused you to respond this way? What was the outcome—did the self-silencing make the situation better or worse? How did the self-silencing make you feel about yourself?

## Turn-Taking in Conversation

For the most part, ordinary, everyday conversations occur in turns: One person speaks or takes a turn, then another person responds (takes a turn), and the back and forth continues (Sacks, Schegloff, & Jefferson, 1978). The turns at talk aren't always clean, meaning that turns often overlap, statements are incomplete, people may try to talk at the same time, and so on. But for the purpose of analysis, it's helpful to view conversation as a series of turns—that is, unless someone dominates the conversation and changes it into a monologue. **Turn-taking,** as a structure for conversation and a means of studying or tracking conversation for the purpose of analysis is a subset of **interaction management,** or how people use verbal and nonverbal communication to conduct or manage their conversations with others (Guerrero & Floyd, 2006). Even a conversation that seems chaotic involves a set of informal, culturally based rules that most people tend to learn over time and through continued social experience. Research on this topic emerged when scholars tried to determine those features of conversation that regularly appear and that give interaction its form (Cappella, 1985; Duncan, 1972, 1973; Duncan & Fiske, 1977; Wiemann & Knapp, 1975; Wilson, Wiemann, & Zimmerman, 1984). Like many other aspects of nonverbal communication, turn-taking cues accompany other nonverbal cues (e.g., eye contact, head nodding, forward or backward lean, facial expressions) to accomplish the desired outcome. Four types of turn-taking cues help us understand how conversations are managed.

**Turn-Requesting Cues.**   How do we let others know that we'd like to speak? Do we simply butt into a conversation, saying, "Excuse me, but I'd like a turn at talk"?

### REMEMBER 9.3

| | |
|---|---|
| **Pause (Vocal Hesitation):** | a break or change in the production of sound. |
| **Fluency:** | how continuously we produce sound. |
| **Filled Pause:** | a vocalization like "um" and "er" that fills a pause, typically as a way of covering silence and giving communicators time to think of what to say, or to encourage others to speak. |
| **Silent Pause:** | breaks in speech that carry no sound. |
| **Audible Pause:** | a pause in which air is taken in and speech is disrupted. |
| **Silence:** | the absence of sound. |
| **Self-Silencing:** | the inhibition of self-expression. |

We doubt it, although something like that might be said if we're having particular difficulty getting the floor. We typically use **turn-requesting cues** to signal that we'd like to engage in conversation, usually beginning with an intake of breath. This intake may or may not cue others that we want to talk, or others may ignore this cue and continue right over us, but turns at talk begin with an intake of breath necessary to carry speech. Another method of requesting a turn at talk is to use a **stutter start,** meaning a repetition of the first word or the first letter of the word that starts the statement we want to make, such as "Well, . . . well, . . . w . . . w . . . .," or the use of a filled pause, such as "ah" or "um" as a means of being recognized as an interactant. We also use **back-channel cues,** such as "hmmm" and "uh-huh," which are responses to others' statements that can encourage others to continue speaking and signal our interest and attentiveness in the conversation, while also indicating that we'd like a turn at talk. Some conversationally impatient people will use rapid-fire back-channel cues in succession, to speed up someone who's talking, so as to gain a turn.

**Turn-Maintaining Cues.** If you're talking and someone obviously wants to say something or respond to you, but you don't want to stop talking, what are you likely to do? Put your hand up in the air and say, "Please be patient; I haven't yet finished my turn at talk"? We doubt it; most people prefer nonverbal cues to verbal statements when we try to correct what we perceive as inappropriate behavior (Burgoon, 1993). When speakers sense that someone wants to interrupt or take a turn, but they want to maintain the floor or simply haven't finished what they want to say, they typically get louder and faster. These vocal strategies are **turn-maintaining cues.** Another oft-used strategy is pausing, either through the use of (1) more filled pauses, which keep your sound going, thus your turn at talk going, while warding off someone else's turn; or (2) fewer and shorter silent pauses, because if you pause too long without saying something, someone will likely jump in and you'll lose your turn at talk. So while filled pauses can maintain a turn, silent pauses tend to cause you to lose your turn.

**Turn-Yielding Cues.** How do you indicate that you've finished a turn at talk— throw your arms up in the air and yell, "ta da!"? We doubt it, but you're likely to use a subtle **turn-yielding cue** to indicate that you wish to relinquish the floor, at least for the time being. The most common form of this cue is to simply drop your pitch, meaning to use a diminishing pattern of intonation as you near the end of your turn. Another yielding cue involves rising intonation, such as ending your turn as a question, which invites others to respond. You can also give up your turn and encourage others to engage through the use of a tag line or filled pause after ending your statement, such as "you know" or "and, um. . . ." Finally, a tactic often used by teachers when they want students to respond to their questions or participate in class discussion is simple silence. If instructors are patient enough to endure a short silence, usually a student will bail them out and offer a comment.

**Turn-Denying Cues.** What if you don't want to engage in conversation, or you just want to listen but not talk? Blurt out, "I pass"? We doubt it; you're more likely to use

**turn-denying cues** to help you indicate to people that you want them to continue talking or don't want to converse at all. (This latter aspect becomes critical when flying on an airplane or in other situations in which talking to strangers isn't preferable.) Mentioned earlier, back-channel cues spoken slowly can reinforce speakers and indicate that their turn at talk should continue. Another common way to avoid taking a turn at talk is simply to be silent, although this can be awkward, especially if only two people are involved in the conversation. Long silent pauses give others the opportunity to take a turn, thus relieving you of having to take a turn when you don't want to.

## Interruptions and Overlaps

Besides turn-taking cues, interruptions and overlaps emerge frequently in conversation. These vocal nonverbal cues can either stand alone or accompany speech. Let's first define these terms and then explore how they operate in conversation. **Interruptions** are abrupt intrusions into someone's speech—they're obvious and they disrupt the flow of speech (West & Zimmerman, 1983). Typically, when one person interrupts another, the first person's speech is halted and the interrupter's speech takes over. However, sometimes interruptions are not acknowledged or accepted, meaning that the first speaker continues to speak, usually faster and louder, to ward off the intrusion. The second speaker either has to reassert the interruption more forcefully or wait for another opportunity to seek a turn at talk. In contrast, **overlaps** tend to occur just as one speaker finishes a turn at talk and another begins a turn. Overlaps are considered less egregious than interruptions because overlapping may be seen as supportive—as trying to reinforce or dovetail off of someone's idea. However, be aware that some people aren't forgiving about overlaps; they may view them as interruptions. Perhaps they grew up with the rule that a listener waits for someone to completely stop talking before engaging in a turn at talk.

Nonverbal scholars have examined the role of power or dominance in interaction management, looking specifically at how speakers establish turns at talk; protect, maintain, and lengthen them; and use interruptions and overlaps to dominate other speakers (Burgoon & Le Poire, 1999; Dunbar & Burgoon, 2005; Lustig, 1977; Mehrabian, 1981). Guerrero and Floyd (2006) suggest that "socially skilled individuals can use [interaction management] behaviors as dominance moves by controlling the floor in such a way that their opinions and ideas are heard" (p. 154). Interruptions and overlaps can be interpreted as indicating disrespect, restricting a speaker's rights, controlling a topic, and revealing an attitude of dominance and authority (Marche & Peterson, 1993; Weiss & Fisher, 1998). Interruptions more often indicate dominance and power play than overlaps because they cut off a speaker in midstream and suggest that the interrupter's comment is somehow more important or insightful.

Communication scholars Zimmerman and West (1975) studied interaction management and found that more overlaps and interruptions occurred in cross-sex conversations than in same-sex conversations, more interruptions occurred than overlaps, and 96 percent of the interruptions were made by males. West and Zimmerman compared their findings for male and female interruptive behavior to that seen in parent–child interaction; they suggest that "the use of interruptions by males is a *display* of dominance or control to the female (and to any witnesses), just as the parent's interruption communicates an aspect of parental control to the child and to others present" (1975, as in Coates, 1998, p. 172). While some research provides evidence of male conversational dominance in terms of initiating topics, maintaining conversation around those topics, talking more often and longer, offering minimal responses to women's comments, and using more statements than questions, other research has not found evidence of sex differences in the use of these behaviors (Dindia, 1987; Edelsky, 1981; Fishman, 1983; Henley, 2001; Kimble & Musgrove, 1988).

How does your experience match up with research findings? Do you find that men interrupt other people more than women, or are women just as likely to interrupt and overlap speech as men? The next time you're in a mixed-sex group setting, like a class when discussion is happening, watch how the conversation flows—how informal, unspoken rules are followed or violated (like people raising their hands to get a turn at talk versus blurting out comments), how conversation gets managed through turn-taking, and how overlaps and interruptions emerge and are handled by members of both sexes.

## Vocal Indications of Deception

When you think about detecting deception, you probably think of lie detector machines that conduct polygraph tests—sophisticated devices that measure all kinds of physiological responses in humans, in order to determine if someone is being truthful or deceptive (Knight, 2004; Ruscio, 2005). While the technology of lie detection has advanced, the results of polygraph tests are still not legally admissible in U.S. courts of law. For our purposes, we're more interested in human lie detectors.

### What Would *You* Do?

You *really* like the girl you're dating, but she constantly interrupts you—when you're on the phone, when you're out on a date and casually talking, when you're at her place or your place having an intimate conversation—*all the time*. The constant interruptions make you feel like she thinks she's superior to you, like she doesn't value or respect what you have to say. But she's a comm major, someone who really likes to talk. That's okay, but you wish she was as good a listener as she is a talker. It's starting to become a problem. But you don't know how you can talk to her about this; again, you *really* like her, but her vocal patterns are making you like her less. It's like every date is a conversational tug-of-war!

*What would you do* in this situation? Would you just suck it up and hang in there, hoping that her interruptions will lessen with time, as she becomes more comfortable with you? Would you try giving her little hints that you don't like the constant interruptions, like saying when she tries to interrupt, "Wait a minute; I wasn't done with what I was saying"? What about giving her a dose of her own medicine—interrupting her so that she realizes what it feels like, hoping that she'll get the hint? Or might you try a more direct method, actually sitting down with her and explaining how her constant interrupting makes you feel? There's no real right answer here; it all depends on what you're comfortable with and how much a vocalic habit like this bugs you.

**REMEMBER 9.4**

| | |
|---|---|
| **Turn-Taking:** | when one person speaks or takes a turn in conversation, then another person responds (takes a turn), and so forth. |
| **Interaction Management:** | how we use verbal and nonverbal messages to conduct or manage our communication with others. |
| **Turn-Requesting Cues:** | vocal nonverbal cues that signal that we would like to engage in conversation. |
| **Stutter Start:** | repetition of the first word or first letter or sound of the word of a statement we want to make. |
| **Back-Channel Cues:** | vocal nonverbal cues that can encourage others to continue speaking and signal our interest in a conversation, while also indicating that we'd like a turn at talk. |
| **Turn-Maintaining Cues:** | vocal nonverbal cues that indicate that we want to maintain the floor or our turn at talk. |
| **Turn-Yielding Cues:** | vocal nonverbal cues that indicate that we want to relinquish the floor. |
| **Turn-Denying Cues:** | vocal nonverbal cues that indicate that we want other people to continue talking or don't want to converse at all. |
| **Interruptions:** | obvious and abrupt vocal intrusions into someone's speech that disrupt the flow. |
| **Overlaps:** | vocalizations that tend to occur just as one speaker finishes a turn at talk and another begins a turn. |

One of the most heavily researched topics within the field of nonverbal communication is deception, or the study of how people use their bodies and voices to deceive others. Research has focused on deceivers' behavior, as well as how receivers detect deception in others (Vrij, 2006). Two examinations reviewed more than 100 studies of nonverbal cues of deception, only to determine this: No one behavioral cue was a dead giveaway of deception (DePaulo, Lindsay, Malone, Muhlenbruck, Charlton, & Cooper, 2003; Vrij, 2000). While we might wish deception revealed itself as simply as a nose growing with a lie, deception and its detection is complicated, with multiple cues attached. However, vocal cues tend to be more reliable indicators of deception than other nonverbal cues, including eye contact, facial expressions, or body movements (Bauchner, Kaplan, & Miller, 1980).

In this section of the chapter, we explore four primary vocal indicators of deception, but we repeat something we mentioned in Chapter 5 when we discussed facial and eye behaviors related to deception: Once information gets publicized as to how deceivers tend to act, people intent on deception *change* that behavior so they won't be caught in their lies. For example, popular word on the street was that liars wouldn't look you in the eye while deceiving you; avoiding eye contact was a telltale sign of deception. Once that finding became public knowledge, good liars changed their ways. The best liars will absolutely look you straight in the eye and lie to your face, and you'll be hard-pressed to know that they're lying. So be forewarned about the information we provide in this section, because people intent on lying or caught in a lie may or may not exhibit these vocal cues.

In general, the best way to detect deception in someone you know fairly well is to compare behavior you think reveals deception to how the person usually acts or speaks, meaning their baseline of normal behavior. Look for aberrant behavior; watch and listen for behaviors that are out of the ordinary for the person. These behaviors could be outgrowths of anxiety or extra energy in the body, usually present when being deceptive. Such anxiety or energy typically leads to altered nonverbal behavior, sometimes described as deception leakage. Altered nonverbal cues have multiple causes, but deception is one thing to consider as you try to interpret what's going on. Again, the nonverbal should outweigh the verbal messages, because nonverbal cues carry the truer meaning behind a message. But as you'll see, deception detection is a tricky endeavor. Researchers estimate that most people's ability to accurately detect deception is below 50 percent (Levine, Park, & McCornack, 1999). When people like police officers and therapists, who are trained to deal with deception, are tested for their detection abilities, their accuracy rates are higher than the average person (Ekman, O'Sullivan, & Frank, 1999; O'Sullivan, 2005). People who attend more to vocal cues than bodily cues are more accurate detectors of deception (Anderson, DePaulo, Ansfield, Tickle, & Green, 1999; Zuckerman, Spiegel, DePaulo, & Rosenthal, 1982).

Read the typical exchange between a mother and child below, and then we'll analyze it for deceptive elements.

**Mother:** Jeffrey, come here this instant and tell me what happened to this cookie jar. It's on the kitchen floor and broken into pieces! Did you break this jar while I was outside talking to the neighbors?

**Jeffrey:** [after a long pause and in a very high-pitched voice] Uh, *NO*, Mom; I didn't break the cookie jar. I didn't go near it 'cuz you told me not to, so I dunno what happened. I'm not 'posed to have cookies before dinner, so I didn't get up there. The jar must've fallen off the counter all by itself, 'cuz I sure didn't do it.

**High Pitch.**    One reliable indicator of deception is unusually high pitch (Anolli & Ciceri, 1997; Ekman & Friesen, 1974; Ekman, Friesen, & Scherer, 1976; Ekman, O'Sullivan, Friesen, & Scherer, 1991; O'Sullivan, 2005). Children, such as Jeffrey in our cookie jar example, often produce high pitches in their speech or vocalizations when trying to deceive. Adults do this, too—in fact it's interesting to watch courtroom testimony when, in the heat of emotions, witnesses, defendants, and plaintiffs may exhibit unusually high pitches as they testify. Pitch variation, with higher than usual peaks, can belie a deceiver's intentions. Most explanations for this phenomenon point to increased tension in the body, and thus in the voice, due to anxiety related to deception; the more stressful the act of deception, the greater the increases in pitch (Andersen, 2004).

**Response Latency.**   In the exchange above, Jeffrey paused a few seconds before answering his mother's questions—a common nonverbal cue when people are challenged or feel cornered. The amount of time it took Jeffrey to answer is termed **response latency** and, again, what you want to listen for if you think you're being deceived is a change in behavior. If someone typically maintains a fast or normal pace of talking and responding, and then that person takes longer than usual to respond to a question or comment, deception is a possibility. Again, we say *possibility*; we urge caution when interpreting nonverbal cues you believe indicate deception—detection is an imprecise activity. Often the response isn't complete silence; it can be masked by an extended filled pause, meaning that a deceiver may use vocalizations during the pause before she or he responds, usually for the purposes of thinking fast and coming up with something to say. People who perceive that they are caught in their lies tend to struggle for creative explanations, and response latencies are telltale signs of this activity.

**Message Duration.**   Look back at the conversation between Jeffrey and his mother; note how short the mother's questions were, compared to the length of Jeffrey's answer. One vocal cue of deception is **message duration** or the length of a verbal message. To repeat, when attempting to determine deception in someone you know, use your baseline of information about the person, then watch and listen for aberrant nonverbal behaviors. If someone tends to be verbose (takes lengthy turns at talk), then listen for unusually short, curt statements or answers to questions. Limiting how much you engage in conversation can be an indication of deception. Conversely, if someone typically gives moderate or short answers to questions, but exhibits out-of-character behavior in conversation by offering unusually long turns at talk, the person might be trying to deceive.

Let's use a stereotypical boyfriend–girlfriend exchange to illustrate this behavior: Mike and Debbie have been dating for several months and were supposed to get together one night to study for finals. When Mike couldn't reach Debbie the night before or even the day of the study session, and when his message on her cell wasn't returned, Mike started to wonder and worry. That evening, Debbie was a no-show. When Mike saw Debbie the next day in the student union, he asked her what happened, reminding her that they'd made plans to study together. Mike asked Debbie, "What happened last night? I thought we were going to study together. I called you a few times; where were you?" Turns out, Debbie chose to go out and party with her girlfriends rather than study with Mike, and she decided not to tell him so he wouldn't think she'd blown him off. Instead of fessing up, Debbie lied to Mike and said: "Last night? Uh, uh.......last night, huh? What happened last night.......? Um, let me think; were we supposed to get together? Oh yeah; sorry, I completely forgot and well, what happened, well you're not going to believe this, but here's the crazy thing that happened and I wasn't able to call you—it was too late and my cell died—anyway, what happened was...." See how long Debbie's communication is, compared to Mike's? She also used response latencies (in the form of "ums" and "uhs") as stalling tactics so that she'd have time to make up an alibi. Once again, use caution in these kinds of situations; don't assume someone is lying when they evidence abnormal response latencies, pitch variations, and message durations. But it's understandable to be suspicious and try to get to the bottom of the situation.

**Speech Disfluencies and Errors.**   Remember that most of us were taught that lying is wrong, so when we attempt to deceive (and we believe that *everybody* attempts to deceive at one time or another, even with "little white lies"), we experience some sort of heightened activation in the body, some extra energy. That energy must travel somewhere, and, as we've said, for many people the nervousness or activation manifests itself in the voice. We overviewed speech fluency in an earlier section on pausing and silence, but realize that speech disruptions (disfluencies) can be evidence of anxiety, possibly generated by or created in anticipation of deception (Anolli & Ciceri, 1997; Cook, 1965; Harrigan, Suarez, & Hartman, 1994; Siegman, 1987). Research suggests that vocal fluency is strongly related to perceptions of competence, as a dimension of credibility, so disfluencies can affect your perception of someone's credibility and, quite possibly, your suspicion that the person is deceptive (Burgoon, Birk, & Pfau, 1990).

If you suspect someone is lying to you, listen for disfluencies, sometimes referred to as **speech errors,** meaning vocalizations that disrupt the flow of speech. Guerrero and Floyd (2006) explain,

> Although the term speech errors may seem to imply a verbal behavior, the markers that are typically measured are vocalic but not verbal. These include vocal disfluencies such as filled pauses (e.g., "um" or "uh") and false starts, excessively long pauses, and long response latencies (the time lapse between when a question is posed and when the recipient begins to answer it). (pp. 178–179)

We explored response latency as its own category, but it can be viewed as a subset of the larger category of speech errors or disfluencies. Granted, speech errors have all kinds of causes—being in a hurry; being tired or not feeling well, such that you slur your words or pause in odd places; and being frustrated, and the words just don't come out right. Many things can cause speech errors, but deception is one of them (Andersen, 2004; Feeley & de Turck, 1998; Vrij & Heaven, 1999).

---

### REMEMBER 9.5

| | |
|---|---|
| **Response Latency:** | a deception cue; amount of time someone takes to respond to another person's communication. |
| **Message Duration:** | a deception cue; length of someone's message or response to another person's communication. |
| **Speech Errors:** | a deception cue; incorrect uses of grammar, mispronounced words, and so forth. |

---

## ■ UNDERSTANDING VOCALICS: APPLYING THE REFLEXIVE CYCLE OF NONVERBAL COMMUNICATION DEVELOPMENT

By now you know what we're going to ask you to do—walk yourself through the Reflexive Cycle with regard to how you use your voice to communicate nonverbally with others, as well as how you perceive others' voices. You may not think much about your voice unless you make a lot of presentations or are a singer, but each of us needs to think about this important channel of nonverbal information. How would you characterize your voice—low and loud? Raspy, breathy, or nasal? Do you like the sound of your own voice, either in your head or on a recording? Do people tell you that you speak too quickly or in a monotone? What kind of feedback have you received about your voice and speech production? Answering these kinds of questions is the first step in the cycle, inventorying your own nonverbal communication.

But this personal inventory goes beyond a mere description of your voice, from your own perspective. How does your voice reveal your emotions? Think of a time when you were really down, sad, or depressed; how did your voice reflect these emotions? Possibly you were successful in masking your emotional state to most people, but people closest to you (intimacy-wise, not proxemically) probably could tell from your voice and other nonverbal cues how you felt. Does nervousness emerge through your voice? When you give a presentation, do you tend to sail through smoothly with little pausing (filled or silent), and no shakiness or dryness in the voice? It probably depends on the situation—whether it's a small or large audience you're addressing, how prepared you are, and so on. But it's important to become more aware of situations that put your voice under duress or that cause you to vary from your normal way of speaking.

Once you've inventoried yourself in terms of your voice and speech patterns, you may have identified some areas you want to improve or change. Perhaps you need to work with a vocal coach, to overcome disfluencies or learn to breathe differently so that you gain more vocal power. Perhaps you need to take a public speaking or voice and diction course, or other communication courses that will require you to work on your vocal production. Still another technique is to work with a recording device, summoning up the courage to record yourself and listen to the playback, noting elements you want to affect or change, then working diligently to make the changes, re-recording yourself and continuing the work. Changing your voice and the way you deliver your verbal communication, both in everyday conversation and presentations, takes time and effort, because you've learned habits over your lifetime that will be hard to alter.

The third phase of the Reflexive Cycle involves inventorying others' vocalic behavior. When you're in professional, educational, and social settings, sharpen your listening skills to attend to the vocal nonverbal behaviors of others, noting things you want to emulate as well as avoid. Perhaps you admire the fluidity with which your boss speaks, or how a teacher's words seem to command attention. Specifically, what contributes to those effects—pausing? Volume? Rate? Pitch? Articulation? Someone at a party might have an interesting sounding voice—what makes it interesting? Pay attention also to the disfluencies you are now more likely to hear than you did before reading this chapter. Note people's uses of pauses and hesitations—do they create interest or bog down the message? Do you detect any deception from the way people use high pitches, response latencies, message durations, or speech errors? You can learn a great deal about vocalics from all of this listening and observation.

Your next step in the Reflexive Cycle is to interact with others, enacting any vocalic changes you've decided are appropriate, and gauge how your nonverbal behaviors transact with others' behaviors. Do you find that your vocalic changes heighten other people's interest in and attention to you? Do you feel that you have more vocalic options at your disposal now?

After you have inventoried yourself, begun to make changes in your vocalic behavior, inventoried others' vocalics, and engaged in mutual transaction of behavior (such that your vocal nonverbal communication affects other people and theirs affects you), the final phase of the Reflexive Cycle involves an evaluation of the whole process. What did you learn about your own and others' voices that makes you a better communicator? As we've said in other chapters and reiterate here, the reflexive process takes an honest assessment of yourself, the willingness to change, keen observational skills, and a sense of "communicator adventure," as you put your new behaviors into action, transact with others, note the results, and re-evaluate.

## SUMMARY ■ ■ ■ ■ ■

This chapter was devoted to vocalics—the study of the voice as a code of nonverbal communication, and how we use our voices to produce messages. We began with an overview of the anatomical and physiological functioning of the voice, to gain an understanding of how the mechanism works to produce voice.

Five properties were explored for their unique contributions to vocal production: pitch, rate, volume, articulation, and pronunciation. We also discussed how our emotions are revealed by the pitches we use, the rate with which we speak, and the varying levels of volume we produce. While vocal properties are easily changeable, vocal qualities are harder to vary. These qualities include breathiness, raspiness, and nasality. The final topic in this section was vocalizations, defined as non-words or sounds that accompany speech or stand alone, as forms of nonverbal communication.

Pausing and silence are vocal nonverbal cues that are often overlooked, but which carry communicative power. We explored three types of pauses and their functions in conversation and presentations, then examined silence for its nonverbal clues. We discussed silence as a reaction or strategy in conflict situations, as well as positive and negative uses of silence. Silencing of Self theory refers to the way people inhibit their self-expression, producing a negative impact on self-esteem and communication in relationships.

We then explored interaction management, in terms of how turn-taking operates to organize conversation. Nonverbal cues associated with four types of turns were provided, including turn-requesting, turn-maintaining, turn-yielding, and turn-denying cues. We contrasted interruptions with overlaps, and investigated how these vocal nonverbal cues can affect people's perceptions of our communication and us, as communicators.

Finally, we delved into the provocative topic of deception, in terms of vocal nonverbal cues deceivers tend to use. Four common vocalic cues included high pitch, response latency, message duration, and speech disfluencies and errors. We discussed the complex process of detecting deception in others' communication, including tips for what to consider when attempting to discover if someone is lying to us or not. In general, the mechanism that enables us to produce vocal nonverbal communication is complex, but understanding how vocalics operate can give average communicators an edge as we interact with others. The chapter closed with an examination of how the Reflexive Cycle of Nonverbal Communication Development can help you enhance your use of vocal cues.

## DISCUSSION STARTERS

1. How do verbal and vocal communication differ? How do we separate out the vocal nonverbal cues from the verbal, for purposes of analysis?

2. Review the five major properties of the voice; then assess your own voice versus the "ideal" voice in terms of these properties. What changes would you like to make in vocal properties, to enhance these important nonverbal cues?

3. What's the best laugh you ever heard? Can you describe it in terms of pitch, duration, or odd noises? Why do you think laughter is contagious? What kind of messages can laughter send to listeners?

4. Recall the three vocal qualities we explored in this chapter. Think of some famous people—celebrities, politicians, musicians, athletes—whose voices correspond with the three qualities.

5. What role do you think pausing and silence should play in conflict? When people in a romantic, intimate relationship argue, what positive uses can they make of pausing and silence? What are some negative uses of pausing and silence?

6. What rules did you learn growing up about interruptions and overlaps? Have you strayed from those rules as you've become an adult and participated in your own social situations?

7. Deception among people is tough; we know it exists, but we wish it didn't. Think about instances in which you were deceived by others—from little white lies to real whoppers. Then analyze those instances for elements of deceivers' voices and speech production that might have been clues that they were deceiving you. If you didn't pick up on those clues then, do you think you will now, if there are future attempts to deceive you?

## REFERENCES

Andersen, P. A. (2004). *The complete idiot's guide to body language.* New York: Alpha.

Anderson, D. E., DePaulo, B. M., Ansfield, M. E., Tickle, J. J., & Green, E. (1999). Beliefs about cues to deception: Mindless stereotypes or untapped wisdom? *Journal of Nonverbal Behavior, 23,* 67–89.

Anolli, L., & Ciceri, R. (1997). The voice of deception: Vocal strategies of naive and able liars. *Journal of Nonverbal Behavior, 21,* 259–284.

Anstendig, K. (1998). Selective mutism: A review of the treatment literature by modality from 1980–1996. *Psychotherapy, 35,* 381–391.

Apple, W., Streeter, L. A., & Krauss, R. M. (1979). Effects of pitch and speech rate on personal attributes. *Journal of Personality and Social Psychology, 37,* 715–727.

Argyle, M. (1988). *Bodily communication.* Reprinted in L. K. Guerrero, J. A. DeVito, & M. L. Hecht (Eds.), *The nonverbal communication reader: Classic and contemporary readings* (1999, 2nd ed., pp. 135–148). Prospect Heights, IL: Waveland.

Barber, N. (1995). The evolutionary psychology of physical attractiveness: Sexual selection and human morphology. *Ethology and Sociobiology, 16,* 395–424.

Bauchner, J. E., Kaplan, E. P., & Miller, G. R. (1980). Detecting deception: The relationship of available information to judgmental accuracy in initial encounters. *Human Communication Research, 6,* 251–264.

Beavin Bavelas, J., & Chovil, N. (2006). Nonverbal and verbal communication: Hand gestures and facial displays as part of language use in face-to-face dialogue. In V. Manusov & M. L. Patterson (Eds.), *The Sage handbook of nonverbal communication* (pp. 97–115). Thousand Oaks, CA: Sage.

Berry, C. (2001). *Voice and the actor* (Rev. ed.). New York: Harrap.

Bloom, K., Moore-Schoenmakers, K., & Masataka, N. (1999). Nasality of infant vocalizations determines gender bias in adult favorability ratings. *Journal of Nonverbal Behavior, 23,* 219–236.

Bloom, K., Zajac, D. J., & Titus, J. (1999). The influence of nasality of voice on sex-stereotyped perceptions. *Journal of Nonverbal Behavior, 23,* 271–281.

Bombar, M. L., & Littig, L. W. (1996). Babytalk as a communication of intimate attachment: An initial study in adult romances and friendships. *Personal Relationships, 3,* 137–158.

Brown, B. L., Strong, W. J., & Rencher, A. C. (1973). Perceptions of personality from speech: Effects of manipulations of acoustical parameters. *Journal of the Acoustical Society of America, 54,* 29–35.

Brown, B. L., Strong, W. J., & Rencher, A. C. (1974). Fifty-four voices from two: The effects of simultaneous manipulations of rate, mean fundamental frequency, and variance of fundamental frequency on ratings of personality from speech. *Journal of the Acoustical Society of America, 55,* 313–318.

Brownmiller, S. (1984). *Femininity.* New York: Simon & Schuster.

Bruneau, T. J. (1973). Communicative silences: Forms and functions. *Journal of Communication, 23,* 17–26.

Buller, D. B. (2005). Methods for measuring speech rate. In V. Manusov (Ed.), *The sourcebook of nonverbal measures: Going beyond words* (pp. 317–323). Mahwah, NJ: Erlbaum.

Buller, D. B., & Burgoon, J. K. (1986). The effects of vocalics and nonverbal sensitivity on compliance: A replication and extension. *Human Communication Research, 13,* 126–144.

Burgoon, J. K. (1993). Interpersonal expectations, expectancy violations, and emotional communication. *Journal of Language and Social Psychology, 12,* 30–48.

Burgoon, J. K., Buller, D. B., & Woodall, W. G. (1996). *Nonverbal communication: The unspoken dialogue* (2nd ed.). New York: McGraw-Hill.

Burgoon, J. K., Birk, T., & Pfau, M. (1990). Nonverbal behaviors, persuasion, and credibility. *Human Communication Research, 17,* 140–169.

Burgoon, J. K., & Le Poire, B. A. (1999). Nonverbal cues and interpersonal judgments: Participant and observer perceptions of intimacy, dominance, composure, and formality. *Communication Monographs, 66,* 105–124.

Caporael, L. R. (1981). The paralanguage of caregiving: Baby talk to the institutionalized aged. *Journal of Personality and Social Psychology, 40,* 876–884.

Cappella, J. N. (1985). Controlling the floor in conversation. In A. W. Siegman & S. Feldstein (Eds.), *Multichannel integrations of nonverbal behavior.* Hillsdale, NJ: Erlbaum.

Christenfeld, N. (1995). Does it hurt to say um? *Journal of Nonverbal Behavior, 19,* 171–186.

Coates, J. (Ed.) (1998). *Language and gender: A reader.* Malden, MA: Blackwell.

Cohan, S. L., Price, J. M., & Stein, M. B. (2006). Suffering in silence: Why a developmental psychopathology perspective on selective mutism is needed. *Journal of Developmental and Behavioral Pediatrics, 27,* 341–355.

Cook, M. (1965). Anxiety, speech disturbances, and speech rate. *British Journal of Social and Clinical Psychology, 4,* 1–7.

Cruttenden, A. (1986). *Intonation.* Cambridge, UK: Cambridge University Press.

Dabbs, J. M. Jr., & Mallinger, A. (1999). High testosterone levels predict low voice pitch among men. *Personality and Individual Differences, 27,* 801–804.

DeGroot, T., & Motowidlo, S. J. (1999). Why visual and vocal interview cues can affect interviewers' judgments and predict job performance. *Journal of Applied Psychology, 84,* 986–993.

DePaulo, B. M., Lindsay, J. L., Malone, B. E., Muhlenbruck, L., Charlton, K., & Cooper, H. (2003). Cues to deception. *Psychological Bulletin, 129,* 74–118.

Dimitrius, J-E., & Mazzarella, M. (1999). *Reading people.* New York: Ballantine.

Dindia, K. (1987). The effects of sex of subject and sex of partner on interruptions. *Human Communication Research, 13,* 345–371.

Dunbar, N. E., & Burgoon, J. K. (2005). Perceptions of power and dominance in interpersonal encounters. *Journal of Social and Personal Relationships, 22,* 207–233.

Duncan, S. (1972). Some signals and rules for taking speaking turns in conversations. *Journal of Personality and Social Psychology, 23,* 283–292.

Duncan, S. (1973). Toward a grammar for dyadic conversation. *Semiotica, 9,* 24–46.

Duncan, S., & Fiske, D. W. (1977). *Face-to-face interaction.* Hillsdale, NJ: Erlbaum.

Edelsky, C. (1981). Who's got the floor? *Language in Society, 10,* 383–421.

Ekman, P. (1965). Communication through nonverbal behavior: A source of information about an interpersonal relationship. In S. S. Tomkins & C. E. Izard (Eds.), *Affect, cognition, and personality.* New York: Springer.

Ekman, P., & Friesen, W. V. (1974). Detecting deception from the body or face. *Journal of Personality and Social Psychology, 29,* 288–298.

Ekman, P., Friesen, W. V., & Scherer, K. R. (1976). Body movement and voice pitch in deceptive interaction. *Semiotica, 16,* 23–27.

Ekman, P., O'Sullivan, M., & Frank, M. G. (1999). A few can catch a liar. *Psychological Science, 10,* 263–266.

Ekman, P., O'Sullivan, M., Friesen, W. V., & Scherer, K. R. (1991). Face, voice, and body in detecting deceit. *Journal of Nonverbal Behavior, 15,* 125–135.

Ellgring, H., & Scherer, K. R. (1996). Vocal indicators of mood change in depression. *Journal of Nonverbal Behavior, 20,* 83–110.

Feeley, T. H., & de Turck, M. A. (1998). The behavioral correlates of sanctioned and unsanctioned deceptive communication. *Journal of Nonverbal Behavior, 22,* 189–204.

Feldstein, S., Dohm, F. A., & Crown, C. L. (2001). Gender and speech rate in the perception of competence and social attractiveness. *Journal of Social Psychology, 141,* 785–808.

Ferguson, C. A. (1964). Baby talk in six languages. *American Anthropologist, 66,* 103–114.

Fishman, P. M. (1983). Interaction: The work women do. In B. Thorne, C. Kramarae, & N. Henley (Eds.), *Language, gender, and society* (pp. 89–101). Rowley, MA: Newbury.

Floyd, K., & Ray, G. B. (2003). Human affection exchange: IV. Vocalic predictors of perceived affection in initial interactions. *Western Journal of Communication, 67,* 56–73.

Fuller, W. (2006, August). Talking points: Five facts about the human voice. *O: The Oprah Winfrey Magazine,* 76.

Georgakopoulos, A. (2004). The role of silence and avoidance in interpersonal conflict. *Peace and Conflict Studies, 11,* 85–95.

Goethals, G. R. (2005). Nonverbal behavior and political leadership. In R. E. Riggio & R. S. Feldman (Eds.), *Applications of nonverbal communication* (pp. 95–115). Mahwah, NJ: Erlbaum.

Graddol, D., & Swann, J. (1989). *Gender voices.* Cambridge, MA: Basil Blackwell.

Grammer, K. (1990). Strangers meet: Laughter and nonverbal signs of interest in opposite-sex encounters. *Journal of Nonverbal Behavior, 14,* 209–236.

Greene, J. O., & Ravizza, S. M. (1995). Complexity effects on temporal characteristics of speech. *Human Communication Research, 21,* 390–421.

Grieser, D. L., & Kuhl, P. K. (1988). Maternal speech to infants in a tonal language: Support for universal prosodic features in motherese. *Developmental Psychology, 24,* 14–20.

Guerrero, L. K., & Floyd, K. (2006). *Nonverbal communication in close relationships.* Mahwah, NJ: Erlbaum.

Harrigan, J. A., Suarez, I., & Hartman, J. S. (1994). Effect of speech errors on observers' judgments of anxious and defensive individuals. *Journal of Research in Personality, 28,* 505–529.

Henley, N. M. (2001). Body politics. In A. Branaman (Ed.), *Self and society: Blackwell readers in sociology* (pp. 288–297). Malden, MA: Blackwell.

Hirano, M., Tanaka, S., Fujita, M., & Terasawa, R. (1991). Fundamental frequency and sound pressure level of phonation in pathological states. *Journal of Voice, 5,* 120–127.

Hummert, M. L., Mazloff, D., & Henry, C. (1999). Vocal characteristics of older adults and stereotyping. *Journal of Nonverbal Behavior, 23,* 111–131.

Izard, C. E. (1991). *The psychology of emotions.* New York: Plenum.

Jack, D. C. (1991). *Silencing the self: Women and depression.* Cambridge, MA: Harvard University Press.

Jaworski, A. (1993). The power of silence in communication. Reprinted in L. K. Guerrero, J. A. DeVito, & M. L. Hecht (Eds.), *The nonverbal communication reader: Classic and contemporary readings* (1999, 2nd ed., pp. 156–162). Prospect Heights, IL: Waveland.

Karpf, A. (2006). *The human voice: How this extraordinary instrument reveals essential clues about who we are.* New York: Bloomsbury.

Kimble, C. E., & Musgrove, J. I. (1988). Dominance in arguing mixed-sex dyads: Visual dominance patterns, talking time, and speech loudness. *Journal of Research in Personality, 22,* 1–16.

Kipper, S., & Todt, D. (2003). The role of rhythm and pitch in the evaluation of human laughter. *Journal of Nonverbal Behavior, 27,* 255–272.

Knapp, M. L., & Hall, J. A. (2006). *Nonverbal communication in human interaction* (6th ed.). Belmont, CA: Thomson/Wadsworth.

Knapp, M. L., & Vangelisti, A. L. (2005). *Interpersonal communication and human relationships* (5th ed.). Boston: Allyn & Bacon.

Knight, J. (2004). The truth about lying. *Nature, 428,* 692–694.

Kooijman, P. G. C., Thomas, G., Graamans, K., & de Jong, F. I. C. R. S. (2007). Psychosocial impact of the teacher's voice throughout the career. *Journal of Voice, 21,* 316–324.

Kramer, C. (1977). Perceptions of female and male speech. *Language and Speech, 20,* 151–161.

Krolokke, C., & Sorensen, A. S. (2006). *Gender communication theories and analyses: From silence to performance.* Thousand Oaks, CA: Sage.

Ladany, N., Hill, C. D., Thompson, B. J., & O'Brien, K. M. (2004). Therapist perspectives on using silence in therapy: A qualitative study. *Counseling and Psychotherapy Research, 4,* 80–89.

Lakin, J. L., Jefferis, V. W., Cheng, C. M., & Chartrand, T. L. (2003). The chameleon effect as social glue: Evidence for the evolutionary significance of nonconscious mimicry. *Journal of Nonverbal Behavior, 27,* 145–161.

Lang, J. M. (2007, May 4). Perfecting your vocal technique. *The Chronicle of Higher Education,* pp. C2–C3.

Laver, J., & Trudgill, P. (1979). Phonetic and linguistic markers in speech. In K. R. Scherer & H. Giles (Eds.), *Social markers in speech.* Cambridge, UK: Cambridge University Press.

Leathers, D. G., & Eaves, M. H. (2008). *Successful nonverbal communication: Principles and applications* (4th ed.). Boston: Allyn & Bacon.

Lessac, A. (1997). *The use and training of the human voice: A bio-dynamic approach to vocal life* (3rd ed.). New York: McGraw-Hill.

Levine, T. R., Park, H. S., & McCornack, S. A. (1999). Accuracy in detecting truths and lies: Documenting the "veracity effect." *Communication Monographs, 66,* 125–144.

Lombard, L. E., & Steinhauer, K. M. (2007). A novel treatment for hypophonic voice: Twang therapy. *Journal of Voice, 21,* 294–299.

Lustig, M. W. (1977). *The relationship between verbal reticence and verbal interaction in triads.* Unpublished doctoral dissertation, University of Wisconsin, Madison.

MacDonald, F. F. (2005). Why do we talk so much? The art of silence in psychotherapy. *Annals of the American Psychotherapy Association, 8,* 43.

Marche, T. A., & Peterson, C. (1993). The development and sex-related use of interruption behavior. *Human Communication Research, 19,* 388–408.

Martin, R. A., & Kuiper, N. A. (1999). Daily occurrence of laughter: Relationships with age, gender, and Type A personality. *HUMOR-International Journal of Humor Research, 12,* 355–384.

McConnell-Ginet, S. (1983). Intonation in a man's world. In B. Thorne, C. Kramarae, & N. Henley (Eds.), *Language, gender, and society* (pp. 69–88). Rowley, MA: Newbury.

Mehrabian, A. (1981). *Silent messages* (2nd ed.). Belmont, CA: Wadsworth.

Miller, N., Maruyama, G., Beaber, R. J., & Valone, K. (1976). Speed of speech and persuasion. *Journal of Personality and Social Psychology, 34,* 615–624.

Nelson, A., & Golant, S. K. (2004). *You don't say: Navigating nonverbal communication between the sexes.* New York: Prentice Hall.

O'Sullivan, M. (2005). Emotional intelligence and deception detection: Why most people can't "read" others, but a few can. In R. E. Riggio & R. S. Feldman (Eds.), *Applications of nonverbal communication* (pp. 215–253). Mahwah, NJ: Erlbaum.

Owren, M. J., & Bachorowski, J. A. (2003). Reconsidering the evolution of nonlinguistic communication: The case of laughter. *Journal of Nonverbal Behavior, 27,* 183–200.

Pfeiffer, J. (1985). Girl talk, boy talk. *Science, 85,* 58–63.

Poyatos, F. (1993). *Paralanguage: A linguistic and interdisciplinary approach to interactive speech and sound.* Amsterdam: John Benjamins.

Provine, R. R. (2000). *Laughter: A scientific investigation.* London: Faber and Faber.

Remland, M. S. (2003). *Nonverbal communication in everyday life* (2nd ed.). Boston: Allyn & Bacon.

Rendle-Short, J. (2005). Managing the transitions between talk and silence in the academic monologue. *Research on Language and Social Interaction, 38,* 179–218.

Riding, D., Lonsdale, D., & Brown, B. (2006). The effects of average fundamental frequency and variance of fundamental frequency on male vocal attractiveness to women. *Journal of Nonverbal Behavior, 30,* 55–61.

Roberts, F., Francis, A. L., & Morgan, M. (2006). The interaction of inter-turn silence with prosodic cues in listener perceptions of "trouble" in conversation. *Speech Communication, 48,* 1079–1093.

Ruark, J. K. (2007, September 7). Voice lessons. *The Chronicle of Higher Education,* p. A88.

Ruscio, J. (2005). Exploring controversies in the art and science of polygraph testing. *The Skeptical Inquirer, 29,* 34–39.

Sacks, H., Schegloff, E. A., & Jefferson, G. (1978). A simple systematic for the organization of turn taking for conversation. In J. Schenkein (Ed.), *Studies in the organization of conversational interaction* (pp. 7–55). New York: Academic.

Scherer, K. R. (1986). Vocal affect expression: A review and model for future research. *Psychological Bulletin, 99,* 143–165.

Scherer, K. R., & Oshinsky, J. S. (1977). Cue utilization in emotion attribution from auditory stimuli. *Motivation and Emotion, 1,* 331–346.

Schuessler Harper, M. (2004). *Keeping quiet: Self-silencing and its association with relational and individual functioning among adolescent romantic couples.* Unpublished doctoral dissertation, University of Tennessee, Knoxville.

Segrin, C. (1998). Interpersonal communication problems associated with depression and loneliness. In P. A. Andersen & L. K. Guerrero (Eds.), *Handbook of communication and emotion: Research, theory, applications, and contexts* (pp. 216–245). San Diego, CA: Academic.

Shaver, P. R., Schwartz, J., Kirson, D., & O'Connor, C. (1987). Emotion knowledge: Further explorations of a prototype approach. *Journal of Personality and Social Psychology, 52,* 1061–1086.

Shute, B., & Wheldall, K. (1989). Pitch alterations in British motherese: Some preliminary acoustic data. *Journal of Child Language, 16,* 503–512.

Siegman, A. W. (1987). The telltale voice: Nonverbal messages of verbal communication. In A. W. Siegman & S. Feldstein (Eds.), *Nonverbal behavior and communication* (2nd ed.). Hillsdale, NJ: Erlbaum.

Street, R. L., Jr., & Brady, R. M. (1982). Speech rate acceptance as a function of evaluative domain, listener speech rate, and communication context. *Communication Monographs, 49,* 290–308.

Thornberg, R. (2006). Hushing as a moral dilemma in the classroom. *Journal of Moral Education, 35,* 89–104.

Toda, S., Fogel, A., & Kawai, M. (1990). Maternal speech to three-month-old infants in the United States and Japan. *Journal of Child Language, 17,* 279–294.

Tracy, K. (2002). *Everyday talk: Building and reflecting identities.* New York: Guilford.

Trainor, L. J., Austin, C. M., & Desjardin, R. N. (2000). Is infant-directed speech prosody a result of the vocal expression of emotion? *Psychological Science, 11,* 188–195.

Tuomi, S. K., & Fisher, J. E. (1979). Characteristics of a simulated sexy voice. *Folia Phoniatrica, 31,* 242–249.

Tusing, K. J. (2005). Objective measurement of vocal signals. In V. Manusov (Ed.), *The sourcebook of nonverbal measures: Going beyond words* (pp. 393–401). Mahwah, NJ: Erlbaum.

Vettin, J., & Todt, D. (2004). Laughter in conversation: Features of occurrence and acoustic structure. *Journal of Nonverbal Behavior, 28,* 93–115.

Vrij, A. (2000). *Detecting lies and deceit: The psychology of lying and its implications for professional practice.* Chicester, UK: John Wiley and Sons.

Vrij, A. (2006). Nonverbal communication and deception. In V. Manusov & M. L. Patterson (Eds.), *The Sage handbook of nonverbal communication* (pp. 341–359). Thousand Oaks, CA: Sage.

Vrij, A., & Heaven, S. (1999). Vocal and verbal indicators of deception as a function of lie complexity. *Psychology, Crime, and Law, 4,* 401–413.

Weiss, E. H., & Fisher, B. (1998). Should we teach women to interrupt? Cultural variables in management communication courses. *Women in Management Review, 13,* 37–44.

Wells, L. K. (2004). *The articulate voice: An introduction to voice and diction* (4th ed.). Boston: Allyn & Bacon.

West, C., & Zimmerman, D. H. (1975). Women's place in everyday talk: Reflections on parent-child interaction. Reprinted in J. Coates (Ed.), *Language and gender: A reader* (1998, pp. 165–175). Malden, MA: Blackwell.

West, C. & Zimmerman, D. H. (1983). Small insults: a study of interruptions in cross-sex conversations between unacquainted persons. In B. Thorne, C. Kramarae, & N. Henley (Eds.), *Language, gender, and society* (pp. 102–117). Rowley, MA: Newbury.

Wiemann, J. M., & Knapp, M. L. (1975). Turn-taking in conversations. *Journal of Communication, 25,* 75–92.

Wilson, T. P., Wiemann, J. M., & Zimmerman, D. H. (1984). Models of turn-taking in conversational interaction. *Journal of Language and Social Psychology, 3,* 159–184.

Woodall, W. G., & Burgoon, J. K. (1983). Talking fast and changing attitudes: A critique and clarification. *Journal of Nonverbal Behavior, 8,* 126–142.

Zebrowitz, L. A., Brownlow, S., & Olson, K. (1992). Baby talk to the babyfaced. *Journal of Nonverbal Behavior, 16,* 143–158.

Zimmerman, D. H., & West, C. (1975). Sex roles, interruptions and silences in conversation. In B. Thorne & N. Henley (Eds.), *Language and sex: Difference and dominance* (pp. 105–129). Rowley, MA: Newbury.

Zraick, R. I., Gentry, M. A., Smith-Olinde, L., & Gregg, B. A. (2006). The effect of speaking context on elicitation of habitual pitch. *Journal of Voice, 20,* 545–554.

Zuckerman, M., & Driver, R. E. (1989). What sounds beautiful is good: The vocal attractiveness stereotype. *Journal of Nonverbal Behavior, 13,* 67–82.

Zuckerman, M., Hodgins, H., & Miyake, K. (1990). The vocal attractiveness stereotype: Replication and elaboration. *Journal of Nonverbal Behavior, 14,* 97–112.

Zuckerman, M., & Miyake, K. (1993). The attractive voice: What makes it so? *Journal of Nonverbal Behavior, 17,* 119–135.

Zuckerman, M., Miyake, K., & Elkin, C. S. (1995). Effects of attractiveness and maturity of face and voice on interpersonal impressions. *Journal of Nonverbal Behavior, 29,* 253–272.

Zuckerman, M., Spiegel, N. H., DePaulo, B. M., & Rosenthal, R. (1982). Nonverbal strategies for decoding deception. *Journal of Nonverbal Behavior, 7,* 171–187.

# Nonverbal Communication and the Internet

## CHAPTER OUTLINE ■ ■ ■ ■ ■

## CHAPTER OBJECTIVES ■ ■ ■ ■ ■

After studying this chapter, you should be able to:

1. Understand the effects of computer-mediation on nonverbal communication.

2. Describe the factors involved in the presentation of self online, with particular emphasis on the role of nonverbal cues in expressing the self to others.

3. Describe the nonverbal dimensions of computer-mediated communication (CMC), with specific regard for email, chat rooms, and Instant Messaging.

4. Explain the use of emoticons, listening, pausing, and silence as forms of nonverbal communication online.

5. Recognize nonverbal cues associated with CMC, in contrast to nonverbal aspects of face-to-face (FtF) communication.

6. Explain the difference between the physical body and the virtual body.

## CASE STUDY  Mr. Wrong

About two years ago I was feeling lonely and decided to enter a chat room. I was never one to think of the Internet as a source of romance, but that night was different. I began talking to a guy in the chat room and then he invited me to a private domain. We chatted for three hours that night and over the next few months we talked more and more every day. He was so easy to talk to and we had so many things in common. Six months passed and we decided it was time to take this chatting to a new level. He invited me to have coffee with him at the local Starbucks. He told me I would recognize him because he would have one long-stemmed red rose laying on his table. I got ready that evening and drove to Starbucks. When I walked in I casually looked around and headed to the counter to order my Double Chocolate Chip Iced Latte. There he was with a single long-stemmed rose on the table by the window; it was Jim, my best friend Nancy's husband.

I stared at him for what seemed like an eternity, then turned to the cashier and paid for my drink. He spotted me and waved; I went over to him just to let him know I was headed home and needed a nightcap. He told me he was waiting for Nancy. I wanted to rip his head off and tell him what a jerk he was, but I didn't. I just smiled and left. The next day I called Nancy, invited her to lunch, and told her the entire story. She hasn't spoken to me since that day, but I feel I did the right thing.

**Daughter:**  "I just broke up with John."

**Mother:**  "When did this happen? Did you talk on the phone?"

**Daughter:**  "No. We were Instant Messaging."

**Mother:**  "What did he say?"

**Daughter:**  "Nothing! He didn't even write me back. Can you believe it? That sure shows how much he cares."

What does this brief conversation reveal about how and where we communicate in the Information Age? In the not-so-distant past, breaking up with a romantic partner was something most people did face to face, out of respect for the other person's feelings and simply because it was the "right thing to do" (although the "Dear John" letter was popular). Giving bad news over the telephone, through a text message, or via a social networking system such Facebook or a MySpace page happens more frequently nowadays, as people take advantage of the distance and impersonality of the Internet (Lawson & Leck, 2006; Starks, 2007). To many of us, the "cyber-dump" is reprehensible, but the increased popularity of this method led a couple of entrepreneurs to develop the website breakupservice.com. People wishing to avoid face-to-face confrontation can simply pay the online service $50 and one of their representatives will do the breaking up for them. Options include making a phone call, writing an old-fashioned letter, or sending an email message to deliver the bad news. As an additional service, an employee of the website will even pick up any possessions left in the care of the ex and make sure they get returned. The service's employees report a significant increase in business just after major holidays!

Analyzing this breakup example in nonverbal terms, mechanisms such as the telephone or an email system reduce or filter out the nonverbal channels that would be present in a face-to-face confrontation. Nonverbal cues of being hurt, dejected, or outraged (e.g., angry facial expressions, tears, emotional vocalizations, increased distance, lack of touch or, worse, violent touch) can be mediated, thus saving the person doing the dumping from having to experience these behaviors "in the flesh" (Li, Jackson, & Trees, 2008). On the other end of the breakup, however, the dumped person will likely feel stunned by the insensitivity of the action, as well as short-changed because her or his nonverbal reactions are being controlled or contained.

Breaking up is just one aspect of relating to others that has changed because of increased accessibility to and affordability of technology. Our ways of communicating with one another continue to change almost daily, such that it's hard to keep up with all the innovation. Do you think technology has helped or hurt communication? Certainly, pros and cons abound when it comes to the use of technology to connect with others and manage our relationships. We've probably all heard wonderful stories of people connecting online, then face to face, and then getting married, but we've also heard stories about online predators targeting young kids and adolescents. One thing is clear: Technological innovation regarding communication isn't going away; it's only going to increase as newer, faster, more convenient, and more affordable approaches and gizmos will continue to be developed for our use.

Many people think that communication facilitated by such systems as email, Instant Messaging, social networking, and texting suffers because of the loss of nonverbal cues. You may remember that in Chapter 1 we discussed how nonverbal communication experts suggest that approximately 65 percent of the way human beings convey meaning in our messages is through nonverbal channels, leaving only 35 percent to be accomplished verbally (Birdwhistell, 1970). Take the nonverbal cues out of interaction, and you've severely impeded successful communication. So is all online communication hampered in this way, or do other nonverbal cues emerge or operate that we don't typically think of as nonverbal cues? Your textbook authors argue the latter, suggesting that we need to change our thinking on this topic to consider how various elements within emailing, chatting online, Instant Messaging, creating web or social networking pages, and other forms of relating to people in the virtual realm can be construed as nonverbal communication. As the Internet has become a part of everyday life, it's not too surprising that the nature of our communication, especially our nonverbal communication, is changing (Andersen, 2004; Hermes, 2008; Yee, Bailenson, Urbanek, Chang, & Merget, 2008). We invite you to explore this chapter with an open mind as to what constitutes nonverbal communication online.

## ■ CYBERSPACE: AN EVOLVING CONTEXT FOR COMMUNICATION

The nonverbal communication codes covered in previous chapters are important to examine when our interaction shifts from face-to-face (FtF) communication to **computer-mediated communication (CMC)**—human communication that is facilitated by a wide range of technologies such as chat rooms, email message systems, message boards, and online games (Arvidsson, 2006; Gibbs, Ellison, & Heino, 2006; Li, Jackson, & Trees, 2008; Martey & Stromer-Galley, 2007; Peter & Valkenburg, 2007; Walther & D'Addario, 2001; Walther, Loh, & Granka, 2005). CMC scholar Susan Barnes (2003) contends that "the driving force behind current changes in communication technologies is the **Internet**—generally defined as a network of networks because it consists of many smaller computer networks that are interconnected to each other" (p. 4).

CMC researchers have argued for many years that computers would reshape human communication; no doubt their predictions have come to fruition (Hiltz & Turoff, 1993; Jones, 1997; Marvin, 1988; Poster, 1990; Sproull & Kiesler, 1991). When human communicators rely on computers as our primary channels for communicating with friends, family members, colleagues, and even strangers, we must understand the effects that this channel has on our verbal and nonverbal communication (Couch & Liamputtong, 2008; Li, Jackson, & Trees, 2008; Pollock, 2006).

Before exploring such particular computer applications as email and chat rooms, we need to situate CMC within a context. You've probably heard and used the term **cyberspace,** but just what is cyberspace? Cyberspace includes "the diverse experiences or space associated with computing and related technologies" (Strate, 1999, p. 383). As a way of accessing or making sense out of something as vast as cyberspace, we tend to think of smaller contexts for CMC, known as **virtual communities** or social aggregations that emerge from the Internet when enough people engage in discussions with sufficient human feeling to form webs of personal relationships in cyberspace (Rheingold, 1993; Riley, Keough, Christianson, Meilich, & Pierson, 1998). As CMC scholar Howard Rheingold (1993) suggests, "We reduce and encode our identities as words on a screen, decode and unpack the identities of others. The way we use these words, the stories (true and false) we tell about ourselves (or about the identity we want people to believe us to be) is what determines our identities in cyberspace" (p. 61). With the growth of the Internet, now thousands of virtual communities exist whose members never or rarely meet to communicate face to face (Baym, 2000; Couch & Liamputtong, 2008; Danet, 2001; Virnoche

*Communication in cyberspace is an increasingly important aspect of our day-to-day existence.*

TABLE 10.1    Internet Genres

| GENRE | DESCRIPTION |
| --- | --- |
| **Simple Email Exchange:** | similar to a phone call; two people exchanging computer-mediated messages. |
| **Listserv/Discussion Group:** | multiple-user online interaction that occurs over an extended period of time, with common core group members who bond as they share a sense of communal space. |
| **Bulletin Boards/Forums/ Newsgroups:** | complicated online social interaction with an increased sense of space. |
| **Real-Time Chat/Internet Relay Chat (IRC):** | computer-mediated, fluid interactions that overlap because they occur in near real time. |
| **Instant Messenger (IM):** | brief online interactions in near real time. |
| **Multi-Player Games/Multi- User Dimensions or Dungeons (MUDs)/Object Oriented (MOOs):** | use of characters and structure that foster complex group dynamics and heighten the element of fantasy in online interactions. |
| **Web Pages:** | Internet sites that offer text plus pictures, graphics, sound, and films to enhance the online experience. |

Table adapted and reproduced with permission of: Barnes, S. B. (2003). *Computer-mediated communication: Human-to-human communication across the Internet.* Boston: Allyn & Bacon.

& Marx, 1997). People who are deaf have benefited tremendously from the move toward more computer-mediated communication and away from face-to-face interaction. Take a moment to review Table 10.1 as a reminder of the various genres important to our application of nonverbal communication codes to the Internet.

## ■ THE NONVERBAL SELF ONLINE

Have you ever thought about how you present yourself nonverbally online? Do you come across through computer-mediated communication in a very similar way as you do when meeting people face to face? Or are you somehow different in your online communication? Have you thought about the effects of absent nonverbal communication cues (e.g., physical appearance, vocalics, facial expression, eye expression, gestures, touch) on the clarity and impact of your message? Do you think your sense of humor is understood by others who read an email message from you?

Scholar Ervin Goffman's (1959) research on how people present or represent themselves in everyday life is applicable to CMC. Goffman suggests that "the expressiveness of the individual (and therefore his capacity to give impressions) appears to solve two radically different kinds of sign activity: the expression that he *gives*, and the expression that he *gives off*" (p. 2). What people *give* refers to our verbal communication, typically occurring in face-to-face settings. However, since CMC relies more heavily on verbal text than nonverbal cues, what people *give* takes on more significance. The *giving off* part is nonverbal, which involves such things as facial expressions, gestures, body movements, and attire (Martey & Strommer-Galley, 2007). What we typically think of as nonverbal cues may be altered in CMC, but we still *give off* these cues to assist in the transmission of the verbal message and to represent ourselves to our online partners (Li, Jackson, & Trees, 2008).

Internet researchers are fascinated with this topic—the way people present themselves online (Hancock & Dunham, 2001; McKenna, Green, & Gleason, 2002; Mitchell, 1995; Ramirez & Burgoon, 2004; Tidwell & Walther, 2002; Walther, Slovacek, & Tidwell, 2001). CMC scholar Sherry Turkle (1995) suggests that "the computer offers us both new models of mind and a new medium on which to project our ideas and fantasies" (p. 1). "Life on the screen," she explains, "makes it very easy to present oneself as other than one is in real life" (p. 228). Another scholar, Mark Poster (1990), observes that in computer-mediated contexts the individual is affected in the following ways: (1) new possibilities for playing with identities emerge; (2) gender cues are removed; and (3) the subject is dispersed and dislocated in space and time. Communication researcher Charles Soukup (2004) confirms this sense of identity play, observing that virtual communities enable people to engage in dramatic performance online through nonverbal communication.

**Avatars** are ways that computer users express themselves using embodiments or manifestations, typically as characters in interactive games (Li, Jackson, & Trees, 2008; Martey & Strommer-Galley, 2007) and, increasingly, as instructors in college classrooms to facilitate distance learning (Bailenson, 2008; Foster, 2008). Avatars allow users to visually and nonverbally express human characteristics and emotions (Barnes, 2003). One study examined how participants in the online community known as *The Palace* used avatars and props to manage space and express themselves (Soukup, 2004). The research determined that the placement and actions of avatars such as "Naughty Guy" and "Zombie Wolf" expressed computer users' closeness of relationship to others. These embodiments of computer users represent extensions of the self—yet another nonverbal

---

### REMEMBER 10.1

| | |
|---|---|
| **Computer-Mediated Communication (CMC):** | human communication facilitated by technologies such as chat rooms, email systems, message boards, and online games. |
| **Internet:** | network of interconnected computers. |
| **Cyberspace:** | diverse experiences or space associated with computing and related technologies. |
| **Virtual Communities:** | social aggregations that form on the Internet when people discuss common topics and form webs of personal relationships in cyberspace. |
| **Avatars:** | ways computer users express themselves and convey emotions through embodiments and manifestations that resemble human characteristics. |

means of expressing oneself in a virtual community. Since many of our daily actions, interactions, and experiences are mediated by technology, it's important to think about how we express ourselves and how this form of expression changes our sense of self, compared to how we communicate our identities to people face to face (Walther, Loh, & Granka, 2005; Wright, 2004).

## SPOTLIGHT on Research

The impressions that others have of us are "facts of life" that we must deal with and manage in our personal and professional relationships. Beyond the impressions that people form as a result of such things as our email style or screen name, personal websites or social networking sites such as MySpace.com advertise people to the general computer-using public. These sites and services are increasingly created to communicate people's identities to a broader audience than face-to-face contact will allow.

One line of research examined the online communication of parents wanting to adopt a child. Communication researchers Wahl, McBride, and Schrodt (2005) studied a new frontier in family communication, specifically how parents use online adoption websites to advertise themselves to birth mothers looking to find a family. Families expressed their identities through verbal and nonverbal channels, primarily through photographs and narratives posted online. Many parents suggested that they made concerted efforts to "clean up" their image as a family. Pictures of suburban homes (often with white picket fences) in nice neighborhoods and children with pets appeared frequently. One can only imagine the potential for deception in some of these presentations.

In terms of the family narratives, many were written in a classified ad style in an attempt to appeal to birthparents seeking a suitable adoption family. In essence, the CMC became a method of impression management, with families selling themselves by creating an image that a birth mother would buy. Three themes emerged in this research: (1) The Suburban Family as Prototype, meaning that families most wanted to present themselves as being typically suburban, as though that would be perceived as ideal by birthparents; (2) Online Adoption as Utopia, meaning that families who utilized this approach to adoption viewed the website service as a cure-all, an expedient means to an end through the wonders of technology; and (3) Child as Cyber Commodity, which refers to the fact that in most instances the child being presented for adoption got lost in this electronic space of exchange, competition, and self-marketing.

You may be thinking: Why focus on families using adoption websites? As Wahl, McBride, and Schrodt's research shows, modifying our physical appearance and image online is simple and done with increasing frequency, for all kinds of purposes. But as consumers, we must be forewarned: What we see online may not be what we get in reality. Can you see any similarities between the strategies parents used in this study and personal ads or profiles posted on dating websites or MySpace pages? Have you ever used or considered using technology to modify a picture of yourself and your surroundings? What aspects of your physical appearance or personality might you modify to impress others? What might be someone's motivation for altering their image in this way? The key question is this: Does the Internet normalize deception?

Do you want to know more about this study? If so, read: Wahl, S. T., McBride, M. C., & Schrodt, P. (2005). Becoming "point and click" parents: A case study of communication and online adoption. *Journal of Family Communication, 5,* 279–294.

# ■ NONVERBAL DIMENSIONS OF COMPUTER-MEDIATED COMMUNICATION (CMC)

In the CMC context, many things we think of as verbal communication actually become nonverbal cues. We don't want this to become confusing, so we're going to explore the basic nonverbal dimensions within some of the most commonly used functions of CMC, realizing that your tendency will probably be to think of these as verbal elements.

## Email and Nonverbal Cues

Research reveals that the primary use for the home computer is relationship maintenance, mainly in the form of emailing to keep in touch with family members and friends (Stafford, Kline, & Dimmick, 1999; Wright, 2004). We know that people working in businesses and professional organizations increasingly rely on their email systems to communicate with colleagues and accomplish their work, including school systems in which parent–teacher email exchanges are becoming more commonplace (Thompson, 2008). Given how prevalent email usage is and will continue to be in our culture, let's examine this form of CMC more closely for its nonverbal properties.

We begin with a basic element—the email address. Have you ever thought about how your email address communicates such things as your personality, personal interests, deviances, and occupation? Granted, the address itself is verbal, but the image it communicates makes it a nonverbal cue. The typical email address for a professor looks something like this: chris.prof@university.edu. The first part of the email address designates the owner's or recipient's name; the last part of the address points to the server or location where the recipient can be found.

As email has become more normalized, people have begun to move away from using a real name that reflects their identity. Instead people are creating names which, upon first inspection, illustrate a sense of play. Instead of using our real names, we can select something about ourselves to provide a more creative email address. For example, Sally is on the basketball team and her athletic participation is a defining factor in her sense of self. Instead of using sally.smith@email.com, Sally can have some fun by creating a different email address, such as supersallystar@email.com. Some people celebrate the fact that a creative email name provides them **anonymity**—the ability to communicate, participate, and have presence without revealing their true identity (Harasim, Hiltz, Teles, & Turoff, 1995; Hiltz, 1994; Hiltz & Turoff, 1993; Rosen, 2000; Sproull & Kiesler, 1991). Reflect on your email address for just a moment. (We're assuming all of our readers have email accounts. Most students have access to university email services, even if they don't have their own accounts through personal computers.) Does your email address reflect your real name or a made-up name? What was the basis of your decision when you set up your email account? Did you give any thought to using your real name versus a made-up name?

While a sense of play or freedom may emerge when setting up an email address, it's important to think about the impressions others will form about us based on such a simple thing as our email address, because email addresses are verbal expressions with nonverbal implications (Byron & Baldridge, 2007). Both authors of this book advise our students to review and possibly change their email addresses when applying for jobs or graduate programs. Consider the reaction a job recruiter or graduate director would have when receiving an email message from islandprincess@university.edu versus jane.doe@university.edu. Which address implies more credibility? Which address communicates a more positive first impression? We need to think about the perceptions that others may form about us from this form of CMC before we meet face to face or talk on the phone.

In addition to being aware of the communicative function of our email address, it's important to recognize the different types of emailers (people regularly using email systems) we've already experienced or will encounter in future professional contexts. If you ask anyone who has a job that requires communication via email, probably she or he will be able to identify at least one experience in which conflict, aggression, or misunderstanding occurred online (Wollman, 2008).

Beyond business and professional contexts, we should also reflect on the communicative function of email in personal relationships and more casual social networks (Hardey, 2004; Starks, 2007). Have you ever received an email message that you perceived as inappropriate? Aggressive? Insulting? Communication scholars continue to study **aggressive communication**—self-serving interaction that does not take a listener's feelings and rights into account (Atkin, Smith, Roberto, Fediuk, & Wagner, 2002; Heisel, La France, & Beatty, 2003; Infante & Rancer, 1996; Infante, Riddle, Horvath, & Tumlin, 1992). In one offshoot of this research, communication scholars study college instructors' aggressive communication for its effects on students' perceptions of instructor behavior and effectiveness, students' apprehension about interacting in class, their perceptions of classroom climate, and their motivation toward achievement (Myers & Rocca, 2001; Rocca, 2004; Schrodt, 2003). Only recently has this form of communication begun to be investigated in the CMC context. Research indicates that with increasing frequency, students use email (as well as other popular tech devices like Twitter and YouTube) as their primary means to communicate with professors (Farrell, 2005; Young, 2008a, 2008b). What are some nonverbal elements within email messages between teachers and students that may be interpreted as aggressive?

Let's first consider the poor student: A student sends a polite request to his or her professor for clarification on a due date or a confusing concept that she or he did not understand in class. How might the aggressive professor respond? The email exchange might look something like this:

(STUDENT)
```
Dear Dr. Toxic,
This is Holly from your nonverbal communication class. Can you
explain the concept of proxemics? I am having a difficult time
understanding the concept. Also, is our exam review next Tuesday?
Thanks for your time.
Sincerely,
Holly
```

(PROFESSOR)

HOW MANY TIMES DO I HAVE TO EXPLAIN?!? PROXEMICS IS ABOUT SPACE AND DISTANCE. MAYBE IF YOU WOULD READ THE BOOK YOU WOULD NOT HAVE TO ASK SUCH SILLY QUESTIONS. BOY DO WE EVER NEED TO REVIEW FOR THIS EXAM.
DR. TOXIC
PROFESSOR OF COMMUNICATION
OFFICE HOURS: BY APPOINTMENT ONLY
EMAIL: TOXIC@EMAIL.EDU

First, we sincerely hope that communication professors rarely send such pathetic email responses to students, but we live in the real world and know that communication professors are human, too, and capable of ineffective communication from time to time. Given that, let's inspect this email exchange, looking especially for nonverbal elements that communicate volumes about the verbal message and the messengers.

To begin, the student's email message includes a greeting or salutation (Dear Dr. Toxic), which communicates a level of professionalism and respect, just as you would include a formal salutation in a business letter. What if the student's message had started with "Hey Doc!"? Would that have sent a different signal? The verbal cues are the words in the greeting, but the presence or absence of a salutation is a nonverbal cue. Next the student identified herself to the professor by which class she's in—always a good idea, given that the "absent-minded professor" is often a reality, not a stereotype. She then asked a question, revealed her confusion over the subject of the question, asked another brief question, thanked the prof for his or her time, ended the email with another polite closing (Sincerely), and added her name. The brevity of the message is another nonverbal signal—in this example, one that conveys respect for the professor's time. In most situations, lengthy email messages that meander wildly before coming to the point, as well as terse or surprisingly short (out of the ordinary) messages, send negative nonverbal cues to email recipients.

Now let's turn our focus to the professor's response, which most people would interpret as negative and aggressive. First, note the lack of any greeting or salutation. Many people begin their email messages without any form of greeting; this practice is frowned upon in professional contexts, but may develop into a form of shorthand that is perfectly acceptable between people who frequently use email to communicate with each other. But in this case, it sets the tone for the impersonality of the professor's response; Dr. Toxic doesn't address the student by name at any point in the message. Second, Dr. Toxic's message is written in all caps, a style known as **shouting**, which experts suggest be used sparingly and only for emphasis in email messages. Reading the message in all caps generates a sense of nonverbal noise, which can be disturbing and distracting for receivers of the message. In this case, it's as though the professor were screaming her or his words at the student.

Another feature is the extraneous and dramatic punctuation at the end of the professor's first statement (?!?). The presence of three punctuation marks instead of one is a nonverbal indicator of exasperation; again, this is an aggressive choice by the professor. Think about how punctuation functions when reading something. It serves as a vocal cue, right? The question mark at the end of that last sentence indicates rising vocal intonation or an upward lift in pitch, which we recognize as a way to convey that a question is being asked. A comma or semi-colon cues us to pause when reading, either in our heads or out loud, so punctuation marks are symbols that cause us to vocalize a certain effect. All our lives we've been using written symbols (verbal elements) to provide nonverbal cues to enhance meaning.

Note the end of Dr. Toxic's message; does the professor end personally or impersonally? Dr. Toxic used a **signature file**—a standard closing that can be programmed into an email system and automatically inserted at the end of every outgoing email message. Typically signature files accompany professional email systems, but they can be used for personal email messages as well. They often contain the person's name, title, address, affiliation, and other general contact information; occasionally people will include a favorite quotation, inspirational message, or graphic image. Some people believe that the signature file is an acceptable closing and that it's redundant to also type your name at the end of a message, before the signature file. Others believe that not typing your name after a message—leaving the signature file to suffice—is cold and inappropriate. Think about the perceptions that your email recipients will form if you forget or choose not to attach your name to a message; will the nonverbal message be positive, negative, or neutral?

Another nonverbal element to analyze in email messages is the general look of the message itself. Granted, some reformatting occurs in the transmission of email messages from computer to computer, but some elements don't reformat. What font (typeface) do you prefer to use for class papers? As we mention in Chapter 11 on nonverbal communication in professional and educational contexts, styles of fonts convey different nonverbal signals about verbal messages (Bringhurst, 2004). Would you use a fancy scrolling script for a research paper, an Old English font that looks like Shakespeare himself penned your paper, or a fairly standard font like Times or Chicago? These are important nonverbal decisions that affect your verbal communication. Just like for a class paper, the font you choose for email messages (given that it doesn't reformat in transmission) sends a nonverbal signal about you. Note that the student, Holly, in our example above used Courier New font—one that resembles a font from an old-fashioned typewriter. In our opinion, this font does not send any particular negative signal, but compare it to the font Dr. Toxic used—Geneva—with its straight-up style, exaggerated when typed in all caps, which conveys a much more terse tone than the font the student chose.

What would your perception be of a professor like Dr. Toxic, after receiving such a verbally and nonverbally aggressive email message? Would you use email to ask your professors questions in the future? How would this type of message influence your FtF communication during class with this professor?

In addition to font choice, other format decisions send distinctive nonverbal messages to people on the other end of the line. Take, for example, an email request from a student to one of this text's authors for a letter of recommendation for graduate school. The message arrived in a hot pink color with italicized, cursive writing and more smiley faces than you can count, and an email address of beachbaby@hotmail.com. Since the message requested a professional letter of recommendation, you can imagine the disconnect the professor felt between the significance of the request and the youthfulness or lack of professionalism of the requester. Some fancy software packages allow creativity in the look and format of email messages, but it's important to think about what nonverbal messages are conveyed along with the clever design features.

Over time and with continued use of email, people tend to develop a style or approach to emailing. We've developed a typology of emailing styles for both personal and professional contexts; see if you recognize your style among the ones listed in Table 10.2.

The types of emailers identified in Table 10.2 are significant because we form perceptions of people based on their style of sending and receiving email messages, especially if we don't also know the person in an FtF context. We may misunderstand someone's intended tone and form a negative impression, which then carries over into future emailing as well as the face-to-face context. Connected with this typology of emailers are behaviors that we may not even think about, but which send messages to people on the other end (Wollman, 2008). For example, are you one of those people who takes your time responding to messages ("turtle")? Or do you feel a mandate, a necessity to return a message immediately after you read it ("jack rabbit")?

Let's say you're emailing a friend who normally returns a message within a couple of days; you send your friend an email message with some questions in it, but don't hear anything for a week. What might you think? Explanations could be perfectly benign, like the person is out of town or her or his email system is down for a few days, causing the inbox to be particularly crowded when the system comes back up. Another explanation might be that you asked questions that require pondering or that

### TABLE 10.2   Types of Emailers

| | |
|---|---|
| **Bully:** | verbally aggressive and usually insulting. |
| **Impersonal Comedian/Watchdog:** | forwards material like jokes, funny stories, and warnings about computer viruses and scams to people in their address book. |
| **Inspirational Speaker:** | forwards messages about medical tribute months, fund raisers, and good causes; also known to send religious information and prayer requests. |
| **Jack Rabbit:** | responds to email messages immediately but hurriedly; often uses incomplete sentences, abbreviations (such as "bc" for "because" and "LOL" for "laugh out loud"), no caps, and no punctuation. |
| **Non-Responder:** | refuses to respond to email messages even when questions are raised. |
| **Over-Talker (AKA, "It's All About Me"):** | sends lengthy self-oriented email messages, often containing vivid, personal self-disclosure, accompanied by numerous recent photos; expects an immediate reply as to what you think about her or him, the disclosure, and the photos. |
| **Sniper:** | passive/aggressive style; uses brief, one-word replies; too busy to write in complete sentences. |
| **Trainee:** | first-time user lacking confidence; usually sends the same message two or three times; neglects or forgets to attach pictures and documents. |
| **Turtle:** | takes two to three weeks to respond to email messages; original message is forgotten by the time the reply is received. |

sparked the person's emotions, and he or she just needs time to think about it or to cool off before responding. Perhaps the lack of response reveals a deeper problem, a beginning of some distance being created between the two of you.

What if one friend's tendency is to send lengthy, detailed messages, perhaps with attachments of photographs, inspirational messages, or links to websites, and the friend on the other end has a completely different emailing style? The receiving friend returns the lengthy message with a short, terse, non-detailed one, perhaps prefaced with "just a short one this time—gotta dash to a meeting." What kind of messages are sent if this pattern is continual? How can these nonverbal cues related to emailing behavior reveal the nature of the relationship between the two friends?

 All kinds of nonverbal signals surround the sending and receiving of email messages—signals that we often take for granted or just don't think much about. As a way of enhancing our awareness of ourselves as communicators, it's advisable to inventory what kind of emailer we are, both in sending and receiving functions, to see what profile of ourselves we extend through our emailing behavior. Might some changes be warranted?

### What Would _You_ Do?

Jamie is graduating from college and has been on several job interviews, but she has her heart set on this one job in particular. She's been through a couple of interviews and it's now down to just her and a couple of other people, and she's really hoping she gets the position. Any day now she should hear from her possible future employers, and she's nervous. Graduation is only two weeks away and Jamie wants to have good news to share with her family when they come to town for the commencement ceremony. She wants to have landed her dream job and announce it to her family and friends at her graduation party.

Much as Jamie would like to get the job, she made one critical error in her job searching process: Jamie included a link to her MySpace page on the electronic version of the resumé she emailed to the company she wants to work for. The link is at the top where she listed her current address, phone number, and email address, so it's hard not to notice it. She included it just like she would any other personal information. Problem is, her MySpace page contains some elements that she didn't remember were there when she started her job hunt. It's the typical stuff—no nude photos or anything like that—but there are several pics of her partying with her friends, complete with beer bottles and cigarettes in the foreground. (She "party smokes" from time to time.) The company Jamie wants to work for is well known for being conservative, which she knew in advance of applying for a job there. She communicated professionally on the various job interviews with the company, but on her MySpace page, she seems to look like a social butterfly, not a serious college graduate.

If you were in Jamie's situation, _what would you do_? Would you quickly redo the MySpace page, replacing the party photos with more serious ones or deleting photos completely, and then email an updated resumé to the potential employer, hoping he or she hadn't yet seen the page? Would you own up to the mistake to your potential boss, apologizing for the situation, stressing your positive qualities as a future employee, and hoping that doing so would demonstrate your integrity?

**REMEMBER 10.2**

| | |
|---|---|
| **Anonymity:** | ability to communicate, participate, and have presence online without revealing one's true identity. |
| **Aggressive Communication:** | self-serving communication that doesn't take into account a listener's feelings and rights. |
| **Shouting:** | typing words in all caps in email or text messages. |
| **Signature File:** | standard closing that can be programmed into an email system and automatically inserted at the end of every outgoing message; often contains an emailer's name, title, address, affiliation, and other general contact information. |

## Chat Rooms, Instant Messaging, and Nonverbal Cues

While email messages occur in **asynchronous time**—messages are posted at one time, then read at another time—CMC also offers more interactive features, such as communication in **synchronous time.** In chat rooms and through the use of such text messaging features as Instant Messenger, people can communicate with little lag time between comments. People's preferences for asynchronous versus synchronous CMC reveal something about them nonverbally. As we mentioned in Chapter 3 on environment, **chronemics** is defined as the communicative aspects of time, and our sense of time can play a role in the online context as well (Ballard & Seibold, 2000). Let's consider some of the prominent nonverbal features of these forms of CMC.

In chat rooms, participants typically use **screen names** or aliases rather than their real names, for the purpose of maintaining anonymity. Again, the name or "nickname" is verbal, but the message sent by a choice of name is also nonverbal. What message is sent by using the screen name "Studly" versus "Brainiac," for example? Similar to having a sense of play with creative email addresses, screen names are one way chat participants can present themselves online (Baym, 2000; Soukup, 1999, 2000, 2004, 2006). Screen names give chatters and Instant Messengers the ability to play with their sex and gender identity—a process termed **gender swapping** (Barnes, 2003). For example, "sallygo" appears to be a screen name of a woman, but through continuous chat room communication with this person or if a private online relationship forms, we may discover that "sallygo" is actually a man. Communication scholar Tim Jordan (1999) believes that this type of fluctuation with our identity in virtual communities is typical of the fluid or constantly emerging formations of the online self. Jordan uses the term **identity-fluidity** to articulate how our online identity may change at any moment with a simple change of screen name. In Table 10.3, different categories of screen names are provided, along with examples to illustrate each category.

Have you ever participated in an online chat room? If you did, what screen name did you create for yourself and in what ways was it an extension of your real (offline)

## TABLE 10.3    Screen Names

| CATEGORY | EXAMPLE | |
| --- | --- | --- |
| People using their real names | <JohnD> | <SueK> |
| Names relating to self or lack of self | <oldbuck> | <justagirl> |
| Technology-oriented names | <blogqueen> | <technophile> |
| Names of objects, flora, and fauna | <fordtruck> | <redrose> |
| Word play and sounds | <gogoboy> | <whathell> |
| Famous people and characters | <forestgump> | <elvis> |
| Sexually oriented or provocative names | <spankchick> | <sexslave> |

Table adapted and reproduced with permission of: Bechar-Israeli, H. (1995). From <Bonehead> to <cLoNehEAd>: Nicknames, play, and identity on Internet Relay Chat. *Journal of Computer-Mediated Communication, 1(2)*. Available: www.ascusc.org/jcmc/vol1/issue2/bechar.html

identity? In what ways did the screen name identity differ from your real identity? Have you ever experimented with altering your sex online—the practice described as gender swapping? Did chatters respond to you differently when you assumed a different sex online?

Because of the anonymity chat rooms afford, verbal aggression is fairly common, but such aggression can insult an entire online community or chat room. **Flaming** is a form of aggressive communication in which people who interact on topics or games of interest are personally attacked, disrupted, or heckled with aggressive comments, repetitive text, or foul language (Quercia, 1997). Flaming can also occur in asynchronous online channels, such as when someone posts a highly charged message to a **listserv** (a computer service that facilitates discussions by linking people who

## REMEMBER 10.3

**Asynchronous Time:**    messages posted at one time, then read at another time.

**Synchronous Time:**    CMC that occurs with little to no lag time between participants' comments.

**Chronemics:**    the communicative aspects of time.

**Screen Names:**    aliases or assumed names that chat participants select, rather than using their real names; the "nicknames" of online communication.

**Gender Swapping:**    through the use of screen names, participants experiment with sex/gender identity.

**Identity-Fluidity:**    how online identities can change at any moment with a simple change of screen name.

share common interests) or an **electronic bulletin board** (an online service in which anyone, not just a subscriber, can access and read postings) (Doyle, 1998; Hult & Huckin, 1999). When repeated comments of this nature "fan the flames," a **flame war** is often the result, with seriously negative consequences to users (Quercia, 1997). Listservs and bulletin boards often employ a "host"—someone connected to the service who edits comments so that participants are warned when flaming messages are about to be transmitted, or so that flaming messages don't get communicated to participants at all.

Another chat room behavior to consider has implications for nonverbal communication, proxemics in particular (Soukup, 2004, 2006). Sometimes participants prefer to enter a chat room and merely read the postings of other chatters—in essence, to follow the conversation without engaging in it, just as you might observe or overhear a conversation at a party from a distance. This form of virtual eavesdropping is termed **lurking** and it has some benefits. First, someone new to a chat room may feel more comfortable at first by being a casual observer, tracking the flow of conversation before deciding whether or not to offer a comment. This practice can be beneficial if you think you're in one sort of chat room, only to find out that your original perceptions about the nature of the chat room were wrong. You can simply exit the chat room without engaging in the flow of postings, so you've not been disruptive. As a second example, you may not be entirely new to the chat room, but you haven't entered it for awhile. Lurking allows you to pick back up the thread of a conversation and decide from a more informed stance whether or not you want to engage.

However, there is a downside to lurking, in that other participants may perceive you as an eavesdropper and may feel violated or deceived as a result. It's as though you watched and waited, manipulating a situation with less-than-honorable intentions. Occasionally, people with deviant or dangerous intentions will lurk in chat rooms, monitor the postings, then call out a certain chatter to enter into a private room—one in which other participants may not enter. We've all no doubt heard or read stories in which unknowing chatters' comments were monitored by a sexual deviant who lurked in a chat room, looked for certain characteristics revealed by someone's comments, and then attempted to develop an online relationship and, in some tragic cases, a face-to-face relationship.

Another area of study in the online arena pertains to deception (Burgoon, 2005; Zhou, Twitchell, Qin, Burgoon, & Nunamaker, 2003). To clarify, this line of research doesn't focus on online deception we tend to think of, like gender-bending or predators who mask their identities. This form of online deception is much more subtle, but likely more common. Information systems specialist Lina Zhou (2005) examined the deceptive behavior of online communicators using Instant Messaging to determine the differences in nonverbal behavior between deceivers and truth tellers. IM-ers were grouped into triads, each person with an individual computer, and each logged on to *Yahoo! Messenger* for the study. Each group's task was a version of the Desert Survival Problem, a problem-solving exercise in which group members must reach consensus on how to cope with a hypothetical life-or-death situation. Two of the three group members were instructed by the researchers to exchange truthful IMs (meaning express their actual opinions) as they worked through the exercise; the third member was told to give opinions that varied from what she or he really thought.

Zhou focused on the following sets of nonverbal cues: (1) Productivity, measured by the total number of words participants used in their online exchanges; (2) Participation, in terms of the number of turns participants took in IM exchanges, pauses between sending continuous messages, and response latency (how long a participant took to send a response to an incoming message); (3) Initiation, meaning if a participant started a discussion; (4) Spontaneous correction (messages that were deleted completely and replaced with new messages); (5) Word diversity; (6) Affect or the participants' expressions of emotions; (7) Cognition complexity, as indicated by thoughts and inferences expressed in messages; and (8) Non-immediacy in the form of such aspects as negative sentences, passive verbs, and self-references. Boiling down such a complicated study is a challenge, but, in essence, here's what Zhou found: Deceivers' nonverbal cues (as defined above) were significantly different from truth tellers' cues. More specifically, compared to truth tellers, deceivers participated more and initiated discussions in the IM exchanges more frequently, erased messages less frequently, took shorter pauses between messages, displayed lower word diversity, and expressed more positive attitudes and emotions during the task. We can't come up with a profile of deceptive IM-ers from this one study, but this research is a fascinating example of a new and growing direction for nonverbal scholars who wish to better understand what constitutes nonverbal cues and how they operate in the online realm.

## Emoticons

Another important nonverbal aspect of communication to be considered in CMC is the expression of emotion (Derks, Bos, & von Grumbkow, 2007; Walther & D'Addario, 2001). Without the usual nonverbal mechanisms in FtF communication that allow us to reveal our emotions to others, how do we let others at a distance know what we're feeling? Have you thought about how you communicate your emotions in an email message or chat room posting? Take a moment to think about how different the expression of emotion is when you don't have your face to smile or frown, your voice to scream or whisper, or the ability to reach out and touch or hug someone. In an effort to combat this deficit, **emoticons** were developed—an ingenious use of the common keyboard in which combinations of typed symbols convey emotions or instructions to readers (Boone & Kurtz, 1997; Derks, Bos, & von Grumbkow, 2007; Quercia, 1997). The most commonly used emoticon is the happy face or smiley, made by combining a colon, dash, and right parentheses mark, as in : – ). Some emoticons that frequently appear in email messages, chat room postings, and Instant Messaging appear in Table 10.4.

Communication scholars Murphy and Collins (1997) studied the CMC of students in instructional chat rooms—chat rooms related to courses students were taking. Their work revealed four interesting categories of nonverbal cues that are often added to the text of a message to enhance the meaning. These include: (1) adding underlining, punctuation, and capitalization to a text; (2) using graphic accents, such as smileys; (3) adding playfulness and humor; and (4) indicating a pause or continuation of a

## TABLE 10.4    Emoticons

**Emoticons** are means of expressing emotions in email or other forms of technological communication, using a common keyboard. Here are some of the most often-used emoticons:

| | |
|---|---|
| : - ) | Happy face or smiley |
| : - o | Surprised |
| : - ( | Depressed or upset by a remark |
| : - l | Indifferent |
| ; - ) | Winking at a suggestive or flirtatious remark |
| : - / | Skeptical |
| : - l | Straight faced or poker faced |
| : - P | Sticking your tongue out |
| : - D | Laughing |
| : - @ | Screaming |
| 8 – ) | Wearing sunglasses |
| :: - ) | Wearing regular glasses |
| ( - : | Left-handed |

Table adapted and reproduced with permission of: Beebe, S. A., Beebe, S. J., & Ivy, D. K. (2007). *Communication: Principles for a lifetime* (3rd ed.). Boston: Allyn & Bacon; Boone, L. E., & Kurtz, D. L. (1997). *Contemporary business.* New York: Dryden Press.

thought or statement through the use of ellipses. Consider the following chat room exchange between classmates after a test:

**Jose:**     Man that was a tough test!

**Matt:**     I *REALLY* DON'T GET IT. WHAT WAS PROF TRYING TO PROVE?!?!?

**Jamie:**    might be easier if you'd <u>actually</u> bought the book or come to class . . . . . : - )

The three chatters in this example employ multiple nonverbal cues to help classmates understand the meaning of their messages. First, punctuation (e.g., exclamation marks, asterisks, question marks) helps decipher the emotion behind the message. The second comment is typed in all caps (shouting), an indication of irritation or exasperation, perhaps even anger. Using all lower case letters, as in the third comment, increases the speed of typing and may communicate a certain informality, intimacy, or friendliness. Underlining a word, as in the third comment, offers emphasis, just as you would increase your volume to stress certain words in conversation. The ellipsis (series of periods) expresses a continuation of a thought, as well as the sarcasm or humor behind a verbal message. The smiley at the end functions to soften the sarcasm, which could be verbally translated as "I'm joking with you" or "just kidding."

These nonverbal techniques not only aid the translation of the verbal message, they add sociability to the exchange and express clues about the relationships between the chatters. One problem, however, is that punctuation beyond periods and commas, as well as other formatting options like underlining and italicizing, often reformat or get omitted in the transmission of a message from computer to computer. This is especially true when PC users communicate with Mac users, so users have to get even more creative when attempting to include such nonverbal elements in their online messages.

## Listening, Pausing, and Silence

How do you know if someone is actually listening to you or receiving your message in a chat room? Does someone's lack of response to your email make you feel like you're not being heard? CMC scholar Annette Markham (1998) wrote about the notions of listening and silence during virtual communication. She described the experience of interviewing online users for information for her book, and how she had to learn to be patient and tolerate pauses and silence in order to give people time to respond to her questions.

 In a world of "instant everything" and immediate communication channels like email and faxes, it's interesting to consider how some everyday experiences and nonverbal cues like silence are being redefined. We mentioned chronemics in the previous section; if you chat with people in an electronic newsgroup format, how do you handle **response latencies,** or how much time someone takes to formulate a response to a statement or question? Does the technology influence how long it takes you to respond to others' comments? Is the amount of time it takes for you to register silence in a face-to-face conversation comparable to an electronic format? A friend of ours recently went on ChristianMingle.com to meet men she might consider dating. One function of the site is similar to chat room interaction or Instant Messaging, in that participants can create an online connection so that they can have private exchanges and explore the potential for a relationship. When one person posts a message to another, while the other is responding an area blinks on the screen to indicate that the other person is typing. The blinking heightens the anticipation of receiving the next message and acts much like an "ah" or "um" in FtF conversation, a nonverbal signal that one is pausing to consider what to say next or how to say it. But what if the online responder gets interrupted or pauses to consider his or her words and the blinking stops? Might the person on the other end of the virtual connection think that her or his contact had a change of heart?

**Voice recognition software** is becoming increasingly popular and accessible. We know from Chapter 9 on vocalics that each human voice has unique qualities, but to think that a computer could hear those qualities and respond to them may seem like the stuff of a futuristic movie or novel. For you *Star Trek* fans, many have longed for the day that you could walk into your office or home, say "computer" out loud, and have that computer recognize your voice and turn itself on or come out of sleep mode. Voice recognition software that can be installed in your home or office computer can do just that—recognize your voice and respond to it. Another feature of this relatively new form of technology is that it allows you to speak into a microphone and the computer will listen to you and post your words on a screen. IBM's *Via Voice Gold* and Dragon System's *Naturally Speaking Preferred* are but two examples of voice recognition software that people are finding increasingly useful and affordable.

But can computers listen empathically? Although voice recognition software permits you to speak words that your computer will then print, computers do not yet have the sophistication to listen and respond with the same sensitivity as people. But computer researchers are working on it. Stanford University professors Byron Reeves and Clifford Nass have been working for more than two decades to discover ways that computers can interact with people more humanistically. Using research results on human interaction, Reeves and Nass first identified four major personality types (dominant, submissive, friendly, and unfriendly) and common communication patterns for each. Next they developed strategies computers can be programmed to use that more closely emulate human responses according to the four personality types. In one provocative outcome from their research, Reeves and Nass (1996) discovered that people react to computers much in the same way that they react to other people. In specific, they found the following:

1. People think they perform better on a computer task when they are flattered by a computer.
2. People like a computer more when they are flattered by it.
3. The appropriateness of praise has no impact on what people think about a computer that has praised them.
4. People like a computer more and believe that a computer is better when it praises them, rather than when it criticizes them.

Although computers may not yet listen with the sensitivity and empathy of your best friend, researchers continue to work on software that can better emulate human interaction. Who knows? Perhaps someday your computer can sit with you and have a good cry.

*The capability of computers to communicate emotional responses may develop over these kids' lifetime.*

![knot icon] **REMEMBER 10.4**

| | |
|---|---|
| **Flaming:** | aggressive online communication that intentionally disrupts, heckles, and harasses others. |
| **Listserv:** | online service that facilitates discussion by linking people who share common interests. |
| **Electronic Bulletin Board:** | online service in which anyone, not just a subscriber, can access and read postings. |
| **Flame War:** | when repeated aggressive comments in an online community, such as a listserv or bulletin board, "fan the flames" and generate increased negativity. |
| **Lurking:** | entering a chat room and merely reading the postings of other chatters without engaging in the interaction. |
| **Emoticons:** | combination of electronic symbols typed out for the recipient of an electronic message. |
| **Response Latency:** | how long it takes someone to formulate a response to a statement or question in online or FtF interaction. |
| **Voice Recognition Software:** | technology that allows computers to recognize voices, respond to commands, and post one's words on a screen. |

# CMC VERSUS FACE-TO-FACE (FtF) COMMUNICATION

Researchers offer several theories to explain the differences between CMC and FtF communication. As summarized by communication theory expert Em Griffin (2006), **social presence theory** suggests that online communication is an isolating activity, in that it reduces users' sense that other people are jointly involved in an interaction. This lack of social presence makes CMC vastly different from FtF communication. **Media richness theory** classifies each communication medium according to the complexity of the messages it can handle effectively. These theories point to the absence of nonverbal cues as a major deficit in CMC, meaning that the lack of nonverbal communication cues during CMC is disadvantageous for the development, maintenance, and termination of relationships (Griffin, 2006). For some of us, understanding the presence or absence of nonverbal communication codes in face-to-face versus computer-mediated communication can be confusing. We've included Table 10.5 to emphasize the differences where nonverbal communication is concerned.

## Social Information Processing Theory (SIP)

Communication scholar Joseph Walther (1995) developed **social information processing theory (SIP)** to explain how CMC and face-to-face communication are equally useful channels for developing close relationships. Walther's SIP theory suggests that relationships grow only to the extent that parties first gain information about each

**TABLE 10.5  Nonverbal Codes in Face-to-Face Versus Computer-Mediated Communication**

| NONVERBAL CODE | FACE-TO-FACE COMMUNICATION (FtF) | COMPUTER-MEDIATED COMMUNICATION (CMC) |
|---|---|---|
| Kinesics (Body Movement, Gestures, and Posture) | Gestures can substitute for or accent verbal communication. | Avatars convey emotion through characters who imitate or portray human characteristics. |
| Facial/Eye Behavior | The face and eyes are instrumental in regulating interaction. Facial features send unintended messages. | Emoticons represent facial expressions which indicate the mood of the user. |
| Vocalics (Paralanguage) | Vocal characteristics such as pitch, rate, and volume influence how others interpret our verbal messages. | Voice technology enables online communication. Typed punctuation, formatting, and font selection indicate inflection. |
| Proxemics/ Territoriality | Territoriality and our use of personal space influence our communication and reveal our thoughts, attitudes, and emotions. | Response time in CMC creates a feeling of distance or closeness. Online journals are private, personal spaces for users. Avatar placement brings attention to space. |
| Touch (Haptics) | Touch is the most powerful and misunderstood nonverbal code, and can convey an array of emotions and meanings. | Verbal immediacy in instant messages, emails, and chat rooms creates a sense of touch, as if the receiver is with us. As with the physical body, the virtual body can be sexualized and abused online (e.g., cybersex, cyber-rape). |
| Environment | Our surroundings communicate who we are and influence how we behave and interact. | Virtual communities, such as MySpace, create webs of personal relationships in cyberspace. Surroundings on web pages can create a constant or variant sense of self, just like physical environments maintained offline. |
| Physical Appearance | Clothing, artifacts, weight, height, tattoos, piercings, and skin color are elements of physical appearance that people observe and judge us by. | We can post digitally modified pictures of ourselves online. We can also describe our idealized, fantasized virtual body. Gender-swapping and the use of avatars alter the virtual body. |

other and then use that information to form impressions or composite mental images. In contrast to other CMC theories, Walther recognizes that nonverbal cues are filtered out of the information exchanged via CMC, but he doesn't believe that this loss is detrimental to the development of successful and satisfying online relationships.

Two features of CMC provide a rationale for SIP theory. The first feature relates to **verbal cues,** in that CMC users can create fully formed impressions of others based solely on linguistic (verbal) content of messages. In essence, Walther doesn't believe that nonverbal cues must be present for communication to facilitate the development of a relationship. The second feature, **extended time,** means that although the exchange of social information is slower through CMC than in face-to-face channels, over time online relationships are not weaker or more fragile than FtF relationships (Walther, 1995, 2002).

Walther claims that people desire attachment and connection just as much online as they do in face-to-face interaction. Given the absence of or diminished nonverbal cues in CMC, which typically signal affinity (liking), users must rely on text-only messages to make connections with other users. In one test of SIP theory, Walther and colleagues examined CMC users' pursuit of social goals and expressions of affinity (Walther, Loh, & Granka, 2005). In this study, participants discussed a moral dilemma with a stranger in either a CMC or face-to-face setting. The stranger was, in actuality, a research associate (confederate) told to pursue a specific communication goal with the study's subjects. Half of the confederates interacted in a friendly manner and half interacted in an unfriendly manner. Results of the study showed that mode of communication (CMC versus FtF) made no difference in the emotional tone perceived by participants. Participants' self-disclosure, praise, and explicit statements of affection successfully communicated warmth in both channels of interaction.

## REMEMBER 10.5

| | |
|---|---|
| **Social Presence Theory:** | CMC theory that suggests that online communication is an isolating activity, in that it reduces users' sense that other people are jointly involved in interaction. |
| **Media Richness Theory:** | CMC theory that classifies each communication medium according to the complexity of the messages it can handle efficiently. |
| **Social Information Processing Theory (SIP):** | CMC perspective that suggests that online relationships grow only to the extent that parties gain information about each other and use it to form impressions or mental images. |
| **Verbal Cues:** | CMC users can create fully formed impressions of others based solely on verbal content of messages. |
| **Extended Time:** | the exchange of social information is slower through CMC than in face-to-face channels, but over time online relationships are not weaker or more fragile than FtF relationships. |

# ■ THE VIRTUAL BODY

One of the most interesting nonverbal codes that has significant impact on the FtF context, but which is diminished or nonexistent in the CMC context, is physical appearance. As we mentioned in Chapter 5, U.S. culture (as well as many other cultures around the world) places a great deal of emphasis on looks. One important aspect within the larger category of physical appearance is the body, a topic increasing in significance in communication research (Corey, 2007).

Researchers have long debated the importance of the **physical body** (the body that is not mediated, but real and existing in face-to-face communication) in human impression formation and relationship development. Examinations of the impact of the **virtual body** (the body that is mediated, represented, or constructed through email, pictures, descriptions, avatars, and emoticons) on computer-mediated communication are increasing (Andersen, 2004; Corey, 2007; Hammers, 2007; Lipka, 2008; McRae, 1996; Whitty, 2003; Whitty & Carr, 2003; Young, 2008b).

Our body and the way we talk about and portray it is important, given the increasing frequency of online relationships (McCown, Fisher, Page, & Homant, 2001; Parks & Roberts, 1998). Have you or has someone you know ever initiated a relationship online? For those of you familiar with this experience, you know that it's not uncommon for some of the first questions to be about age, sex, appearance, and location. So, it seems that one of the first things that interests people who seek a potential romantic partner is the body. In fact, researchers have studied the development of online relationships and have found that some of the first questions between interactants focus on physical appearance (Whitty & Gavin, 2001).

## Cyber-Flirting

One aspect of CMC that is particularly interesting to think about is **cyber-flirting**—representing the body online in order to attract others (Whitty, 2004). But you may be thinking: How can someone flirt online? Some of you may be experienced with this skill, others of you may just now be ready to step up to the keyboard and give it a try, and still others of you will never engage in this activity. (Play at your own risk is our best advice.) For flirting to occur online, the body needs to be represented through text. For example, instead of preparing to look good for a face-to-face date, individuals online create a first impression by describing through text how attractive they appear. One important difference between FtF and CMC encounters is that there are no restrictions to the way the virtual body looks, since the Internet allows a person to create a new and improved body through text (McRae, 1996; Whitty, 2003, 2004; Whitty & Carr, 2003). This new and improved body can have an ideal weight, perfect skin, a good job, confidence—a whole array of characteristics and attributes that may or may not be the reality.

Cyber-flirting and Internet dating give people an alternative to more traditional meeting places (e.g., bars, coffee shops, parties). Online relationships do decrease the emphasis on physical appearance—an aspect of attraction many deem unimportant, but with which society seems obsessed. But it's important to realize some drawbacks to this form of connecting. Specifically, the research team of McCown, Fisher, Page, and Homant (2001) found in their study of Internet relationships that a substantial number of men and women reported lying online about their age and physical appearance. Men in the study revealed a higher rate of lying (77 percent), compared to women (46 percent). What does this teach us? If you are going to try Internet dating, realize that the people you're connecting with onscreen may not have the beautiful body they describe. A brother of one of your textbook's authors has been divorced for more than 10 years and has tried Internet dating. His testimony sums up the dark side of this experience: "I met seven women in an online dating forum. All of them lied about their age and body weight."

## Internet Dating and Online Love

While Internet dating can be filled with deception, increasingly many men and women in both heterosexual and homosexual relationships are going online to seek romance (Couch & Liamputtong, 2008; Eharmony patents, 2004; McKenna, Green, & Gleason, 2002). In fact, Internet dating services have become normalized to the extent that web services like eharmony.com and match.com are commonly advertised on television (Arvidsson, 2006; Gibbs, Ellison, & Heino, 2006; Lawson & Leck, 2006; Peter & Valkenburg, 2007). Ads focus on successful relationships that begin on the Internet—couples who experience "love at first *site*."

In fact, many major newspapers, including *USA Today*, have featured the popularity and success of Internet relationships. On a smaller scale, both authors of this book have been interviewed by our local newspaper about gender issues, romantic relationships, and cyber-dating. For a special Valentine's Day article on Internet dating several years ago, a reporter from the local paper wanted to interview an academic expert on communication, whom she assumed would support her slant in the story. She didn't receive the response she was looking for, because one of your authors talked about the negative aspects of Internet dating for at least 10 minutes! After listening patiently, she kindly asked, "Dr. Wahl, can you talk about some of the positive things about Internet dating?"

## Cybersex: Getting "Virtually" Physical

As online relationships develop, it's not uncommon for people to have sexual experiences (Couch & Liamputtong, 2008; Hammers, 2007; Lee & Wahl, 2007). **Cybersex**—sexual experiences, fantasies, and interactions that are exchanged in real time through the Internet—is a topic important to the study of online relational development, even though many online relationships develop successfully without sexual activity. Cybersex is very personal and intimate for people in Internet relationships; it can serve an important maintenance function for people who are geographically separated (i.e., in long-distance relationships) (Booth & Jung, 1996). Many people who participate in cybersex view it as just as satisfying and essential as face-to-face sexual activity. For some, it's preferable because cybersex lacks the complications that FtF sex may evoke. However, many people who participate in cybersex do not use their real names and view it as entertainment.

If people are in face-to-face, monogamous relationships and they have cybersex with someone else online, do you consider that to be cheating, meaning computer adultery or infidelity? Interestingly, researchers have reported varying reactions to cybersex with someone other than one's partner. Some people view it as adultery and fair grounds for divorce (Averyt, 1997; Fiely, 2003; Kennedy, Ben-Ali, & Bertrand, 1996), while others compare it to reading a sexy novel (Turkle, 1995). The physical body versus the virtual body comes into play here. Nonverbal communication codes, such as physical appearance and touch, are important in making a distinction between sexual experiences with the physical body in FtF settings versus those experiences with the virtual body online.

## Cyber-Rape: Abusing the Virtual Body Versus the Physical Body

This is not an easy or comfortable topic, but it's important to understand. Consider the step into an area that goes beyond cybersex. If we consent to cybersex, we're agreeing for our body, whether we think of it as physical or virtual, to engage in a particular experience (Corey, 2007; Hammers, 2007). But what happens if we're coerced or forced to do something online that we don't consent to? One view is that we can simply "log off" or exit the space if we're uncomfortable. However, some Internet communities have reported unwanted sexual acts and coercion of the body, so obviously interactants merely leaving the exchange isn't as simple as it sounds. What we are referring to is **cyber-rape**—the use of online communication to force virtual characters or participants to unwillingly perform sexual acts. Whether or not you've heard of this phenomenon, cyber-rape is a real, emotional experience and some people have evidenced post-traumatic stress after the rape (Michals, 1997).

According to Barnes (2003), behind virtual communities and online games "are actual people with real emotional responses. Rape in cyberspace illustrates how people can blur the distinctions between on and offline experience and exemplifies how the emotional content of cyberspace can bleed into the real world" (pp. 257–258). You may be thinking: What does a cyber-rape look (or read) like? Free-lance author Debra Michals (1997) wondered the same thing, and so she entered into an America Online (AOL) chat room, where she observed her first online gang rape. Here's an excerpt of what appeared on her screen, but be forewarned—this is graphic material you're probably not used to reading in a textbook (or anywhere). The names have been changed, but are similar to those used online.

**Greg0987:** Hold her down, guys.
**Panther:** I got her legs.
**Robodude:** I got her pinned.
**Greg0987:** She wants it bad. Don't ya bitch?
**Bigone:** Like it rough? Hit her in the face, Greg. Smash her.
**Tiger:** Don't move or I'll cut you with this knife.
**Greg0987:** Me first, then the rest of you go. Stop moving or I'll hit you, bitch!
**Meg:** What the hell is going on in here?
**Greg0987:** Chill out. We're just playing.
**Meg:** Playing? Women are raped and beaten every day, and it isn't play.
**Greg0987:** If you don't like it, get out of here. You don't have to stay.

---

### REMEMBER 10.6

| | |
|---|---|
| **Physical Body:** | the body that is not mediated, but real and existing in face-to-face communication. |
| **Virtual Body:** | the body that is mediated, represented, or constructed through email messages, pictures, descriptions, avatars, and emoticons. |
| **Cyber-Flirting:** | representing the body online in order to attract others. |
| **Cybersex:** | sexual experiences, fantasies, interactions, and descriptions that are exchanged in real time through the Internet. |
| **Cyber-Rape:** | use of online channels to force virtual characters to unwillingly perform sexual acts. |

---

In this scenario, an unsuspecting female user (someone presenting herself online as female, at least) engaged in chat room communication, only to witness the conversation take a turn at her expense and the pace of the postings increase dramatically. This excerpt of cyber-rape text shows the blending of the experience of the physical body and the virtual body. At times, such blending can be liberating, but at other times, such as the cyber-rape example illustrates, it can be confusing, perhaps even terrifying. If and when you communicate online, be aware of the differences between CMC and FtF communication, be particularly aware of the role of online nonverbal cues, and take just as many precautions (maybe more) with who you meet and spend time with online as you do in your non-virtual life. While many positive aspects of CMC exist, some aspects are quite troubling.

## SUMMARY ▪ ▪ ▪ ▪ ▪

In this chapter, we provided an application of nonverbal communication to the Internet. We defined computer-mediated communication (CMC), including virtual communities, and discussed how nonverbal communication codes are an important aspect of presenting oneself online. Recall the nonverbal communication cues that are altered in CMC (e.g., physical appearance, vocalics, gestures, distance, time), some of which can be represented online with text and graphics.

Next we discussed the nonverbal dimensions of email as a channel for communication. Factors such as email addresses, font choice, signature files, and stylistic features of email messages are important considerations when communicating online. While anonymity can be empowering, remember the potential consequences of anonymity and the impressions that others may form about you, both personally and professionally, as a result of such simple choices you make in your online communication. We also examined verbal aggression—self-serving communication that does not take a receiver's feelings or rights into account—which is particularly ineffective in online contexts.

In the next section of this chapter, we examined the significance of nonverbal communication in chat rooms and Instant Messaging contexts, with special attention to the exploration of identity that the Internet allows. You may also recall that emoticons are often used to express emotions and provide nonverbal context in CMC. As a conclusion to this section, we explored nonverbal indications of listening, pausing, and silence in CMC.

Differences between CMC and face-to-face (FtF) communication are informed by a number of communication theories. We discussed more in depth social information processing theory (SIP) to explain how CMC and FtF communication are equally useful channels for developing close relationships. Two features of CMC—verbal cues and extended time—provide a rationale for SIP theory, leading some researchers to conclude that FtF and online relationships form and maintain themselves in similar ways.

In the final section of this chapter, we contrasted the physical and the virtual body. Nonverbal communication is an important part of cyber-flirting, which you should recall is representing the body online through text in order to attract others. We also examined other experiences of the virtual body, including Internet dating and cybersex, both of which are significantly related to how physical appearance is managed in CMC. We ended the chapter by exploring a more sinister extension of the virtual body—cyber-rape. This aspect of CMC shows that behind the screen are real people who can have emotional reactions to what happens to the body online. We trust that your reading of this chapter has provided you with an understanding of some of the more important aspects of nonverbal communication and how they influence CMC.

## DISCUSSION STARTERS

1. What are the primary differences between face-to-face (FtF) communication and computer-mediated communication (CMC)? What nonverbal cues are missing or altered in CMC, and how do they affect online interaction?

2. How do you feel when you send an email message and get no response? What nonverbal impression do you get about the person you emailed? What if the person takes a long time to reply to your message (response latency)—might your feelings or impressions of the person be altered by the delay?

3. Do you think using a smiley face or other emoticon helps you communicate your feelings when emailing or posting in a chat room, or have emoticons become just mere expected punctuation or adornments? Is it easier for you to communicate your personal feelings online as opposed to face to face? Why?

4. Have you ever been misunderstood during or as a result of an online exchange? If so, what was the cause of the misunderstanding? Were you at fault, the other person, or both? Did you or the other person change your online behavior to avoid future misunderstandings?

5. Do you believe that online relationships are just as strong and important as face-to-face relationships? Why?

6. What is the difference between the physical body and the virtual body? Does your physical body differ from your virtual body?

## REFERENCES

Andersen, P. A. (2004). *The complete idiot's guide to body language*. New York: Alpha.

Arvidsson, A. (2006). "Quality singles": Internet dating and the work of fantasy. *New Media and Society, 8*, 671–690.

Atkin, C. K., Smith, S. W., Roberto, A. J., Fediuk, T., & Wagner, T. (2002). Correlates of verbally aggressive communication in adolescents. *Journal of Applied Communication Research, 30*, 251–268.

Averyt, L. (1997, September 21). Caught in adultery's new 'net. *Corpus Christi Caller Times*, pp. A1, A10.

Bailenson, J. N. (2008, April 4). Why digital avatars make the best teachers. *The Chronicle of Higher Education*, p. B27.

Ballard, D. I., & Seibold, D. R. (2000). Time orientation and temporal variation across work groups: Implications for group and organizational communication. *Western Journal of Communication*, *64*, 218–242.

Barnes, S. B. (2003). *Computer-mediated communication: Human-to-human communication across the Internet.* Boston: Allyn & Bacon.

Baym, N. (2000). *Tune in, log on: Soaps, fandom, and online community.* Thousand Oaks, CA: Sage.

Bechar-Israeli, H. (1995). From <Bonehead> to <cLoNehEAd>: Nicknames, play, and identity on Internet Relay Chat. *Journal of Computer-Mediated Communication [Online]*, *1(2)*. Available: www.ascusc.org/jcmc/vol1/issue2/bechar.html

Beebe, S. A., Beebe, S. J., & Ivy, D. K. (2007). *Communication: Principles for a lifetime* (3rd ed.). Boston: Allyn & Bacon.

Birdwhistell, R. L. (1970). *Kinesics and context.* Philadelphia: University of Pennsylvania Press.

Boone, L. E., & Kurtz, D. L. (1997). *Contemporary business.* New York: Dryden.

Booth, R., & Jung, M. (1996). *Romancing the net.* Rocklin, CA: Prima Publishing.

Bringhurst, R. (2004). *The elements of typographic style* (3rd ed.). New York: Harts and Marks.

Burgoon, J. K. (2005, November). *Truth, lies and virtual worlds.* The Carroll C. Arnold Distinguished Lecture, National Communication Association. Boston: Allyn & Bacon.

Byron, K., & Baldridge, D. C. (2007). E-mail recipients' impressions of senders' likability: The interactive effect of nonverbal cues and recipients' personality. *Journal of Business Communication*, *44*, 137–160.

Corey, A. M. (2007). Body politics in online communication. *Texas Speech Communication Journal*, *32*, 21–32.

Couch, D., & Liamputtong, P. (2008). Online dating and mating: The use of the Internet to meet sexual partners. *Qualitative Health Research*, *18*, 269–279.

Danet, B. (2001). *Cyberpl@y: Communicating online.* Oxford, UK: Berg Publishers.

Derks, D., Bos, A. E. R., & von Grumbkow, J. (2007). Emoticons and social interaction on the Internet: The importance of social context. *Computers in Human Behavior*, *23*, 842–849.

Doyle, T. A. (1998). *Allyn & Bacon quick guide to the Internet for speech communication.* Boston: Allyn & Bacon.

Eharmony patents its formula for romance. (2004, May 30). *Corpus Christi Caller Times*, p. A2.

Farrell, E. F. (2005, September 2). Logging on, tuning out. *The Chronicle of Higher Education*, p. A46.

Fiely, D. (2003). Cyber-infidelity: Internet access implicated in growing number of divorces. *The Columbus Dispatch*, Health and Medicine Week [Electronic Version].

Foster, A. L. (2008, April 4). What happens in a virtual world has a real-world impact, a scholar finds. *The Chronicle of Higher Education*, p. A14.

Gibbs, J. L., Ellison, N. B., & Heino, R. D. (2006). Self-presentation in online personals: The role of anticipated future interaction, self-disclosure, and perceived success in Internet dating. *Communication Research*, *33*, 152–177.

Goffman, E. (1959). *The presentation of self in everyday life.* Garden City, NJ: Doubleday Anchor Books.

Griffin, E. (2006). *A first look at communication theory* (6th ed.). New York: McGraw-Hill.

Hammers, M. L. (2007). Desire and fantasy in online RPGs: Bridging the gap between self and other. *Texas Speech Communication Journal*, *32*, 44–52.

Hancock, J. T., & Dunham, P. J. (2001). Impression formation in computer-mediated communication revisited: An analysis of the breadth and intensity of impressions. *Communication Research*, *28*, 325–347.

Harasim, L., Hiltz, S. R., Teles, L., & Turoff, M. (1995). *Learning networks.* Cambridge, MA: MIT Press.

Hardey, M. (2004). Mediated relationships, authenticity, and the possibility of romance. *Communication and Society*, *7*, 207–222.

Heisel, A. D., La France, B. H., & Beatty, M. J. (2003). Self-reported extraversion, neuroticism, and psychoticism as predictors of peer rated verbal aggressiveness and affinity-seeking competence. *Communication Monographs*, *70*, 1–15.

Hermes, J. J. (2008, April 25). Colleges create Facebook-style social networks to reach alumni. *The Chronicle of Higher Education*, p. A18.

Hiltz, S. R. (1994). *The virtual classroom: Learning without limits via computer networks.* Norwood, NJ: Ablex.

Hiltz, S. R., & Turoff, M. (1993). *The network nation: Human communication via computer.* Reading, MA: Addison-Wesley.

Hult, C. A., & Huckin, T. N. (1999). *The new century handbook.* Boston: Allyn & Bacon.

Infante, D. A., & Rancer, A. S. (1996). Argumentativeness and verbal aggressiveness: A review of recent theory and research. *Communication Yearbook 19*, 319–351.

Infante, D. A., Riddle, B. L., Horvath, C. L., & Tumlin, S. A. (1992). Verbal aggressiveness: Messages and reasons. *Communication Quarterly*, *40*, 116–126.

Jones, S. G. (1997). The Internet and its social landscape. In S. G. Jones (Ed.), *Virtual culture: Identity and communication in cybersociety* (pp. 7–35). Thousand Oaks, CA: Sage.

Jordan, T. (1999). *Cyberpower: The culture and politics of cyberspace and the Internet.* London: Routledge.

Kennedy, H., Ben-Ali, R., & Bertrand, D. (1996, February 3). Cybersuit to trash: Experts. *The New York Daily News,* p. 5.

Lawson, H. M., & Leck, K. (2006). Dynamics of Internet dating. *Social Science Computer Review, 24,* 189–208.

Lee, R., & Wahl, S. T. (2007). Justifying surveillance and control: An analysis of the media framing of pedophiles and the Internet. *Texas Speech Communication Journal, 32,* 1–15.

Li, N., Jackson, M. H., & Trees, A. R. (2008). Relating online: Managing dialectical contradictions in massively multiplayer online role-playing game relationships. *Games and Culture, 3,* 76–97.

Lipka, S. (2008). The digital limits of in loco parentis: Colleges avert gaze from students' posts on social-network sites. *The Chronicle of Higher Education,* p. A1.

Markham, A. N. (1998). *Life online: Researching real experience in virtual space.* Walnut Creek, CA: Alta Mira Press.

Martey, R. M., & Stromer-Galley, J. (2007). The digital dollhouse: Context and social norms in The Sims Online. *Games and Culture, 2,* 314–334.

Marvin, C. (1988). *When old technologies were new: Thinking about electronic communication in the late nineteenth century.* Oxford, UK: Oxford University Press.

McCown, J. A., Fisher, D., Page, R., & Homant, M. (2001). Internet relationships: People who meet people. *Cyberpsychology and Behavior, 4,* 593–596.

McKenna, K. Y. A., Green, A. S., & Gleason, M. E. J. (2002). Relationship formation on the Internet: What's the big attraction? *Journal of Social Issues, 58,* 9–31.

McRae, S. (1996). Coming apart at the seams: Sex, text, and the virtual body. In L. Cherny & L. R. Weise (Eds.), *Wired women: Gender and new realities in cyberspace* (pp. 242–263). Seattle: Seal Press.

Michals, D. (1997, March/April). Cyber-rape: How virtual is it? *Ms.,* 68.

Mitchell, W. J. (1995). *City of bits: Space, place, and the infobahn.* Cambridge, MA: MIT Press.

Murphy, K. L., & Collins, M. P. (1997). Communication conventions in instructional electronic chats. *First Monday, 2(11).* Available: www.firstmonday.dk/issues/issue2_11/murphy/index.html

Myers, S. A, & Rocca, K. A. (2001). Perceived instructor argumentativeness and verbal aggressiveness in the college classroom: Effects on student perceptions of climate, apprehension, and state motivation. *Western Journal of Communication, 65,* 113–137.

Parks, M. R., & Roberts, L. D. (1998). "Making MOOsic": The development of personal relationships on-line and a comparison to their offline counterparts. *Journal of Social and Personal Relationships, 15,* 517–537.

Peter, J., & Valkenburg, P. M. (2007). Who looks for casual dates on the Internet? A test of the compensation and the recreation of hypotheses. *New Media and Society, 9,* 455–474.

Pollock, S. L. (2006). Internet counseling and its feasibility for marriage and family counseling. *The Family Journal: Counseling and Therapy for Couples and Families, 14,* 65–70.

Poster, M. (1990). *The mode of information: Post-structuralism and social context.* Cambridge, MA: Polity.

Quercia, V. (1997). *Internet in a nutshell.* Cambridge, MA: O'Reilly.

Ramirez, A. J., & Burgoon, J. K. (2004). The effect of interactivity on initial interactions: The influence of information valence and modality and information richness on computer-mediated interaction. *Communication Monographs, 71,* 422–447.

Reeves, B., & Nass, C. (1996). *The media equation: How people treat computers, television, and new media like real people and places.* Stanford, CA: CSLI Publications.

Rheingold, H. (1993). *The virtual community. Homesteading on the electronic frontier.* Reading, MA: Addison-Wesley.

Riley, P., Keough, C. M., Christianson, T., Meilich, O., & Pierson, J. (1998). Community or colony: The case of online newspapers and the web. *Journal of Computer-Mediated Communication, 4(1).* Available: http://jcmc.huji.ac.il/issue4/riley.html

Rocca, K. A. (2004). College student attendance: Impact of instructor immediacy and verbal aggression. *Communication Education, 53,* 185–195.

Rosen, J. (2000). *The unwanted gaze: The destruction of privacy in America.* New York: Random House.

Schrodt, P. (2003). Students' appraisals of instructors as a function of students' perceptions of instructors' aggressive communication. *Communication Education, 52,* 106–121.

Soukup, C. (1999). The gendered interactional patterns of computer-mediated chat rooms: A critical ethnographic study. *The Information Society: An International Journal, 15,* 169–176.

Soukup, C. (2000). Building a theory of multimedia CMC: An analysis, critique, and integration of computer-mediated communication theory and research. *New Media and Society, 2,* 407–425.

Soukup, C. (2004). Multimedia performance in computer-mediated community: Communication as a virtual drama. *Journal of Computer-Mediated Communication, 9(4).* Available: http://jcmc.indiana.edu/vol9/issue4/soukup.html

Soukup, C. (2006). Computer-mediated communication as a virtual third place: Building Oldenburg's great good places on the world wide web. *New Media and Society, 8,* 421–440.

Sproull, L., & Kiesler, S. (1991). *Connections: New ways of working in the networked organization.* Cambridge, MA: Nelson Hall.

Stafford, L., Kline, S. L., & Dimmick, J. (1999). Home e-mail: Relational maintenance and gratification opportunities. *Journal of Broadcasting and Electronic Media, 43,* 659–669.

Starks, K. M. (2007). Bye bye love: Computer-mediated communication and relational dissolution. *Texas Speech Communication Journal, 32,* 11–20.

Strate, L. (1999). The varieties of cyberspace: Problems in definition and delimitation. *Western Journal of Communication, 63,* 382–412.

Thompson, B. (2008). Characteristics of parent-teacher e-mail communication. *Communication Education, 57,* 201–223.

Tidwell, L. C., & Walther, J. B. (2002). Computer-mediated communication effects on disclosure, impressions, and interpersonal evaluations: Getting to know one another a bit at a time. *Human Communication Research, 28,* 317–348.

Turkle, S. (1995). *Life on the screen: Identity in the age of the Internet.* New York: Simon & Schuster.

Virnoche, M. E., & Marx, G. T. (1997). "Only connect." E. M. Forster in an age of electronic communication: Computer-mediated association and community networks. *Sociological Inquiry, 67,* 85–100.

Wahl, S. T., McBride, M. C., & Schrodt, P. (2005). Becoming "point and click" parents: A case study of communication and online adoption. *Journal of Family Communication, 5,* 279–294.

Walther, J. B. (1995). Relational aspects of computer-mediated communication: Experimental observations over time. *Organizational Science, 6,* 186–202.

Walther, J. B. (2002). Time effects in computer-mediated groups: Past, present, and future. In P. J. Hinds & S. Kiesler (Eds.), *Distributed work* (pp. 235–257). Cambridge, MA: MIT Press.

Walther, J. B., & D'Addario, K. P. (2001). The impact of emoticons on message interpretation in computer-mediated communication. *Social Science Computer Review, 19,* 324–347.

Walther, J. B., Loh, T., & Granka, L. (2005). Let me count the ways: The interchange of verbal and nonverbal cues in computer-mediated and face-to-face affinity. *Journal of Language and Social Psychology, 24,* 36–65.

Walther, J. B., Slovacek, C. L., & Tidwell, L. C. (2001). "Is a picture worth a thousand words?" Photographic images in long-term and short-term computer-mediated communication. *Communication Research, 28,* 105–134.

Whitty, M. T. (2003). Cyber-flirting: Playing at love on the Internet. *Theory and Psychology, 13,* 339–357.

Whitty, M. T. (2004). Cyber-flirting: An examination of men's and women's flirting behavior both off-line and on the Internet. *Behavior Change, 21,* 115–126.

Whitty, M. T., & Carr, A. N. (2003). Cyberspace as potential space: Considering the web as a playground to cyber-flirt. *Human Relations, 56,* 861–891.

Whitty, M. T., & Gavin, J. K. (2001). Age/sex/location: Uncovering the social cues in the development of on-line relationships. *Cyberpsychology and Behavior, 4,* 623–630.

Wollman, D. (2008, March). Get ahead: Don't be an email ass. *Laptop,* pp. 120–121.

Wright, K. (2004). On-line relational maintenance strategies and perceptions of partners with exclusively Internet-based and primarily Internet-based relationships. *Communication Studies, 55,* 239–253.

Yee, N., Bailenson, J. N., Urbanek, M., Chang, F., & Merget, D. (2008). The unbearable likeness of being digital: The persistence of nonverbal social norms in online virtual environments. In L. K. Guerrero & M. L. Hecht (Eds.), *The nonverbal communication reader: Classic and contemporary readings* (3rd ed., pp. 203–208). Prospect Heights, IL: Waveland.

Young, J. B. (2008a). Forget e-mail: New messaging service has students and professors atwitter. *The Chronicle of Higher Education,* p. A15.

Young, J. B. (2008b). YouTube professors: Scholars as online video stars. *The Chronicle of Higher Education,* p. A19.

Zhou, L. (2005). An empirical investigation of deception behavior in Instant Messaging. *IEEE Transactions on Professional Communication, 48,* 147–160.

Zhou, L., Twitchell, D., Qin, T., Burgoon, J. K., & Nunamaker, J. F., Jr. (2003). An exploratory study into deception detection in text-based computer-mediated communication. *Proceedings of the 36th Hawaii International Conference on System Sciences.* Los Alamitos, CA: IEEE.

# Nonverbal Communication in Professional and Educational Contexts

## CHAPTER OUTLINE ■ ■ ■ ■ ■ ■

## CHAPTER OBJECTIVES ■ ■ ■ ■ ■ ■

After studying this chapter, you should be able to:

1. Understand the importance of nonverbal communication in professional life.

2. Distinguish between direct and indirect nonverbal communication with regard for the job search process.

3. Identify and describe key nonverbal communication codes to be aware of in job interviewing.

4. Apply nonverbal communication codes to the superior–subordinate relationship in professional settings.

5. Understand the importance of coworker nonverbal communication.

6. Describe nonverbal behaviors most important to customer relations personnel.

7. Identify the nonverbal essentials of leadership.

8. Define emotional intelligence as an essential quality of leaders, and describe its similarities to nonverbal communication sensitivity.

9. Understand the importance of nonverbal communication in educational settings.

10. Apply nonverbal communication codes to learning environments and teacher behavior.

11. Define teacher immediacy and offer examples of immediate teacher nonverbal behavior in the college classroom.

12. Describe the most common student nonverbal cues, including adapting behavior, misbehavior, and cues related to students with disabilities.

## CASE STUDY   Jordan's Performance Review

Jordan works as a client relations representative for a large company—his first job since graduating from college with a business degree. Jordan's professional goal is to work his way up into management; he's confident that his degree and track record will fast track him to higher positions. He feels that things are going well at work, but here's the problem: Jordan's perception of himself differs from perceptions most everyone else has about him. He's not the most sensitive communicator, nor is he particularly open to feedback, so Jordan's opinion of himself and his potential may not be grounded in reality.

He's been on the job six months and has his first performance review with his supervisor. Client relations reps are reviewed on three primary aspects: communication skills, attitude, and courtesy. He isn't nervous, because he believes he's done a first-rate job and is certain his boss will agree; he's looking forward to a conversation about how well he's done and how he's ready for a promotion. What Jordan doesn't know is that he's about to get a cold dose of reality from his boss.

Jordan was completely floored by the discussion that took place during his review. His boss informed him that numerous customers had filed complaints about his sarcasm, rude behavior, and bad attitude. Customer service surveys contained comments about how Jordan rolled his eyes, sighed at customer questions, and turned his back to customers while they were trying to get help with their issues. The most serious complaint described how Jordan talked inappropriately about his personal life, telling details to coworkers within easy earshot of customers, some of whom had their children with them. The boss explained that, *if Jordan were to stay with the company*, he would have to make major improvements in all performance areas or he would be let go.

# ■ NONVERBAL COMMUNICATION IN TWO EVERYDAY CONTEXTS

In this chapter, we explore nonverbal communication that occurs in two settings we commonly encounter in our lives. We begin with a discussion of critical nonverbal cues in *professional settings*, like organizations and companies in which nonverbal cues are important to getting a job as well as succeeding in a job. In addition, we examine the role of nonverbal communication in developing leadership abilities. Finally, we overview nonverbal communication in *educational settings*. Sound like a huge task? We understand; it can be overwhelming to think about getting a job or where we're going to be in a few years. However, our study of nonverbal communication is incomplete without applying the codes to everyday contexts. Let's first look at nonverbal communication in professional settings.

# ■ THE IMPORTANCE OF NONVERBAL IN PROFESSIONAL CONTEXTS

We've all heard our parents, teachers, friends, and neighbors ask the daunting question "What are you going to do with your degree?" This question can be really annoying. At the same time, when coming from the right person at the right time and place, any question about our future, our occupation, or what we dream about is open for discussion. While it can be challenging and emotional to think about what we're going to do when we get out of school, it's important to think about communication skills, especially our nonverbal communication skills, as we approach any professional context.

One of the first situations in which we can use our nonverbal communication skills is the job search process. Many people make the mistake of approaching their job search with too much confidence. After all, they have their degree in a given area of study, have technical skills and competencies, and feel like they can get the job done better than their competition. While many people have certifications, undergraduate degrees, and professional training, many struggle with job placement. We wonder, "Why can't Bobby Joe get a job? He's such a smart guy." Sure, Bobby Joe *is* a smart guy, but what if Bobby Joe is inept when it comes to verbal and nonverbal communication skills? Bobby Joe may have no awareness of how he comes across in job interviews. What can we do to save Bobby Joe? Well, that's going to be up to him, but what we can do is take a look at some nonverbal communication skills that are important in any professional setting.

# ■ GETTING THE JOB

Nonverbal communication is critical to job applicants in any hiring situation (Adler & Elmhorst, 2008; O'Hair, Friedrich, & Dixon, 2008). You may think that nonverbal cues related to the hiring process only occur face to face or in a direct manner. However, nonverbal communication in a job search is both direct and indirect, in terms of the impression we establish in professional situations and the impact of nonverbal behavior on the hiring process (Beebe, Beebe, & Ivy, 2007; Crane & Crane, 2002; Remland, 2006). **Direct nonverbal communication** refers to what we do during a live interview with a hiring committee, manager, or business owner, whether it's accomplished through face-to-face interaction, telephone communication, or perhaps even an online interview that might occur via a web cam. In contrast, **indirect nonverbal communication** refers to those job interviewing decisions or actions that tend not to occur face to face. In other words, indirect nonverbal communication comes before or after the actual interview, but it's just as important as the direct cues. We explore both of these forms in the sections to follow.

## Direct Nonverbal Communication

Direct nonverbal communication can be best understood by applying many of the nonverbal communication codes we've examined in previous chapters to the job interview context. One primary code is **physical appearance**—the way our bodies and overall appearance communicate to others and impact our view of ourselves in everyday life. Physical appearance has a direct impact because it communicates something about us to people in hiring positions (Cash, Gillen, & Burns, 1977; Dipboye, Arvey, & Terpstra, 1977; Hamermesh & Biddle, 1994). With an increasing emphasis on communicating a professional image in the job search process, more and more employers are searching for people who have "the look" that will build business (Nai-kuo, 2005; Pante, 2006; Thornbory & White, 2006; White, 1995).

The connection between physical appearance and nonverbal communication in a job interview is important for two reasons: (1) Our physical appearance as well as the decisions we make to maintain or alter our physical appearance communicate powerful nonverbal signals to other people; and (2) the physical appearance of other people impacts our perceptions of them (and, in this case, the organization with which we interview), how we communicate with them, how approachable they are, and so on. The nonverbal code of coworkers' and bosses' physical appearance directly clues us about such things as workplace culture, what to wear in terms of clothing or a uniform, and what types of people work there.

A central component of physical appearance is clothing. We all know that clothing communicates something to people, so it's no surprise that it's a critical nonverbal signal in a job interview (Pante, 2006; Rainey, 2006; Roach, 1997; Rosenfeld & Plax, 1977; Thornbory & White, 2006). Before going further, we need to mention something that students ask us about constantly when this topic comes up in class: Students often believe that, because people who work at a certain business or organization dress casually, applicants should also dress casually for job interviews. They think that doing so will show they've done an "audience analysis," meaning they've researched the company and are dressed casually for the interview so they'll be perceived as fitting in. This viewpoint couldn't be more wrongheaded, but we understand that sometimes it's also a justification for lacking the funds to purchase proper interviewing attire. We're sympathetic to the economics of the situation, but remember this: An applicant for a job is on the outside, looking in and wanting in. Job candidates don't work at the business or for the organization yet, but are selling themselves to land a position. It's not a good idea to try to match workers' style of dress until you land the

*Professional attire is a significant nonverbal cue.*

job, because *you aren't yet one of them.* You need to look like you want the job, that you're competing for the job, and that you care enough about getting the job to go out of your way to look impressive.

In terms of apparel, clues such as "business casual," "professional attire," or "dressing down" give us a sense of what's expected, but we don't always get those clues provided to us prior to a job interview (McPherson, 1997; Peluchette, Karl, & Rust, 2006). Can clothing help us get a job? The answer is "you bet" (Peluchette, Karl, & Rust, 2006). While we're not the fashion police or Tim Gunn from *Project Runway*, we do want to mention a couple of nonverbal cues related to appearance that potential employers look for. This information mainly applies to career-type job interviews, not as much to interviews for part-time summer jobs or other kinds of opportunities (although the same standards can apply):

1. In general, go for a conservative look: Like we said, even if the company is a casual place, don't dress casually until you get the job. Going conservative for men means a dark suit, white shirt, and nice, serious tie (no stains, no cartoon characters), dark socks (that match the color of the suit), and dress shoes (polished and clean). For women, a dark suit with a skirt is still preferable, although pantsuits are now more acceptable than they used to be. (Watch the hemlines of

the skirts and sit down in them before you purchase them; some skirts don't work well or show more than you want when you sit in them.) A light colored blouse under the suit works best; avoid bright colors. Hose and nice dress shoes (clean and polished, with a low heel) are still expected.

2. Pay attention to artifacts (e.g., jewelry, piercings, fingernail polish, makeup, briefcases) so that you don't wear or carry too much of anything that might be distracting to an interviewer. Nice leather or microfiber accessories (portfolios, briefcases) make a good impression.

3. The best guideline is to find out ahead of the interview what is standard or typical dress at the organization you're interviewing with, and go one step higher or more professional than that. You can tone it down once you get the job.

Hair length is another factor to consider as a nonverbal cue related to physical appearance. Young men who want to be viewed at job interviews as more mature and seasoned are often advised by stylists to let their hair grow out to a traditional length in order to avoid showing a baby face (Masip, Garrido, & Herrero, 2004). Men with longer hair (below the collar) are advised to cut or trim their hair for interviews so that they will be viewed as professional, serious, and credible. We do recognize that hair length and style may not be important in certain industries, so you can do what you want with your hair *once you land a job*. But when you're *wanting* the job, again, as we've said, your best bet is to go conservative. If you are male and have long hair, at least pull it back for the interview. What about men's facial hair? Job interviewers' perceptions of facial hair vary, so it can depend on the situation as to whether facial hair will work for or against you in an interview. The most conservative look is clean-shaven.

Body smell during a job interview is another form of direct nonverbal communication. Nonverbal communication scholars use the term **olfaction** to refer to the role of smell in human interaction (Andersen, 2004; Dimitrius & Mazzarrella, 1999; Riley, 1979). For both women and men, it's a balancing act in terms of how much scent, body powder, or cologne to use, since smell is closely connected to our overall appearance. As we mentioned in Chapter 5 on physical appearance, nonverbal scholar Robert Baron (1983) studied artificial scents and the evaluation of job applicants. Male interviewers in his study struggled when they tried to ignore applicants' smell, more so than female interviewers. Male interviewers rated applicants who wore cologne less favorably than those who did not, while female interviewers rated applicants wearing cologne more favorably. You might think that cologne would be a good thing to wear at an interview, since it could help create a positive impression of you. The converse is actually true: We suggest to students that they not wear any cologne when interviewing for a job because nervousness or activation in the body enhances the strength of a scent. You could overwhelm an interviewer and lose a job opportunity, all because your cologne was too strong.

What other direct nonverbal communication cues do we need to be aware of when trying to get a job? In addition to physical appearance, our **kinesics** (defined as human movement, gestures, and posture), in particular our body posture, serve as  direct nonverbal communication since posture is attached to many attractive attributes in U.S. culture, such as confidence, positivity, and high self-esteem (Guerrero & Floyd, 2006). We make personality judgments based on something as subjective as posture, so it's worth thinking about. How aware are you of your posture? Do you tend to stand in a dominant position, or does your stance typically give off signs of weakness, timidity, or low self-esteem? In a job interview, an interviewer tends to be much more relaxed than an applicant who puts herself or himself on the line to get hired. So even if the interviewer looks relaxed, maintain your professional, erect body posture. The level of relaxation or tension you feel will tend to show up in body posture and movement, which can be clues to potential employers (Nelson & Golant, 2004).

What about your tone of voice and how well you articulate during an interview? Remember that when we study how people express themselves through their voices, we're studying **vocalics,** sometimes referred to as paralanguage. Besides being able to identify someone from his or her voice, we can also come to detect physical, emotional, and attitudinal states through **tone of voice,** which is a non-technical term for all the elements that the human voice can produce and manipulate. Think about the direct impact your tone of voice can have in an interview setting. What does your voice say about you to potential employers? Vocalics are particularly critical in telephone interviews, which these days are often precursors to face-to-face interviews. Phone interviews save employers money and time, and they're often a weeding-out tool. That means you have the use of only one nonverbal code—vocalics—to help you make a positive impression.

We've heard some humorous, as well as horror, stories from faculty colleagues who went through phone interviews for their positions. A few years ago, a graduate student friend of ours was on a phone interview and the technology wasn't as good as it is today. He had a five-second delay between what his interviewers would say and when he would hear it, as well as between what he would say in response and what the interview committee members would hear. Our buddy used his typical humorous approach in the interview, but when he'd say something funny, all he heard was dead air at the other end. Nervously thinking he'd messed up and forgetting about the five-second delay, he'd get ready to try and cover what he'd done when he'd hear the  group break into laughter. The time lag was unsettling, to say the least; he never felt like he got into a rhythm in that interview. Thankfully, most phone systems are so sophisticated now that you can avoid this, unless perhaps you're interviewing with people who are overseas. In general, you want your voice to come across strong and confident. You may need more volume with a phone or web cam interview, especially a group interview when someone puts you on speaker phone. Watch filled pauses (e.g., "uh," "er," "um") even if you're trying to come up with an answer to an interview question, because pauses are exaggerated in a phone situation where there are no other nonverbal cues (like physical appearance or facial expressions) to accompany the voice. In phone, web cam, and face-to-face interviews alike, watch interrupting the interviewers (another vocalic cue). While interrupting may be your general style in interpersonal settings, it'll likely be seen as rude behavior in an interview.

One very important aspect of direct nonverbal communication to consider within the category of **haptics** (or touch) is the **professional handshake,** which can be distinguished from the social handshake (Hiemstra, 1999). In professional settings in the U.S., the handshake is critical to making a good first impression (Chaplin, Phillips, Brown, Clanton, & Stein, 2000). Here's how author Bruce Campbell (2002) talked about handshakes while on tour to promote his book *If Chins Could Kill: Confessions of a B Movie Actor*:

*A good deal of information about people is conveyed through a simple handshake.*

To shake, or not to shake—that is the question. The act of interfacing with fans (I prefer the term "clients") in person always provides hours of awkward quirkiness. I have found, after shaking enough hands to land a seat in Congress, a person's handshake is as unique as their fingerprints—no two people do it the same way. A short-and-simple handshake was very popular during the book tour, particularly in Middle America. I enjoy how straightforward it is, but if a handshake is too short, it can be misinterpreted as "Sick, this guy has cooties," or perfunctory, as in "Okay, I'll shake this guy's hand because everyone else is…." Conversely, a long handshake tends to get a little too intimate for me. I've had thirty-second handshakes, during which an enthusiastic sort would tell an entire story while squeezing the blood out of my fingers. No handshake discussion would be complete without mentioning the grip. To me, a person's grip is a "key indicator," it lets you know who you're dealing with. A firm grip says, "Hi pal, nice to make your acquaintance." However, if you grip too firmly, it can be intrusive, suggesting, "You want a handshake? Huh? Okay—let's do it!" A weak grip, for my money, signifies disinterest. Every time I encountered a weak handshake, and I'm talking about the real dead fish ones, the person's interest level was pretty much the same. Much like driving, you are how you shake. (p. 317)

In the professional handshake, here's what needs to happen: The hands need to meet fully, firmly, and equally (meaning palm-to-palm; locked or hooked around the space between the thumb and forefinger; and with no turn of the hands, i.e., hands stay straight up and down), with definite but brief shaking. Social handshakes don't usually turn out this way; they often aren't equal, meaning that people may only take the time to grab part of the hand or a few fingers. They're often accomplished with a quick touch and no shake, and this may or may not create a negative impression. However, getting a social handshake when a professional one is expected will not serve you well. And don't assume that a good handshake is "natural" or something everyone can do, because we've received some pretty lousy handshakes in our years of interviewing people for faculty and administrative positions.

Because of our experience, we encourage students in our nonverbal communication classes to practice shaking hands with each other. Read over the explanation of a good professional handshake above, and see if you can extend this kind of shake to classmates and they to you. Are certain handshakes better than others? Why? Do some handshakes creep you out? Why? Here a few handshake types to avoid:

1. *The Crusher:* A person can give you a painful experience by squeezing your hand too tightly. Some men exhibit this behavior, as though handshaking were a precursor to arm wrestling or some other form of competition. (This sounds funny, but it can be a serious offense if your interviewer has arthritis, which many people do. You can actually hurt someone with arthritis in their hands if you grip too tightly.)
2. *The Pumper:* A person who shakes too long can leave you rattled—physically and emotionally. Too much shaking can be a nonverbal sign that you're overeager.
3. *The Taker:* A person who takes your hand to shake it before you've even extended it can send aggressive signals. Most often, this is a nonverbal dominance move.
4. *The Frenchie:* No international stereotypes intended, but some men (French as well as American) have seen too many old movies in which a man took a woman's hand, turned it palm down, raised it, and kissed it. You know this form of greeting is unprofessional, but you may run into this kind of shaker socially.
5. *The Gapper:* One handshake that tends to give people a creepy or empty, unfulfilled feeling occurs when you can't feel the palm of the other person. The credibility in a handshake mostly lies in the palms. If you extend your hand straight to people and they cup their hand instead of responding with a flat palm, it creates a hollow in the handshake and tends to give people negative impressions. People may deem you weak, untrustworthy, or insecure with a "gapped" handshake.

Have you experienced any of these handshakes? What was your reaction or impression of the person? As we've established, direct nonverbal communication, such as a handshake, may not come to mind immediately when approaching the professional interview, but it's something to think about and work on.

One final form of direct nonverbal communication critical to successful job interviewing is **eye gaze** (commonly referred to as eye contact), defined as looking at the general eye area of other people. Eye gaze is extremely important in U.S. culture, because we make all kinds of judgments about people—particularly about trustworthiness and sincerity—on the basis of whether they make or avoid eye contact. In fact, research has found that of all the nonverbal cues, eye contact is the most critical to judgments of credibility (Beebe, 1974). So if you want to make a positive impression within the first few seconds of meeting a potential employer, you will stand with good posture, extend your hand to give a firm, professional handshake, while at the same time making good eye contact.

What exactly is *good* eye contact? As we talked about in Chapter 7 on facial expressions and eye behavior as critical nonverbal codes, in U.S. culture, good eye contact occurs when one person looks in the general eye area of another person, then breaks to briefly look elsewhere—up, down, around the room, or other places on the person's face (like the forehead)—then returns to the eyes. But you have to reach a balance here: Too little eye contact (not meeting someone's gaze) is perceived negatively, as though you might have something to hide; too much eye contact is an invasion we call staring in this culture, and it's definitely viewed negatively. In an interview setting, the best approach is to match the eye contact you receive from an interviewer; if the person gives a lot of eye contact (almost to the point of staring), try to mirror that behavior. If the interviewer looks around a lot and doesn't make much eye contact, then it won't matter much because the interviewer won't see what you're doing anyway. But if the person tends to give average or a modicum of eye contact, try to match that. Now we turn our attention to indirect nonverbal communication or the more subtle cues that impact getting a job.

## REMEMBER 11.1

| | |
|---|---|
| **Direct Nonverbal Communication:** | nonverbal cues related to telephone, face-to-face, or online communication, as in a live interview with a hiring committee, manager, or business owner. |
| **Indirect Nonverbal Communication:** | decisions or actions that tend not to occur face to face, but before or after a job interview. |
| **Physical Appearance:** | how our bodies and appearance communicate to others and impact our view of ourselves. |
| **Olfaction:** | role of smell in human interaction. |
| **Kinesics:** | human movement, gestures, and posture. |
| **Vocalics:** | how people express themselves through voices. |
| **Tone of Voice:** | elements that the human voice can produce and manipulate. |
| **Haptics:** | human touch. |
| **Professional Handshake:** | full, firm, and equal handshake that makes a good first impression as a professional. |
| **Eye Gaze (Eye Contact):** | looking at the general eye area of other people. |

## Indirect Nonverbal Communication

In review, many of the nonverbal communication codes discussed in previous chapters such as physical appearance, vocalics, kinesics, touch, and so on are *direct* forms of nonverbal communication that impact the professional interview. What about more subtle, *indirect* nonverbal communication? We tell our students that indirect nonverbal communication can make all the difference when it comes to standing out among other applicants. As we said earlier, **indirect nonverbal communication** refers to decisions or actions that tend not to occur face to face; these are the nonverbal cues that speak volumes about you before or after the actual interview, and they're just as important as the direct cues.

Let's begin with the **cover letter** (letter of introduction to a potential employer) and **resumé** (a document that details your educational and professional experience). You've probably not thought of it this way before, but cover letters and resumés serve as nonverbal reflections of who you are and what you have to offer. We know that many job applications nowadays are conducted entirely online, but some companies and organizations still prefer receiving hard copies of documents. Plus it's wise to take hard copy backups of documents with you to interviews so that if your interviewer misplaced your materials, you have extras to provide.

Plenty of books on resumés and cover letters offer tips, such as Richard Wallace's (2008) *The Only Resumé and Cover Letter Book You'll Ever Need*, Michael Farr's (2007) *The Quick Resumé and Cover Letter Book,* and Scott Bennett's (2005) *The Elements of Resumé Style*. But here are a few things to think about, with regard for nonverbal aspects. Besides introducing yourself, expressing your interest in the job, listing your education, career goals, experience, references, and so on, think about what your documents communicate nonverbally about you. Given that a cover letter and resumé are a bunch of words on pieces of paper, how can they communicate something nonverbally? Here are some nonverbal aspects of cover letters and resumés that you need to consider, so that you communicate yourself to potential employers in the best manner possible.

1. *Paper Quality:* People who submit cover letters and resumés on traditional white (cheap) printer paper run the risk of having their documents look like everyone else's. In contrast, documents printed on high quality paper in a light color, like creme or grey, say something about the applicant's interest in establishing a positive first impression. This trend can vary year to year; if everyone is using nice colored paper, use nice white paper to make your documents stand out.

2. *Print Quality, Font, and Ink Color:* In addition to the quality of cover letter and resumé paper, it's also important to consider print quality, font, and color. Poorly printed documents can send a message that an applicant is sloppy or doesn't care about details. The font you choose to use communicates nonverbal signals as well, or attributes about the words you use that shape people's impressions of you (Bringhurst, 2004). One of your co-authors once received a final research paper from a student typed in a font called Kidplay, one that mimicked children's writing. Some letters were turned backward; others were printed above and below the line, so that the letters zig-zagged across the page. This choice of font communicated an immature feel to the research

paper—not what you want for a work of this sort. Think also about ink color for your cover letter and resumé. It's unwise to try to squeeze out the last bit of ink from a cartridge to print job interview documents; if your typeface is too faint to be easily read, your papers will most likely wind up in File 13 (the trashcan), so make sure your print is dark and readable. While most of us print important documents in traditional black, some people print resumés in blue, red, or even pink ink! What kind of signal does ink color send? Some employers may see the use of ink colors other than black as creative or distinct, while others will see it negatively, as though you're "off the wall." We recommend staying with traditional black because of the potential indirect nonverbal message other colors might send.

3. *Typos and Misspellings:* While words are verbal, **typos** (mistakes in typing) and **misspellings** (mistakes in spelling) speak volumes nonverbally. These are probably the most common mistakes students make with their cover letters and resumés. Resumés with even a single typo can get sent to the garbage can so fast your head will spin. We recognize that people *do* make mistakes, but the job search or interview process is a critical time in your life to be extra careful with communication. Misspellings, typos, and sending something to the wrong address are indirect forms of nonverbal communication that can prevent you from getting an interview or proceeding beyond the first level. Don't rely solely on a computer spellcheck program; get a second set of eyes to proof your resumé before copying it and certainly before sending it out.

4. *Length:* The general rule used to be, and still is to a great extent, to keep your cover letter short and sweet and your resumé to a single page. However, for some of us who have years of experience, a one-page resumé is hard to manage and doesn't really sell us in the best way. You may encounter a reason to do a more extended resumé, but just realize that some potential employers will hurl your resumé to the trash heap without reading it—just because it's longer than one page.

What are some other factors that serve as indirect nonverbal communication? Since so much pre-interview communication takes place via email, it's important to think about nonverbal elements of email exchanges. While we addressed these topics in more depth in Chapter 10, let's explore a few features of online communication that serve as nonverbal cues about us. For starters, have you ever thought about how your email address communicates such things as your personality, interests, occupation, and even your deviances? Granted, the address itself is verbal, but the image it communicates makes it a nonverbal cue. The typical email address for a professor might look like this: richard.prof@university.edu. The first part of the email address designates the owner's or recipient's name; the last part of the address points to the server or location where the recipient can be found.

As email has become more utilized, people have begun to move away from providing their real name that reflects their identity in their email address (Barnes, 2003; Flynn & Flynn, 2003). Instead, now many people select something about themselves to include, so that they communicate a more creative email address. For example, Rachel is on the swim team and her athletic participation is a defining factor in her sense of self. Instead of using rachel.garcia@email.com, Rachel can have some fun by creating a different email address, such as swimmingdolphin@email.com. Reflect on your email address for just a moment. Does it contain your real name or a made-up name? What was the basis of that decision when you set up your email account?

While there is a sense of play or freedom when setting up an email address, it's important to think about the impressions others will form about us based on such a simple thing as our email address (Wahl, McBride, & Schrodt, 2005; Waldvogel, 2007; Walther, 2006). We advise students to reconsider their email addresses when applying for jobs or graduate programs. Think about the reaction a job recruiter or graduate director might have when receiving an email message from tigertemptress@university.edu or sexonthebeach@hotmail.com versus penny.student@university.edu. Which address implies more credibility and communicates a more positive first impression, professionally speaking?

One of your textbook authors participated as a panelist at a business etiquette dinner recently. The other panelists were from major corporations; their job was to give students tips for landing a job in their company and to educate in general about presenting oneself on the job market. One question that a student posed to the panel was: "Is it true that many companies are now looking at applicant MySpace accounts and running Google searches to see what comes up?" Representatives from each company responded that they did in fact run Internet searches on potential applicants. One recruiter indicated that her company was especially interested in how potential applicants represent themselves online. So, in addition to the email address we use in our job search process, it's also important to be mindful about what we post on the web related to our personal life.

Ever thought about how to start or end an email message? The opening or closing of an email message might seem really minor, yet researchers have explored such nonverbal dimensions of email, as this chapter's Spotlight on Research Box describes.

In addition to pre-interview nonverbal communication (e.g., resumé paper, print details, email addresses), think about post-interview decisions that can send nonverbal signals. Business etiquette specialists and personal effectiveness consultants advise people always to send a thank-you note after such encounters as job interviews (Post & Post, 2005; Whitmore, 2005). If you have a group of people interviewing you, the suggestion is to thank each person individually, not just the chair or head of the group. But will an email message of thanks suffice? Email has evolved into a norm for our everyday communication, especially in professional contexts. Many of us have gotten away from sending hand-written thank-you notes via traditional mail since email is faster and cheaper. After all, isn't an email message sent hours or the day after a job interview more impressive than a hand-written card received days or weeks later? While sending a thank-you email is indeed faster, it doesn't take much time or effort, and employers know that (because they use email a lot too). What nonverbal signal about you and your professionalism is conveyed when a potential employer receives a nice-looking, hand-written thank-you note within a few days of your interview? Such attention to detail and the care involved can communicate many positive things about you.

# SPOTLIGHT on Research

In today's fast-paced world of technology, most people send and receive email messages on a daily or almost daily basis. In workplace settings, emails may go back and forth several times a day, forming a virtual conversation between colleagues. Most email users probably don't pay much attention to their style of writing in email contexts. However, as recent research points out, employee email style may reflect more than we think. You may not have thought of email style as a form of nonverbal communication, but remember that nonverbal is more about *how* you communicate, not *what* you communicate. Email style relates to the *how* of communication.

During a hectic day, the type of greeting or closing we use in an email message may be the last thing on our mind. When sending a quick, informal message to a good friend or colleague, we may be less inclined to bother with a greeting or closing; we're likely to just start in with our message or reply. But what about with people we know less well or who are higher status than we are in the professional realm? A study by communication scholar Joan Waldvogel (2007) examined email greetings and closings used by employees in two different workplaces. One company was an educational organization; the other was a manufacturing plant.

First, Waldvogel calculated the percentage of greetings provided in emails by workers at each company. At the educational organization, 59 percent of emails contained no greeting. Twenty-one percent contained a greeting of just the recipient's name, and another 20 percent of emails contained a greeting such as "Hi," "Dear...," "Hello," and the like. At the manufacturing plant, 58 percent of emails that were sent contained some form of greeting that usually included the recipient's name.

Next, Waldvogel examined the closings in employees' emails and found similar results to the percentages of greetings included in email messages from employees at each company. At the educational organization, most employees preferred a closing, but 34 percent used no closing, and 38 percent ended with the sender's first name only.

Employee status was another factor Waldvogel considered. At both the educational organization and the manufacturing plant, higher-status employees were more likely to be greeted or acknowledged by name within the emails they received than were lower-status individuals. Higher-status receivers were also more likely to see a closing in their emails than their lower-status colleagues.

The interpersonal relationship between colleagues was also indicated by the styles of emails they sent and received. Distant colleagues (in terms of social relationship, not geographical location) were more likely to use the recipient's name in emails sent to each other. Conversely, closer workers were less likely to use greetings when they sent emails to each other, but when they did use greetings, they were predominantly in the form of first names only. Based on all of these results, the educational facility employees seemed less friendly and close-knit than the manufacturing plant employees.

Finally, Waldvogel found a difference between men and women according to the inclusion of greetings or closings in workplace emails. At the educational organization, women included greetings and closings more often than men in their emails. However, men who included greetings did so more often in emails they sent to groups of people or other men, rather than to women only. These results have many implications regarding the workplace culture in each of the two organizations studied.

Take a moment to think about the greetings and closings you use regularly in emails you send. Does your use or lack of a greeting or closing pertain to the type of relationship

*(continued)*

**SPOTLIGHT on Research** *(continued)*

you have with the recipient of your message, or is more a matter of general style or preference? Is the recipient's status within the organization a factor?

For more information on this research, read: Waldvogel, J. (2007). Greetings and closings in workplace email. *Journal of Computer-Mediated Communication, 12(2),* article 6.

# ON THE JOB

Congratulations, you've landed a job! Now it's time to go to work. So, what do you do *now*? You've been fortunate enough to impress the hiring committee and/or manager and now they're bringing you in as part of their team. What can you expect on the job? Who are you going to talk to? Are you going to get along with your boss? Are your coworkers going to be nice? These are important questions to think about. Remember the huge impact nonverbal communication played in *getting the job*? Nonverbal communication may be even *more* important once you're *on the job*. This section of the chapter focuses on the important role of nonverbal communication with bosses, coworkers, and the customers or clients you're expected to impress. After all, your successful verbal and nonverbal skills are what got you here in the first place!

## Superior–Subordinate Nonverbal Communication

The first thing to think about in terms of nonverbal communication on the job concerns your employer or boss, because remember: You want to *keep* this job (in most

## REMEMBER 11.2

| | |
|---|---|
| **Indirect Nonverbal Communication:** | decisions or actions that tend not to occur face to face, but before or after an interview. |
| **Cover Letter:** | letter of introduction to a potential employer. |
| **Resumé:** | document indicating educational and professional experience that serves as a reflection of who people are and what they can offer a potential employer. |
| **Typos:** | mistakes in typing. |
| **Misspellings:** | mistakes in spelling. |

cases). How does nonverbal communication impact employer-employee interaction? One way to prepare for this interaction is by understanding **status**—a person's rank or position in an organization. In most situations, those people who hold higher status have more years of experience, training, education, and rank. In the language of the workplace, the **superior** (supervisor/employer) is typically the higher-status person and the **subordinate** (employee) is the lower-status person (Adler & Elmhorst, 2008; Carney, Hall, & LeBeau, 2005; Cashdan, 1998; Glick, Larsen, Johnson, & Branstiter, 2005; O'Hair, Friedrich, & Dixon, 2008). Let's apply some of the nonverbal communication codes from previous chapters to the superior-subordinate relationship.

**Environment.**   One of the first nonverbal codes that impacts employer–employee relationships is **environment**—the built or natural surroundings that serve as the contexts in which people interact. We know from Chapter 3 on environment as nonverbal communication that people are influenced by such factors as office architecture, design, colors, lighting, smell, seating arrangements, temperature, and cleanliness (Harris & Sachau, 2005; Jackson, 2005; McElroy, Morrow, & Ackerman, 1983; Morrow & McElroy, 1981; Salacuse, 2005; Teven, 1996; Vilnai-Yavetz, Rafaeli, & Schneider-Yaacov, 2005; Vogler & Jorgenson, 2005; Zweigenhaft, 1976).

What might a person in a leadership or high-status role have in his or her professional environment or office, compared to subordinates? The professional environment is important because it communicates status, credibility, and organizational skills, all of which impact **impression management**—the formation of an impression, perception, or view of a person (Goffman, 1971; Harris & Sachau, 2005). Names on the door; diplomas, awards and plaques on the wall; and the presence of expensive office furnishings provide nonverbal reinforcement that the occupant of that office is in charge. In addition, professional environments are important to employers because job interviews, important meetings, and private conversations often take place in bosses' offices (DeMeuse, 1987). These offices are usually situated in the most status-oriented locations within the larger company environment, such as corner areas of buildings with large windows and private elevators, flanked by assistants' desks protecting the boss from foot traffic. In contrast, the lowest-ranking workers tend to have their offices, cubicles, or desks located near restrooms and high-traffic areas, with usually no buffer from noise or people (Farrenkopf & Roth, 1980; Sandberg, 2003).

**Proxemics.**   **Proxemics,** defined as the way distance and space play a communicative role in everyday life, also apply to superior–subordinate communication (Smeltzer, Waltman, & Leonard 1991). Superiors can more readily invade their subordinates' space and privacy (a concept we studied in Chapter 4 called a **violation** or the use of people's territory without their permission) than the reverse. In many organizational settings, subordinates have their own desks, cubicles, or offices where they keep personal belongings and other professional items. It can be unsettling to realize that the boss has access to subordinates' offices and can choose to re-locate employees or take over or violate their spaces because of higher status. (This isn't good management style, but it happens.) On the other hand, if subordinates violate their superiors' space without permission, reprimand or termination may occur.

*Diplomas and certificates in an office are nonverbal cues about a person's status.*

**Physical Appearance.**   As we discussed previously in this chapter, physical appearance serves as direct nonverbal communication in professional settings; our appearance can also convey our status within an organization. For superiors (higher-status people), conservative, solid-colored, well-fitting and well-made clothing often communicate power and success. It's not uncommon to see supervisors "dress the part" of their position. For example, executives of large corporations tend to dress in expensive business suits with the best looking accessories, like high quality leather shoes. (We know this depends on the corporation, because someone like Bill Gates is an exception at Microsoft, where casual dress rules the day, every day.) Perhaps you've heard male professionals talk about wearing a "power" tie and looking sharp. This isn't a hard and fast rule, but typically higher-status employers dress better (more formally and expensively) than their employees, so as to stand out and convey their dominance (Schmid Mast & Hall, 2004). Clothing is often an indicator of rank, because at some places of business, organizational standards are in place that communicate to employees and customers alike who does what. For example, you often see counter and kitchen employees at fast food restaurants dressed alike, but the manager is dressed differently—usually more conservatively or formally—so that she or he is recognizable.

**Kinesics.**   The pace at which a person walks is also a fascinating nonverbal aspect to observe and study, because some people believe pace correlates with power and status. Do higher-status or "power" people tend to walk faster, as though they've got many places to be, lots to do, tons of people wanting to meet them, and they're cutting their arrival at every meeting too closely? Or do higher status people tend to move more leisurely because, simply put, they *can*? Their time is more their own, so they can control the pace of their movement because much in their lives is in their control. Here's the answer: If you watch a busy office complex, you will likely see the lower employees on the totem pole scurrying around to retrieve things for their bosses, while their bosses wouldn't be caught dead "scurrying." Instead, they may stroll, causing associates around them—particularly those of lower status—to slow down to match their pace. Let's be clear: The higher-status person calls the nonverbal shots; lower-status people are expected to adapt their nonverbals to parallel or remain subordinate to the higher-status person's cues (Carney, Hall, & LeBeau, 2005; Cashdan, 1998; Hall, 2001).

**Vocalics.** Another nonverbal code applied to our study of superiors and subordinates is vocalics. Higher-status professionals tend to sound authoritative, using pitch, rate, and volume properties of the voice to convey status and dominance. Some even hire vocal coaches and communication consultants to help them sound more credible (Krapels, 2000). In addition, vocal behaviors of higher-status people include a less anxious tone, few disfluencies, and the use of silence to communicate authority. In contrast, subordinates may sound submissive yet engaged in what their superiors say. Subordinates usually have more anxious tones of voice and filled pauses, and may use silence to protect themselves if their superiors "call them on the carpet." As we explored in Chapter 9 on vocalics, nonverbal communication scholars have examined the role of power or dominance in interaction management (how conversation gets accomplished), looking specifically at how higher-status speakers establish turns at talk; protect, maintain, and lengthen them; and use interruptions and overlaps to dominate other communicators (Burgoon & Le Poire, 1999; Dunbar & Burgoon, 2005; Mehrabian, 1981).

**Touch.** What role does touch play in the superior–subordinate relationship? People with higher status tend to initiate more touch with subordinates (rather than the reverse), control how touch occurs in professional settings, and in general have more freedom to express themselves through touch than do subordinates (Hall, 1996). Subordinates usually receive touch from superiors and are inclined to accept the touch. Typically, a subordinate will not initiate touch toward a higher-status person, and will only reciprocate touch if it seems appropriate.

Now, we grant that this is a "touchy" topic—more difficult now than in years past. While some touches, such as a handshake or pat on the back (we said back, not backside), may convey respect from bosses to employees, we all know by now that touch can be misused. One boss's affectionate or appreciative touch is one employee's sexual harassment, so this is a difficult area to deal with. Many employers walk on eggshells around the office, because the nonverbal power of touch evokes very individualized interpretations of what a touch means (Haunani Solomon & Miller Williams, 1997; Keyton & Rhodes, 1999). Today's supervisors are leery of touch toward subordinates due to a fear of lawsuits and sexual harassment claims (Adler & Elmhorst, 2008; Eisenberg, Goodall, & Trethewey, 2006; Gruber, 2006; O'Hair,

Friedrich, & Dixon, 2008; Remland, 2006; Rogers & Henson, 2006). While today's climate may seem restrictive, think about it: An office climate that's a bit more restrictive in terms of how bosses and employees treat each other is preferable to one in which boundaries about touch and proxemics are violated on a daily basis, with no repercussions.

As we strive for successful relationships as superiors or subordinates, we need to remember the power of nonverbal communication; appropriate nonverbal behavior often makes or breaks our chances of being viewed positively on the job, such that we create opportunities for advancement. Now that we've applied several of the nonverbal codes to superior–subordinate communication on the job, let's consider coworker nonverbal communication.

## Coworker Nonverbal Communication

We'll be the first to admit it—communication with bosses is important. But we can't forget the importance of interpersonal relationships with our colleagues. Nonverbal cues play a huge role in making impressions on others, which underlies the formation of relationships in both personal and professional life. In fact, research suggests that we make judgments based on nonverbal information about other people very quickly, even as quickly as the first ten seconds within meeting them (Bernieri, as in Burch, 2001; Bert & Piner, 1989). You may decide whether you like a fellow employee just as quickly, before your colleague has had time to utter more than "hello." Nonverbal cues are important not only in the early stages of relationships, but also as we maintain, deepen, and sometimes terminate those relationships. This is true for our personal relationships *at* as well as *away* from work.

---

### REMEMBER 11.3

| | |
|---|---|
| **Status:** | a person's rank or position in an organization. |
| **Superior:** | supervisors or employers in professional situations who typically rank higher than others in terms of hierarchy. |
| **Subordinate:** | employees in professional situations who typically rank lower than others in terms of hierarchy. |
| **Environment:** | built or natural surroundings that serve as the contexts in which people interact. |
| **Impression Management:** | formation of an impression, perception, or view of another person. |
| **Proxemics:** | the way distance and space play a communicative role in everyday life, such as in the development of coworker relationships. |
| **Violation:** | use of people's territory without their permission. |

## *What Would <u>You</u> Do?*

Kimberly has worked at a law firm for the past three years. She's married, has a newborn son, and just returned to work from maternity leave. Her boss, Tim, has "made eyes" at her in the office, but he's never said or done anything more than that. She's felt uncomfortable at times, but doesn't want to blow anything out of proportion, so she doesn't say anything and just goes on working.

Last week as she got on the elevator to leave for the day, Tim ran up just in time to put his briefcase between the doors and open them. He got on the elevator and acted normally until he and Kimberly were one floor above the parking level, when he pushed the emergency stop button for the elevator. He turned to Kimberly, moved closer to her, and told her that he'd missed her while she was gone. While Kimberly's stomach turned, she stepped away from Tim, released the stop button, and simply mumbled "thanks." When the elevator doors opened Tim asked Kimberly if he could walk her to her car, but she just said "see you tomorrow" and walked away quickly.

After learning about nonverbal communication applied to superior–subordinate interaction, *what would you do* if you were in Kimberly's position? Would you act as if nothing happened? Would you confront Tim the following day—either alone or while other people were around the office? Would you quit your job rather than confront a person like this?

From what research has discovered about sexual harassment, this situation definitely qualifies as harassment—inappropriate, unwelcome, unsolicited behavior of a sexual nature, intended to make a target person feel uncomfortable. Sexual harassment is about power, not sex, as you probably know. Unfortunately, in this situation Kimberly will have difficulty winning a court case against Tim, if she decided to go that route, for two reasons: (1) Courts typically look for a pattern of behavior, not just one incident; and (2) the incident happened in private, not in view of anyone, so a court case could turn into a "he said/she said" situation. But Kimberly (or *you*, if you're ever in a similar situation) might think about checking the law firm's policy on sexual harassment, to see if the firm has a mechanism for reporting this kind of behavior. She might or might not want Tim fired and might not have grounds if this is a one-time incident, but she could try to expose the behavior to Tim's superiors and ask them to make his behavior stop.

As we build coworker relationships, the more we understand the nonverbal cues of our colleagues (Remland, 2006). The more we get to know our colleagues the more likely we are to use nonverbal cues to convey negative messages than to announce our explicit dislike of something or someone (Burgoon, Stern, & Dillman, 1995). In fact, it's safer to let our friends at work know through our nonverbal cues of our disagreement with a decision or policy or our dislike of another person, especially the boss; we wouldn't want to risk being overheard.

Related to proxemics, which we discussed in the previous section, is **proximity,** which refers to physical and spatial closeness. Proximity is an important factor in the development of coworker relationships. The closer we are to people physically, meaning sheer proximity, the more likely we are to form relationships. Colleagues who work in adjacent desks, cubicles, or offices are more likely to develop closer relationships than people who work for the same company, but on different floors or opposite ends of a building. Of course, people who work for the same company or with teams of people on connected projects can create virtual proximity through technology, such as email exchanges or video conferencing. This form of proximity is being increasingly studied by communication experts (Riggio, 2005). Communication scholars O'Hair, Friedrich, and Dixon (2008) have explored communication in professional settings; they offer the following characteristics of coworker relationships:

1. *Shared Interests and Common Tasks:* People like to be around others who share their interests. Working in an organization prompts a number of common interests that help work relationships form. Coworkers share a professional identity, work location, similar tasks, and, in many cases, a boss.
2. *Satisfaction of Needs:* Coworkers develop relationships to satisfy their basic needs. Our needs for affiliation, social exchange, and the sharing of ideas are just as important in professional life as they are in personal life.
3. *Difficult Coworkers:* Almost all professional settings contain employees who are difficult to work with. Our knowledge of nonverbal communication should provide us some clues as to who is difficult.

## Nonverbal Communication with Customers and Clients

Nonverbal communication is critical to successfully interacting with customers, clients, or potential business contacts (Leigh & Summers, 2002; Pugh, 2001; Riggio, 2005). **Customer relations,** also known as customer service, is the interaction between employees or representatives of an organization or business and the people the organization sells to or serves. Retail centers, restaurants, banks, insurance companies, movie theatres, and so on are but a few examples of locations in which we experience service. Nonverbal communication helps professionals fine tune their relations with customers who expect and demand excellent service (Krapels, 2000; Mausehund, Timm, & King, 1995). In today's competitive business environment, consumers expect to be served by professionals who are competent about their products and services, and who communicate with dignity, respect, and courtesy. Sad to say, many times that's not what we experience.

Let's explore some basic functions of nonverbal cues, relating them to the customer service arena. Remember from Chapter 1 that nonverbal cues can work independently or in tandem with verbal language to convey meaning. First, nonverbal cues can *substitute* for verbal messages. You're at a baseball game and see a guy going up and down the aisles of the stadium, selling hot dogs. (Yes, the hotdog salesperson is actually a customer service rep.) He gets near your row and your hunger kicks in, but you know he can't hear you way down the row. You simply call on your nonverbal powers, wave to get his attention, make eye contact, and hold up one or two fingers, depending on how hungry you are. These kinesic and eye behaviors substitute when verbal communication won't do the trick. In customer relations, nonverbal cues often substitute for verbal messages; that's why it's important for

*What kind of nonverbal messages is this customer service rep—in this case, a bartender—conveying to his customer?*

customer service reps to work to develop and improve their nonverbal sending and receiving abilities.

We often use nonverbal cues in connection with words, to *complement* our communication or to clarify or extend the meaning of our words. This complementary function allows us to convey more information, leading to a more accurate interpretation by receivers of our communication (McNeill, 2000). Complementary cues also help color our expressed emotions and attitudes. For example, a long, heavy sigh may reveal how tired or bored we are—something we definitely want to avoid if we work in customer relations. We've probably all placed an order at a fast-food restaurant and heard the voice of an employee sigh, "Whenever you're ready...." The likely downward pitch and sigh accompanying the speech act cue us as to the emotional (bored) state of the employee.

On occasion, our nonverbal cues *contradict* rather than complement our verbal cues. Have you ever dealt with someone behind a counter when you have a real problem with something you bought, that now won't work? While the verbal communication the employee says might be acceptable or rote, the nonverbal facial expressions, body postures, vocalic indications of exasperation, and other cues belie the verbal message. Sometimes customer service reps get frustrated or sick of dealing with complainers all day, but that doesn't mean their behavior as professionals shouldn't be at its best. Those of us who work in customer relations, either part-time while in college or as a career, need to remember that our nonverbal and verbal communication need to coordinate so as to represent our organization professionally.

Nonverbal behaviors may also serve a *repeating* function. Say you're working as a flight attendant and the airline you work for only allows passengers to bring one carry-on item onto the plane. A passenger has violated the carry-on rule, made it past the ticket counter workers, and now wants to stow all his or her stuff. The first time you speak to the person, you (the customer service rep) explain that she or he needs to gate check extra bags. When you realize that the passenger is too far away from you or too wrapped up in the "stowing" activity and can't hear you, you hold up baggage claim tickets and point to the excessive bags. In this example, your verbal communication comes first, followed by a nonverbal signal that repeats the message, thus clarifying the communication that's exchanged between the two of you. Customer service personnel often use this repeating function, because many times customers won't understand or accept a verbal message alone.

One of the more fascinating functions of nonverbal communication in customer relations is its ability to *regulate* conversation (Ekman, 1965). As we know from the chapter on vocalics, most conversations occur in a series of turns at talk by the interactants, and this is true of the customer service rep/customer exchange as well. Those turns are negotiated by a series of regulator cues. For example, the customer service rep may lean toward the customer, make eye contact, raise the eyebrows, and take in a breath—all before uttering a word. These nonverbal cues are important, because when customers perceive positive conversational regulators—bodily, facial, and vocal cues of patience and concern—the entire exchange is affected in the right direction. But when customers are belligerent (as we sometimes are), our negative nonverbal conversational regulators may rouse the same kind of behavior in the employee. The whole point of the exchange is likely defeated as a result.

Finally, nonverbal behaviors in customer relations often *accent* or provide emphasis for a verbal message. Customer relations professionals have to be very careful on this point, because certain accenting cues can be perceived negatively and can escalate a bad encounter with a member of the public. For example, if an angry or frustrated customer slams down a receipt on a counter, yelling, "Just give me my money back!" a customer service rep shouldn't follow suit or the exchange will escalate, possibly causing other disgruntled customers to become involved. Many customer relations personnel work entirely over the phone. Nonverbal vocalic accents—like raising the pitch or volume of the voice—are tricky too, because such cues typically intensify a bad situation. Telephone service reps need to be trained in how to use their voices to calm and reassure customers, but not patronize or appease them.

Communicating effectively with customers is essential in professional contexts (Pugh, 2001). If you work in customer service, we recommend taking responsibility for the excellent service you're expected to provide. Customers and clients want to do business with organizations and professionals who employ effective verbal and nonverbal communication skills—those who are empathetic and responsive to their concerns. **Unresponsive behavior,** defined as verbally and nonverbally communicating an apathetic or uncaring attitude, is deadly in customer service. Many of us have experienced bad service agents who are unresponsive; they give off that blank stare that tells us they could care less and hate their jobs. They've seen enough crabby people all day and we're just the next person in a very long line. As people, they may not be aggressive or rude, but the facial expressions, lack of eye contact, and flat vocal tone say it all.

So in sum, customer relations professionals should employ affiliative nonverbal communication behaviors such as smiling, making eye contact, and exhibiting a positive attitude through tone of voice (Pugh, 2001). Your male book author maintains a professional consulting practice. He uses his expertise as a communication scholar and assists in the design and delivery of customer service trainings, orientation programs, and leadership seminars. One of the most requested workshop topics—from professionals in the health care industry to real estate—is customer service, because companies know the value of excellent customer service for new and repeat business. Some of the most highly trained professionals in industries of all kinds need a reminder that their communication skills, especially their nonverbal skills, are crucial in fostering a work environment in which people treat others with respect (Krapels, 2000; Pugh, 2001; Timm & Schroeder, 2000).

## ■ LEADERSHIP AND NONVERBAL COMMUNICATION

So far, we've applied nonverbal communication codes to important professional situations—getting a job and functioning on the job. This discussion brings us to our next point of study—nonverbal communication and leadership. We have no doubt that many readers of this textbook are currently in leadership positions in their educational, professional, social, or personal lives. Many of us will emerge into leaders as we finish school and pursue our career interests. No matter where you are in the process of developing leadership, attention to nonverbal communication will only enhance what you can achieve.

Scholars have long studied the topic of leadership and communication, providing typologies of leadership styles, strategies, and approaches (Hackman & Johnson, 2004). In this section, we examine nonverbal communication as an essential leadership quality. Here are some questions to get us started: Do you join clubs as a college student and remain just a member, or do you tend to become a leader of those clubs? If you admire leadership as a quality in people, but you don't view yourself as a leader, why is that? What are some qualities and nonverbal communication skills of good leaders?

### The Nonverbal Essentials of Leadership

Many people make the mistake of viewing leadership as a title. Once they're promoted or elected into a particular position of leadership, they think that's it—job over,

I've arrived. We emphasize that leadership is a skill, one that needs to be developed and fostered throughout life. One particular skill set that helps leaders emerge is nonverbal communication (Remland, 1981, 1984, 2006). Think about the qualities of leaders who are successful at what they do. What makes them great? How do they communicate, nonverbally? As we've established in this chapter, many nonverbal communication codes are germane to success in professional situations, which is especially true for leadership roles.

**Impression Management.** One of the essential leadership abilities is impression management, which we defined earlier in this chapter as the formation of an impression, perception, or view of a person. Effective leaders work on creating the desired impression of themselves on other people, so that they are perceived as they want to be perceived. They also recognize others' efforts at impression management. Nonverbal communication scholars Crane and Crane (2002) provide specific impression management strategies for leaders:

1. Effective leaders should recognize a variety of factors that lead to the use of impression management strategies by employees. In other words, leaders should be effective receivers and interpreters of the verbal and nonverbal cues their employees, coworkers, superiors, and customers/clients give off as they attempt to affect perceptions that are formed about them.
2. Some level of impression management is always going to be present in professional settings. Leaders should differentiate between honest versus manipulative strategies used by employees to shape perception.
3. Effective leaders should become keenly aware of the image they wish to project to their audience, and work to actually project the desired image, staying open to feedback about image. (That audience includes customers/clients, subordinates, fellow leaders, superiors, and rivals.)
4. Before using an impression management strategy, it's important for leaders to know their audience, the situation, and the goal of any encounter.
5. Leaders should lead through honest performance. The best impression a leader can make is to be a high performer.
6. Leaders should present their real selves and not a false front to their various audiences; reality makes the best impression.

**Dress to Impress.** Another essential for leaders is to wear clothing and use accessories (artifacts) that signal to others that they're leaders. Many of the tips we provided for appropriate interview attire apply to leaders' appearance as well. However, leaders may need to strategically "dress down" when a situation calls for it, such as in situations where they're expected to build rapport with clients or employees or informally celebrate an organization's accomplishments (McPherson, 1997; Peluchette, Karl, & Rust, 2006).

**Business and Social Etiquette.** Leaders should strive to enact the following business and social etiquette skills:

1. Know how to make an entrance and work a room; understand appropriate proxemics (the amount of space between people in conversation) (Remland, Jones, & Brinkman, 1995).
2. Be well versed in first-meeting (initial interaction) strategies, in which such nonverbal cues as the professional handshake are critical (Hiemstra, 1999; Whitmore, 2005).
3. Practice making business and social introductions with confidence and poise, making the best use of vocalics and other important nonverbal codes (Adler & Elmhorst, 2008).
4. Attend to others' nonverbal cues, as well as the related emotions and attitudes driving those cues. Apply sensitivity and caution when attempting to decipher complex nonverbal cues, rather than relying on stereotypes or past experience.
5. Make use of the skill of perception checking. Check your perceptions of others' nonverbal cues with trusted people, so as to formulate appropriate responses and realistic expectations for future behavior (Beebe, Beebe, & Ivy, 2007).

**The Posture of Leadership.** As we discussed in the kinesics chapter, Albert Mehrabian is a major contributor to our understanding of many nonverbal behaviors, among them kinesics. His work on posture set an early standard for nonverbal research and applies to our focus on the nonverbal essentials of leadership. Mehrabian (1968, 1969a, 1969b, 1972, 1981) contended that two primary dimensions of posture exist, through which we communicate our attitudes and feelings to others. The first dimension he termed **immediacy,** which refers to the degree of perceived physical or psychological closeness between people (Mehrabian, 1966). (We return to this concept in the last half of this chapter, when we explore teacher and student nonverbal behaviors.) The more immediacy behavior someone exhibits, generally the more we like that person or are interested in what she or he has to say or conveys nonverbally. Postural cues related to immediacy include forward lean of the body, symmetric positioning (meaning that arms or legs are in correspondence with the general body position), and a direct body orientation (meaning that the body is positioned towards someone, rather than in an indirect or side configuration). **Relaxation** is Mehrabian's second dimension, which refers to a backward lean of the body, asymmetric positioning, rocking movements, and reduced tension in the body, specifically the arms and legs. Mehrabian suggested that a keen observer of nonverbal behavior could tell how much interest, liking, and activation occurred among people just by watching their posture, positioning, and body movement. Effective leaders know when to exhibit immediate and relaxed body postures and to detect these stances in others, because they understand the power of nonverbal cues.

**Hiring Good People.** Effective leaders not only pay attention to their own nonverbal communication, they also pay attention to the nonverbal cues of people they hire and who others hire to work for them, from the initial interview to performance on the job. Leaders set the tone in job interviews: If they look beyond the basic information presented during an employment interview and see through applicant anxiety, which is often communicated nonverbally, they will be more likely to hire and retain good people (McCarthy & Goffin, 2004). On the job, many employers now look beyond technical training and basic competencies in hirees; organizations seek people to join their ranks who are aware of and proactive with their current level of communication skill, open to receiving communication skills training so that they can improve, and focused on contributing to a positive organizational culture (Krapels, 2000; Pugh, 2001; Timm & Schroeder, 2000).

 **Emotional Intelligence.**   Effective leaders strive for **emotional intelligence**—our ability to monitor our own and others' feelings and emotions, to discriminate among them, and to use this information to guide our thinking and action (Engelberg & Sjoberg, 2004; O'Sullivan, 2005; Salovey & Mayer, 1990). While the study of emotional intelligence originated from the discipline of psychology, the concept is particularly applicable in business and leadership contexts (Morand, 2001). In fact, people in leadership positions as well as those interested in mastering emotional intelligence have supported the sales of best-selling books on the topic (Bradberry & Greaves, 2005; Goleman, 1995). Obviously, our interest is the connection between emotional intelligence and nonverbal communication. We've included emotional intelligence as a leadership essential since it incorporates nonverbal communication as a skill—specifically, the ability to recognize emotional expressions displayed by oneself and others. Developing our powers of emotional intelligence helps us regulate our own emotions and better understand the emotions of others. In addition, emotional intelligence encourages us to utilize our emotions for flexible planning, creative thinking, redirecting our attention, and motivating ourselves to accomplish goals and finish tasks (Mayer & Salovey, 1993; Morand, 2001).

## REMEMBER 11.4

| | |
|---|---|
| **Proximity:** | physical or spatial closeness. |
| **Customer Relations:** | also referred to as customer service, the interaction between employees or representatives of an organization or business and the people the organization sells to or serves. |
| **Unresponsive Behavior:** | verbally and nonverbally communicating an apathetic or uncaring attitude. |
| **Immediacy:** | degree of perceived physical or psychological closeness between people. |
| **Relaxation:** | nonverbal behaviors that may include backward lean of the body, asymmetric positioning, rocking movements, and reduced tension, especially in the arms and legs. |
| **Emotional Intelligence:** | ability to monitor one's own and others' feelings and emotions, to discriminate among them, and to use this information to guide one's thinking and actions. |

## ■ NONVERBAL COMMUNICATION IN EDUCATIONAL CONTEXTS

We know how critical nonverbal communication is in professional contexts, so we now turn to the second major topic of this chapter—nonverbal communication in educational contexts. In this section, we examine critical nonverbal communication codes that inform the teaching–learning process. This information is relevant to you, the student, because you spend a good deal of your life in classrooms as you work on your degrees. Attention is given to student nonverbal behavior to help you think about or reflect on your current experience. We also provide information about nonverbal communication in the educational arena, in case you ever decide to take on the role of a teaching professional or currently serve in that capacity.

 Now, some of us may be thinking, "I'm not going to be a teacher; why do I have to read this?" That's a fair question, but we want to encourage those of you with a view of yourselves as non-teachers to keep an open mind. While it might not be realized now, an awareness of nonverbal communication in educational contexts can help us understand our own learning experiences as students. Such an awareness can also help prepare us for life experiences, such as raising children and being involved with their learning and development, or other situations where we take on the role as teacher, trainer, facilitator, mentor, or coach. We may not immediately think of ourselves as teachers, but we never know when our responsibilities in life may require us to take on a new role.

## ■ LEARNING ENVIRONMENTS

What type of learning environments do you prefer? Think about colors, lighting, temperature, and seating comfort. These are all characteristics of **learning environments**— spaces and locations within which learning occurs. Typical learning environments exist in the form of seminar rooms, lecture halls, labs, and classrooms. These spaces establish communication contexts that influence perceptions of safety, comfort, attitude, and character (Bowen & Kilmann, 1975; Holley & Steiner, 2005; Jackson, 2005; McCroskey & McVetta, 1978; Stires, 1980; Teven, 1996; Winchip, 1996; Wollin & Montagre, 1981). Believe it or not, learning environments are nonverbal because they influence our performance, comfort, mood, attitude, and even our ability to pay attention or participate. What preferences do you have for learning environments? What do you view as a conducive learning environment versus a disruptive one?

### From the Sunshine Room to the Lecture Hall

Let's think back to our first classrooms, perhaps in kindergarten or elementary school. What were the dominant room colors? What was the seating like—in rows of individual desks or in groups of tables with small chairs? How did our teachers organize the room? Now fast forward to your junior high and high school years. Think about how the learning environments changed. When your textbook authors planned this chapter, we talked about the bright colors and vivid images of animals, plants, and people present in our lower grades. The male co-author

*Some design features of college classrooms, like lighting and comfortable seating, enhance learning. Some features detract from learning.*

recalls different classroom themes from the first grade. He was lucky enough to be assigned to the "Sunshine Room," while a kid from down the street was proud to report daily to the "Green Room."

What kind of classrooms do you have now, as college students? Things really change when you get a little older and move past general education! Think about most of your college classroom environments—kind of boring, aren't they? (They're no "sunshine rooms.") We realize that classrooms come in different sizes, configurations, and colors, but here are some features of this particular category of physical environment you should pay attention to (Cooper & Simonds, 2006; Kougl, 1997):

1. *Colors:* Elementary-aged students respond better to warm colors (yellow and pink) in classrooms, while secondary students respond better to cool colors (blue and green). Research isn't specific when it comes to colors and college students, but as you've no doubt noticed, most college classrooms are painted your basic white, beige, or grey.
2. *Lighting:* Limited light or lighting that is too bright or that produces glare can create eye strain and fatigue, and contributes to poor concentration, thus poor learning.

3. *Temperature:* Students have trouble learning if they're too hot or cold, but many times establishing a comfortable temperature in a classroom is beyond much of anyone's control. (Many faculty have taught in a room that's too cold or too hot, where it's hard to remember your purpose and keep teaching.)

4. *Spatial Arrangement:* The way classroom furniture is arranged determines what communicative relationships are possible and affects the teaching and learning process. Some seating in large lecture halls involves seats attached to long desks, such that communication beyond a few people around you is pretty near impossible. For communication classes that often involve group work, flexible classrooms with movable chairs and tables tend to work the best.

5. *Furnishings:* Due to a lack of funding or attention, some college classrooms look like something right out of the depression years. The rooms look dingy, as though they haven't been painted in a century, with stained floors or carpet, broken or missing desks or chairs, antiquated chalkboards, peeling walls, and an obvious lack of technology. These kinds of unkempt environmental features can send negative signals to teachers and students who attempt to teach and learn in such surroundings.

## Online Learning Environments and Distance Education

When you move beyond face-to-face classroom settings, you see huge growth in online learning environments—computer-mediated, web-based educational forums. Online learning environments are also referred to as **distance education**—courses taught via computer, such that students don't have to be present in traditional classrooms (Wang & Reeves, 2006). Distance education courses use computer-mediated tools to offer students a wider array of courses than their home campuses can offer; they also enable students to take courses from remote locations. For example, our university offers many nursing courses to students working in hospitals at a distance.

Since online learning environments and distance education programs have proliferated with the emergence of new technologies, communication researchers continue to explore how these new learning environments affect the student and teacher experience (Lee & Busch, 2005; Mottet, 2000). Much of this scholarly attention focuses on the role of nonverbal communication in online learning environments and distance education. Communication scholars Witt and Wheeless (1999) explain that students have particular nonverbal expectations of their teachers in distance learning, because teachers must attempt to overcome the distance and replicate the face-to-face situation students are more used to. Over the years we've grown to understand students' preferences in traditional learning environments, but the emergence of distance education and other online learning forums are causing teachers to think about nonverbal communication in a different way.

With the growth of online learning and distance education, many colleges and universities are establishing **wired environments**—built environments that are conducive to the use of laptop computers and other web-based technologies, without the need for plugging into an electrical outlet. This is an important trend, since laptop computers and wireless Internet access play an increasingly integral role in the education process at all levels (Worley & Chesebro, 2002). Technology has promoted more flexibility in open spaces with movable desks and chairs, since so many students are now bringing laptop computers to campus and maintain MySpace pages, Facebook websites, or other weblog services (Mazer, Murphy, & Simonds, 2007). The days of planning for a large computer lab on campus are changing with the arrival of students like you, the "Net Generation" (Carlson, 2006). Computer labs are still prevalent, but more attention is being given to how Internet environments and the profuse use of technology are changing the way we design and renovate spaces in modern schools, colleges, and universities.

## ◼ TEACHER NONVERBAL COMMUNICATION

A variety of the nonverbal communication codes we've explored earlier in this chapter, as well as in previous chapters in this book, pertain to teaching effectiveness. In fact, many teachers turn to nonverbal communication teacher training forums to become masters in the classroom (Cooper & Simonds, 2006; Elfenbein, 2006; Kougl, 1997; McCroskey, Richmond, & McCroskey, 2006; Mottet & Beebe, 2006a; Richmond, McCroskey, & Hickson, 2008; Timm & Schroeder, 2000). In this section, we explore specific nonverbal cues that research suggests positively influence student learning.

### Teacher Immediacy

What are some specific nonverbal cues teachers use in the classroom? Teacher nonverbal cues communicate more than their simple like or dislike of students or of teaching, as an activity; teacher nonverbal cues display attitudes toward subject matter and one's job (Chamberlin, 2000; Chesebro, 2003; McCroskey, Richmond, & McCroskey, 2006). Researchers have devoted specific attention to verbal and nonverbal behaviors that create an open classroom environment and have a positive impact on student learning (Christophel, 1990; Gorham, 1988; Harris & Rosenthal, 2005; Montgomery, 1982; Moore, Masterson, Christophel, & Shea, 1996; Powell & Harville, 1990).

As we mentioned in the first half of this chapter, Mehrabian (1971) first conceptualized **immediacy**—behavior that enhances psychological and physical closeness between people. Since this conceptualization, the immediacy behavior of classroom teachers has been studied, specifically for its impact on student attitude and learning (Frymier, 1993; Menzel & Carrell, 1999; Rocca & McCroskey, 1999). **Teacher nonverbal immediacy** is the use of nonverbal cues (e.g., eye contact, smiling, vocal expressiveness, gestures, relaxed body positions, movement around the classroom, appropriate touch) to signal to students a teacher's approachability, availability, closeness, and warmth. When teachers exhibit nonverbal immediacy behaviors, a number of positive effects emerge (McCroskey, Richmond, & McCroskey, 2006; Richmond, McCroskey, & Hickson, 2008): (1) higher student enjoyment of the subject matter and content; (2) increased student–teacher and student–student communication; and (3) enhanced learning opportunities, because students' attention spans are increased. Since teacher nonverbal communication is important in any educational setting, we offer some typical nonverbal teacher behaviors (immediate and not-so-immediate) that researchers have documented (adapted from Cooper & Simonds, 2006, pp. 79–80).

1. *Accepts student behavior:* Smiles, affirmatively shakes head, pats on the back, winks, places hand on shoulder or head.
2. *Praises student behavior:* Places index finger and thumb together ("okay" sign), claps, raises eyebrows and smiles, nods head affirmatively and smiles.
3. *Displays student ideas:* Writes comments on board, puts students' work on bulletin board, holds up papers, provides for nonverbal student demonstration.
4. *Shows interest in student behavior:* Establishes and maintains eye contact.
5. *Moves to facilitate student-to-student interaction:* Physically moves into the position of group member, physically moves away from the group.
6. *Gives directions to students:* Points with hands, looks at specified area, employs predetermined signal (such as raising hands for students to stand up), reinforces numerical aspects by showing a number of fingers, extends arms forward and beckons with the hands, points to students for answers.
7. *Shows authority toward students:* Frowns, stares, raises eyebrows, taps foot, rolls book on desk, negatively shakes head, walks or looks away from students, snaps fingers.
8. *Focuses students' attention on important points:* Uses pointer, walks toward students or objects, taps on something, thrusts head forward, thrusts arms forward, employs a nonverbal movement with a verbal statement to add emphasis.
9. *Demonstrates and/or illustrates:* Performs a physical skill, manipulates materials and media, illustrates a verbal statement with a nonverbal action.
10. *Ignores student behavior:* Fails to provide a nonverbal response when one is ordinarily expected.

## Teacher Touch: Too Close for Comfort

As we've made clear, teachers use nonverbal communication to establish approachability and connection with their students. At the same time, teachers must strive for balance between their personal and private lives, as well as manage the notion of teaching as a mode of friendship (McBride & Wahl, 2005; Rawlins, 2000). It's also important to be aware of **excessive immediacy,** defined as offensive and inappropriate comments, gestures, physical proximity, and touch that can occur in classrooms, hallways, and faculty offices. In some cases, excessive immediacy may be viewed as sexual harassment (Rester & Edwards, 2007; Weiss & Lolonde, 2001). **Teacher misbehaviors**—offensive or disruptive actions by teachers (e.g., yelling, insulting, and harassing students; telling offensive jokes; chronically arriving to class late) are detrimental to student learning (Kearney, Plax, Hays, & Ivey, 1991; McPherson, Kearney, & Plax, 2003).

Communication scholars Cooper and Simonds (2006) have a view of teacher touch that we think says it best: "Good teacher touch is *appropriate*. One way to define appropriateness is by location, duration, and intensity. The touch should be on a neutral part of the body, specifically the hand, forearm, shoulder, or upper back" (p. 89). Of course, the amount of teacher and student touch will vary with age and grade level, but we urge caution with this particularly powerful form of nonverbal communication. One teacher's sign of affection is one student's interpretation of sexual harassment.

Another type of touch in educational settings comes in the form of discipline. Perhaps you have participated in the corporeal punishment debate. **Corporeal punishment**—also referred to as striking a student with a paddle or other object as a form of reprimand—has been a controversial issue in U.S. public schools for some time now (Flynn, 1998). From appropriate touch to the paddle, teachers have to be aware of the positive and negative impact touch can have in educational settings.

## Teacher Appearance and Attire

Physical appearance is another nonverbal communication code that applies to educational contexts, especially student ratings of teacher attractiveness (Edwards & Edwards, 2001; Edwards, Edwards, Qing, & Wahl, 2007). For example, teachers viewed as attractive by their students are perceived as more approachable (Rocca & McCroskey, 1999).

Just as clothing has an impact in professional situations, the same holds true for teacher attire. The way that teachers dress does communicate something to students in classrooms, from elementary to college (Pante, 2006; Rainey, 2006; Roach, 1997; Rosenfeld & Plax, 1977; Thornbory & White, 2006). What reaction do students have when teachers wear informal or casual attire, compared to when they're dressed formally? Research shows that formally dressed teachers and teaching assistants are generally perceived as organized, competent, and prepared, while informally dressed teachers are viewed as friendly, fun, understanding, and flexible (Cooper & Simonds, 2006; Roach, 1997). A tension seems to exist between what to wear and what not to wear as a teacher; this can be somewhat of a conundrum for less-experienced or beginning teachers who want appear hip or "on the students' level," while also establishing their credibility. If a beginning teacher or assistant dresses in formal attire, he or she may be viewed as credible, but not approachable. On the other hand, if she or he dresses informally, he or she may be viewed as "on the students' level" and approachable, but students may lack respect for the teacher and be prone to misbehavior (e.g., talking out of turn, distracting other students, leaving class early, arriving late). As teachers, we may seek to establish **homophily**—perceived similarity in appearance, background, and attitudes—so that our relationship and level of popularity in our students' eyes is enhanced, but there are downfalls to this approach.

## Teacher Chronemics

In the chapter on environment, we explored **chronemics** or the communicative aspects of time. Some teachers have strict rules about time, meaning they're very punctual to classes and meetings, as well as demanding with regard for students arriving on time and not wasting time. You may not normally think of the management of time as a form of nonverbal communication, but time management and rules communicate a great deal about a person. In U.S. culture, we tend to be rigid about time compared to other cultures, such as European cultures who have more flexible views of time than Americans. What nonverbal messages are sent by a teacher who consistently arrives to class early, just to greet and chit-chat with students? How about a

## REMEMBER 11.5

| | |
|---|---|
| **Learning Environments:** | spaces and locations where learning occurs. |
| **Distance Education:** | courses in which students don't have to be physically present in traditional classrooms. |
| **Wired Environments:** | built environments conducive to the use of laptop computers and other web-based technologies without the need for plugging into an electric outlet. |
| **Immediacy:** | behavior that enhances psychological and physical closeness between people. |
| **Teacher Nonverbal Immediacy:** | nonverbal cues that reflect a teacher's approachability, availability, closeness, and warmth. |
| **Excessive Immediacy:** | offensive and inappropriate comments, gestures, physical proximity, and touch that can occur in classrooms, hallways, and faculty offices. |
| **Teacher Misbehaviors:** | teachers' offensive or disruptive actions that are detrimental to student learning. |
| **Corporeal Punishment:** | striking a student with a paddle, belt, or other object as a form of reprimand. |
| **Homophily:** | perceived similarity in appearance, background, and attitudes. |
| **Chronemics:** | the communicative aspects of time. |

teacher who is consistently 10 to 15 minutes late to class? A teacher who won't let you out on time to get to your next class on time? A teacher who demands that you be on time, but isn't on time him/herself? You can probably now see how teacher chronemics, among other nonverbal cues, communicate a great deal about the person.

## ■ STUDENT NONVERBAL COMMUNICATION

Another factor to consider in educational contexts is student nonverbal behavior. Ever been distracted by what other students are doing around you in class? Have you thought about how much student nonverbal communication takes place in the classroom? Student nonverbal communication is important for us to explore, so that you can be more aware of your own behavior as well as the behavior of other students in your classrooms and other campus settings. Your classmates' behavior affects your own, but you probably knew that. At the same time, this information about student nonverbal cues helps prospective teachers become more aware of what may go on in their classrooms.

While researchers have given teacher nonverbal behavior specific consideration, they've also examined student nonverbal communication (Andersen, Andersen,

Murphy, & Wendt-Wasco, 1985; Baringer & McCroskey, 2000; Mottet, 2004; Mottet & Beebe, 2006b; Mottet, Beebe, Raffeld, & Paulsel, 2005; Paulsel, 2004; Titsworth, 2001). We now turn our attention toward *you*—yes, you, the one sleeping in the back row of our classroom.

## Student Adapting Behaviors

Ever thought about the nonverbal cues students send in educational settings? There are so many we could cover, but let's focus on the more obvious ones. One category of nonverbal cues, mostly associated with kinesics, are termed **adaptors**—nonverbal behaviors that help us to satisfy a personal need, cope with emotions, or adapt to an immediate situation. As professors, we know that our students prefer to bolt the classroom as soon as they've finished an exam, but as a nonverbal experiment, the next time you finish a test and some of your classmates are still in the room finishing theirs, stick around and watch the nonverbals. You'll see interesting examples of nervous tension in the bodies of your classmates—frequent shifts of posture in chairs, hair twirling, pencil chewing or tapping on desktops, running the hands through the hair repeatedly, and long stares up at the ceiling (hoping for a vision of the right answer)—because most students exhibit some sort of nonverbal signal of test anxiety. Then there's the thigh shaker. Some students can make one of their legs quiver up and down at a very high speed, and they don't usually realize they're doing it.

Another common nonverbal category is termed **leave-taking behavior**—nonverbal cues that indicate a departure is imminent, such as sighing or breathing hard, looking at a clock or watch, sitting on the edge of a chair, packing up a backpack or laptop computer, and so on. These cues tell the teacher that students are ready to hit the road! Students engage in these behaviors consciously and unconsciously, as a means of nonverbally masking their desire to run out the door because they want class to be over. Other students choose to leave class early or arrive late. What's the nonverbal message sent to a professor and your fellow classmates if you leave class early or arrive late? While some teachers aren't bothered by these behaviors, others find them to be disrespectful, so much so that they post rules in their course syllabi forbidding or penalizing late arrivals or early departures. (One of our former colleagues used to lock the door of her classroom when class started, as sort of a "public shaming" for students arriving late.) In contrast, some students arrive to class early, wait outside the door for the classroom to become available, or sit in the classroom studying their notes (or catching up on emails and text messages) before the professor and other students arrive. What nonverbal signal is sent by students who arrive to class early? Do teachers view them as smarter? More involved and interested in course content? Our point is this: Student nonverbal behavior in educational settings *does* play a role in helping form positive or negative impressions.

## Student Misbehaviors

Just as teachers exhibit misbehaviors, students are capable of behaving badly too. Student behaviors in the classroom that are perceived by teachers and other students

*The loading of a bag as class is ending can send a negative nonverbal signal to an instructor.*

to be negative, such as talking out of turn, interrupting the teacher or other students, over-talking (meaning monopolizing class discussion), arriving late to class, and leaving class early have been termed in research **student misbehaviors.** Take a moment to think of student misbehaviors that really bother you (but that, of course, you would *never* do). How many of these misbehaviors are nonverbal?

Students and teachers alike use more and more technology in the classroom these days. Laptop computers, personal digital assistants (PDAs), cell phones, and pagers are the beginning of a long list of electronic devices that help us manage our everyday lives. But where do we draw the line when the use of such technology invades the classroom? Consider your teacher's syllabus or class rules for this course you're taking in nonverbal communication. Does the syllabus address the use of technology in the classroom? Should teachers permit cell phone usage during class, in your opinion? As textbook authors and communication professors, we've experienced this dilemma first hand, and we still grapple with it. Here's our current cell phone and laptop policy reprinted from one of our undergraduate course syllabi:

> **CELL PHONE POLICY:** Please avoid cell phone discussions and texting during class. This policy is in place to create a context conducive to learning. Please turn all phones off or turn them to vibrate. I will stop and ask students who take phone calls to leave the classroom. If you're expecting an emergency call during class, please inform your instructor and set your phone or pager to vibrate so that class disruption is minimalized.

**LAPTOP COMPUTER POLICY:** Laptop computers are for note taking purposes ONLY. Students who are caught surfing the web, sending emails, or playing computer games during class will be asked to leave.

What's your reaction to these policies? Do you think they're fair or unreasonable in this day and age? Not too many years ago, teachers hoped that students would "raise their hand" to be called on. Now, they worry about cell phones going off and wonder if students with their faces and eyes buried in laptop computers are taking notes or looking at MySpace pages. What's the nonverbal message sent when students are preoccupied with texting their friends instead of looking at the teacher or participating in class discussion? What impression do teachers have of students who take a cell phone call in the middle of class? What impressions do other students have of this behavior? Have classroom norms evolved along with the growth of technology?

## Students with Disabilities

In previous chapters we've discussed the importance of developing nonverbal competency when communicating with people with disabilities. Nonverbal communication skills of teachers and students are critical to the formation of inclusive, respectful learning environments for students with disabilities. Have you ever had social contact with a student with a disability? Perhaps you, as a student, are living with a disability or have a family member or friend who comes to mind. Our knowledge or clue that a student is living with a disability is often based on their physical appearance (Braithwaite & Thompson, 2000). Sadly, the physical appearance of a person with a disability sometimes causes us to make assumptions about her or his communicative capability, and to interact with the person (or not) based on our assumptions (Braithwaite, 1990, 1991, 1996; Braithwaite & Braithwaite, 1997; Braithwaite & Thompson, 2000). If you have a classmate with a physical disability, you may need that person to clue you as to what is needed or expected in educational settings (e.g., holding open the classroom doors; trading seats so that someone in a wheelchair or on crutches can more comfortably fit in the room; offering special assistance, like carrying books and materials; moving out of the way). But it's important for all of us to be careful that we don't assume that a physical disability means a person has diminished mental, intellectual, or communicative capacity; students with disabilities face and overcome daily obstacles that often don't even register with people who do not have disabilities.

Consider how nonverbal communication awareness can help accommodate students with learning disabilities, such as test anxiety, dyslexia, Attention Deficit Disorder (ADD), and Attention Deficit Hyperactive Disorder (ADHD) (Rieffe, Terwogt, & Kotronopoulou, 2007; Sprouse, Hall, Webster, & Bolen, 1998). For the most part, learning disabilities aren't revealed through nonverbal means (like physical appearance); students with learning disabilities occasionally reveal their status to their teachers but seldom to classmates. Sometimes you might notice a student's absence on test days, which indicates that she or he takes tests in a more private, often proctored environment, so that distractions common to classroom settings are

---

**REMEMBER 11.6**

| | |
|---|---|
| **Adaptors:** | nonverbal behaviors that help a person satisfy a personal need, cope with emotions, or adapt to an immediate situation. |
| **Leave-Taking Behavior:** | classroom nonverbal cues that indicate to teachers that students are ready to leave. |
| **Student Misbehaviors:** | negative student behaviors in the classroom that can disrupt learning. |

---

reduced. You might overhear a student talk to a teacher about disability accommodation or, as happened very recently to the female author of this book, a student was quite disclosing about her learning disability. She explained to everyone in her communication class about her ADHD and dyslexia, and actually taught everyone a good deal about her issues and how best to respond to her. Students with learning disabilities—the hidden or masked kind of disabilities—remind us all that we need to take care with our nonverbal cues in educational settings, as well as sharpen our powers of nonverbal observation, so that we function and communicate more effectively in instructional contexts.

## SUMMARY ■ ■ ■ ■ ■

In this chapter, we provided an application of nonverbal communication to two key contexts in daily life: professional and educational settings. We discussed the importance of direct and indirect nonverbal communication in trying to get a job. Recall the impact of direct nonverbal communication cues during job interviews (e.g., physical appearance, clothing, hair length, body smell, professional handshake) and be aware of the more subtle, indirect forms of nonverbal communication before and after an interview (e.g., resumé, hand-written thank-you notes, email addresses, web postings). Further, we applied several nonverbal communication codes to on-the-job experiences, such as superior–subordinate relationship development, coworker nonverbal communication, and nonverbal communication with customers and clients.

Next we discussed the important role of nonverbal communication as a leadership quality in people. Factors such as impression management, hiring good people, and being aware of one's own and others' verbal and nonverbal communication are essential to leadership. Effective leaders not only pay attention to their own nonverbal communication, they also pay attention to the nonverbals of people they hire. Effective leaders work to develop emotional intelligence—the ability to monitor one's own and others' feelings and emotions, to discriminate among them, and to use this information to guide one's thinking and action.

In the next section of this chapter, we examined the significance of nonverbal communication in educational settings, with special attention to learning environments, teacher nonverbal behavior, and student nonverbal behavior. We discussed how wired environments and other instructional technologies shape how students and teachers use space on college campuses. We also addressed the effect of teacher nonverbal immediacy on student learning. In addition, we examined teacher misbehaviors—offensive or disruptive actions by teachers that are often detrimental to learning and the creation of a supportive, safe classroom environment.

In the final section of this chapter, we overviewed student nonverbal behavior. Specifically, we examined student misbehaviors, such as talking out of turn, interrupting a teacher or other students, monopolizing class discussions, arriving late to class, and leaving class early for their negative impacts in an instructional setting. We ended the chapter with a discussion of the important role of nonverbal cues when communicating with students with disabilities. We trust that your reading of this chapter has provided you with an understanding of some of the more important aspects of nonverbal communication in two critical contexts in which our need to succeed and be perceived as effective communicators are essential.

## DISCUSSION STARTERS

1. What forms of direct nonverbal communication do you think are most important when trying to get a job? What indirect nonverbal strategies are most important?

2. In a professional situation, have you ever shaken hands with someone who violated your expectations? Do you think that a professional handshake is an important skill for you to work on, or do you have this nonverbal cue down?

3. Think about your current email address and what nonverbal cues it sends about you. Are you going to change your email address for professional contexts or keep the same one you've had as a college student? Why or why not? Will you remove information posted on the web about yourself once you're out on the job market?

4. If you currently have a job, how do you nonverbally manage difficult coworkers? Identify some specific nonverbal communication codes and explain how you use them to help resolve or avoid conflict at work.

5. Review the nonverbal essentials of leadership discussed in this chapter. Are these nonverbal qualities something you're capable of? Make a list of people you look up to for their leadership skills. Are they masters of nonverbal communication? In what ways?

6. Have you ever enrolled in distance education or taken an online course? If so, how important was nonverbal communication in that course? How was the nonverbal communication different in the online course, compared to a traditionally delivered course?

7. What's your view of student technology use in classroom environments? Do you find cell phone and laptop usage distracting? What do you think of students who text message their friends during class?

8. Make a list of student nonverbal misbehaviors you find distracting in the classroom. Are most of the behaviors verbal or nonverbal in nature?

# REFERENCES

Adler, R. B., & Elmhorst, J. M. (2008). *Communicating at work* (9th ed.). New York: McGraw-Hill.

Andersen, J. F., Andersen, P. A., Murphy, M. A., & Wendt-Wasco, N. (1985). Teachers' reports of students' nonverbal communication in the classroom: A developmental study in grades K–12. *Communication Education, 34,* 292–307.

Andersen, P. A. (2004). *The complete idiot's guide to body language.* New York: Alpha.

Baringer, D. K., & McCroskey, J. C. (2000). Immediacy in the classroom: Student immediacy. *Communication Education, 49,* 178–186.

Barnes, S. B. (2003). *Computer-mediated communication: Human-to-human communication across the Internet.* Boston: Allyn & Bacon.

Baron, R. A. (1983). Short note: "Sweet smell of success"? The impact of pleasant artificial scents on the evaluations of job applicants. *Journal of Applied Psychology, 68,* 709–713.

Beebe, S. A. (1974). Eye contact: A nonverbal determinant of speaker credibility. *Speech Teacher, 23,* 21–25.

Beebe, S. A., Beebe, S. J., & Ivy, D. K. (2007). *Communication: Principles for a lifetime* (3rd ed.). Boston: Allyn & Bacon.

Bennett, S. (2005). *The elements of resumé style.* New York: AMACOM.

Bert, J. H., & Piner, K. (1989). Social relationships and the lack of social relations. In S. W. Duck & R. C. Silver (Eds.), *Personal relationships and social support.* London: Sage.

Bowen, D. D., & Kilmann, R. H. (1975). Developing a comparative measure of the learning climate in professional schools. *Journal of Applied Psychology, 60,* 71–79.

Bradberry, T., & Greaves, J. (2005). *The emotional intelligence quick book.* New York: Simon & Schuster.

Braithwaite, D. O. (1990). From majority to minority: An analysis of cultural change from able bodied to disabled. *International Journal of Intercultural Relations, 14,* 465–483.

Braithwaite, D. O. (1991). "Just how much did that wheelchair cost?": Management of privacy boundaries by persons with disabilities. *Western Journal of Speech Communication, 55,* 254–274.

Braithwaite, D. O. (1996). "I am a person first": Different perspectives on the communication of persons with disabilities. In E. B. Ray (Ed.), *Communication and disenfranchisement: Social health issues and implications* (pp. 257–272). Mahwah, NJ: Erlbaum.

Braithwaite, D. O., & Braithwaite, C. A. (1997). Understanding communication of persons with disabilities as cultural communication. In L. W. Samovar & R. Porter (Eds.), *Intercultural communication: A reader* (8th ed., pp. 154–164). Belmont, CA: Wadsworth.

Braithwaite, D. O., & Thompson, T. L. (2000). *Handbook of communication and people with disabilities: Research and application.* Mahwah, NJ: Erlbaum.

Bringhurst, R. (2004). *The elements of typographic style* (3rd ed.). New York: Harts and Marks.

Burch, P. (2001, July 15). Silent judgment: Experts say you have 10 seconds to project your true image. *Corpus Christi Caller Times,* pp. C4, C5.

Burgoon, J. K., & Le Poire, B. A. (1999). Nonverbal cues and interpersonal judgments: Participant and observer perceptions of intimacy, dominance, composure, and formality. *Communication Monographs, 66,* 105–124.

Burgoon, J. K., Stern, L. A., & Dillman, L. (1995). *Interpersonal adaptation: Dyadic interaction patterns.* Cambridge, UK: Cambridge University Press.

Campbell, B. (2002). *If chins could kill: Confessions of a B movie actor.* New York: Thomas Dunne Books/St. Martin's Griffin.

Carlson, S. (2006, July 21). The campus of the future: Financially sound and well-designed, with potato-starch cutlery. *The Chronicle of Higher Education,* p. A25.

Carney, D. R., Hall, J. A., & LeBeau, L. S. (2005). Beliefs about the nonverbal expression of social power. *Journal of Nonverbal Behavior, 29,* 105–123.

Cash, T. F., Gillen, B., & Burns, S. (1977). Sexism and "beautism" in personnel consultant decision making. *Journal of Applied Psychology, 62,* 301–310.

Cashdan, E. (1998). Smiles, speech and body posture: How women and men display sociometric status and power. *Journal of Nonverbal Behavior, 22,* 209–228.

Chamberlin, C. R. (2000). Nonverbal behaviors and initial impressions of trustworthiness in teacher-supervisor relationships. *Communication Education, 49,* 352–364.

Chaplin, W. E., Phillips, J. B., Brown, J. D., Clanton, N. R., & Stein, J. L. (2000). Handshaking, gender, personality, and first impressions. *Journal of Personality and Social Psychology, 79,* 110–117.

Chesebro, J. L. (2003). Effects of teacher clarity and nonverbal immediacy on student learning, receiver apprehension and affect. *Communication Education, 32,* 135–147.

Christophel, D. M. (1990). The relationships among teacher immediacy behaviors, student motivation, and learning. *Communication Education, 39,* 323–340.

Cooper, P., & Simonds, C. J. (2006). *Communication for the classroom teacher* (8th ed.). Boston: Allyn & Bacon.

Crane, E., & Crane, F. G. (2002). Usage and effectiveness of impression management strategies in organizational settings. *International Journal of Action Methods, 55,* 25–34.

DeMeuse, K. (1987). A review of the effects of nonverbal cues on the performance appraisal process. *Journal of Occupational Psychology, 60,* 207–226.

Dimitrius, J., & Mazzarella, M. (1999). *Reading people: How to understand people and predict their behavior—anytime, anyplace.* New York: Ballantine.

Dipboye, R. L., Arvey, R. D., & Terpstra, D. E. (1977). Sex and physical attractiveness of raters and applicants as determinants of resume evaluation. *Journal of Applied Psychology, 62,* 288–294.

Dunbar, N. E., & Burgoon, J. K. (2005). Perceptions of power and dominance in interpersonal encounters. *Journal of Social and Personal Relationships, 22,* 207–233.

Edwards, A., & Edwards, C. (2001). The impact of instructor verbal and nonverbal immediacy on student perceptions of attractiveness and homophily. *Journal on Excellence in College Teaching, 12,* 5–16.

Edwards, C., Edwards, A., Qing, Q., & Wahl, S. T. (2007). The influence of computer-mediated word-of-mouth communication on student perceptions of instructors and attitudes toward learning course content. *Communication Education, 56,* 255–277.

Eisenberg, E. M., Goodall, H. L., Jr., & Trethewey, A. (2006). *Organizational communication: Balancing creativity and constraint* (5th ed.). New York: Bedford/St. Martin's.

Ekman, P. (1965). Communication through nonverbal behavior: A source of information about an interpersonal relationship. In S. S. Tomkins & C. E. Izard (Eds.), *Affect, cognition, and personality.* New York: Springer.

Elfenbein, H. A. (2006). Learning in emotion judgments: Training and the cross-cultural understanding of facial expressions. *Journal of Nonverbal Behavior, 30,* 21–36.

Engelberg, E., & Sjoberg, L. (2004). Emotional intelligence, affect intensity, and social adjustment. *Personality and Individual Differences, 37,* 533–542.

Farr, M. (2007). *The quick resumé and cover letter book.* St. Paul, MN: JIST Works.

Farrenkopf, T., & Roth, V. (1980). The university faculty office as an environment. *Environment and Behavior, 12,* 467–477.

Flynn, C. P. (1998). To spank or not to spank: The effect of situation and age of child on support of corporeal punishment. *Journal of Family Violence, 13,* 21–37.

Flynn, N., & Flynn, T. (2003). *Writing effective e-mail: Improving your electronic communication.* Boston: Thomson Course Technology.

Frymier, A. B. (1993). The impact of teacher immediacy on students' motivation: Is it the same for all students? *Communication Quarterly, 42,* 454–464.

Glick, P., Larsen, S., Johnson, C., & Branstiter, H. (2005). Evaluations of sexy women in low- and high-status jobs. *Psychology of Women Quarterly, 29,* 389–395.

Goffman, E. (1971). *Relations in public: Microstudies of the public order.* New York: Harper Colophon.

Goleman, D. (1995). *Emotional intelligence.* New York: Bantam.

Gorham, J. (1988). The relationship between verbal teacher immediacy behaviors and student learning. *Communication Education, 37,* 40–53.

Gruber, J. E. (2006). The impact of male work environments and organizational policies on women's experiences of sexual harassment. In P. J. Dubeck & D. Dunn (Eds.), *Workplace/women's place: An anthology* (3rd ed., pp. 110–117). Los Angeles: Roxbury.

Guerrero, L. K., & Floyd, K. (2006). *Nonverbal communication in close relationships.* Mahwah, NJ: Erlbaum.

Hackman, M. Z., & Johnson, C. E. (2004). *Leadership: A communication perspective.* Longrove, IL: Waveland.

Hall, J. A. (2001). Status roles and recall of nonverbal cues. *Journal of Nonverbal Behavior, 25,* 79–100.

Hall, J. A. (1996). Touch, status and gender at professional meetings. *Journal of Nonverbal Behavior, 20,* 23–44.

Hamermesh, D. S., & Biddle, J. E. (1994). Beauty and the labor market. *American Economic Review, 84,* 1174–1194.

Harris, M. J., & Rosenthal, R. (2005). No more teachers' dirty looks: Effects of teacher nonverbal behavior on student outcomes. In R. E. Riggio & R. S. Feldman (Eds.), *Applications of nonverbal communication* (pp. 157–192). Mahwah, NJ: Erlbaum.

Harris, P., & Sachau, D. (2005). Is cleanliness next to godliness? The role of housekeeping in impression formation. *Environment and Behavior, 37,* 81–99.

Haunani Solomon, D., & Miller Williams, M. L. (1997). Perceptions of social-sexual communication at work: The effects of message, situation, and observer characteristics on judgments of sexual harassment. *Journal of Applied Communication Research, 25,* 196–216.

Hiemstra, K. M. (1999). Shake my hand: Making the right first impression in business with nonverbal communications. *Business Communication Quarterly, 62,* 71–74.

Holley, L., & Steiner, S. (2005). Safe space: Student perspectives on classroom environment. *Journal of Social Work Education, 41,* 49–64.

Jackson, H. (2005). Sitting comfortably? Then let's talk! *Psychologist, 18,* 691.

Kearney, P., Plax, T. G., Hays, E. R., & Ivey, M. J. (1991). College teacher misbehaviors: What students don't like about what teachers say and do. *Communication Quarterly, 39,* 309–324.

Keyton, J., & Rhodes, S. C. (1999). Organizational sexual harassment: Translating research into application. *Journal of Applied Communication Research, 27,* 158–173.

Kougl, K. (1997). *Communicating in the classroom.* Prospect Heights, IL: Waveland.

Krapels, R. H. (2000). Communication training in two companies. *Business Communication Quarterly, 63,* 104–110.

Lee, J., & Busch, P. E. (2005). Factors related to instructors' willingness to participate in distance education. *Journal of Educational Research, 99,* 109–115.

Leigh, T. W., & Summers, J. O. (2002). An initial evaluation of industrial buyers' impressions of salespersons' nonverbal cues. *Journal of Personal Selling and Sales Management, 22,* 41–53.

Masip, J., Garrido, E., & Herrero, C. (2004). Facial appearance and impressions of credibility: The effects of facial babyishness and age on person perception. *International Journal of Psychology, 39,* 276–289.

Mausehund, J. A., Timm, S. A., & King, A. S. (1995). Diversity training: Effects of an intervention treatment on nonverbal awareness. *Business Communication Quarterly, 58,* 27–30.

Mayer, J., & Salovey, P. (1993). The intelligence of emotional intelligence. *Intelligence, 17,* 433–442.

Mazer, J. P., Murphy, R. E., & Simonds, C. J. (2007). I'll see you on "Facebook": The effects of computer-mediated self-disclosure on student motivation, affective learning, and classroom climate. *Communication Education, 56,* 1–17.

McBride, M. C., & Wahl, S. T. (2005). To say or not to say: Teacher communication boundary management. *Texas Speech Communication Journal, 30,* 8–22.

McCarthy, J., & Goffin, R. (2004). Measuring job interview anxiety: Beyond weak knees and sweaty palms. *Personnel Psychology, 57,* 607–637.

McCroskey, J. C., & McVetta, W. R. (1978). Classroom seating arrangements: Instructional communication theory versus student preferences. *Communication Education, 27,* 99–110.

McCroskey, J. C., Richmond, V. P., & McCroskey, L. L. (2006). Nonverbal communication in instructional contexts. In V. Manusov & M. L. Patterson (Eds.), *The Sage handbook of nonverbal communication* (pp. 421–436). Thousand Oaks, CA: Sage.

McElroy, J. C., Morrow, P. C., & Ackerman, R. J. (1983). Personality and interior office design: Exploring the accuracy of visitor attributions. *Journal of Applied Psychology, 68,* 541–544.

McNeill, D. (2000). (Ed.). *Language and gesture.* New York: Cambridge University Press.

McPherson, M., Kearney, P., & Plax, T. G. (2003). The dark side of instruction: Teacher anger as classroom norm violations. *Journal of Applied Communication Research, 31,* 76–90.

McPherson, W. (1997). "Dressing down" in the business communication curriculum. *Business Communication Quarterly, 60,* 134–146.

Mehrabian, A. (1966). Immediacy: An indicator of attitudes in linguistic communication. *Journal of Personality, 34,* 26–34.

Mehrabian, A. (1968). Inference of attitudes from the posture, orientation, and distance of a communicator. *Journal of Consulting and Clinical Psychology, 32,* 296–308.

Mehrabian, A. (1969a). Measures of achieving tendency. *Educational and Psychological Measurement, 29,* 445–451.

Mehrabian, A. (1969b). Significance of posture and position in the communication of attitude and status relationships. *Psychological Bulletin, 71,* 359–372.

Mehrabian, A. (1971). *Silent messages.* Belmont, CA: Wadsworth.

Mehrabian, A. (1972). *Nonverbal communication.* Chicago: Atherton.

Mehrabian, A. (1981). *Silent messages: Implicit communication of emotions and attitudes* (2nd ed.). Belmont, CA: Wadsworth.

Menzel, K. E., & Carrell, L. J. (1999). The impact of gender and immediacy on willingness to talk and perceived learning. *Communication Education, 48,* 31–40.

Montgomery, B. M. (1982). Verbal immediacy as a behavioral indicator of open communication content. *Communication Quarterly, 30,* 28–34.

Moore, A., Masterson, J. T., Christophel, D. M., & Shea, K. A. (1996). College teacher immediacy and student ratings of instruction. *Communication Education, 45,* 29–39.

Morand, D. A. (2001). The emotional intelligence of managers: Assessing the construct of validity of a nonverbal measure of "people skills." *Journal of Business and Psychology, 16,* 21–33.

Morrow, P. C., & McElroy, J. C. (1981). Interior office design and visitor response: A constructive replication. *Journal of Applied Psychology, 66,* 646–650.

Mottet, T. P. (2000). Interactive television instructors' perceptions of students' nonverbal responsiveness and their influence on distance teaching. *Communication Education, 49,* 146–164.

Mottet, T. P. (2004). The effects of student verbal and nonverbal responsiveness on teacher self-efficacy and job satisfaction. *Communication Education, 53,* 150–163.

Mottet, T. P., & Beebe, S. A. (2006a). The relationship between student responsive behaviors, student socio-communicative style, and instructors' subjective and objective assessments of student work. *Communication Education, 55,* 295–312.

Mottet, T. P., & Beebe, S. A. (2006b). Foundations of instructional communication. In T. P. Mottet, V. P. Richmond, & J. C. McCroskey (Eds.), *The handbook of instructional communication: Rhetorical and relational perspectives* (pp. 3–32). Boston: Allyn & Bacon.

Mottet, T. P., Beebe, S. A., Raffeld, P. C., & Paulsel, M. L. (2005). The effects of student responsiveness on teachers granting power to students and essay evaluation. *Communication Quarterly, 53,* 421–436.

Nai-kuo, H. (2005, August 28). Physical appearance an important factor in job hunting: Survey. *Central News Agency* (Taiwan).

Nelson, A., & Golant, S. K. (2004). *You don't say: Navigating nonverbal communication between the sexes.* New York: Prentice Hall.

O'Hair, D., Friedrich, G. W., & Dixon, L. A. (2008). *Strategic communication in business and the professions* (6th ed.). Boston: Allyn & Bacon.

O'Sullivan, M. (2005). Emotional intelligence and deception detection: Why most people can't "read" others, but a few can. In R. E. Riggio & R. S. Feldman (Eds.), *Applications of nonverbal communication* (pp. 215–253). Mahwah, NJ: Erlbaum.

Pante, R. (2006). Image builds business. *Today's Chiropractic, 34,* 73–75.

Paulsel, M. L. (2004). Using behavior alteration techniques to manage student behavior. *Communication Teacher, 18,* 44–48.

Peluchette, J. V., Karl, K., & Rust, K. (2006). Dressing to impress: Beliefs and attitudes regarding workplace attire. *Journal of Business and Psychology, 21,* 45–63.

Post, P., & Post, P. (2005). *Emily Post's the etiquette advantage in business: Personal skills for professional success* (2nd ed.). New York: Collins.

Powell, R. G., & Harville, B. (1990). The effects of teacher immediacy and clarity on instructional outcomes: An intercultural assessment. *Communication Education, 39,* 369–379.

Pugh, D. (2001). Service with a smile: Emotional contagion in the service encounter. *Academy of Management Journal, 44,* 1018–1027.

Rainey, A. (2006). Tress for success. *The Chronicle of Higher Education,* p. A6.

Rawlins, W. K. (2000). Teaching as a mode of friendship. *Communication Theory, 10,* 5–26.

Remland, M. (1981). Developing leadership skills in nonverbal communication: A situational perspective. *Journal of Business Communication, 18,* 17–29.

Remland, M. (1984). Leadership impressions and nonverbal communication in a superior-subordinate interaction. *Communication Quarterly, 32,* 41–48.

Remland, M. (2006). Uses and consequences of nonverbal communication in the context of organizational life. In V. Manusov & M. L. Patterson (Eds.), *The Sage handbook of nonverbal communication* (pp. 501–519). Thousand Oaks, CA: Sage.

Remland, M., Jones, T., & Brinkman, H. (1995). Interpersonal distance, body orientation, and touch: Effects of culture, gender and age. *Journal of Social Psychology, 135,* 281–297.

Rester, C. H., & Edwards, R. (2007). Effects of sex and setting on students' interpretation of teachers' excessive use of immediacy. *Communication Education, 56*, 34–53.

Richmond, V. P., McCroskey, J. C., & Hickson, M. L. III. (2008). *Nonverbal behavior in interpersonal relations* (6th ed.). Boston: Allyn & Bacon.

Rieffe, C., Terwogt, M. M., & Kotronopoulou, K. (2007). Awareness of single and multiple emotions in high-functioning children with autism. *Journal of Autism and Developmental Disorders, 37*, 455–465.

Riggio, R. E. (2005). Business applications of nonverbal communication. In R. E. Riggio & R. S. Feldman (Eds.), *Applications of nonverbal communication* (pp. 119–138). Mahwah, NJ: Erlbaum.

Riley, J. (1979). The olfactory factor in nonverbal communication. *Communication, 8*, 159–168.

Roach, K. D. (1997). Effects of graduate teaching assistant attire on student learning, misbehaviors, and ratings of instruction. *Communication Quarterly, 45*, 125–141.

Rocca, K. A., & McCroskey, J. C. (1999). The interrelationship of student ratings of instructors' immediacy, verbal aggressiveness, homophily, and interpersonal attraction. *Communication Education, 48*, 308–316.

Rogers, J. K., & Henson, K. D. (2006). "Hey, why don't you wear a shorter skirt?" Structural vulnerability and the organization of sexual harassment in temporary clerical employment. In P. J. Dubeck & D. Dunn (Eds.), *Workplace/women's place: An anthology* (3rd ed., pp. 272–283). Los Angeles: Roxbury.

Rosenfeld, L., & Plax, T. (1977). Clothing as communication. *Journal of Communication, 27*, 24.

Salacuse, J. (2005). Your place or mine? Deciding where to negotiate. *Negotiation, 11*, 3–5.

Salovey, P., & Mayer, J. (1990). Emotional intelligence. *Imagination, Cognition, and Personality, 9*, 185–211.

Sandberg, J. (2003, March 2). Want to know someone's job status? Look at desk location. *Corpus Christi Caller Times*, p. D4.

Schmid Mast, M., & Hall, J. A. (2004). Who is the boss and who is not? Accuracy judging status. *Journal of Nonverbal Behavior, 28*, 145–165.

Smeltzer, L., Waltman, J., & Leonard, D. (1991). Proxemics and haptics in managerial communication. Reprinted in L. K. Guerrero & M. L. Hecht (Eds.), *The nonverbal communication reader: Classic and contemporary readings* (2008, 3rd ed., pp. 184–190). Prospect Heights, IL: Waveland.

Sprouse, C. A., Hall, C. W., Webster, R. E., & Bolen, L. M. (1998). Social perception in students with learning disabilities and attention-deficit/hyperactivity disorder. *Journal of Nonverbal Behavior, 22*, 125–134.

Stires, L. (1980). Classroom seating location, student grades, and attitudes: Environment or self selection? *Environment and Behavior, 12*, 241–154.

Teven, J. J. (1996). The effects of office aesthetic quality on students' perceptions of teacher credibility and communicator style. *Communication Research Reports, 13*, 101–108.

Thornbory, G., & White, C. (2006). How to project a professional image. *Occupational Health, 58*, 24.

Timm, S., & Schroeder, B. L. (2000). Listening/nonverbal communication training. *International Journal of Listening, 14*, 109–127.

Titsworth, B. S. (2001). The effects of teacher immediacy, use of organizational lecture cues, and student note taking on cognitive learning. *Communication Education, 50*, 283–297.

Vilnai-Yavetz, I., Rafaeli, A., & Schneider-Yaacov, C. (2005). Instrumentality, aesthetics, and symbolism of office design. *Environment and Behavior, 37*, 533–551.

Vogler, A., & Jorgensen, J. (2005). Windows to the world, doors to space: The psychology of space architecture. *Leonardo, 38*, 390–399.

Wahl, S. T., McBride, M. C., & Schrodt, P. (2005). Becoming "point and click" parents: A case study of communication and online adoption. *Journal of Family Communication, 5*, 279–294.

Waldvogel, J. (2007). Greetings and closings in workplace email. *Journal of Computer-Mediated Communication, 12(2)*, article 6.

Wallace, R. (2008). *The only resumé and cover letter book you'll ever need.* Cincinnati: Adams Media.

Walther, J. B. (2006). Nonverbal dynamics in computer-mediated communication, or :(and the net :('s with you, :) and you :) alone. In V. Manusov & M. L. Patterson (Eds.), *The Sage handbook of nonverbal communication* (pp. 461–479). Thousand Oaks, CA: Sage.

Wang, S., & Reeves, T. C. (2006). The effects of a web-based learning environment on student motivation in a high school earth science course. *Educational Technology, Research and Development, 54*, 597–621.

Weiss, D. S., & Lolonde, R. N. (2001). Responses of female undergraduates to scenarios of sexual harassment by male professors and teaching assistants. *Canadian Journal of Behavioral Science, 33*, 148–163.

White, S. E. (1995). A content analytic technique for measuring the sexiness of women's business attire in media presentations. *Communication Research Reports, 12,* 178–185.

Whitmore, J. (2005). *Business class: Etiquette essentials for success at work.* New York: St. Martin's.

Winchip, S. (1996). Academic environments: Internal analysis. *College Student Journal, 30,* 340–345.

Witt, P. L., & Wheeless, L. R. (1999). Nonverbal communication expectancies about teachers and enrollment behavior in distance learning. *Communication Education, 48,* 149–154.

Wollin, D. D., & Montagre, M. (1981). College classroom environment: Effects of sterility versus amiability on student and teacher performance. *Environment and Behavior, 13,* 707–716.

Worley, D., & Chesebro, J. (2002). Goading the discipline towards unity: Teaching communication in an Internet environment—A policy research analysis. *Communication Quarterly, 50,* 171–191.

Zweigenhaft, R. (1976). Personal space in the faculty office: Desk placement and the student-faculty interaction. *Journal of Applied Psychology, 61,* 529–532.

# Nonverbal Communication

## Chapter 12

## Gender, Intimate Relationships, and Sexuality

## CHAPTER OBJECTIVES ■ ■ ■ ■ ■

After studying this chapter, you should be able to:

1. Distinguish between the terms sex and gender.

2. Define the terms androgyny, sexual orientation, and gender identity as subsets of the larger concept of gender.

3. Identify key sex differences in nonverbal sending and receiving abilities.

4. Discuss major research findings regarding men's and women's behavior within the nonverbal codes of proxemics, physical appearance, kinesics, facial expressions and eye behavior, touch, and vocalics.

5. Identify Scheflen's four stages of quasi-courtship behavior and the relevant nonverbal cues present in each stage.

6. Overview Mehrabian's immediacy research, in terms of the most relevant nonverbal cues associated with immediacy.

7. Identify and provide examples of nonverbal cues within Jones and Yarbrough's three categories of intimate touch.

8. Review major research findings on nonverbal cues and relationship maintenance, conflict, and dissolution.

9. Define sexuality, sexual orientation, and gaydar, and identify the primary nonverbal codes associated with each.

10. Discuss the impact of nonverbal cues before, during, and after sexual activity.

## CASE STUDY   Kelly and Chris Get Into It

Last semester I took a gender communication class, as well as a nonverbal communication class. I got lucky, in that I actually got to witness in action a lot of what I studied in both courses when I went to a holiday party at the end of the semester. Two friends of mine who've been dating for quite awhile, Kelly and Chris, got into a huge fight at the party, and it was really interesting to watch. (Okay, so I don't like to see my friends fighting, but it *was* fascinating, in a sick kind of way.)

I guess they'd been arguing for a few weeks, or at least before the party, but that night it went like this: Kelly asked Chris to refresh the drinks they were having—a simple request, right? But Chris said in response, "What do I look like? Your own personal slave? You have two legs; use them." A couple of us laughed and someone said, "Wow, that was rude," but we also knew that Kelly can kind of be like that—sorta bossy. You should have seen the look on Kelly's face when Chris said that. Kelly was obviously embarrassed, because that face got redder and redder, as Chris just stood up and went to the bar, ignoring Kelly's request. Then Kelly stood up, apologized to the group of us right there who were witnessing the exchange, then followed Chris to the bar area, where they proceeded to have a little "chat." The chat soon turned into a full-out fight, with both yelling, in full view of everyone at the party. Chris had a grip on Kelly's arm that was pretty aggressive, as they stared at each other and yelled. I'd really never seen them fight like this; they've been together for a long time and they usually get along well, so this was unusual (to say the least).

Well, to make a long story longer, they realized everyone was looking at them and that conversation at the party had come to a virtual stop, so they went their separate ways. Kelly headed outside, Chris headed into a back room somewhere. We didn't see them together at all the rest of the night; I heard that Kelly left with some guy, probably because Chris took off in the car they came in.

All the nonverbals were there, related to power and dominance: Chris' proxemics created distance from Kelly at first, but Kelly wouldn't have any of that. Kelly's and Chris' walk and posture showed anger, as well as their flushed faces and intense eye contact. As they stood almost nose-to-nose during the argument, Chris' aggressive touch toward Kelly revealed an intensifying level of anger, as did the increasing volume with what they were saying to each other. Then proxemics kicked in again, as the couple parted ways at the party. In terms of who was the aggressor or who "won" the fight, I guess I'd say it was a draw.

Did I forget to mention that Kelly and Chris are a gay couple I've known for several years?

"That girl over there is really hot, and she knows she's hot, too. She's not looking at anybody, but everybody's sure looking at her."

"Check out that cute guy; do you think he's gay or straight? Got any gaydar on him?"

"We've been out a couple of times, and I keep thinking he's going to make a move, then he doesn't. I think he's attracted to me, but I can't figure out if he's just being polite, if he's shy, or 'just not that in to me.'"

Sex, gender, relationships, sexuality. If those words aren't enough to pique your interest in this chapter, check your pulse.

When deciding what application chapters to write for this book, your co-authors felt that this chapter was a "no brainer"; this topic *had* to be covered. Everyone has a sex and a gender (and we'll discuss later why those are different things), as well as relationships, ranging at different times in our lives from to very casual and non-intimate to very close and intimate. But perhaps you've not stopped to think about how nonverbal communication facilitated your establishment of those relationships. And have you ever considered the role nonverbal communication plays in developing or deepening your relationships, or just keeping them going? What about how nonverbal affects the way relationships end?

In order for you to get the most you can out of this reading, we challenge you to insert people (including yourself) into the descriptions of the various relationships and experiences we explore here. Try not to read this *objectively* or at an emotional distance, as you might if you were merely preparing to be tested over the material. Read this chapter *subjectively*, putting yourself, your relationships, and your experiences into every page, so that you get the most out of this information. Compare your experience to what research has discovered; if your experience is similar, then you'll see yourself in these pages. But if your experience differs, try not to dismiss the information out of hand, as in "this stuff doesn't apply to me." Relationships are unique entities—each with their own lessons to be learned—so we can't possibly cover all circumstances and types of relationships in this chapter. Trust that there is something to be gained in this information, something that can be applied to at least one of your relationships to help you better understand its dimensions or affect it in a positive direction.

We also broach the important, but "ticklish" subject of sexuality in this chapter. Nonverbal cues are a critical part of how we view ourselves as sexual beings, how we communicate our sexuality to other people, and how we express how we feel about certain people in our lives. But we feel the need for a disclaimer for an intense topic like this one: Please don't think that by tackling the topic of sexuality and relationships we're assuming that, (1) all our readers are sexually active, (2) all readers are equally interested in sexuality and relationships, and (3) all readers are involved in relationships in which sexual activity may or may not be an integral part. Not everyone is part of an intimate relationship at present; some people are single and celibate. We do believe that all human beings are sexual creatures, but how you choose to express your sexuality (or not) is not subject to our judgment. We hope that the information in this chapter is relevant for those of you who look forward to sexual activity within the confines of one committed relationship, such as marriage or a monogamous partnering, as well as those of you with whom sexual activity is a more frequent occurrence within multiple relationships.

So let's begin this provocative chapter by examining nonverbal communication as affected by sex and gender, then explore the role of nonverbal communication in the initiation, maintenance, and sometimes termination of relationships. Finally, we'll close with a discussion of sexuality, including sexual orientation, in terms of how we express our sexual selves nonverbally.

# ■ EFFECTS OF SEX AND GENDER ON NONVERBAL COMMUNICATION

We know "it takes two to tango" and that for some people, differences between the sexes "make the world go 'round,'" but are the sexes more alike than different when it comes to nonverbal communication, or are the differences more pronounced? How can we possibly address such huge generalizations inherent in this topic? Let's first begin by getting on the same page regarding terminology; then we'll explore the sexes and nonverbal cues.

## Sex Versus Gender

In the world outside the walls of your classroom, the terms **sex** and **gender** are used interchangeably. For the sake of clarity, we use them in this chapter with exclusive meanings. The term **sex** refers to the biological/physiological characteristics that make us female or male. Sex is binary, meaning that, apart from a very few anatomical aberrations of nature, human beings have two options in terms of their sex: female and male. At some points in this chapter we use the term sex to refer to sexual activity between men and women, but we'll try to make it as clear as possible whether we mean the term as a categorization of persons or an activity.

The term **gender** refers, first, to psychological and emotional characteristics of individuals. Commonly these characteristics pertain to masculinity, femininity, or **androgyny** (a combination of both feminine and masculine traits) (Bem, 1974). But gender encompasses more than this. Unlike sex, gender isn't binary; it is far more complicated. Gender includes the following: biological sex; personality traits and psychological makeup; attitudes, beliefs, and values; **sexual orientation** (related to the sex of a person with whom we wish to engage in sexual activity); and **gender identity** (our view of self relative to feminine and masculine traits, as well as our view of appropriate roles for men and women in society) (Lippa, 2006).

While sex is biologically or genetically derived, gender is socially and culturally constructed, meaning that our femaleness or maleness is much more extensive than the fact of being born anatomically and hormonally female or male (LaFrance, Paluck, & Brescoll, 2004; Marecek, Crawford, & Popp, 2004). What's attached to or interpreted from our biological sex is taught to us through our culture, virtually from the time we're conceived. Culture, with its evolving customs, rules, and expectations for behavior, has the power to affect our perceptions of gender. When we encounter members of other cultures (or our own culture, for that matter) who view sex and gender differently or who operate from rules that contrast with our own, the notable difference may reinforce our original conception of gender or cause it to change (Ivy & Backlund, 2008).

Thinking of gender as culturally constructed allows us to change or reconstruct gender, meaning that the way we view masculinity and femininity is not the way we *have* to view them. We can learn to understand gender differently and more broadly if we break through the boundaries of binary sex. Viewing gender through a broader lens helps us understand nonverbal cues that can be construed as masculine or feminine and realize how culture overlays such interpretations. Then we can choose to accept or reject the interpretations for ourselves. So when studying nonverbal communication, it's

## REMEMBER 12.1

| | |
|---|---|
| **Sex:** | biological/physiological characteristics that make us female or male; sexual activity between people. |
| **Gender:** | our psychological and emotional characteristics. |
| **Androgyny:** | combination of feminine and masculine traits. |
| **Sexual Orientation:** | related to the sex of persons with whom we wish to engage in sexual activity. |
| **Gender Identity:** | view of self relative to feminine and masculine traits; view of appropriate roles for men and women in society. |

important to remember the biological constraints of sex, as well as the cultural constructions of gender, that have a profound effect on how we learn to express ourselves and interpret others' nonverbal cues.

## Women, Men, and Nonverbal Codes

Now that we've discussed how gender is a broader construct than sex, which makes it the more interesting concept to explore, we must now admit that this section of information will seem illogical to you. Here's why: Most of the research and literature on nonverbal behaviors of men and women focus on biological sex, not psychological/ cultural gender. Perhaps the reason for this is because gender, with all its interesting complications, is harder to study than binary sex. Imagine you're a researcher: Is it easier to categorize a group of people by sex—female or male—or by gender, which involves many variables? While we would learn more from studying gender and all its complexities, studies of gender are harder to accomplish, therefore they are less prevalent than studies of sex. In this section, we progress through various codes of nonverbal behavior to explore sex effects, as research has investigated them.

**Nonverbal Sending and Receiving Ability.** Research on this topic has shown consistently that the sexes have varying abilities when it comes to sending and receiving nonverbal cues, with women having the edge, in general. At least three explanations can be offered for the variation: (1) genetics, (2) brain functioning, and (3) modeling (i.e., socialization). In terms of genetics, biological factors affect our development, which affects our nonverbal behavior (Richmond, McCroskey, & Hickson, 2008). For example, our physicality in terms of body shape, type, and structure are genetically determined, and these characteristics affect how our physical appearance communicates to others, as well as our kinesics, like walk, stance, gesturing behavior, and facial expression. Studies suggest that our brains function differently, in terms of how men and women process and interpret stimuli, as well as how we respond verbally and nonverbally to others, although this area of research is controversial (Begley, 1995; Gur et al., 1995; Halpern, 2000; Kimura, 1987, 2000; Kohlberg, 1966; Paul, 2002). Some experts conclude that brain studies actually show

*In your experience, do women and men behave differently, in terms of nonverbal cues?*

minimal differences (indicating that the sexes' brains are actually more similar than different) and that these research results are used primarily to engender divisiveness and create unnecessary drama (Bleier, 1984; Gibbons, 1991; Tavris, 1992).

In terms of the third explanation, modeling (which some view as a subset of the larger force of socialization), researchers contend that children model the thoughts, emotions, and actions of others, and that this role modeling has a powerful effect on how children see themselves in terms of sex and gender (Bandura, 1971, 1986; Lippa, 2006; Mischel, 1966; Peach, 1998). These modeling experiences are most potent in childhood and adolescence, but they continue to affect us as adults, as we continue to redefine ourselves as men and women.

In American culture, women and femininity are more associated with affiliation, meaning that women are socialized to emphasize connectedness and culturally shaped to behave in ways that enhance social interaction (Mehrabian, 1981). Women are generally more expressive of emotion than men, which relates to approachability and the skills of listening, responding, and connecting with others (Burgoon, Buller, & Woodall, 1996; Cegala & Sillars, 1989). In general, women's nonverbal behaviors— from body positioning to eye and facial expressions to tone of voice—are enacted out of a motivation to be congruent with other people. Thus, women and girls have been found in studies to be better encoders of emotional information, meaning that they more readily display nonverbal cues of emotion than men and boys (Buck, Miller, & Caul, 1974; Friedman, Riggio, & Segall, 1980; Hall, 2006; Wagner, Buck, & Winterbotham, 1993; Zaidel & Mehrabian, 1969).

In contrast, men are socialized toward independence (versus interdependence), and masculinity is associated with status, power, and dominance (Eccles, 1987; Henley, 2001; Pleck, 1977). Men's nonverbal behaviors primarily serve the purpose of commanding attention and asserting their ideas and identities (Guerrero, 1997; Major, Schmidlin, & Williams, 1990). These socialization trends affect a great deal of what we are taught, from very young ages, regarding appropriate behavior for a person of our sex.

In addition to being more nonverbally expressive than men, women tend to be more sensitive receivers and decoders of others' nonverbal cues, especially those associated with emotions (Baron-Cohen, Wheelwright, Hill, Raste, & Plumb, 2001; Guerrero & Reiter, 1998; Hall, 1998; Scherer, Banse, & Wallbott, 2001; Vogt & Colvin, 2003). On various tests of nonverbal receiving ability measured over decades of studies, girls and women typically outscore boys and men—a differential that begins in grade school and continues into adulthood. What this means is that a female advantage exists not only when it comes to expressing one's own emotions, but also when interpreting others' nonverbal cues, such as processing minute facial expressions and eye behavior, attending to subtle changes in vocal cues, remembering people's appearance, and so forth (Burgoon & Bacue, 2003; Hall, 1984; Horgan, Schmid Mast, Hall, & Carter, 2004; McClure, 2000; Schmid Mast & Hall, 2006). This sex difference is consistent across U.S. and non-U.S. subjects and across age groups (Dickey & Knower, 1941; Hall, 1978; Izard, 1971; Rosenthal, Hall, DiMatteo, Rogers, & Archer, 1979). However, two exceptions have been documented in research: Women tend to be less adept than men when it comes to decoding nonverbal expressions of anger (Rotter & Rotter, 1988; Wagner, MacDonald, & Manstead, 1986) and nonverbal cues of deception (Hurd & Noller, 1988; Zuckerman, DePaulo, & Rosenthal, 1981).

**Proxemics.**   In Chapter 4, we defined **proxemics** as the way that distance and space play a communicative role in everyday life. While proxemic behavior reflects our culture more than our sex, some interesting differences exist in how women and men tend to use and relate to space. Sociologist Judith Hall summarized the research on this topic in 2006, as an update to her review of 1984; surprisingly little has changed during this period. In general, women's personal space bubble seems to be smaller than that of men. Research conducted in public settings shows that female dyads stand and sit closer together than male dyads, with the male–female dyad standing and sitting the closest (Aiello & Jones, 1971; Mehrabian & Diamond, 1971). Women and girls interact with others more closely than men and boys, and are less likely to view intrusions into their personal space as violations. But this tendency is affected by whether the other people in the interaction are perceived as friendly or hostile. In situations where people are perceived as possibly hostile or threatening, women tend to keep as great a distance as men (Bell, Kline, & Barnard, 1988).

Have you ever noticed at a movie theatre how men and boys who come together typically don't sit side by side—they tend to leave a seat between them? One time one

*Have you ever detected a difference in how female friends use space, versus male friends?*

of your co-authors saw three boys around the age of 11 or 12 come into a movie theatre together, only to split up and sit in three different rows, in seats right in front of one another.

Various explanations for proxemic differences have been rendered over the years. One is that males tend to be physically larger than most females, thus they require more space. (We think that explanation is rather bogus, but we do come across it from time to time.) Another explanation relates to how children play and what they play with (Blakemore & Centers, 2005; Campenni, 1999; Hughes, 1994; Leaper, 1994). Typically, girls play with dolls and small objects, which don't take much space; conversely, boys play with trucks, balls, and larger objects, which encourage play away from the home and often take more room. As we mentioned earlier, the female orientation toward affiliation and connection also offers insight into sex differences in proxemics, in that girls and women may feel that getting physically closer to people facilitates psychological closeness. Yet another explanation relates to traditional roles for men and women in U.S. culture, meaning that, even in this day and age, women are more often the primary homemakers, men the primary breadwinners. These roles translate into women more often being in the home with children who invade their spaces at will, while men are more often in the public sphere, which affords more space and less invasion (Riesman, 1990; Wood, 1994). A final explanation is this: Since expansive, highly protected and defended spaces are correlated with higher power and status, particularly in U.S. culture, the tendency is for men to be afforded more personal space since they hold more economic, political, and social power than women (Henley, 2001; Spain, 1992; Weisman, 1992).

**Physical Appearance, Attractiveness, Clothing, and Artifacts.**   In Chapter 5, we explored physical appearance as a significant code of nonverbal behavior, and some obvious differences exist in terms of cultural displays of biological sex. For example, in most cultures, men do not wear dresses or skirts, but there are always exceptions (like Scottish kilts or tribal sarongs worn by members of both sexes). What's more interesting for our discussion are men's and women's attitudes toward attractiveness and how their choices regarding physical appearance, clothing, and artifacts (e.g., jewelry, cosmetics, cologne) serve as nonverbal communication.

What's the first question most people in the U.S. ask when they learn a baby has been born—ten fingers and ten toes? No; usually they ask "boy or girl?" After the sex of the baby is learned, pink and blue clothing and accessories are often lavished on the infant (as well as a whole array of sex-typed behavior) (Ivy & Backlund, 2008). Parents who dress their boy baby in pink will no doubt be ridiculed (as will the baby), but that boy baby may grow up to be as self-confident as Donald Trump, who is known for his pink power ties. Girls dressed in blue don't face as much ridicule as boys in pink, but for infants, the colored clothing serves as a nonverbal cue to people who wouldn't be able to otherwise detect the sex of the infant.

In U.S. culture, as well as many cultures around the world, more emphasis is placed on the physical attractiveness of females than males. Girls are given toys related to appearance more often than boys. Grooming sets (toy brushes, combs, and mirrors), makeup and fingernail kits, tutus and other "dress up" items, and dolls with endless outfits and accessories can communicate an "appearance is everything" message to young girls (Caldera, Huston, & O'Brien, 1989; Kuther & McDonald, 2004; Messner, 2000; Pomerleau, Bloduc, Malcuit, & Cossette, 1990). Is the most important thing about G.I. Joe the outfits he wears and the gun he carries? We can see a trend that begins in childhood and that carries over into adulthood. Granted, more emphasis has been placed in recent decades on men's fashion and accessories, and it has become more acceptable, even encouraged, for men to pay serious attention to their attractiveness and how they look and dress (hence the term "metrosexual"), but fashion is still predominantly a "woman's world." We can look to cable television for an example of this, in that the hit show *Project Runway* on the Bravo cable network involves male and female designers, designing almost exclusively women's clothing.

While clothing has become more generic, fashions for men and women still differ significantly in most cultures around the world. Clothing for men primarily serves as body protection, cultural display, and, for many, as an extension of their personalities. Men's clothing and artifacts are less often chosen for their conveyance of masculinity and their ability to attract members of the opposite sex, but for women clothing is quite often an extension of their sexuality and a device for attracting attention. As gender communication scholar Julia Wood (2005) explains, "Women's clothing is designed to call attention to women's bodies and to make them maximally attractive to viewers. Form-fitting skirts, clingy materials, and details in design encourage seeing women as decorative objects. Most women's shoes are designed to flatter legs at the cost of comfort and safety—how fast can you run in two-inch heels?" (p. 134) (Try four-inch stilettos and a tight mini skirt.) Researchers continue to examine the connection between clothing choices, the pressure women feel to conform to current standards, and women's physical and sexual safety (Crawford & Unger, 2004).

Volumes have been written on this subject; it is beyond the parameters of this chapter to explore it more thoroughly. But we should all be encouraged to take this information and relate it to our own experiences and observations. Is it your opinion that women are more concerned with, as well as more often judged by, their appearance and attractiveness than men in American culture? Or think about it this way: Do women and men take equal heat when they seem not to care about their appearance? How often do you hear, in reference to a married couple, that the wife has "let herself go," compared to the husband? In our experience, it seems that men can put a few pounds on around the middle without people thinking that they've "let themselves go," but the scrutiny and criticism of women who gain weight or seem to lose interest in their appearance is pronounced.

**Kinesics.**   In Chapter 6, we explored **kinesics** or the study of human movement, gestures, and posture. With regard for movement in general, researchers have obtained mixed results when observing members of both sexes (Bente, Donaghy, & Suwelack, 1998). Some studies have found that men tend to be more active (or restless), in that they move and gesture more than women, which runs opposite to the stereotype that most women couldn't talk if you tied their hands together. Yet other studies have found that women tend to use more gestures than men (Hall, 2006). What may distinguish the sexes is not the amount of gesturing, but the type of gesture or the purpose for its use. Men often use commanding gestures for the purpose of indicating dominance, while women more often use gestures in acquiescence or affiliation with other people (Hall, 1984; Richmond, McCroskey, & Hickson, 2008). For example, you're more likely to see a man use a pointing gesture to make a point, while a woman is more likely to use a palms up or other less confrontational gesture to make the same point.

In terms of walking behavior, some sex differences have been detected (Hickson, Stacks, & Moore, 2004). For example, nonverbal communication scholar Peter Andersen (2004) explains that men's bodies are somewhat motionless while walking, in that their hips and torso tend to stay frontward, their feet move about one foot apart in stride, and their arms swing significantly. In contrast, women have more swing or side-to-side motion in their walks. Women's hips tend to move more than men's, mostly due to the fact that women often put one foot in front of the other when walking, which engages the hip action.

Sex differences in sitting behavior have also been observed with regularity in American culture. Typically, men assume open sitting positions, meaning that the legs are often extended and spread apart rather than close together. A man is more likely to cross his leg over his knee in a 90-degree angle to the floor, while a woman is more likely to cross her legs at the knee with the crossed leg hanging down, or to cross her legs at the ankles (Andersen, 2004; Hall, 1984). While some women like the comfort of the 90-degree angle seating position, sitting this way tends to give off a masculine connotation.

*See if you can detect sex differences in sitting behavior as you go about your everyday life.*

**Facial and Eye Expressions.**    A subset of kinesics, the facial and eye expressions of the sexes have long been a fascination of nonverbal research. A key difference between women and men has been detected in how often and why they smile. A comprehensive review of more than 400 studies revealed that women smile more than men (LaFrance, Hecht, & Levy Paluck, 2003). Women tend to use more facial animation than men; they smile as a common facial expression in social interaction, whereas men's smiles are more purposeful and used to reveal their emotions (Briton & Hall, 1995; Burgoon, Buller, & Woodall, 1996; Hall, Carney, & Murphy, 2002). Apparently, women smile more, even when they are alone (Trees & Manusov, 1998) and they receive more smiles from others than men (Hinsz & Tomhave, 1991). Watch a mixed-sex group in interaction some time and note the smiling behavior. Might you see more of the men using rather blanked expressions, until they wish to make a point or convey a particular emotion, whereas the women smile, seemingly for no reason?

In terms of eye contact, research shows some sex differences in that women tend to maintain more eye contact in conversation than men; men tend to hold eye gaze while they are speaking, but not while listening (Bate & Bowker, 1997; Hall, 2006; Hall & Halberstadt, 1986; McCormick & Jones, 1989). As we explained in Chapter 7, in research terms this is called the **visual dominance ratio,** which is the amount of time looking while speaking versus looking while listening (Hall, 2006). Individuals, particularly men, who wish to assert dominance will make eye contact when they have something to say, but break eye contact when spoken to. However, the athletics context may be an exception to this trend, in that athletes often make direct, continuous eye contact with opponents, as a way of "psyching them out" and asserting their dominance (Pearson, 1985). Ever seen two prize fighters face off before the fight and stare each other down?

**Touch (Haptics).**   The study of touch behavior in humans and animals is often referred to as **haptics,** as we explored in depth in Chapter 8. Studies document some sex differences in terms of how women and men give and receive touch. Research shows that, in general, parents extend more affection to daughters than to sons, and touches they extend to daughters are more gentle (Condry, Condry, & Pogatshnik, 1983). Rough-housing or "rough and tumble" play is often enacted differently between parents and male versus female children (Lindsey & Mize, 2001; Ross & Taylor, 1989).

Many nonverbal researchers have deemed touch more of a "female-appropriate" behavior, primarily because studies from the 1970s through the 2000s have concluded the following: (1) women express more nonverbal affection than men; (2) women receive more touch, from both men and other women, than men; (3) women engage in more frequent and more intimate same-sex touch than men; (4) women are more comfortable with touch in general, and same-sex touch in specific, than men; (5) women in heterosexual stable or married relationships are more likely to initiate touch than their male partners; and (6) women perceive themselves as being more affectionate than men (Andersen & Leibowitz, 1978; Bombar & Littig, 1996; Burgoon & Walther, 1990; Derlega, Lewis, Harrison, Winstead, & Costanza, 1989; Emmers & Dindia, 1995; Floyd, 1997, 2000; Floyd & Morman, 1997; Greenbaum & Rosenfeld, 1980; Guerrero & Floyd, 2006; Hall & Veccia, 1990; Jones, 1986; Major, Schmidlin, & Williams, 1990; Roese, Olson, Borenstein, Martin, & Shores, 1992; Wallace, 1981; Willis & Rawdon, 1994). In their study of touch in sporting contexts, Kneidinger, Maple, and Tross (2001) found that females enacted significantly more touching behavior than males, even after negative events (like losing a point or a game).

Certainly, factors other than sex influence our touching behavior, such as age, culture, what we witnessed and modeled after in the homes in which we grew up, our personalities, and our life experiences in general. But, just as we mentioned in Chapter 8, it's important for all of us to remember that touch is a complicated nonverbal cue. Touch is the most powerful, yet also the most misunderstood, of the nonverbal cues we study. Research has shown convincingly and consistently that men often misinterpret touches they receive from women, and this can prove detrimental in our relationships, as well as day-to-day interactions. We've all heard about sexual harassment in the workplace and educational settings, and many sexual harassment incidents begin as misunderstandings about the boundaries of propriety related to touch behavior. So we all need to learn as much as we can about this topic, about how the sexes may view and enact touch differently, and how one person's expression of affection or interest is another's sexual harassment.

**Vocalics (Paralanguage).**   The study of how people express themselves through their voices is termed **vocalics,** sometimes referred to as **paralanguage.** Some sex differences in vocal production can be attributed to physiology, meaning how male and female vocal anatomy is structured and the influence of hormones on its functioning. But physiology doesn't tell the whole story. Granted, men's typically thicker vocal folds produce lower pitches; changes in hormones (specifically, a depletion of estrogen as women age) deepen the average pitch of female voices (Krolokke & Sorensen, 2006; Tracy, 2002). But cultural/societal factors (and resulting stereotypes) affect voice production as well (Addington, 1968; Brownmiller, 1984; Graddol & Swann, 1989). We understand the association of low pitch with masculinity and high pitch with femininity, but why turn this aspect into a stereotype and then ridicule people who don't adhere to what's expected? As we mentioned in Chapter 9 on this topic, research indicates that women and men have equal abilities to produce high pitches, but that men have been socialized not to use higher pitches lest they sound feminine (Henley, 2001; Viscovich, et al., 2003). Masculinity is associated with greater volume, while femininity is associated with a softer-sounding voice, but men and women are equally capable of generating volume when they want to or the situation demands. See how the stereotypes come into play?

One ill-effect that stems from the pitch tendency is a monotone problem, which refers to the effect produced when people don't vary their pitches when they speak. Men often go monotone when giving presentations, primarily due to the lack of emphasis on and practice in vocal variation, stemming from what we just mentioned— the tendency to see variation as feminine. But a monotone voice is deadly for an audience (as many of our students can attest, having listened to monotonic lectures delivered by well-meaning professors). Perhaps men should experiment with more vocal variety for the sake of their listeners, in everyday conversation as well as presentations to audiences, because a modicum of variety is pleasant to the ear. Women might do well to monitor their vocal variety, listening for an appropriate use of variation, because too much variation can sound "sing-songy" and diminish credibility.

One other vocal characteristic relates to sex—male conversational dominance, primarily in the form of interruptions in conversation. Research on this phenomenon is extensive, beginning with communication scholars Zimmerman and West (1975) who studied interaction management and found that more interruptions occur in mixed-sex conversations than in same-sex conversations, and the predominance (96 percent in their studies) of interruptions are made by males. Other evidence of

## REMEMBER 12.2

| | |
|---|---|
| **Proxemics:** | the way that distance and space play a communicative role in everyday life. |
| **Kinesics:** | study of human movement, gestures, and posture. |
| **Visual Dominance Ratio:** | amount of time looking while speaking versus looking while listening. |
| **Haptics:** | study of touch behavior in humans and animals. |
| **Vocalics (Paralanguage):** | study of how people express themselves through their voices. |

male conversational dominance includes initiating topics, maintaining conversation around those topics, talking more often and longer, offering minimal responses to women's comments, and using more statements than questions (Hall, 1984; Marche & Peterson, 1993; Tannen, 1994, 1995; Weiss & Fisher, 1998; West & Zimmerman, 1983). The next time you're in a group of men and women in conversation, see if you can detect any of these sex-typed vocalic behaviors. What impressions do you receive about the interactants who correspond to or defy stereotypes?

## ■ NONVERBAL CUES IN INTIMATE RELATIONSHIPS

Relationships: fascinating, compelling, satisfying, mystifying, thrilling, terrifying, puzzling. For most of us, relationships are what give us life's greatest joy. Sure, we may like our work, enjoy sports, and have hobbies, but if asked what makes life most worth living, most of us would answer "other people." So let's start out this section of the chapter with the premise that relationships of all types—family members, friends, coworkers, intimate loved ones—create both satisfaction and frustration in our lives. Given the importance of relationships, it's only natural that we should study the role of nonverbal communication in the initiation, maintenance, and sometimes even termination of relationships.

Many relationships can be intimate, such as those with close friends, family members, possibly even coworkers, ministers, therapists, attorneys, doctors, or bosses, because the quality of the relationship and the communication within it is of an intimate nature. Because this topic is huge, we've chosen to focus only on the romantic or loving intimate relationship, which may or may not be sexual. What exactly do we mean by **intimacy**? Couples therapist Jeffrey Fine (2001) defines it this way: "To be intimate is to be totally transparent, emotionally naked in front of another who is equally transparent. You want to see into the other's heart. What people should mean when they say *intimacy* is in-to-me-see" (p. 225). As nonverbal communication scholars Andersen, Guerrero, and Jones (2006) explain, intimacy has been conceptualized in a myriad of ways; however, we agree with their view of intimacy as "an experience consisting of felt emotions and perceptions of understanding, or as a relationship that is characterized by affection and trust" (p. 260). These authors locate intimacy within interaction, suggesting that interaction is the "vehicle through which people exchange intimate actions, thoughts, and feelings"; further, they suggest that "nonverbal communication is intimacy's primary vehicle" (p. 260). Whether or not you currently have an intimate relationship in your life, these relationships are what most of us seek and hope to experience in our lifetimes, so it's important to consider the role of nonverbal cues in this context.

### Relationship Initiation

It may sound old-fashioned, but the activity of getting a relationship going is termed **courtship** in research; the more common term is **dating.** To begin this discussion, we rely on the longstanding work of Albert Scheflen (1965), who studied interpersonal encounters and noted patterns of nonverbal behavior over time—patterns that formed into a courtship ritual. (Scheflen's observations were about western cultures in specific, so understand that courtship in African or Middle-Eastern cultures, for example, is enacted differently.) Scheflen distinguished between **courtship,** which he defined as romantic attraction and an interest in some form of sexual intimacy, and **quasi-courtship behavior,** which he was much more keen on and known for among nonverbal scholars. To make it confusing, the same set of behaviors can indicate courtship—a more serious level of interest—as well as quasi-courtship, in which behavior is flirtatious and not to be taken seriously. Scheflen believed that quasi-courtship behavior was useful, in that it could breathe life into dull interactions or settings, or reinvigorate someone's waning attention. We can see the problems that could arise if someone interprets nonverbal cues as courtship while someone else views the behavior as harmless flirtation or seduction—with no intention of forming a deeper connection. The onus is on the receiver of such nonverbal cues to judge the motivation or intent of the behavior, as to whether it indicates serious interest or "just kidding around" or "having fun." In their book on nonverbal communication in relationships, Guerrero and Floyd (2006) explain that "there is often little distinction in the flirtation behaviors used by courters and quasi-courters; where the groups differ is often only in the eventual outcomes they seek" (p. 81).

Scheflen's quasi-courtship ritual includes four categories or stages, summarized in Table 12.1. First are *courtship readiness* cues or the ways we nonverbally communicate to others that we're open to being approached. Women and men alike engage in these behaviors, which include erect posture (no slouching), reduced eye bagginess and jowl sag (meaning alert eyes and a lifted chin), higher general muscle tone, and a tucked-in stomach. In this phase we accentuate our best physical features instead of camouflaging or downplaying them, so as to attract people to us. In the second category, *preening behavior* occurs, which involves self-adaptors such as stroking, twirling, or moving our hair; fixing makeup (especially when women reapply lipstick); smoothing or rearranging clothing (e.g., tugging on a bra strap, adjusting a tie); checking ourselves in a mirror; and unbuttoning or leaving unbuttoned parts of shirts or blouses.

**TABLE 12.1   Scheflen's Quasi-Courtship Behavior**

| STAGE | DESCRIPTION | NONVERBAL CUES |
|---|---|---|
| **Stage 1: Courtship Readiness** | Cues of approachability; behavior that shows readiness for an interpersonal encounter | Erect posture; alert eyes; high muscle tone; tight stomach; emphasized physical features |
| **Stage 2: Preening** | Use of self-adaptors | Touching hair; fixing makeup; touching clothing |
| **Stage 3: Positional Cues** | Partitioning oneself toward someone and away from others | Blocking proxemics; kinesics that keep someone's focus and that keep someone away from others |
| **Stage 4: Actions of Appeal or Invitation** | Cues that suggest progress toward a more intimate, private encounter | Extended eye gaze; exposing of the skin; rolling the pelvis; muscle flexing; revealing wrists, palms, and neck |

*Applying lipstick in public is categorized as preening behavior.*

In the third phase, *positional cues* partition us toward someone and away from others. We can see this happen at social gatherings where people use proxemics as well as their arms, legs, and seating/standing positions to section themselves off from a group, thereby signaling interest in each other and creating a barrier to ward off intruders. It's also interesting to see one person attempt to "corner" someone in conversation, but the other person doesn't wish to be cornered. What is the cornered party likely to do? That person may adjust her or his nonverbal behavior by shifting eye gaze to others in the room, signaling others with facial expressions that equate to "help me" or just to show that he or she isn't glued to that one conversation. The person may also shift body position—either seated or standing—by turning more outward and away from a direct orientation to the other person. A more obvious behavior is to excuse oneself from the conversation or to simply walk away (rude, but expedient).

Scheflen termed his fourth category *actions of appeal or invitation.* These actions typically occur later in the ritual and involve more engaged behaviors, like holding eye gaze longer than in previous phases; looking at a partner flirtatiously (e.g., looking down, then back up quickly and repeatedly; looking at facial and body parts other than the eyes; "batting" the eyelashes); exposing more of the skin (e.g., rolling back sleeves, removing jackets, shifting or crossing the legs to expose a thigh); rolling the pelvis forward (which sounds odd, but is a subtle subconscious move that reveals attraction); flexing muscles or moving in a way that emphasizes those body parts we're most proud of or that will arouse our partner; and revealing the wrists, palms, or neck (which are considered fairly intimate body parts at this stage in a relationship).

Other systems for understanding courtship behavior have been developed. For example, one of the founders of the modern day study of nonverbal communication, Ray Birdwhistell (1970), suggested 24 steps in male–female courtship (which he termed "the courtship dance"), ranging from initial contact to sexual intimacy. Behavioral scholar Desmond Morris (1971) developed a 12-step typology for courtship, which also begins with initial contact and proceeds through sexual intimacy. Anthropologist David Givens (1978) viewed courtship in five stages, beginning with the *Attention Phase* in which people appear alternatively interested and ambivalent. This stage is characterized by such behaviors as making and breaking eye contact and moving close, then away. In the second phase, *Recognition*, people acknowledge their interest and signal their availability. In the *Interaction Phase*, nonverbal cues take a back seat to verbal interaction; nonverbal behavior reinforces the conversation and prevents interruption. If phases one through three are successful, Phase 4 (*Sexual Arousal*) occurs, in which partners communicate sexual interest through such behaviors as touching and kissing. The final stage (dependent on the success of the previous four) Givens labeled the *Resolution Phase*, which involves sexual activity beyond simple touching and kissing.

A fascinating approach to understanding courtship comes from British psychologist Peter Collett, who provided commentary for years on the BBC's equivalent of the *Big Brother* TV show. As he explains in his work, *The Book of Tells*, Collett (2004) views nonverbal cues as **tells**—highly informative attributes or actions that reveal a great deal about a person. (If you're a poker player, you'll recognize the language of "tells" immediately.) Of the heterosexual courting context, Collett explains:

> When it comes to romance, men like to think that they're the ones who make the first move and who decide how fast the relationship should progress. All the research on human courtship shows that this is simply not the case. . . . In nightclubs, bars and at parties, it's the woman who invariably makes the first move. She does this by producing an *approach tell*—a signal which is not too explicit, but which is sufficiently clear to show a man that he may approach her. It's her way of giving him "clearance." (p. 253)

Table 12.2 details six behaviors within Collett's category of *Approach Tells*. According to Collett, the nonverbal tells must be enacted subtly, in a muted fashion, because broader, more obvious behaviors convey very different meanings.

One important thing we all need to remember about this information is this: Nonverbal behavior is complex; if we observe some of these courtship behaviors in various social settings—particularly in early phases—we shouldn't necessarily leap to the interpretation that courtship is going on. For instance, review the behaviors related to Scheflen's Phase 1 (courtship readiness), and then think of the job interview setting. A job applicant might show some of these same behaviors during an interview, because they reflect an *invitation* to communication, not necessarily courtship. What's most important is that Scheflen found certain behaviors consistently present in courtship and quasi-courtship rituals, but such cues can be enacted for other purposes.

## TABLE 12.2   Collett's Approach Tells

| TYPE | DESCRIPTION |
|------|-------------|
| **The Strobe Glance** | A woman will stare at a man to whom she is attracted until she catches his eye. Then she will hold his gaze, avert her eyes, then turn her eyes back to the man and repeat the cycle. |
| **The Eye-Lock** | Instead of several glancing sequences, a woman will hold a man's gaze longer than normal, indicating her interest. |
| **The Eye-Flicker** | Once eye contact is made, a woman will raise her upper eyelids slightly and briefly, causing the eyes to open more widely. This indicates that she's only looking at him and that she's posing a question as to what might follow. |
| **The Hair-Flick** | Once eye contact is made, a woman will run her fingers through her hair or toss her head so that her hair moves. |
| **The Pout** | To draw attention to her femininity (meaning the fact that women tend to have larger lips than men), a woman will protrude her lips (pout) or lick them. This is a sexual cue, since the lips become engorged with blood during sexual arousal. |
| **The Smile** | The most often used approach tell, a woman will offer a partial smile to a man as a sign of attraction, because full smiles tend to be given only to friends and acquaintances. Full smiles convey recognition more than attraction. |

Another approach to this topic of relationship initiation is to examine nonverbal behaviors relevant to **flirting,** or the act of attracting romantic attention. Studies of this topic among heterosexuals have found upwards of 50 gestures and related nonverbal cues that people use to signal their interest (Grammer, Kruck, Juette, & Fink, 2000; Knox & Wilson, 1981; Moore, 1985, 1995; Muehlenhard, Koralewski, Andrews, & Burdick, 1986; Renninger, Wade, & Grammer, 2004). Among the top flirting cues are smiling, surveying a crowded room with the eyes, and increased proxemics. Other flirting behaviors include prolonged and mutual eye gaze; brief, darting glances; looking at specific body features of another person; animated facial expressions; touching behavior (both purposeful and accidental touches); head tosses (sometimes including the infamous "hair flip"); caressing objects such as a glass or keys; movement to music (not dancing, but keeping time to some rhythm one hears); animated vocal inflection, increased rate of speaking, and changes in volume (louder voices to command attention, whispered voices to convey intimacy); and the adjustment of clothing (McCormick & Jones, 1989; Moore, 1985; Perper & Weis, 1987).

Research has found that men tend to view flirting as more sexual than women do, and, as we referenced in the opening section on nonverbal cues and gender, heterosexual men often misinterpret women's friendly behaviors as signs of sexual attraction and interest (Henningsen, 2004; Koeppel, Montagne, O'Hair, & Cody, 1992; Koukounas & Letch, 2001; Moore, 2002). Studies have found that the likelihood for this kind of misinterpretation greatly increases as alcohol consumption increases (Abbey, Zawacki, & Buck, 2005; Delaney & Gluade, 1990).

One other line of research is informative on this topic. Nonverbal scholar Albert Mehrabian, whose work we reference many times in this book, used the term **immediacy** to mean the degree of perceived physical or psychological closeness between people (Mehrabian, 1966). Immediate behaviors indicate liking or a positive feeling (affect) between people. Specifically, Mehrabian (1972) found the following nonverbal cues illustrative of positive affect: forward body lean; symmetric positioning (arms or legs correspond with the general body position); more direct body orientation (body is positioned towards someone, rather than in an indirect or side configuration); relaxed body posture; increased openness of arms and body; close proximity; increased eye gaze; increased touching; and animated facial expression. It's fairly easy to spot two people who like each other, isn't it? Do their behaviors show they like each other but are just flirting, or that their attraction is more serious? If we sharpen our nonverbal observational powers, we might be able to tell *how much* they like each other, if their attraction is serious, and what stage their relationship is in at that particular moment. For example, watch couples in the hallway before class, the student union, or the library. Watch to see if they wall themselves off from others, as though they don't want anyone to talk to them, so engrossed they are in their own conversation. Check out their body positioning, eye gaze, close proximity, touch behavior, and facial expressions, such as prolonged smiling. In general, couples' immediacy behavior is much more pronounced or obvious in the early stages of a relationship than the middle or latter stages.

## Relationship Maintenance

Once an intimate relationship has been launched, it's equally (if not more) challenging to maintain it. What codes of nonverbal communication are most central to the effective maintenance of an intimate relationship? Perhaps the nonverbal code most relevant

### REMEMBER 12.3

| | |
|---|---|
| **Intimacy:** | an experience involving emotions and perceptions of understanding within a relationship characterized by affection and trust. |
| **Courtship (Dating):** | process of trying to get a relationship going; romantic attraction and an interest in some form of sexual intimacy. |
| **Quasi-Courtship Behavior:** | patterns of nonverbal communication that form a ritual of flirtatious behavior. |
| **Tells:** | highly informative attributes or actions that reveal a great deal about a person. |
| **Flirting:** | act of attracting romantic attention. |
| **Immediacy:** | degree of perceived physical or psychological closeness between people; behaviors that indicate liking or a positive feeling between people. |

to the intimate relationship is touch. Psychologist Karen Prager (1995) points to the importance of touch in a relationship, suggesting that it "eliminates the space between people" and "may intensify experiences of intimacy" (p. 348). We turn to the work of Jones and Yarbrough (1985) who identify three categories of touch integral to intimacy. The first category is *Inclusion Touch*, which refers to sustained touches that draw attention to the fact that two people are together and in a relationship. These touches mostly involve the lower body parts, such as sitting hip to hip with someone or entwining the legs. The second category, *Sexual Touch*, includes touches that convey attraction and sexual interest, such as caresses or prolonged holds that involve multiple body parts and that typically move from one part of the body to another. The third category is termed *Affection Touch*, because such actions as placing a hand on a shoulder or squeezing someone's arm in a positive way communicates affection between the parties. Affection touches are just that—pure affection—and they do not convey inclusion or sexual interest. Touches in each of the three categories foster an intimate relationship.

However, research suggests that touch and several other nonverbal cues tend to be more prevalent in the beginning stages of a relationship (relationship escalation), as opposed to the middle or latter stages (Emmers & Dindia, 1995; Guerrero & Andersen, 1991; McDaniel & Andersen, 1998; Noller, 1980). We've probably all felt that rush of excitement a new relationship brings, along with that feeling that we just can't keep our hands off our beloved. When we're with that special person, we want to be close and touching, so as to express and confirm the growing intimacy between us, as well as to shout it to the mountain tops that "we're together." But what happens when the "dew is off the rose"? What happens over time, if the closeness and touching (and, in some relationships, sexual fever) wanes a bit (or a lot)? Within the context of a sexual relationship, the "wane" could be the first time a couple sleeps together—actually *sleeps*—without engaging in sexual activity. We're not saying all relationships experience this kind of change, but many do. Is this sort of change natural or to be expected in an intimate relationship?

Yes and no. From one point of view, becoming more comfortable or used to a partner can be a positive sign that a relationship is maturing, that the outward signals of closeness are no longer necessary or are less important. We no longer have a statement to make to the public; we're just comfortable being together and with who we are as a couple. But if the outward or public displays of affection, as well as the inward or private displays change, that might signal a problem. Research shows that relational partners perceive a variety of nonverbal cues, including vocal expressions, to be indications of intimacy (Le Poire, Shepard, Duggan, & Burgoon, 2002); a lack of attention to and inaccurate decoding of nonverbal cues are related to marital dissatisfaction and can be a sign of waning intimacy (Gottman & Porterfield, 1981; Koerner & Fitzpatrick, 2002; Noller, 1992, 2006). In his book *My Guy: A Gay Man's Guide to a Lasting Relationship*, psychiatrist Martin Kantor (2002) discusses one particular change in an intimate relationship—sexual dissatisfaction, more specifically, boredom—in a gay male relationship:

> Boredom with sex is not inherent in gay relationships, new or old. Overfamiliarity is often cited as the culprit, but with good relationships sex gets less, not more, boring. When a relationship is solid, lust, although not necessarily in its original form, actually increases over the days, months, and years. In simple behavioral terms, having your cake makes you want another slice. (p. 183)

*The nonverbal code of touch, commonly known as affection, is critical in intimate relationships.*

If changes in intimate nonverbal cues aren't handled effectively, it can be alarming and conflict can be the result. But here again, it depends on the people in the relationship. Perhaps a more "normal" or "natural" level or amount of touch, proximity, eye contact, and other nonverbal cues is understandable as a relationship matures, and nothing is wrong. We put those words "normal" and "natural" in quotes because their definitions really depend on the relational partners. No appropriate levels of these behaviors (within the boundaries of a decent society, that is) can be measured and published for all couples to understand and adhere to; it's not that simple.

Think about your parents or an older (meaning older than you) couple for a moment, especially a couple who has been together for many years, perhaps decades. How do the partners behave nonverbally around each other? We've seen such couples operate like a well-oiled machine, without the need for much close proximity, touch, eye contact, or other nonverbal behaviors typically associated

### What Would *You* Do?

Desiree has been with her live-in boyfriend, Justin, for almost three years and she really loves him. But lately—like over the six months or so—Justin has become distant. They rarely have sex anymore, much less touch, other than the perfunctory kiss as they head out the door for the day or say goodnight as they try to fall asleep. Desiree comes from a "touchy" family and considers herself an affectionate person—one who gives touch freely and who needs a lot of affection from her significant other. She wonders if the change in Justin is because he just started a new job, he's stressed, and his attention is on other things—not her. She wonders if she's just being self-absorbed when she thinks about the lack of closeness she feels, or if she's justified in being upset or feeling lonely. In the back of her mind, a little voice makes her wonder if Justin has lost interest in her and, worse, if he's gained interest in someone else.

If you were in this situation, *what would you do?* Would your feelings of loneliness over the loss of closeness be justified, such that you would feel the right to confront your partner about his or her distance? Might you try some nonverbal means of fixing the situation, like increasing your affection to your significant other, in hopes that she or he would get the hint and reciprocate? Or might you just wait out the situation, hoping that as new circumstances become more familiar and stress reduces, your significant other will become affectionate again?

with intimacy. Many of these couples gave up sleeping in the same bed or even the same room years ago, yet if you asked them they would say truthfully that their relationship is as intimate as they come. What we're trying to express here is that the forms of intimate nonverbal behaviors and the frequency and duration with which they are enacted within a relationship is up to the couple to decide. The key is to agree on the decision. When one partner dictates the levels and the other doesn't agree or is disappointed or resentful, intimacy between the two will most definitely be hampered.

Other nonverbal codes besides touch are critical to the successful maintenance of an intimate relationship. Four important proxemic cues are interpersonal distance, body lean, body orientation, and the physical plane (meaning the vertical and horizontal distance between people) (Andersen, et al., 2006). Interpersonal distance means the physical space between partners; research shows that people tend to sit closer to their romantic partners than their friends (Guerrero, 1997). Forward lean, a face-to-face body orientation, and interacting on the same physical plane (as opposed to above or below someone) are all associated with enhanced intimacy (Andersen, et al., 2006). Kinesic behaviors including smiling, facial animation, general facial pleasantness, increased eye contact, and synchronized gestures of immediacy, affection, closeness, and warmth are all important in an intimate relationship (Burgoon & Newton, 1991; Kleinke, 1986; Tickle-Degnen, 2006). As people remain intimate over time, they tend to mimic or acquire each other's nonverbal behaviors, such that they come to look, sound, and behave alike.

Certain vocal behaviors are associated with intimacy and demonstrations of affection between partners (Farinelli, 2008). In terms of pitch, research shows that high-pitched female voices and low-pitched male voices communicate affection rather than the reverse; for both sexes, varying the inflection (i.e., avoiding a monotone delivery) conveys affection as well (Collins & Missing, 2003; Floyd & Ray, 2003). Vocal pleasantness and warmth, as well as laughter, communicate affection between intimates (Burgoon & Newton, 1991; Guerrero, 2004). And finally, intimate partners, especially women, occasionally use babytalk as a show of affection (Bombar & Littig, 1996).

## Relational Conflict and Relationship Dissolution

Some people believe that if we've ever had a connection to someone, that relationship supercedes time, meaning that there's no such thing as an ending to a relationship because these connections and their impact on us are too profound to be considered "terminated." Others believe that many, if not most, relationships end at some point or another, but the truly intimate ones transcend everything, even death. No matter our view of relationship dissolution—lofty, existential, pragmatic, or spiritual—nonverbal communication plays a role in the final cycle of relationship development as well as the initiation and maintenance phases.

Interestingly enough, more information exists about the role of nonverbal communication in relationship initiation than relationship termination or disengagement—perhaps because people like to look on the bright side. Fairy tales are all about the courting stage, but seldom deal with what happens once people start "living happily ever after" or break up. Getting us to think about our breakups or researching the "terminal" can be depressing, but it's important to examine what happens as relationships come apart. We approach this topic in two parts: First, let's examine nonverbal cues and conflict, with the understanding that conflict can be constructive in a relationship; conflict doesn't necessarily signal a relationship's demise (Beebe, Beebe, & Ivy, 2007). But conflict is usually present in a relationship that's on its last legs. Second, let's focus on nonverbal communication and the "parting of ways."

**Relational Conflict.**   Not surprisingly, nonverbal cues are ever-present in conflict situations, often appearing prior to verbal cues (Galvin & Brommel, 1991). But conflict is wide-ranging, in that it can take the form of a simple disagreement without much emotional toll, an ongoing feud with patterns of emergent nonverbal cues, all the way up to a full-blown, knock-down, drag-out, with all the heightened nonverbal cues to boot. One way to tame this beast of a topic is to examine some of the most prevalent nonverbal cues that emerge within conflicts of all shapes and sizes, then discuss how nonverbal cues change depending on the ferocity of the conflict. We know that many conflicts take place over the phone, through text-messaging, and via email and other online ways of connecting, but for simplicity's sake, we frame this discussion around face-to-face conflict.

If we were to ask you what romantic relational partners look and sound like when they fight, you might begin with the nonverbal category of proxemics, because couples in conflict use distance in interesting ways. The most obvious use of proxemic cues is to put physical distance (that parallels the psychological or emotional distance partners feel) between us and our partner (Guerrero & Floyd, 2006). The boxing reference of "going to separate corners" often applies to arguing couples as well, as we attempt to "get some space" from our partners when we disagree.

But the reverse behavior—getting in the face of someone when arguing—is also prevalent. Sometimes we decrease distance in order to appear menacing or get some sort of advantage. We may try to back our partners into a corner or tight space, so that we control the situation by intimidating our partners physically or keeping them from leaving the scene. It's common to witness a sort of push–pull between two partners in conflict, as one advances and one retreats, then they reverse these actions. Sometimes we leave the scene of the conflict altogether, preferring time and distance before we can approach our partners again. However, a withdrawal or avoidant response to conflict is seldom effective (Cloven & Roloff, 1993; Gross, Guerrero, & Alberts, 2004). The more heightened the emotion within a conflict, the more dramatically the nonverbal behaviors will be enacted, unless there is a point when everything shuts down, one person leaves the scene, or someone tries a different tactic (like calming down).

Another relevant nonverbal cue related to proxemics is touch—its decrease or absence, or touch that is increasingly controlling, overbearing, even abusive. When we're in conflict with an intimate partner, most of us decrease our affectionate touch with that person as we increase our distance from him or her. Even once a conflict has been resolved, it may be hard for partners to express affection for each other because the sting of the conflict still hangs in the air. While we may need a hug or prefer to "kiss and make up" once an argument is over, our partner may not be comfortable with this, preferring to stew a bit or process what happened before resuming a normal level of affection with us. It's wise for us all to remember that we have to let people heal at their own pace, rather than force patterns of nonverbal behavior on our partners or make them feel guilty because they're not letting go of the incident or getting beyond it as quickly as we are. If we don't return to equilibrium as quickly as our partner, we have a right to our feelings and to a period of time to recover, but it's unwise to withhold nonverbal cues of intimacy (like eye contact, close proximity, and touch) as a power trip over our partner.

In terms of touch turned abusive in a conflict, it's beyond our scope here to provide a full discussion of dating or domestic violence. But we know that in the heat of an argument, men and women alike may let touch escalate into physical violence when their emotions get out of control (Christopher & Lloyd, 2000). One thing is for sure though, and it warrants mention: Touches that are extended with more force than usual in a relationship can definitely be characterized as abusive (Ivy & Backlund, 2008). We often hear or read in the news about women (gay and straight) who, when asked if their partners physically abuse them, reply no, saying such things as "he just grabbed my shoulders hard and held me against the wall" or "she held my arms down and it left bruises." Abusers (and often their targets) don't like to term such actions abusive, preferring to think of and excuse the behavior as "force" or "pressure." There are too many psychological factors related to partner violence to discuss here, but make no mistake: Touches that arise during conflict and that cause pain to someone are, in all but the rarest of cases, abusive. Excusing someone for pinning you down on the floor or against furniture because "I made him angry" and "she just went too far" are cover-ups for an abusive partner.

What other nonverbal cues are typically present in conflict situations? How about kinesics? Research shows that some conflict partners experience animated gestures,

*People in conflict are likely to use animated gestures.*

head shaking, and random movement in the heat of battle (Newton & Burgoon, 1990). For some of us, our energy builds to such a degree in an argument that our gestures fly about uncontrollably when we're angry; others of us pace and gesture in a repetitive fashion, often pointing accusedly at our partner while placing a hand on our chest to signify that we're blameless. A common gesture, besides pointing, is with arms up, bent at the elbows, with palms facing out, as if to say "stop; I can't take any more" or "back off." Some of us can't sit and argue—we have to stand, as though towering over our partners will give us an edge.

Facial expressions are usually animated in conflict, although some of us put on a stone face and stay that way until the conflict is over. Some of us use continuous eye contact—staring like we want to burn a hole into our partner—while others break eye contact in an argument, preferring to look down or stare off into space. These behaviors are highly individualistic; they depend on the person, the situation, the relationship, and the level of intensity of the conflict.

Vocalic behaviors in conflict are very revealing, but again, quite individualistic. Some of us are vocally aggressive; the more the conflict, the faster our rate of speaking, the greater the volume, the more varied the pitch, and the longer our turns at talk. Heightened vocalic cues rarely diffuse a conflict; they tend to escalate it. Others of us have learned the value of the pause and use a dramatic volume, pitch, and rate decrease to reveal the intensity of our emotions. Still others "suffer in silence," preferring not to engage vocally in an argument at all (Wilmot & Hocker, 2001). But sometimes an even, level, calm way of speaking can enrage a partner because it seems manipulative and controlling.

So if we want to improve our conflict management skills, what does the research suggest we do, nonverbally speaking? First, it's helpful to realize that emotion is almost always a factor in conflict; our nonverbal communication will be affected by the emotion we feel during a disagreement or argument. Second, it's wise to inventory ourselves in terms of how anger affects our nonverbal cues, then work to mediate those displays so that we don't "lose it" in conflict situations, so that we can make constructive conflict out of what potentially could be destructive conflict. Third, it's important to monitor our nonverbal behaviors, as well as those of the person (or people) involved in the conflict, rather than getting caught up in what's being said. Fourth, demonstrating our involvement in conflict resolution means that we show nonverbally that we're in the situation, not checked out of it (Feeney, Noller, Sheehan, & Peterson, 1999). Silence rarely resolves anything, so we should try to speak calmly and normally, modulating the rate, volume, and pitch of our voice and avoiding interrupting our partner (Sillars, Coletti, Parry, & Rogers, 1982). Condescending or irritating cues like eye rolling, accompanied by a "hmmph" or "tsk" kind of vocalization, are clear signals of disdain that won't help mediate or resolve a conflict. We should use direct eye contact, but at normal levels—not staring or avoiding gaze, which send negative signals. Maintaining a calm facial expression and body position and placing ourselves physically on the same plane as the other person, so that we don't give off power cues, are also effective behaviors. A respectful, non-antagonistic distance from our partner in conflict is advisable, recognizing that movements toward or away send definite signals and will likely not help diffuse the conflict (Beebe, Beebe, & Ivy, 2007).

**Relationship Dissolution.** So what happens, nonverbally speaking, when a relationship "tanks"? Communication scholars Knapp and Vangelisti (2005) provide a five-stage framework for relationship disengagement (de-escalation), summarized in Table 12.3. One thing to remember is that a couple may enter one or more stages of the de-escalation process, only to revive their relationship and save it from termination. In general, the stages are characterized by avoidance and increased distance, so nonverbal cues related to general avoidance pertain to the phases. If you review Mehrabian's (1966, 1972) concept of immediacy, discussed earlier in this chapter, the opposite or reverse of immediate behaviors is what typically occurs as a relationship ends.

Knapp and Vangelisti's first stage, *differentiating*, occurs when the differences between relational partners begin to outweigh the similarities. At this point, partners' identities as individuals become more important than their identity as a couple. Nonverbally, partners begin to increase physical distance, use fewer affirming cues (e.g., smiling, head nodding, forward body lean, direct body orientation), and decrease both public and private touch. In the second stage, *circumscribing*, partners become superficial in their communication with each other and generally are more restrictive in their nonverbal expressions of emotion and affection. If we were at a

TABLE 12.3    Knapp & Vangelisti's Stages of Relationship Disengagement

| STAGE | DESCRIPTION | NONVERBAL CUES |
|---|---|---|
| **Stage 1: Differentiating** | Differences between partners begin to outweigh similarities. | Increased distance, fewer affirming cues, decreased touch |
| **Stage 2: Circumscribing** | Superficial communication and restricted expressions of emotion and affection occur. | Significantly increased distance, few affiliative cues (e.g., facial and vocal expressiveness) |
| **Stage 3: Stagnating** | Verbal communication and nonverbal cues of closeness cease. | Little to no touch, almost nonexistent facial and vocal expressiveness |
| **Stage 4: Avoiding** | Couples experience physical separation. | Little to no contact, pains taken to avoid partner |
| **Stage 5: Terminating** | Couples end their relationship. | No contact, pains taken to avoid partner |

party and saw a couple in this phase of their relationship, we could hardly tell from their verbal and nonverbal communication that they were a couple.

*Stagnating* is the third stage, in which communication virtually stops and nonverbal behaviors of closeness and affiliation (e.g., eye contact, physical proximity, touch, facial expressiveness, vocal engagement) shut down. According to news reports, Bill and Hillary Clinton experienced relationship dissolution to this point (the third stage) in the aftermath of the sex scandal that plagued the former president's second term of office. A now-famous piece of footage emerged of President and Mrs. Clinton walking across the White House lawn toward Marine One (the helicopter that would take them to Air Force One)—with their daughter, Chelsea, between them—each holding one of her hands. As President Clinton stopped at the door of the helicopter, he turned to smile and wave to the press while Mrs. Clinton breezed past him and into the copter, not saying a word, making no eye contact nor physical contact with her husband.

The fourth stage of relationship de-escalation is *avoiding*, in which couples physically separate and aren't seen in public together anymore. They tend to avoid going to places where they might run into each other; almost all communication ceases. In the final phase, *terminating*, couples end their relationship. While we don't encourage that you stage a breakup just to study the relevant nonverbal cues, it's fascinating to explore how nonverbal cues change as an intimate relationship comes apart. Those nonverbal cues that were so important to our expression of how we felt about our partner seem to do an about-face once the relationship is in trouble. Probably most of us have had an intimate relationship go south and, painful as it is to remember that experience, it's worth it to take some time and think about how our nonverbal communication was affected when a relationship started to unravel. Did we notice the change in the nonverbal cues at the time—both our own cues and those of our partner? Were there cues we should have picked up on, but didn't—things that might have made a difference and perhaps saved the relationship? Are there things we want to do differently the next time?

# ■ NONVERBAL CUES AND SEXUALITY

Did the word "sexuality" in the heading of this section catch your eye, when you were paging through this chapter, trying to decide what to read and what to skip (er, we mean postpone reading for another time)? What exactly do we mean by "sexuality"— how you view yourself as a sexual being? Your sexual orientation? How you express yourself sexually? Your attitudes about sexual activity? Here's our answer: all of the above. There's no way to do a full treatment of this topic here; volumes of books are written on it and TV and radio shows are dedicated to it, not to mention the pornography industry, because sexuality has fascinated human beings since the beginning of time. So what might we possibly add to the discussion? Our purpose in this final section of the chapter is to overview or hit the high points regarding nonverbal cues and the communication of sexuality. Some of the language you'll read in this section may not be what you're used to in your college textbooks, but we ask you to forge ahead with us, for the greater purpose of learning something, rather than being embarrassed, shocked, or offended by language you may be unaccustomed to reading. Let's begin by defining a few key terms that will be critical to our discussion.

## Sexuality, Sexual Orientation, and Gaydar

The online Encarta World English Dictionary offers three definitions for **sexuality**: (1) the state of being sexual; (2) involvement or interest in sexual activity; and (3) sexual appeal or potency. In their article about sexuality, authors DeLamater and Shibley Hyde (2004) discuss the difficulty in conceptualizing sexuality, because research on this topic is hampered by a narrow view that tends to focus on how sex is accomplished, how often, and, to a lesser degree, with what effect. Much of the research has honed in on penile-vaginal intercourse, which DeLamater and Shibley Hyde believe to be constraining, as though only certain behaviors count as "real sex" (p. 8). They suggest that "in daily life and relationships, by contrast, a wide range of behaviors may contribute to the experience of physical/sexual intimacy by a person, including prolonged contact, holding hands, hugging, dancing, and massage, in addition to behaviors that involve the sex organs" (p. 8). They call for a broader conceptualization of sexuality, with an emphasis on *outercourse* instead of intercourse—one that includes the role of thought, emotions, psychological factors (such as aversion or inhibition), identity, and sociocultural factors (such as social norms, family influences, and access to information). In 2001, Surgeon General David Sacher described sexuality this way: "Sexuality encompasses more than sexual behavior....the many aspects of sexuality include not only the physical, but the mental and spiritual as well. Sexuality is a core component of personality....[it is] a fundamental part of human life" (Office of the Surgeon General, 2001, p. ii, as in DeLamater & Shibley Hyde, 2004, p. 8). So, for the purposes of clarity in our discussion here, let's view **sexuality** as including sexual behavior, as well as cognition, emotion, and psycho-sociocultural factors.

We can operate from an assumption that all human beings are sexual creatures, but the choice of how to communicate our sexuality, if we choose to do so at all, is very individualistic. How do we convey the sexual part of our being? Granted, some of us believe in abstinence, meaning we hold the belief that sexual activity should be within the confines of a monogamous, committed partnering, like marriage. But just because we're not *having* sex doesn't necessarily mean that we don't express our sexuality. But just how does a person nonverbally convey who she or he is sexually? The best way to address this question is to simply ask our friends or acquaintances: Who do you think is sexy and why? Sure, we might get some answers like "he's really intelligent" or "she has a great sense of humor and I find that sexy," but we're more likely to hear comments about physicality and behavior.

This won't surprise you one bit: Physical appearance (which includes attractiveness as well as choices about clothing and artifacts) is the most central nonverbal code related to sexuality. Physical features that we're born with, that we influence by eating right (or not) and working out (or not), that may be altered by illness or accident, and that we accentuate are key conveyers of sexual information. Secondarily, all the things we do to enhance our physical appearance and attractiveness—from clothing choices to alterations to our hair, skin, and bodies to adornments like tattoos, piercings, and jewelry—send sexual messages to other people, whether we intend to do so or not. We're not saying that everyone gets up each day, looks in the closet, and says "How can I look sexy today?" (Although we acknowledge that some people are motivated this way.) What we're saying is that, even if we don't intend to send signals about our sexuality through our appearance, those messages may be conveyed and people may receive them.

All of the other nonverbal codes can relate to sexuality as well. For example, aspects of kinesics like our walk, stance, and posture (i.e., how we "carry" ourselves) may attract others to us because we look confident. Or these cues may repel others because we look like we're carrying the weight of the whole world on our shoulders. Some nonverbal cues are flirtatious, such as the way we use eye contact to show interest in another person, how closely we sit or stand by someone in conversation, how we animate our facial expressions, what kind of touch occurs between us and other people, and how our vocal inflection reveals our interest. All of these elements reveal our sexuality, even if acting sexy or seeking sexual activity is not our intent.

A key element within the larger construct of sexuality is **sexual orientation,** defined in the first section of this chapter as being related to the sex of persons with whom we wish to engage in sexual activity. Since this isn't a human sexuality textbook, we won't go into detail about theories of the origins of sexual orientation, social and political views, and so forth, but will instead focus on the role of nonverbal behavior in the communication of a person's orientation.

Since homosexuality is still largely discriminated against and negatively viewed within U.S. culture and other cultures around the world, many gay, lesbian, bisexual, and transgender people have long felt that they must be "closeted" in order to safely function in society. Briefly, bisexuality refers to people who are attracted to members of both sexes—those who emphasize the whole individual over the biological sex of the individual. Transgender individuals cross over or transcend the traditional boundaries of sex and gender, to develop their own unique expression of their sexuality (Ivy & Backlund, 2008). The United States is more open about gay relationships now than ever, in fact when the president of Iran gave a speech at Columbia University in the fall of 2007, he made the statement that there were no gays in Iran—that homosexuality simply didn't exist in his country. This was met with laughter by the American audience because it was such a ludicrous and politically driven statement, but we must remember that the openness we experience in the U.S. isn't paralleled in all countries around the world. So because of the danger—perceived and real—that homosexual people face, a "sixth sense" or way of perceiving someone's sexual orientation has emerged. You've probably heard the term **gaydar,** referring to an ability to detect the sexual orientation of another person (Leap, 2007). But did you know that gaydar, which is based primarily on nonverbal cues, developed within the homosexual community first, and then was co-opted by heterosexuals as a way of detecting whether someone was gay?

Is gaydar something intuitive, like extrasensory perception (ESP), something a few blessed individuals are born with—this uncanny way of detecting that someone is gay? Yes and no. While some people may have a natural sixth sense about such things, most gaydar is based on keen nonverbal observation, enhanced listening skills, and experience over time in varied social encounters. (As an aside, the ability to sense whether someone is heterosexual has been termed **breedar,** after the derogatory term "breeder," coined to refer to heterosexual people.) Scholar Cheryl Nicholas (2004) defines gaydar as "a folk concept used within the gay community to name the recognition of verbal and non-verbal behavior associated with gay identity" (p. 60). She elaborates: "Gaydar suggests that members of the gay and lesbian culture along with straight people *familiar* with gay/lesbian culture have an innate remote detector that picks up the behavior of individuals within a specified range. The receiver of the stimuli is then of the opinion that the person whose behavior caused the 'blip' in gaydar is gay" (pp. 60–61). Nicholas contends that gaydar is necessary for homosexual people's survival in a world where heterosexuality is the norm or dominant paradigm for relationships. Gaydar protects the invisibility many homosexuals feel is necessary to survive in a discriminatory world. She adds, "Gaydar is possible because gay people believe that it is possible" (p. 66).

Before we take a more in-depth look at how gaydar functions in relation to nonverbal communication, we feel the need to get some stereotypes about gays and lesbians out in the open—to "un-closet" them, so to speak. For one thing, so many of the stereotypes stem from nonverbal behavior. Second, if we expose the stereotypes, then we can see how ludicrous they are and be done with them. Here are some stereotypes about gay men's nonverbal behavior: (1) Gay men have high-pitched voices, use a lot of vocal variety for emphasis and to draw attention to themselves, and talk with a lisp; (2) they have limp wrists, so their hands flap around a lot while they're talking; (3) they're over-sexed, so they touch people a lot more than straight people do, meaning they're overly and inappropriately affectionate; (4) they're over-sexed, so they're promiscuous; (5) they dress flamboyantly or in the most expensive designer clothing, so as to call attention to themselves and how "different" or "special" they are; (6) they make sexually suggestive eye contact, especially with the sexual body parts of any man they meet; (7) they secretly despise themselves and wish they were women, so many of them dress in drag and become drag queens; (8) they secretly despise themselves and wish they were women, so they adopt feminine looks and behaviors; (9) they want to turn straight men gay, so they come on to straight men by using increased proximity, inappropriate touch, and direct and steady eye contact (which would be considered staring in any other context), so that the straight man succumbs to their charms;

(10) they're artistic with a great sense of style, so they dress extremely well and are terrific decorators; (11) they use exaggerated facial expressions in interaction, which is related to the need for attention and to appear different; (12) they're obsessed with looking good and attracting men because sex is very important, so they work out constantly and have beautiful, virtually flawless bodies; (13) they sit or stand in ways that highlight their crotches or buttocks, so that other men will notice and be attracted; (14) when they walk, they sashay, using lots of hip action (like women do); and (15) they like to have women around as camouflage.

Here's the list of stereotypes for lesbians: (1) They're unattractive, both facially and bodily; (2) they wear drab, masculine clothing (like flannel shirts, trucker caps, boots, and pants—never dresses or skirts) in order to appear more "butch" and dominant; (3) they use few accessories and prefer to keep a wallet in a pocket rather than carry a purse, or simply carry a nondescript book bag or briefcase; (4) they secretly despise themselves and want to be men, so they have short haircuts, don't wear makeup, and don't shave their armpits or legs; (5) they're drawn to sports so that they can keep in physical contact with other women; (6) they're over-sexed, so they're overly and inappropriately affectionate; (7) they're over-sexed, so they're promiscuous; (8) they make sexually suggestive eye contact, especially with the sexual body parts of any woman they meet; (9) they want to turn straight women into lesbians, so they come on to straight women by using increased proximity, inappropriate touch, and direct and steady eye contact; (10) they like performing sex acts for the pleasure of straight men; (11) they can't possibly fully enjoy sex since they don't have penises, because everyone knows that the only "true" sex involves penile-vaginal intercourse (and "toys" are no substitute); (12) they have a lousy sense of style, both in dress and home decoration; (13) they appear stone-faced (inexpressive), because too much facial expression looks feminine; (14) they talk in a monotonic fashion, using little vocal variety so as to not seem feminine; and (15) they're overly aggressive and are quick to resort to physical violence to protect their "woman" or their lesbian friends.

That was an exhausting exercise. Do you have some stereotypes that are equally ridiculous to add to either or both lists? Are you appalled or surprised at the length of the lists? What does all this mean?

While *some* of the behaviors listed here might be descriptive of *some* gays and *some* lesbians *some* of the time, since stereotypes typically arise from some observation or experience, you can no doubt see the problem. We run into trouble when we superimpose a stereotype onto new people we meet, expecting them to behave according to type, not as the individuals that they are. But if these descriptions are stereotypes, not the "truth," then just how do gays and lesbians act, nonverbally speaking? Do patterns of nonverbal behavior actually emerge among gays and lesbians and are they detectable with regularity, thus proving the existence and reliability of gaydar?

Scholars have studied gaydar for some time, but they are divided on these questions: While some researchers argue against a distinct set of behaviors for gays and lesbians that would distinguish them from heterosexuals (Van Newkirk, 2006), other studies have produced interesting results that speak to the existence and utility of gaydar. Over a period of three years and with numerous observations and interviews, Nicholas (2004) examined eye gaze as a cue of identity recognition among gay men and lesbians. She noted two persistent forms of eye gaze that she deemed components of gaydar: the **direct stare** and the **broken stare.** The direct stare lasts much longer than typical eye contact made in social circles, and is accomplished by two people in different conversational groups. Nicholas explains:

> Eye contact associated with gaydar is direct, prolonged, curious yet purposeful. The assumptions behind the "direct stare" is that eye-gaze is maintained for a period of time that is considered longer than what would be customary in a social context. If the interactants are moving in different directions, then the body or head would turn to accommodate the eye-gaze. (p. 74)

The second type of eye gaze Nicholas detected with regularity was the broken stare, described in two forms: a "stare-look-away-stare-again" phenomenon and a "peek-a-boo" behavior, which means flashing a look at someone out of the corner of one's eyes (p. 75). Nicholas contends that these forms of eye gaze trigger gaydar and, thus, reinforce and validate its existence. Often the gaze is accompanied by other nonverbal cues, especially facial expressions, hand/body gestures, and turning of the head to follow a gaze. These behaviors work in conjunction with eye gaze to symbolically ask such questions as, "Are you gay?" and "Are you interested in me?"

In another study, researchers Johnson, Gill, Reichman, and Tassinary (2007) investigated how body shape and motion affect perceptions of sexual orientation. In two experiments, they used computer-generated animations, manipulated for body shape and motion, and found that both nonverbal categories affected subjects' perceptions of female figures' sexual orientation. Female figures with hourglass bodies that moved with hips swaying were perceived as heterosexual, whereas female figures who did not look or move this way were perceived as homosexual. For men, body shape wasn't as much a factor as movement; male animated figures who moved with "shoulder swagger" were perceived as heterosexual while those that did not were perceived as homosexual (p. 321). In a third study, the researchers replicated the earlier studies, but used outlines of real people and achieved the same results. People perceived sexual orientation based on body shape and movement, which does not mean that they were accurate in these perceptions, but that people make inferences from what they observe. Are stereotypes operating here or patterns of behavior that can feed into gaydar?

Other studies have investigated whether observation of nonverbal cues enhances the accuracy of judgments regarding sexual orientation (Gowen & Britt, 2006; Lawson, 2005; Shelp, 2002). In one study, subjects indicated the most helpful characteristics they relied on when attempting to identify a person as straight or gay (Carroll & Gilroy, 2002). The most predominant cue was eye contact; other helpful cues included clothing style and fit, jewelry, facial expressions, posture, body type, walk or gait, and gesture type and frequency of use. Another investigation determined that judgments of sexual orientation were more accurate when dynamic stimuli (movement depicted in short video clips) were presented, rather than static stimuli (still photographs) (Ambady & Hallahan, 2002; Ambady, Hallahan, & Conner, 1999).

Perhaps you've seen some cable TV shows in recent years that feature homosexuals, such as *Boy Meets Boy* and *Gay, Straight, or Taken?* Shows of this sort tap into the fascination with gaydar by posing situations in which the goal is to correctly identify people's sexual orientation (Fonseca, 2003). Some social critics (as well as regular old TV watchers like us) react negatively to such attempts to popularize gaydar abilities, as though gaydar was something merely to be measured on a game show with contestants and prizes (Bennett, 2006). When we remember that gaydar grew out of a need to protect people's safety in a society in which hate crimes, isolation, and discrimination exist, we may view these pop cultural artifacts more critically.

## SPOTLIGHT on Research

In this day and age, interaction between gay and straight individuals is quite common, especially on college campuses. More college students now say that they know someone who is openly gay, or are openly gay themselves, than 20 years ago, certainly than 50 years ago. But have you ever stopped to consider whether nonverbal behavior changes when heterosexuals communicate with or are in the presence of homosexual individuals, versus in all-hetero gatherings?

That's the focus of an intriguing study by Knofler and Imhof (2007), who hypothesized that "the patterns of nonverbal behavior displayed in dyads with and without an individual with an open homosexual orientation are different from those in dyads with heterosexual participants only" (p. 189). Twenty-four individuals—12 women and 12 men in their mid-twenties—formed 12 dyads (pairs) of subjects for the purpose of interacting with a stranger of their same sex. In half of the dyads, partners were of the same sexual orientation (four pairs were heterosexual; three pairs were homosexuals who were openly gay). In the other half of the dyads, partners were of differing sexual orientations; however, partners weren't informed of each other's orientation, nor did they perceive that their own orientations were relevant to the experiment. Participants were told to talk about a topic of their choosing, except that the topic needed to be "something serious and/or personal" (p. 190). (Sexuality was not a topic of conversation.) Conversations were videotaped and analyzed according to body posture, body orientation, self-touch, and eye gaze.

Do you think nonverbal patterns of behavior were affected by the sexual orientation of participants in this study? Indeed, differences emerged across the dyads, even though participants did not know the orientation of their conversational partners. Mixed-orientation dyads exhibited more neutral body positions, meaning that these participants didn't sit with their shoulders parallel (a more feminine, affiliative posture), nor did they sit with one shoulder at an angle to their partners (a more masculine, dominant posture). Mixed dyads also maintained less eye contact and produced more self-touches to the face and other parts of the body than concordant dyads (same orientation, gay or straight).

Granted, this study used a small group of people, but the findings are interesting. For one thing, the authors explain that "contrary to popular belief, it was not found that homosexual individuals 'mimic' the behavior pattern of the opposite sex. Homosexual individuals in this study adopted a neutral posture while heterosexual individuals acted within the respective gender stereotype" (p. 201). This counteracts the stereotypical thinking that, in mixed-orientation settings, gays and lesbians act differently (i.e., act straight) so that they "pass" or fit in. From this study Knofler and Imhof observed that "quite distinct patterns of nonverbal expression were visible in the interactions when a homosexual person was involved in the interaction" (p. 201). While they don't go as far as to suggest that homosexuals

*(continued)*

SPOTLIGHT on Research *(continued)*

give off such distinctive nonverbal cues as to affect heterosexuals' behaviors, they generate some possible explanations for their findings and suggest that further study is needed.

Do you want to know more about this line of research? If so, read: Knofler, T., & Imhof, M. (2007). Does sexual orientation have an impact on nonverbal behavior in interpersonal communication? *Journal of Nonverbal Behavior, 31,* 189–204.

---

## REMEMBER 12.4

| | |
|---|---|
| **Sexuality:** | sexual behavior, as well as cognition, emotion, and psycho-sociocultural factors that affect one's sexual being. |
| **Sexual Orientation:** | related to the sex of persons with whom one wishes to engage in sexual activity. |
| **Gaydar:** | ability to detect the homosexual orientation of another person. |
| **Breedar:** | ability to detect the heterosexual orientation of another person. |
| **Direct Stare:** | a cue of attraction involving sustained, atypical eye contact, accomplished by people in different conversational groups. |
| **Broken Stare:** | a cue of attraction in which one person flashes a look at another out of the corner of the eyes. |

## Sexual Activity

Like we mentioned at the beginning of this chapter, we know that not all of us are currently sexually active; some are celibate by choice, believing that sexual activity is only appropriate in a committed, monogamous partnering. Others are celibate for certain periods of time, like those times when we're not in a relationship, our relational partner is at a distance, or we're simply concentrating on other aspects of our life. Sexual expression ebbs and flows for most people (even married people or committed partners); this discussion of nonverbal behavior and sexual activity can be applicable to whatever period of life we experience.

What we present in this section sounds contradictory to other information in this book. But in the realm of sex, it's wise to rely more on *verbal* information than *nonverbal* cues. That's not a typo: We explore some nonverbal cues related to sexual interest and activity, but in this context, verbal communication is key, and here's why: While nonverbal cues are important in the sexual context, too much sexual behavior involves reading signals, looking for "body language" (ugh, but that's a commonly used term in society), "getting vibes," sensing what our partner wants, giving our partner exactly what we sense is needed, and so forth. A mythology exists which suggests that people are supposed to be so "in tune" with their own and their partners' bodies, that they're supposed to somehow read nonverbal cues accurately (while in the midst of their own arousal), and interpret the cues appropriately so that they respond perfectly. Sorry, but what world are these folks living in?

Sexual experience and education can help us develop enhanced nonverbal sending and receiving abilities, so that we can send clear signals of interest, attraction, and arousal to a potential sexual partner, as well as receive and interpret such cues more accurately. But the opportunity for misunderstanding is so great and the consequences so dire that we encourage a little more talking, a little less "guessing." (And more verbal communication means more than such statements as, "Ouch; you're on my hair.") If more talk about, during, and after sexual activity sounds non-romantic to you, we encourage you to begin to think about it differently, because we still advocate for clear communication over media-concocted romance any day. *Real* romance can be highly communicative. Spontaneity and "picking up a vibe" have their definite downsides. It's advisable to use nonverbal cues as an *initial* or *partial* gauge of someone's interest and attraction, but wiser, first, to look for a *pattern* or the *totality* of the nonverbal information, rather than jumping to conclusions from one or two cues in isolation. Then use your verbal communication skills to complete the picture.

**Nonverbal Cues: Before Sexual Activity.** Which nonverbal codes are most related to sexual arousal, meaning the stage before sexual activity might take place or as it is beginning to occur? Certainly physical appearance, sometimes referred to as sex appeal, is a primary factor (Regan, 2004). In the U.S. as well as other cultures around the world, many people go to great lengths to enhance their physical attractiveness. Kantor (2002), whose book on gay male relationships we cited earlier, devotes an entire chapter to "Step Six: Look Great for Mr. Wonderful." He describes in detail physical appearance concerns that gay men should attend to if they want to attract a wonderful mate—from paying attention to hygiene, complexion, physical fitness, and style, down to specific nonverbal behaviors to avoid so that one doesn't draw unnecessary attention. Specifically, Kantor advises the following:

> Avoid broadcasting your deep anxieties in body language. Try not to slump as you walk as if you are depressed, convey feelings of anxiety by nail biting or hair twirling, or manifest distancing behaviors by neck craning to see everyone that walks in the room when you should instead be looking at Him. Try not to make a nonverbal statement about your special fantasy of what it means to be gay. Instead, try to make a nonverbal statement about being good husband material. Mugging, swishing, or any other behavior that gets you attention and laughs instead of admiration and love detracts from the quiet refinement that makes an eligible man think he can introduce you to his mother without having to make excuses for his choice, and without making the mother feel that she is not losing a son, but gaining a rival. (pp. 82–83)

In the section on sex, gender, and nonverbal cues in the first section of this chapter, we referenced cosmetic surgery as but one way that people attempt to alter physical features so as to be perceived as more attractive. In Chapter 5 on physical appearance and attractiveness, we explored alterations like breast augmentation, face lifts, butt lifts, and tummy tucks for the nonverbal messages such procedures convey, but one question related to appearance and sexuality should be addressed here: "Does size really matter?" (If you're saying to yourself, "I can't believe they're going there," our view is that *someone* needs to address this issue—someone besides the popular media and the pornographers.) You may not be satisfied with the answer, but the best answer really is "it depends." When we refer to size, we're equal opportunists, in that many women struggle with breast and vagina size just as men struggle with penis size. The best answer to the size question is that, for some people, the size of sexual parts does matter, but others find that their bodies and attitudes about sexuality accommodate any partner and that focusing on anatomical size misses the point and ruins the enjoyment. Yet another response is to focus on compatibility of sexual partners, meaning whether people's body parts fit well together sexually. This topic makes some people squeamish, but it's important to focus on how compatible sexual partners are or can become, rather than on some societally concocted notion of what is "enough" or desirable.

In addition to physicality, the way people adorn their bodies can be clues of sexuality. But here's a caution we've all probably heard before, about assumptions regarding appearance and sexual interest: *Just because someone is dressed in what we deem to be a sexy manner doesn't mean the person is looking for sexual activity.* We emphasize this point because the claim "she was asking for it" or "he wanted it" in relation to sexual assault and rape trials is common, when perpetrators of these crimes claim that a victim was dressed or acting provocatively, thereby somehow asking for sex. We can dress in a sexy manner because we want to feel sexy, because we want to express that part of our personality, but that doesn't mean we necessarily give our consent or want to have sexual activity. *Dressing and behaving in a sexy way doesn't equate to an invitation.*

Other nonverbal cues, including kinesic behaviors such as walk, posture, and sitting position may reveal sexual arousal as well, such as when heterosexual women tend to exaggerate their hip action when they walk past men, so as to indicate sexual interest, get men's attention, and possibly arouse the men sexually. Likewise, men may accentuate their body parts and move in ways that emphasize their masculinity, hoping to attract attention and sexual interest from onlookers. You may not have thought of dancing as a form of nonverbal communication, but people often reveal their sexuality and attraction to other people through the way they move to music.

We briefly mentioned the following behavior in the kinesics chapter, but an interesting phenomenon to observe when two people are attracted to each other is **interactive synchrony,** defined as a coordination of speech and body movement or a "social rhythm" between people (Knapp & Hall, 2006, p. 246). It's fun to watch a couple who appear interested in each other; as their interest and attraction develop over time, their body positions, gestures, touch, facial expressions, and eye behavior will mirror one another, such that they develop a rhythm of behaving. If we happen to find ourselves in such a situation, it can be exciting and confirming—to be in synch with another person. But again, it's helpful to apply a bit of caution and use all our powers of communication (verbal and nonverbal) to determine if sexual activity should be the outcome of such synchrony.

Proxemics reveal attraction too, in that decreased distance between people can be a signal of sexual interest, but it's just as likely the music is too loud. We have to watch leaping to an interpretation of sexual interest just because someone gets close to us.

Eye behavior is a fascinating thing to watch among persons of all sexual orientations, because it's a key indicator of interest and attraction. We've already talked about eye contact and its role in gaydar, but in U.S. culture, we rarely give our attention to people without looking at them. Someone "undressing you with their eyes" certainly communicates a pointed message, but this can really backfire, making the other person feel objectified and degraded. (Women get tired of men who make eye contact with only their breasts.) Eye contact—both continuous or the kind that stops and starts (the double take)—often reveals interest and sexual attraction. We've all heard of lovers staring deeply into each other's eyes, or of people whose eyes meet "across a crowded room." (Okay, we're ripping off the musical *South Pacific* here, but you get the point.) Eyes are often the very first signals of sexual interest. But again, we have to use caution to make sure the other person is actually looking at us, not someone over our shoulder. When in doubt, we can ask a question or seek more information before leaping to a conclusion from a simple nonverbal cue.

Increased frequency and intimacy of touch may indicate arousal as well, but again we emphasize the word *may* in this sentence. As we mentioned earlier, research over several decades shows that heterosexual men tend to misinterpret women's touches as being more intimate than women intend (Abbey, 1982, 1987, 1991; Henningsen, 2004; Koukounas & Letch, 2001; Moore, 2002). While women may intend their touch to be an indication of friendship or warmth, men may interpret those touches as indications of love and intimacy (or romantic interest and attraction), leading to sexual arousal (Guerrero & Andersen, 1999; Heslin & Alper, 1983; Heslin, Nguyen, & Nguyen, 1983). Part of the problem is that some heterosexual men believe that women send mixed signals regarding intimacy, and we grant that this does happen. Women may believe they're

*A whole host of nonverbal cues reveal sexuality and attraction in social settings.*

just flirting harmlessly and "having a good time," but when their actions are viewed differently than they intend, the result can be devastating.

A final, important topic warrants discussion in this section—the issue of sexual consent. Research shows that people usually indicate their consent to sexual activity nonverbally, rather than verbally (Beres, Herold, & Maitland, 2004). But how are people likely to indicate that they *don't* consent? We've probably all heard the admonition, "no means no," but sometimes the sexual waters get murky and it isn't all that simple (Ivy & Backlund, 2008; Schulhofer, 1998). We're going to repeat what many sources say about this point: When anyone says "no" to sex, that means "no"—no matter what the body is saying or if he or she expresses it without conviction in the voice. When anyone says "no" at any point in sexual activity, activity *must stop*. Throughout this book, we've advised you that when the verbal and the nonverbal contradict, believe the nonverbal because it usually carries the truer weight of the message. However, in this context, the verbal should override the nonverbal. Translation: If someone's words say "no" but her or his body says "yes," the "no" should take precedence, sexual activity should stop, and partners should seek clarification before any further action. Beware of sending mixed signals, because it's hard to stop sexual activity when our partner seems like he or she is still into it. But if our partner verbally or nonverbally requests for either a "breather" or for the activity to stop, that request simply *must* be heeded, no matter if any sort of physical affection continues.

Some heterosexual men report being conditioned to view a woman's "no" as **token resistance,** a casual or faked attempt to resist a sexual advance that someone may believe is expected before agreeing to sexual activity (Muehlenhard & Cook, 1988; O'Sullivan & Allgeier, 1994). In such a situation, men may believe that "no" actually means try harder, try something else, or try again later. Some women have been conditioned to say "no" as a tactic of "playing hard to get" or a way of heightening their partner's arousal, as though sexual activity should be some kind of chase or game. A few of our female students have been honest enough to reveal that they sometimes say "no" before they actually agree to or initiate sexual activity, just so that the men they're with won't think them "easy" or "slutty." If their bodies and nonverbal actions contradict their lack of verbal consent, the message is that they actually want the activity to continue (Muehlenhard & Rodgers, 2005). Saying "no" can be a ploy to make a partner work harder or pay more attention—another form of game playing. Sexual game playing is inadvisable because it creates confusion at best and conflict, hurt feelings, and possibly even abuse at worst (Anderson, Schultz, & Staley, 1987; Baxter, 1987; Harvey & Weber, 2002). So the bottom line is this: If we say "no" to sexual activity, we must say "no" with our voice *and* our body. We shouldn't say "no" just to fake people out, mess with their minds, or manipulate their emotions. If we do so, we make "no" meaningless *for all of us*. If we hear "no" from a partner, we have to take it at face value, stop what we're doing, and seek clarification.

This discussion reinforces our earlier remarks about needing clear verbal communication to help explain nonverbal cues, because all of this "reading cues" and "sensing what each other wants" can lead to embarrassment and maybe even heartbreak. In many social settings where "checking each other out" is likely to occur, equally likely is the presence of drugs and alcohol, which seriously warp our ability to give off accurate nonverbal cues as well as to decipher them. If you've ever had an embarrassing "morning after" experience, then you understand firsthand how impaired judgment affects the interpretation of nonverbal cues.

**Nonverbal Cues: During Sexual Activity.** Sexual intimacy is a significant development within a relationship (Mongeau, Serewicz, Henningsen, & Davis, 2006). But saying that this topic is "ticklish" isn't just a pun, it's the reality of delving into such personal waters. It's important to discuss this subject for many reasons, most of which we've already articulated (e.g., misunderstanding, embarrassment, hurt feelings, abusive behavior). Here's another reason: quality. We wholeheartedly believe, as research, therapists, and self-help books suggest, that sexual activities will be of better quality for both partners if the communication between them is enhanced (Baus & Allen, 1996; Cupach & Metts, 1991; Edgar & Fitzpatrick, 1988; Wheeless & Parsons, 1995). That's probably no great revelation to you, but it may be quite a challenge to find a more honest treatment of this topic in other resources on nonverbal communication. Why is that? For one, it's a challenging topic to tackle—not for the faint of heart. Second, the media has done us all a disservice here, with films, TV shows, song lyrics, and romance novels depicting sexual encounters primarily in two ways: either as (1) blissful, smooth, perfectly coordinated events, wherein partners don't talk much but seem to know exactly what to do, what feels best, how to gauge how their partner feels, and how to react appropriately, or (2) the complete opposite—awkward, embarrassing, uncoordinated, horrible, unsatisfying, and sometimes even abusive encounters.

So what nonverbal codes are most important in a sexual encounter? Research has revealed the following nonverbal cues to be related to courtship and seduction: flashing an eyebrow, licking the lips, touching a thigh, tossing the head, presenting one's neck, coming close, making continuous eye contact, and flipping one's hair (Abbey & Melby, 1986; Anolli & Ciceri, 2002; Grammer, 1990; Kendrick & Trost, 1987; Moore, 1985, 1995). One of the more obvious codes is haptics (touch behavior) (Jones & Yarbrough, 1985; Prager, 1995; Thayer, 1986). Probably touch is the most integral nonverbal behavior between sexual partners, but some of us make the mistake of assuming a lot with a sexual partner. We may assume, for one thing, that our current partner will behave and react like our past partner; another assumption is that what we may have read or heard about sex works the same way for every partner. Yet another assumption that can cause difficulty is that our partner wants what we want. Sure, we can learn some things from books, Internet sites, and other people's experiences, but we also have to learn to treat our partner as a unique human being who will likely desire and react to us differently than other people, than what the books say, or than we will. That lack of predictability can be viewed as a positive, not a negative.

For some people, eye contact and facial expressions during sexual activity are very important. Most of us would agree that making love to someone who won't look at us would be a major turnoff (or a dead giveaway that the person would rather be somewhere else or with someone else). What if someone cries during sex? In nonsexual situations, people may cry because they're sad or afraid, but some people cry when they're happy. How do we know what's going on with a sexual partner who's crying if we don't ask? Should we ignore the crying or assume we did something wrong? Some people—men and women alike—cry when they climax, but if we don't understand this reaction, it can be confusing and disconcerting (to say the least).

In terms of kinesics, body positioning and movement are other central aspects of the sexual encounter. Those of us who are comfortable enough to talk about our preferred sexual positions or what feels best to us are more likely to have positive sexual encounters than those of us who just hope for the best or who are too afraid or intimidated to discuss our preferences (Sprecher & Cate, 2004). Again, nonverbal cues are important but they don't replace the power of the good old conversation. Studies show that, in general, the more partners talk about sex (and we mean a *quality* conversation), the greater their satisfaction with both sexual and nonsexual aspects of their relationship (Byers & Demmons, 1999; Chesney, Blakeney, Cole, & Chan, 1981; Wheeless, Wheeless, & Baus, 1984; Yelsma, 1986).

One other nonverbal code warrants brief note—vocalics. As we mentioned earlier when discussing nonverbal cues essential in the maintenance of intimate relationships, such aspects of vocal production as volume, pausing, rate, breathiness, and pitch can enhance a sexual situation (Farinelli, 2008). In Chapter 9 we explored a subcategory of vocalics termed **vocalizations,** defined as non-words or sounds not tied to speech, including those that can substitute for speech (Andersen, 2004; Argyle, 1988; Mehrabian, 1981). Some sexual messages can be conveyed through vocalizations and the inflection and volume that accompany them. Vocalizations are quite individualistic, so over time a sexual partner can come to understand what certain sounds mean from his or her partner. As for other cues, it's unwise to assume that a sound one partner makes means the same thing when a different partner produces it.

You may chuckle while reading this, but consider the scenario of two people who meet at a party. They're attracted to each other, are drinking heavily or taking drugs, and end up in a sexual situation. What if one or the other partner is too drunk or high to give verbal consent to sex, much less resist what's being done to her or him physically? What if that person moans? Should the other person assume that the moan means the person is sexually aroused, or might that moan be related to being drunk, feeling like the room is spinning, and wanting to be left alone or taken home? Some people get so drunk or stoned that they can't form words; a moan or groan is all they can produce. Should we base the appropriateness of a whole sexual encounter on such flimsy nonverbal cues? We can see how serious mistakes (even criminal behavior) can occur in such a situation, based on an inaccurate interpretation of a simple nonverbal behavior.

One final word on this topic: If certain nonverbal cues heighten our sexual arousal and pleasure, it's important to learn to ask for them rather than expecting or hoping that a partner will read our mind. If we like to be touched in a certain way, how will our partner know? Touching him or her the way we like to be touched may have an impact, but this form of hinting or indirect method often doesn't work. Better to be explicit and verbalize our desires, but not like a drill sergeant barking out orders, either. Too much instruction can kill the mood, but too little can kill the enjoyment. Nonverbal cues are important, but we shouldn't rely on them to carry sexual messages for us; clear verbal communication is critical.

**Nonverbal Cues: After Sexual Activity.** People are as varied in their preferences and approaches for after-sex activity as they are in other phases. So it isn't wise to assume or buy into such stereotypical notions as "all women like to be held" and "if you don't sleep over after sex, it's rude." The intent here is not to take all the spontaneity out of sexual activity—before, during, or after—but again, we shouldn't try to read our partner's mind if we're unsure of what to do after sexual activity has subsided. It's okay to ask a few simple questions, keeping in mind our own desires and preferences, and we'll know better how to behave. Some people like a little physical distance after sex, which shouldn't necessarily be interpreted negatively. Not wanting to be touched or finding our own side of the bed when sex has wound down aren't necessarily judgments about the quality of the sex or clues as to feelings between partners. Some people like to cuddle and maintain psychological as well as physical closeness, but these kinds of preferences are very individualistic. If we have certain needs or preferences for nonverbal behavior (and verbal, for that matter) after engaging in sexual activity, the best tactic is to make our desires known explicitly, but sensitively. Pushing someone out of bed and yelling "get out" isn't what we have in mind.

As we've said before in this section, the best preconceived plans can fly out the window when you mix alcohol, drugs, and sex. If you haven't experienced this, you've likely heard the jokes or seen a scenario depicted in a movie or TV show—the scene *after* the passion, when sexual partners realize their buzz is wearing off, look at each other like "who *are* you again?", and generally want to exit the scene as quickly as possible. While this may be funny in the media, it's actually making fun of a pretty tragic circumstance. Needless to say, you don't want to be one of these people.

One of the things you may not have thought of regarding the after-effects of sex is this: Being in the throes of passion takes many of us to a different plane, where logic and the best advice pounding in our head have to fight to be heard. But once that passion and lust subsides, reality sets back in and things can get *really* awkward. (Talk about nonverbal cues becoming strange.) So, while we don't want to provide a laundry list of dos and don'ts regarding sexual activity and its aftermath, it's important to take some time to think about these issues, whether or not you're currently sexually active or imagine yourself someday becoming active. Ask yourself, what kind of sexual encounter do I want? How do I want to nonverbally communicate my sexuality, before, during, and after sexual activity? How do I want to verbally communicate? What kind of nonverbal and verbal communication do I want, need, and expect from my partner?

### REMEMBER 12.5

| | |
|---|---|
| **Interactive Synchrony:** | coordination of speech and body movement or a nonverbal rhythm between people. |
| **Token Resistance:** | a casual or faked attempt to resist a sexual advance, which someone may believe is expected before agreeing to sexual activity. |
| **Vocalizations:** | non-words or sounds not tied to speech, including those that can substitute for speech. |

# SUMMARY ■ ■ ■ ■ ■

In this chapter we explored three important aspects of nonverbal communication within our social world. First, nonverbal communication as affected by sex and gender was examined. We began by distinguishing between the terms sex and gender, and discussed how each formed a part of our identity. We then overviewed key research findings regarding how the sexes are both similar and different in their displays of nonverbal codes of behavior.

Since relationships are what gives most of us life's greatest joy, we turned our attention in this chapter to the role of nonverbal cues in the initiation, maintenance, and sometimes termination (dissolution) of intimate relationships. We first explored various meanings for the term intimacy, then highlighted nonverbal cues associated with the establishment and development of intimacy in a romantic relationship. Most of us would agree that conflict is inevitable in intimate relationships, but it can also be healthy or constructive if partners are attuned to their own and each other's nonverbal communication. Not all relationships are successful, so we concluded this section of the chapter by looking at predominant nonverbal cues associated with relationship dissolution or disengagement.

Finally, and arguably, saving the best for last, we explored the important subject of nonverbal cues and the expression of sexuality. We first defined some key terms, including sexuality and sexual orientation, then explored the phenomenon of gaydar, since this ability or sensation relies predominantly on nonverbal cues. We exposed some common stereotypes about the behavior of gays and lesbians and the pitfalls of relating to someone through a stereotype rather than as a unique human being. We closed the chapter with a discussion of the most critical nonverbal codes of behavior that typically occur before, during, and after sexual activity.

# DISCUSSION STARTERS

1. How do sex and gender differ? If you consider yourself to be androgynous, is that part of your sex or your gender, or both?

2. In your experience, are men and women more alike than different, nonverbally? If you believe the sexes are different, what nonverbal behaviors differ the most, from your perspective and observation?

3. Define quasi-courtship behavior, in terms of its four stages, and provide some examples of nonverbal communication that might occur in each stage.

4. What nonverbal cues do you use to flirt with someone you find attractive? What nonverbal cues of flirtation have you seen friends or

acquaintances enact, that you'd like to try or wish you could pull off in social situations?

5. If you have had an intimate relationship in the past, think about the nonverbal cues present when that relationship first began. Then think about how those nonverbal cues changed, diminished, or disappeared over time (if they did change, diminish, or disappear). What do you believe caused the change in behavior? Did your behavior change more than your partner's? Why or why not? What do you want to try to do differently the next time?

6. What's the worst breakup story you've ever heard? Was the breakup done via a sticky

note left on the nightstand next to the bed (as happened to the Carrie Bradshaw character in one episode of the TV show *Sex and the City*)? Was it done via text message or email? What nonverbal cues can help ease the pain of breaking up with someone? What nonverbal cues are inappropriate in a breakup situation?

7. In your experience, does gaydar exist? What nonverbal cues are most integral to gaydar?

How reliable is gaydar, in general, and *your* gaydar, in specific?

8. In this chapter, we discussed the role of nonverbal communication in sexual activity. What things might you have discovered about yourself in reading this part of the chapter, in terms of how you nonverbally express your sexual self (or not) to other people? What changes do you think you need to make in this regard?

# REFERENCES

Abbey, A. (1982). Sex differences in attributions for friendly behavior: Do males misperceive females' friendliness? *Journal of Personality and Social Psychology, 42*, 830–838.

Abbey, A. (1987). Misperception of friendly behavior as sexual interest: A survey of naturally occurring incidents. *Psychology of Women Quarterly, 11*, 173–194.

Abbey, A. (1991). Misperception as an antecedent of acquaintance rape: A consequence of ambiguity in communication between men and women. In A. Parrot & L. Bechhofer (Eds.), *Acquaintance rape: The hidden crime* (pp. 96–111). New York: Wiley.

Abbey, A., & Melby, C. (1986). The effects of nonverbal cues on gender differences in perceptions of sexual interest. *Sex Roles, 15*, 283–298.

Abbey, A., Zawacki, T., & Buck, P. O. (2005). The effects of past sexual assault perpetration and alcohol consumption on reactions to women's mixed signals. *Journal of Social and Clinical Psychology, 25*, 129–157.

Addington, D. W. (1968). The relationship of selected vocal characteristics to personality perception. *Speech Monographs, 35*, 492–503.

Aiello, J. R., & Jones, S. E. (1971). Field study of the proxemic behavior of young school children in three subcultural groups. *Journal of Personality and Social Psychology, 19*, 351–356.

Ambady, N., & Hallahan, M. (2002). Using nonverbal representations of behavior: Perceiving sexual orientation. In A. M. Galaburda & S. M. Kosslyn (Eds.), *The languages of the brain* (pp. 320–332). Cambridge, MA: Harvard University Press.

Ambady, N., Hallahan, M., & Conner, B. (1999). Accuracy of judgments of sexual orientation from thin slices of behavior. *Journal of Personality and Social Psychology, 77*, 538–547.

Andersen, P. A. (2004). *The complete idiot's guide to body language.* New York: Alpha.

Andersen, P. A., Guerrero, L. K., & Jones, S. M. (2006). Nonverbal behavior in intimate interactions and intimate relationships. In V. Manusov & M. L. Patterson (Eds.), *The Sage handbook of nonverbal communication* (pp. 259–277). Thousand Oaks, CA: Sage.

Andersen, P. A., & Leibowitz, K. (1978). The development and nature of the construct touch avoidance. *Environmental Psychology and Nonverbal Behavior, 3*, 89–106.

Anderson, J., Schultz, B., & Staley, C. C. (1987). Training in argumentativeness: New hope for nonassertive women. *Women's Studies in Communication, 10*, 58–66.

Anolli, L., & Ciceri, R. (2002). Analysis of the vocal profiles of male seduction: From exhibition to self-disclosure. *Journal of General Psychology, 129*, 149–169.

Argyle, M. (1988). *Bodily communication.* London: Peters Fraser & Dunlop Group Ltd.

Bandura, A. (1971). Social-learning theory of identificatory processes. In D. A. Goslin (Ed.), *Handbook of socialization theory and research.* Chicago: Rand McNally.

Bandura, A. (1986). *Social foundations of thought and action: A social cognitive theory.* Englewood Cliffs, NJ: Prentice-Hall.

Baron-Cohen, S., Wheelwright, S., Hill, J., Raste, Y., & Plumb, I. (2001). The "Reading the Mind in the Eyes" Test Revised Version: A study with normal adults, and adults with Asperger Syndrome or high-functioning autism. *Journal of Child Psychology and Psychiatry, 42*, 241–251.

Bate, B., & Bowker, J. (1997). *Communication and the sexes* (2nd ed.). Prospect Heights, IL: Waveland.

Baus, R. D., & Allen, J. L. (1996). Solidarity and sexual communication as selective filters: A report on intimate relationship development. *Communication Research Reports, 13*, 1–7.

Baxter, L. A. (1987). Cognition and communication in the relationship process. In R. Burnett, P. McGhee, & D. Clarke (Eds.), *Accounting for relationships: Explanation, representation, and knowledge* (pp. 192–212). London: Methuen.

Beebe, S. A., Beebe, S. J., & Ivy, D. K. (2007). *Communication: Principles for a lifetime* (3rd ed.). Boston: Allyn & Bacon.

Begley, S. (1995, March 27). Gray matters. *Newsweek*, 48–54.

Bell, P. A., Kline, L. M., & Barnard, W. A. (1988). Friendship and freedom of movement as moderators of sex differences in interpersonal spacing. *Journal of Social Psychology, 128*, 305–310.

Bem, S. L. (1974). The measurement of psychological androgyny. *Journal of Consulting and Clinical Psychology, 42*, 155–162.

Bennett, J. A. (2006). In defense of gaydar: Reality television and the politics of the glance. *Critical Studies in Media Communication, 23*, 408–425.

Bente, G., Donaghy, W. C., & Suwelack, D. (1998). Sex differences in body movement and visual attention: An integrated analysis of movement and gaze in mixed-sex dyads. *Journal of Nonverbal Behavior, 22*, 31–58.

Beres, M. A., Herold, E., & Maitland, S. B. (2004). Sexual consent behaviors in same-sex relationships. *Archives of Sexual Behavior, 33*, 475–486.

Birdwhistell, R. L. (1970). *Kinesics and context: Essays on body motion communication.* Philadelphia: University of Pennsylvania Press.

Blakemore, J. E. O., & Centers, R. E. (2005). Characteristics of boys' and girls' toys. *Sex Roles, 53*, 619–634.

Bleier, R. (1984). *Science and gender: A critique of biology and its theories on women.* New York: Pergamon.

Bombar, M. L., & Littig, L. W. (1996). Babytalk as a communication of intimate attachment: An initial study in adult romances and friendships. *Personal Relationships, 3*, 137–158.

Briton, N. J., & Hall, J. A. (1995). Gender-based expectancies and observer judgments of smiling. *Journal of Nonverbal Behavior, 19*, 49–65.

Brownmiller, S. (1984). *Femininity.* New York: Simon & Schuster.

Buck, R., Miller, R. E., & Caul, W. F. (1974). Sex, personality and physiological variables in the communication of affect via facial expression. *Journal of Personality and Social Psychology, 30*, 587–596.

Burgoon, J. K., & Bacue, A. E. (2003). Nonverbal communication skills. In J. O. Greene & B. R. Burleson (Eds.), *Handbook of communication and social interaction skills* (pp. 179–219). Mahwah, NJ: Erlbaum.

Burgoon, J. K., Buller, D. B., & Woodall, W. G. (1996). *Nonverbal communication: The unspoken dialogue* (2nd ed.). New York: McGraw-Hill.

Burgoon, J. K., & Newton, D. A. (1991). Applying a social meaning model to relational message interpretations of conversational involvement: Comparing observer and participant perspectives. *Southern Communication Journal, 56*, 96–113.

Burgoon, J. K., & Walther, J. B. (1990). Nonverbal expectancies and the evaluative consequences of violations. *Human Communication Research, 17*, 232–265.

Byers, E. S., & Demmons, S. (1999). Sexual satisfaction and sexual self-disclosure within dating relationships. *Journal of Sex Research, 36*, 180–189.

Caldera, Y. M., Huston, A. C., & O'Brien, M. (1989). Social interactions and play patterns of parents and toddlers with feminine, masculine, and neutral toys. *Child Development, 60*, 70–76.

Campenni, C. E. (1999). Gender stereotyping of children's toys: A comparison of parents and nonparents. *Sex Roles, 40*, 121–138.

Carroll, L., & Gilroy, P. J. (2002). Role of appearance and nonverbal behaviors in the perception of sexual orientation among lesbians and gay men. *Psychological Reports, 91*, 115–122.

Cegala, D., & Sillars, A. (1989). Further examination of nonverbal manifestations of interaction involvement. *Communication Reports, 2*, 39–47.

Chesney, A. P., Blakeney, P. E., Cole, C. M., & Chan, F. A. (1981). A comparison of couples who have sought sex therapy with couples who have not. *Journal of Sex and Marital Therapy, 7*, 131–140.

Christopher, F. S., & Lloyd, S. A. (2000). Physical and sexual aggression in relationships. In C. Hendrick & S. S. Hendrick (Eds.), *Close relationships* (pp. 331–343). Thousand Oaks, CA: Sage.

Cloven, D., & Roloff, M. E. (1993). The chilling effect of aggressive potential on the expression of complaints in intimate relationships. *Communication Monographs, 60*, 199–219.

Collett, P. (2004). *The book of tells.* London: Bantam.

Collins, S. A., & Missing, C. (2003). Vocal and visual attractiveness are related in women. *Animal Behaviour, 65*, 997–1004.

Condry, S. M., Condry, J. C., & Pogatschnik, L. W. (1983). Sex differences: A study of the ear of the beholder. *Sex Roles, 9*, 697–704.

Crawford, M., & Unger, R. (2004). *Women and gender: A feminist psychology* (4th ed.). New York: McGraw-Hill.

Cupach, W. R., & Metts, S. (1991). Sexuality and communication in close relationships. In K. McKinney & S. Sprecher (Eds.), *Sexuality in close relationships* (pp. 93–110). Hillsdale, NJ: Erlbaum.

DeLamater, J., & Shibley Hyde, J. (2004). Conceptual and theoretical issues in studying sexuality in close relationships. In J. H. Harvey, A. Wenzel, & S. Sprecher (Eds.), *The handbook of sexuality in close relationships* (pp. 7–30). Mahwah, NJ: Erlbaum.

Delaney, H. J., & Gluade, B. A. (1990). Gender differences in perception of attractiveness of men and women in bars. *Journal of Personality and Social Psychology, 16,* 378–391.

Derlega, V. J., Lewis, R. J., Harrison, S., Winstead, B. A., & Costanza, R. (1989). Gender differences in the initiation and attribution of tactile intimacy. *Journal of Nonverbal Behavior, 13,* 83–96.

Dickey, E. C., & Knower, F. H. (1941). A note on some ethnological differences in recognition of simulated expressions of emotions. *American Journal of Sociology, 47,* 190–193.

Eccles, J. S. (1987). Adolescence: Gateway to gender-role transcendence. In D. B. Carter (Ed.), *Current conceptions of sex roles and sex typing* (pp. 225–241). New York: Praeger.

Edgar, T., & Fitzpatrick, M. A. (1988). Compliance-gaining in relational interaction: When your life depends on it. *Southern Speech Communication Journal, 53,* 385–405.

Emmers, T. M., & Dindia, K. (1995). The effect of relational stage and intimacy on touch: An extension of Guerrero and Andersen. *Personal Relationships, 2,* 225–236.

Farinelli, L. (2008). The sounds of seduction and affection. In L. K. Guerrero & M. L. Hecht (Eds.), *The nonverbal communication reader* (3rd ed., pp. 160–168). Long Grove, IL: Waveland.

Feeney, J. A., Noller, P., Sheehan, G., & Peterson, C. (1999). Conflict issues and conflict strategies as contexts for nonverbal behavior in close relationships. In P. Philippot, R. S. Feldman, & E. J. Coats (Eds.), *The social context of nonverbal behavior* (pp. 348–371). Paris: Cambridge University Press.

Fine, J. (2001, October). Intimacy. *O: The Oprah Winfrey Magazine, 225.*

Floyd, K. (1997). Communicating affection in dyadic relationships: An assessment of behavior and expectancies. *Communication Quarterly, 45,* 68–80.

Floyd, K. (2000). Affectionate same-sex touch: The influence of homophobia on observers' perceptions. *Journal of Social Psychology, 140,* 774–788.

Floyd, K., & Morman, M. T. (1997). Affectionate communication in nonromantic relationships: Influences of communicator, relational, and contextual factors. *Western Journal of Communication, 61,* 279–298.

Floyd, K., & Ray, G. B. (2003). Human affection exchange: VI. Vocalic predictors of perceived affection in initial interactions. *Western Journal of Communication, 67,* 56–73.

Fonseca, N. (2003, June 6). You've got males. *Entertainment Weekly, 12.*

Friedman, H. S., Riggio, R. E., & Segall, D. O. (1980). Personality and the enactment of emotion. *Journal of Nonverbal Behavior, 5,* 35–48.

Galvin, K. M., & Brommel, B. J. (1991). *Family communication: Cohesion and change* (3rd ed.). New York: HarperCollins.

Gibbons, A. (1991). The brain as "sexual organ." *Science, 253,* 957–959.

Givens, D. B. (1978). The nonverbal basis of attraction: Flirtation, courtship, and seduction. *Psychiatry, 41,* 346–359.

Gottman, J. M., & Porterfield, A. L. (1981). Communicative competence in the nonverbal behavior of married couples. *Journal of Marriage and the Family, 43,* 817–824.

Gowen, C. W., & Britt, T. W. (2006). The interactive effects of homosexual speech and sexual orientation on the stigmatization of men: Evidence for expectancy violation theory. *Journal of Language and Social Psychology, 25,* 437–456.

Graddol, D., & Swann, J. (1989). *Gender voices.* Cambridge, MA: Basil Blackwell.

Grammer, K. (1990). Strangers meet: Laughter and nonverbal signs of interest in opposite-sex encounters. *Journal of Nonverbal Behavior, 14,* 209–236.

Grammer, K., Kruck, K., Juette, A., & Fink, B. (2000). Nonverbal behavior as courtship signals: The role of control and choice in selecting partners. *Evolution and Human Behavior, 21,* 371–390.

Greenbaum, P. E., & Rosenfeld, H. M. (1980). Varieties of touching in greetings: Sequential structure and sex-related differences. *Journal of Nonverbal Behavior, 5,* 13–25.

Gross, M. A., Guerrero, L. K., & Alberts, J. K. (2004). Perceptions of conflict strategies and communication competence in task-oriented dyads. *Journal of Applied Communication Research, 32,* 249–270.

Guerrero, L. K. (1997). Nonverbal involvement across interactions with same-sex friends, opposite-sex friends, and romantic partners: Consistency or change? *Journal of Social and Personal Relationships, 14,* 31–58.

Guerrero, L. K. (2004). Observer ratings of nonverbal involvement and immediacy. In V. Manusov (Ed.), *The sourcebook of nonverbal measures: Going beyond words* (pp. 221–235). Mahwah, NJ: Erlbaum.

Guerrero, L. K., & Andersen, P. A. (1991). The waxing and waning of relational intimacy: Touch as a function of relational stage, gender, and touch avoidance. *Journal of Social and Personal Relationships, 8,* 147–165.

Guerrero, L. K., & Andersen, P. A. (1999). Public touch behavior in romantic relationships between men and women. In L. K. Guerrero, J. A. DeVito, & M. L. Hecht (Eds.), *The nonverbal communication reader: Classic and contemporary readings* (2nd ed., pp. 202–210). Prospect Heights, IL: Waveland.

Guerrero, L. K., & Floyd, K. (2006). *Nonverbal communication in close relationships.* Mahwah, NJ: Erlbaum.

Guerrero, L. K., & Reiter, R. L. (1998). Expressing emotion: Sex differences in social skills and communicative responses to anger, sadness, and jealousy. In D. J. Canary & K. Dindia (Eds.), *Sex differences and similarities in communication* (pp. 321–350). Mahwah, NJ: Erlbaum.

Gur, R. C., Mozley, L. H., Mozley, P. D., Resnick, S. M., Karp, J. S., Alavi, A., Arnold, S. E., & Gur, R. E. (1995). Sex differences in regional cerebral glucose metabolism during a resting state. *Science, 267,* 528–531.

Hall, J. A. (1978). Gender effects in decoding nonverbal cues. *Psychological Bulletin, 85,* 845–857.

Hall, J. A. (1984). *Nonverbal sex differences: Communication accuracy and expressive style.* Baltimore: Johns Hopkins University Press.

Hall, J. A. (1998). How big are nonverbal sex differences? The case of similarity and sensitivity to nonverbal cues. In D. Canary & K. Dindia (Eds.), *Sex differences and similarities in communication: Critical essays and empirical investigations of sex and gender in interaction* (pp. 155–178). Mahwah, NJ: Erlbaum.

Hall, J. A. (2006). Women's and men's nonverbal communication: Similarities, differences, stereotypes, and origins. In V. Manusov & M. L. Patterson (Eds.), *The Sage handbook of nonverbal communication* (pp. 201–218). Thousand Oaks, CA: Sage.

Hall, J. A., Carney, D. R., & Murphy, N. A. (2002). Gender differences in smiling. In M. H. Abel (Ed.), *An empirical reflection on the smile: Mellen studies in psychology* (Vol. 4, pp. 155–185). Lewiston, NY: Edwin Mellen.

Hall, J. A., & Halberstadt, A. G. (1986). Smiling and gazing. In J. S. Hyde & M. Linn (Eds.), *The psychology of gender: Advances through meta-analysis* (pp. 136–158). Baltimore: Johns Hopkins University Press.

Hall, J. A., & Veccia, E. M. (1990). More "touching" observations: New insights on men, women, and interpersonal touch. *Journal of Personality and Social Psychology, 59,* 1155–1162.

Halpern, D. (2000). *Sex differences in cognitive abilities* (3rd ed.). Mahwah, NJ: Erlbaum.

Harvey, J. H., & Weber, A. L. (2002). *Odyssey of the heart: Close relationships in the 21st century* (2nd ed.). Mahwah, NJ: Erlbaum.

Henley, N. M. (2001). Body politics. In A. Branaman (Ed.), *Self and society: Blackwell readers in sociology* (pp. 288–297). Malden, MA: Blackwell.

Henningsen, D. D. (2004). Flirting with meaning: An examination of miscommunication in flirting interactions. *Sex Roles, 50,* 481–489.

Heslin, R., & Alper, T. (1983). Touch: A bonding gesture. In J. M. Weimann & R. P. Harrison (Eds.), *Nonverbal interaction* (pp. 47–75). Beverly Hills: Sage.

Heslin, R., Nguyen, T. D., & Nguyen, M. L. (1983). Meaning of touch: The case of touch from a stranger or same-sex person. *Journal of Nonverbal Behavior, 7,* 147–157.

Hickson, M., III., Stacks, D. W., & Moore, N. J. (2004). *Nonverbal communication: Studies and applications* (4th ed.). Los Angeles: Roxbury.

Hinsz, V. B., & Tomhave, J. A. (1991). Smile and (half) the world smiles with you, frown and you frown alone. *Personality and Social Psychology Bulletin, 17,* 586–592.

Horgan, T. G., Schmid Mast, M., Hall, J. A., & Carter, J. D. (2004). Gender differences in memory for the appearance of others. *Personality and Social Psychology Bulletin, 30,* 185–196.

Hughes, F. P. (1994). *Children, play, and development.* Boston: Allyn & Bacon.

Hurd, K., & Noller, P. (1988). Decoding deception: A look at the process. *Journal of Nonverbal Behavior, 12,* 217–233.

Ivy, D. K., & Backlund, P. (2008). *GenderSpeak: Personal effectiveness in gender communication* (4th ed.). Boston: Allyn & Bacon.

Izard, C. E. (1971). *The face of emotion.* New York: Appleton-Century-Crofts.

Johnson, K. L., Gill, S., Reichman, V., & Tassinary, L. G. (2007). Swagger, sway, and sexuality: Judging sexual orientation from body motion and morphology. *Journal of Personality and Social Psychology, 93,* 321–334.

Jones, S. E. (1986). Sex differences in touch communication. *Western Journal of Speech Communication, 50,* 227–241.

Jones, S. E., & Yarbrough, A. E. (1985). A naturalistic study of the meanings of touch. *Communication Monographs, 52,* 19–56.

Kantor, M. (2002). *My guy: A gay man's guide to a lasting relationship.* Naperville, IL: Sourcebooks Casablanca.

Kendrick, D. T., & Trost, M. R. (1987). A biosocial theory of heterosexual relationships. In K. Kelley (Ed.), *Females, males, and sexuality: Theories and research* (pp. 59–100). Albany: State University of New York Press.

Kimura, D. (1987). Are men's and women's brains really different? *Canadian Psychology, 28,* 133–147.

Kimura, D. (2000). *Sex and cognition.* Boston: MIT Press. [Excerpt derived from Paul, E. L. (2002). *Taking sides: Clashing views on controversial issues in sex and gender* (2nd ed., pp. 94–96). New York: McGraw-Hill/Dushkin.]

Kleinke, C. L. (1986). Gaze and eye contact: A research review. *Psychological Bulletin, 100,* 78–100.

Knapp, M. L., & Hall, J. A. (2006). *Nonverbal communication in human interaction* (6th ed.). Belmont, CA: Thomson/Wadsworth.

Knapp, M. L., & Vangelisti, A. L. (2005). *Interpersonal communication and human relationships* (5th ed.). Boston: Allyn & Bacon.

Kneidinger, L. M., Maple, T. L., & Tross, S. A. (2001). Touching behavior in sport: Functional components, analysis of sex differences, and ethological considerations. *Journal of Nonverbal Behavior, 25,* 43–62.

Knofler, T., & Imhof, M. (2007). Does sexual orientation have an impact on nonverbal behavior in interpersonal communication? *Journal of Nonverbal Behavior, 31,* 189–204.

Knox, D., & Wilson, K. (1981). Dating behaviors of university students. *Family Relations, 30,* 255–258.

Koeppel, L. B., Montagne, Y., O'Hair, D., & Cody, M. J. (1992). Friendly? Flirting? Wrong? Reprinted in L. K. Guerrero, J. A. DeVito, & M. L. Hecht (Eds.), *The nonverbal communication reader* (1999, 2nd ed., pp. 290–297). Prospect Heights, IL: Waveland.

Koerner, A. F., & Fitzpatrick, M. A. (2002). Nonverbal communication and marital adjustment and satisfaction: The role of decoding relationship relevant and relationship irrelevant affect. *Communication Monographs, 69,* 33–51.

Kohlberg, L. (1966). A cognitive-developmental analysis of children's sex-role concepts and attitudes. In E. E. Maccoby (Ed.), *The development of sex differences* (pp. 82–173). Stanford, CA: Stanford University Press.

Koukounas, E., & Letch, N. M. (2001). Psychological correlates of perception of sexual intent in women. *Journal of Social Psychology, 141,* 443–456.

Krolokke, C., & Sorensen, A. S. (2006). *Gender communication theories and analyses: From silence to performance.* Thousand Oaks, CA: Sage.

Kuther, T. L., & McDonald, E. (2004). Early adolescents' experiences with and views of Barbie. *Adolescence, 39,* 39–51.

LaFrance, M., Hecht, M. A., & Levy Paluck, E. (2003). The contingent smile: A meta-analysis of sex differences in smiling. *Psychological Bulletin, 129,* 305–334.

LaFrance, M., Levy Paluck, E., & Brescoll, V. (2004). Sex changes: A current perspective on the psychology of gender. In A. H. Eagly, A. E. Beall, & R. J. Sternberg (Eds.), *The psychology of gender* (2nd ed., pp. 328–344). New York: Guilford.

Lawson, W. (2005, November/December). Gay men and women really do find it easier to spot other gays. *Psychology Today,* 30.

Leap, W. (2007). Language, socialization, and silence in gay adolescence. In K. E. Lovaas & M. M. Jenkins (Eds.), *Sexualities and communication in everyday life: A reader* (pp. 95–106). Thousand Oaks, CA: Sage.

Leaper, C. (1994). Exploring the consequences of gender segregation on social relationships. In C. Leaper (Ed.), *Childhood gender segregation: Causes and consequences* (pp. 76–86). San Francisco: Josey-Bass.

Le Poire, B., Shepard, C., Duggan, A., & Burgoon, J. (2002). Relational messages associated with nonverbal involvement, pleasantness, and expressiveness in romantic couples. *Communication Research Reports, 19,* 195–206.

Lindsey, E. W., & Mize, J. (2001). Contextual differences in parent-child play: Implications for children's gender role development. *Sex Roles, 44,* 155–176.

Lippa, R. A. (2006). *Gender, nature, and nurture* (2nd ed.). Mahwah, NJ: Erlbaum.

Major, B., Schmidlin, A., & Williams, L. (1990). Gender patterns in social touch: The impact of setting and age. *Journal of Personality and Social Psychology, 58,* 634–643.

Marche, T. A., & Peterson, C. (1993). The development and sex-related use of interruption behavior. *Human Communication Research, 19,* 388–408.

Marecek, J., Crawford, M., & Popp, D. (2004). On the construction of gender, sex, and sexualities. In A. H. Eagly, A. E. Beall, & R. J. Sternberg (Eds.), *The psychology of gender* (2nd ed., pp. 192–216). New York: Guilford.

McClure, E. B. (2000). A meta-analytic review of sex differences in facial expression processing and their development in infants, children, and adolescents. *Psychological Bulletin, 126,* 424–453.

McCormick, N. B., & Jones, A. J. (1989). Gender differences in nonverbal flirtation. *Journal of Sex Education and Therapy, 15,* 271–282.

McDaniel, E., & Andersen, P. A. (1998). International patterns of tactile communication: A field study. *Journal of Nonverbal Behavior, 21,* 59–75.

Mehrabian, A. (1966). Immediacy: An indicator of attitudes in linguistic communication. *Journal of Personality, 34,* 26–34.

Mehrabian, A. (1972). *Nonverbal communication.* Chicago: Aldine.

Mehrabian, A. (1981). *Silent messages: Implicit communication of emotions and attitudes* (2nd ed.). Belmont, CA: Wadsworth.

Mehrabian, A., & Diamond, S. G. (1971). Seating arrangement and conversation. *Sociometry, 34,* 281–289.

Messner, M. (2000). Barbie girls versus sea monsters: Children constructing gender. *Gender and Society, 7,* 121–137.

Mischel, W. (1966). A social learning view of sex differences in behavior. In E. E. Maccoby (Ed.), *The development of sex differences* (pp. 56–81). Stanford, CA: Stanford University Press.

Mongeau, P. A., Serewicz, M. C. M., Henningsen, M. L. M., & Davis, K. L. (2006). Sex differences in the transition to heterosexual romantic relationship. In K. Dindia & D. J. Canary (Eds.), *Sex differences and similarities in communication* (2nd ed., pp. 337–358). Mahwah, NJ: Erlbaum.

Moore, M. M. (1985). Nonverbal courtship patterns in women: Context and consequences. *Ethology and Sociobiology, 6,* 237–247.

Moore, M. M. (1995). Courtship signaling and adolescents: "Girls just wanna have fun?" *Journal of Sex Research, 32,* 319–329.

Moore, M. M. (2002). Courtship communication and perception. *Perceptual and Motor Skills, 94,* 97–105.

Morris, D. (1971). *Intimate behavior.* New York: Random House.

Muehlenhard, C. L., & Cook, S. W. (1988). Men's self-reports of unwanted sexual activity. *Journal of Sex Research, 24,* 58–72.

Muehlenhard, C. L., Koralewski, M. A., Andrews, S. L., & Burdick, C. A. (1986). Verbal and nonverbal cues that convey interest in dating: Two studies. Reprinted in L. K. Guerrero & M. L. Hecht (Eds.), *The nonverbal communication reader* (2008, 3rd ed., pp. 353–359). Long Grove, IL: Waveland.

Muehlenhard, C. L., & Rodgers, C. S. (2005). Token resistance to sex: New perspectives on an old stereotype. In J. K. Davidson & N. B. Moore (Eds.), *Speaking of sexuality* (2nd ed., pp. 280–289). Los Angeles: Roxbury.

Newton, D. A., & Burgoon, J. K. (1990). Nonverbal conflict behaviors: Functions, strategies, and tactics. In D. D. Cahn (Ed.), *Intimates in conflict: A communication perspective* (pp. 77–104). Hillsdale, NJ: Erlbaum.

Nicholas, C. L. (2004). Gaydar: Eye-gaze as identity recognition among gay men and lesbians. *Sexuality and Culture: An Interdisciplinary Quarterly, 8,* 60–86.

Noller, P. (1980). Misunderstanding in marital communication: A study of couples' nonverbal communication. *Journal of Personality and Social Psychology, 41,* 272–278.

Noller, P. (1992). Nonverbal communication in marriage. In R. S. Feldman (Ed.), *Applications of nonverbal behavioral theories and research* (pp. 31–59). Hillsdale, NJ: Erlbaum.

Noller, P. (2006). Nonverbal communication in close relationships. In V. Manusov & M. L. Patterson (Eds.), *The Sage handbook of nonverbal communication* (pp. 403–420). Thousand Oaks, CA: Sage.

O'Sullivan, L. F., & Allgeier, E. R. (1994). Disassembling a stereotype: Gender differences in the use of token resistance. *Journal of Applied Social Psychology, 24,* 1035–1055.

Paul, E. L. (Ed.). (2002). *Taking sides: Clashing views on controversial issues in sex and gender* (2nd ed.). New York: McGraw-Hill/Dushkin.

Peach, L. J. (1998). Women in culture: Introduction. In L. J. Peach (Ed.), *Women in culture: A women's studies anthology* (pp. 1–12). Malden, MA: Blackwell.

Pearson, J. C. (1985). *Gender and communication.* Dubuque, IA: William C. Brown.

Perper, T., & Weis, D. L. (1987). Proceptive and rejective strategies of U.S. and Canadian college women. *Journal of Sex Research, 23,* 455–480.

Pleck, J. H. (1977). The psychology of sex roles: Traditional and new views. In L. A. Cater, A. F. Scott, & W. Martyna (Eds.), *Women and men: Changing roles, relationships, and perceptions* (pp. 181–199). New York: Praeger.

Pomerleau, A., Bloduc, D., Malcuit, G., & Cossette, L. (1990). Pink or blue: Environmental stereotypes in the first two years of life. *Sex Roles, 22,* 359–376.

Prager, K. J. (1995). Nonverbal behavior in intimate interactions. Reprinted in L. K. Guerrero & M. L. Hecht (Eds.), *The nonverbal communication reader* (2008, 3rd ed., pp. 346–352). Long Grove, IL: Waveland.

Regan, P. C. (2004). Sex and the attraction process: Lessons from science (and Shakespeare) on lust, love, chastity, and fidelity. In J. H. Harvey, A. Wenzel, & S. Sprecher (Eds.), *The handbook of sexuality in close relationships* (pp. 115–133). Mahwah, NJ: Erlbaum.

Renninger, L. A., Wade, T. J., & Grammer, K. (2004). Getting that female glance: Patterns and consequences of male nonverbal behavior in courtship contexts. *Evolution and Human Behavior, 25,* 416–431.

Richmond, V. P., McCroskey, J. C., & Hickson, M. L. III. (2008). *Nonverbal behavior in interpersonal relations* (6th ed.). Boston: Allyn & Bacon.

Riesman, C. (1990). *Divorce talk: Women and men make sense of personal relationships.* New Brunswick, NJ: Princeton University Press.

Roese, N. J., Olson, H. M., Borenstein, M. N., Martin, A., & Shores, A. L. (1992). Same-sex touching behavior: The moderating role of homophobic attitudes. *Journal of Nonverbal Behavior, 16,* 249–259.

Rosenthal, R., Hall, J. A. DiMatteo, M. R., Rogers, P. L., & Archer, D. (1979). *Sensitivity to nonverbal communication: The PONS test.* Baltimore: Johns Hopkins University Press.

Ross, H., & Taylor, H. (1989). Do boys prefer daddy or his physical style of play? *Sex Roles, 20,* 23–31.

Rotter, N. G., & Rotter, G. S. (1988). Sex differences in the encoding and decoding of negative facial emotions. *Journal of Nonverbal Behavior, 12,* 139–148.

Scheflen, A. E. (1965). Quasi-courtship behavior in psychotherapy. *Psychiatry, 28,* 245–257.

Scherer, K. R., Banse, R., & Wallbott, H. G. (2001). Emotion inferences from vocal expression correlate across languages and cultures. *Journal of Cross-Cultural Psychology, 32,* 76–92.

Schmid Mast, M., & Hall, J. A. (2006). Women's advantage at remembering others' appearance: A systematic look at the why and when of a gender difference. *Personality and Social Psychology Bulletin, 32,* 353–364.

Schulhofer, S. (1998, October). Unwanted sex. *The Atlantic Monthly,* 55–66.

Shelp, S. G. (2002). Gaydar: Visual detection of sexual orientation among gay and straight men. *Journal of Homosexuality, 44,* 1–14.

Sillars, A. L., Coletti, S. F., Parry, D., & Rogers, M. A. (1982). Coding verbal conflicts: Non-verbal and perceptual correlates of the "avoidance-distributive-integrative" distinction. *Human Communication Research, 9,* 83–95.

Spain, D. (1992). *Gendered spaces.* Chapel Hill: University of North Carolina Press.

Sprecher, S., & Cate, R. M. (2004). Sexual satisfaction and sexual expression as predictors of relationship satisfaction and stability. In J. H. Harvey, A. Wenzel, & S. Sprecher (Eds.), *The handbook of sexuality in close relationships* (pp. 235–256). Mahwah, NJ: Erlbaum.

Tannen, D. (1994). *Gender and discourse.* New York: Oxford University Press.

Tannen, D. (1995). *Talking 9 to 5: Women and men at work.* New York: Harper.

Tavris, C. (1992). *The mismeasure of woman.* New York: Simon & Schuster.

Thayer, S. (1986). Touch: Frontier of intimacy. *Journal of Nonverbal Behavior, 10,* 7–11.

Tickle-Degnen, L. (2006). Nonverbal behavior and its functions in the ecosystem of rapport. In V. Manusov & M. L. Patterson (Eds.), *The Sage handbook of nonverbal communication* (pp. 381–399). Thousand Oaks, CA: Sage.

Tracy, K. (2002). *Everyday talk: Building and reflecting identities.* New York: Guilford.

Trees, A. R., & Manusov, V. (1998). Managing face concerns in criticism: Integrating nonverbal behaviors as a dimension of politeness in female friendship dyads. *Human Communication Research, 24,* 564–583.

Van Newkirk, R. (2006). "Gee, I didn't get that vibe from you": Articulating my own version of a femme lesbian existence. *Journal of Lesbian Studies, 10,* 73–85.

Viscovich, N., Borod, J., Pihan, H., Peery, S., Brickman, A. M., & Tabert, M. (2003). Acoustical analysis of posed prosodic expressions: Effects of emotion and sex. *Perceptual and Motor Skills, 96,* 759–777.

Vogt, D., & Colvin, C. R. (2003). Interpersonal orientation and the accuracy of personality judgments. *Journal of Personality, 71,* 267–295.

Wagner, H. L., Buck, R., & Winterbotham, M. (1993). Communication of specific emotions: Gender differences in sending accuracy and communication measures. *Journal of Nonverbal Behavior, 17,* 29–53.

Wagner, H. L., MacDonald, C. J., & Manstead, A. S. R. (1986). Communication of individual emotions by spontaneous facial expressions. *Journal of Personality and Social Psychology, 50*, 737–743.

Wallace, D. H. (1981). Affectional climate in the family of origin and the experience of subsequent sexual-affectional behaviors. *Journal of Sex and Marital Therapy, 7*, 296–396.

Weisman, L. K. (1992). *Discrimination by design: A feminist critique of the man-made environment.* Chicago: University of Chicago Press.

Weiss, E. H., & Fisher, B. (1998). Should we teach women to interrupt? Cultural variables in management communication courses. *Women in Management Review, 13*, 37–44.

West, C., & Zimmerman, D. H. (1983). Small insults: A study of interruptions in cross-sex conversations between unacquainted persons. In B. Thorne, C. Kramarae, & N. Henley (Eds.), *Language, gender, and society* (pp. 102–117). Rowley, MA: Newbury.

Wheeless, L. R., Wheeless, V. E., & Baus, R. (1984). Sexual communication, communication satisfaction, and solidarity in the developmental stages of intimate relationships. *Western Journal of Speech Communication, 48*, 217–230.

Wheeless, L. R., & Parsons, L. A. (1995). What you feel is what you might get: Exploring communication apprehension and sexual communication satisfaction. *Communication Research Reports, 12*, 39–45.

Willis, F. N., & Rawdon, V. A. (1994). Gender and national differences in attitudes toward same-gender touch. *Perceptual and Motor Skills, 78*, 1027–1034.

Wilmot, W. W., & Hocker, J. L. (2001). *Interpersonal conflict* (6th ed.). New York: McGraw-Hill.

Wood, J. T. (1994). Engendered identities: Shaping voice and mind through gender. In D. R. Vocate (Ed.), *Intrapersonal communication: Different voices, different minds* (pp. 145–168). Hillsdale, NJ: Erlbaum.

Wood, J. T. (2005). *Gendered lives: Communication, gender, and culture* (6th ed.). Belmont, CA: Wadsworth.

Yelsma, P. (1986). Marriage vs. cohabitation: Couples' communication practices and satisfaction. *Journal of Communication, 36*, 94–107.

Zaidel, S., & Mehrabian, A. (1969). The ability to communicate and infer positive and negative attitudes facially and vocally. *Journal of Experimental Research in Personality, 3*, 233–241.

Zimmerman, D. H., & West, C. (1975). Sex roles, interruptions and silences in conversation. In B. Thorne & N. Henley (Eds.), *Language and sex: Difference and dominance* (pp. 105–129). Rowley, MA: Newbury.

Zuckerman, M., DePaulo, B. M., & Rosenthal, R. (1981). Verbal and nonverbal communication of deception. In L. Berkowitz (Ed.), *Advances in experimental social psychology* (Vol. 14). New York: Academic Press.

# AUTHOR INDEX

# SUBJECT INDEX

# PHOTO CREDITS

Kathryn Anderson, p. 405

Ashley K. Billig, pp. 3, 8, 11, 18, 25, 30, 32, 35, 37, 65, 66, 79, 86, 101, 104, 107, 111, 115, 133, 141, 147, 149, 159, 175, 176, 177, 178, 184, 187, 207, 209, 214, 219, 224, 230, 234, 247, 253, 255, 266, 272, 285, 294, 299, 303, 322, 338, 354, 357, 366, 371, 378, 385, 400, 402, 410, 415, 419, 431

Bruce G. Billig, p. 96

Diana K. Ivy, pp. 63, 188, 194, 195, 290

Kathy Pengelly, p. 260

Amanda Smith, p. 140

Shawn T. Wahl, p. 206

Walk Street Restaurant, Inc., p. 70